J. BURKE SEVERS
GENERAL EDITOR

A Manual of the Writings
in Middle English

1050-1500

J. BURKE SEVERS
GENERAL EDITOR

A Manual of the Writings
in Middle English

1050-1500

*By Members of the Middle English Group of the
Modern Language Association
of America*

Based upon
A Manual of the Writings in Middle English 1050–1400
by John Edwin Wells, New Haven, 1916
and Supplements 1–9, 1919–1951

THE CONNECTICUT ACADEMY OF ARTS AND SCIENCES
MDCCCCLXX

ISBN 0 208 00894 2

Printed in the United States of America

Order from

ARCHON BOOKS
The Shoe String Press, Inc.
995 Sherman Ave.
Hamden, Connecticut 06514

Volume 2

II. THE *PEARL* POET

by

Marie P. Hamilton

III. WYCLYF AND HIS FOLLOWERS

by

Ernest W. Talbert and S. Harrison Thomson

IV. TRANSLATIONS AND PARAPHRASES OF THE BIBLE, AND COMMENTARIES

by

Laurence Muir

V. SAINTS' LEGENDS

by

Charlotte D'Evelyn and Frances A. Foster

VI. INSTRUCTIONS FOR RELIGIOUS

by

Charlotte D'Evelyn

PREFACE

This manual of Middle English literature is a collaborative project of the Middle English Group of the Modern Language Association of America. It is appearing in parts, as the various chapters of the work are completed. Volume 1,* on the Romances, has already appeared. The present Volume 2 deals with the *Pearl* Poet, Wyclyf and His Followers, Translations and Paraphrases of the Bible, Saints' Legends, and Instructions for Religious. The Bibliography is intended to be complete for all serious studies down through 1955 and to include all important studies from 1955 to the date of going to press (March 1968 for Volume 2). A full account of the principles followed by the editors of the work will be found in the Preface to Volume 1.

For help in the editorial work on this second volume, the General Editor wishes to express appreciation to his colleagues, Professors Albert E. Hartung and Peter G. Beidler. His able secretary, Elizabeth J. Salay, was of considerable help in preparing copy for the printer. The Editor is indebted also to Lehigh University and to the Lehigh Institute of Research for released time and financial support. Finally, the Middle English Group is deeply grateful to the Connecticut Academy of Arts and Sciences for undertaking the publication of this revised *Manual,* as it had undertaken the publication of the original.

J. Burke Severs

General Editor

November 30, 1968

*Previously called Fascicule 1.

CONTENTS

II. THE *PEARL* POET

by

Marie P. Hamilton

THE PEARL POET [1]. A single quarto volume in the British Museum, MS Cotton Nero A.x. + 4, has preserved four untitled poems of unknown authorship which as a group illustrate the variety and quality of the Alliterative Revival at its best. In the order of their position in the manuscript the poems are *Pearl*, a mystical, elegiac dream-vision; *Purity* (or *Cleanness*) and *Patience*, both homilies with Biblical paraphrases as exempla; and *Sir Gawain and the Green Knight*, the finest of the Middle English romances. (See Romances, I [25], for Helaine Newstead's bibliography and commentary on *Sir Gawain and the Green Knight*.) The manuscript is accompanied by crude and sometimes inaccurate colored illustrations of scenes described in each of the poems, the sole surviving medieval commentaries on them.

The manuscript, written in a late fourteenth-century hand, is in a Northwest Midland dialect; and the poems apparently were composed sometime within the period 1360–95, by a poet, or poets, who grew up in the vicinity of south Lancashire or northwest Derbyshire, though he has also been assigned to Cheshire and recently to north Staffordshire. The presence of the four pieces in the same unique manuscript and the same dialect, reflecting similar attitudes, preoccupations, and tastes, and sharing certain distinctive features of vocabulary and style, has seemed to most commentators to indicate authorship by the same person, commonly known as the *Pearl* poet or the *Gawain* poet. The evidence is not conclusive, however; the theory of single authorship has been contested by a number of competent scholars. Nevertheless, for convenience in the present survey all four poems will be regarded as the work of one person. The alliterative poem *St. Erkenwald* has also been attributed to the *Pearl* poet, but persuasive evidence against the attribution has recently been provided by Larry Benson.

The practice, once popular, of assembling a biography of the poet from internal evidence, with *Pearl* as the starting point and chief source, is now restricted to the legitimate procedure of noting indications of his interests, tastes, convictions, education, and probable status. With the authority of a Middle English scholar who was also trained in theology Carleton F. Brown, in an influential essay in 1904, maintained that the treatment of Scripture and religious matters in the four poems is the work of an ecclesiastic, well versed in the Bible and theology and acquainted with the controversy about predestination, free will, and divine grace which was a leading issue among English intellectuals during the middle years of the fourteenth century and later. This view of the poet, which seemed to run counter to the prevailing conception of *Pearl* as a father's poem about his daughter, has been slow in gaining acceptance. On the other hand, Brown's contention in the same essay that the poet was heretical in *Pearl*, in his apparent belief in equal as against graded rewards in heaven, was readily accepted for a time, but has now been refuted by various commentators, to the satisfaction of most students of the poems.

Attempts to identify the author with writers known by name (e.g., Huchown, Ralph Strode, Friar John de Erghome) or to associate him with one of the royal households (as a retainer of John of Gaunt, e.g., or of one of Gaunt's brothers-in-law, the Earl of Pembroke or the French Earl of Bedford) have necessarily proved inconclusive, but are illuminating in their by-products. A full century of scholarship has brought no certain clues to the poet's identity, but it has enlarged our knowledge of the society for which he wrote and the probable circumstances of his life. A more sharply focused and authentic image of him has emerged from an objective scrutiny of his work and an increasingly accurate knowledge of life in his period. A perceptive analysis of him as man and poet is Henry L. Savage's estimate in Chapter I of his book *The Gawain Poet*.

In vocabulary, style, and meter the four poems attributed to him exhibit in varying degrees the distinctive techniques of the alliterative school, handled with originality, imagination, and superior skill. The tradition demanded a vocabulary often elevated in style, marked by rare

and archaic words and by stereotyped alliterative phrases with aristo-
cratic connotation. At the same time the free rhythms of the native verse
in its late Middle English phase were hospitable to the use of colloqui-
alisms and homely expressions, with easy shifts from formal to informal
diction. In addition to these stylistic features, the verbal ingenuity of
the alliterative poets appears to advantage in the work of the *Pearl* poet,
and their fondness for oblique expression is seen at its best in the stylistic
subtleties of *Sir Gawain* and the cryptic manner of passages in *Pearl*.
The pronounced northerly complexion of the vocabulary in the four
poems is due in part to a high proportion of Scandinavian words, but
the French element also bulks large.

Evidence for dating the four poems with any precision, or for determining their chronological order, is almost non-existent. For *Pearl* and
Sir Gawain we have only the uncertain evidence of costume and other
current fashions; for *Patience* and *Purity*, as will appear below in the
accounts of them, the evidence from literary relationships is conclusive
only in the case of *Purity*.

PEARL [2] is as remarkable in its kind as *Sir Gawain* is among the romances. Though it is composed of elements well established in medieval
tradition, they are so combined that *Pearl* in its total effect is unlike
anything else in Middle English. In a moving story of personal loss, leading to a visionary journey to the other world and a conversion, the
author employs scholastic debate, Biblical paraphrase, pervasive Biblical
symbols, and a vocabulary of extraordinary range, as he seeks to justify
eternal providence in the Christian doctrine of the Atonement, with
emphasis on the efficacy of sacramental grace. He conveys the whole in
the rhythms of an intricate metrical pattern which, in its varied movement and its echoing rimes and refrains, is in harmony with the deep
and changing emotions with which the poem is charged. The reasons
given by John Edwin Wells for judging *Pearl* to be "the best of the
lyrical-narrative English pieces of the fourteenth century" may well
stand: "Because of its elaborate and finished artistic form, the brilliance
and vigor of its imagination, and the sincerity and profundity of its
passion, it has a force and depth of appeal, encountered not at all in
kind, and scarcely ever in degree, in other writings of the period."

In metrical form *Pearl* probably is the most elaborate poem of its length in the language. The poet chose native rhythms and a stanzaic pattern long familiar in West Midland verse, but gave these a swifter movement and a more complex and finished scheme of stanza-linking and refrains than are found elsewhere. The poem consists of 101 twelve-line stanzas, each line having four stresses, heavily but not systematically alliterated, and preserving the old rhythmic variety of the alliterative long line, only slightly modified by adaptation to riming stanzas. These (riming ababababbcbc) are arranged in twenty clusters, each cluster with one exception having five stanzas. Each group is marked by a refrain, running through the five stanzas and yielding to a different refrain for the next group. Echo-words link each stanza throughout with the pre-ceding stanza, and the last line of the poem echoes the first line, thus completing the concatenation with circular effect (cf. *Patience* and *Sir Gawain*, in which the last lines echo the first lines).

Even though the rhythms, style, and diction of *Pearl* are mainly de-rived from the native tradition, these, and more especially the diction, are modified by the elaborate patterns of rime, echo-words, and refrains. These demanded an uncommonly rich vocabulary and encouraged the use of strange and difficult words and levels of diction ranging from homely idiom to archaic, aureate, and rare learned words. The resulting obscurity is increased for the modern reader by oblique expression, a stylistic mannerism of the alliterative school which was appropriate to the theological paradoxes and symbolism of *Pearl*. The Middle English vocabulary of religion and of courtly society being rich in French words, these are consequently numerous in the poem. The Scandinavian ele-ment, though considerable, is proportionately lighter than in the com-panion pieces.

Brief accounts of the action in *Pearl* are especially unsatisfactory, for the plot, approached in an atmosphere of mystery, is disclosed gradually, and then often in the cryptic language of paradox and symbol which was traditional for the portrayal of sacred mysteries intended for an enlightened audience.

The narrator in *Pearl* relates his loss of a matchless pearl which had been the main-spring of his health and happiness. Through grass to earth it sprang from him in a garden. Mortally wounded by Love's power, he watches in loneliness, longing for his precious pearl without spot (which he refers to in turn as "she" and "it"). As he broods over the thought of her color "clad in clay," a song of rare sweetness is wafted to him, bearing the promise that from the dark earth, enriched by his jewel in decay, spice plants are bound to spread. Flowers and fruits of unfailing lustre will shine there in the sunlight.

During a high feast at harvest time in August, the bereaved man, entering the garden, finds the "hill" where the pearl had descended to earth indeed shaded by spice-bearing herbs in flower, bright and fragrant. Yet in spite of reason's counsel of peace, the appeal of the garden, and the comfort imparted by Christ, the wilful mourner persists in obstinate grief. Prostrate on the hill in sorrow for his loss, he falls into a deep slumber, induced by the fair scent of the spices, and "in God's grace" journeys in spirit to a land of shimmering cliffs, exotic woodlands, and singing birds of flaming hues.

As he wanders blissfully along the jeweled banks of a jewel-studded stream, he looks out across the water to a region of supernal loveliness which he takes to be paradise. Soon he is startled by the appearance there of a child, or young maiden, of angelic beauty and mien, wearing a crown of pearls, her dazzling white vesture trimmed with pearls, and her breast adorned by a single wondrous pearl without blemish. He recognizes her and watches with mingled exultation and awe as she approaches and stands facing him on the farther side of the stream, "fresh as fleur de lis." "She was nearer to me than aunt or niece," he explains; "my joy therefore was much the more."

In the ensuing dialogue the dreamer inquires whether the maiden is indeed the jewel he has mourned, and what fate conveyed her to this paradise, leaving him in great duress and pain. Pearl then points out false assumptions underlying his speech. His gem was not entirely "away," but secure in a treasure chest, as (if?) in the bright garden. The loss of the jewel which he has lamented was a matter of brief concern, and the fate which he has accused of theft actually has brought him profit, a remedy for his misfortune. What he lost was but a rose that withered naturally, and now by virtue of the chest in which his pearl is enclosed it is "put in proof" for a pearl of price.

The enraptured dreamer now proposes to remain with Pearl in the festive groves and must therefore be reprimanded again for his presumption, for trusting his fallible powers of vision in supposing that she is actually present there, while doubting God's promise to raise up his "life" (soul), in spite of the mortality of the flesh. The desperate man, after avowing that if he is again to be deprived of his jewel, he cares not what fate may await him, ruin or exile far from earth, is persuaded to heed the maiden's counsel that he submit to God's will, and prayerfully throws himself upon the divine mercies. Piteously he seeks comfort from Pearl also. Before they parted they had been at one and she was the ground of his bliss, he reminds her. God forbid that they should now be at odds.

In his new submissiveness and humility, the dreamer asks for an account of Pearl's happy state. He rejoices in her good fortune; it is the highway of his own felicity. After her fall at a tender age, Pearl explains, Christ espoused her, crowned her queen, and endowed her with his heritage. To the startled dreamer, she disclaims any rivalry with Mary, Queen and Empress of Heaven. All who enter God's kingdom enjoy royal rank and pay glad homage to Mary, she says. No rivalry exists in the mystical body of Christ, to which each Christian soul belongs. The dreamer is disturbed nevertheless by a system of preferment in which a child can achieve the highest rank upon initiation into a social order; for Pearl by her own testimony was made Queen "on the first day" of her entrance into God's kingdom, though she was not yet two years old and was ignorant of Paternoster, Creed, or how to please God.

The maiden begins the defense of her rank by a paraphrase of the Parable of the Laborers in the Vineyard (Matthew 20:1–16) adapted to the case of baptized children, whom she associates with those who enter the vineyard at the last hour of the workday and yet are paid the full day's wage, though they have done little or no work.

Babes are rewarded, not for labor performed, but for obedience to God's command, "Go into my vineyard." After all, she points out to the skeptical dreamer, considerations of "more" and "less" are irrelevant in the kingdom of God, who pours out his gifts like streams from unfailing springs. The debate resolves itself into an argument about the Law vs. Grace, the dreamer insisting upon justification by works, as Pearl upholds the orthodox Christian view of salvation as the free gift of God. Her special concern is to demonstrate the efficacy of grace bestowed in the sacrament of infant baptism, by which she had entered the vineyard, God's kingdom (lines 625–28). She was paid the full wage at once, in advance of some who had labored long, of some indeed who have not yet been rewarded, and may not be rewarded soon (lines 577–88).

The eligibility of infants for the full measure of grace bestowed in baptism is further defended as Pearl balances the relative claims of the righteous and the innocent to the heavenly prize. Both are saved, but those "who to guile have never swerved aside," having no personal sin to remit but original sin only, which is cleansed in baptism, have the surer claim. For such as they the kingdom of heaven is prepared. Let them but knock for entrance and the gate is promptly opened to that realm where the bliss without end is to be found, the Pearl of Price for which the jewel-merchant of old gave all that he possessed. The maiden then identifies the wondrous pearl which adorns her own breast with the precious *margarita* of the parable. It was placed there in token of peace, she says, by the Lamb who shed his blood. Pearl, at this climactic moment, urges the dreamer to forsake the mad world and purchase his pearl without blemish.

The debate is now at an end. The dreamer, no longer rebellious but still naive, questions Pearl further about her status, her transcendent beauty, her vesture, her angelic mien. These, she replies, were gifts of Christ when he espoused her, cleansed her robes, and crowned her in virgin purity, for she is one among the brides of the Lamb whom St. John saw on Mount Sion, as he records in the Apocalypse. In response to further questions, Pearl describes the Lamb of God in rhapsodic paraphrase of the Biblical accounts, concluding with the description in the Apocalypse of Christ and his retinue, the joyous throng of virgins, 144.000 strong.

The dreamer, further humbled, protests that he is "but muck and dust" in the presence of "so rich a rose" as Pearl, a being of simple (uncompounded) essence. Nevertheless, he would ask one last boon of her, a glimpse of the dwellings in manor or castle wall which she shares with her royal companions. He may not enter the heavenly Jerusalem, she replies, but she by special favor has gained permission for him to look upon it from a lofty hill-top apart, to which she guides him. Thus the dreamer beholds the New Jerusalem as John of Patmos, also rapt "in the spirit" to a high mountain, saw it "in ghostly dream": the golden city, filled with the radiance of God and of the Lamb; the River of Life flowing out from the throne of God, brighter than sun or moon; and seated on the throne, encircled by Elders and angelic hosts, the High God's Self. At the wonder of it all the dreamer experiences a moment of pure ecstasy in which he has no sensation of exertion or of rest. Then suddenly he is aware of the immaculate procession of the Lamb, thousands moving in rhythmic unison towards the throne, as though the vast city were filled with hosts of virgins, all attired and crowned like Pearl, and wearing at their breasts "the blissful pearl of great delight." The dreamer, supposing that Pearl is still near him, is amazed to recognize her in the procession, "so white among her peers." Overcome by love-longing, he madly attempts to swim across the stream which divides them and join her at all hazards, but before he reaches the bank his dream is suddenly brought to an end. His impulsive action was not in accord with his Prince's pleasure.

Awake and alone once more in the garden where the pearl had "strayed to ground," the man meditates ruefully upon the folly of striving against God's will and resolves: "Now all be to that Prince's pleasure." He concludes at last that all is well with him

in this earthly "dungeon of sorrow" if Pearl, as the vision has indicated, is in truth
pleasing to that Prince. He therefore commits his jewel to God and finds sustaining
joy in friendship with him who, in the Blessed Sacrament in memory of Christ, has
permitted us to be his household servants and precious pearls according to his
pleasure.

No other Middle English poem, not even *Piers Plowman*, has during
the last half century aroused more lively speculation and controversy
than *Pearl*. The view that it is a personal elegy, which was presented as
simple fact by its first editor a century ago, went unquestioned for thirty
years. The poet, in a word, recalls his sorrow over the loss of a daughter
who died before she was two years old, his anguished vigils beside her
grave, and the reassuring vision of her as a follower of the Lamb, which
leads to his own reconciliation and friendship with God. This reading
has, with considerable modifications, been accepted by all but two editors
of *Pearl*, by most modernizers, and by many commentators.

Courthope, dissenting from the prevailing interpretation, described
the poem in 1895 as "allegory made the vehicle of contemplation" and
employing "such common heirlooms of Platonic allegory" as the dream,
the *Itinerarium mentis*, and the apocalyptic vision, by a poet with "a
passion for riddles and conceits." In an article published in 1903
William H. Schofield argued in similar vein that *Pearl* is to be classed
among didactic vision-poems and allegories, that the elegiac frame is
merely a device for introducing the allegorical vision, with its theological debate, that Pearl herself is a purely fictitious character meant to
typify clean maidenhood, with which pearls were traditionally associated. Such an equation of the Pearl-maiden with a mere abstract virtue
has had no great appeal, but some interpreters have followed Schofield
and Courthope in rejecting the reality of the seemingly autobiographical
elegiac element. Notable among the dissenters was Sister Mary Madeleva,
who in a lively book published in 1925 denied any possibility of elegy
and favored total allegory. *Pearl* in her view is a monastic poet's account
of an experience in interior desolation, spiritual dryness, the withdrawal
of "the sensible sweetness of God," a jewel much prized by young religious. Pearl, the maiden encountered in the vision, is therefore not to
be identified with the lost gem; she is the personification of the poet's
own soul in a state of potential perfection, or in the state of sanctifying
grace; that is, as it would be in heaven. The Pearl of Price which adorns

her breast is the poet's own hope of heaven, revealed to him as evidence that his dejection is unwarranted. As a whole this reading has not been widely accepted, but Sister Madeleva's conception of the dialogue in the Earthly Paradise as the poet's "supernatural intercourse with his own soul" has appeared in several later analyses. It is defended by Stanley P. Chase, for example, and has been adopted by Sister Mary V. Hillman, both editors of *Pearl* who have also turned it into modern English. Since the advent of Sister Madeleva's exegesis, students of the poem have been divided among those who regard the lost pearl as a person, those who regard it as a spiritual value, and those who think it might be both. Those for whom it is a spiritual quality or endowment are not agreed on a single key to the allegory, but a measure of agreement appears in some recent interpretations.

The undeniable symbolic element in *Pearl* has received increased attention from those for whom it is a genuine elegy, as from others. The point was made some years ago, and notably by J. B. Fletcher, that the elegiac hypothesis need not preclude the possibility of systematic allegory, nor even of multiple symbolism. Conversely the view has been expressed that even though the poem is primarily an allegory, it may owe its elegiac form and emotional urgency to some bereavement deeply felt by the poet. A spirit of accommodation is thus apparent in recent studies. Dorothy Everett in *Essays in Middle English Literature* asserts that most likely *Pearl* is a personal elegy, but disclaims the idea that its emotional quality may not be otherwise explained. The case for personal elegy is ably restated in the Oxford edition by Eric V. Gordon and Ida L. Gordon. Though ruling out the possibility of systematic allegory, they describe the symbolism as dominating and illuminating the whole and deepening its significance, and yet they are convinced that a directly autobiographical basis can best account for the form and poetic quality of the poem.

Whereas the native English tradition is foremost in the verse, style, and technique of *Pearl*, no clear trace has been found of its indebtedness to any known English writing, nor of its influence on any. The Vulgate Bible is the poet's main source, accounting for about a third of his lines. In addition to the theme of the Fall and Atonement, the Scriptures provide the matter for homiletic and descriptive passages and for the pervasive symbols of the Pearl of Price (*pretiosa margarita*, Matthew 13:45–6) and of the redeemed soul, or soul in the state of sanctifying grace, as the bride of Christ. Important use is made of Psalms and Pauline Epistles, with special attention to the Parable of the Workers in the Vineyard (Matthew 20:1–16) and to the vision of the New Jerusalem and the procession of the Lamb, in what M. R. James calls the best of all paraphrases of the Apocalypse (Apocalypse 14, 21, 22).

The citation of certain Biblical texts in association with others may be reminiscent of liturgical services in which the same texts were associated, and the poet specifically designates some of his key passages from the Bible as belonging to the services of the Mass (*Pearl* 497, *Patience* 9, *Purity* 51). The texts cited in the discourse on Grace and pedobaptism in *Pearl* are in several instances the same as those used by St. Augustine in support of the same arguments. The poet must have been familiar with Augustine's anti-Pelagian writings at least. One who studies the Scriptural and theological content of *Pearl* in relation to the treatment of the same themes by the Fathers and Doctors of the Church will agree with Henry L. Savage that the poet was acquainted with "a considerable body of patristic writing on theology and symbolism."

Yet the learned poet does not parade his learning. Apart from Biblical authors, only two writers are named in any of the four poems. One is Aristotle, referred to in *Pearl*, line 751, in what must surely be an allusion to his treatise *On the Soul*, the source of St. Thomas Aquinas's conception of the soul as the form of the body. The other non-Biblical writer is Jean de Meun, mentioned in *Purity* as an author of the *Roman de la Rose* (see [4] below). The direct influence of the *Roman* on *Pearl* also is altogether likely, though it is probably less extensive than was once assumed by scholars who, overlooking some of the features shared by *Pearl* with other religious visions, assigned those parallels to the *Roman*.

There is no valid evidence that our poet knew the work of any of the Italians whose poetry enriched Chaucer's. Resemblances of *Pearl* to Dante's *Commedia*, and especially to scenes laid in the Terrestrial Paradise, have been noted by various critics, but such resemblances are perhaps not remarkable in the work of poets impelled by similar motives, reflecting the same medieval modes of thought and feeling, and drawing upon a common tradition. No direct connection is now thought to have existed between *Pearl* and Boccaccio's brief Latin eclogue, *Olympia*, written in memory of a daughter who died in her sixth year, though the two poems exhibit certain similarities. For students of *Pearl* the disclosure of Boccaccio's poem at least weakened the argument that an elegy on the death of a child would have been without precedent in the fourteenth century.

Somewhat the same contribution to our understanding of *Pearl*, and of *Purity*, is afforded by Thomas Usk's prose *Testament of Love*, which has no known direct connection with these poems, but which in its elaborate Margarite-pearl allegory indicates that the *pretiosa margarita* symbolism of the Vulgate was alive in other vernacular writings of the period. It appears also in Gower's *Mirour de l'omme* (16837–48) and is expounded in more than one passage of *Le livre du Chevalier de la Tour Landry*, which must have circulated in England by the latter 1370's, at least, and rapidly became popular there. Here again no direct connection need be assumed between the *Pearl* poet and the Chevalier's use of the pearl in his advice to his daughters, in spite of Sir Israel Gollancz's contention that the English poet was the debtor. As has been demonstrated recently by C. A. Luttrell, such parallels attest rather to the dissemination of Scriptural pearl-symbolism by descent from patristic commentaries and homilies, through the media of the Roman liturgy, Latin manuals of religious instruction, and eulogistic saints' legends, to vernacular sermons and writings for a wider audience.

PATIENCE [3]. The homiletic poems *Patience* and *Purity* are in unrimed alliterative long lines, which are thought to have been grouped originally in four-line stanzas. The handling of the verse in each poem is that of a master at ease in his craft. Certain individual mannerisms of style are found in both poems, as also in *Sir Gawain and the Green Knight*, but not in *Pearl*. The two homilies follow the same orderly plan: (1) statement of theme, (2) announcement of the text from the New Testament, (3) discussion of another passage from the New Testament in elucidation of that text, (4) elaborate paraphrase of an *exemplum*, or of *exempla*, from the Old Testament. The poet in each homily usually adheres to his Scriptural sources with scrupulous fidelity, but reveals his familiarity with them by the freedom and independence with which he sometimes transforms them in homely adaptations, and all but disguises them by renderings in the racy idiom of the vernacular. Both homilies display the poet's vigor and originality in story-telling and his descriptive power, notably in graphic scenes boldly realistic in details and in scenes depicting wild and awesome aspects of nature.

Patience, in 531 lines, begins with a commendation of that virtue and proceeds to an account of the Beatitudes (Matthew 5:3–10). The homilist's text is the eighth Beatitude, *Beati qui persecutionem patiuntur propter iustitiam*, which he renders "Blessed are they who are able to steer their hearts." This text he relates to the first of the *happes*, "Blessed are the poor in spirit"; for Dame Patience and Dame Poverty are of one kind, teammates by necessity. As one "brought to a condition called Poverty," the narrator will provide himself with Patience, and play with both ladies, thus making the best of his lot. Willingly he will bow to the bidding of his Liege-lord and run or ride on his missions, lest he fare worse, as did Jonah of Judea.

The body of the sermon is a lively paraphrase of the book of *Jonah*, cited as an example of the folly of impatience: the refusal to "suffer for righteousness' sake" and rebellion against divine commands. Jonah, the reluctant missionary, that "witless wretch," would not suffer and thereby "placed himself in a plight of far greater peril." By contrast we have the patience and courtesy of God in dealing with the repentant Ninevites. The story is told with graphic elaboration of the storm at sea, Jonah's journey in the whale, his brief repentance, and his anger against God for sparing the Ninevites after dispatching him on the perilous mission to proclaim their doom and thereby causing him to lose face. The homily is rounded off by a statement of the moral and application to the narrator's own case.

Patience, the slightest of the four poems, is a gem in its kind. It is well-proportioned and skilfully executed, as though the poet, relishing his theme, composed in high spirits. With creative imagination and psychological insight he depicts Jonah as seeking by rationalizing excuses to justify himself for his flight from the face and commands of God. The circumstantial retelling of the adventure with the whale reveals the poet's appreciation of its comic as well as its terrifying aspects, and his own gentleness is reflected in his attribution to God of a special concern for innocent babes, "witless women," and dumb beasts, when he decides to spare "such a sweet place" as Nineveh. A first-hand knowledge of sea-faring seems to have gone into the report of Jonah's brief voyage by ship, and the account of the storm is fresh and compelling.

The Vulgate Bible is the only manifest source of *Patience*. Resemblances to *Piers Plowman* and to Tertullian's homily *De patientia* probably are too general to indicate indebtedness. The influence of Tertullian's poem *De Jona et de Ninive* also has been urged, denied, and quite recently defended anew. A striking parallel between *Patience* 319 and the *Wars of Alexander* (Alexander C) 1154 can hardly be accidental, but the slender evidence for dating either poem is insufficient for determining which is the debtor. (See Bibliography, under *Sources and Literary Relations* in [1] below, on the *Wars* and the *Pearl* poet). If, as seems likely, the *Siege of Jerusalem*, which was written about the year 1390, was influenced by *Patience*, that approximate date would be the downward limit for the homily.

PURITY (CLANNESSE, CLEANNESS) [4]. (See [3] above, introduction to *Patience* and *Purity*.)

Purity, in its 1812 alliterative long lines, follows on a grand scale the same homiletic pattern as *Patience*: (1) statement of theme, (2) text from the New Testament, (3) elucidation of text by reference to another New Testament passage, (4) paraphrases of Old Testament narratives as exempla.

The theme is the supreme value of purity in the eyes of God, who searches the heart and abominates all manner of defilement in his followers, as when sinful priests receive or administer the sacrament of his own Body. The text is the sixth Beatitude, *Beati mundo corde quoniam ipsi Deum videbunt* (Matthew 5:8), rendered: "Happy is the man who is clean in his heart, for he shall look joyfully on our Lord." Beware, then, says the homilist, of rushing to heaven with unwashed hands, in ragged clothes and a beggar's hood. Such a guest would be "hurled to the hall door" and "shoved without" if he visited an earthly prince, and "the high King would be more severe."

Thus the poet leads up to his paraphrase of the parable of the Guest without a Wedding Garment (Matthew 22:1–14; Luke 14:16–24) in illustration of his text. With homely elaboration he pictures the Marriage Feast in a great medieval hall, with a marshal in charge and a genial host who, nevertheless, is imperious in his rejection of the thrall "in foul weeds" who dishonors the feast by his presence. All who were ever baptized are invited to the heavenly banquet, the homilist explains; but before appearing there, let everyone take care that his clothes are clean and honest for the holiday, for clean garments betoken good works. Whoever would see God must be "clean as the polished beryl, . . . without spot or blemish as the margery-pearl."

The poet teaches by contraries. As the case of Jonah, the impatient man who was unable to steer his heart, illustrates by contrast the value of that equanimity which results from settled loyalty to a noble cause, so also in *Purity* the text of the sermon is elucidated by the stories of the Flood, the destruction of Sodom and Gomorrah, and Belshazzar's feast, as examples of those whose impurity has provoked divine vengeance. These exempla are prefaced by brief accounts of the falls of Lucifer and Adam to enforce the point that even their disloyalty did not arouse the wrath of the Creator as did "the filth of the flesh," the sins against nature, which led first to the near annihilation of mankind in the Deluge and later to the wholesale destruction of the Sodomites and the dwellers in three neighboring cities. It is clear from the text that the poet follows the traditional commentators on Genesis 6:1–8 in imputing unnatural sins to the descendants of Adam and linking their vice to the union between "the daughters of men" and "fiends" (*filii Dei*), which (according to the same tradition) produced the race of giants and contributed to the moral turpitude leading to the Flood.

The "filth of the flesh" cited by the homilist is, then, not merely unchastity, nor is the purity he recommends confined to chaste living; it is freedom from defilement. The soiled garments of the presumptuous wedding guest are not said to symbolize any one type of sin, and the poet's last example of impurity is the desecration by Belshazzar (Baltasar) of the holy vessels from Solomon's Temple, which had been seized among the spoils in the wake of the capture of Jerusalem by Nebuchadnezzar (Nabugodenozar), but had not been put to sacrilegious use until Belshazzar added them to the ornaments and drinking vessels for his vainglorious feast.

The homilist expressly enlarges his definition of uncleanness to comprise the defilement of anything, be it a human soul, a cup, or a basin, which has been consecrated to God. It would have been strange, therefore, if "the Lord of the heavens" had not been angered to see vessels which had been "blessed by bishops' hands" for his sacrifices now being used by that "boaster on bench" to serve wine to his concubines; or to see the great candelabrum which had stood before the *sanctum sanctorum*, where he had spoken to his chosen prophets, adorning a festivity where thanks were offered to gods of silver and gold. For such "frothing filth," Daniel tells Belshazzar, he has incurred the terrible judgment announced by the handwriting on the wall. He had witnessed the blasphemous pride of his father, Nebuchadnezzar, his degradation as a brute, his repentance and reconciliation to God; and yet, as Daniel reminds Belshazzar, he has not profited, as Nebuchadnezzar did, by those warning signs, but has ever "lifted up his heart against the Most High," who now proclaims the collapse of his kingdom and his glory.

Purity in its epic scope is marred by a certain unwieldiness and disproportion. For modern tastes the narrative preambles to the main stories are rather long and full of detail. Yet the design of the whole is clear and carefully worked out, with skilful transitions and frequent, but varied, reminders of the central theme. In the exhortations to pure living which precede each of the examples of impurity, the doctrine of the Beatific Vision is mentioned again and again, and the imagery of the Marriage Feast and "the bright weeds" required of its guests is a recurrent *motif.* God's kingdom, as in *Pearl*, is envisioned as a royal court; and courtesy, which presupposes purity, is the ideal of conduct exemplified by Christ and his followers.

Purity in its imaginative vigor and passionate earnestness has undeniable power, and its prevailing austerity is relieved by lyrical passages of tenderness and beauty: the description of Mary's great joy in the birth of her Son, which was shared by an orchestra of angels; the passages exalting the purity of Christ and Mary; and the exposition of the pearl as a type of the pure soul, and again as a symbol of the soul cleansed and polished in the sacrament of Penance, as a pearl is cleansed and brightened in wine. The description of the various stages in the progress of the Deluge and the frantic efforts of its victims to escape from the mounting waters is an example of the poet's ability to take an action which is merely outlined in his source and so visualize and recreate it in its essential details as to make it come vividly alive. His presentation of the insolent splendor of Belshazzar's feast is brilliant in its pictorial detail and its irony; and the swiftly moving narrative of Sodom and Gomorrah, pursued by the "hounds of heaven" and swallowed up by the abyss, is hardly surpassed in English for terror and grandeur.

The poet's familiarity with the Bible, the ultimate source of four-fifths of *Purity*, is indicated by the freedom with which he on occasion chooses from it only what serves his purpose, and the skill with which he harmonizes matter from different accounts of the same incidents as, for instance, his blending of information from Chronicles, Jeremiah, and Daniel for his treatment of Nebuchadnezzar and Belshazzar. (See [3] above for his handling of Scripture.) It is of some interest that *Purity*, alone among the Cotton-Nero poems, draws upon religious apocrypha in presenting, for example, the Ark's carrion-eating crow, the disobedience of Lot's wife in serving salt to guests, the adoration of the ox and ass at the Nativity, and Christ's miraculous skill in breaking bread.

Only *Purity* among the three poems offers clear internal evidence of dependence on known secular writings. In support of his precept that a follower of Christ must conform to his nature in order to please him, the author cites Jean de Meun (Clopinel) in the *Roman de la Rose*, where he advises a lover to observe and conform to his lady's tastes in order to win her favor (*Purity* 1057). The description of the Dead Sea (*Purity* 1022–48) is derived from the early French version of *Mandeville's Travels*, as are details in the description of Belshazzar's table adornments (lines 1464 ff.). The French version of the *Travels* having circulated in England probably as early as 1360, that year might be taken as the upward limit in dating *Purity*. However, if, as has been argued, the poem was influenced also by *Le livre du Chevalier de la Tour Landry*, which was completed by the year 1373, the earliest date for *Purity* would of course be after that time; but it has recently been demonstrated by Luttrell that the parallels cited in support of indebtedness are either non-existent or commonplace, and hence must be dismissed in reckoning the dates for *Purity*. Its indebtedness to *Cursor Mundi* has also been suggested, and parallels to the *Wars of Alexander* in *Purity*, as in the companion pieces, indicate a close connection, the precise implications of which have not been determined. (See Bibliography, under *Sources and Literary Relations* in [1] below, on the *Wars* in relation to the *Pearl* poet.)

III. WYCLYF AND HIS FOLLOWERS

by

Ernest W. Talbert and S. Harrison Thomson

John Wyclyf (Wyclif, Wycliffe) [1] was born in Hipswell near Richmond in 1320 or soon thereafter, probably the eldest son of the lord of the manor of Wyclyf. He early went to Oxford, and matriculated at Balliol College, then patronized by north-country and Scots students. He certainly heard the lectures of Bradwardine and FitzRalph, as his works show beyond any doubt. He may have been, for a brief period, a Fellow of Merton College, but he certainly was Master of Balliol for a year or more, resigning in March 1361 to accept the living of Fillingham, Lincolnshire, in the gift of the college. For a few years, between 1363 and 1366, and at two later periods, he rented rooms at Queen's College. By 1360 he appears to have gained some academic repute as a lecturer on logic and philosophy, and his earliest treatises must date from this period. In 1362 the Pope provided him with the prebend of Aust, near Bristol, which he retained to his death without residence— a usual practice for an academic person. In 1365 he was appointed by Archbishop Islip as Warden of Canterbury Hall. The appointment was protested, on the ground that, as Wyclyf was a secular, he could not properly be put over a monastic chapter. Another cleric was then named to the post. Wyclyf made a formal appeal to the Pope, but his case was weak and the judgment went against him. In later life he expressed no resentment at the adverse decision. By about 1370 he must have finished his great philosophical *summa*. He took his B. D. some time before May 1370 and his D. D. in 1372. In 1368 he had exchanged the living of Fillingham for the cure of Ludgershall, which was nearer Oxford, and in 1371 he received from the Pope a canonry in Lincoln.

By 1372 he was recognized as one of the leading scholars of the University, and in his lectures he must have expressed nationalistic opinions. In April 1374 he was given, by royal act, the rectory of Lutterworth, which he kept to the end of his life. In July of the same year the king chose him to be a member of a royal commission which would discuss and negotiate with papal envoys on matters in dispute between England and the Curia. The negotiations, held in Bruges, were quite fruitless. The papal negotiators, we are to understand, were so cynically grasping as to disgust Wyclyf. In any event, on his return to England in the autumn of 1374, he began writing his *De dominio divino*, which was the opening blow in his attack upon the Roman control of the English Church. It is to be doubted that he knew at this time where the logic of his position, that God was the "lord" of all, and that dominion over any worldly thing was of grace alone, would lead him. There followed, in the next seven years, eleven more militant books, making together his theological *summa*. The separate works in this *summa* can almost be dated by a measurement of their growing bitterness against the Papacy. In the last volumes he concludes that the Papacy is quite unnecessary and the Pope might even be the Antichrist, while the English Church should be under the control of the King.

Before he reached his final positions, however, he suffered increasingly sharp attacks on his orthodoxy. In February 1377 he was summoned before Courtenay, Bishop of London, to be questioned on his views concerning church property. In the brawl that broke out between John of Gaunt, who wished to defend Wyclyf, and Bishop Courtenay, Wyclyf went unquestioned. Courtenay sent reports of Wyclyf's pronouncements to Rome and in May 1377 Pope Gregory XI issued five bulls against Wyclyf's erroneous teaching, specifying eighteen errors from his works. Meantime Edward III died (June 21, 1377) and Gregory's bulls were not published until December. Summoned to appear at St. Paul's, Wyclyf did not obey until March, when he appeared before the bishops at Lambeth Palace. This hearing was inconclusive. In the summer of 1378 Wyclyf defended before Parliament the royal cause against the Church in the case of a violation of sanctuary. This was probably his last participation in national politics. The outbreak of the Great Schism turned his thoughts to the theoretical bases of the Church. In the *De ecclesia* (written 1378–79) he attacked the Petrine supremacy, pronounced for

the *convencio predestinatorum*, and asserted that the Pope was not necessarily the head of the Church. His realist philosophy led him further
to question the doctrine of transubstantiation probably as early as 1379.
This error made the opposition more determined to shut him up, and he
was haled before a sort of court, set up by Berton, the Chancellor of Oxford, and threatened with excommunication if he taught the remanence
of the bread and wine, or denied the real presence. He replied with a
spirited defense of his views. On May 17, 1382, a synod at Blackfriars,
London, condemned ten conclusions from his works as heretical and
fourteen more as erroneous. An earthquake adjourned the synod. In the
summer of this year, perhaps after a slight stroke, he retired to Lutterworth. His production in the last two years of his life (d. December 31,
1384) was prodigious, and though his influence may have waned at
Oxford under the pressure exerted by the hierarchy against his followers,
he still had many loyal adherents among the academicians and the common people.

His voluminous Latin writings are his greatest work, and make an
imposing corpus covering philosophy in all its branches from logic to
metaphysics, political thought, to a degree Erastian, in any case royal
and nationalistic, theology both dogmatic and pastoral, homiletics and
exegesis. His English works, [2], [6]ff., important as they may be for
linguistic and literary reasons, are largely derivative, to such a degree
that we must often use the authenticated Latin work to prove genuine-
ness of attribution of a given English tract or sermon.

The assignment to him of the translation of the Bible is now restricted
to the idea of such an enterprise and the first translation of the New
Testament, begun probably in 1382 and left unfinished at his death (see
IV [52] below) [3]. Wyclyf's high repute as a scholar, his aggressive approach to the problems of church and state that then disturbed almost
every thinking Englishman, attracted to him a great following, particularly among the idealistic youth of Oxford, and it was from this group
that there grew up the "pore preachers" who were soon identified as
Lollards and carried the master's teachings to the highways and byways
of England. To them must also be assigned, in all probability, a large
proportion of the anonymous vernacular sermons, tracts, and pamphlets
which have at one time or another been ascribed to Wyclyf or called

simply Wyclyfite. In some cases it is easy to show that they are obviously translations or close abridgements of some authentic Latin work of Wyclyf. The content is indisputably his. A few of these followers were men of great ability. Among them were Philip Repingdon, who recanted in 1382, Nicholas of Hereford, the leading collaborator in the first translation of the Bible, who recanted in 1390, and John Purvey, who worked with Hereford on the first translation and continued on the revision in 1387–88. He recanted in 1401. Of the less academic followers there was William of Swinderby, "the Hermit," who, after recanting in 1382, was again tried (in 1391), found guilty of heresy, and excommunicated. All these and some lesser characters wrote tracts for the times in the Wyclyfian manner, and some of the anonymous works mentioned above may well be by one or other of these like-minded followers [4].

The consistent efforts by the hierarchy to stamp out the heresy of Wyclyf and his Lollard followers met ultimate success. In 1401 Henry IV was persuaded—not unwillingly—to issue an edict *De heretico comburendo* which effectively discouraged further dissemination of these obnoxious teachings. What Lollardy survived was driven underground or into such obscure corners of the country as the Chiltern Hills.

The English works ascribed to Wyclyf and his followers are mentioned in this chapter under the heads: 1. Works Generally Ascribed to Wyclyf; 2. Works Ascribed to Purvey; 3. Other Wyclyfite Writings; 4. Accounts of Lollard Trials and Related Writings.

Although a careful examination of the manuscripts, particularly of those giving the Sermons ([7] below), is necessary before Wyclyf's authorship of any English work can be established, yet Wyclyf's impact upon his contemporaries and upon the immediately succeeding generations undoubtedly will preserve his stature. In addition to the translations of the Bible and their glosses (IV [52]) and in addition to the writings listed below, the Lollards seem to have edited and augmented Rolle's *Psalter* and *Canticles* (see under Rolle and His Followers), Clement of Llanthony's *Harmony* (IV [37] and [51] below), the English translation of the Anglo-Norman Apocalypse (IV [49]), as well as Thoresby's *Catechism* (see under Works of Religious Instruction and [12], [64] below) and the English *Elucidarium* (see under Dialogues, Debates, and Catechisms). Their hands have been seen in versions of *The Pore Caitif* (see under Works of Religious Instruction; also *Poem against the Friars* under Works Dealing with Contemporary Conditions); and there is a Lollard *Chronicle of the Papacy* (see under Chronicles). In the fifteenth century, one writer apparently would circulate Lollard doctrine by making the Sunday Gospel sermons covnentionally ascribed to Wyclyf an integral part of a cycle otherwise orthodox except for two short passages (see the *Sidney Sussex Cambridge 74 Sermons* under Homilies). Other English works have been given to Wyclyf and his followers (see e.g., Dan Jon Gaytryge's *Sermon* and the *Pater Noster* under Works of Religious Instruction; see *Of Three Arrows on Doomsday* under Rolle and His Followers; and see [11], [12], [67] below), as have some sermons and tracts as yet undiscussed and apparently unedited [6]. As a result, a Lollard campaign to promulgate Wyclyfite doctrine in English is referred to frequently, although earlier writers have sometimes considered comment and criticism that was essentially orthodox to be Wyclyfite.

Of Wyclyf's followers John Purvey, Wyclyf's "secretary," and Nicholas of Hereford have received most attention (see IV [52] and below, Part 2, as well as [19], [22], [36], [37], [90], [98]). In addition, however, Philip Repington (or Repton) was a particularly stalwart Oxford follower, and others were noted as leaders of the first "academic" group: John Aston (see [66], [97] below), Lawrence Bedeman (or Bedmond), Thomas Brightwell, Robert Rigg, Richard Fleming, William James, Thomas Hilman (or Hulman), John Ashwardby of Oriel, and Robert Alington. Like Hereford, but unlike Purvey and Bedeman, most of this group rose in the Church after recanting or otherwise establishing their orthodoxy. Later prominent Oxford Lollards were Richard Lychlade (or Lechlade); Peter Pattishull, the Augustinian (see [49] below); David Gotray of Pakring (Pickering); Ralph Mungyn; and Peter Clark or Payne, or Peter the Clerk (see [55] below), who after 1415 was prominent at Prague. Associated with at least some of the early Oxford group were men of the Leicester "conventicle"; the hermit Swinderby (see [99] below), Stephen Bell, Walter Brute (see [92], [100] below), Richard Waytestathe, and William Smith, a "parchemyner." Much of the information about the activity and the intent of such individuals and of later Lollards must be gleaned from, e.g., Wilkins's *Concilia* and Foxe's *Acts and Monuments*; from the attacks by Thomas Gascoigne, Thomas Netter of

Walden, and Reginald Pecock; from episcopal registers; and even from Nicholas Love's references to Lollard errors (see his *Myrrour of the Blessed Lyf* under Works of Religious Instruction). In this respect, the Croxton *Sacrament* may also be pertinent (see under Dramatic Pieces). Characteristic emphases in fifteenth-century Lollardy can be found in the examination of the poor priest William Thorpe (see [101] below; and [93], [94]); but except for Murdock Nisbet's translation of Purvey's New Testament (1513–22), apparently no writings have survived from the considerable Lollardy in Scotland during the fifteenth century.

With the exception of the Pseudo-Augustine Translations, the Four Cambridge Tracts, and the Tenison Tracts ([65–76] below), Lollard writings are listed separately in a conventional manner. It is unlikely, however, that questions of authorship can be settled until the composition of the Lollard manuscripts has been examined carefully and the texts collated thoroughly. The outstanding Lollard compilations seem to be MSS Corpus Christi College Cambridge 296 (C.6), Trinity College Dublin 244 (C.iii.12), and Trinity College Dublin 245 (C.v.6).

Although they probably had little or nothing to do with the composition of the treatises considered here, one should also note the "political" Lollards gathered about Oldcastle, whose condemnation, revolt, and execution (1413–17) brought about a systematic attack on humbler Lollards as well as upon his immediate followers ([102] below). Proceedings after the condemnation of Pecock's anti-Lollard apologetic in 1457 also caused "Lollards" to recant their errors ([103] below). In the next century the trials of the Wyclyfites would gain fame in England especially through Foxe's *Acts and Monuments*.

1. WORKS GENERALLY ASCRIBED TO WYCLYF

by

Ernest W. Talbert

Writings generally ascribed to Wyclyf fall into four groups: I, Sermons; II, Didactic Works; III, Statements of Belief, etc; IV, Controversial Works.

I. Sermons

THE SERMONS [7]. 1375—ca. 1412; 788 pages; in five groups: (1) 54 sermons on Sunday Gospels, (2) 31 on Gospels for the Commune sanctorum, (3) 38 on Gospels for an irregular Proprium sanctorum, (4) 116 on Ferial Gospels, (5) 55 on Sunday Epistles. Only nine manuscripts give all five groups, which, with the exception of the Proprium sanctorum, show only slight variations from Sarum use. An appreciable part of each sermon gives the Biblical text in English but agrees with none of the Wyclyfite Bible versions so far encountered (IV [52]). The Biblical text is usually handled in a manner which precludes any sharp division between the translation and the postilling, and the importance of this literal sense of the Bible is emphasized constantly—a feature which leads to attacks on Wyclyf's opponents and upon abuses in the Church.

The sermons, consequently, reflect Wyclyf's point of view constantly. Although frequently, as with the contemplative life, the Wyclyfite attitude may agree with that held by many of Wyclyf's contemporaries, yet his attack on pseudo-contemplatives is expressed much more insistently and directly. Assaults are made on the value and selling of pardons, on the value of pilgrimages and dispensations, on the granting and issue of indulgences, on endowments of the clergy, and on the Church's holding

of property. The same is true for the "new" consistory law by which
the law of Christ is supplanted, the Pope's right to legislate for the
Church, Papal infallibility, and the Church's use of the temporal sword.
Also attacked are auricular confession, the methods of canonization, the
Church's right of absolution, and the Church's and the friars' false doctrine of the Eucharist. Constant are comments and applications attacking the Pope as Antichrist and the friars as children of Cain. They not
only speak heresy; they also silence faithful priests.

The schism and the crusade of le Spencer also are utilized to attack
the Papacy; and by such reflections of contemporary events portions of
the sermons throughout MS Bodleian 2628 (Bodley 788) have been dated
from 1377 to 1412, with most of the references indicating 1382–83. The
suggestion that even the Sunday Gospel group (in seventeen MSS) represents the Lollards' version of Wyclyf's notes may be substantiated
thereby (see also [49] below). A possible chronology of the sermons is
not discordant, but emphasizes 1375–84. At any rate, one may err in
using the sermons in MS Bodleian 2628 as a touchstone to determine
Wyclyf's authorship of other English writings.

In accordance with their emphasis on the literal sense of the Bible,
the sermons exemplify Wyclyf's contribution to medieval literary criticism. His concepts in this respect are derived, probably, from Augustine;
and the sermons clearly show Wyclyf's rejection of the ideal of ornate-
ness, his demand for simplicity (*plana locucio*), his abhorrence of *titil-
lans delectacio*.

The relation between the Biblical passages as the literal sense of the
sermons and the Wyclyfite Bible versions (IV [52]) may be closer than
has been realized, when all manuscripts of the latter and of the related
glosses have been examined. The Bible versions roughly correspond to
the normal medieval pattern of translation (a commentator and sometimes a second translator working with a crude, ungrammatical rendering); and since both sermons and translations were part of a planned
endeavor, at some point in the process there may have been an appreciable overlapping.

WYCKLYFFE'S WYCKET [8]. Extant in no manuscript. It presents
Wyclyf's doctrine of the Eucharist, and its attack upon rival theories may

explain its popularity with the "known men" and "Christian Brothers" contemporary with Tindale.

VAE OCTUPLEX [9] and OF MINISTERS IN THE CHURCH [10]. Ten to eleven pages; twenty-seven pages; found in a majority of the manuscripts having the complete cycle of the Sermons. *Vae Octuplex* divides Matthew 23:13–33 into its eight woes and applies them to friars and prelates. *Of Ministers in the Church* is an exposition of Matthew 24. The text was chosen because it was "not al red" in the service; thus much of its wisdom had been hidden. In it a detailed but characteristic application is made to current conditions in the Church.

An additional set of fifty-four sermons [11] and five others on great festivals have been ascribed incorrectly to Wyclyf.

II. Didactic Works

THE TEN COMMANDMENTS [12]. Ten pages. It is related to existing non-Wyclyfite tracts on the same subject (see also [13], [16–18], [20], [22] below); and it apparently exists in at least three major versions: that attributed to Wyclyf, those that have been expanded, and those that have been condensed. The version attributed to Wyclyf states that selling "leve to synne" and not preaching breaks the fifth commandment; that dominion rests on grace (the seventh); that God's law, not the emperor's or the Pope's, should be read and followed (the tenth). When it was edited, its author's possible use of a longer non-Wyclyfite version was noted (e.g., MS Bodleian 1049)—a suggestion reinforced when MS Bibliothèque Ste. Geneviève Paris 3390 was described. The passages in the Kraus Codex which were thought to indicate that it contained Wyclyf's "true" work, subsequently condensed, are found in MS Trinity College Dublin 245 (a manuscript with a non-Wyclyfite "tone"). MS M. 861, Pierpont Morgan Library, which is related to Thoresby's *Catechism* (see under Works of Religious Instruction) and uses Biblical citations found elsewhere in such discussions, is not as close to the version attributed to Wyclyf as is that in MS Rylands English 85, in which the Exodus translations show a verbatim correspondence with the Late Version of the Wyclyfite Bible.

EXPOSITION OF THE PATER NOSTER (BODLEY) [13] and (HARLEY) [14]. Four pages; twelve pages. Both are ascribed to Wyclyf primarily because of their inclusion in Wyclyfite compilations and because the shorter Bodley version also occurs in a MS giving Wyclyf's name (Harley 2385). (See [12] above, [15] below.) The longer Harley version attempts a rather original scheme (omitting the Gifts of the Holy Ghost and doubling the Virtues), contains characteristic Wyclyfite diatribes, and attacks those who "pursuwe" preachers of the Gospel. It may be revealing that the latter passage occurs at the end of the tract. (See also [57] below.)

THE AVE MARIA [15]. Two pages. It is found in manuscripts with the Bodley Pater Noster and criticizes indulgences that make a pope Antichrist. It is ascribed to Wyclyf in MS Harley 2385. (See also [58] below.)

EXPOSITION OF THE APOSTLES CREED [16]. Two to three pages. MS Bibliothèque Ste. Geneviève Paris 3390 may be this Wyclyfite commentary altered by a Wyclyfite commentator.

EXPOSITIONS OF THE FIVE OUTER WITS [17] and THE FIVE INNER WITS [18]. A half page each. See [12] above.

A COMMENT ON THE SEVEN DEADLY SINS [19]. Forty-eight pages. A reworking of a tract identical with, or very similar to, that in MS Royal 17.A.xxvi, this treatise has been connected stylistically and doctrinally with Wyclyf, but stylistically and dialectically with Hereford also (see [36] below).

TREATISES ON THE SEVEN WORKS OF MERCY BODILY and THE SEVEN WORKS OF MERCY GHOSTLY [20]. Ca. 1382; fourteen pages. These works refer, i. a., to the Earthquake Council (Courtenay's London Synod, May 19, 1382). Stylistic evidence "strongly" indicates Wyclyf's authorship. (See also [12] above.)

FIVE QUESTIONS ON LOVE [21]. Two pages. It may be Wyclyf's

own "halting" translation of a short Latin tract of his. It notes, i. a., the necessity for all to study the Bible in the tongue clearest to them.

OF FAITH, HOPE, AND CHARITY [22]. Eight pages. It is essentially evangelical, even though the Friars' Eucharistic teaching is attacked. The fourth chapter utilizes Antinomian opinions. The corresponding tract in MS Bibliothèque Ste. Geneviève Paris 3390 may be the original or a Wyclyfite adaptation of this Wyclyfite commentary. It is ascribed usually to Wyclyf, even though it is one of four tracts associated by alliteration with Hereford (see [36] below and also [12] above.)

CONFESSION AND PENITENCE [23]. Nineteen pages. It cites abuses of confession, admits silent confession, but urges public confession and the study and teaching of God's law, which is superior to Peter's keys. Predestinarian doctrines are accepted in passing, and transubstantiation is attacked at the end. (See Wyclyf's *De Eucharista et poenitentia.*)

ON THE SUFFICIENCY OF HOLY SCRIPTURES [24]. A "flyleaf." It defends the supremacy of the Bible against Antichrist's clerks.

THE HOLI PROPHET DAVID SAITH [25]. 1378–84; ten pages. It emphasizes Bible study and a poor and holy life. It is ascribed to Wyclyf because of its style and an outlook similar to that in the *De veritate Sacrae Scripturae.*

OF WEDDID MEN AND WIFIS AND OF HERE CHILDREN ALSO [26]. Twelve to thirteen pages. It states, i.a., that marriage of priests is allowed by God and that wives' wasting money on begging friars is one of three great failings in marriage. In general, it is quite conventional (see [67–76] below).

DE STIPENDIIS MINISTRORUM [27]. One and a half pages. It discusses what laymen should look for in finding priests, e.g., knowledge and preaching of Scriptures and not incensing and intoning.

A SHORT RULE OF LIFE [28]. Three pages. It is quite conventional except that it warns lords not to support Antichrist's disciples in their errors, whereby true men who teach the Gospels are slandered and "pursued."

III. Statements of Belief, A Letter, A Petition

STATEMENT OF BELIEF CONCERNING THE EUCHARIST (KNIGHTON) [29] and (BODLEY) [30]. A half page; two pages. The short account in Knighton's Chronicle is orthodox, perhaps an abstract of Wyclyf's Latin confession made in May, 1381. The Bodley statement refers to the sacrament as God's body, not bread ("for hit is bothe togedir"), and calls upon the King and the realm to punish all of the clergy who believe it to be an accident without subject. The relationship, here and elsewhere, to Berengar's thought has been noted. The immediate occasion has been interpreted diversely.

A LETTER TO POPE URBAN [31]. Two pages. It argues that since the Gospel is God's law, the Pope should be supreme in following it; if he does not, he is not to be followed. It seems to have been derived, but heightened and enlarged, from Wyclyf's Latin letter dated variously from before 1379 to 1384.

A PETITION TO KING AND PARLIAMENT [32]. Usually dated May 1382; fourteen pages. It makes four points: members of religious orders can leave their rule and join Christ's; secular power can take temporalities from the Church; tithes and offerings depend on merit; teaching the Wyclyfite doctrine of the Eucharist is legitimate. Comparison with the Latin version shows it to be complete and a common source probable.

IV. Controversial Works

SIMONISTS AND APOSTATES [33]. One and a half pages. It condemns simony from Pope to priest and is perhaps an early tract.

CHURCH TEMPORALITIES [34]. Ca. 1377–78; four and a half pages. The tract argues that the secular power should control worldly monks and priests by depriving them of temporal holdings, but friars are not attacked.

DE PRECATIONIBUS SACRIS [35]. Perhaps before 1379; nine to ten pages. It declares the efficacy of prayers by righteous priests, the inefficacy of those by evil priests, and attacks intoning.

LINCOLNIENSIS [36]. Two pages. The tract calls upon knights especially to release poor priests imprisoned by friars who have been shamed because of the priests' pure lives, their preaching, and their sounder faith about the Eucharist. This tract is one of four sometimes assigned to Hereford because of alliteration ([19], [22] above; [37] below), a few "unusual words," a Western dialect ([19] and [37] only), and a knowledge of the gentry. (See also [90] below.) It was issued perhaps with *Vita sacerdotum* ([37] below) after Blackfriars Synod (1382) to reaffirm six of the fourteen conclusions condemned as erroneous.

VITA SACERDOTUM [37]. Eight pages. It reaffirms aspects of Wyclyf's doctrine of dominion: the clergy's possession of temporalities violates Christ's law; to remedy that sin, lords and great men have a God-given power to deprive the Church gradually. It is sometimes ascribed to Hereford (see [36] above).

DE PONTIFICUM ROMANORUM SCHISMATE [38]. Twenty-four pages. Its author utilizes the Schism to attack the temporal aims and means of the Church, and especially plenary indulgences.

THE GRETE SENTENCE OF CURS EXPOUNDED [39]. Sixty-six pages. It specifies the counts upon which the clergy, and especially the Pope, are subject to anathema. Because of its "exasperation," Wyclyf's authorship has been questioned. Purvey has been suggested because of similarities to the *Fifty Heresies* ([49] below). It refers to le Spencer's crusade as current (1383) but also to earlier current events.

THE CHURCH AND HER MEMBERS [40]. Twenty-six pages. It attacks, i.a., the Pope as Antichrist, and has been admired for its lucidity and precision in attacking religious orders along lines which later generations did little more than follow.

DE BLASPHEMIA, CONTRA FRATRES [41]. Twenty-seven pages. Its author utilizes scholasic logic effectively while attacking the friars' doctrine of the Eucharist, their begging, and their letters of fraternity. It refers incidentally to the right way to answer inquisitorial questions.

DE APOSTASIA CLERI [42]. Eleven pages. It attacks religious orders and Church endowments but lacks the precision of the immediately preceding tracts.

SEVEN HERESIES [43]. Five pages. It points out how the friars and the clergy at Rome sin against the seven petitions of the Lord's prayer.

OCTO IN QUIBIS SEDUCUNTUR SIMPLICES CHRISTIANI [44]. Six pages. It repeats the attacks noted above but is presented as if it were a didactic tract.

DE DOMINIO DIVINO [45]. Ten pages. It argues that dominion (whether possession or jurisdiction) belongs to lay rulers, who may not alienate it without God's leave. The corollary is that Church endowments are unlawful. Signs of translation from the Latin have been seen in the tract.

DE SACRAMENTO ALTARIS [46]. One page, apparently incomplete. It argues that Wyclyf's adversaries accuse the Pope and the Roman curia of an heretical Eucharist doctrine. Perhaps the author had appealed to the oath of Berengar (see [29], [30] above).

TRACTATUS DE PSEUDO-FRERIS [47]. Twenty-eight pages. Its author utilizes incidentally Wyclyf's doctrine of dominion and predestination while censuring friars in detail. He recognizes a tendency to vindictiveness and distinguishes good friars from the usually evil ones.

DE PAPA [48]. Twenty-three pages. The tract is concerned with dominion, utilizing arguments and illustrations that occur frequently in Wyclif's Latin works.

See also [57–63] below.

2. Works Ascribed to Purvey

by

Ernest W. Talbert

See also [39] above; [77], [90] below.

FIFTY HERESIES AND ERRORS OF FRIARS [49]. Thirty-five pages. It repeats familiar points of attack and may have been inspired by the twenty-four accusations against Wyclyf. It has been dated 1384; but it contains a possible reference to some anti-vernacular statute comparable to a reference in the sermon on the Gospel for Palm Sunday ([7] above). Purvey, rather than Peter Pateshull, seems to be the author.

DE OFFICIO PASTORALI [50]. 1382–95, probably before 1387; fifty pages. It is translated probably from Wyclif's Latin tract of that name. Purvey seems the likely author in view of: (1) Thomas Netter of Walden's description of Purvey's activity, (2) the insertion of Chapter XV to defend the English translation of the Bible, (3) relationships between that chapter and the General Prologue to the Wyclyfite Bible versions.

TWELVE TRACTS OR SERMONS [51]. 1382–95, probably before 1390; 158 manuscript pages. They seem to be addressed to a vulgar audience. All emphasize the lawfulness and necessity of vernacular Bibles, references to which become increasingly explicit. The second tract agrees with a prologue to Clement of Llanthony's *Harmony: inc.* "Our Lord Jesu Christ, very God and very man" (see IV [37]). The tenth largely coincides with Purvey's epilogue to his comment on St. Matthew (see IV [52]), without the special explanation of Purvey's authorities or the discussion of his Acquinas gloss. The tracts begin: (1) "All Christian people stand in three manner of folk"; (2) as above; (3) "Our Lord Jesu Christ made the gospel"; (4) "Another sentence commending the gospel in our mother tongue"; (5) "Another sentence shewing that the people may have Holy Writ"; (6) "This that sueth sheweth that all those be in great peril"; (7) "This treatise that followeth proveth"; (8) "Another chapter strengthening the sentences"; (9) "These be the arms of Antichrist's disciples"; (10) "A dere God, lord of truth"; (11) "A commendation of holy writ in our own language"; (12) "A dialogue of a wise man and a fool."

ECCLESIAE REGIMEN (REMONSTRANCE AGAINST ROMISH CORRUPTIONS or THIRTY-SEVEN CONCLUSIONS) [52]. Ca. 1395; eight pages. It appears in a shorter Latin version and has passages in common with the General Prologue (IV [52]). Considered a political pamphlet of 1395, it states that the clergy's temporal possessions and power are temporary and should be revoked when necessary by the state and the people. Readers of the Twelve Conclusions ([53] below) are referred to this *libellum*, used also by Lavenham for his list of Purvey's heresies and errors in Thomas Netter of Walden's *Fasciculi Zizaniorum*.

TWELVE CONCLUSIONS OF THE LOLLARDS [53]. 1395; nine pages. It appears also in a Latin version, which was nailed to the doors of Westminster Abbey and St. Paul's. Details of the presentation of the English version to Parliament (Jan. 27 - Feb. 15) are debatable (see [52] above).

SIXTEEN POINTS BROUGHT AGAINST THE LOLLARDS [54]. 1400–07; eight manuscript pages. The tract elucidates a via media for each accusation, in contrast with *On the Twenty-five Articles* ([90] below) and the General Prologue (IV [52]). As a consequence, it has been dated after Purvey's recantation.

THE COMPENDYOUS TREATISE (ON TRANSLATING THE BIBLE INTO ENGLISH) [55]. 1400–14, ca. 1405, 1407; six and a half pages. Apparently it resulted from an Oxford debate in which Peter Payne took part, sometime between 1399 and 1405. It supports its position by surveying Bible translations and citing authorities (i.a., Grosseteste, John of Gaunt, Arundel). The editor of the "Hans Luft" edition was probably Tindale, in controversy with More.

THE LOLLARD DISENDOWMENT BILL [56]. 1410; four pages. According to contemporaries, it was presented in Parliament. It specifies the income to king and realm that would result from seizing some of the Church temporalities from worldly clergy, who have been "longe vicious" to all, including lords and "symple comvnes." Lavenham's list of Purvey's errors and the provision for universities indicate Purvey's authorship. When revived by Jack Sharpe in 1431, the second half varied considerably from that of 1410.

3. Other Wyclyfite Writings

by

Ernest W. Talbert

Modified by consideration of possible authorship ([57–63], [77–85] below) and of date (e.g., [67] below), the order of the works listed here moves in general from didactic writings to controversial ones.

AN EXPOSITION OF THE PATER NOSTER [57]. Four to five pages. It shows less Lollardy than the Harley version noted above (see [14]); but its relationship to the *Ave Maria* ([58] below) leads its editor to give it to Wyclyf.

A TRACT ON THE AVE MARIA [58]. Five to six pages. It develops lessons which attack especially the frivolity of the gentry and gross amusements at court. It has been given to Wyclyf by its editor largely because of its expressing the immanence of God. (See [15] above.)

SPECULUM DE ANTICHRISTO [59]. Three pages. The author meets the arguments of Antichrist and his clerks against preaching, refers to predestination as a recognized truth, but does not attack transubstantiation when the sacrament of mass is mentioned. Its editor considers it by Wyclyf before the poor priests were repressed.

OF FEIGNED CONTEMPLATIVE LIFE [60]. Eight pages. It criticizes contemplation because it hinders preaching. A style "better" than that apparent in other polemical tracts, and "finer" touches, lead its editor to give it to Wyclyf.

OF SERVANTS AND LORDS [61]. Ca. 1382; seventeen pages. It expounds the duty of servants, disclaiming for poor priests the accusation that they encourage rebelliousness; but it also attacks false conduct in lords, lawyers, merchants, and the clergy. Matthew gives it to Wyclyf soon after Tyler's riots.

HOW SATAN AND HIS PRIESTS . . . CAST BY THREE CURSID HERESIES TO DESTROY ALL GOOD LIVING AND MAINTAIN ALL MANNER OF SIN [62]. Eleven pages. The author declares heretical the statements: (1) that the literal sense of scripture can be ignored, (2) that a lie is lawful, (3) that attacking the sins of prelates and Antichrist's clerks is uncharitable. Its editor considers it possibly by Wyclyf.

THE RULE AND TESTAMENT OF ST. FRANCIS [63]. Twelve pages. The Franciscan rule is translated to show how friars break it. The tract was given to Wyclyf by its editor primarily because the *Fifty Heresies* (see [49] above) seemed "an amplification" of this tract.

SPECULUM VITAE CHRISTIANAE [64]. Matthew believes it may have had bits inserted, probably by Wyclyf; but articles 1 and 7 are from Thoresby's *Catechism* (see under Works of Religious Instruction).

TRANSLATION OF FOUR PSEUDO-AUGUSTINIAN TRACTS [65]. Seventy-six manuscript pages. They are described as (1) *De salutaribus documentis*, an exhortation to one Julian to lead a Christian life and spread Christian doctrine; (2) *De vita Christiana*; (3) *De creatione*; (4) *De duodecim abusionibus*. The method of translation is said to agree with the principles of the Early Bible Version except for added explanatory matter, which is "intermediary" between the second stage of the Early Version and the Late Version (see IV [52]).

FOUR CAMBRIDGE TRACTS [66]. In a hand of 1380–1400; fifty-one manuscript pages; appearing after the *Holy Prophet David Saith* ([25] above). They are (1) *Meekness*, (2) *Here Sueth the Sayings of Divers Doctors* (on Matthew 26), (3) *Chrisostom and Some Other Doctors*, (4) *Four Errors Which Letten the Very Knowing of Holy Writ*. Their style accords with their Biblical quotations, which use the Early Version and suggest authorship by one of the original circle, e.g., John Aston.

THE BRITISH MUSEUM TRACTS (THE TENISON WYCLYFITE TRACTS) [67]. They seem to vary in date of composition, from before

1390 (see [68] below) to a time when an emphasis characteristic of later Lollardy would be appropriate (see [73] below and, e.g., [101]). The twelve tracts, dealt with separately ([68] to [76] and 8, 10, 11 below), are as follows:

1. THE BISCHOPES OTHE THAT HE SWERIS TO THE POPE [68]. Twenty-six manuscript pages. It refers apparently to Urban VI (1378–89) and has condemnatory remarks on the oath and its twenty-three articles.

2. A TREATISE OF MIRACLIS PLEYINGE [69]. Fourteen manuscript pages. Expressing an attitude similar to one found in *Against the Minorite Friars* (see under Works Dealing with Contemporary Conditions) the tract enumerates arguments in favor of the performances in order to refute each. The author does not show the precision and clarity found in some Wyclyfite tracts (e.g., [40], [41] above), and his treatment of the argument that performances are "quick" paintings reminds one of attitudes among later Lollards (see [99] below).

3. AGAINST DICE [70]. Eight manuscript pages.

4. AGAINST EXPOSING RELICS FOR GAIN [71]. Two manuscript pages.

5. ON THE KNOWLEDGE OF THE SOUL [72]. Two manuscript pages.

6. A TRETYSE OF IMAGES [73]. Five manuscript pages. It opposes their use.

7. A TRETISE OF PRISTIS [74]. One manuscript page.

8. OF WEDDID MEN AND THEIR WYUIS AND THER CHILDERE. Generally given to Wyclyf ([26] above).

9. ON TITHES AND OFFERINGS [75]. One manuscript page.

10, 11. THE SEVEN SACRAMENTIS and THE SEVEN UERTUES. Parts of Dan Jon Gaytryge's Sermon (see under Works of Religious Instruction).

12. A TREATISE PRINCIPALLY AGAINST THE RELIGIOUS ORDERS [76]. Fragmentary. It begins within a sixteenth chapter and ends at the beginning of a thirty-ninth one; but Wyclyf is cited, along with other favorite Lollard authorities (Grosseteste, Bradwardine, Fitz-Ralph, Kilmington).

OF THE LEAVEN OF PHARISEES [77]. Ca. 1383; twenty-six pages. The author attacks the religious orders, who, like the Pharisees, show all sins of omission and commission. Its style, described diversely as "weak" and "exceedingly bitter," has caused it to be ascribed, nevertheless, to the author of the next tract and, possibly, the next eight ones. Similarities to *Fifty Heresies* (above, [49]) has caused it to be ascribed to Purvey.

OF PRELATES [78]. Ca. 1383–84; fifty-two pages. It has been given, with the preceding tract, and possibly the next seven, to one author (see [77] above). It lacks precision and is inclined to repetition.

DE OBEDIENTIA PRELATORUM [79]. Ten pages. It is a bitter attack on prelates which has been thought to emanate from its author's experience as a poor priest. On stylistic grounds it has been included in a group of seven ([80–85] below) that may have been written by the author of *Of the Leaven of Pharisees* ([77] above).

OF CLERKS POSSESSIONERS [80]. Twenty-four pages. The author attacks worldly clergy in forty short chapters, some of which overlap. It has been included in a group of seven showing stylistic similarities (see [79] above).

HOW THE OFFICE OF CURATES IS ORDAINED BY GOD [81]. Nineteen to twenty pages. One of the same stylistically related group (see [79] above), it attacks the worldliness of curates but has been dated by its editor after 1383.

THE ORDER OF PRIESTHOOD [82]. Fourteen pages. It enumerates abuses; and the final exhortation, developed from the nobleness of priesthood, calls on lords and great men to amend those evils (see [79] above).

THREE THINGS DESTROY THE WORLD [83]. Six pages. The author attacks false confessors, who are friars; wicked, ecclesiastical lawyers; and cheating, usurious merchants. Of these, the first is worst (see [79] above).

HOW SATAN AND HIS CHILDREN TURN WORKS OF MERCY UPSIDE DOWN [84]. Nine pages. It develops a series of antitheses between Christ and Satan, emphasizes the viciousness of imprisonment for debt, and shows an intimate realization of the suffering of the poor (see [79] above).

THE CLERGY MAY NOT HOLD PROPERTY [85]. Forty-two to forty-three pages. The tract is in general orderly and restrained, although it has been placed on stylistic grounds in this group of seven (see [79] above). Its appendix lists authorities in Latin on the wrongfulness of clerics in secular office.

HOW RELIGIOUS MEN SHOULD KEEP CERTAIN ARTICLES (HOW MEN OF PRIVATE RELIGION SHOULD LOVE MORE THE GOSPEL) [86]. Six pages. It attacks religious orders by some forty-four suggestions, mainly negative, including the persecution of true preachers.

OF POOR PREACHING PRIESTS [87]. 1377–1400; five pages. The author gives three general points and thirty-one special ones for amending the realm. The first three apply to poor priests, the next thirteen to the clergy, the last eighteen to king, lords, and commons.

WHY POOR PRIESTS HAVE NO BENEFICE [88]. Nine pages. The author vigorously explains why there are poor priests.

HOW ANTICHRIST AND HIS CLERKS TRAVAIL TO DESTROY HOLY WRIT [89]. Seven to eight pages. It justifies an insistence upon the Gospels by refuting four points: (1) that the Church is of more authority than Scriptures, (2) that Augustine would not believe the Gospel unless told to by the Church, (3) that men know the Gospel only by the Church's approval, (4) that men have no reason to believe anything in the Gospel.

ON THE TWENTY-FIVE ARTICLES [90]. Ca. 1388; forty-one pages. The author refutes accusations against Lollards which are dated by Knighton and said to have been the basis of a Parliamentary petition.

The tract usually is dated also by a reference to Urban VI (d. 1389). Traces of a North Midland dialect have been thought to indicate that Purvey was not the author; its effective prose, to indicate Hereford in part, though its "language" is not his.

ANTICHRIST AND HIS MEYNEE [91]. Twenty-one manuscript pages. The author develops a contrast between (1) Christ and his disciples and (2) the clergy, from the Pope through pardoners; and attacks, i.a., intoning, tithes, mass-pennies, offerings. Reference to the killing of "true men" seems to indicate a fifteenth-century date.

THE LAST AGE OF THE CHURCH [92]. Five manuscript pages. It is a short apocalyptic demonstration of the tribulations of the Church, emphasizing the worldliness of prelates and priests and the fact that the year 1400 marks the era of Antichrist. The similarity of its manner to one of Walter Brute's conclusions has been noted (see [100] below), as has a possible influence from the pseudo-Joachim of Floris. It was formerly considered one of the earliest of Lollard tracts.

AN APOLOGY FOR LOLLARD DOCTRINES [93]. 113 pages; Northern characteristics. Its author explains thirty points. They range from attacks on the Pope, on indulgences, and on cursing, and from a denial of the efficacy of the priestly office when the priest is sinful, to doctrine about fasting, canonical hours, marriage, images, begging. Each point is supported by authorities, mainly Biblical. Frequently it is linked with *The Lanterne of Liȝt* to illustrate emphases in late Lollard doctrine (see also [101] below).

THE LANTERNE OF LIȜT [94]. 1410–15; 136–37 pages. Its author differentiates between Antichrist's church, the church spiritual, and the church material; points out by contrasting descriptions how Christ's Church and Antichrist's can be perceived in the material church; and describes the union of the good in the material church with the spiritual, and its persecution by the evil. Throughout, Lollard doctrine is apparent in the author's insistence: (1) that Scripture is the supreme authority, (2) that it should be available in the vernacular, (3) that the Pope and his ministers are Antichrist's, (4) that preaching is the priest's chief duty, (5) that pilgrimages and indulgences, e.g., are contrary to God's law, as are temporal possessions and swearing in any form. Apparently written during persecutions, it is moderate in tone with no heretical opinions about the sacraments. Its author gives his own Biblical translations and relies for his other authorities upon Gratian, Lombard, and Strabo. Its manuscript shows fewer Northern forms than does *The Apology* ([93] above), and the language accords with a date between the promulgation of Arundel's constitutions and a reference to this tract at John Claydon's trial, August 17, 1415. The treatise was well-known to fifteenth-century Lollards.

JACK UPLAND [95] and UPLAND'S REJOINDER [96]. 1390–1420; ca. 1450. Eighteen pages; 340 alliterative lines, plus Latin quotations. Single authorship is improbable, although both works are related to *Friar Daw's Reply* (see under Works Dealing with Contemporary Conditions). The authors repeat Lollard commonplaces, and a Lollard interpolater has added forty-seven lines to the *Rejoinder*.

4. Accounts of Lollard Trials and Related Writings

by

Ernest W. Talbert

THE CONFESSION OF JOHN ASTON [97]. 1382; one page. It gives Aston's belief about the Eucharist and is similar to the first point in Hereford's confession ([98] below). It also denies that Aston taught or preached "Materiale brede leves in þe Sacrament aftur þe consecration." Dated ca. June 19, the document may have been circulated for propaganda while Aston was imprisoned. (See an unedited *Protestation* [6], by Hereford, Aston, Repington.)

THE CONFESSION OF NICHOLAS OF HEREFORD [98]. 1382; one page. It states that through the sacramental words the bread becomes Christ's body, that the whole body is present in every part of the Eucharist, that His bodily presence is to the salvation of those who worthily receive it but to the damnation of others. Purportedly made before Courtenay on June 19, but probably soon after June 27, the statement may have been written for propaganda purposes (see [97] above; and [6], an unedited *Protestation*).

DOCUMENTS CONNECTED WITH WILLIAM SWYNDERBY'S TRIAL [99]. 1390–91; twenty-nine to thirty pages. These concern Swynderby's trial at Hereford after his trial at Lincoln in 1382, and consist of his articles, his excuse for not appearing in the Church of Ledebury North, his defense, his appeal, and his letter to the knights in Parliament. The emphasis at this trial apparently was upon the Lollards' unlicensed preaching and their insistence upon the literal sense of Scriptures, in contrast to the earlier emphasis upon the efficacy of the priestly office.

WALTER BRUTE'S SUBMISSION [100]. 1393; one page. It consists only of the brief statement that Trefnant required Brute to read before assembled clergy and laymen on October 3; but in the Latin account surrounding it, this Welsh layman defends Swynderby and himself with a multitude of Apocalyptic arguments and subsequently attacks Hereford, then present, as a traitor.

THE EXAMINATION AND TESTAMENT OF MASTER WILLIAM THORPE [101]. *Examination*, 1407; *Testament*, Sept. 19, 1460; seventy-four pages. The *Examination* is useful for comments about other Lollard leaders and other Lollard trials, e.g., that of Sawtry. It is particularly revealing both as to Lollard beliefs and the orthodox attitude toward them. The account of this examination, of which no official record survives, is said to have been written by Thorpe, who describes himself as a Wyclyfite since 1377 and as one who had preached, especially in the North Midlands, since 1387. The following ideas appear in the examination: listening to preaching is more important than attending mass; after consecration the bread is not accidents without a subject; pilgrimages are objectionable; worship of man-made images is against God's law; tithes should not be paid to unrighteous priests; none should swear by a "creature"; confession to God without shrift is sufficient. Constantly Thorpe appeals to the literal sense of the Bible. The *Examination*, which shows Thorpe's knowledge of scholastic terminology, has real literary merit, particularly in representing the thrust and parry of disputants. Its popularity is attested, i.a., by a Latin version and by Tindale's edition. The *Testament* is largely polemical.

THE EXAMINATION OF THE HONOURABLE KNIGHT, SIR JOHN OLDCASTLE [102]. September 1413; fourteen pages. For the most part it concerns the doctrine of the Eucharist; but the viciousness of worldly possessions among Pope and clergy, and Lollard doctrine about shrift, pilgrimages, and the worship of images also appears.

THE RECANTATION OF ROBERT SPARKE OF RECHE [103]. 1457; six pages. Although the proceedings against Sparke apparently resulted from an inquiry about owners of Pecock's writings, Sparke recanted as a Lollard. His heresy involved disbelief in pilgrimages, fasts, burial in churchyards, most of the sacraments, and the veneration of images. His opinions should be viewed in the light of those held by other Lollards who were tried after 1413. Their trials continued throughout the fifteenth century and are reported mainly in episcopal registers, a considerable number of which are not printed. The persons examined are, for the most part, skilled artisans, and their beliefs show a variety of traditions. Some of their opinions are clearly derived from Wyclyfite doctrines; others may represent garbled versions; some express extreme doctrinal positions; others are derived from the disendowment proposals [56]; some cannot be related to any teaching of the Lollards. Although these later Lollards can be called a sect, their opinions represent attitudes rather than a series of carefully formulated doctrines. Denial of transubstantiation, in some form or another, and a dislike of pilgrimages and images appear consistently. Even more frequent are references to heretical English "books" and, especially, to translations of the Bible. At least one confession (that of John Walcote, October 1425) reads almost like a Lollard martyrology. There are only a few well-attested cases of Lollardy in Scotland. John Knox's account of the so-called Lollards of Kyle (1494) is the most detailed. They were gentry and men having connections with the court. The English trials continued into the sixteenth century; and since the thought of these Lollards was strongly antipapal, it may have contributed to popular acceptance of Henry VIII's break with Rome. Lollard doctrine also gave the sanction of "antiquity" to the reformers' purposes, especially in the central matters of scriptural authority and ecclesiastical possessions. Other opinions of these Lollards vaguely anticipate post-reformation puritanism.

IV. TRANSLATIONS AND PARAPHRASES OF THE BIBLE, AND COMMENTARIES

by

Laurence Muir

Discussion of the translations and paraphrases of the Bible and the Scriptural commentaries is arranged in four parts: the Old Testament, the New Testament, the Old and New Testaments, and the Southern Temporale. The individual pieces within each part are arranged so far as possible according to the order of the books of the Bible.

1. THE OLD TESTAMENT

GENESIS AND EXODUS [1]. About 1250; 4162 four-stress verses in couplets (*Genesis* 2536 verses, *Exodus* 1626); East Midland, probably based on a Northern original of 1150–1200. In its present dialectal form the poem belongs to the southern part of the East Midlands. It appears to be the work of one author. Its main source has generally been thought to be Peter Comestor's *Historia scholastica*, a popular epitome and commentary of about 1170, although the question has been raised whether it may not depend upon an original earlier than Comestor. At any rate, there were other sources besides Comestor, and perhaps little was taken directly from the Bible. The poem paraphrases, in a simple but uninspired style, the chief events from the Biblical Genesis and Exodus, with portions of Numbers and Deuteronomy included to round out the story of Moses. The prologue suggests that the work was prepared for the instruction of the laity, for those who were unlearned in books, and that by it Christian men might hear of God's love, of man's bliss and sorrow, and of salvation through Christ. The poem contains a few legendary details, but on the whole it is a straightforward narrative, without moralizing, of the chief incidents from early Biblical history. It lacks the poetic merit of the Old Testament metrical paraphrases in Old English.

STROPHIC VERSION OF OLD TESTAMENT PIECES [2]. Later fourteenth century or beginning fifteenth; 18,372 lines in twelve-line stanzas, with alliteration; Yorkshire. The stanzaic form is ababababcdcd, the first eight lines having four stresses and the last four having three. This form is found also among the York plays (see under Dramatic Pieces). The two extant copies are said to be independently derived from a common source, which itself was not the original. A source of the original, in addition to the Bible, was Peter Comestor's *Historia scholastica*, and several passages in the poem are taken from the York plays. The poem paraphrases Genesis through II Kings, III and IV Kings, Job, Tobias, Esther, Judith, and portions of 2 Maccabees. Impressive mainly for its magnitude, the poem nevertheless narrates the Biblical stories faithfully and straightforwardly, with a certain poetic skill. It contains direct speeches, dramatic incidents, and some details of medieval setting.

IACOB AND IOSEP [3]. 1250–75; 538 lines (not counting a missing leaf) in riming couplets; Southwestern. The poem contains a mixture of six-stress and seven-stress lines, with medial caesura and some alliteration. It represents a blending of religious and minstrel traditions, and was possibly composed by a traveling friar for recitation in hall or market-place. Thus it differs from the Scriptural and legendary poems of the nearly contemporary *South English Legendary* (see under Legends V [1], with which it has certain minor similarities, but which had a didactic, ecclesiastical function. *Iacob and Iosep* has the characteristics of ballad poetry: narrative simplicity, direct speeches, repetition of line and phrase, rapidity of movement and concentration on vivid incident, popular idiom and imagery, and romantic detail of castle, court, and bower. It was clearly created for entertainment. The poem recounts the Biblical story of Joseph from the dream of the sheaves to the final settling of Jacob and his family in Egypt. Jacob holds a place of prominence throughout almost equal to Joseph's; his sufferings and joys are dramatically depicted. The poem contains a number of modifications and additions to the Biblical story, as, for example, the transference

of the attempted seduction from Potiphar's wife to Pharaoh's wife, the
Queen. Parallels for these alterations are found variously in the Joseph
legends of Hebrew and Mohammedan tradition, in Josephus, in certain
of the writers of the early Church, in Old French verse translations,
and in other medieval sources including the English *Genesis and Exodus*
(see above [1]). As a ballad based on Biblical and religious material,
Iacob and Iosep may represent a tradition of popular poetry of which
few evidences remain.

JOSEPH AND ASENATH [4]. Poem of 933 lines, 901 in rime royal
and 32 of a prologue (ababcdcd, etc.). Written probably just before or
after 1400 in the West Midlands. Begins "As I on hilly halkes logged
me late,/Beside ny of a ladi sone was I war." The romantic and apocryphal story of the love of Asenath (see Genesis 41:45, 50) for Joseph, her
conversion to the Jewish faith, and their marriage. Pharaoh's son sought
to carry her off, but Joseph's brothers, Benjamin, Simeon, and Levi,
rescued her.

HISTORYE OF THE PATRIARKS [5]. Fifteenth century. A literal
prose translation of the Genesis portion of Peter Comestor's *Historia
scholastica*. As far as is known, it is the only existing early English translation of this commentary. Its frequent condensations and omissions of
passages in the original, together with the substitutions of Biblical text,
suggest that it may have been based on Desmoulins' version in French,
rather than directly on the *Historia* and the Vulgate.

LESSONS OF THE DIRIGE I [6]. Also called "Pety Iob." Beginning of fifteenth century; 684 irregular four-stress verses in stanzas
ababababbcbc; East Midland. A paraphrase of the "Lamentations of
Job," nine passages from the Biblical book that were used in the Matins
of the Office of the Dead. They are Job 7:16–21, 10:1–12, 13:23–28,
14:1–6, 14:13–16, 17:1–2, 17:11–15, 19:20–27, 10:18–22. Before each
stanza appears one of the Vulgate verses, and the stanza paraphrases and
enlarges upon it in lyrical fashion, ending with the refrain "Parce michi
domine." The poetry has power and beauty. Notwithstanding a heading
in three manuscripts attributing the work to Rolle, Rolle is not the

author; nor is the work related to Rolle's Latin Job, except in being concerned with the same passages. The suggestion that Richard Maidenstone was the author is largely speculative.

LESSONS OF THE DIRIGE II [7]. Early fifteenth century; 418 four-stress lines in stanzas abababab (stanza no. 26 with an extra couplet); West or Southwest Midland. This is another paraphrase of the Dirige, here divided into ten lessons. Its language shows it to be based on the prose lessons of Dirige III (see below [8]). It incorporates into its stanzas some of the responsories and versicles, as well as the Canticle of Judgment, found in Dirige III.

LESSONS OF THE DIRIGE III [8]. Beginning of fifteenth century; Midland. A prose version of the nine lessons of the Matins of the Office of the Dead from the book of Job, with the responsories and versicles and the Canticle of the Last Judgment, following the Sarum Use. The text is that of the Office found in certain manuscripts of the English Primer (see under Works of Religious Instruction). In other Primer manuscripts the text of the Lessons is that of the Later Wyclyfite Version. Although our piece agrees fully with neither the Early nor the Later Wyclyfite, and although it may be an independent adaptation of one or the other, it is possible that it represents an intermediate Wyclyfite revision (see below [52]).

METRICAL LIFE OF JOB [9]. Probably middle of fifteenth century; 26 seven-line stanzas, ababbcc (rime royal). This brief narrative of events in the life of Job owes some of its detail to the ancient folktale tradition about Job, as well as to the Biblical book. It concentrates on outward incident and largely ignores the reflective and dialectic content of the book of Job. Frequent passages parallel the Vulgate text, but the narrative also contains apocryphal elements, such as the minstrels who visit Job on his dunghill and are rewarded with scabs from his afflicted body, which at once turn into gold. Apparently the poem was originally composed to accompany miniatures depicting events in Job's life, as evinced by lines like the following:

"Here, lo, holy Job his children doth sanctifie." (15)
"Lo, here, the envy of this serpent and devyll Sathan." (29)

The original manuscript is lost, however, and in the one extant manuscript relevant passages from the Vulgate appear to replace the illustrations. In style the poem tends to be flowery and melodramatic, but within its limits it conveys the lesson of Job with a certain direct effectiveness.

SURTEES PSALTER [10]. 1250–1300. The hundred and fifty Psalms in rimed couplets, with predominantly four-stress lines; in the manuscripts other than Cotton Vespasian D.vii, the couplets occasionally give way to quatrains abab. Generally considered Northern, Yorkshire, although this has not been proved with certainty and an argument has been made for a Midland origin. The Psalter derives its name from the edition issued by the Surtees Society in 1843–47. The work is a translation, not a paraphrase, and it is written for the most part in good, idiomatic English, with some vigor and flexibility of style. Certain peculiarities, such as archaic diction, Latinized constructions, and a relative rarity of French terms, suggest a source in an earlier Latin Psalter with English glosses. Especially striking are the large number of similarities in wording to Rolle's somewhat later English Psalter (see below [12]). The hypothesis has been convincingly defended that both Rolle and the author of the Surtees Psalter referred to an early Middle English interlinear gloss on the Vulgate, probably Northern, which was itself a modernized version of an Old English glossed Psalter.

MIDLAND PROSE PSALTER [11]. 1325–50; Northamptonshire. A translation of all the Psalms with eleven canticles and the Athanasian Creed (see below [14]), accompanied, verse by verse, by a glossed version of the Vulgate. At one time erroneously attributed to William of Shoreham because of the presence of his poems in one of the manuscripts, this work cannot with certainty be designated the "earliest" English prose Psalter, since Rolle's version (see below [12]) may possibly antedate it. The English consistently renders the Latin glosses rather than the Vulgate itself. It has been shown, however, that the English translator depended upon a French glossed version as well as the glossed text of the Vulgate. Many of the discrepancies between the Latin text and the English rendering can be explained by reference to the French version (perhaps found in Bibliothèque Nationale fr 6260, a manuscript some hundred years later than the one the English translator must have used). One manuscript of the English Psalter (Pepys 2498) attributes the Latin glosses to "Gregory," and the French manuscript attributes both the Latin and French versions to "St. Gregory." The Gregory in question has never been identified. The glosses, which frequently introduce allegorical interpretations, in general diminish the force and vividness of the Vulgate. But the English version as a whole has literary merit.

ROLLE'S ENGLISH PSALTER AND COMMENTARY [12]. 1337–49; Yorkshire. A verse-by-verse English prose rendering of the Vulgate Psalms, each verse accompanied by the Latin text and by a commentary in English. A prologue in English prose introduces the work. The translation of the Psalms is close and literal. It nevertheless contains some felicitous renderings and some phrasings that seem not only to connect it with earlier versions (see above [10]), but even to anticipate modern ones. The commentary is based on Peter Lombard's catena on the Psalter, and Rolle's selections from his source and his own interpolations reflect his personality and mysticism. The English Psalter is in the main independent of the author's Latin Commentary on the Psalter, although the two naturally show many similarities. As is stated in a later verse prologue found in MS Bodleian 1151 (Laud 286), the English Psalter was written for a friend, Margaret Kirkeby, a nun of Hampole and later a recluse. In its literal rendering of the Vulgate, the English translation was intended to be accompanied by the gloss or commentary, and in such form was orthodox enough in an age when free Scriptural renderings were in disfavor with the Church. It enjoyed a long period of influence, and many fifteenth-century copies remain. In addition to its use by the orthodox, however, it was interpolated by Lollards, and a number of these revised copies are extant. They include many of the ideas and doctrines of Lollardy, with typical attacks on the clergy and on ecclesiastical practices. Although it is not known who the Lollard revisers were, there were at least three of them whose methods can be distinguished.

CANTICLES I (In Rolle's Psalter with Commentary) [13]. A regular part of the medieval Psalter, indicating its liturgical use, are the twelve

Canticles (the "cantica" of the Roman *Breviary*), consisting of Old and New Testament hymns, the Te Deum, and the Athanasian Creed. They generally follow the Psalter without a break, and in Rolle's they are arranged in the same pattern of Latin and English texts and commentary as is the Psalter itself. Canticles I to VII appear in most of the Rolle manuscripts and are doubtless Rolle's work. They are the Song of Isaiah (Isaiah 12), the Song of Hezekiah (Isaiah 38:10–20), the Song of Hannah (1 Kings 2:1–10 in the Vulgate), the first Song of Moses (Exodus 15:1–19), the Prayer of Habakkuk (3:2–19), the second Song of Moses (Deuteronomy 32:1–43), and the Magnificat (Luke 1:46–55). In several manuscripts five more Canticles are added, probably the work of Lollard revisers. These are the Te Deum, the Benedictus (Luke 1:68–79), the Nunc Dimittis (Luke 2:29–32), the Benedicite (Daniel 3:57–88; called in some manuscripts "Canticum 3^m Puerorum"), and the Athanasian Creed.

CANTICLES II (In Midland Prose Psalter without Commentary) [14]. The Twelve Canticles (see above [13]) which accompany the Midland Prose Psalter (see above [11]).

JEROME'S ABBREVIATED PSALTER [15]. Probably 1350–1400. An English prose translation of the *Psalterium abbreviatum* ascribed to St. Jerome. It is an abridgement of the Psalter containing selected verses from various Psalms. Some Psalms are omitted entirely, and a few are included fully. In MS Bodleian 4050 (Hatton 111), the work occupies fourteen pages. The versions in this manuscript and in Bodleian 2315 (416) are closely similar, but are not closely related to that in Huntington HM 501. The three differ in completeness, and none represents the full Latin text as printed by Horstmann. The Latin version is headed by a rubric telling how Jerome was inspired to prepare the brief Psalter for the salvation of the souls of those who, for various reasons, were unable to say the entire Psalter daily. The English versions are headed by a special prayer.

ST. BERNARD'S EIGHT-VERSE PSALTER [16]. About 1400; eight stanzas of eight four-stress lines, ababab. Each stanza, preceded by a portion of the verse in Latin, paraphrases a verse of the Psalter. The rubric in English explains that the Devil revealed to St. Bernard these eight verses, which, if said daily, would save a man from damnation. A Latin source is found in MS Harley 1845, ff 15, 16.

PRIMER VERSION OF CERTAIN PSALMS [17]. Late fourteenth century. An English Primer in which the text of the Scriptural passages differs from that of either the Early or the Late Wyclyfite, although it is probably contemporary with them. The Wyclyfite text is found in most Middle English Primers. The Scriptural passages in the Primer are the seven Penitential Psalms, the fifteen gradual Psalms, the Psalms of Commendation, and other Psalms and Biblical passages regularly used in the Offices. (See The Primer under Works of Religious Instruction).

MAIDSTONE PENITENTIAL PSALMS [18]. 1350–1400; 952 four-stress lines in eight-line stanzas, abababab; East Midland with marks of a Southeastern influence. A prologue or introductory stanza occurs in eight manuscripts, in one of which is included the name of Richard Maidstone, a Carmelite friar, as author of the poem. Although there is no verification for this ascription, there is no good reason for doubting it. Each stanza of the poem follows and paraphrases a Vulgate verse from the seven Penitential Psalms, the paraphrase frequently expanding in a lyrical style on the theme of salvation through Christ's sacrifice. There are a number of differences in the text of the poem among the manuscripts, due probably not only to scribal error and misinterpretation, but also to varying devotional tastes. The poem was evidently often copied.

BRAMPTON'S PENITENTIAL PSALMS [19]. Early fifteenth century; 124 stanzas of eight four-stress lines, ababbcbc. A paraphrase of the seven Penitential Psalms. There are two versions, which, although clearly from one original, vary in places all the way from brief phrases to entire stanzas. The attribution to Thomas Brampton, a Doctor of Sacred Theology and a Franciscan friar who lived in the West of England, is found in two of the manuscripts. After six introductory stanzas, the poem proceeds with a stanza of paraphrase for each verse (or at times half-verse) of Biblical text. Each stanza ends with "Ne reminiscaris, Domine." Some of the stanzas are mainly paraphrases of the text; others treat relevant

subjects of church doctrine. Of the two versions, the original was probably anti-Lollard in tone, while the revision may have been pro-Lollard.

COMMENTARY ON THE PENITENTIAL PSALMS [20]. Fifteenth
century. A long work in prose translated from the French. A note at the
end attributes the translation to Eleanor Hull. Phrases of the Vulgate
text accompanied with snatches of Latin commentary, both in a large
script, are followed by a lengthy English exposition in smaller script.

PARAPHRASE OF FIFTY-FIRST PSALM (VULGATE 50th) I [21].
Probably early fourteenth century; each Latin verse followed by a four-
line stanza aabb, except for three verses that are followed by six-line
stanzas. Two stanzas within the poem are illegible, and the last two
paraphrase the Gloria Patri. There are eighty-six extant English lines.
The verse is somewhat crude, and the poem seems to reflect a simple
piety.

PARAPHRASE OF FIFTY-FIRST PSALM (VULGATE 50th) II [22].
Probably fifteenth century; six-line stanzas of alliterative verse; 67 verses,
ends imperfectly.

COMMENTARY ON PSALMS 91, 92 (VULGATE 90, 91) [23]. 1350–
1400; Northern or North Midland. A verse-by-verse exposition of the
Psalms *Qui habitat* and *Bonum est* in English prose. The literal English
rendering of each verse, following the Latin, shows many similarities to
Rolle's version (see above [12]), doubtless partly because both are close
renderings of the Vulgate. The lengthy commentary is orthodox in tone
and suggests the mysticism of Rolle and his school of thought. In it
there is the flavor of the author's personality and experience. No source
for it has been found. Walter Hilton was probably the author of at least
Psalm 91. Psalm 92 differs in style and may have been written by Hilton
at a later period or by a pupil of his. None of the five manuscripts is
the original, and from linguistic evidence they all seem to have been
written in the South, though deriving from a Northern original.

PARAPHRASE OF PSALM 130 (VULGATE 129) [24]. Probably sixteenth century. An expanded verse paraphrase of De Profundis in eleven
twelve-line stanzas.

PARAPHRASE OF ECCLESIASTES [25]. Middle fifteenth century; lowland Scottish. A free prose paraphrase. As the author proceeds through the book, he introduces each successive passage with a reference to King Solomon as the original composer: "Item, he sais—." The style is straightforward and vigorous.

SUSANNA OR THE PISTEL OF SWETE SUSAN [26]. 1350–80; 28 alliterative stanzas of ababababcdddc, being eight long lines followed by the bob and wheel; Northern or Northwest Midland. The story of Susanna and the Elders from the Vulgate Book of Daniel, not included in the Authorized Version. The question of authorship is bound up with the whole problem of Huchown (see below [27]). There is no certainty that Huchown was the author of this poem, or for that matter who Huchown was or where he lived. On the other hand, it is not necessary to react so vigorously to the rather extravagant hypotheses of Huchown enthusiasts as to deny any likelihood of a Huchown as the poet of the Pistel. It is as probable an attribution as many that are accepted from these early times. The story is faithful to the Biblical narrative in its main features, but not slavish. There are some divergences, such as the added description of the garden with its details from the *Roman de la rose*, and Susanna's parting from her husband. The poem is a pleasing product of the alliterative revival.

HUCHOWN DISCUSSION [27]. A number of Middle English alliterative poems have been associated with the name of Huchown. The only reference in Middle English literature to Huchown occurs in Wyntoun's *Cronykil* (ca. 1420), where Wyntoun attributes to "Huchown of the Awle Ryale" the following three poems: the *Geste of Arthur*, the *Awntyre of Gawayn*, and the *Pistel of Swete Susan*. The first two of these have been supposed to be the extant *Morte Arthure* (see I [16]) and *Awntyrs of Arthure* (see I [30]), respectively. These identifications are very doubtful. That the extant *Pistel of Swete Susan* (see above [26]) is the poem referred to by Wyntoun is a reasonable conjecture. Huchown has been thought by some, without much evidence, to be Sir Hugh of Eglinton, a Scottish statesman and reputed poet of the fourteenth century. Elaborate and unlikely theories have been built about Huchown and his work.

Some 40,000 lines of extant alliterative Middle English verse have at various times been assigned to Huchown, including, in addition to the three poems mentioned, the *Gest Historiale of the Destruction of Troye, Golagrus and Gawain, Gawayne and the Grene Knight,* the *Wars of Alexander, Titus and Vespasian, Purity, Erkenwald, Patience,* the *Pearl, Wynnere and Wastoure,* and the *Parlement of the Thre Ages.* The theories have been as vigorously attacked as defended. The only reliable material on Huchown is still what is in Wyntoun. That he is Sir Hugh is unlikely; that he wrote any of the other extant Middle English pieces has been supported by no good evidence.

For other treatments of Old Testament material, see

Legends of Adam and Eve, under Legends, V, Section 4.

Cursor Mundi, under Works of Religious Instruction.

The Ten Commandments (III, [12]), and under Works of Religious Instruction, and under Rolle and His Followers.

The Southern Temporale, below Section 4.

Wyclyfite Versions, below [52].

Dramatic Pieces.

Patience (II [3]).

Purity (II [4]).

2. THE NEW TESTAMENT

LA ESTORIE DEL EUANGELIE [28]. 1250–1325; 1876 four-stress lines (in MS Bodleian 30236, Additional C.38), aaaa (with occasional aabb); East Midland. A paraphrase of the Gospel narrative with apocryphal and homiletic materials. The earliest manuscript, Dulwich College XXII, which is a fragment containing only 519 lines, represents a fuller text than the others. If its scale had been followed in the complete text, MS Bodleian 30236, the poem would have run to some 3000 lines. In an opening address to Christ, the poet declares his devotion, his intention to write Christ's story in English, and Christ's superior worth over ancient moral wisdom and over the wonders of nature. Bestiary material on the hart, the serpent, and the eagle appears here in the Dulwich manuscript. The Gospel story proceeds from the annunciation to Pentecost, with final homiletic material on the last judgment and Christ's suffering and saving grace. There are some important omissions from the Gospel story, as well as a few apocryphal additions. The sources for the Biblical and apocryphal materials were evidently compilations rather than the Vulgate itself or the apocryphal Gospels. The same is true of the homiletic passages, which were ultimately derived from the Church fathers. Among these intermediate sources, the only one that can be identified with probability is Peter Comestor for the apocryphal material. The bestiary material seems to derive, through an intermediary, from Augustine's *Commentaries on the Psalms*.

FALL AND PASSION [29]. 1275–1325; 216 four-stress verses abab. One of the "Kildare poems" of MS Harley 913, probably copied and possibly composed in Ireland. In a homiletic framework, the poem rapidly narrates the fall of the angels, the creation and fall of man, the incarnation and crucifixion (with only one stanza on the life of Christ before his betrayal), the harrowing of hell, and the ascension.

STANZAIC LIFE OF CHRIST [30]. Fourteenth century; 10,840 four-stress lines grouped in quatrains abab, with the same rimes often carrying over to the following quatrain; West Midland. The matter extends from the incarnation and the visitation to Elizabeth through Pentecost. Although the *Life* was aimed ostensibly at the unlearned layman, there are allusions in it also to clerks and learned men who might be listening to it or reading it. In general the contents consist of matters in which the Church wished to instruct its laity. In its arrangement, and with its introduction of Old Testament stories, apocryphal legends, and Church festivals, it resembles the Temporale (see below Part 4). The *Legenda aurea* was, in fact, the prime source for the author, although he depended much also on Higden's *Polychronicon*, and less upon the Vulgate and minor sources. The poem seems to have strongly influenced some of the Chester plays. In arrangement and selection of legendary material as well as in details, a number of the plays show the influence of this vernacular source, although there is no word-for-word borrowing and the plays re-arrange incidents as needed for effectiveness. Linguistic evidence of a Northwest Midland provenance, probably Cheshire and possibly South Cheshire, confirms the other indications of relationship with Chester. It has been suggested that the author may well have been a monk of St. Werburgh's Abbey there.

PROSE LIFE OF CHRIST [31]. Late fourteenth or early fifteenth century; southern variety of East Midland. One hundred thirteen prose sections varying in length from a dozen lines to well over a hundred, each section with a descriptive title. A harmony of the Gospels, of the sort that weaves the accounts of the four evangelists into one continuous narrative. It shows evidence of being a translation of a French source. After a brief introductory section, the work proceeds from the visitation to Elizabeth and the conception of Jesus through the Gospel events of Christ's life and crucifixion to the ascension. Deviations from the sources include some few omissions, some condensations, some brief explanations, and some modifications for the purpose of reconciling apparent discrepancies among the Gospels. These changes tend always in the direction of greater simplicity, just as the usual aim of this type of harmony is to give Christ's life as an organic whole in direct and simple fashion. The piece evidently was prepared for daily readings and meditation.

METRICAL LIFE OF CHRIST [32]. Fourteenth century; 5520 four-stress lines in rimed couplets; Northeast Midland. Begins imperfectly, and about 80 lines are missing after line 803. Edited in an unpublished dissertation. It is followed in its manuscript by miracles of the Virgin. In its present state, the *Life* begins with the nativity, continues with the Gospel story with many accretions, and ends with the apparitions and Pentecost. Although in places the narrative is fairly direct and rapid, the verse generally is rough and uninspired.

PASSION OF OUR LORD [33]. Thirteenth century; 706 seven-stress lines with caesura, in rimed couplets with the rime sometimes extending through quatrains; Southwestern. After a short summary of Christ's preaching following the temptation in the wilderness, the poem gives the events of the passion from Palm Sunday through Pentecost. The whole is prefaced by twenty lines in which the poet states his subject, noting that this is not a tale of Charlemagne and his knights. The poem has, however, qualities of a romance, as, for example, in the dramatic emphasis on action, the emotional telling of the betrayal and suffering, the participating Roman "knights," and the direct dialogue. It is free of homiletic amplification.

WALTER KENNEDY'S PASSION OF CHRIST [34]. Late fourteenth or early fifteenth century; Scottish; 1715 lines in rime royal. The seventy-line prologue opens with "Hail, Cristin knycht, haill, etern confortour." The poem proper covers in summary fashion man's fall, the annunciation, the nativity, and a few events in Christ's life, and then proceeds to a greatly expanded account of the betrayal, judgment, and crucifixion. The ten apparitions of Christ and the ascension follow. Although lengthy, the poem is well-constructed, and at times the style is strong and effective.

FIFTEENTH-CENTURY PASSION OF CHRIST [35]. Scottish poem, anonymous, of fifteenth century, consisting of eight eight-line stanzas, ababbcbc, and extant in three manuscripts. Begins "Compatience persis, reuth and marcy stoundis." Addressing Christ directly, the poet alludes successively to the events of the passion while lyrically focusing attention on his own emotional response. An artistic unity and a sense of controlled energy result from this concentration.

RESURRECTION AND APPARITIONS [36]. Fifteenth century; 605 lines in six-line stanzas, aabccb, the third and sixth lines with three stresses and the others with four. There are a number of gaps and defects in the only extant copy. The story is told as a medieval romance: Pilate selects four knights with medieval names to guard the tomb; bishops and palmers and castles appear; speeches and dialogue abound. The story is told with vigor and some skill. The poem begins with Sir Pilate and the four knights and at the end comes back again to them, with the tomb now empty, Christ risen, and the story completed.

CLEMENT OF LLANTHONY'S HARMONY OF THE GOSPELS [37]. 1375–1400. A translation of Clement of Llanthony's *Unum ex quattuor*, existing in an undetermined number of manuscripts. Clement was a prior of Llanthony in Gloucestershire during the latter part of the twelfth century. His *Harmony* was one of the popular theological works of medieval times. The translation was probably made by a Lollard, and the text is said to be close to that of the Earlier Wyclyfite Version (see below [52]). Its exact relationship to the Wyclyfite versions has not been determined. In addition to Clement's prologue, two other prologues occur in some of the manuscripts. These, which were printed by Forshall and Madden, have been connected with Purvey, and contain arguments for the existence of the Scriptures in English. (See III [51], "Twelve Tracts or Sermons.") The text of the *Harmony* consists of fairly long passages from the Vulgate arranged chronologically. In some manuscripts Epistles and other Scriptural passages on the subject of Christian doctrine are added to the *Harmony*.

COMMENTARY ON THE FOUR GOSPELS [38]. 1375–1400. Called also the "Glossed Gospels," the work contains the Gospel text in English accompanied by lengthy commentaries. The commentaries are mainly derived from the *Catena aurea* of Thomas Aquinas. No more than two of the Gospels occur in any one of the extant manuscripts. The commentaries accompany passages of the Biblical text of from one to twelve verses in length. Some of the commentaries are brief and some greatly expansive. They appear in abridged forms in some of the manuscripts, and there occur two different commentaries for Matthew. The English text of the Biblical passages agrees closely with that of some of the Wyclyfite Bible manuscripts (see below [52]), and the commentaries correspond with marginal glosses in some manuscripts of the Wyclyfite New Testament. Purvey, usually accepted as the chief reviser of the Wyclyfite Version, may have been author of this version of the Gospels. The version was likely made after the completion of the Earlier Wyclyfite; but in the absence of original copies, both of the marginal glosses in Wyclyfite manuscripts and of the Gospel Commentaries, the exact relationship of our piece to the Wyclyfite revisions has not been worked out. The prologues and epilogues to the different Gospels discuss both authorities used and the Lollard problem of clerical opposition to the multiplication of the Scriptures in English.

COMMENTARY ON MATTHEW, MARK, AND LUKE [39]. 1325–1375; North Midland. Composed in the following pattern: a passage of the Latin, an English translation, and a patristic comment or gloss translated from Peter Lombard. *Matthew* occurs alone in two manuscripts, and *Mark* and *Luke* in a third. In a prologue to the *Commentary on Matthew* there are suggestions, but no real evidence, of a connection between the author and the Lollards or even Wyclyf himself. Actually, however, the *Commentary* is quite orthodox and uncontroversial, and the work may have been undertaken and carried out entirely within the pale of clerical conservatism. The Biblical translation is literal and awkward.

COMMENTARY ON THE BENEDICTUS [40]. Fourteenth century. A prose translation and commentary of about 3000 words, verse by verse or phrase by phrase, of the canticle in Luke 1:68–79. Its attribution to Walter Hilton has met with some opposition. The author apparently was a contemplative, he was concerned for the peace and unity of the Church, and he was probably acquainted with the mystical commentaries such as Rolle's Psalter. There are internal hints that he wrote rather late in the century.

BODLEY VERSE PIECES [41]. Fourteenth century; four short pieces in four-stress lines rimed in couplets. The pieces paraphrase the following Gospel passages: John 1:1–14 ("In beginning worde it was," 40 lines); the annunciation, Luke 1:26–28 ("In þat time, als was ful wel," 48 lines); the nativity, Matthew 2:1–12 ("When þat Iesus was born yhing," 50 lines); the commission of the eleven apostles, Mark 16:14–20 ("In þat time and in þat lande," 34 lines). These four excerpts from the Gospels were popular, frequently standing first in medieval *Horae* and primers. The first of them especially, *In Principio,* is important both liturgically and doctrinally. All are evidently metrical versions of the Gospels for certain days. They correspond in verse-form, dialect, matter, and expression to certain pieces of the Northern Homily Cycle (see under Homilies), and may have come from a common original. (See below [42]).

RAWLINSON STROPHIC PIECES [42]. The same four Gospel passages as in [41], here paraphrased in stanzas with six four-stress lines riming aaaaaa with usually three stresses alliterated. The refrain "With an O and an I" repeated in the first half of line 5 in each stanza places the poems in the O-and-I-refrain group (see under Poems Dealing with Contemporary Conditions). Their manuscript is Northern and four-teenth century. The pieces are as follows: "Luke in his lesson," 48 lines; "Mathew his manhede," 48 lines; "Marke of his myghtes," 30 lines; "John of his heghnes," 30 lines. Their style is more lyrical than that of the Bodley Verse Pieces, and they reflect considerable poetic art. It has been held that in origin these pieces are connected both to the Bodley Verse Pieces and the Northern Homily Cycle (see under Homilies), the Bodley Pieces representing an intermediate stage of development from the stage represented by the Homilies. The Homilies, however, cannot be a direct source for either.

BALLAD OF TWELFTH DAY [43]. Thirteenth century; ten stanzas of eight four-stress lines riming abababab. "Wolle ye iheren of twelte day." The subject is the journey of the three kings to the Christ child. It occurs in MS Trinity Cambridge 323 just before the *Trinity Poem on Biblical History* (see [50]), with evidence on the pages of the *Trinity Poem* that the writer or scribe of that poem was working on the com-position of the *Ballad of Twelfth Day*. These fragments of a first draft reveal elements of the poem in the process of composition. The affinity of subject matter in the two poems offers the possibility that the *Trinity Poem* suggested the *Ballad* to the writer. The same scribe wrote the *Ballad of Judas* (see under Ballads) in the manuscript, listed by Child as by several centuries the earliest recorded English ballad. With its more sophisticated metrical pattern, and further removed as it is from the true ballad tradition, the *Ballad of Twelfth Day* might be looked upon as a thirteenth century imitation of a popular ballad. Character-istics of this manuscript indicate that it may have been compiled in a religious house whose members from time to time wrote in it pieces they wished to preserve for their use.

WOMAN OF SAMARIA [44]. Thirteenth century, perhaps before or near 1250; 77 septenary verses in riming couplets, with two quatrains at the end, aaaa; Southwest Midland. "þo ihesu crist an eorþe was." A paraphrase of John 4:4–30. It has been suggested that the piece is an antecedent of the *South English Legendary* (see under Legends, V [1]).

Like other medieval paraphrases of Biblical narrative, the poem has a homely simplicity in its incidents, persons, and dialogue that quite effectively domesticates the New Testament material.

PARABLE OF THE LABORERS [45]. 1300–25; five stanzas aabaabccbccb, except the last stanza, which rimes aabaabccbddb; the lines predominantly have three stresses; Southern with Midland traits. "Of a mon Matheu þohte." It paraphrases Matthew 20:1–16, with the last stanza expressing the restlessness of the poet over his sins and those of the blameworthy people in the parable who desired more than their penny.

A LERNYNG TO GOOD LEUYNGE [46]. 1400–25; twenty stanzas of eight four-stress lines, abababab; Midland, probably South or Southwest. So entitled in MS Bodleian 1703, the poem begins, "Pore of spirit, blessed be." It is a free paraphrase in skilful verses of a portion of the Sermon on the Mount, in particular of Matthew 5:3–16. It has been attributed to the same author as the poems associated with it in the manuscript, poems in which there are believed to be numerous political and social allusions to the reigns of Henry IV and V. The author was probably a priest, or an abbot or prior.

PROSE VERSION OF EPISTLES, ACTS, AND MATTHEW [47]. More accurately "versions," for it is only by combination in single manuscripts that two different versions are associated. One is Southern, its chief character being Southwestern but with deviating forms suggesting a Kentish original or the work of Kentish scribes. This probably formed the original collection. It is represented by a "Prologue" or tract; the Catholic Epistles of 1–2 Peter, James, and 1 John; and the Pauline Epistles. The other is Northern or Northeast Midland, and it is represented by all the Catholic Epistles, Matthew 1–6, and the Acts. The copies of this version are southernized, although the Acts, and Matthew to a lesser degree, occur in a form closer than the Epistles to a North Midland original. It is likely that all these translations were made during the time of Wyclyf, between 1380 and 1400, with perhaps the

Northern version slightly the earlier, and the Southern somewhere in the neighborhood of 1388.

The portion of Matthew in these versions seems to be related to the version in the "Glossed Gospels" (see above [38]), but is a freer rendering. It is possible, but by no means probable, that this unglossed North Midland version, the Glossed Gospels, and the North Midland Pauline Epistles (see below [48]) are all connected in origin.

The compiler of the Prose Version as it appears in two manuscripts (Corpus Christi Cambridge 434 and Selwyn Cambridge 108.L.1) combined the Northern version of 2–3 John and Jude, the Acts, and Matthew 1–6 with the Southern version of 1–2 Peter, James, 1 John, and the Pauline Epistles. The Southern translator possibly discovered the Northern version only after his own work had progressed through the Epistles up to 2 John. All the Catholic Epistles in the Northern version appear in another manuscript (Bodleian 21824).

The long Prologue that occurs with the Southern Epistles is a tract that makes no mention of the translation following. It contains a discourse on Old Testament matters, and a dialogue between two "brothers," and then between a "brother" and a "sister." A brother is requested to teach those things necessary for the salvation of the soul, and in the course of his reply he emphasizes the dangers he will run in translating Biblical matters. The Prologue ends with the brother's discourse on the moral and ceremonial laws of the Old Testament. The brother and sister converse again more briefly before the start of the Pauline Epistles, and at several points in the version the sister is directly addressed. The characters and dialogue are probably a literary framework. Nevertheless, the version may have been prepared at least partly for the benefit of nuns. There is no evidence that the writer was a convinced Lollard.

NORTHERN PAULINE EPISTLES [48]. Later fourteenth century; mainly Northeast Midland. A prose translation of the Pauline Epistles. The Latin Vulgate accompanies the English, and the English text contains a few short glosses, amplifications, and alternative renderings. The alternating passages in Latin and English vary in length from part of a verse to an entire chapter, becoming longer in the latter part of the work. The translation is literal and awkward, its English style being inferior to that of most fourteenth-century versions, including the Early Wyclyfite. The glosses appear to have been made by the original translator, and many of them aim merely to make the English clearer. No sources are clearly identifiable for the few glosses that might be dependent on a commentary. Although the translation dates from about the period of the Wyclyfite, it bears no marks of Lollardy, and was quite likely made by a monk or secular cleric for the purposes of teaching.

APOCALYPSE AND COMMENTARY [49]. Fourteenth century; earliest version probably North Midland. The Middle English *Apocalypse and Commentary* was translated from the French of the Norman or Anglo-Norman version of the preceding century and a half, a version that was adopted into the French Bibles of the thirteenth and fourteenth centuries. These Norman versions survive in many copies, and the manuscripts of the Middle English versions number some seventeen. There are three classes of Middle English text. The first two, the earlier of them dating probably from about 1340–70, are based on differing French forms. The translator of the second probably was acquainted with the first. The third Middle English class, based on the second, is the version of the Later Wyclyfite (see below [52]). Eight of the manuscripts have been identified by Paues (1902 edition) as belonging to the first class, some of them containing numerous mistranslations and omissions. The Biblical text of the two manuscripts of the second class agrees frequently with the Later Wyclyfite. One manuscript represents the third class. These relationships suggest a possible interesting use by the Wyclyfite translators of earlier existing versions. Until, however, more is known about the varieties and stages of the Wyclyfite versions themselves, the relationship to them of the successive forms of the Middle English *Apocalypse* cannot be definitely stated.

All the Middle English texts are accompanied by a commentary, which is virtually the same in all, and which for long was ascribed to Wyclyf. Text and commentary come in sections of three to five verses each. The commentary translates the French quite faithfully. Most of the manuscripts begin with a prologue deriving from Gilbert de la Porée. The commentary has also been said to be that of Gilbert, although Paues

(1902 edition, pages xxii and xxiv) asserts the Latin original "has not yet been discovered."

For other treatments of New Testament material, see

Groups of Homilies, under Homilies.

Legends of Jesus and Mary, under Legends.

Gospel of Nicodemus, under Legends (V [312]).

Cursor Mundi, under Works of Religious Instruction.

The Pater Noster (III [13], [14], [57]), also under Works of Religious Instruction, also under Rolle and His Followers.

Works on the Passion of Christ, under Works of Religious Instruction, also under Rolle and His Followers.

The Southern Temporale, below Section 4.

Wyclyfite Versions, below [52].

Dramatic Pieces.

Pearl (II [2]).

3. THE OLD AND NEW TESTAMENTS

TRINITY POEM ON BIBLICAL HISTORY [50]. Thirteenth century; 344 seven-stress verses in quatrains, usually aaaa; Southwestern. Beginning with the fall of Lucifer, the poem treats briefly some of the events of Old and New Testament history, dwelling more fully on the coming of the Magi, the acts of Herod, and the flight into Egypt, with mention of apostles and martyrs. The material is general and universal, pointing to no specific sources.

BIBLE SUMMARY [51]. In prose, probably later fourteenth century; four leaves of the original 216 lost at the end, twelve others throughout. Summarizes the Bible book by book and chapter by chapter, with 2 Maccabees, the Apocalypse, and most of the Catholic Epistles missing. The summaries from Genesis to Job are very short, the book of Ruth being summarized in the equivalent of four biblical verses. Thereafter the summaries are longer. Where the Bible is quoted directly, as it is most often in the Psalms, the text sometimes agrees with one or the other of the Wyclyfite versions and sometimes with neither. It contains a summary of the fourth book of Ezra, which is not found in the Wyclyfite or in many Latin Bibles. Notes on the flyleaves by an early nineteenth-century owner attribute the work to Trevisa. There appears to be no further evidence of this authorship, and David C. Fowler reports that "the language is very different from Trevisa's."

WYCLYFITE VERSIONS [52]. 1380–95. The first complete translation of the Bible into English, made at Oxford or nearby by associates and followers of John Wyclyf from the Latin Vulgate. More than 170 extant manuscripts contain the version entire or in part. There are at least two distinct versions, possibly three, and the stages of revision are complexly mingled in many of the copies. In its earlier forms the translation is literal and unidiomatic; in its later ones it is a smooth and effective rendering, with many verses anticipating the phrasing of the modern versions of the sixteenth and seventeenth centuries.

The only complete edition is that of Forshall and Madden (FM), published in 1850, which contains in parallel columns an Early and a Late Version (EV and LV). This edition has served as the basis for most of the studies done on Wyclyfite Bibles since 1850, and thus has been the base for most of the conclusions drawn about them. The editors made use of some 59 manuscripts, basing EV on five manuscripts and LV mainly on one. FM's view that Nicholas Hereford and perhaps Wyclyf himself were mainly responsible for EV, and John Purvey for LV, was accepted for many years. Later opinion has discounted Wyclyf's own participation in the actual work of translation, although recently one scholar, Sven L. Fristedt, on rather doubtful evidence, has returned to the belief that Wyclyf may have engaged personally in the work. It is still generally accepted that Hereford was one of the translators of EV and that Purvey was a leader in the work of revision resulting in LV.

Cardinal Gasquet's argument in 1897, that the Middle English Bible as we have it is not Wyclyf's at all but an older translation stemming from orthodox sources, found little acceptance.

Recent studies of the manuscripts tend to reveal a more complicated process of revision and copying than is represented by FM's EV and LV. In particular, extensive exploratory studies by Fristedt (1953), including a review of FM's methods of editing, throw doubt on some of FM's central findings, as, for example, the identification of the original manuscript of EV. Instead of one revision, Fristedt believes there were at least two. Other recent limited studies have produced further evidence both of the complexity of the problem and of the likelihood of more than one revision. At this writing, the number of uncollated manuscripts, together with the confusion of revisions, corrections, and errors throughout all, necessitates further intensive investigation before questions about text, date, and authorship can be answered with any degree of confidence.

As a step in such an investigation, MS Bodleian 959, which contains EV from Genesis to Baruch 3:20 and which FM believed to be an original manuscript, is being edited by Conrad Lindberg (vols 1, 1959; 2, 1961; 3, 1963; 4, 1965). Lindberg believes with Fristedt that this manuscript is a direct copy of the original, although his findings do not agree completely with Fristedt's. His tentative conclusions in the 1961 volume are in part that Hereford was very likely the translator of this part of EV, and that it was probably completed about 1390 instead of 1382 as FM conjectured.

The connection of the Wyclyfite versions with the Lollard movement is little apparent in the Biblical text, but rather in the General Prologue, appearing in some of the manuscripts. This Prologue constitutes an introduction to the books of the Old Testament, and it includes statements of the Lollard views about the translating and reading of Scripture. In addition it includes an enlightened set of principles for translating, principles exemplified and justified by the revisions themselves.

4. The Southern Temporale

THE SOUTHERN TEMPORALE [53], as it occurs in the *South English Legendary*, is a composite of Scriptural materials on the birth, life, death, and resurrection of Christ, of certain Old Testament narratives, and of expositions of the chief festivals in the Church year. In its provenience, its language and versification, and its point of view and purpose, it is a part of the *Legendary*, and the reader is referred to that section (Legends V [1]) for a discussion of these subjects.

The homogeneity of the *Legendary* characterizes the Temporale. What were probably the latest additions to the Temporale, the *Long* and *Short Lives of Christ* and the *Old Testament History,* drew on earlier materials and maintained the original serious didactic spirit and simplicity of presentation. Although the question of authorship in the *Legendary* is unsettled, single authorship could apply to much of the Temporale as to the Sanctorale.

Probably the earliest pieces in the Temporale were the expositions of the Church festivals, with their clear purpose of informing and instructing the laity, the "lewede" folk, concerning important matters in their religion. The *Southern Passion* may have followed soon. The *Concepcio Marie,* in one form a piece serving as a life of St. Anne, developed into a partial life of Christ. The materials centering on the two great feast days, Christmas and Easter, became blended into full Gospel narratives. The desire to instruct further in the Scriptural sources for other seasons of the Church year perhaps led finally to the introduction of the Old Testament materials. Such may have been the structural development of the Southern Temporale.

The various manuscripts reflect the conflicting principles on the one hand of distributing the Temporale through the *Legendary* according to the calendar and on the other of collecting it as a unit at the beginning. The early Corpus Christi Cambridge 145 and Harley 2277, for example, distribute it according to the calendar, while Lambeth 223 groups all the Temporale material (except for the immovable feasts) at the beginning. Some manuscripts, as Egerton 1993, place all the Old and New Testament pieces at the beginning, but distribute the pieces on festivals, both movable and immovable, throughout the year. One manuscript, St. John's Cambridge 28, contains the Temporale almost exclusively and in a complete form. We may assume that as the Temporale grew in content the tendency developed to separate it from the Sanctorale.

I. Old Testament

OLD TESTAMENT HISTORY [54]. Probably one of the later additions to the Temporale. Begins: "Whan hit comyth in my þouȝt, þe meche sorwe and synne." As it appears in MSS Egerton 1993, Bodleian 3938, and St. John's College Cambridge 28, it contains some 1800 lines;

there are expanded texts. It gives Old Testament narrative from the creation to Habakkuk, following the *Historia scholastica* of Peter Comestor. It opens with a brief prologue, melancholy in tone, on man's sorrow and sin. It has been suggested that the joyful prologue to the *Concepcio Marie* (see below [57]) may have suggested to the poet this contrasting one. There is no Old Testament history in the *Legenda aurea*. Quite possibly this material, like other Biblical matter in the *Southern Temporale*, arose from the need and desire for Scriptural knowledge among the unlearned.

II. New Testament

LONG LIFE OF CHRIST [55]. In ten manuscripts of the *South English Legendary*, in most of them partially. In its complete form in MS St. John's Cambridge 28, it runs to nearly 3900 lines. Beginning with the account of Joachim and Anna as it appears in *Concepcio Marie* (see below [57]), it follows that poem to where the *Concepcio*, in two of its manuscripts, ends. From there on the *Long Life* makes varying use of the *Concepcio Marie* and the *Southern Passion* (see below [58]). There are identical passages, and there is frequent verbal agreement. But the author of the *Long Life* added new contents and rearranged and abridged material from the others, with the apparent intent of creating one complete life of Christ. The inclusion of apocryphal matter, such as the wonders happening on the flight into Egypt or the three kinds of blood spilled by Jesus at the crucifixion, indicates that the composer was probably not the same as the scrupulous author of the *Southern Passion*.

SHORT LIFE OF CHRIST [56]. Appears only in Egerton 1993; 472 lines. Includes lines and couplets taken directly from the other Gospel pieces of the Southern Temporale and from the *Origin of the Festival of the Conception of Mary* (see under Legends V [319]). It opens with the introductory five lines of the *Long Life* (see above [55]), beginning "þe prophetes tolden while, in here prophecie." The events of the birth of John the Baptist, the annunciation, and the nativity are told in detail, but the subsequent events of Christ's life are treated briefly up to an abrupt termination in the midst of the crucifixion.

CONCEPCIO MARIE [57]. This poem of the Southern Temporale, occurring in five manuscripts, begins with Isacar, the father of Anne the mother of Mary, and treats the conception, birth, and early life of Mary, up to her wedding with Joseph. In MSS Pepys 2344 and Bodleian 6924, the poem is associated mainly with St. Anne, and contains about 277 lines. MS Egerton 1993, however, continues the poem some 900 lines farther, covering the birth of John the Baptist, the nativity, and the flight into Egypt, to the incident of the boy Jesus in the temple. This represents the matter of the advent and Christmas Gospels. With this addition the piece definitely takes its place among the Temporale pieces on the life of Christ and is closely related to the others. An eighty-line lyrical introduction begins: "Of ioie and blisse is now mi þouʒt, care to bi leue." The poem proper begins: "A god mon þat het Isacar was bi olde dawe." An entirely different version of the *Concepcio Marie* is said to be found in MS Trinity Cambridge 605.

SOUTHERN PASSION [58]. Appearing in some completeness in ten manuscripts, the poem weaves into a continuous narrative the Gospel events from Palm Sunday, through the crucifixion and resurrection, to the Pentecost. At its fullest it contains about 2550 lines. It was probably a very early or contemporary addition to the original Temporale material of the *South English Legendary*, assimilating a brief exposition of Easter which occurs separately in some manuscripts of the *Legendary*. It in turn was used in the composition of the *Long Life of Christ* (see above [55]). There is no reason to question a common authorship with the other parts of the *Legendary*, or to doubt its original preparation for the *Legendary*. Sources are the Vulgate and Peter Comestor, although, as with the *Legendary* as a whole, the main direct source may have been Jacobus de Voragine's *Legenda aurea*. It has also been held that significant resemblances, especially in the lyrical and hortatory tone of the *Southern Passion*, link the poem with the *Meditationes vitae Christi* as a source. The didactic spirit of the *Southern Passion*, its faithful, sober, and discriminating use of Scriptural material, and its skillful composition of the matter from the four Gospels, distinguish it among the Middle English renderings of the story of Christ.

EUANGELIUM IN PRINCIPIO [59]. This consists of 190 lines of extended paraphrase and exposition of the first fourteen verses of St. John's Gospel. It appears in three manuscripts of the *South English Legendary*, and begins: "Among holy gosspelles alle, hit is nouʒt goed to byleue." The passage in John is one of the Gospels for the mass on Christmas Day, and was in the Middle Ages considered one of the most significant of all Scriptural passages for the Christian Church. (See above [41]).

III. Movable Feasts

Explanations of the movable festivals in the Church year appear as a part of the Temporale in the *South English Legendary*. They occur in a majority of the Temporale manuscripts, some more often than others. Certain ones were probably a part of the *Legendary* in its earliest form. In some manuscripts they appear distributed according to the seasons, while in others they are gathered in a group. The first one, *Septuagesima*, includes six introductory lines naming the five movable feasts. It begins: "Festen mouable þer beoþ icluped viue in þe ʒere."

SEPTUAGESIMA [60]. After the six introductory lines on movable feasts, six more follow, beginning "Septuagesime is icluped wanne, me loukeþ alleluye." On this Sunday the singing of Alleluia is discontinued until Easter, in preparation for the penitence of Lent.

LENT (QUADRAGESIMA [61]. "Leinte comeþ þer afterward, þat six wike ilasteþ." An explanation, in 175 lines, of the length of the Lenten period, with examples of fasting under the Old and New Law, and with lengthy monitions about fasting, shriving, and penance.

EASTER [62]. A piece containing 58 lines, beginning "þe holy feste of Ester comþ, after Leinte anon." It identifies the actual day of the crucifixion with the anniversary of the annunciation, which in that year was on the day of the full moon. Thereafter the day of the full moon determined the date of Good Friday.

LETANIA MINOR (ROGATION) [63]. "þe feste of þe Rouysons, þe lasse Letanie is." An explanation of Rogation Days and the processions, in 22 lines.

ASCENSION [64]. The feast of Holy Thursday, as incorporated into the *Southern Passion*, occupies 50 lines. It begins: "ʒut com Ihesus þe teoþe tyme, ar he wente to heuene." It is an account of Jesus' last appearance, his promise of the gift of the Holy Ghost to his disciples, and his ascension into heaven.

WHITSUNDAY [65]. Account in some 30 lines of the gift of tongues to the disciples at Pentecost, as included in the *Southern Passion*. It begins, "At hondern a wytsonday, as þe apostles stode and sede."

CORPUS CHRISTI [66]. This consists of 268 lines, occurring in two manuscripts. Beginning "þe hyʒe feste of goddus blood, þat late was I-founde," the piece tells of the founding of the Feast of Corpus Christi by Pope Boniface IV and the virtue attendant on its observance. It explains why the manna of the Jews is in no way to be compared to the body and blood of Christ. The miracle of transubstantiation is expounded at length, together with Christ's words when he instituted the Eucharist and a statement of the significance of the Eucharist to man.

IV. Immovable Feasts

Explanations of the Immovable Feasts appear as a part of the Southern Temporale. They generally are distributed through the *South English Legendary* according to the calendar.

CIRCUMCISION (YEAR'S DAY) [67]. A piece of twenty-eight lines in some eighteen manuscripts, beginning "ʒeresday þe holy feste, hey day is and god." It explains three significances of the day, the three names Christ had on earth, and four reasons for Christ's circumcision. In MS Bodleian 1486 (Laud 108) is found an entirely different notice about the feast, five lines in length, beginning "þe furste feste þat in þe ʒere comez, we cleopiez ʒeres-dai." It follows six lines of general introduction to the feast days.

EPIPHANY (TWELFTH DAY) [68]. Following directly on the Feast of the Circumcision, Epiphany is explained in some seventeen manuscripts in a short piece of twelve lines. It begins, "Twelþe day þe heiȝe feste, noble is to holde." Four things are named that make this day holy. An entirely different version of this feast occurs in MS Bodleian 1486 (Laud 108). This too is twelve lines long, and recounts a comparable list of significances for the day. It begins, "He was Nyne and twenti ȝer, and þrettene dawes old."

ANNUNCIATION [69]. "Seinte Marie day in Leinte, among oþer dawes gode." This piece of 24 lines occurring in many of the manuscripts of the *South English Legendary* cites this day as one of the highest feasts. In addition to celebrating the annunciation, it is the anniversary of several other events of the Old and New Testaments, including Christ's death (see above [62]).

LETANIA MAJOR (ST. MARK'S DAY) [70]. The Greater Litany is treated in conjunction with the Lesser (see above [63]). It occupies 30 lines. The distinction between the two Litanies is given, and also the reason for the celebration of St. Mark's Day. The opening line reads, "Letanie is a song, as ȝe moweþ ofte iseo."

ALL SAINTS [71]. About 80 lines, beginning "Alle Halewe day schulle holde, o tyme in þe ȝere." The piece explains the several reasons for having All Saints' Day. It tells about the building of a church in Rome by Pope Boniface in honor of Mary and All Saints, about the changing of the date of the feast by Pope Gregory, and about a vision of Christ and Mary and the saints in heaven, as seen by the warden of St. Peter's.

ALL SOULS [72]. A long piece of some 380 lines, beginning "Alle Soulen day an vrþe, riȝt is to holde heȝe." It treats the subject of purgatory and tells how men on earth may help souls in purgatory and how some souls go straight to heaven. It ends with a condemnation of a sinful priest, which is followed by two anecdotes.

V. SAINTS' LEGENDS

by

Charlotte D'Evelyn and Frances A. Foster

Wells's use of the term legend as a literary classification is embracive and indefinite, as a glance at his Table of Contents shows. His chapter on Romances has as subheadings Arthurian Legends, Charlemagne Legends, and Legends of Troy. His chapter on Homilies and Legends has the subdivisions Legends of Saints, and Other Legends, including the Saga of Adam and Eve. Legend, in other words, is equated with Romance, with Homily, with Saga. The vagueness of the term legend is an inheritance from the Middle Ages, as one may note in Chaucer's titles: the *Romaunt of the Rose* and the *Legend of Good Women*. Modern critics have been well aware of the difficulty of isolating the essential quality of legend as a type of narrative. It must suffice here to refer to the discriminating opening chapter on Definition and Use in Gerould's *Saints' Legends* (1916) and to the lucid learning of Father Helehay's *The Legends of the Saints* (see the translation by V. M. Crawford issued by the University of Notre Dame, 1961), in his initial chapter on Preliminary Definitions. One seeks nowadays not the definition but the genre of the legend as a narrative form. The specific hereditary element of this type of narrative still escapes modern microscopic investigation. A comparatively recent discussion of saints' legends in the Middle Ages,— Theodor Wolpers, *Die englischen Heiligenlegenden des Mittelalters* (Buchreihe der Anglia Zeitschrift für Englische Philologie 10 Band, Tübingen, 1964)—reviews with much learning and understanding the more important analyses of the genre legend made by Horstmann, ten Brink, Gerould (pp. 14–17), and offers his own analysis of the factor which distinguishes legend from history or biography or allegory. (For fuller discussion of Wolpers see Spec 42.213). Wolpers accepts the saint's legend as a narrative with the double purpose of honoring the saint and instructing the audience or reader in the significance of the saint for Christian faith. Without this second element the saint's legend is only history or biography. The legend of the specific saint reflects the condition of the saintliness of his period. The retelling of a saint's legend over periods of time would, presumably, reflect changes in the most fundamental factors of Christian belief. Wolpers does not work out his theory in detail for any one saint, but his is a challenging idea that could give new significance to the investigation of successive versions of the lives of the more universally honored saints. As the use of the concept of genre in defining legend reflected the dominating concept of evolution in the nineteenth century, so the attempt to analyze the quality of a saint's saintliness involves the concepts of grace and faith and reflects the twentieth-century willingness to accept concepts of psychology such as ESP in the explanation of saintliness rather than physical endurance of suffering or mental patience under persecution. The saint is born, not made.

Wolpers is interested also in less tenuous aspects of legend, such as artistic representations. He has had the advantage of studying the fairly recently (1923) recovered fifteenth-century wall paintings in the Chapel of Eton College. He studies grouping, shading, gesture, spacing, and the movement of the painted curve as well as the flow of the written line of verse. Whether or not one accepts all his comparisons, he makes one aware of the opening up of new fields of investigation and appreciation of the legends of saints and of the vitality of their narratives even today.

In this chapter are treated not only Saints' Legends but also related religious legends dealing with Adam and Eve, the Cross, Jesus and Mary, and the After-Life. Several changes have been made from Wells's arrangement of the material on the Legends (Wells V). The legends are here separated from the homilies; the latter will be dealt with in a later chapter. The Temporale material in the *South English Legendary* (Wells V [67–69], [71]) has been transferred to Translations and Paraphrases of the Bible (see below, IV [28], [29], [36], [53–71]). English Translations of the *Legenda aurea* (Wells V [21], [25–26]) are grouped here in a new Section 2. Lydgate's legends (Wells V [23]) are merely listed here in Section 3 (Legends of Individual Saints). They will be treated in detail in a later chapter dealing with Lydgate. The four legends in MS Douce 114 (Wells V [28]) have been distributed alphabetically in Section 3. Capgrave's *Nova legenda Anglie* (Wells V [29]) is omitted since it is a Latin, not a Middle English, text. Its English summary, *Kalendre of the new legende of Englande*, printed by Pynson, 1516, is not included partly because of its late date, partly because of its wide coverage of well over a hundred saints whose legends apparently are not extant in Middle English. Again because of its date—early seventeenth century—the Stowe *Lives of Women Saints* (Wells V [30]) is omitted. On the other hand, Caxton's translation of *Vitae patrum*, printed by Wynkyn de Worde, 1495, has been added to Section 1 and its separate items with some exceptions have been included in Section 3.

1. Collections of Saints' Legends

by

Charlotte D'Evelyn

THE SOUTH ENGLISH LEGENDARY (SEL) [1]. In the comprehensiveness of its plan and anonymity of its execution the *SEL* is a typical specimen of medieval moral and religious instruction by narrative example, the narrative example of Biblical history and saint's legend. The plan, a combined Temporale and Sanctorale, is discernible in the earliest surviving manuscript, Bodleian 1486 (Laud Misc. 108) of the late thirteenth century. It is worked out by accretion rather than by development in later manuscripts extending from the early fourteenth through the late fifteenth centuries. By present count the total number of manuscripts, not including those containing single items, is fifty-one, a number which in the Brown-Robbins table of Preservation of Texts (p. 737) puts the *SEL* in fourth place, outnumbered only by the *Prick of Conscience*, the *Canterbury Tales*, and *Piers Plowman*.

The very nature of the material of the *SEL* increases the difficulty of making clear-cut statements on such fundamental matters as authorship and source and even purpose of the work. Many of the question-marks implied in Wells's careful and cautious summary of Horstmann's work and particularly that on manuscripts are still unresolved. Horstmann's comparison of the manuscripts known to him is based primarily on contents and arrangement of contents. Wells has formalized Horstmann's statement of his results and has drawn up eight groups of manuscripts. The first six groups illustrate stages in the growth of the work. The seventh group lists manuscripts which contain small portions of the *SEL*; the eighth, manuscripts which contain usually single items, in no case more than four. The first six groups furnish material for a study of the *SEL* as a whole; the last two are, naturally, of importance for the study of separate legends. Wells points out that the first six groups are not mutually exclusive: cross-cutting is frequent. That fact together with the imperfect condition of most of the manuscripts complicates further the establishment of a satisfactory manuscript tradition for the *SEL* as a whole. In any such attempt, however, the following manuscripts are generally recognized as offering important clues.

(1) Bodleian 1486. The first seven items are missing. The eighth, so numbered in the manuscript, is a fragment of the *Life of Christ*, written in the septenary verse of the *SEL*. That fact suggests that the lost items were also Temporale material and that the *SEL* was indeed originally planned as a combination of Temporale and Sanctorale. The disarray of the Sanctorale material in this manuscript is sufficiently illustrated by the fact that the legend of Thomas Becket (December 29) is followed by a brief prologue announcing

Al þis bok is i-maked of holi dawes: and of holie mannes liues . . .
þei ich of alle ne mouwe nouȝt telle: ichulle telle of some,
Ase euerech feste after oþur: In þe ȝere doth come. —
þe furste feste þat in þe ȝere comeȝ: we cleopieȝ ȝeres-dai . . .

(EETS 87.177)

This misplaced statement is valuable evidence for the early arrangement of the *SEL* according to the secular, not the ecclesiastical, year.

(2) Harley 2277, ca. 1300, and Corpus Christi Cambridge 145, early fourteenth century (group 2.a) were paired by Horstmann as preserving between them the earliest extant arrangement of the *SEL* according to the secular year. Harley 2277 begins imperfectly; Corpus Christi Cambridge 145 is intact. It is assumed that Harley originally contained the Prologue or Banna Sanctorum and the following twenty-four items with which Corpus Christi begins. Both manuscripts continue in the order of the secular calendar through the legend of Thomas Becket (December 29). Both then add the legends of Judas and Pilate, a popular addition to be found frequently in later manuscripts, not necessarily as a mere appendage but incorporated with Temporale material.

(3) Bodleian 2567 (Bodley 779), ca. 1400 (group 5) represents the fullest extent of the Sanctorale material. It adds twenty-seven legends—eleven of popes, sixteen of saints other than popes. Of these twenty-seven legends, the following fourteen are found in no other Middle English ver-

sion: *Anicet, Damasus, Emerentiana,*[1] *Evaristus, Felix "III," Firmin,*[2] *Innocent I, Leo II, Marius and Martha, Melchiades, Oswin King of Deira, Silverius, Sother, Vitalis and Agricola.*

Besides these twenty-seven additions to the contents of the *SEL,* Bodleian 2567 introduces variant septenary texts of *Faith* (Brown-Robbins, no. 1397), *Francis* (Brown-Robbins, no. 3494), and *Silvester* (Brown-Robbins, no. 318), and a stanzaic version of *Margaret of Antioch* (Brown-Robbins, no. 2672) in place of the usual septenary text (Brown-Robbins, no. 2987). Neither the Temporale nor the Sanctorale material in this manuscript follows any recognizable order,—a feature shared notably with the earliest extant manuscript Bodleian 1486.

(4) St. John's Cambridge 28 (B.6), late fourteenth century (group 6). Like the Sanctorale material, the Temporale material of the *SEL* also increased in amount and shifted in position. The most complete version of the Temporale is preserved in St. John's Cambridge 28, without any accompanying Sanctorale. The only traces of Sanctorale material are the legends of Longinus and of Pilate, no saint, which occur between the account of Pentecost and the Harrowing of Hell, and at the end of the manuscript four moveable feasts usually found in the *SEL* Sanctorale. The inclusion and location of these six items, however, are apt to shift from Temporale to Sanctorale.

Two other manuscripts closely studied in more recent work on the *SEL* should be noted:

(5) Bodleian 6924 (Ashmole 43), second quarter of the fourteenth century (group 2.b). This manuscript has been selected as the basic text for editions of *Brendan* (Bälz), *Juliana* (Schleich), and *Thomas Becket* (Thiemke); see under Legends of Individual Saints in the Bibliography. The problem here is the selection of the best text for a single legend and involves a different approach to the manuscripts (see EETS 244.14).

(6) Pepys 2344, second quarter of the fourteenth century. This manuscript is not classified by Horstmann or Wells. It was selected as the basic text for the edition of *The Southern Passion* (EETS 169). It has been

---

[1]In CCC 145, f. g^b, opposite line 129 of the legend of Agnes is the marginal note, Agneta secunda; EETS 235.23. This is the name used for Emerentiana's feast-day in *Legenda aurea,* which combines the legends of Agnes and Emerentiana; Graesse LA, p. 116. But the text of CCC 145 at this point makes no reference to Emerentiana.

[2]Caxton GL, Temple 2.216 records only the *Invention* of Firmin, which is not included in Bodleian 2567.

claimed, further, as offering better evidence than Harley 2277 of direct use of the *Legenda aurea* (M. E. Wells, JEGP 51.337).

Even this small sampling makes clear the diversity of the *SEL* manuscripts. It is obvious the *SEL* had no rigid plan. Its material offered every opportunity to individual scribes to add, to omit, to re-order. Each extant manuscript is, in fact, an individual version of the *SEL* which may offer important clues to the process of its growth as a whole or to its adaptation to local needs or preferences. This evaluation of the manuscripts is still in progress.

The fact that the language of the earliest manuscripts of the *SEL* shows clear marks of Southern and Southwest Midland dialect and that certain verbal parallels with the text of Robert of Gloucester's *Chronicle* occur, led early critics to propose the Abbey of St. Peter's in Gloucester as the probable home of the *SEL* and Robert of Gloucester, singly or in collaboration, as its author. Both claims have been successfully challenged. As to verbal parallels, close comparison of similar passages in the *SEL* and the Chronicle version of the legend of *Brendan* shows that the *SEL* makes independent use of a source common to both, William of Malmesbury's *Gesta regum Anglorum* (see B. D. Brown, MLN 41.19). Fruitful also for the further investigation of the *SEL* has been the reappraisal of that text not as the work of monks but of friars (EETS 169.xciii). It is now generally accepted that the *SEL* was intended for the public instruction of the unlettered laity rather than for the use of monks. The relative claims, however, for the Dominicans or the Franciscans, as its authors, are still being argued. Recognition of the *SEL* as a work directed to the populace has apparently sparked a growing interest in the relation between the *SEL*, both Temporale and Sanctorale, and the cycles of miracle plays.

The determination of the model for the *SEL* as a whole and of the sources for individual legends presents another complex problem. Some connection between the *SEL* and its slightly older contemporary, Jacobus de Voragine's *Legenda aurea* (ca. 1255–1266), seems inevitable. Yet Horstmann (AELeg 1881, p. xlv; EETS 87.viii) maintained from the first that the *SEL* had no direct dependence on the *Legenda aurea*. Later writers have questioned his position and have offered evidence of dependence in general plan, in contents, and in the phrasing of particular legends. The diversity of the source material traceable in the *SEL* is demonstrated in the four detailed studies of separate legends already published, of *Brendan, Juliana, Thomas Becket,* and *Ursula and the Eleven Thousand Virgins* (see under Legends of Individual Saints in the Bibliography). Bälz (ix) concludes that the *SEL Brendan* is based on both the Latin prose *Navigatio S. Brendani Abbatis* and the Anglo-Norse verse version. After examination of a wide range of versions including Cynewulf's and the early prose *Liflade*, G. Schleich (pp. 41, 48) finds none that contains all the material of the *SEL* version and concludes that its author may have welded together several versions. Thiemke's study of the sources of the *SEL Thomas Becket* legend reaches a more certain conclusion. He claims (p. lii) that the *SEL* text is a direct free translation of the Latin prose *Quadrilogus,* itself a "harmony" of four earlier accounts, dating in its first form from 1198–99. In the case of the legend of *Ursula,* results are again uncertain. Schubel (p. 104) accepts the *Legenda aurea* as apparently the model of the *SEL* text.

The term, saint's legend, covers a variety of narrative forms. A typical pattern—conversion (or efforts to convert others), trial, torture and triumphant death—underlies many of the stories of early Christian martyrs. But the accretion of apocryphal material and of miracles turns the legend of a St. Thomas of India or a St. Katherine of Alexandria into a romance of religious adventures. Again, legends such as those in the *SEL* of St. Thomas Becket and St. Edmund Rich have some claim to be called biographies. This variety of subject-matter has been one of the permanent sources of interest in the *SEL* for the hearer or reader, medieval or modern.

The *SEL* makes some uncommon additions to its legendary material. The legend of St. Michael is the outstanding example. A large section of Part II is concerned with the status and powers of the fallen angels in this world after their expulsion from Heaven by St. Michael. Some have become harmless elves and fairies, some evil incubi and nightmares. In particular the unheroic temptations now practiced by the chief of devils on the ordinary fallen man are described with every-day realism. This is the material of folklore and of moral instruction. St. Michael is biding his time until Doomsday. Part III of the same legend has still less to do with St. Michael. It contains a "pseudo-scientific" explanation of the structure of earth and of the cosmos, of the phenomena of weather with its rain and dew and frost, of the four humors of man, and of the development of the human embryo and its three souls. This is the material of common knowledge and experience of the natural world mingled with inherited conceptions of the outer and the other worlds. The only connection of Part III with the preceding material is a neat verbal transition from the last line of Part II ("þat hi [the fallen angels] þe bernynge of helle. wiþ hom ne bereþ aboute") and the first line of Part III (þe riȝte put of helle is . amidde eorþe wiþinne") (EETS 236.414). The irrelevance of Part III to the legend of St. Michael is emphasized by the fact that this section circulated independently and is extant, in whole or in part, in nine manuscripts (Brown-Robbins 3453; Arch 98.401).

A study of the technique of oral delivery in the *SEL* assumes a new interest and importance if one accepts that work as fundamentally preaching material for the use of friars. Evidence for speaker and hearer rather than writer and reader is suggested if not proved in the conventional ending of most of the legends; e.g.,

> Nou God for þe loue of seint Edmund? þat war so noble kyng
> Grante ous þe ioye þat he is inne? after oure ending. Amen
>   (EETS 236.515)

More positively indicative of the presence of an audience are the quips, the taunts, the asides which lose their point if they are not intended to call out reaction on the part of an audience; e.g., this comment on St. Francis's habit of giving away whatever was given to him:

> Wel ich wot þat þer nys non: among vs alle her
> þat gladlich wolde tak his good: to eny soch spenser!—
>   (Arch 82.315, line 155).

However, not all apparently personal and spontaneous comments can be attributed without question to the author or scribe of the *SEL*. Some comments may be taken over from his sources. The sceptical remark about the devil's swallowing of St. Margaret (EETS 235.297, line 165) has its counterpart in the *Legenda aurea*, where the incident is characterized as "apocryphum et frivolum" (Graesse LA, p. 401). Whatever their source, such comments are a trade-mark of the *SEL* and mark it as a work of popular instruction.

THE SCOTTISH LEGENDARY (ScL) [2]. The *ScL* is extant in a single manuscript, Cambridge University Gg.2.6 (first half of the fifteenth century), a defective text with couplets dropped and folios missing. Its contents consist of a general prologue of 171 lines and 50 legends in tetrameter couplets totaling well over 33,000 lines. The legends, as Horstmann pointed out (AELeg 1881, p. lxlvii), are arranged in no conventional order such as that of the ecclesiastical or secular calendar but in eight groups. This arrangement is arbitrary but apparently not haphazard. In his general prologue the author himself outlines the composition of the first group: legends of the twelve apostles headed by Peter and Paul, followed by the remaining ten in the order of the article of the Apostles' Creed which each traditionally sponsored. In the prologue to the legend of *Mark* the author again explains his order. He plans next to give the legends of the evangelists who were not apostles, *Mark* (no. 13) and *Luke* (no. 14). Then follows *Barnabas* (no. 15), whom the author includes at this point because "some men" think, though wrongly, that he, too, was an Apostle. For later groups the arrangement is not so clearly explained, if explained at all, nor so easily discernible. Horstmann's classifications—confessors, martyrs, virgins—are not necessarily the labels the original writer might have supplied. The loss of beginning and ending for several of the legends helps further to obscure the connection between legend and legend or between group and group. The arrangement in any case is obviously elastic.

With the modern discovery of the *ScL*, announced in 1866 by Henry Bradshaw, was coupled the ascription of the work to John Barbour, author of *The Bruce* and Archdeacon of Aberdeen. The writer of the *ScL* speaks of himself as "mynistere of haly kirke" (General Prologue, line 34); the two Scottish saints, Ninian and Machor, whose legends he includes, are associated with Aberdeen; Horstmann claimed that the language of the manuscript of the *ScL* was without doubt the dialect of Aberdeen (Horstmann ScL, p. 305).[3] Early criticism centered in this dispute over the author's identity. The claims for Barbour, based principally on linguistic and stylistic grounds, seem to have been successfully countered. The author of the *ScL* remains anonymous. In fact, it has

---

[3]It is of interest to note that the author himself says: ". . . I haf translat / þe story . . . / In ynglis townge" (no. 18, line 1468).

been questioned whether one author only is responsible for this obviously expanding collection.

The little that is known about this unnamed author he himself has recorded in various scattered remarks. To the commonplace explanation that he writes to avoid idleness for himself and others, he adds a personal reason for the idleness that threatens him: " . . . sene I ma nocht wirk / as mynistere of haly kirke, / for gret eld & febilnes," (General Prologue, line 33). In several other places age and feebleness are his excuse for shortening his story or refusing to argue a point. He will not add to the praises of St. Andrew (no. 3, line 1139) or St. Matthew (no. 10, line 585); he will not record further miracles of St. James the Greater (no. 4, lines 381, 390); he will not set down the genealogy of St. James the Less (no. 7, line 12). It is noteworthy that these references to age and feebleness occur in the first group of legends.

Another commonplace, the formal prayer that customarily ends a legend, becomes in the *ScL* a kind of personal signature, personal because of the constant use of the same or very similar formula and because of the content of that formula. The writer prays that he may depart this world: "bot schame, or deit, or dedly syne." The first occurrence of this formula is in the legend of *Paul* (no. 2, line 1136), the last in *Katherine* (no. 50, line 1211). Variations in the wording are slight, in some cases merely a change of order. The last use of the formula is also the most variant: "out of lyf but dedly syne."[4] The formula itself with its seeming concern for posthumous reputation as well as future reward accords with that impression of the writer's sense of fact and unpretentiousness that one finds throughout the *ScL*.

Definitely personal are the lines in the prologue to the legend of *Julian the Hospitaler* (no. 25, line 1) where the author recalls that he, too, had been a traveler in his youth and had observed how travelers in sight of a hostelry uncovered and said aloud a Pater Noster in honor of St. Julian and in hope of good entertainment. From the literary point of view the most valuable of these personal passages is the writer's detailed account of his previous earlier work: "I hafe translatit symply / sume

4It should be noted that in several cases this formula does not mark the end of the legend as a whole, but rather the end of a section or of an incident. The most conspicuous example of this usage occurs in the legend of *Ninian* where the line appears three times (no. 40, lines 634, 814, 1358). The actual conclusion is lost.

part, as I fand in story, / of Mary & hir sone Ihesu" (General Prologue, line 37). From his following summary it is clear that he has completed a full account of the apocryphal and Biblical story of Mary and Jesus beginning with the conception and birth of the Virgin and ending with her assumption and coronation in heaven; and to this story he has appended sixty-six miracles of the Virgin. This lost work is linked closely to the extant *ScL*. In the legend of *John the Baptist* (no. 36, lines 989, 1214) the writer refers twice to material in the lost work which he will not need to repeat. Critics have noted that these two works would have offered that combination of Temporale and Sanctorale subject matter already familiar in the *SEL* and in the *Cursor Mundi*.

The chief source of the *ScL* is the *Legenda aurea*. That work is named only once, as the source for the legend of *Blasius*. The writer promises to "undo" it " . . . but ony ekine set þare-to, / as in sentence mare ore les" (no. 20, line 17). Closeness of translation, however, and adherence to content of the *Legenda aurea* differ from legend to legend. Again, the legend of St. Thadee (= *Thais*, no. 35) begins: "Of haly faderis in þe lyfe / one wthyre tale I fand ryfe,"—a clear reference to *Vitae patrum*. But since *Legenda aurea* also names this source (Graesse LA, p. 677), both modern editors of the *ScL* quote *Legenda aurea* rather than *Vitae patrum* as the source of the *ScL* legend. No other written sources are directly named. For three legends, however, basic sources have been satisfactorily determined: for *Machor* (no. 27), a lost Latin *Vita S. Macharii* which is also the source of the Lectiones for the office of St. Machor in the Aberdeen Breviary and for the chapters on Machor included in O'Donnell's *Vita S. Columbae*; for *Ninian* (no. 40), Ailred of Rievaulx's *Vita Nianiani*; for *Tecla* (no. 49), *Acta Pauli et Theclae*.

The writer of the *ScL* throughout his work has shown himself a selector and arranger of legends. And books were not his only source of information. He reports a contemporary miracle of St. Ninian, the cure of John Balormy, on his own authority: "& þis mare trastely I say, / for I kend hyme weile mony day" (no. 40, line 1365; see Metcalfe, PSTS 3.410).

Only two "Scottish" saints are included in the *ScL*: Ninian (no. 30, ca. 432), reputedly born in Scotland and the earliest recorded missionary to the southern Picts; Machor (no. 27, sixth century), reputedly born in Ireland, disciple of St. Columba and with him missionary to the northern Picts. St. Margaret, Queen of Scotland (d. 1093) is mentioned briefly in a list of men and women who lived chastely (*Alexis,* no. 24, line 53). None of these three appears in Middle English legendaries. No native English saints are included in the *ScL.* To its author the St. George (no. 33) of whom he writes is St. George of Cappadocia, not the St. George recently named patron saint both of England and of the Order of the Garter.

The question of one or more authors set aside, the author of the *ScL* has been commended by critics particularly for his mastery of the tetrameter couplet in the use of which he varies closed and run-on couplets, and also for his skill in phrase-making within the line and from line to line. In a passage of balanced phrases, for example, he characterizes St. Ninian as follows: "I treu, þare lifis nane / þat al cane say of sancte Ninian, / þat wes sa mek a confessoure / & of vicis persecutore, / lofare of vertu & dyspysare / of þe warld, of hewine ʒarnar, / & for he studit here to be / pouer, in hewine rike is he"/ (no. 40, line 719). But especially the brisk movement of his narrative has been praised. Wells concludes his account of the *ScL* with the comment: "Each piece (however many authors wrote the items) begins with the story, holds to the story, ends with the story" (p. 306).

OSBERN BOKENHAM, THE LIVES OF SAINTS, OR LEGENDS OF HOLY WOMEN [3]. Like the *ScL,* Bokenham's metrical *Lyvys of Seyntys or Legendys of Hooly Wummen* is also extant in a single manuscript, British Museum Arundel 327. On the last page, f. 193ᵃ, is a table of contents, followed by a note identifying the author as "Osbern Bokenam frere Austyn of the convent of Stokclare" and identifying this copy of the text as one written by order of Friar Thomas Burgh at Cambridge in 1447. An interlined note in a hand later than any of the three used in the text further describes the author as "a suffolke man." Within the text Bokenham has provided the date September 7, 1443 for the beginning of his work on the legend of St. Margaret, the first in the series (EETS 206.xix and 6, line 187). *The Legends of Holy Women,* therefore, is to be dated between 1443 and 1447.

The manuscript begins without a title. In the list of contents on the last page, already noted, the collection is described as "þe seyntys Lyuys" and this phrase furnished the name, *Lives of Saints*, used in the Roxburghe and Horstmann editions. Miss Serjeantson has based her "more distinctive title Legendys of Hooly Wummen," on lines within the text: "dyuers legendys . . . Of hooly wummen" (EETS 206.xix, 138, lines 5038–40).

Bokenham's collection includes thirteen legends in the following order: *Margaret, Anne, Christina, the Eleven Thousand Virgins, Faith, Agnes, Dorothy, Mary Magdalen, Katherine of Alexandria, Cecilia, Agatha, Lucy, Elizabeth of Hungary.* Most of the legends were written by request for patrons having a particular devotion to the saint in question or bearing that saint's name. The legend of *Mary Magdalen*, for example, owes its inclusion to Lady Isabel Bourchier, Countess of Eu, who had long cherished "a singular devotion" to this "apostyllesse" (EETS 206.xxi and 139, line 5063); the legend of *Katherine*, to Katherine Denston, wife of John Denston, a man of local reputation, and to Katherine Howard, probably wife of John Howard, future Duke of Norfolk (EETS 206.xx and 174, line 6365).

As to the language both of the author and of the extant text, Bokenham confirms the late inserted description of himself as "a suffolke man" by his own statement in the legend of *Agnes*:

. . . spekyn & wrytyn I wyl pleynly
Aftyr þe language of Suthfolk speche .

(EETS 206.111, line 4063)

The manuscript is accepted as a valuable dated specimen of Southeast Midland dialect.

Bokenham employs a variety of meters: stanzaic forms of seven, eight, or sixteen lines and rimed couplets. Rime royal stanzas and rimed couplets indifferently tetrameter and pentameter are the forms most frequently used. Different versification for the prologue and for the life in the same legend is a constant usage with Bokenham.

The source most often mentioned by him is the *Legenda aurea* of Jacobus de Voragine. He refers to this work sometimes by title, in English or Latin, e.g., "goldene legende," "legenda aurea" (lines 281, 5273) and sometimes by author. The latter is always designated simply as

Ianuence, of Genoa, in reference to Jacobus de Voragine's position as Archbishop of that city (lines 5734, 8544). As his source for the legend of *Anne* he names the life by St. Ambrose, whom he finds "full hard" to follow (line 4711). Whatever his source his method of translation is stated in the familiar formula, not word for word but from sentence to sentence (cf. line 4713).

With all the personal comment which Bokenham has introduced into his Legends of Holy Women, he has not supplied definitely the name of his birthplace, and only indirectly the date of his birth. His surname would presumably be derived from that of his birthplace. Of various attempts made to identify the place, the latest, that of Miss Serjeantson, who equates Bokenham with the modern Old Buckenham in South Norfolk (EETS 206.xiv), seems to fit best with the author's own statements and is now generally accepted. In the legend of *Faith*, Bokenham notes that he was born on her feast-day, October 6. The probable year date, ca. 1392, is calculated from two statements in the General Prologue and in the prologue to the legend of *Margaret* (lines 187, 248) that he was fully fifty years old at the time he began that legend on September 7, 1443 (EETS 206. xv).

The usual assumption that Bokenham died ca. 1447 was based principally on the final note in Arundel 327 stating that this manuscript was copied by order of Thomas Burgh in 1447. The fact that in the General Prologue (line 200) Bokenham had asked Thomas to keep his authorship of the legendary secret and that in the appended note the authorship was openly announced seemed to support the assumption that Bokenham had died. Bokenham, moreover, had scattered throughout his work reference to himself as aged: e.g., fully fifty years (line 248), far run in age (line 1409), now in my last age (line 5040). This dating, however, has been questioned recently on the evidence of official documents of the *OESA*, including a chartulary of Clare Priory, in which Bokenham is named as still active as late as 1464. The new dating proposed for his death is, therefore, "after 1464."

Bokenham wrote other works in English besides the *Legends of Holy Women.* The treatise *Mappula Angliae*, a prose translation in seventeen chapters of Higden's *Polychronicon*, Book I, Chapters 39–60, was written ca. 1443. It is authenticated as his by the signature of his full name

Osbernus Boken[h]am given in an anagram composed of the initial letters of Chapters 2–17. The H has been lost through loss of a folio. Furthermore, in the first chapter of this treatise Bokenham records important information about an earlier work, "the englische boke the whiche y have compiled of legenda aurea and of oþer famous legendes." The *Mappula*, in fact, was written to supply geographical information "fulle herd to knowene" for the English saints in the earlier work. Bokenham names specifically Sts. Chad, Felix, Edward, and Oswald. He is therefore not referring to his metrical *Lives of Holy Women*. Horstmann (EStn 10.2) called attention to several manuscripts of the 1438 *GL* but rejected that text as Bokenham's work. The later investigations of Sister Mary Jeremy, however, have strengthened the case for Bokenham's authorship (see [6] below).

Again, if the revised dating for Bokenham's death "after 1464" is accepted, a third work in English may be assigned to him. This is *A Dialogue betwix a Seculer asking and a Frere answeryng at the grave of Dame Johan of Acres* . . . , dated 1456 and first printed without indication of its provenance in Dugdale, *Mon. Angl.* VI, Part III, p. 1600. This work was accepted as Bokenham's in the Roxburghe Club edition of the *Legends of Holy Women*, but rejected by Horstmann in his edition because of its late date (Horstmann Bokenham, p. 269, note 1). The *Dialogue* is written in rime royal and is paralleled with a metrical Latin translation. Stoke Clare Priory is obviously the setting. In his *Mappula Angliae* Bokenham has described in detail the location of Dame Iohan's (or Jone's) tomb: "in þe frires queere of clare one the sowthe side" (Angl. 10.11). As another possible link with Bokenham may be noted the use in the last line of the *Dialogue* of a familiar phrase, "aftir this outelary," one which in slightly variant forms occurs in the concluding lines of a majority of Bokenham's prologues and legends as a synonym for "this wicked world" (e.g., EETS 206.7, 86, 203, 288).

As a writer Bokenham shows the marks both of scholastic learning and of post-Chaucerian rhetoric. He begins his *Legends of Holy Women* as the learned clerk he is with a promise to explain in orderly procedure the "what" and the "why" of his book. Although he disclaims for himself any eloquence or skill in rhetoric, he is fully aware of the poetic fashions and poetic reputations of his day. To Chaucer, Gower, and

Lydgate he pays the customary undiscriminating homage of the post-Chaucerians. But he also pays to Lydgate and to Capgrave a more knowledgeable tribute. He has read Lydgate's *Life of Our Lady* and Capgrave's *Life of St. Katherine* (EETS 206.55, line 2005; 173, line 6354). For help in his work he invokes Christian grace and the inspiration of the Muses. And when as a humble Christian he repudiates the help of these pagan muses he does so in a roll-call of classical names typical of aureate rhetoric EETS 206.143, line 5214). Bokenham is at his best writing familiarly about himself and his friends,—and the saints, too, were his friends,—about the children of Lady Isabel at their Twelfth Night revels (EETS 206.138, line 5021), or about his jesting with Thomas Burgh on the authorship of his *Legends* (EETS 206.6, line 199), or in his concluding prayer to St. Cecilia reminding her that she and St. Faith and St. Barbara were long ago chosen to be his "valentyns" (EETS 206.225, 8275).

CAXTON, VITAS PATRUM (Caxton VP) [4]. Caxton's *Vitas Patrum* or "the lyfe of olde auncyent faders," is a translation of a contemporary French text published at Lyon in 1486/7, which was itself translated from the *Vitas patrum* traditionally attributed to St. Jerome. Caxton finished his work in 1491 on the last day of his life. Wynkyn de Worde published it at Westminster in 1495. These basic facts are given, presumably by Wynkyn de Worde, in the opening and closing lines of this 1495 edition.[5] Attention was again called to Caxton's translation and its French source by the seventeenth-century scholar Rosweyd (cf. Migne PL 73, col. 79), then at work on a critical edition of the Latin *Vitas patrum*. On the basis of Caxton's text Rosweyd stated that the French text of 1486, which he himself had not seen, was based on the second Latin edition of 1478. But the complicated history of the development of the *Vitas patrum*, which dates back to the fifth century, is not essential to an understanding of Caxton's text. Working in 1491 as an old man, Caxton was apparently no longer interested, as he had been in 1483 when he translated the *Legenda aurea*, in comparing variant texts—French, Latin and English. His *Vitas patrum* is a close rendering of the

---

[5]For the Caxton *VP* a microfilm of the British Museum copy, STC no. 14507, has been used; for the French *VP*, a microfilm of the Huntington Library copy.

French work before him. Even the occasional comments on conditions "nowadays" are not his but the French writer's.

The *Vitae Patrum*, to use the more common form of the title, is a long, composite work unified only by the fact that it is concerned throughout with the lives, the ascetic practices, and hard-won wisdom of the early Christian hermits and monks, especially with those dwelling in the deserts of Egypt.

The work is divided into five parts. On this point the general table of contents in both translations is misleading. In the French text the first folios of this table are missing but an original leaf giving the contents of Part 4 reads: "Consequemment sensuiuent les chappitres contenuz en la quarte et derniere partie de ce volume. . . ." After listing the contents of Part 4 the table reads: "Et finablement sensuiuent les rubriches des chappitres contenuz en ung petit traictie faisant mencion de la louenge des vertuz. Compose por monseigneur saint machaire: et adiouste en la fin dudit quatriesme volume." This is Part 5 but it is not numbered as such here or in the text. The English general table of contents begins: "Here foloweth the declaration of the table of þe chapytres of this present volume conteynyng in it four partyes. . . ." (Sig Aaii[b]). After listing the contents of Parts 1, 2 and 3, the table continues: "Here begynneth þe prologue of saynt Paschayse upon the fourth parte of the lyfe of holy faders as well of Egypte as of Grece." There follows a list of fourteen admonitions discussed in Part 4 and then the statement: "Here after folowen some smale treatyse & the fyfth parte." Caxton never refers to Part 4 as the last part; Part 5 is always definitely numbered both in the general table and in the text. Caxton's copy of the 1486 French text may have differed from the copy here quoted.

Only Part 1 is in any sense a legendary, and even some of its chapters belong rather among the anecdotes and admonitions of the later parts of the book. Part 1 is an undisguised combination of two works: the *Historia monachorum* of Rufinus of Acquileia (ca. 343–410) and the *Vitas patrum* of St. Jerome (ca. 342–420). Part 1 begins with a prologue ascribed to St. Jerome in which he eulogizes the sanctity of the desert fathers. Then follows—not St. Jerome's work, but the *Historia* of Rufinus in thirty-two chapters. The conclusion of chap. 32 together with chap. 33 serves as a link between the work of Rufinus and that of St. Jerome.

They describe the seven perils through which St. Jerome passed on his visit to the desert fathers. At the conclusion of chap. 33 the French writer added a special note, duly translated by Caxton as follows:

Here folowen the lyues and fayttes of holy faders of Egypte that dwelleden in Syrye and Thebayde / Lyke as Saynt Jherome fonde theym ancentyely [sic] wreten in Greke / And after by him translated in to Latyn / To whom he adiousted many other dedes of the sayde holy faders / Whyche by other translatours had be verytably translated /

And fyrst folowith shortly þe Prologue of saynt Jherom in þe lyf of saynt Poul the fyrst hermyte / & the forsayd Prologue begynnyth in Latin / Inter multos. Caplm xxxiiii (f. xxviii).

This is the prologue to St. Jerome's separate work, *Vitas patrum*, and the second prologue supplied by him for Part 1 of this late composite version. This second section extends from chap. 34 through chap. 165. In both sections of Part 1, that based on Rufinus and that based on St. Jerome, the lives vary in length from a single paragraph to a series of chapters. The briefer records are more common in the first section and are often of saints no longer familiar or even identifiable; e.g., Ammon the hermit (chap. 8), John the holy father (chap. 32). Among the legends attributed to St. Jerome, on the other hand, are some of the most widely known; e.g., St. Antony (chap. 36), St. Simeon Stylites (chap. 46), St. John the Almoner (chaps. 106–57). Not all the saints included can be properly classified as "desert fathers"; e.g., St. Paula (chap. 40), St. Mary of Egypt (chap. 42). And one, St. Christian the religious of Maine, who flourished in France ca. 1160, is out of both time and place among the desert fathers.[6]

Some of the material was not new to Caxton in 1491. He had already translated eleven of these legends in his *Golden Legend* of 1483. These are of Sts. Antony, Basil, Eugenia, John the Almoner, Macarius of Alexandria, Marina, Mary of Egypt, Paul the Hermit, Paula, Pelagia, Simeon Stylites. But again Caxton was not now going beyond the French text on his desk to compare his earlier and later translations. They are two different versions.

The French translator on occasion introduced comments of his own. These Caxton appropriated without change or further comment. For

[6]See Migne PL 73, col. 76. The French text has the title (chap. 105, f. 105ᵃ): "De la vie saint crestien religieus commencant. Quidam Cenomanensis . . ." and within the text: "Saint Crestien du pays du maine. . . ."

example, in the legend of *Mary of Egypt* the French text (chap. 42, f. 56ª) describes the custom of the desert fathers of leaving their abbeys to spend Lent in solitude, and then adds:

> Enuie de obtenir benefices et prieurez pour auoir occasion de saillir hors de leur monastere ny estoit point logee, et ne ressembloyent point le moyneau qui vole tousiours autour de la cage pour trouuer vng partuys cestadire vne abbaye ou prieure pour voler parmy les champs. Pour retourner doncquez a nostre propos. . . . .

Caxton's translation (chap. 42, f. 66ᵇ) is like a gloss:

> Enuye for to opteyne benefyces and pryouryes for to haue occasyon to lepe oute of theyr monasterye was not lodged there. / And they resembled not þe birde that fleeth alwaye abowte the cage for to fynde an hole. That is to say an Abbaye or Pryorye, for to flee thorugh the feeldes and countree. / For to retorne thenne to our purpose. . . .

Caxton's only changes are indefinite *birde* for concrete *moyneau* and the doublet *feeldes and countree*. It was accomplishment enough at the very end of a busy life to have carried through this long and exacting task.

2. English Translations of Legenda Aurea

by

Charlotte D'Evelyn

VERNON GOLDEN LEGEND (Vernon GL) [5]. The Vernon *Golden Legend* is not properly a translation of the *Legenda aurea* but rather a translation of selections from that work. Its meager number of items, eight—a ninth, *Euphrosyne*, is from *Vitae patrum*—covers a small percentage of the 182 chapters in Graesse's edition, smaller still if the sixty or so chapters of his appendix are included. But although the number of items is small the total number of lines in all nine items adds up to over 7,000, even without the several hundred lines lost because of missing folios. The choice of the particularly long legends from the *Legenda aurea* of *Ambrose, Augustine of Hippo, Barlaam and Josaphat,* and *Bernard* is responsible for this large total.

Incomplete as it is, the Vernon *Golden Legend* is by no means negligible. Of its eight items six, *Ambrose, Augustine, Bernard, Paula, Savinian and Savina, Theodora,* are the earliest extant Middle English versions of those legends; one, *Virgin of Antioch,* is the only extant Middle English version. The legend of *Barlaam and Josephat* is included in one manuscript, Bodleian 2567 (ca. 1400), of the *South English Legendary* and in one manuscript, Harley 4196 (fifteenth century), of the *Northern Homily Cycle,* both later than the Vernon text (ca. 1385). The ninth item, *Euphrosyne,* is represented in only one other Middle English version, Caxton's translation (1491) of *Vitae patrum.* The unknown translator of the Vernon collection has been decidedly individual and eclectic in his choice and arrangement of his limited legendary. Unfortunately the opening lines of the first item in which he might have explained his purpose have been lost, and the conclusion of the last item makes no reference to the collection as a whole.

The Vernon *Golden Legend* is written in somewhat irregular tetrameter couplets. Occasionally the translator incorporates a Latin couplet or a bilingual couplet riming Latin and English words. Occasionally he indulges in word-play. These points may be illustrated in a short passage in his translation of the "Tolle, lege" incident in the legend of *Augustine*:

> þen tok he hit to him for þe nones,
> þe book of þe apostles pistles,
> And opened hit—þer weore þistles!—
> He fond iwriten hol and sum:
> Induimini dominum Jhesum Cristum (AELeg 1878, p. 67, line 364)

The translator follows his Latin source closely and with a few exceptions, correctly. His use of naturalized Latin words, however, is not excessive. Clerkly lines such as these explaining Theodora's change of name are rare:

> Hire name, þat was femynyn
> Of gendre, heo turned in to masculyn (AELeg 1878, p. 36, line 109)

More characteristic of the easy vernacular of his work is his translation of the self-accusing words of Josaphat's master: "quia et oculos sanos non habeo et in peccatis sordesco" by the English couplet: "ffor myn eiȝen. beo not al hole / And of sunnes.I. have a mole" (AELeg 1875, p. 219, line 317; Graesse LA, chap. 180, p. 814). Apart from mere filling out of lines and adding tag-ends for rime, the translator's additions usually take the form of a more specific statement than that in the Latin or of a homely touch. Reference to the monastic orders usually calls forth a complimentary or a knowledgeable comment: the phrase "fratres cartusienses" becomes "þe freres of charthous —/ þat is an ordre glorious" (AELeg 1878, p. 52, line 639); the monks of Clairvaux are "Gode men and religious" (p. 46, line 307); Theodora takes refuge specifically in "a munstre of monkes blake" (p. 36, line 101). The translator's comment on the task to which she is assigned is perhaps his most interesting addition:

> þen of þat mon þe monkes were glad
> And token him in wiþ chere ful sad.

þat tyme monkes neih lewed men were.
þis man þei dude among hem schere. . . .
þei putten him to an offyce—
þat nouþe schulde bi holde nyce—:
To ȝoke þe oxen, so mot i þe,
And fette oyle at þe cite (p. 36, line 113)

To this fourteenth century commentator, perhaps himself a monk, the monks of "that time" were almost ignorant rather than learned, some of their duties rude rather than refined.

The Vernon *Golden Legend* is addressed to a mixed audience of lay-folk. In the legend of *Ambrose* line 1 begins: "Herkeneþ, sires: for my purpose/ Is ou to telle of seint Ambrose"; line 53 widens its audience: "Herkneþ nou, hosbonde and wyf" (AELeg 1878, p. 8, line 1; p. 9, line 53). Most of the legends, however, have no address at the beginning and make short work of the customary concluding prayers for mutual benefit from this act of devotion. The sense of the presence of an audience is kept vivid by the translator's comments, such as those already noted, and by the exclamatory passages already supplied in the Latin text and effectively enlivened by the translator's quick couplets.

1438 GOLDEN LEGEND (1438 GL) [6]. It was Caxton who first centered attention on the existence of an English translation of *Legenda aurea* earlier than his own. In the much-quoted preface to the first (1483) edition of his *Golden Legend* he anticipates possible objections to a second English translation:

. . . ageynst me here myght somme persones saye that thys legende hath be translated tofore and trouthe it is/ but for as moche as I had by me a legende in frensshe/ another in latyn/ & the thyrd in englysshe whiche varyed in many and dyuers places/ and also many hystoryes were comprysed in the two other bookes/ Whiche were not in the englysshe book and therefore I haue wryton one oute of the sayd thre bookes/ which I haue ordryd otherwyse than the sayd englysshe legende is/ whiche was to tofore made. . . . (Crotch, EETS 176.72).

The identification of Caxton's English source with the 1438 *Golden Legend* is now generally accepted. But Caxton's translation, continuously reprinted between 1483 and 1527 and revived in 1892 in the sumptuous Kelmscott edition, has completely overshadowed the 1438 translation. That work as a whole has not yet been printed. It has been studied chiefly in connection with Caxton's text. Recent investigations, however, are establishing its independent interest and value in the long history of saints' legends in English.

The 1438 *Golden Legend* is extant in seven comparatively complete manuscripts, all of the fifteenth century. An eighth manuscript, Trinity College Dublin 319, contains a small group of nineteen legends. Several manuscripts of miscellaneous contents include single items from the 1438 *Golden Legend*, e.g., Cotton Titus A.xxvi, f. 180, *Katherine*; Durham University Cosin V.ii.14, f. 106, *Mary Magdalen*. The 1438 *Golden Legend* in common with *Legenda aurea* and with Jean de Vignay's *Légende dorée* contains both saints' lives and material on feast days, such as Circumcision and Ember Days, together with more extraneous subject matter, the Dedication of a Church and a section of Lombardic history introduced under the somewhat ambiguous title: "the life of S. Pelagien, with Geestis of Lumbardie" (Harley 4775, chap. 172, f. 243[b]). In other words, the 1438 *Golden Legend* is the kind of collection that invites variations in contents. No two copies are alike in the number and order of their items; moreover, their original differences are now augmented by loss and mutilation of folios. The most complete manuscript, British Museum Additional 35298, contains 199 items, beginning, after a prologue, with *Andrew* and ending with *Advent*.[7]

Of particular interest for the history and literary relations of the 1438 *Golden Legend* is the addition of a large number of "English" saints in three manuscripts: British Museum Additional 11565 and 35298 and Lambeth 72. Butler (LA, pp. 70, 151) discussed these additions in some detail; Kurvinen (NM 60.357) with fuller knowledge of the manuscripts in question has carried the comparison of their contents further. The subject is too complicated and as yet incomplete to be reviewed here. But one or two points should be noted. Kurvinen has listed the contents of British Museum Additional 35298 and given in parallel columns the corresponding chapter numbers of Harley 4775 and of Caxton's *Golden*

---

[7]For the list of contents see Kurvinen, NM 60.358. Kurvinen is correct in noting that BM Addit 35298 omits chap. 66 of Harley 4775 entitled ". . . the lyfe of S Jerome." But the title is wrong. Chap. 66 contains the legend of *Malchus* written by St. Jerome. Both Harley 4775 and Addit 35298 have a proper legend of *Jerome* later in the text, respectively at f. 181[b] and 124[b]. MS Bodl 21947 (Douce 372) makes the same mistake in the title of its chap. 65, f. 51[a].

Legend. Conspicuous in these lists is a group of nineteen chapters, 95 through 113, for which there are no corresponding chapters in Harley 4775. With the exception of four legends, 105 *Theopilus,* 110 *Faith,* 111 *Dorothy,* 112 *Leger,* the remaining fifteen are "English" saints.[8] Furthermore, British Museum Additional 35298 contains three legends not found in any other known manuscript of the 1438 *Golden Legend:* 79 *Edward the Confessor,* 80 *Winifred,* 81 *Erkenwald.* These additions certainly sharpen the national flavor of the whole collection.[9] For further information on the classification according to contents and also to textual readings, one awaits the announced publication of Kurvinen's edition of the 1438 *Golden Legend* version of *Katherine.*

On other aspects of the 1438 *Golden Legend,*—title, author, sources,— MS Bodleian 21947 (Douce 372) furnishes if not exact information at least important clues. Its colophon reads: " . . . Here endith the Lives of Seintis that is callid in latynne Legenda Aurea, and in Englissh the Gilte Legend, the which is drawen out of Frensshe into Englisshe. The yere of our Lorde M.CCCC. and xxxviij bi a synfulle wrecche. . . ."[10] This title, the *Gilte Legend,* not found in other manuscripts, has been adopted by Kurvinen to distinguish the 1438 translation of *Legenda aurea* from Caxton's. The date of the manuscript, 1438, furnishes the date "before which" for the whole collection. The characterization of the translator as "a synfulle wrecche," and the general statement that the text is taken from a French translation of the Latin *Legenda aurea* need further clarification.

As to author, the possible claim of Osbern Bokenham to that title was rejected by Horstmann (EStn 10.2) and then persuasively restated by Sister M. Jeremy (MLN 59.181). The claim rests primarily on the open-

---

[8] 95 *Edmund of Canterbury,* 96 *Bridget,* 97 *Edmund King and Martyr,* 98 *Frideswithe,* 99 *Edward King and Martyr,* 100 *Alphege,* 101 *Augustine of Canterbury,* 102 *Oswald of Worcester,* 103 *Dunstan,* 104 *Aldhelm,* 106 *Swithum,* 107 *Kenelm,* 108 *Chad,* 109 *Cuthbert,* 113 *Brendan.*

[9] It is a point of interest, perhaps of significance, in the tradition of saints' lives in English that of the fifteen additional legends just noted, six, *Edmund of Canterbury, Bridget, Frideswide, Oswald of Worcester, Chad, Brendan,* are found elsewhere in Middle English only in the *SEL;* six others, *Edward King and Martyr, Alphege, Dunstan, Aldhelm, Swithun, Kenelm,* only in *SEL,* the 1438 *Golden Legend* and Caxton's *Golden Legend*—in other words in the earliest and latest Middle English collections.

[10] F. Madan, *Summary Catalogue of Western MSS,* 4.610; for the complete colophon see AELeg 1881, p. cxxxii.

ing statement made by Bokenham in his prose *Mappula Angliae*, where he refers to " . . . the englische boke whiche y have compiled of legenda aurea and of oþer famous legendes . . ." (EStn 10.6). He names specifically *Chad, Felix, Edward,* and *Oswald.* These saints are not included in manuscripts of the 1438 *Golden Legend* known to Horstmann, but with the exception of *Felix* they are found in more recently identified manuscripts of that work. Moreover, the date of the 1438 *Golden Legend* fits in with Bokenham's, ca. 1393 to "after 1464" (see [3] above.) And the self-deprecating description, "synfulle wrecche," would not be out of keeping for that scholarly and unassuming Augustinian monk, author of the *Lives of Holy Women.*

As to the source, the statement in Bodleian 21947 that the 1438 *Golden Legend* was "drawen out of Frensshe" has been amply supported by modern investigation. Its principal source is the *Légende dorée* of Jean de Vignay, translated from the *Legenda aurea* ca. 1333 at the request, as it is usually said, of the patroness of his earlier work, Jeanne de Bourgoyne, Queen of Phillippe of Valois (d. 1348). In both manuscript and printed texts the translator usually records his name at the end of the legend of *Dominic* ". . . ie frere iehan de vignay, translateur de ce liure, ne veult cy plus mettre ceste vision car elle est deuant en ce meisme chappitre (f. ccxxij^a2 of 1480? edition; Butler LA, p. 45).[11] This statement, with the translator's name badly corrupted but recognizable, has even been carried over into the 1438 translation (Butler LA, p. 146). It also reappears in Caxton's *Golden Legend* (Temple 4.199) but with the name correctly given, an indication that Caxton's source in this case is the French text.

Jean de Vignay's French text was twice revised, the last revision involving both addition and rearrangement of material. This fact complicates the relationship between the 1438 *Golden Legend* and its sources. The English text is not, as Horstmann first described it, a word-for-word translation of the French. Butler offered evidence showing that the 1438 *Golden Legend* made direct use of both the French and the Latin text (Butler LA, pp. 70, 146). Again, in her investigation of Caxton's sources, Sister M. Jeremy worked out in greater detail similarities

---

[11]The provenance of this edition, formerly given as Paris?, is now marked in handscript, Low Countries; see *BM General Catalogue of Printed Books* (1962), 133.594.

and differences between the 1438 *Golden Legend* and Caxton's *Golden Legend* in their use of the revised French text (MS 8.101). The problems of the 1438 *Golden Legend* and the evaluation of that text as a translation are far from settled. They are also closely bound up with similar problems in the study of the Caxton *Golden Legend*.

CAXTON'S GOLDEN LEGEND (Caxton GL) [7]. Caxton's statement about his French, Latin, and English sources, quoted under [6], is correct in every detail. He had the books before him; he had noticed their differences in contents and arrangement. But his statement is incomplete. It remains incomplete even after the three sources have been identified as Jean de Vignay's revised *Légende dorée*, Jacobus de Voragine's *Legenda aurea* and the 1438 *Golden Legend*. Neither Caxton nor modern researchers have as yet identified which particular text of each version, in manuscript or printed form, Caxton followed. Moreover, Caxton used other sources, named and unnamed. The legend of St. Rock, for instance, is not in de Vignay or in the 1438 *Golden Legend* or in any other Middle English version; it is found much abbreviated in the appendix (p. 933) of Graesse's *Legenda aurea*. Caxton makes a special point of informing the reader that this "life is translated out of Latin into English by me William Caxton." But out of which Latin text he does not say. Similarly, Caxton's legends of the English saints, Bede and Hugh of Lincoln, are not included in any known manuscript of the 1438 *Golden Legend*, his usual source for English saints. This interweaving of new strands of material complicates still further the already complex pattern of making three books into one and emphasizes the incompleteness of Caxton's statement on his sources.

That statement was written in part, as Caxton says, as a justification for another English translation of the *Legenda aurea*. Therefore he notes certain differences between the earlier English translation and the French and Latin versions, differences which would also distinguish his English translation from the 1438 text. As to content in general, the Latin and French texts, he writes, "comprised" many more histories than the 1438 English text. As to arrangement in general, Caxton stated definitely that his own translation he had "ordered otherwise than the said English is."

Caxton's version is in fact ordered according to the revised de Vignay text. This is a major variation from both the Latin and the earlier English versions. After a prologue, which Caxton has skilfully adapted and augmented to fit his own work, both de Vignay and Caxton continue with fourteen items covering the feast days of the Church calendar from Advent (1) to Pentecost (14). At this point the French and English texts diverge: the French gives next an exposition of the four parts of the Mass (15–18), the Ten Commandments (19) and the Twelve Articles of the Faith (20); Caxton gives the Feast of the Holy Sacrament (15) and the Dedication of the Temple (16).[12] This item in Caxton is followed by a series of Bible stories beginning with Adam (17)[13] and ending with Judith (31). Then with the legend of St. Andrew (de Vignay 21, Caxton 32) the parallel arrangement of the French and English texts is renewed. But at this point this order of legends is also that of the Latin and 1438 *Golden Legend* texts and no longer indicates a special relationship between Caxton and de Vignay.

The new arrangement, initiated in the revised de Vignay text and augmented by Caxton with his Bible stories, is in fact a separation of Temporale and Sanctorale material. In the de Vignay text the last item in the new arrangement (20) is followed by the statement, "Cy fine du temps" (1480? edition, f. xlix[ni]). Column 2 and the entire verso of this folio are left blank, a gap appearing in a decidedly questionable shape, since it is at this point that Caxton introduces his own addition with the note, "Here follow the stories of the Bible" (Temple 1.168). The Sanctorale in the de Vignay text is preceded by the statement: "Apres les festes de nre seigneur ihu crist cy devant mises par ordre sensieuent les legendes des sains/ Et premierement de saint andreieu" (f. 1[ai]). This note Caxton translates exactly without any reference to the Bible stories

---

[12]These items are not omitted by de Vignay or Caxton. They are merely rearranged. De Vignay's items 15–18 and his item 20 are the concluding items of Caxton's whole book (Temple 7.225). De Vignay's item 19 is similar to Caxton's item 24, following the history of Moses (Temple 1.281). Caxton's item 15 on the Holy Sacrament or Corpus Christi Feast (Temple 1.141) is found in the 1480? edition of de Vignay on f. 398; Caxton's item 16 on f. 362 of the same edition.

[13]The *Life of Adam and Eve* in the 1438 *Golden Legend* (cf. Harley 4775, chap. 175; ML Roto 343, 2.513) is a purely apocryphal legend including Seth's journey to Paradise to fetch the oil of mercy; see Legends of Adam and Eve below. Caxton (Temple 1.180) ends his account of Adam with a brief reference to Seth's journey, warning the reader, however, that ". . . it is said, but of none authority, that he sent Seth his son into Paradise for to fetch the oil of mercy. . . ."

he has added (Temple 2.94). One recalls that the same process of rear-rangement into Temporale and Sanctorale material occurs in other collections such as the *South English Legendary* and the *Northern Homily Cycle*.

In choosing the contents of his *Golden Legend,* Caxton used again a method of selective borrowing with additions of his own. According to Butler's count, about thirty-five new legends of French or Dutch saints probably came from his French source (Butler LA, p. 148). The 1438 *Golden Legend* is the source for about fifteen new legends of English saints.[14] On the other hand, as already noted, Caxton adds from a Latin source not the *Legenda aurea,* the legend of St. Rock, and to his English saints, the legends of the venerable Bede and St. Hugh of Lincoln, not found in any extant text of the 1438 *Golden Legend.* Again, given a legend in one or all of his three named sources, he may present material not found in any of them, as he does in the legend of St. Patrick (see Butler LA, p. 86). Of particular interest are Caxton's personal comments and pieces of information gathered at first hand: his account, for instance, of the miracle of St. Augustine of Hippo and the disguised angel at the seashore, which he had "seen painted on an altar of S Austin at the black frirs at Antwerp" but had not found "in the legend, mine examplar, neither in English, French, ne in Latin" (Temple 5.65). He reports a discussion about King David's penance which he had heard "beyond the sea riding in the company of a noble knight named Sir John Capons . . . " (Temple 2.33). For the literary history of Caxton's book the most informative of these personal additions is his prologue, already noted, skilfully adapted from de Vignay's but unmistakably stamped as his own by the vigorous account of his trials as translator and printer and of his happy rescue by my lord William, Earl of Arundel.[15]

---

[14]See Butler LA, pp. 83, 148, 151; Kurvinen, NM 60.358, 364. Their results are in practical agreement. Butler's comparison of the contents of the 1438 *Golden Legend* and Caxton's *Golden Legend* was finished before he knew of the more complete manuscripts, BM Addit 35298 and Lambeth 72. His conjectures that the source of many of Caxton's legends would be supplied by some fuller text of the 1438 *Golden Legend* were largely confirmed by these newly available manuscripts, but his comparison of their contents with Caxton's, given in an appendix, p. 149, is rather difficult to correlate with his earlier listings of content.

[15]For the text of this prologue and of all the personal additions see Crotch, EETS 176.70.

A detailed study of the correspondence between the text of Caxton's *Golden Legend* and the texts of the Latin, French, and English versions is of first importance for any final determination of his direct sources, of his proficiency in Latin and in French, and of the characteristics of his own English style. As Butler long ago emphasized (Butler LA, p. 98) such a study needs to be carried out legend by legend.

Caxton's *Golden Legend* is the last of the Middle English collections. Yet it introduces, chiefly from the revised de Vignay version, a comparatively large number of legends, about twenty-five, not extant in any other Middle English legendary. As the following sampling shows, these new legends cover a wide range in time, place, and relative popularity: Sts. Polycarp of Smyrna, ca. 155; Victor with Corona in Syria, ca. 177; Fiacre of Ireland and France, ca. 670; King Louis IX of France, 1200; Clare of Assisi, 1252; Ives of Kermartin in Brittany, 1303. The English saints Bede and Hugh of Lincoln are also unique to Caxton's *Golden Legend*.

Caxton's interest in saints was not antiquarian. It was personal and contemporary. The frequent reprinting between 1483 and 1527 of the *Golden Legend*,—in every sense Caxton's largest undertaking,—is a sure sign that the book found a matching interest among English readers of the period.

3. Legends of Individual Saints

by

Charlotte D'Evelyn

LEGENDS OF INDIVIDUAL SAINTS [8–296] are dealt with in the Bibliography one by one, alphabetically.

4. Legends of Adam and Eve

by

Frances A. Foster

The eighth-century Latin *Vita Adae et Evae* goes back to a first-century Greek version, based on the Jewish Apocalypse of Moses. The story begins with the penance of Adam and Eve for their sin. When Adam is near death, he sends Seth and Eve to the Garden to seek the oil of mercy. The angel Michael promises that Christ will bring the oil of mercy to all. After Adam's death and burial, Seth writes the story on stone tablets, which are found and read by Solomon. Many versions add details from the Bible and from the Cross legend.

In Middle English we have an incomplete version in the Auchinleck couplets, a stanzaic version in *Canticum de Creatione*, and three in prose.

Episodes from the *Vita Adae* are also incorporated in *Cursor Mundi*. Michael's promise to Seth at the gates of Paradise that the oil of mercy would be given, is in the Gospel of Nicodemus. In the enlarged *Northern Passion* Cross story of two fifteenth-century manuscripts and in the expanded *Northern Homily Collection*, the Adam story is prefixed to the legend of the Cross, which originally began with David. Adam's story is, of course, also found in Old Testament narratives, in the drama, and in homiletic material of the *South English Legendary*. For the creation of Adam, see *Questiones by-tweene the Maister of Oxenford and his Clerke.*

AUCHINLECK COUPLETS [297]. These 780 lines, written in the North Midlands about 1300–25, contain two portions of the story. The first tells the Fall of Man and the penance of Adam and Eve; the second begins near Adam's death, gives Seth's journey to the Garden, Adam's death and burial, the revelation to Solomon of the tablets bearing the record, and a short account of Noah's flood.

CANTICUM DE CREATIONE [298], 400 stanzas rimed aabccb, written in the East Midlands in 1375, is preserved in a manuscript before 1400. Added to the Adam and Eve story are the Revolt of the Angels, and episodes from the Cross Legend: Seth's vision at the gate of Eden, the finding of the three rods by Moses, and their later history under David and Solomon, with the scenes of Maximilla and Sybilla. The Cross Legend comprises about a third of the poem.

THE VERNON PROSE NARRATIVE [299], seven printed pages, about 1385, adds to the *Vita Adae* story a brief mention of the three apple seeds that afterwards became the cross. Some passages suggest that this was originally a poem in long lines like the *South English Legendary*; and parallels in phrasing have been noted to the *South English Legendary* and to the *Ancrene Riwle*.

THE BODLEIAN 2376 PROSE VERSION [300] is in two fifteenth-century manuscripts, about eight and a half printed pages. It is similar to the 1438 *Golden Legend* version, but based on a better Latin text.

1438 GOLDEN LEGEND ADAM AND EVE [301] (eleven printed pages) is in five manuscripts of the collection and in six other manuscripts. The text is similar to Bodleian 2376, with a few added details.

5. LEGENDS OF THE CROSS

by

Frances A. Foster

Around the Cross clustered a body of legends known widely in various tongues of the Middle Ages. They concern the Early History of the Cross, the Invention of the Cross by St. Helena with the martyrdom of St. Quiriac, and the Exaltation of the Cross under the Emperor Heraclius.

Versions of the Early History, which took shape in the eleventh century, fall into two groups: The Rood-Tree group and Meyer's Latin *Legend* group, both probably from one original. Most of the English stories are derived from the Latin *Legend: South English Legendary, Northern Passion, Northern Homily Collection,* and *Worcester Early History*; only the twelfth-century prose *History of the Rood-Tree* belongs to the Rood-Tree group.

The story of the Latin *Legend* is in brief as follows:

Adam as he neared death sent Seth to Paradise for the oil of mercy. There Seth saw three visions: a dry tree, a serpent about the trunk, and a babe at the top. The angel promised the oil of mercy ultimately to all and gave Seth three kernels from the tree of knowledge to place in Adam's mouth when he was buried in Hebron. From these grew three rods. Moses found them and recognized the sign of the Trinity; he carried them with him and used them to strike the rock at Meribah. They remained near his grave on Mount Tabor. A thousand years later David found them and brought them to Jerusalem, with miracles. Planted in his garden they grew into one tree, around which he placed a silver ring for each of thirty years. When Solomon was building the temple, the tree would not fit in. It was left in the temple, and Maximilla, attempting to sit on it, prophesied the Savior and suffered martyrdom. It was thrown into the Probatica Piscina, where the sick were healed; then made a bridge over the brook Siloe. The Queen of Sheba refused to set foot on it and prophesied. At the time of the Crucifixion the Jews took a third of it to make the Cross.

Portions of the Early History are included in *Cursor Mundi*, in *Canticum de Creatione*, and in the ancient Cornish drama; it is alluded to in *Travels of Sir John Mandeville*.

The Invention of the Cross and the Exaltation of the Cross, as told in the *Legenda aurea,* are found in the great English collections: *South English Legendary, Northern Homily Collection,* Mirk's *Festial, Speculum Sacerdotale,* 1438 *Golden Legend,* and Caxton's *Golden Legend.*

The Invention of the Cross tells how after the Crucifixion the Jews buried the three crosses on Calvary, Hadrian built a heathen temple there, and the place was forgotten. When Constantine had a vision of the Cross and conquered under its sign, he sent his mother St. Helena to find the Cross. A certain Judas, brother of Stephen, was at length induced to show her where the three crosses were buried. The true Cross was discovered by a miracle and enshrined by Helena. Judas also found the nails. His name was changed to Quiriac; he became bishop of Jerusalem and was martyred under the Emperor Julian. The virtue of the Cross was attested by two miracles concerning notaries. (This is, of course, the legend of Cynewulf's *Elene,* and episodes from it are included in *Cursor Mundi.*)

The Exaltation of the Cross deals with the heathen Cosroe, who conquered Jerusalem, stole the Cross, and set himself up on a tower as God the Father. The Emperor Heraclius overcame the pagan army and beheaded Cosroe. He brought the Cross in great pomp to Jerusalem, and when he had humbled himself, he placed the Cross in the temple. Six miracles follow, showing the power of the Cross over unbelievers.

SOUTH ENGLISH LEGENDARY [302]. The Cross story (about 520 lines) normally comprises three parts in the order Early History, Invention, Exaltation; the Early History is in twenty-one manuscripts and the other two parts in eighteen. In some manuscripts the Exaltation (September 19) is separated from the Invention (May 3) and set in its proper place in the calendar; and in one the three legends are condensed. Two manuscripts, Bodleian 1486 and Winchester Cathedral 33ᵃ, begin the series with the Invention and insert the Early History between incidents; the arrangement is given the title *Historia Sanctae Crucis* (614 lines) in the Winchester MS.

The Early History mostly follows the Latin *Legend;* but it begins with a thirty-line prologue on Adam's life; there is no Maximilla; when the tree will not fit into the temple, the Jews make it a bridge, which the Queen of Sheba refuses to walk on; the Jews bury the tree and a healing well appears; at the time of the Crucifixion the tree floats to the top, and the Cross is made from it. In the Invention and the Exaltation the miracles of the *Legenda aurea* are not present.

NORTHERN PASSION [303]. Five fourteenth- and fifteenth-century manuscripts include the Early History, 142 lines expanded from twenty-six lines in the Old French *Passion.* It begins with David's finding the three rods and narrates the building of the temple, the bridge, and the healing pool (no Sibilla or Maximilla). Two *Northern Passion* manuscripts lengthen the Cross story: the late fourteenth-century Cambridge Gg.5.31 has 299 lines relating the Latin *Legend* beginning with Seth's quest, except that the visions at Eden are omitted; and in the fifteenth-century Thornton MS a longer version begins with ninety lines on the early life of Adam, and after a blank that might hold a hundred lines, there follow the visions of Seth and the rest of the Latin *Legend* story (595 lines).

NORTHERN HOMILY COLLECTION [304]. The two manuscripts of the Expanded Collection contain Early History (798 lines), Invention (359 lines), and Exaltation (306 lines). The Early History is part of the *Northern Passion*, which is assigned to Good Friday; the same text is also in the *Northern Passion* of the mid-fourteenth century MS Bodleian 14667. Beginning with Seth's quest, it covers about the same ground as the Thornton MS, but in an independent translation of the Latin *Legend*. The Invention and the Exaltation do not have the appended miracles of the *Legenda aurea*.

HISTORY OF THE ROOD-TREE [305] (of seventeen printed pages, fifteen are Early History), in an early twelfth-century manuscript, belongs to the Rood-Tree group, allied to the episodes in the *Cursor Mundi*, to the Andrius French prose, and to other continental versions.

Moses found three rods, which he knew betokened the Trinity. He planted them and they stayed the same till David, warned in a vision, came to beg them. By the help of Moses' servant Robii, David obtained the rods, which performed miracles on the way to Jerusalem. In his garden the three rods grew into one tree, with thirty silver rings about it (these became the thirty pieces of silver given to Judas). The tree would not fit into Solomon's temple; the priest Cericium who tried to remove it was destroyed by fire. The Meretrix Sibilla who sat on it prophesied Jesus' death, and was martyred. Part of it was used for Jesus' Cross.

MIRK'S FESTIAL [306]. The Invention and the Exaltation are much condensed. The Invention (four printed pages) is followed by two Narraciones, one of them about the Jew in Beritus, adapted from the Exaltation of the *Legenda aurea*. The Exaltation (two printed pages) ends with one of the Latin miracles.

SPECULUM SACERDOTALE [307]. The Invention (three printed pages) and the Exaltation (two and a half printed pages) are condensed from the *Legenda aurea*. The Invention includes stories of Julian the Apostate and of Ciprian and Justina. The Exaltation has one of the Latin miracles.

1438 GOLDEN LEGEND [308]. The Invention and the Exaltation keep close to the Latin.

CAXTON'S GOLDEN LEGEND [309]. The Invention is somewhat condensed. The Passion of St. Quiriacus also occurs in a more extended form as a separate item toward the close of the collection. The Exaltation is close to the Latin.

WORCESTER EARLY HISTORY [310]. This prose in a late fifteenth-century manuscript covers eight folio pages, as one of two appendages to the Gospel of Nicodemus. It follows the Latin *Legend*, beginning with the Quest of Seth and ending when Simon takes up Jesus' cross.

6. LEGENDS OF JESUS AND MARY

by

Frances A. Foster

This section deals with legendary material under the following headings: Childhood of Jesus, Gospel of Nicodemus, Harrowing of Hell, Devils' Parliament, Holy Blood of Hayles, Mirror of Man's Salvation, The Life of the Virgin Mary and the Christ, Assumption, and Origin of the Festival of the Conception of Mary.

The story of Jesus and Mary is of course found in the Translations and Paraphrases of the Bible (chap. IV). The Passion of Christ and the Compassion of Mary are themes of Contention pieces, of Lyrics, and of Meditations. Legends of Jesus and Mary are frequent in *Cursor Mundi*, and in the Drama. They are also dealt with in appropriate items of the Homily Collections: examination of Advent, Christmas, and Easter pieces, of those on Circumcision, Epiphany, and Ascension, as well as on the Nativity, Annunciation, and Assumption of Mary afford the matter on Jesus and Mary. The Miracles of the Virgin are treated in the chapter on Tales.

THE CHILDHOOD OF JESUS [311], a series of legendary miracles based ultimately on *Infantia Salvatoris*, is found in two poems. The first, in the *South English Legendary* of Bodleian 1486 (Laud Misc. 184), consists of 1854 lines in short couplets, carrying the story from Manger to the Miracle of Cana. A second poem, mostly in twelve-line stanzas rimed somewhat irregularly abababababcdcd, appears in three fifteenth-century manuscripts, varying in length and content. Harley 2399 (842 lines) is from the North Midland, and British Museum Additional 31042 (925 lines) from the North. A shorter version from the North Midlands in Harley 3954 (694 lines) includes a passage (lines 195–328) from *A*

Disputisun bi-twene Child Ihesu and Maistres of the Lawe, of the Vernon MS.

THE GOSPEL OF NICODEMUS [312], composed of two parts, *Acta Pilati* and *Descensus Christi ad Infernos*, had a great influence on medieval faith, on medieval art of all kinds, and on medieval drama. It includes the incidents of the Passion from the accusation of the Jews to the death of Jesus, the activity of Joseph of Arimathea, the Resurrection and Ascension, the account of the Harrowing of Hell written by Leucius and Karinus, the reception of the document by Pilate, Annas and Caiaphas, and Pilate's letter to Emperor Claudius.

Though no version is found before 400 A.D., it was important in controversies between the Greek and Roman churches as to the purpose of Christ's mission to Hell. Practically every one of the extant Easter Cycles of miracle plays contained a version of the Harrowing of Hell. Caught from such versions, Satan and his satellites were stock figures of the stage and prepared the way for some of the comic personages in later drama. Hell-mouth became a regular part of the stage equipment.

Besides an Old English translation and two poems on the Harrowing of Hell treated in the next section, Early English has two verse translations of the Gospel of Nicodemus and ten manuscripts in prose.

(a) The stanzaic version (1752–1812 lines rimed abababcdcd) is in four fifteenth-century manuscripts: Cotton Galba E.IX and Harley 4196 are Northern, and closer to the original than British Museum Additional 32578 and Sion College Arc L.40, which show a Northern tendency. The poem was composed before 1325. It was known to the reviser of the *Northern Passion*, who used it in the expanded *Northern Homily Collection*; and its influence is clear on a group of York plays written in similar stanza.

(b) A couplet Gospel of Nicodemus, as yet unprinted, is in British Museum Additional 39996, among the eighty folios that tell the story of Mary and Christ. After the Resurrection and "How þe apostles made þe crede," two folios give "How God delyuered Ioseph of aramathie out of prisoun," followed by "How þe vernycle was broght to Rome," and the Assumption.

(c) Of the ten manuscripts of prose translation, Bodleian 2021, Eger-

ton 2658, and Stonyhurst College B.xliii form a group; British Museum
Additional 16165 and Salisbury Cathedral 39 are by Trevisa. Bodleian,
Egerton, Harley 149, Stonyhurst, Library of Congress, and probably
Worcester Cathedral F.172 (before some leaves were lost) have the whole
Gospel. The others present a fairly close translation of parts especially
connected with Joseph of Arimathea. Black letter editions by Julian
Notary 1507, de Worde 1509, and John Skot 1529 are evidence of its
popularity.

THE HARROWING OF HELL [313]. The Descent into Hell as
elaborated in the Gospel of Nicodemus forms part of many Passion and
Resurrection pieces (see [312] above) and is also treated in two poems.
The first, probably written in the East Midland during the second half
of the thirteenth century, is in short couplets, preserved in three manuscripts all before 1350: Bodleian 1687, (Digby 86, 250 lines), Harley 2253
(248 lines), and Advocates 19.2.1 (201 lines, beginning and ending gone).

After a short narrative introduction, the piece proceeds as a drama, with speeches
assigned by name to the personages, Christ, Satan, the Door Keeper, and the persons
in Hell—Adam, Eve, Abraham, David, John, and Moses. Christ tells of his sufferings
on earth, is threatened by Satan, reproves Satan for the Fall, and claims Adam as his
own. Satan threatens to seduce as many men as Christ takes away patriarchs. Christ
retorts that he will bind Satan so that he will be impotent till Doomsday. He breaks
in the door, and binds the Devil. Adam and Eve confess their guilt, and are freed.
Abraham is promised release. John declares he has died in advance to announce the
freeing of souls in Hell. Christ states to John and Moses that all his servants shall
dwell with him, but unbelievers shall remain evermore with Satan. A prayer closes
the piece.

Early critics hailed this as a drama, but modern scholars agree that it
was meant for recitation.

The septenary Harrowing (322 lines) is included in the St. John's College Cambridge MS of the Southern Temporale.

THE DEVILS' PARLIAMENT [314], 504 lines in three manuscripts
of the fourteenth and fifteenth centuries, is written in stanzas riming
ababbab.

When Mary gave birth to Jesus, all the devils held a parliament to know who his
father was. Satan tells how he tempted Jesus in the wilderness. At a second Parliament
the devil recalls miracles and sayings of Jesus; he failed to catch Jesus' soul at the
Crucifixion, and chains the gates of hell. After argument with Jesus, the gates burst
open and Jesus rescues Adam, Noah, Abraham, Moses, David, Zacharias, Simeon, and

John. Hell, Satan, and Beelzebub blame each other. Jesus rose on the third day, was seen by many, and ascended on Holy Thursday. Mary was taken into heaven. In the concluding two stanzas the poem is called a song, recently made to be read on the first Sunday in Lent.

THE HOLY BLOOD OF HAYLES [315] (100 quatrains) is preserved in one manuscript of the early fifteenth century. The dialect is West Midland.

In the first part, stated to be from the Latin of Pope Urban, a Jew (unnamed) caught some of the crucified Jesus' blood in a vessel; the Jews locked him up with it in a stone house. Forty-two years later at the destruction of Jerusalem, Titus and Vespasian found him alive; but when they took the blood from him, he fell dead. The blood was placed with the Vernicle in the Temple of Peace at Rome. Charlemagne took some of it to his castle at Triuelence. The second part of the poem tells how Edmund, son of Richard Earl of Cornwall, found it and brought a portion of it to England. It was lodged at Hayles Abbey in 1270, and seven years later Robert Gifford, Bishop of Worcester, hallowed the shrine, where many miracles are performed.

THE MIRROR OF MAN'S SALVATION [316], a fifteenth-century translation of *Speculum humanae salvationis,* is found in a former Huth MS, now owned by Mr. W. A. Foyle of Beeleigh Abbey, Maldon, Essex. The Latin *Speculum,* an early fifteenth-century collection of sermon material, is in long prose lines (5241), rimed in pairs. It opens with a summary of the work in 300 lines; the main body is 45 chapters, each, except the last three, 100 lines long. After two chapters on Lucifer and Adam, it begins with the Conception of the Virgin, and ends with the Last Judgment, followed by three hymns. The English translation in rimed Alexandrines keeps pretty close to the Latin.

THE LIFE OF THE VIRGIN MARY AND THE CHRIST [317], on twenty-four folios of a fifteenth-century manuscript in Trinity College Dublin, has a one-chapter prologue on the Fall of Adam, then in twenty-five chapters tells the life of Mary and Jesus from the Conception of Mary to the Raising of Lazarus. The author bases his narrative on Pseudo-Bonaventura *Meditationes vitae Christi,* supplemented by Pseudo-Matthaei *Evangelium,* and the Vulgate. The Allegory of the Four Daughters of God (chapters 7 and 8) precedes the Annunciation.

THE ASSUMPTION OF THE VIRGIN [318], a legend that took shape in the East probably in the fourth century, is the basis of a Blickling Homily and a narrative by Wace. In the South of England as early as 1250 the story was effectively told in four-beat couplets (some 900 lines). Our six manuscripts range from late thirteenth century to late fifteenth; in one it is incorporated in the *Northern Homily Collection*; and in two it occurs among romances. This early couplet version forms the basis of the tail-rime stanzas in the Auchinleck MS (736 lines with the beginning gone); of the unique Assumption in the Lambeth MS of the *South English Legendary* (364 lines); of the Assumption in the two manuscripts of the expanded *Northern Homily Collection* (542 lines); and is incorporated almost line for line in the *Cursor Mundi*. Fourteen manuscripts of the *South English Legendary* have a version based on the *Legenda aurea* (246 lines). Unprinted are the unique text in the Huntington MS of the *Northern Homily Collection*, and the late couplets of Additional MS 39996, both former Phillipps MSS. Prose versions, all related to the *Legenda aurea* story, are in Mirk's *Festial*, the *Speculum Sacerdotum*, the 1438 *Golden Legend*, and Caxton's *Golden Legend*.

THE ORIGIN OF THE FESTIVAL OF THE CONCEPTION OF MARY [319]. The legend is first found in the *Miraculum de Concepcione Beatae Mariae* inserted by Gerberon in the Benedictine edition of the works of Anselm. Wace wrote *L'Établissement de la Fête de la Conception Notre Dame* (ca. 1125–1150).

It tells how Helias, returning from an embassy to placate the King of Denmark on behalf of William the Norman, was almost lost in a storm at sea; how an angel offered him safety if he would vow with all his monks to celebrate annually the conception of the Virgin, and urge others to do so; how he learned that the feast should be on December 18, the Nativity of Mary, the service being the same, the word Conception displacing Nativity; and how he kept his vow at Ramsay.

The legend is present with a 114-line prologue in two manuscripts of the *South English Legendary*, Vernon and Bodleian 2567; in the *Cursor Mundi* (241 lines); and in the prose of Mirk's *Festial*, the *Speculum Sacerdotale*, and the two translations of the *Golden Legend*.

7. Legends of the After-Life

by

Frances A. Foster

Widespread throughout the period was the interest in legends of the after-life. In the twelfth century we have in English prose a brief *Vision of Leofric* and a *Vision of St. Paul*. From the middle of the century on, elaborate Latin visions of Purgatory and Paradise were popular (*Vision of Tundale, St. Patrick's Purgatory, Vision of the Monk of Eynsham*). Early in the thirteenth century, the first two of these appeared in English verse, along with the *Vision of Paul*. In the next century Robert Manning told Bede's *Vision of Fursey* in *Handlyng Synne*. And in fifteenth-century English prose, we have the *Revelation of Purgatory*, and a printed version of the *Vision of the Monk of Eynsham*.

Related material is also abundant: see for example *Harrowing of Hell; Cursor Mundi; Pricke of Conscience*, which includes a brief *Vision of Lazarus*; the *Adulterous Falmouth Squire*; and the legend of *Brendan*. With these English pieces should be compared such Latin accounts as Bede's *Vision of Drihthelm*, the *Vision of Thurcill* in Roger of Wendover's *Chronicle*, and the *Vision of the Boy William* in Vincent de Beauvais' *Speculum historiale*, as well as Dante's *Divine Comedy* and other continental works.

THE VISION OF ST. PAUL or THE ELEVEN PAINS OF HELL [320] goes back to a fourth-century Greek original, and was widely popular in Latin. Middle English has six versions, of which four are in verse: (a) an early short couplet version in two late thirteenth-century manuscripts, 290 lines, Southwestern, and 308 lines Southern; (b) an early stanzaic version in the late thirteenth century, 252 lines, Southern; (c) the Vernon couplet version, 346 lines, Southern; and (d) Audelay's fifteenth-century stanzaic version, 365 lines. In prose there are two: (e) a Lambeth Homily, three pages in print; and (f) a version of a fifteenth-century manuscript, also three pages.

The story as it appears in the Vernon Couplet and Audelay versions is as follows: Paul visited hell in the company of Michael and viewed its torments. On burning trees sinners were suspended by different portions of the body. In a heated caldron wherein were plagues of snow, ice, clotted blood, poisonous reptiles, lightning, and stench, suffered those who would not repent. On a burning wheel were punished others. In a horrible lake full of venomous reptiles suffered backbiters, wedlock-breakers, whores and whore-mongers, rejoicers in others' ill, brawlers in church, and the like, each submerged according to his guilt. In a deep pit, gnawing their tongues, were usurers. In another place, boiling in pitch, bitten by serpents, and tormented by devils, were unchaste women who had slain their offspring. Those who broke fasts were subjected to starvation. Devils tormented an old man who was unchaste, covetous, and proud. In a deep stinking pit sealed with seven seals suffered those who did not believe in Christ's birth from Mary, or in Baptism, or in the Eucharist. Paul saw tormented a soul who despised God's commands and lived in foolishness and then the soul of a righteous man welcomed by angels, brought before God, and borne to Paradise. The damned called to Paul and Michael, who prayed to the angels. In response Christ granted that the lost souls should have rest each week from Saturday at noon until the second hour on Monday. He who hallows Sunday shall have part in the angels' eternal rest.

The early stanzaic version and the two in prose are shortened by the omission of many details. The early couplet version has the opening lines in French and was probably based on a French original; no mention is made of the Sabbath rest; and the torments, described by an escaped soul to Satan with a bare mention of Paul, differ in details from those of the other English versions.

ST. PATRICK'S PURGATORY [321] is described in six English verse accounts of the knight Owayn's visit; and in two prose accounts, the visit of Nicholas and the vision of William Staunton.

Owayn's visit was written down some time after 1155 in the Latin of Henry, a Benedictine monk of Saltrey in Huntingdonshire. Many manuscripts of the twelfth to the fifteenth century are extant, and the story was frequently retold in other languages, from Marie de France to Calderon.

In Middle English the *South English Legendary* has Owayn's visit in ten manuscripts (varying in length up to 712 verses); and five other versions are known: a stanzaic version of 198 stanzas, incomplete, in the Auchinleck Manuscript; an early couplet version (342 short couplets,

fifteenth century); a later couplet version (341 similar couplets); the
Harley fragment, two folios of fifteenth century quatrains, based on the
South English Legendary; and the Hearne fragment, nine quatrains from
his edition of the *Scoti-Chronicon*.

St. Patrick drove the poisonous snakes from Ireland and did other wonders. Then
he drew a circle on the ground. In it was formed a great pit, which is his "Purgatory." Hereabout he set up a great religious establishment. The sinful while alive
might purge themselves by descending into the pit. But few who made the attempt
returned. Sir Owayn, guilty of all the deadly sins, despite remonstrances of the clergy,
went into the pit. He came upon a splendid hall, where a group of fair men warned
him that he would soon be tempted and tormented by devils and that his salvation
lay in prayer. Yawning and grinning, the devils beset and tortured him and dragged
him bound from world's end to world's end. Then he was taken through the various
places of torment—first into a waste, where men and women were spiked out prone,
with nails of fire driven through their bodies; next where, spiked to the earth, souls
were devoured by serpents and tortured with awls and scourges; then where the souls
were full of burning nails and played upon by a bitter wind; then where souls were
hung up by arms and feet and neck, etc., and burned in fire and brimstone; then
where souls were fixed on a wheel that whirled about, burning and stinking of brimstone; and to several other places of torture. To all the torments the knight was subjected; but he escaped each by prayer. Then he was borne into a pit which the devils
declared to be Hell; his prayers caused him to be expelled by a blast of wind. Then
he was forced to cross a narrow, sloping, high bridge, under which was really Hell.
Now the devils left him, and he entered the Earthly Paradise with its sweet odors
and flowers and gem-paved roads, where a procession welcomed him to a great hall.
After a time he was directed to return to earth. At the opening of the pit, the ecclesiastics welcomed him with joy. He became a holy man.

The account of Nicholas' journey appears first in the *Legenda aurea*,
and is translated in the 1438 *Golden Legend*, based on Jean de Vignay's
French. It is similar to Owayn's, but much shorter (ca. 250 words).

The 1409 visit of William Staunton (Additional MS Stranton) is recorded in two fifteenth-century manuscripts.

He was placed in the cave and fell asleep. Then there appeared to him St. John of
Bridlington and St. Ive (Additional MS, St. Hilda of Whitby), who encouraged him.
Left to himself, he escaped a group of fiends by prayer. He was then led by St. John
to a fire, crowded with people who had loved vanity in dress; then to the appropriate
punishments of blasphemous swearers, breakers of holy days, dishonorers of parents;
robbers; those who had born false witness; murderers; the unchaste; those who did
not chastise their children; backbiters, evil bishops, ecclesiastics who had lived a
worldly life and who had neglected their parish duty. Left alone by his guide, William
came to a grisly water, with a tower on the other side. At length a lady in the tower
let down a ladder, up which he climbed to a fair company of clergy. From there he
was sent back to his earthly life.

St. Patrick's Purgatory as visited by Owayn and Nicholas bears a resemblance to the Vision of Paul; but there is no guide and, except for the final pit, the torments are clearly purgatorial, not eternal; the visitor suffers something of each pain, and is rescued by prayer. While William Staunton enters the traditional cave of St. Patrick, his account draws freely on other medieval purgatories: his journey seems to be a vision; he has a guide who occasionally leaves him; the different punishments, his guide tells him, are adjusted to sins against seven of the ten commandments and against the failings of the clergy; and except at the beginning and end, he does not suffer the pains he sees.

THE VISION OF TUNDALE [322], is one of the best known and certainly one of the most elaborate of the medieval visions. There are many manuscripts in Latin, French, German, and other languages. The prologue to the piece says it was composed by Marcus, probably an Irish monk, at Ratisbon in 1149. An English version in short couplets is in five fifteenth-century manuscripts. The composite text of Wagner contains 2354 lines. The English original was probably of the North and belongs to the end of the fourteenth or beginning of the fifteenth century.

Tundale, a rich knight of Cashel, living a riotous and evil life, went to collect money due him for three horses. Angered that the debtor could not pay, Tundale was stricken at dinner and lay almost dead four days. Horrid demons gathered about his spirit and reviled him: where was now his pride and wealth? A bright star, his guardian angel, came to him as guide and expositor. They pass a gloomy valley stinking and strewn with hot coals, over which murderers are melted on iron plates, to trickle through and reform, and again be melted; a mountain, one side covered with fire and smoke, the other with ice and snow, between which thieves are tossed back and forth; a stinking abyss spanned by a bridge, where the proud and boastful are tormented. The next five torments are suffered by Tundale himself for a brief time: a huge beast Acheron, who swallows the covetous, and torment by adders and fire and ice; a lake full of terrible creatures, where Tundale has to lead a wild cow he has stolen over a bridge a handsbreadth wide and set with spikes; an oven where fiends mutilate the gluttons; a great beast in the midst of a frozen lake, who swallows and casts out the unchaste; and the vale of the smiths, where souls are beaten and welded on anvils. Hell itself for the eternally damned is a noisome fiery pit, with Satan's fingers crushing souls like grapes.

Leaving the foul air behind, Tundale is led within a wall where the neutrally good, who did not give to the poor, wait in hunger and thirst till they are ready for salvation. Passing through a door in the wall, he finds himself in the Earthly Paradise, filled with those who are not yet ready for heaven: King Cormac receives courtiers, but spends three hours a day in pains for breaking his marriage vow and for perjury. Beyond a silver wall is the Paradise of those who have lived righteous lives; and beyond a golden wall those who gave their lives to God dwell under a beautiful tree with fruit and birds, which is the Church. Beyond the last wall of precious stones is a ladder leading up to God: He sees St. Ruadan, St. Patrick, Celestine and Malachy, archbishops of Ardmach, Christian of Lyon, Neeman of Cluny, and an empty throne awaiting its occupant.

Returning to his body, Tundale lived a devout life.

Friar Marcus drew on many sources for his details: Christian visions and classical authors. Like Furseus, Tundale suffers some of the purgatorial pains. And, as in earlier continental visions, he sees in the Earthly Paradise his contemporaries, Irish prelates and kings.

THE VISION OF FURSEY [323], first narrated by Bede, is expanded in *Handlyng Synne* from the twenty-five lines of *Manuel des péchés* to 117 lines, and is also found in the *Golden Legend* of 1438 and in Caxton's *Golden Legend*. As exemplum, it appears in an English translation of *Manuel des péchés*, in *Alphabetum Narrationum*, and in *The Floure of the Commandmentes of God*, printed by Wynkyn de Worde.

Fursey's spirit, parted from his body, is taken by three angels toward heaven. Devils dispute with the angels for his soul, and his shoulder is burned when the devils throw a tormented soul at him. He sees a deep valley flaming with the four fires of falsehood, covetousness, discord, and iniquity. Returning to himself, he ever after lived a good life.

THE VISIONS OF LEOFRIC [324] occur in one West Saxon manuscript of about 1100. Leofric, Earl of Mercia, died in 1057. The first (about 225 words) of the four visions tells how he passes over a narrow bridge above horrible water, being led to a glorious company, where St. Paul has just pronounced the blessing at the end of mass. He is told that he will return later. The bridge seems to be from the *Dialogues* of Gregory.

In A REVELATION OF PURGATORY [325], found in three fifteenth-century manuscripts, a holy woman tells her ghostly father of visions she saw on three nights beginning St. Lawrence Day, 1422 (ten printed pages). Reference to the "recluse of Westemynster" suggests that the dreamer lived nearby.

She sees the pains suffered by her friend Margaret, lacerated and burned, and led about by a fiery cat and dog, whom she had been too fond of in her life. Margaret asks to have thirteen masses said for her, and repetitions of the psalm *Miserere mei Deus*, and the hymn *Veni Creator Spiritus*. She says that of the three great purgatorial fires, the hottest purges of the seven deadly sins, the second purges of venial sins, and the third completes the cleansing. Devils are active with knives and hooks, and, most painful of all, the worm of conscience. While Margaret suffers her worst penance, the dreamer sees the punishment of priests and prelates, of wedded folk, and of single men and women. Margaret's penance is shortened by masses and prayers, and by the pilgrimage to Southwark which she had vowed and the dreamer had performed for her. At length the Virgin weighs Margaret in the scales, the devil departs with his worm; and Margaret, wrapped in white, is led across a strong bridge, cleansed in a fair well, and brought to mass in a white chapel. Then with the crown of grace and the scepter of victory, she passes to the golden gate of the Paradise "þat Adam was ine."

THE VISION OF THE MONK OF EYNSHAM [326], sometimes confused with Evesham, was printed (some 30,000 words) by William of Machlinia in London about 1482. No English manuscripts have survived, but the Latin appears in seven manuscripts, and extracts in two manuscripts, in the *Chronicle* of Roger of Wendover, and elsewhere. It was made into a French poem and retranslated into Latin before 1400. The author was Adam, sub-prior of Eynsham, who also wrote a life of St. Hugh of Lincoln; and the monk was named Edmund.

In the year 1196, during a trance after illness and prayer, the monk is guided by St. Nicholas to the first Purgatory, a region of mud and marshes, where souls suffer torments of burning, gnawing by serpents, etc. In the second Purgatory souls are tossed from hot to cold in a dark valley; a woman's soul is helped by St. Margaret, and a goldsmith tells his story. The monk then comes to the most severe Purgatory, a field with stench, "worms," clawing demons, and fire; he recognizes a doctor of law who had lived in sodomy. He then describes interviews with seven souls from the first Purgatory, monks, a bishop, a poor man's wife, and two knights. From the second Purgatory he specifies sins and sinners, some generalized, as poisoners, usurers, and fugitives from religion; some individualized, as an Archbishop of Canterbury, a King of England, and a bishop who died just after he was elected archbishop. At length he reaches the abode of the blessed, a flowery field with a vision of the crucified Christ. Beyond a crystal wall guarded by a cross, a ladder is seen with eager souls mounting toward the glory of God. And to the pealing of sweet bells, the monk's soul returns to his body.

Unlike other twelfth-century visions, this one has no pit of hell; and unlike Fursey and Tundale and Owayn, the visitor suffers no torments as he passes through. The vision was intended primarily for the monks of Eynsham: twenty-eight of the forty-four chapters following the prologue are interviews with individuals, most of whom, though unnamed, were probably recognized by the monks. Among them are a few of the laity (a King of England, a goldsmith, a poor man's wife and two knights), but most are religious: Baldwin, Archbishop of Canterbury; Reginald Fitz Jocelyn, archbishop-elect; a prior who died "this same yere," etc. In Paradise the four spirits named are all from the Church.

VI. INSTRUCTIONS FOR RELIGIOUS

by

Charlotte D'Evelyn

1. Ancrene Riwle

ANCRENE RIWLE [1]. The medieval popularity of the *Ancrene Riwle* as a rule of life is attested by the surviving manuscripts in English, Latin, and French. Since the publication in 1853 of Morton's edition of the English MS British Museum Cotton Nero A.xiv, that popularity has been extended in other directions to include the literary and cultural aspects of the work. Interest in the *AR* on the part of both lay and ecclesiastical students shows no signs of diminishing.

The fundamental problem of the original language of the *AR* was introduced by Morton and decided in favor of English; Bramlette argued for Latin; Macaulay, for French. Miss Dymes brought the argument back full turn to English and there it has come to rest.

The English manuscripts of the *AR* date from ca. 1230 through the fifteenth century. None of them is unrevised. After a detailed study of textual problems within the group of English manuscripts and between the groups of English, French, and Latin texts, English MS Corpus Christi Cambridge 402, *Ancrene Wisse*, emerges as probably the best surviving representative of the original.

The *AR* was originally written as a personal guide for three sisters, of one father and one mother, who wished to withdraw from active to contemplative life. Miss H. E. Allen's proposed identification of these three sisters with the three historical anchoresses of Kilburn—Gunhilda, Emma, and Christina, daughters of Deor—may no longer be accepted as proved. But her minute researches and subtle deductions have made it clear that the *AR* reflects concrete and localized circumstances and conditions. So simple-seeming a statement as "Nu easki ӡe hwet riwle ӡe ancren schulen halden" (EETS 249.7) gains added significance in the face of the contemporary controversy between liberal Benedictine and conservative Cistercian over the theory and practice of the ruled life. Adaptation of the *AR* soon set in. The Latin text frequently and inconsistently addresses its admonitions to "religiosus vel religiosa"; the Trinity French text, to "hommes et femmes de religion"; the late fifteenth-century English extract in British Museum Royal 8.C.1 has become apparently a homily addressed to a lay congregation.

The author of the *AR* remains unknown. A note in Latin MS Magdalen Oxford 67 (ca. 1400) attributes the work to Bishop Simon of Ghent (d. 1315), and that attribution as far as the Latin text is concerned may be allowed. Bishop Richard Poore (d. 1237), Dominican Roger Bacon (d. 1294), and Gilbert of Sempringham (d. 1189) have each been proposed unconvincingly as author.

But if modern scholarship has divested the author of a name, it has recognized him as a personality whose understanding of his world, human sympathy, and literary skill have turned what might have been a routine manual into "a living persuasion toward perfection." No direct source for his rule has been traced. His references to other writings of this class and his obvious understanding of the theory and practice of the contemplative life make his work representative of the age in its substance, individual in its presentation.

The *AR* is not a manual of the mystic way. These three anchoresses are at the very beginning of the preparatory journey toward the contemplative life. They have much to learn. As their spiritual guide suggests, at times it may be more profitable for them to read than to pray: "Ofte leoue sustren ӡe schulen uri lease? forte reden mare" (EETS 249.148). The treatise begins and ends with the routines, devotional and practical, of religious life: Part I, On Divine Service; Part VIII, On Domestic Matters. The intervening parts deal with the fundamental disciplines of guarding against temptation in all or any of the five senses, with the fundamental duties of confession and penance, and with Christian love as the central motive and final goal of all their disciplines. The "annesse" for which the writer of the *Ancrene Wisse* in a unique passage praises his charges (EETS 249.130) is not the oneness of mystic union but the unity of love which binds them into a Christian community.

2. BENEDICTINE ORDER

RULE OF ST. BENET [2]. If Chaucer's Monk had known the rule of St. Maure or St. Beneit in his native tongue he would have condemned it not only as "olde and somdel streit," but as barbarous also. Throughout the medieval period the *Rule* remained a textbook of regulations, didactic, impersonal, and unadorned. Even in its fifteenth-century versions no glint appears of that aureate English which might have caught the eye of such a lover of pomp and style as Chaucer's Monk. Richard Fox, early sixteenth-century Bishop of Winchester and last in the direct line of translators from Aethelwold, characterized the language of his version in these words: "We have translated the sayd rule into oure moder's tongue/commune/playne/rounde englysshe/easy and redy to be understande."

Omitting versions in Old English which were still being copied in the eleventh and twelfth centuries, there are five extant Middle English translations, dating from the early thirteenth through the fifteenth century. For particular reasons to be noted later, Richard Fox's translation may be included in this group as a sixth version. All of these translations except that in Version c, Cotton Vespasian A.xxv, are in prose. Scraps of verse have been detected in Version b, the Northern Prose version. Version d, the Library of Congress MS 4, ends with five couplets, highly irregular in meter, with the peculiar rime-scheme a (lines 1–8) b (lines 9–10). The single metrical translation, Version c, is written throughout in the familiar short couplet.

Like the *Ancrene Riwle* the *Rule of St. Benet* was adapted in time for both men and women. This shift in gender is already apparent in Old English versions. The six translations here considered are addressed, not always consistently, to men, to women, or to both men and women. Specifically the Winteney text, following the example of the Latin version which accompanies it, is addressed to nuns: "myncenes or geswustren"; the Northern Prose version is addressed to monks in the beginning and then to nuns. In the Northern Metrical version an original preface explains that the work is translated for women who, unlike monks, do not learn Latin in their youth. In the metrical epilogue of the Library of Congress MS, already mentioned, the writer states that this translation is made from the French for those hampered by their lack of French. The text itself is addressed throughout to women. Caxton's extract is intended for men and women "the whyche understonde lytyll laten or none." By a skillful use of plural pronouns no longer indicative of gender, and of generalizations such as "religious people," this version usually, but not always, avoids inconsistency in sex. Finally, Richard Fox writes his translation for nuns, whom he still calls "mynchins," but unlike any of the other translators he makes no compromise either of change or omission for those chapters which could not be properly applied to women. Chapter 60, for instance, is headed: "The lx chapiter treateth of seculer prestes that desyre to entre into religion in any monastery." Then follows Fox's comment: "Albeit that this lx chapiter nor no part thereof may touche or concerne the congregacion of Mynchins/yet for the cause above rehersed in the other chapitres of this rule not towchynge them/and especially for the instruction of som monkes meynly lettered/we have translated the sayde lx chapitre in fourme folowing." Fox continues with a "masculine" text.

None of the extant Middle English versions is directly dependent on one of the others, or translates literally a known Latin or French text. Omissions, shifts, and changes of material make each Middle English text a different version. The obvious similarity of their contents, even their verbal echoings, are rather the natural result of the common source behind them, itself modified by centuries of use. In contents these translations represent the chief subject matter of the original rule: qualifications and duties of abbot or abbess, process of admission to the order, directions for divine service by canonical hours and by ecclesiastical seasons, cultivation of obedience with an enumeration of the twelve rungs of the ladder of humility, and practical regulations on dress, food, and manual duties. All this is stated in general and impersonal terms without exempla or concrete instances to point up the moral. But since this was and is a way of life, the reality of the human situation is still discernible under the formulas of the *Rule*. The elaborate ritual which marked the Saturday change of kitchen service is in substance a thankful "Praise the Lord" on the part of the outgoing kitchener and an apprehensive "God help me" on the part of her (or his) successor in office.

It is a matter of interest, historical and literary, that Bishop Fox's version, like the earliest Middle English version, was intended for the nuns of Winteney. In his preface the Bishop states that he has undertaken this task at the instant request of "the Abbasses of the Monasteris of Rumsay/wharwel/Seynt Maries within the citie of Winchester/and the Prioresse of wintnay: oure right religious diocesans." Close comparison of the two versions should bring out interesting changes in the mother tongue written for Winteney nuns of the early thirteenth century and for those of the early sixteenth century. Bishop Fox's preface calls attention to another significant change: "And by cause we wolde not/ that there shulde be any lacke amongis them of the bokis of this sayd translation/we haue therfore/aboue and besyde certayne bokes ther of/ which we haue yeven to the said monasteris: caused it to be emprinted by our wel beloued Richarde Pynson of London printer. The xxii day of the Monethe of January. The yere of oure lorde M.CCCCC.XVI. and the .VIII. yere of the Reigne of our soverayne lorde kynge Henry the .VIII. and of our translation the XVI." The Winteney nuns of 1516, unlike their thirteenth-century sisters, read their *Rule* in print, not in script. But the greatest change of all the Bishop did not anticipate: that within a few years, through the dissolution of the monastic houses, there would be no further reading of his *Rule of St. Benet* by the nuns of Winteney.

RITUAL FOR ORDINATION OF NUNS [3]. This *Ritual for Ordination of Nuns* has close connections internally and externally with the *Rule of St. Benet*. It is, in fact, based on Chapter 58 of that *Rule*, outlining the ceremony in which the novice after her period of probation makes her final profession. Two manuscripts of the *Ritual*, Lansdowne 378 and Cotton Vespasian A.xxv, also contain the *Rule*; another, Cambridge University Mm.3.13, ca. 1500, has a note in Latin stating that this copy belongs to the nunnery of St. Mary's in Winchester and is the gift of Bishop Richard Fox, the same bishop who translated the *Rule* at the request of the Abbess of this same nunnery.

The extant copies of the *Ritual* differ in amount of detail of the ceremony which each includes, in the length of quotations from the service, and in the combination of Latin and English which each uses in rubrics and in text. Comments or explanations are few; Lansdowne 388, one of the fuller texts, notes that the ceremony is a symbolic marriage and adds a comment that the professed nun may now be fittingly called "madame and ladye."

3. AILRED OF RIEVAULX, INFORMACIO

AILRED OF RIEVAULX, INFORMACIO AD SOROREM SUAM INCLUSAM [4]. Ailred's rule shares with the *Ancrene Riwle* that added interest which a close personal link between writer and reader naturally gives to subject matter otherwise impersonal. Ailred wrote his rule at the request of his sister, like himself of mature age and of long experience in the ruled life. This treatise is at once more intimate and more conventional than the *Ancrene Riwle*.

The title of the original Latin differs from text to text. The two extant English translations also differ in this respect. Bodleian 2322 is headed: *A tretys that is a rule and a forme of lyvynge perteyning to a Recluse*; its colophon: *Here endith the Reule of a Recluse that seynt Alrede wrote to his suster*. The heading of the Vernon text combines title, author, and translator: *Informacio Alredi Abbatis Monasterii de Rieualle ad sororem suam inclusam: translata de Latino in Anglicum per Thomam N.*

The two English translations seem to be related only indirectly through their common source. Since the Latin source itself varies in arrangement and amount of material it is not surprising to find similar differences in the translations. Bodleian 2322 begins with Ailred's prologue and divides his material into sixteen chapters; Vernon, omitting the prologue and several of the early chapters, covers the remaining material in nineteen chapters. In the present state of information on Latin and English texts one cannot judge finally the accuracy of Horstmann's description of Vernon as a "literal translation," or Miss Clay's of Bodleian 2322 as a "paraphrase," of Ailred's rule.

Language apart, it is clear that the translator, Thomas N., is not adapting the thirteenth-century original to his own day or to different readers. "Suster" is the word of address throughout. Ailred's well-known warning against over-ornamentation of the recluse's cell is translated vigorously indeed, but without a hint of any possible difference between the thirteenth- and fifteenth-century attitudes on that subject: "And vurþermor I nel not be no wey þat as it where vndur colour of deuovioun and holynesse þu delite þe in veyne peyntyngges, kyttyngges and in grauyngges in þy celle, noþer in cloþys gaylyche yweue ne steyned wᵗ bryddes or bestes or diuerse trees or floures or oþer babounrye. Let hem haue swych aray þat noon or litul ioye hauyngge wᵗ-ynne, sechyþ al here ioye wᵗ-oute" (EStn 7.314).

As befitted the maturity both in age and religious experience of Ailred and his sister, his rule emphasizes the spiritual rather than the practical aspects of the recluse's life. The latter part of the work is patterned as a three-fold meditation on things past, present, and future. Incidents in the life of Christ furnish the subject for meditation on things past. The second and highly personal meditation on things present centers upon the gratitude both brother and sister owe to God for their having been born sound, not deformed, in a Christian, not a pagan, land, and for their having by God's guidance chosen and persevered in their religious vocations. In the third meditation, things future, the subjects are death as at once dreaded and desired, the Last Judgment as at once full of suspense and of hope, and the ultimate joy of Salvation, when the soul shall be parted finally from the unsavory multitude "þat shall be damp-ened." In the meditations both the greater intimacy and conventionality of Ailred's rule in comparison with the *AR* are evident. Ailred writes as equal to equal; the author of the *AR* as older to younger, experienced to inexperienced. Ailred ends in all seriousness and humility, asking only that his effort may find him favor with his Maker and his Judge. That touch of wry humor that led the author of *AR* to exclaim, "Got hit wot, me were leouere uorto don me toward Rome þen uorte biginnen hit eft forto donne" (Morton's edition, p. 430), is foreign to Ailred's tempera-ment.

4. ENGLISH BRIGITTINE ORDER

RULE OF ST. AUGUSTINE [5]. The *Rule of St. Augustine*, the *Rule of St. Saviour, Additions to the Rule of St. Saviour,* and the *Mirror of Our Lady* (see [6], [7], and [8] below) have a close relationship through their association with the Brigittine Monastery of Syon at Isleworth, established by Henry V in 1415. St. Bridget (Birgitta) of Sweden, founder of the Order, based her *Rule of St. Saviour* (fourteenth century) on the *Rule of St. Augustine* (fifth century); the *Additions to the Rule of St. Saviour* (fifteenth century) were drawn up for the English Brigittines of Syon; the *Mirror of Our Lady*, though not in fact a rule, but an exposition of the Office of the Virgin as sung at Syon, reflects an important aspect of the way of life in that particular community. All of these works of instruction and admonition should have been thoroughly familiar to the inmates of Syon. Every candidate for admission in making final vows promised "to kepe obedience after the rewle of Seynt Austyn and constitucions of Saynt Birgitt Ande to observe the addicions . . . addyd and annexid to the seyd constitucions or rewle"; a similar promise was made by each Sister at the installation of a new Abbess, and in addition the two rules were read once a week to the assembled Sisters at meal-time (see EETSES 19.xxii note, xxiv, xxxiii). Richard Whytforde in translating the *Rule of St. Augustine* into English was making doubly sure that the Sisters of Syon should not only hear but understand the basic regulations of their Order.

The *Rule of St. Augustine* was translated into Middle English at least twice. The first translation is not extant; its author is not known. When Richard Whytforde (fl. 1495–1555?), "Wretch of Syon" as he liked to style himself, was asked by the Sisters of Syon either to revise their old translation or to make a new one, he chose the second alternative. His reason for this choice is stated with characteristic directness in the prefatory note to the first edition addressed to his "Good Deuout relygyous doughters: . . . to amende your translacyon passed my power and wyt. It semeth unto me so scabrouse/ rughe/ or rude/ and not after the commune englysshe of this countree." For his own translation he aimed at "a playne style/ without ynkehorne termes. If ony suche be here after the commune vse/ yet doeth an other terme folowe/ or twayne of more playne englysshe/ to declare that goeth before" (quotations from microfilm of Bodleian Douce A. 277).

In the same prefatory note Whytforde promised to add to his translation of the *Rule* a translation of the exposition of the *Rule* made by Hugo of St. Victor (ca. 1096–1141), "which ye shal haue as shortly as we may brynge it vnto ende." There is a curious ambiguity between Whytforde's statement here and his statement in the prefatory note to the second edition addressed "unto the deuoute and ghostely reders." It begins: "Instauntly required vii yeres ago to translate this holy rule of saynt Augustyne out of the latyn into englysshe. I (the rather and more lyghtly) dyd graunt therunto/ that I had not before ye tyme seen or herde of ony other translacyon/ but that was olde/ scabrouse/ rough/ & not of the englysshe comynly vsed in these partyes." The prefatory note continues with a description of the contents and method of printing used in the second edition. What is the connection of this seven-year period with Whytforde's writing of the *Rule*? Did he put off for seven years his agreement to translate the *Rule* or did he put off for seven years the performance of his additional promise, "shortly" to give the Sisters a translation also of Hugo's exposition? In other words, how long was the interval between the actual printing of the first and second editions? The second edition is dated in the colophon, November 28, 1525. The first edition is undated. Bibliographers, if they date it at all, date it 1525, with or without parenthesis. This dating does indeed leave a "short" interval between the two editions and by implication a long interval, seven years, between Whytforde's promises and their fulfillment. The point cannot be argued further here. Whatever the interval between first and second editions, Whytforde in the second edition more than fulfilled his promise to the Sisters.

This second edition is an elaborate piece of work both in its contents and in its method of printing. It contains the Latin text of St. Augustine's *Regula ad servos Dei*, Whytforde's translation and exposition of Augustine and Whytforde's translation of Hugo of St. Victor's *Expositio in regulam beati Augustini*. These four texts are arranged as follows: Whytforde quotes a passage of the Latin rule and translates it. Then follows his own exposition of that passage, ending with some such phrase as "Now here Saynt Hugh." St. Hugh's name in capitals is centered in the next line and then follows Whytforde's translation of this exposition. Occasionally Whytforde also explains Hugh's text. Such interpolations are carefully indicated in the margin, e.g., "a note of the translatour," or within the text by parenthetical remarks, e.g., "(I tell you)". The interweaving of Whytforde's own exposition with his translation of Hugo's makes for repetition and diffuseness but it has the effect, also, of a lively running comment and interchange of views.

Accepting Migne's texts as standard for the Latin texts of Augustine and Hugh, it is evident that Hugo follows Augustine's text more closely than Whytforde does. Hugo keeps Augustine's division into twelve sections or chapters, usually with the same or similar headings. Whytforde cuts across these divisions, condensing the material into seven chapters. Hugo is the more formal commentator and draws his illustrations from Holy Scripture and the Fathers. Whytforde is writing primarily for the Sisters of Syon, obviously not scholars. He points up his remarks with colloquial phrases and familiar saws: e.g., "Your commune englysshe prouerbe hath here good place. Better is ynough/ than a feest" (f. 33ᵃ). Whytforde's comments, moreover, reflect conditions within Syon Monastery, contemporary practices in the outer world, and his own forceful opinions on a variety of subjects. One example will sufficiently illustrate his localization of Augustine's concise, general statements, in this case a regulation for the borrowing of books. Augustine (Migne PL, 32, col. 1383) writes: "Codices certa hora singulis diebus petantur: extra horam qui petierit, non accipiat." Hugo (Migne PL, 176, col. 911) makes no comment on the phrase "certa hora" but adds a long and eloquent passage on reading as one of the three fundamental duties of the ruled life. Whytforde's comment (f. 67ᵃ) is practical and contemporary: "He [Augustine] begynneth fyrst with the offyce of the library & bokes/ whiche yᵗ tyme were of grete pryce/ and therfore very scarce & rare. Yet wolde he yᵗ of those bokes yᵗ were to be had/ none shold be denyed/ so they were axed at the tyme appoynted/ as is in dyuers libraryes in bothe the uniuersytees/ & also in London/ yᵗ from viii of the clocke unto x or xi or other lyke tymes/ the libraryes be at lyberty open/ but in other tymes not so."

Finally it should be noted that Whytforde's translation of the *Rule of St. Augustine* in the first edition is not identical with that in the second edition. Small differences in the arrangement of words and phrases, numerous changes in diction, and minor omissions occur throughout the two translations. But without doubt Whytforde had a copy of his first translation before him as he worked out the new arrangement of interwoven Latin text, translation and two expositions.

RULE OF ST. SAVIOUR [6]. The Brigittine Order is officially Ordo sanctissimi Salvatoris. Its founder, St. Bridget (Birgitta) of Sweden, claimed that the official *Rule* was revealed to her by the Saviour himself. Some of the Latin manuscripts and both the English texts record the Saviour's words in terms of direct address. These nightly revelations St. Bridget wrote down in Swedish, presumably about the year 1345. They were then translated into Latin by her confessor, Peter Olafson, and submitted to the Holy See. To meet the requirement that new orders must be based on one of those already approved, the *Rule of St. Augustine* was acknowledged as the basis of the *Rule of St. Saviour*. The latter was recognized by Urban V in 1370 and finally confirmed by Urban VI in 1378. It provided for the establishment of a double community to consist of 85 members: 60 sisters, 13 priests, 4 deacons, and 8 laymen, representing numerically the 12 Apostles with St. Paul added as a thirteenth and the 72 Disciples.

The English translation of the *Rule of St. Saviour* is extant in two fifteenth-century manuscripts: Cambridge University Ff.vi.33 and St. Paul's Cathedral Library MS, both of which also contain the English translation of the *Rule of St. Augustine*. None of the numerous Latin texts so far examined proves to be the direct source of either English text, nor is either English text copied from the other. But in general the English translation reproduces carefully its Latin counterpart.

The *Rule*, Latin and English, is preceded by a brief Preface presumably written by Alphonse of Vadstena, confirming the authenticity of its revelation. Next follows a Prologue in which the Saviour announces to St. Bridget his purpose to plant a new vineyard to which she shall "bere the brawnches of [his] wordes." [Passages from the *Rule of St. Saviour* are quoted by kind permission of H. S. Waltzer, Mrs. E. P. Sheridan.] This new order "I wyll sette, ordeyne fyrst and principally by women to the worshippe of my most dere beloued modir, whose ordir and statutys I shall declare most fully with myn owne mowthe" (Waltzer's edition, p. 14). In the twenty-four chapters of the *Rule* itself both general directions and particular details covering the material and spiritual life of the community are prescribed.

This is a rule strict and demanding in its requirements, but recognizing the need for discretion in their application. Certain distinctive, even unique, features of the *Rule* show St. Bridget's concern for the intellectual as well as the devotional growth of her community. It was not sufficient to say and sing the offices; they must be understood. Hence that later, elaborate production of Syon Abbey, the *Mirror of Our Lady* (see [8] below). The number of service-books, for instance, was limited to "as many as be necessary to doo dyvyne office and moo in no wyse." But "thoo bookes they shall have as many as they wyll in whiche ys to lerne or to study" (chap. 18). Like the author of the *Ancrene Riwle*, St. Bridget recognized reading in the proper time as an acceptable good work. Two brief ceremonies performed daily are unique to this Order: after Tierce the ceremony held at an open grave in the cloisters, symbolic of death and doomsday (chap. 24); before Evensong the ceremony of Indulgete held in the choir when each side alternately asked and granted forgiveness for offenses done that day (chap. 4). The sense of proportion and the need for discretion which underlie this *Rule* find characteristic expression in the concluding statement of Chapter 21: "Of the measure of metys to be sette: . . . ther must be ordeyned an even mesure to all, noble and unnoble, to pore and to riche, the quantite of which mesure he can ordeyne that hath nowe lernyd infirmitees in hymself by sadde experience in gostly lyfe. For to kon to ordeyn a mesure is lerned be preef and fulfilled with paciens and discrecion."

ADDITIONS TO THE RULE OF ST. SAVIOUR [7]. In anticipation of the spread of her *Ordo S. Salvatoris* to other communities and other lands St. Bridget provided for modifications and additions to the original *Rule*. The English version of that *Rule,* which follows its source closely, states: "Who that woll make a monastery of this religion, he must in no wyse presume it withoute wyll and licence of the prince. Farthermore, thes constitucions confermyde [by the Pope], ther must be sowȝte som devoute bretheren of the rewlys of Benett or Bernard, whiche addying to thes constitucions muste wryte in howe excesses are to be amendide in the monastery" (chap. 23). There follows a list of provisions and regulations to which additions might or should be made.

This statement and the fact that the *Rule* for the use of the mother-monastery had already been amended provided the authority for Henry V's appointment in 1416 of a group of regular clergy—Benedictine, Cluniac, and Cistercian—to draw up additions to the *Rule of St. Saviour* for Syon. The negotiations involved in this undertaking, which included consultation with the mother-monastery at Vadstena, extended over several years. The English translation of the Latin text has been dated about 1431. It is extant in two fifteenth-century manuscripts: British Museum Arundel 146, written for the Sisters of Syon; St. Paul's Cathedral Library MS, written for the Brothers.

This document, like its Latin source, extends to fifty-nine chapters. It fills in with much concrete detail the subject matter of the original *Rule of St. Saviour* on such topics as the qualifications and duties of the Abbess, the Chambress, the Chantress, and the Serches or monitors; and the proper behavior at table, in the choir, in the garden, and in the dorter. Nothing is insignificant in the ruled life. The list of "light defawtes" to be confessed (chap. 2) matches in its homely variety that better known list of "sins" in the *Ancrene Riwle* (EETS 249.175). Among "more grevous defautes" (chap. 4) an unexpected item appears, doubt of the divine origin of the *Rule*: "if any afferme the revelacions of saynte Birgitta as dremes, or else detracte them." Apparently the undercurrent of scepticism and heresy in fifteenth-century thought might find its way even into Syon, center of orthodoxy.

MIRROR OF OUR LADY [8]. The chief duty of the Sisters of Syon was to sing daily, "as well festys as private days," the Hours of the Virgin. The chief function of the *Mirror of Our Lady* was to explain in English both the letter and the sentence of this Latin service. As the author says, "And therfore that ye shulde haue some maner of vnderstondynge of youre seruyce, yf ye lyste to laboure yt; causeth me to begyn thys worke" (Blunt's edition, p. 49). But the words and their meaning are not the writer's only concern. The singer and her state of grace are of equal importance. The *Mirror*, therefore, reflects both the Hours of the Virgin as a service of praise and the *Rule of St. Saviour* as the Sisters' avowed way of life. These two form one unity: "all ought to synge togyther and accorde togyther, that as ye oughte to be all of one harte, so ye prayse god, as yt were wyth one voyce" (p. 57).

The *Mirror* is extant in two manuscripts, Bodleian 12772 (Rawlinson C.941) and Aberdeen University WPR.4.18, both unprinted. Richard Fawkes's edition, printed in 1530, is also extant in several copies, one of which is edited in EETSES 19. Three men associated with Syon Monastery have been accepted or suggested as author: Richard Whytford (fl. 1495–1555?), Thomas Gascoigne (1403–58), and Clement Maidstone (fl. 1410). The authorship, however, remains unproved. The *Mirror* itself dates from the first half of the fifteenth century.

The *Mirror* is introduced by two Prologues. In the first the author explains his reasons for and methods of translation, and outlines in general terms the subject matter of the three parts into which the treatise is divided. Notable is his comment (p. 3) that he has made few "drawings" of the Psalms since the Sisters may use Richard Rolle's translation. The second Prologue is a brief but knowledgeable statement of the difficulties of translation, difficulties increased by those would-be censors who have "a lytel latyn and scarcely that well" (p. 8). Following this Prologue is a table of contents of the twenty-four chapters of Part I.

Part I is a history and exposition of the Syon Hours of the Virgin: of its origin (like that of the *Rule of St. Saviour*, by divine revelation), of the significance of its sevenfold division, of the technique required for its proper saying and singing, and, more important, of the attitude of mind and conscience necessary for its full acceptance as a service of praise. In his exposition the author speaks as historian, as choirmaster, as exegete, and as director of conscience. The goal of his teaching, as of the Sisters' singing, is the increase of devotion: "that ye shulde haue the more sprytuall loue, & inwarde delyte and deuocyon, in thys holy seruyce" (p. 3).

Part II is by far the longest of the three parts. It begins with an essay on the right reading of holy books, which is fully in accord with the place given to reading in the Syon *Rule*. Reading is a part of contemplation: "in redynge god spekyth to man" (p. 66). But the Sisters of Syon were by no means all scholars. It is to the author's credit that without condescension he provided an English exposition for those unable to cope with Latin. The main subject matter of Part II is the exposition of the seven "stories" of the Virgin as they are set forth in the seven Hours of the seven days in the week. The Sunday Hours are expounded in fullest detail. In this part the author includes also a statement of the form and symbolism of the two ceremonies, at Tierce and at Evensong, unique to the Brigittine Order (pp. 142, 150; see also under *Rule of St. Saviour* [6] above).

In contrast to the Sunday Hours, the weekday Hours and the Hours for special feasts of the Virgin are explained with relative brevity. Part III in equally brief fashion comments on the Sisters' Masses. It is not surprising that in some extant copies of the *Mirror* Part III is omitted entirely.

The *Mirror* is of interest and significance from several points of view: that of the historian of Syon Monastery specifically and of the ruled life in general; that of the student of liturgy and ecclesiastical symbolism; and, not least, that of the student of Biblical translation and its effect on English vernacular. The author's own English is competent and varied in its simple and orderly exposition (p. 148, "rorate"), in its homely illustrations (p. 38, "that like as man"), and in its occasional burst of eloquence (p. 97, "now ioyne to all thys").

5. Franciscan Order

RULE OF ST. FRANCIS (First Order of St. Francis) [9]. Material in Middle English on the Franciscan orders is meagre and late. Each of the three Orders—the Friars Minor (dealt with here), the Poor Clares or Minoresses (see [11] below), and the Penitents (see [12] below)—is represented by a version of its *Rule*; one of the reformed group of the first Order, the Observants, is represented by a summary of its *Rule* (see [13] below). The *Testament of St. Francis* (see [10] below), with its last plea for the preservation of both word and spirit of his *Rule*, accompanies the Middle English versions of the *Rule* itself and rightly belongs with that document. One or two of these haphazard survivals—there must be others unrecorded or unnoticed—acquire an additional interest from their associations with people and places: with Wyclyf, for instance, and with the first house of Poor Clares established in England, outside London, in the Minories.

The *Rule of St. Francis* is extant in Middle English in two versions. Version a, ascribed doubtfully to Wyclyf, is known in three manuscripts of the late fourteenth and early fifteenth centuries. It begins directly —"þis his þe reule of seynt Frauncis"—and contains twelve chapters. The thirteenth chapter is the *Testament of St. Francis*. That chapter finished, Wyclyf, if the writer is Wyclyf, begins his attack: "But here þe menours seyn." In rapid and pungent phrases he points out both their false logic in repudiating the *Testament* as still binding, and their unfranciscan practices in carrying out the commitments of the *Rule*. The writer obviously understood and sympathized with the founder and his original *Rule*. In fact, his last accusation, that the *Rule* is misnamed—it should be called not "fraunseis reule but reule of crist or of the gospel"—is the highest possible commendation he could give.

The later Middle English Version b is extant in one manuscript, British Museum Cotton Faustina D.iv, described as a portuary (or, more colloquially, a porthous) and owned by John Howell, probably a Franciscan friar. Its text, also in twelve chapters, is interlarded with brief notations classifying the separate statements of the *Rule* as "An Admonicioun" or as "A libertee" or as "Hauyng the strenght of a commaundement." At two other places in the manuscript, f. 34 and f. 56, much longer comments discuss various interpretations of such fundamental requirements of the *Rule* as poverty and manual labor.

Both the Wyclyfite and the Howell versions are based on the *Regula bullata* of 1223, confirmed by Pope Honorius III.

TESTAMENT OF ST. FRANCIS [10]. As already noted, a translation of the *Testament of St. Francis* follows each of the Middle English versions of the *Rule* (see [9] above). In Version b (Howell), however, the *Testament* is not incorporated as the concluding chapter of the *Rule*. Alike in contents, both Middle English translations follow that group of Latin manuscripts which, as one distinguishing feature, read, "Feci misericordam cum illis" (i.e. with lepers), rather than "Feci moram cum illis." The Middle English texts, in modern spelling, read, "I did mercy with them." However, the English texts are two distinct translations, as a fuller quotation from this passage clearly shows:

Version a (Wyclyf): " . . . whanne I was 'in ouere' myche synnes it semyd to me bittrere to see leprous men, and þe same lord brouʒte me among hem and I dede mercy wiþ hem" (EETS 74.45).

Version b (Howell): " . . . when I was in bondage of synne yt was bitter to me and lothesomme to see and loke uppon persounys enfect with leopre; but that blessid Lord browghte me amonge them, and I did mercy with them" (Brewer, Monumenta Franciscana, 1.562).

The *Testament of St. Francis* is a testimony as well as a testament: a testimony of his own conversion and of his experiences as a friar; a testament, also, bequeathing "under obedience" the safekeeping of his *Rule* in word and spirit to his brethren, both clerk and layman. Ironically, the *Testament* is a gloss on the *Rule*, forbidding further glossing—with what effect the history of the *Rule* sufficiently illustrates. Both Middle English versions are glossed. The Wyclyfite comment or gloss (Version a) is in fact a spirited plea for the preservation of the original *Rule*; the Howell gloss (Version b) is a cool dissection of the letter of the *Rule*, and of the later interpretations of the *Rule*, made point by point in the accepted manner of scholastic exposition.

RULE OF ST. CLARE (Second Order of St. Francis) [11]. The Second Order of St. Francis, that of St. Clare, was introduced into England under royal patronage in the late thirteenth century. The earliest extant document connected with this English establishment is a charter of Edward I, dated June 28, 1293, which grants permission to his brother Edmund, Duke of Lancaster, to convey a piece of property to the Order. It was Edmund's wife, Blanche, formerly Queen of Navarre, who founded the English convent as a daughter-house of the French Monastery of nuns at Longchamp in the diocese of Paris. The English establishment was settled outside the walls of London in the district later to be known as the Minories.

This English house inherited the so-called *Isabella Rule*, named for Blessed Isabella, sister of St. Louis and founder of the Monastery of Longchamp. In the complicated history of the *Rule of St. Clare*, the *Isabella Rule* marks one stage in the modification of the vow of strict poverty, both communal and private, for which St. Clare had fought to her last day. Under the *Isabella Rule* the nuns as a community could own property. It is obvious from the charter of Edward I, mentioned above, that the daughter-community was to be endowed with property from the start. Compensating in part for this defection from the original *Rule*, the *Isabella Rule* reaffirmed its Franciscan origin by adding "Minorissae" to its official name. The *Rule* as drawn up for the Longchamp community was approved by Pope Alexander IV and confirmed with slight alteration by his successor Urban IV in the bull, *Religionis*

augmentum, July 27, 1263. Other alterations were added later by Boniface VIII (1294–1303). It is the *Isabella Rule* in this amended form that
supplies the text for the surviving English translation.

As it is preserved in Bodleian 2357, the English version is divided
into two parts, both written in the same fifteenth-century hand. Part I,
ff. 48ᵃ–72ᵃ, is the *Rule* proper, without title but with the colophon, *Here
endiþ þᵉ Rewle of Sustris Menouresses enclosid.* Part II, ff. 72ᵃ–101ᵃ, also
without title, is a series of additions to the *Rule,* ending with the colophon, *This gode werke is ful complete blessid be þᵉ holi Trinite . . .
Amen.* As its editor notes, the *Rule* and the first pages of the additions
preserve the form of a papal bull, using the first person plural pronouns
of direct address. The latter part of the additions, with two exceptions,
uses the third person pronouns of narrative and statement. Again according to the editor, the English *Rule* is probably a translation from
a French version of the original Latin. In his notes, however, he quotes
only from the Latin text. Occasional French words (e.g., "reddure") and
French plurals (e.g., "demures . . . Sustris, certeines wommen") suggest
a French text in the background. No source has been discovered for the
English additions to the *Isabella Rule.*

The English translation, whatever its direct source, is artless, often
awkward and unidiomatic in its phrasing and construction, and occasionally even unintelligible.

RULE OF THE ORDER OF PENITENTS (Third Order of St.
Francis) [12]. As in the case of the First and Second Orders of St. Francis,
the Third Order has been known by various names and its *Rule* has
undergone various revisions. The only extant Middle English version,
that preserved in the Pennant MS, has the following heading: *Here
begynnyth the Chapituris of the iiiᵈᵉ order of Seynt franceys for the
Brethren and Susters of the order of Penitentis.* The phrases, *iiiᵈᵉ order*
and *order of Penitentis* are later designations of this group. As its editor
makes clear, the text of the English translation is based on a copy of
the third version of the Latin *Rule,* similar to but not identical with that
given in the bull, *Supra montem,* August 18, 1289, issued by Pope
Nicholas IV.

The Third Order was established and its earliest *Rule* drawn up in the lifetime and under the supervision of St. Francis. Traditionally St. Francis and Ugolino, Cardinal Bishop of Ostia, later Pope Gregory IX, were the "authors" of the version of the *Rule* dated 1221. This Third Order was instituted for lay men and women who, remaining in the world, wished to conform their lives to the fundamental principles of the Franciscan rule: chastity, poverty, obedience, and charitable works. Wives were not admitted to the Order without the consent of their husbands. Franciscan poverty was practiced in the form of simple living, temperate eating and drinking, and the wearing of clothes "meek" in price and color. Before admission, would-be members were diligently examined in their faith and obedience to the Church of Rome. After admission they were under obedience to the official Visitor. If they rebelled three times against his authority, they were dismissed from the Order. As to works of charity, members made regular contributions of money and service to the sick and the poor. There was one charity, however, they might not indulge in: they were not to "geue enything to Joglers or mynstrellis for loue of ther vaniteis" (chap. 6). This, along with certain other restrictions put upon the members as lay people, reflects the "world" in which they still took active part. Bearing of weapons, for instance, was forbidden to the Brothers except—and the exceptions were generous—in defense of the Church, of the Christian faith, and of their own land, or by license of the Ministers (chap. 10). Within these limitations a layman might still pick a good quarrel. But peacemaking between Brothers and Sisters and between strangers (chap. 13) was the more characteristic concern of the Order. It goes without saying, also, that a member was expected to carry out a daily program of public and private worship and to assign himself private penance for the day's indiscretions, "at euyn when he remembrithe hym selfe" (chap. 14).

RULE OF THE OBSERVANTS (First Order of St. Francis, Reformed) [13]. The Middle English material on the *Rule of the Observants* needs little comment. It consists only of a brief summary of their *Rule* as set forth in the Statutes of the Order brought together at a general chapter held in Barcelona in 1451. The Observants were reformers seeking to recover the simplicity and strictness of the early

Franciscan Order. Before the middle of the fifteenth century they had already won papal recognition and the right to elect their own vicar-general. The Statutes of Barcelona include not only a rule for the inner and outer "conversation" of the Brothers, but extracts from the papal bulls confirming their privileges.

The Latin text in both incipit and explicit designates this document as an *abbreviatio statutorum tam papalium quam generalium*. The Middle English summary, extant in the Howell portuary (see [9] and [10] above), is indeed a further abbreviation of an abbreviation. It condenses the nine chapters of the Latin text into fewer than ten of its duodecimo folios. All quotation from papal documents is omitted, together with discussion of possible offenses against the *Rule* and their punishment, and the detailed account of procedures in the election of officers. Nevertheless, some material from each of the nine chapters is touched upon, however lightly, in the English summary.

The brevity of the English text disguises much of the complexity and particularity which, with the growth of the Order, have become unavoidable. There are now more contacts and relationships within and without the community to be regulated. Among grievous offenses, for instance, the early *Rule* says nothing about penalties for the unauthorized opening of official letters from the royal court or the papal court. Again, on a less serious subject, the regulations about the friar's vesture have become uniform and standardized—a tailor's specifications for the proper breadth and length of each article. But specifications occasionally clash with facts. The official breadth for the friar's "habit" is not to exceed sixteen spans, "nisi notabilis corpulentia alicuius," or in the Middle English version, unless "the gretnes of the brodre" requires it. These complex regulations for the maintenance of simplicity are sufficient evidence of the difficulties inherent in St. Francis's ideal for his Order in any age.

6. RULES FOR HERMITS AND RECLUSES

RULE OF ST. CELESTINE [14]. An extreme form of withdrawal from the world is represented by the way of life of the hermit and the recluse. As one indication that this form of living was particularly popular in England Father Oliger has noted (Antonianum 9.48) that of nine rules dating from the ninth through the thirteenth centuries whose provenance is known, Germany supplied one, France three, England five.

Both the hermit and the recluse were exceptions among the "regulars." Their rules cut across those of the communal orders and yet included their basic requirements of chastity, poverty, and obedience. But poverty, for instance, had to be interpreted differently for the friar who returned to his community, the hermit who returned to his retreat, and the recluse who never left his cell. Both the friar and the hermit might be abroad by day. The friar would bring back the day's offering to his community; the hermit was obliged each day before sunset to distribute to the poor everything beyond his own immediate needs. For the recluse neither the gathering nor the distributing of alms was a major subject for instruction. In fact, a rule for recluses tended to become a devotional treatise, a guide for the inner life rather than a series of directions for the outer life. The two *Rules* for hermits listed here, [14] and [15], recall and often repeat directives from the Benedictine and Franciscan Orders. The *Rule* for recluses [16], as its editor notes, in addition to such directives, has its proper affiliations with the writings of Hilton and Rolle and, one should add, even more closely with the *Ancrene Riwle* [1] and St. Ailred's letter to his sister [4].

The English *Rule of St. Celestine* is extant in three manuscripts, one dating from the late fifteenth century, two from the early sixteenth century. Of the three, the fifteenth-century British Museum Additional 34193 is the most complete. It gives a table of contents and, omitting the brief prologue, divides the twenty-two sections of the Latin text into seventeen chapters. The language of this manuscript, like that of British Museum Sloane 1584, has a slight Northern tinge.

The source of this English *Rule* is the *Regula eremitarum* or *Oxford Rule*, so called from the only extant manuscript, Bodleian 11937. The *Oxford Rule* in turn is derived from the *Regula hermitarum* or *Cambridge Rule*, also named from the only extant manuscript, Cambridge University Mm.vi.17. Furthermore, scholars have long recognized and recently reemphasized the fact that the *Cambridge Rule* is based on St. Ailred's letter to his sister (see [4] above). And, finally, the *Cambridge Rule* has some slight claim to be counted among the possible works of

Richard Rolle. It is this complex heritage of material, involving such outstanding medieval writers as Ailred, Rolle, and also the author of the *Ancrene Riwle*, that has centered attention on the *Oxford* and *Cambridge Rules* and their direct and indirect offshoots, the Latin and the English *Rules of St. Celestine*. The interweaving of material in the *Rule of St. Celestine* will be obvious to any reader of medieval instructions for the religious.

The three texts of the English *Rule of St. Celestine* are independent translations of their common source. All three ascribe the original to Pope Celestine V, an ascription for which there is no historical basis. Like the Latin source, the English text makes special mention of the hermit's independence of the usual ecclesiastical authorities, often a sore point in disputes over the status of hermits, and emphasizes that independence in an appropriate metaphor: "An hermite also owes to make his Obedience all only to allmgyht god ffor he is abote prior and þe gouernour of his cloyster þat is to say of his hert" (British Museum Additional 34193, f. 132ª). In the same spirit of consecrated independence, the *Rule* leaves it to the hermit to decide whether or not he shall wear a hairshirt, adding the comment that it would be better to give up the physical hairshirt than to "forsake þe heyre of his conscience" (f. 133ª). In spite of the brevity and generality of the *Rule*, the English version with its simple vernacular phrases manages to suggest a certain concreteness in its outline for the daily life of a medieval hermit.

RULE OF ST. LINUS [15]. The *Rule of St. Linus* is preserved in the fifteenth-century MS Lambeth 192, on a flyleaf, f. 46ª, preceding Thomas Scrope's English translation of Ribot's *Speculum Carmelitarum*. According to its editor, the *Rule of St. Linus* shows in its brief text no Carmelite associations, nor is there any evidence to support its ascription of authorship to St. Linus (ca. 79 A.D.). Rather, from liturgical evidence, the editor concludes that the lost Latin source probably dated from the late thirteenth century. Thomas Scrope (d. 1491), he suggests, may have been either the scribe or the author of the English translation.

Anticipating the regulations he is about to set down, the writer of the English *Rule* states simply that the hermit binds himself "thus to spende the nyght and the day to the louyng of god." He concludes equally simply, "This is þe charge of an Hermyȝtis Lyffe." The word "charge" or "officium," as the editor translates it, is an adequate characterization of the skeletal contents of this *Rule*. It is a bare statement of the number of Paternosters, Aves, and Credos which the hermit shall recite each day at the canonical hours, of the fasts and feasts he shall observe throughout the year, of the habit he shall wear by day and by night and at his burial. The final statement of his duties is given in figures, the sum total of the day's prayers. This is the type of "office" prescribed for the layman, not for the clerical hermit. In this faithful routine of acts of devotion the uneducated layman could give adequate proof of his "louyng of god."

SPECULUM INCLUSORUM [16]. The Latin *Speculum inclusorum* is a borderline rule more concerned with the inner than with the outer life. Its unknown author was a scholar well read in the Scriptures and the Fathers and also a man of letters well trained in the refinements of medieval rhetoric. To him the inclosed life was a high calling, high in the demands it made on those who would pursue it, high in the reward of spiritual joys it promised them even in this life. On the basis of the English provenance of the two extant manuscripts of the Latin text, of possible literary reminiscences of Richard Rolle within the text, and of certain features of the inclosed life recommended in this *Rule*, Father Oliger suggests that its author might be found among English Carthusians of the second half of the fourteenth century (Lateranum ns 4.43).

The author of the Latin text made two requests about his work: first, that for those who did not know Latin it should be read in English or French or one's own mother tongue; second, that it should be read aloud, "quia maxime solet corda conpungere vox viva legentis" (p. 106). It is unfortunate that the work of the writer who undertook to translate the text into English has survived only in one badly damaged manuscript, British Museum Harley 2372, ca. 1450, associated with "Straunford" in the diocese of Lincoln. Father Oliger describes this translation as faithful and literal with occasional additions and omissions. A full appraisal of the translator's ability to match the literacy and humane qualities of his Latin original must await the publication of the English text, desirable in spite of its damaged state.

7. OTHER ORDERS

FOUNDING OF THE ORDER OF HOLY TRINITY [17]. This brief and somewhat vague account of the founding of the Order of Holy Trinity is chronicle rather than rule. In the only extant manuscript, British Museum Egerton 3143, it follows directly after the *Life of St. Robert of Knaresborough* and is written in the same couplet form. In the EETS edition the *Founding* is numbered consecutively with the *Life*. In fact, after a formal four-line prologue, the *Founding* does indeed continue the preceding narrative by recounting how St. Robert's Chapel and Cave came into possession of the Order of Holy Trinity. Then, as would be appropriate in a rule, the writer explains the symbolism of the three-fold division of the Order's rents, of which the third part is devoted to the ransom of Christian captives in the Holy Land, and next the symbolism of their white habit (the Order is basically Augustinian) and of the parti-colored cross which is their badge. After that he turns again to chronicle, giving a brief account of the founding of the Order. The general impression of vagueness which obscures his story is understandable when one reads his own prefatory statement that every head has a different opinion of the founding of the Order and that he himself has seen it in no book.

Available information concerning three unprinted items—the FOUNDING OF THE CARTHUSIAN ORDER [18], the ORDINANCE AND CUSTOMS OF THE HOSPITAL OF ST. LAWRENCE, CANTERBURY [19], and T. SCROPE'S INSTITUTIONS AND SPECIAL DEEDS OF RELIGIOUS CARMELITES [20]—will be found in the Bibliography.

Bibliography

Table of Abbreviations

AAGRP	Ausgaben und Abhandlungen aus dem Gebiete der romanischen Philologie
AC	Archaeologica Cantiana
Acad	Academy
AEB	Kölbing E, Altenglische Bibliothek, Heilbronn 1883–
AELeg 1875	Horstmann C, Altenglische Legenden, Paderborn 1875
AELeg 1878	Horstmann, C, Sammlung altenglischer Legenden, Heilbronn 1878
AELeg 1881	Horstmann C, Altenglische Legenden (Neue Folge), Heilbronn 1881
AESpr	Mätzner E, Altenglische Sprachproben, Berlin 1867–
AF	Anglistische Forschungen
AfDA	Anzeiger für deutsches Alterthum
AHR	American Historical Review
AJ	Ampleforth Journal
AJA	American Journal of Archaeology
AJP	American Journal of Philology
ALb	Allgemeines Literaturblatt
ALg	Archivum linguisticum
Allen WAR	Allen H E, Writings Ascribed to Richard Rolle Hermit of Hampole and Materials for His Biography, MLA Monograph Series 3, N Y 1927
Angl	Anglia, Zeitschrift für englische Philologie
AnglA	Anglia Anzeiger
AnglB	Beiblatt zur Anglia

AN&Q	American Notes and Queries
Antiq	Antiquity
APS	Acta philologica scandinavica
AQ	American Quarterly
AR	Antioch Review
Arch	Archiv für das Studium der neueren Sprachen und Literaturen
Archaeol	Archaeologia
Ashton	Ashton J, Romances of Chivalry, London 1890
ASp	American Speech
ASR	American Scandinavian Review
ASt	Aberystwyth Studies
Athen	Athenaeum
BA	Books Abroad
BARB	Bulletin de l'Académie royale de Belgique
Baugh LHE	Baugh A C, The Middle English Period, in A Literary History of England, N Y 1948
BB	Bulletin of Bibliography
BBA	Bonner Beiträge zur Anglistik
BBCS	Bulletin of the Board of Celtic Studies (Univ of Wales)
BBGRP	Berliner Beiträge zur germanischen und romanischen Philologie
BBSIA	Bulletin bibliographique de la Société internationale arthurienne
Bennett OHEL	Bennett H S, Chaucer and the Fifteenth Century, Oxford 1947
Best BIP	Best R I, Bibliography of Irish Philology, 2 vols, Dublin 1913
BGDSL	Beiträge zur Geschichte der deutschen Sprache und Literatur
BHR	Bibliothèque d'humanisme et renaissance
BIHR	Bulletin of the Institute of Historical Research
Billings	Billings A H, A Guide to the Middle English Metrical Romances, N Y 1901
Blackf	Blackfriars

Bloomfield SDS	Bloomfield M W, The Seven Deadly Sins, Michigan State College of Agriculture and Applied Science Studies in Language and Literature, 1952
BNYPL	Bulletin of the New York Public Library
Böddeker AED	Böddeker K, Altenglische Dichtungen des MS Harl 2253, Berlin 1878
Bossuat MBLF	Bossuat R, Manuel bibliographique de la littérature française du moyen âge, Paris 1951; supplément Paris 1955; deuxième supplément Paris 1961 [the item numbers run consecutively through the supplement]
BPLQ	Boston Public Library Quarterly
BQR	Bodleian Quarterly Record (sometimes Review)
Brandl	Brandl A, Mittelenglische Literatur, in Paul's Grundriss der germanische Philologie, 1st edn, Strassburg 1893, 2^1.609 ff, Index 2^2.345
Brown ELxiiiC	Brown C F, English Lyrics of the 13th Century, Oxford 1932
Brown Reg	Brown C, A Register of Middle English Religious and Didactic Verse, parts 1 and 2, Oxford (for the Bibliographical Society) 1916, 1920
Brown RLxivC	Brown C F, Religious Lyrics of the 14th Century, Oxford 1924
Brown RLxvC	Brown C F, Religious Lyrics of the 15th Century, Oxford 1939
Brown-Robbins	Brown C and R H Robbins, The Index of Middle English Verse, N Y 1943; see also Robbins-Cutler
Bryan-Dempster	Bryan W F and G Dempster, Sources and Analogues of Chaucer's Canterbury Tales, Chicago 1941
BrynMawrMon	Bryn Mawr College Monographs, Bryn Mawr 1905–
BSEP	Bonner Studien zur englischen Philologie
BUSE	Boston University Studies in English
CASP	Cambridge Antiquarian Society Publication
CBEL	Bateson F W, Cambridge Bibliography of English Literature, 5 vols, London and N Y 1941, 1957
CE	College English

Chambers   Chambers E K, The Mediaeval Stage, 2 vols, Oxford 1903

Chambers OHEL   Chambers E K, English Literature at the Close of the Middle Ages, Oxford 1945

CHEL   Ward A W and A R Waller, The Cambridge History of English Literature, vols 1 and 2, Cambridge 1907, 1908

CHR   Catholic Historical Review

ChS   Publications of the Chaucer Society, London 1869–1924

Ch&Sidg   Chambers E K and F Sidgwick, Early English Lyrics, London 1907; numerous reprints

CJ   Classic Journal

CL   Comparative Literature

CMLR   Canadian Modern Language Review

Comper Spir Songs   Comper F M M, Spiritual Songs from English Manuscripts of Fourteenth to Sixteenth Centuries, London and N Y 1936

Conviv   Convivium

Courthope   Courthope W J, History of English Poetry, vol 1, London 1895

CP   Classical Philology

Craig HEL   Craig H, G K Anderson, L I Bredvold, J W Beach, History of English Literature, N Y 1950

Cross Mot Ind   Cross T P, Motif Index of Early Irish Literature, Bloomington Ind 1951

Crotch PEWC   Crotch W J B, The Prologues and Epilogues of William Caxton, EETS 176, London 1928

CUS   Columbia University Studies in English and in Comparative Literature, N Y 1899–

DA   Dissertation Abstracts

DANHSJ   Derbyshire Archaeological and Natural History Society Journal

de Julleville Hist de Julleville L Petit, Histoire de la langue et de la littérature française, vols 1 and 2, Paris 1896–99

de Ricci Census	de Ricci S and W J Wilson, Census of Medieval and Renaissance Manuscripts in the United States of America and Canada, vols 1–3, N Y 1935, 1937, 1940
Dickins and Wilson	Dickins B and R M Wilson, Early Middle English Texts, Cambridge 1950
DLz	Deutsche Literaturzeitung
DNB	Stephen L and S Lee, Dictionary of National Biography, N Y and London 1885–1900, and supplements
DomS	Dominican Studies: An Annual Review, Blackfriars Publications, London
DUJ	Durham University Journal
EA	Études anglaises
EBEP	Erlanger Beiträge zur englischen Philologie
EC	Essays in Criticism
EETS	Publications of the Early English Text Society (Original Series), 1864–
EETSES	Publications of the Early English Text Society (Extra Series), 1867–
EG	Études germaniques
EGS	English and Germanic Studies
EHR	English Historical Review
EIE, EIA	English Institute Essays (Annual), N Y 1939–
EJ	English Journal
ELH	Journal of English Literary History
Ellis EEP	Ellis G, Specimens of Early English Poetry, 3 vols, London 1811
Ellis Spec	Ellis G, Specimens of Early English Metrical Romances, 3 vols, London 1805; rvsd Halliwell, 1 vol, Bohn edn 1848 (latter edn referred to, unless otherwise indicated)
Enc Brit	Encyclopaedia Britannica, 11th edn
Engl	English: The Magazine of the English Association
E&S	Essays and Studies by Members of the English Association, Oxford 1910–

E&S Brown	Essays and Studies in Honor of Carleton Brown, N Y 1940
EStn	Englische Studien
ESts	English Studies
ETB	Hoops J, Englische Textbibliothek, 21 vols, Heidelberg 1898–1935?
Expl	Explicator
FFC	Foklore Fellows Communications
FFK	Forschungen und Fortschritte: Korrespondenzblatt der deutschen Wissenschaft und Technik
Flügel NL	Flügel E, Neuenglisches Lesebuch, Halle 1895
FQ	French Quarterly
FR	French Review
FS	French Studies
Furnival EEP	Furnivall F J, Early English Poems and Lives of Saints, Berlin 1862 (Transactions of Philological Society of London 1858)
Gautier Bibl	Gautier L, Bibliographie des chansons de geste, Paris 1897
Gayley	Gayley C M, Plays of Our Forefathers, N Y 1907
GdW	Gesamtkatalog der Wiegendrucke, Leipzig 1925–
Germ	Germania
Gerould S Leg	Gerould G H, Saints' Legends, Boston 1916
GGA	Göttingische gelehrte Anzeiger
GJ	Gutenberg Jahrbuch
GQ	German Quarterly
GR	Germanic Review
Greene E E Carols	Greene R L, The Early English Carols, Oxford 1935
GRM	Germanisch-Romanische Monatsschrift
Gröber	Gröber G, Grundriss der romanischen Philologie, Strassburg 1888–1902, new issue 1897–1906, 2nd edn 1904– (vol 2^1 1902 referred to, unless otherwise indicated)
Gröber-Hofer	Hofer S, Geschichte der mittelfranzösischen Literatur, 2 vols, 2nd edn, Berlin and Leipzig 1933–37

Hall Selections	Hall J, Selections from Early Middle English 1130–1250, 2 parts, Oxford 1920
Hammond	Hammond E P, Chaucer: A Bibliographical Manual, N Y 1908
Hartshorne AMT	Hartshorne C H, Ancient Metrical Tales, London 1829
Hazlitt Rem	Hazlitt W C, Remains of the Early Popular Poetry of England, 4 vols, London 1864–66
Herbert	Herbert J A, Catalogue of Romances in the Department of MSS of the British Museum, London 1910 (vol 3 of Ward's Catalogue)
Hermes	Hermes
Hibbard Med Rom	Hibbard L, Medieval Romance in England, N Y 1924
HINL	History of Ideas News Letter
Hisp	Hispania
HispR	Hispanic Review
HJ	Hibbert Journal
HLB	Harvard Library Bulletin
HLF	Histoire littéraire de la France, Paris 1733–; new edn 1865–
HLQ	Huntington Library Quarterly
Holmes CBFL	Cabeen D C, Critical Bibliography of French Literature, vol 1 (the Medieval Period), ed U T Holmes jr, Syracuse N Y 1949
HSCL	Harvard Studies in Comparative Literature
HSNPL	Harvard Studies and Notes in Philology and Literature, Boston 1892–
HudR	Hudson Review
IER	Irish Ecclesiastical Review
IS	Italian Studies
Isis	Isis
Ital	Italica
JAAC	Journal of Aesthetics and Art Criticism
JBL	Journal of Biblical Literature
JCS	Journal of Celtic Studies

JEGGP	Jahresbericht über die Erscheinungen auf dem Gebiete der germanischen Philologie
JEGP	Journal of English and Germanic Philology
JEH	Journal of Ecclesiastical History
JfRESL	Jahrbuch für romanische und englische Sprache und Literatur
JGP	Journal of Germanic Philology
JHI	Journal of the History of Ideas
JPhilol	Journal of Philology
JPhilos	Journal of Philosophy
JRLB	Bulletin of the John Rylands Library, Manchester
Kane	Kane G, Middle English Literature: A Critical Study of the Romances, the Religious Lyrics, Piers Plowman, London 1951
Kennedy BWEL	Kennedy A G, A Bibliography of Writings on the English Language from the Beginning of Printing to the End of 1922, Cambridge Mass and New Haven 1927
Kild Ged	Heuser W, Die Kildare-Gedichte, Bonn 1904 (BBA 14)
Körting	Körting G, Grundriss der Geschichte der englischen Literatur von ihren Anfängen bis zur Gegenwart, 5th edn, Münster 1910
KR	Kenyon Review
Krit Jahresber	Vollmüller K, Kritischer Jahresbericht über die Fortschritte der romanischen Philologie, München und Leipzig 1892–1915 (Zweiter Teil, 13 vols in 12)
KSEP	Kieler Studien zur englischen Philologie
Lang	Language
LB	Leuvensche Bijdragen, Periodical for Modern Philology
LC	Library Chronicle
Leeds SE	Leeds Studies in English and Kindred Languages, School of English Literature in the University of Leeds

Legouis	Legouis E, Chaucer, Engl trans by Lailvoix, London 1913
Legouis HEL	Legouis E and L Cazamian, trans H D Irvine and W D MacInnes, A History of English Literature, new edn, N Y 1929
LfGRP	Literaturblatt für germanische und romanische Philologie
Libr	The Library
Litteris	Litteris: An International Critical Review of the Humanities, New Society of Letters
LMS	London Medieval Studies
Loomis ALMA	Loomis R S, Arthurian Literature in the Middle Ages, A Collaborative History, Oxford 1959
LP	Literature and Psychology
LQ	Library Quarterly
Lund SE	Lund Studies in English
LZ	Literarisches Zentralblatt
MÆ	Medium ævum
Manly CT	Manly J M, Canterbury Tales by Geoffrey Chaucer, with an Introduction, Notes, and a Glossary, N Y 1928
Manly Spec	Manly J M, Specimens of the Pre-Shakespearean Drama, vol 1, 2nd edn, Boston 1900
Manly & Rickert	Manly J M and E Rickert, The Text of the Canterbury Tales Studied on the Basis of All Known Manuscripts, 8 vols, Chicago 1940
MBREP	Münchener Beiträge zur romanischen und englischen Philologie
MED	Kurath H and S M Kuhn, Middle English Dictionary, Ann Arbor 1952– (M S Ogden, C E Palmer, and R L McKelvey, Bibliography [of ME texts], 1954, p 15)
MH	Medievalia et humanistica
MHRA	MHRA, Bulletin of the Modern Humanities Research Association

Migne PL	Migne, Patrologiae Latinae cursus completus
Minor Poems	Skeat W W, Chaucer: The Minor Poems, 2nd edn, Oxford 1896
MKAW	Mededeelingen van de Koninklijke akademie van wetenschappen, afdeling letterkunde
ML	Music and Letters
MLF	Modern Language Forum
MLJ	Modern Language Journal
MLN	Modern Language Notes
MLQ (Lon)	Modern Language Quarterly (London)
MLQ (Wash)	Modern Language Quarterly (Seattle, Washington)
MLR	Modern Language Review
Monat	Monatshefte
Moore Meech and Whitehall	Moore S, S B Meech and H Whitehall, Middle English Dialect Characteristics and Dialect Boundaries, University of Michigan Essays and Studies in Language and Literature 13, Ann Arbor 1935
Morley	Morley H, English Writers, vols 3–6, London 1890
Morris Spec	Morris R (ed part 1), R Morris and W W Skeat (ed part 2), Specimens of Early English, part 1, 2nd edn, Oxford 1887; part 2, 4th edn, Oxford 1898
MP	Modern Philology
MS	Mediaeval Studies
MSEP	Marburger Studien zur englischen Philologie, 13 vols, Marburg 1901–11
MUPES	Manchester University Publications, English Series
NA	Neuer Anzeiger
Neophil	Neophilologus, A Modern Language Quarterly
NEQ	New England Quarterly
NLB	Newberry Library Bulletin
NM	Neuphilologische Mitteilungen: Bulletin de la Société neophilologique de Helsinki
NMQ	New Mexico Quarterly
NNAC	Norfolk and Norwich Archaeological Society
N&Q	Notes and Queries
NRFH	Nueva revista de filología hispánica

NS	Die neueren Sprachen, Zeitschrift für der neusprachlichen Unterrecht
OMETexts	Morsbach L and F Holthausen, Old and Middle English Texts, 11 vols, Heidelberg 1901–26
Oxf Ch	Skeat W W, The Works of Geoffrey Chaucer, Oxford 1894–1900 (6 vols; extra 7th vol of Chaucerian Poems)
Palaes	Palaestra, Untersuchungen und Texte
PAPS	Proceedings of the American Philosophical Society
Paris Litt franç	Paris G P B, La littérature française au moyen âge, 4th edn, Paris 1909
Patterson	Patterson F A, The Middle English Penitential Lyric, N Y 1911
Paul Grundriss	Paul H, Grundriss der germanischen Philologie, 3 vols, 1st edn, Strassburg 1891–1900; 2nd edn 1900–
PBBeitr	Paul H and W Braune, Beiträge zur Geschichte der deutschen Sprache und Literatur, Halle 1874–
PBSA	Papers of the Bibliographical Society of America
PBSUV	Papers of the Bibliographical Society, Univ of Virginia
PFMS	Furnivall F J and J W Hales, The Percy Folio MS, 4 vols, London 1867–69; re-ed I Gollancz, 4 vols, London 1905–10 (the earlier edn is referred to, unless otherwise indicated)
Philo	Philologus
PMLA	Publications of the Modern Language Association of America
PMRS	Progress of Medieval and Renaissance Studies in the United States and Canada
PP	Past and Present
PPR	Philosophy and Phenomenological Research
PPS	Publications of the Percy Society
PQ	Philological Quarterly
PR	Partisan Review
PS	Pacific Spectator

PSTS   Publications of the Scottish Text Society, Edin-
                        burgh 1884–
PULC   Princeton University Library Chronicle
QF   Quellen und Forschungen zur Sprach- und Cultur-
                        geschichte der germanischen Völker
QQ   Queen's Quarterly
RAA   Revue anglo-américaine
RadMon   Radcliffe College Monographs, Boston 1891–
RB   Revue britannique
RC   Revue celtique
RCHL   Revue critique d'histoire et de littérature
REH   The Review of Ecclesiastical History
Rel Ant   Wright T and J O Halliwell, Reliquiae antiquae,
                        2 vols, London 1845
Ren   Renascence
Renwick-Orton   Renwick W L and H Orton, The Beginnings of
                        English Literature to Skelton 1509, London 1939;
                        rvsd edn 1952
RES   Review of English Studies
RevP   Revue de philologie
RF   Romanische Forschungen
RFE   Revista de filología espanola
RFH   Revista de filología hispánica
RG   Revue germanique
RHL   Revue d'histoire littéraire de la France
Rickert RofFr,   Rickert E, Early English Romances in Verse: Ro-
    RofL   mances of Friendship (vol 1), Romances of Love
                        (vol 2), London 1908
Ritson AEMR   Ritson J, Ancient English Metrical Romances, 3
                        vols, London 1802, rvsd E Goldsmid, Edinburgh
                        1884 (earlier edn referred to, unless otherwise indi-
                        cated)
Ritson APP   Ritson J, Ancient Popular Poetry, 2nd edn, Lon-
                        don 1833

Ritson AS	Ritson J, Ancient Songs from the Time of Henry III, 2 vols, London 1790, new edn 1829; rvsd W C Hazlitt, Ancient Songs and Ballads, 1 vol, London 1877 (last edn referred to, unless otherwise indicated)
RLC	Revue de littérature comparée
RLR	Revue des langues romanes
RN	Renaissance News
Robbins-Cutler	Supplement to Brown-Robbins, Lexington Ky 1965
Robbins HP	Robbins R H, Historical Poems of the 14th and 15th Centuries, Oxford 1959
Robbins SL	Robbins R H, Secular Lyrics of the 14th and 15th Centuries, 2nd edn, Oxford 1955
Robson	Robson J, Three Early English Metrical Romances, London (Camden Society) 1842
Rolls Series	Rerum Britannicarum medii aevi scriptores, Published by Authority of the Lords Commissioners of Her Majesty's Treasury, under the Direction of the Master of the Rolls, London 1857–91
Rom	Romania
RomP	Romance Philology
RomR	Romanic Review
Root	Root R K, The Poetry of Chaucer, Boston 1906
Rot	Rotulus, A Bulletin for MS Collectors
Roxb Club	Publications of the Roxburghe Club, London 1814–
RSLC	Record Society of Lancashire and Cheshire
RUL	Revue de l'Université laval
SA	The Scottish Antiquary, or Northern Notes and Queries
SAQ	South Atlantic Quarterly
SATF	Publications de la Société des anciens textes français, Paris 1875–
SB	Studies in Bibliography: Papers of the Bibliographical Society of the University of Virginia

SBB	Studies in Bibliography and Booklore
ScanSt	Scandinavian Studies
Schipper	Schipper J, Englische Metrik, 2 vols, Bonn 1881–88
Schofield	Schofield W H, English Literature from the Norman Conquest to Chaucer, N Y 1906
SciS	Science and Society
Scrut	Scrutiny
SE	Studies in English
SEER	Slavonic and East European Review
SEP	Studien zur englischen Philologie
ShJ	Jahrbuch der deutschen Shakespeare-Gesellschaft
SHR	Scottish Historical Review
Skeat Spec	Skeat W W, Specimens of English Literature 1394–1579, 6th edn, Oxford
SL	Studies in Linguistics
SN	Studia neophilologica: A Journal of Germanic and Romanic Philology
SP	Studies in Philology
Spec	Speculum: A Journal of Mediaeval Studies
SR	Sewanee Review
SRL	Saturday Review of Literature
STC	Pollard A W and G R Redgrave, A Short-Title Catalogue of Books Printed in England, Scotland, and Ireland and of English Books Printed Abroad 1475–1640, London 1926
StVL	Studien zur vergleichenden Literaturgeschichte
Summary Cat	Madan F and H H E Craster, A Summary Catalogue of Western Manuscripts Which Have Not Hitherto Been Catalogued in the Quarto Series, Oxford 1895–1953
SUVSL	Skriften utgivna av Vetenskaps-societeten i Lund
SWR	Southwest Review
Sym	Symposium
Ten Brink	Ten Brink B A K, Early English Literature, English Literature, trans Kennedy et al, vol 1, vol 2 (parts 1–2), London and N Y 1887–92 (referred to as vols 1–3)

Texas SE	Texas Studies in English
Thompson Mot Ind	Thompson S, Motif Index of Folk-Literature, 6 vols, Helsinki 1932–36
Thoms	Thoms W J, A Collection of Early Prose Romances, London 1828; part ed Morley, Carlsbrooke Library, whole rvsd edn, London (Routledge); new edn, Edinburgh 1904
TLCAS	Transactions of Lancashire and Cheshire Antiquarian Society
TLS	[London] Times Literary Supplement
TNTL	Tijdschrift voor nederlandse taal- en letterkunde
TPSL	Transactions of the Philological Society of London
Trad	Traditio, Studies in Ancient and Medieval History, Thought, and Religion
TRSL	Transactions of the Royal Society of Literature
TTL	Tijdschrift voor taal en letteren
Tucker-Benham	Tucker L L and A R Benham, A Bibliography of Fifteenth-Century Literature, Seattle 1928
UKCR	University of Kansas City Review
UQ	Ukrainian Quarterly
Utley CR	Utley F L, The Crooked Rib: An Analytical Index to the Argument about Women in English and Scots Literature to the End of the Year 1568, Columbus O 1944
UTM	University of Toronto Monthly
UTQ	University of Toronto Quarterly
VMKVA	Verslagen en mededeelingen der Koninklijke vlaamsche academie
VQR	Virginia Quarterly Review
Ward	Ward H L D, Catalogue of Romances in the Department of MSS of the British Museum, 2 vols, London 1883–93 (see Herbert for vol 3)
Ward Hist	Ward A W, A History of English Dramatic Literature to the Death of Queen Anne, 3 vols, new edn, London 1899
Wehrle	Wehrle W O, The Macaronic Hymn Tradition in Medieval English Literature, Washington 1933

WBEP	Wiener Beiträge zur englischen Philologie
Weber MR	Weber H W, Metrical Romances of the 13th, 14th, and 15th Centuries, 3 vols, Edinburgh 1810
Wessex	Wessex
WHR	Western Humanities Review
Wilson EMEL	Wilson R M, Early Middle English Literature, London 1939
WMQ	William and Mary Quarterly
WR	Western Review
Wright AnecLit	Wright T, Anecdota literaria, London 1844
Wright PPS	Wright T, Political Poems and Songs from the Accession of Edward III to That of Richard III, 2 vols, London (Rolls Series) 1859–61
Wright PS	Wright T, Political Songs of England from the Reign of John to That of Edward III, Camden Society, London 1839 (this edn referred to, unless otherwise indicated); 4 vols, rvsd, privately printed, Goldsmid, Edinburgh 1884
Wright SLP	Wright T, Specimens of Lyric Poetry Composed in England in the Reign of Edward I, Percy Society, 2 vols, London 1896
Wülcker	Wülcker R P, Geschichte der englischen Literatur, 2 vols, Leipzig 1896
YCGL	Yearbook of Comparative and General Literature
YFS	Yale French Studies, New Haven 1948–
Yksh Wr	Horstmann C, Yorkshire Writers, Library of Early English Writers, 2 vols, London 1895–96
YR	Yale Review
YSCS	Yorkshire Society for Celtic Studies
YSE	Yale Studies in English, N Y 1898–
YWES	Year's Work in English Studies
YWMLS	Year's Work in Modern Language Studies
ZfCP	Zeitschrift für celtische Philologie (Tübingen)
ZfDA	Zeitschrift für deutsches Alterthum und deutsche Litteratur
ZfDP	Zeitschrift für deutsche Philologie

ZfFSL	Zeitschrift für französische Sprache und Literatur
ZfÖG	Zeitschrift für die österreichischen Gymnasien
ZfRP	Zeitschrift für romanische Philologie
ZfVL	Zeitschrift für vergleichende Litteraturgeschichte, Berlin

Other Commonly Used Abbreviations

ae	altenglische	AN	Anglo-Norman	OF	Old French
af	altfranzösische	c	copyright	ON	Old Norse
engl	englische	ca	circa	pt	part
f	für	crit	criticized by	re-ed	re-edited by
me	mittelenglische	f, ff	folio, folios	rptd	reprinted
u	und	ME	Middle English	rvsd	revised
z	zu	n d	no date	unptd	unprinted

II. THE *PEARL* POET

by

Marie P. Hamilton

[1] THE PEARL POET.

Entries in this section either deal with the four poems commonly attributed to the poet or provide information applicable to all of them. For bibliographies of the individual poems see [2], [3], [4] below for **PEARL, PATIENCE, PURITY (CLEANNESS)**, and for **SIR GAWAIN AND THE GREEN KNIGHT** see Romances, I [25].

MS. BM Cotton Nero A.x $+$ 4, ff 41–130, including illustrations (1375–1400).

Brown-Robbins, nos 635, 2739, 2744, 3144; Brown Reg, 1.274, BM Cotton Nero A.x.

Modern Language Assoc of America Collection of Photographic Facsimiles no 2, British Museum MS Cotton Nero A.x, containing Pearl, Cleanness, Patience, Sir Gawain.

Pearl, Cleanness, Patience, and Sir Gawain, Reproduced in Facsimile from the unique MS Cotton Nero A.x in the British Museum, with Introd by Sir I Gollancz, EETS 162, London 1923; rptd 1931 (crit W W Greg, MLR 19.223).

BM Harley 1879 (earliest listing of MS Cotton Nero A.x).

Madden F, Syr Gawayne, A Collection of Ancient Romance-Poems by Scotish and English Authors, ed with introd, notes, and glossary, London 1839, p xlvii (description of MS Cotton Nero A.x).

Morris R, Early English Alliterative Poems, EETS 1.xxvii (as under *Editions* below).

Fick W, Zum me Gedicht von der Perle, eine Lautuntersüchung, Kiel 1885 (Part 1, emendations; Part 2, the scribe's dialect vs the poet's).

Holthausen F, Zur Textkritik me Dichtungen, Arch 90.144.

Cook A S, Pearl 212ff, MP 6.197 (spelling of final or, our, er in the MS).

Knott T A, The Text of Sir Gawayne and the Green Knight, MLN 30.102 (errors, corrections, offsets in the MS).

Menner R J, Purity, A ME Poem, YSE 61, New Haven 1920, p vii.

Oakden J P, Alliterative Poetry in ME, vol 1, Manchester 1930; Appendix 3: The Scribes of the Poems of the Cotton MS Nero A.x (detects seven scribes).

Greg W W, A Bibliographical Paradox, Libr 13.188 (rejects Oakden's seven scribes).

Oakden, The Scribal Errors of MS Cotton Nero A.x, Libr 14.353 (replies to Greg).

Magoun F P, Kleine Beiträge zu Sir Gawain, Angl 61.129 (final us, ous in the MS).

Day M, Sir Gawain and The Green Knight, ed I Gollancz, EETS 210, London 1940, Introd, p ix.

Smyser H M, Sire Gauvain et le chevalier vert (E Pons), Spec 22.94 (the MS spelling — tȝ).

McLaughlin J C, A Grahemic-Phonemic Study of a ME, MS, The Hague, 1963 (Cotton Nero A.10).

(On the dialect of the MS see Serjeantson under *Language* below).

Editions and Word Lists. Morris R, Early English Alliterative Poems in the West-Midland Dialect of the Fourteenth Century (Pearl, Purity, Patience), EETS 1, London 1864; rvsd 1869; rptd 1885, 1896, 1901; film reproduction of 1st edn: Z A, E 12, no 1, NY Public Library.

(For separate editions of the poems see [2], [3], [4] below).

Chapman C O, An Index of Names in Pearl, Purity, Patience, and Gawain, Cornell Univ Press 1951 (crit R W Ackerman, JEGP 50.538; T A Kirby, MLN 68.582; A Macdonald, RES ns 4.276; H L Savage, Spec 27.364).

Markman A, A Computer Concordance to ME Texts (Cotton Nero A.x poems and Erkenwald), SB 17.55 (on the making of the concordance below).

Kottler B and A Markman, A Concordance to Five Middle English Poems: Cleanness, St Erkenwald, Sir Gawain and the Green Knight, Patience, and Pearl, Univ of Pittsburgh Press 1966.

Modernizations. Gardner J, The Complete

Works of the Gawain-Poet in a Modern English Version (Erkenwald included), Univ of Chicago Press 1965 (crit L D Benson, JEGP 65.38; D Miehl, Angl 85.88; R M Wilson, MLR 62.108).

Williams M, The Pearl Poet, His Complete Works, trans with introd, N Y 1967 (Erkenwald included).

Language. Morris, EETS 1.viii, xviii.

Schwahn F, Die Conjugation in Sir Gawain und den sogenannten Early English Alliterative Poems, Strassburg 1884.

Fick, Zum me Gedicht von der Perle (as under *MS* above).

Knigge F, Die Sprache des Dichters von Sir Gawain and the Green Knight, der sogennanten Early English Alliterative Poems, und de Erkenwald, Marburg 1885.

Morsbach C, Mittelenglische Grammatik, Halle 1896, pp 9, 15.

Kaluza M, Historische Grammatik der englischen Sprache, Part 2, Berlin 1901; 2nd edn 1906–07, §§ 201, 350.

Wyld H C, The Treatment of OE $\breve{y}$ in the Dialects of the Midland and SE Counties in ME, EStn 47.1, passim, especially p 47 (dialect of Pearl, Patience, Purity assigned to Derbyshire).

Brandl A, Zur Geographie der ae Dialekte, Berlin 1915 (supplements Wyld above).

Stidston R O, The Use of Ye in the Function of Thou in ME Literature from MS Auchinleck to MS Vernon, Stanford Univ Publ 1917, pp 44, 47, 93.

Day M, The Weak Verb in the Works of the Gawain Poet, MLR 14.413 (preterites with final d omitted; cf PMLA 37.52, MÆ 1.126).

Hulbert J R, The West Midland of the Romances, MP 19.9, 11.

Menner R J, Purity (as above under *MS*), p lviii; Sir Gawain and the Green Knight and the West Midland, PMLA 37.503 (W Midland in Cotton Nero A.x, vs Hulbert above); Four Notes on the West Midland Dialect, MLN 41.454.

Jordan R, Handbuch der me Grammatik, Teil 1: Lautlehre, Heidelberg 1925; 2nd edn rvsd 1934 (dialect boundaries, texts).

Serjeantson M S, The Dialects of the West Midlands in ME, RES 3.54, 186, 319 (assigns MS Nero A.x to Derbyshire, east of original dialect of Gawain); The Dialect of MS Cotton Nero A.x, in Sir Gawain and the Green Knight, ed I Gollancz, London 1940, EETS 210.xli (detailed analysis).

Andrew S O, The Preterite in North-Western Dialects, RES 5.432, 435, 436.

Whitehall H, A Note on North-West Midland Spelling, PQ 9.1 (qu, qw; crit D Everett, YWES 11.122).

Oakden, Allit Poetry in ME, 1.5, 72, 155 and passim, 261 and passim (crit A Brandl, Arch 159.293; D Everett, YWES 11.92; C T Onions, RES 9.89 [goude, gawle]); vol 2, chaps 8, 11 (crit J R Hulbert, MP 34.198; M S Serjeantson, YWES 16.121).

Koziol H, Grundzuege der Syntax der me Stabreimdichtungen, Vienna and Leipzig 1932.

Luttrell C A, The Gawain Group: Cruxes, Etymologies, Interpretations, Neophil 39.207, 40.290.

Versification. Trautmann M, Über Verfasser und Entstehungszeit einiger alliterierender Gedichte des Altenglischen, Halle 1876; Der Dichter Huchown und seine Werke, Angl 1.119.

Rosenthal F, Die alliterierende englische Langzeile im 14 Jahrhundert, Angl 1.414.

Schipper J, Englische Metrik, Bonn 1881–88, 1.195, 223, 317, 421.

Schipper J, Grundriss der englischen Metrik, Vienna 1895, §§ 47, 332; expanded English trans: J Schipper, A History of English Versification, Oxford 1910, pp 93, 332.

Guest E, A History of English Rhythms, 2nd edn, ed W W Skeat, London 1882, p 458.

Fuhrmann J, Die alliterierenden Sprachformeln in Morris's Early English Alliterative Poems and in Sir Gawayne and the Green Knight, Hamburg 1886.

Luick K, Die englische Stabreimzeile im 14, 15, und 16 Jahrhundert, Angl 11.392, 553, 572, 583.

Trautmann M, Zur Kentniss und Geschichte der me Stabzeile, Angl 18.83.

Fischer J, Die stabende Langzeile in den Werken des Gawaindichters, Darmstadt 1900, and in BBA 11.1 (detects seven stresses to the line; crit K Luick, AnglB 12.48; A Schroer, AnglB 17.41).

Fischer and F Mennicken, Zur me Stabzeile, BBA 11.139 (reply to Luick's criticism).

Thomas J, Die alliterierende Langzeile des Gawayn-Dichters, Coburg 1908.

Kaluza M, Englische Metrik in historischer Entwicklung, Berlin 1909 (trans A C Dunstan, A Short History of English Versification, London and N Y 1911), §§ 156, 158 and passim.

Schumacher K, Studien über den Stabreim in der me Alliterationsdichtung, Bonn 1914.

Menner, Purity, p liii (summary of scholarship on the poet's prosody).

Saintsbury G, A History of English Prosody, London 1923, 1.102.

Oakden, Allit Poetry in ME, 1.153 and passim, 251 (metrical evidence of common authorship for poems in Cotton Nero A.x and for Erkenwald).

Day M, Strophic Division in ME Alliterative Verse, EStn 66.245 (crit D. Everett, YWES 12.99).

Hulbert J R, Quatrains in ME Alliterative Poems, MP 48.73.

Ohye S, Metrical Influences in the Grammar of the Four Poems Preserved in MS Cotton Nero A.x, St Paul's Review (Tokyo), 11.75–97.

Dates and Chronology. See under *MS* above; [2], [3], [4] below.

Morris, EE Allit Poems, p viii (dialect, earlier part of 14 cent).

Thomas M C, Sir Gawayne and the Green Knight, A Comparison with the French Perceval, preceded by an Investigation of the Author's Other Works, Zurich 1883, pp 12, 27.

Ten Brink, 1.336, 350, 351.

Brown C F, The Author of the Pearl, PMLA 19.123n2, 153 (relation to Piers Plowman, Mandeville).

Schofield W H, The Nature and Fabric of the Pearl, PMLA 19.165.

Hulbert J R, Gawain and the Green Knight, MP 13.710 (connection with the Order of the Garter).

Menner, Purity, p xxvii.

Day, EETS 210.xiii.

Authorship. For the ascription of the four poems to Huchown, see Gollancz, Pearl (1921), p xxxvii; H N MacCracken, PMLA 25.507; and studies listed below by Trautmann (Angl 1.109), C F Brown, Gollancz, Morris. For other efforts to identify the Pearl poet see *Authorship* under [2] below.

Morris, EE Allit Poems, EETS 1.v, viii.

Trautmann, Über Verfasser (as above under *Versification*); Der Dichter Huchown und seine Werke, Angl 1.109, 112.

Thomas, Sir Gawayne and the Green Knight, p 1.

Knigge, Die Sprache des Dichters von Sir Gawain, p 1.

Fuhrmann, Die Alliterierenden Sprachformeln in Morris's EE Allit Poems.

Ten Brink, 1.348 (fanciful biography).

Kullnick M, Studien über den Wortschatz in Sir Gawayne and the Grene Knyʒt, Berlin 1902 (vocabulary cited as evidence of common authorship of the four poems).

Brown, PMLA 19.115 (an ecclesiastic, Augustinian in theology), 115, 118 (Huchown, Strode).

Schumacher, Studien über den Stabreim, pp 26, 56, 120.

Wells, p 578 (questions common authorship).

Menner, Purity, p xi (summary of evidence of common authorship; crit G Binz, LfGRP, vol 42, col 376 [doubts common authorship]); PMLA 37.505n9.

Wyld, EStn, 47.47 (excepts Gawain from common authorship).

Savage H L, St Erkenwald, A ME Poem, YSE 72, New Haven 1926, p xliii (attributed to the Pearl poet).

Serjeantson, RES 3.327 (excepts Gawain from common authorship).

Oakden, Allit Poetry in ME, 1.72, 153, 251, 257; 2.78, 88, 90, 179 (evidence of common authorship; crit H L Savage, MLN 52.432 [the Pearl-poet: dialect, audience, relation to London, to St Erkenwald]).

Chapman C O, The Musical Training of the Pearl Poet, PMLA 46.177 (crit D Everett, YWES 12.101).

Gollancz I, CHEL, 1.368 (poet's identity, hypothetical biography).

Olivero F, La Perla, 2nd edn, Bologna 1936, p xxxvii (survey of opinion).

Day, EETS 210.x, xviii (common authorship, poet's identity).

Koziol H, Zur Frage der Verfasserschaft einiger me Stabreimdichtungen, EStn 67.169, 170, 171, 173 (affirmative tests of common authorship).

Pons E, Sire Gauvain et le chevalier vert, traduction avec le text en regard, Paris 1946, p 47 (questions common authorship).

Clark J W, Observations on Certain Differences in Vocabulary between Cleanness and Sir Gawain and the Green Knight, PQ 28.261 (marshals evidence vs common authorship in this series); The Gawain Poet and the Substantival Adjective, JEGP 49.60; Paraphrases for God in the Poems Attributed to the Gawain-Poet, MLN 65.232; On Certain Alliterative and Poetic Words in the Poems Attributed to the Gawain-Poet, MLQ 12.387.

Chapman, Index of Names, under Jeweller.

Everett D, Essays on ME Literature, ed P Kean, Oxford 1955, pp 68, 73 (common authorship; poet's outlook, opinions, learning; crit B J Timmer, YWES 36.66).

Savage H L, The Gawain-Poet: Studies in His Personality and Background, Chapel Hill and Oxford, 1956.

Spearing A C, Patience and the Gawain Poet, Angl 84.305 (distinctive view of man's predicament suggests single authorship).

Brewer D S, The Gawain-Poet: A General

Appreciation of the Four Poems, EC 17.130 (similarities in theme and outlook suggest single authorship).

Sources and Literary Relations. Trautmann, Über Verfasser (as above under *Versification*; relation to Piers Plowman).

Bradley H, The English Gawain-Poet and the Wars of Alexander, Acad Jan 14 1888, p 27 (assigns Wars to the Gawain poet).

Henneman J B, Untersuchungen über das me Gedicht Wars of Alexander, Berlin 1889, p 30 (opposes Bradley above on linguistic grounds, but cf Andrew, RES 5.267).

Brandl, § 75.

Brown, PMLA 19.115 (Huchown), 119 (Scripture, homiletic sources), 126n2 (Erkenwald), 127 (Augustinian theology, Bradwardine), 143 (Wyclyf), 149 (Mandeville).

Gollancz I, The Parlement of the Thre Ages, London 1915, Introd (relation of the Pearl poet to the Parlement and to Winner and Waster).

Menner, Purity, p xi, xix, xxx.

Savage H L, St Erkenwald, p xliii.

Benson L D, The Authorship of St Erkenwald, JEGP 64.393 (persuasive evidence against the Pearl poet's authorship). (For other editions and discussion of the poet's relation to St Erkenwald, see Knigge above and Oakden below).

Hulbert J R, A Hypothesis, MP 28.405 (Gawain, Patience, Purity; cf S Moore, PMLA 28.103; crit D Everett, YWES 12.98).

Oakden, Allit Poetry in ME, 1.392 and passim (stylistic resemblances to other alliterative verse), 1.394 (Death and Life); 1.253, 2.47 (Erkenwald), 2.87 (Wars of Alexander).

Gerould G H, The Gawain-Poet and Dante: A Conjecture, PMLA 51.31.

Day, EETS 210.xiii (Wars of Alexander), xxx (Le livre du Chevalier de la Tour Landry, Le roman de la Rose, Mandeville, Cursor Mundi).

Chapman C O, Virgil and the Gawain-Poet, PMLA 60.16 (Virgilian echoes and similes).

Everett, Essays on ME Literature, p 52 (Parlement of the Thre Ages), p 57 (Wars of Alexander).

Salter E, The Alliterative Revival, MP 64.146, 233 (cf Hulbert, A Hypothesis, MP 28.405 above).

See also *Editions* and *Literary Relations* under [2[,]3], [4] below.

Literary Criticism. See [2], [3], [4] below.

Morris, EE Allit Poems, EETS 1.viii, xvii.

Weichardt C, Die Entwicklung des Naturgefühls in der me Dichtung vor Chaucer (einschliesslich des Gawain-Dichters), Kiel 1900, p 77 (the poet anticipates Shakespeare's nature-portrayal).

Moorman F W, The Interpretation of Nature in English Poetry from Beowulf to Shakespeare, QF 95.95 (chap 7).

Oakden, Allit Poetry in ME, 2.76, 107 and passim; style: 2.263, 343 and chaps 13, 14 passim.

Glunz H H, Die Literarästhetik des europäischen Mittelalters, Bochum-Langendreer 1937, pp 329, 507, 566.

Clark, MLQ 12.387 (style); MLN 65.232; JEGP 49.60 (style and diction).

Everett, Essays on ME Literature, pp 73, 93 (formal rhetoric). See below for her criticism of the individual poems.

Ebbs J D, Stylistic Mannerisms of the Gawain-Poet, JEGP 57.522.

Spearing A C, Patience and the Gawain-Poet, Angl 84.305.

Brewer D S, The Gawain-Poet, EC 17.130.

General References. Ten Brink, 1.336, 348, 350; Brandl, §§ 74, 75; Courthope, 1.349, 366; Morley, 4.144; Wülcker, p 107; Körting, § 105; Schofield, pp 20, 23, 378, 402 and passim; Gollancz, CHEL 1.357, 362, 367 (chap 15); Renwick-Orton, London 1939, pp 66, 67, 76 (literary art, prosody).

Saintsbury G, A Short History of English Literature, N Y and London 1900, p 78.

Thomas P G, English Literature before Chaucer, London 1924, p 136.

Anderson G K, A History of English Literature, ed H Craig, N Y 1950, p 140.

Bibliography. Brown-Robbins, nos 635, 2739, 2744; Kennedy BWEL, nos 4577–91; CHEL, 1.525; Renwick-Orton, London 1939, p 289; CBEL, 1.IX (a), (b), (c), (d) and Supplement, IX.

Schlauch M, English Medieval Literature and Its Social Foundations, Warsaw 1956, p 218.

[2] PEARL.

MS. BM Cotton Nero A.x + 4, ff 43^a–59^b.

Brown-Robbins, no 2744; Brown Reg, 2.248, no 1694.

Fick W, Zum me Gedicht von der Perle, Kiel 1885, Part 1.

Gollancz I, Pearl (as below under *Editions*), 1st edn 1891, pp xxi, xxvii; 2nd edn 1921, pp xiii, xxix.

Osgood C G, The Pearl (as below under *Editions*), p ix.

Cook A S, Pearl 212ff, MP 6.197.

Emerson O F, Imperfect Lines in Pearl and the Rimed Parts of Sir Gawain, MP 19.131 (scribal errors in riming words); Some

Notes on the Pearl, PMLA 37.52 (scribal errors); More Notes on Pearl, PMLA 42.807 (more errors).

Pearl, Patience, Cleanness, and Sir Gawain, Reproduced in Facsimile from the Unique MS with Introd by Sir I Gollancz, EETS 162, London 1923; rptd 1931, pp 7, 9, 12, 45.

Gordon E V, Pearl (as below under *Editions*), p ix.

Editions. Morris R, Early English Allit Poems, EETS 1, London 1864; rvsd 1869; p ix (analysis), p 1 (text). See [1] above for film reproduction.

Gollancz I, Pearl, An English Poem of the Fourteenth Century, ed with Modern Rendering, London 1891 (rvsd 1897, privately printed; crit Athen Aug 8 1891, p 184 [textual notes]; F Holthausen, Arch 90.144 [textual notes]; JEGP 13.353; E Kolbing, EStn 16.268 [textual notes]; R Morris, Acad 39.602, 40.76 [textual notes]; Gollancz replies, Acad 40.36, 117); Pearl, An English Poem of the Fourteenth Century, ed with Modern Rendering together with Boccaccio's Olympia, London 1921 (rptd 1936; crit F Holthausen, ESts 5.133 [textual notes]; A Ricci, Nuovi studi medievali 2¹.188; TLS May 18 1922, p 319 [textual notes]; Gollancz replies, TLS May 25 1922, p 343; June 1, p 364).

Osgood C G, The Pearl, A ME Poem, ed with Introd, Notes, and Glossary, Boston and London 1906; Belles Lettres Series, Boston 1910 (crit F Holthausen, Arch 123.241 [textual notes]; J R Hulbert, MP 18.499; E H Tuttle, MLR 15.298).

Chase S P et al, The Pearl (Bowdoin Edition). The Text of the Fourteenth Century Poem, ed members of the Chaucer Course . . . in Bowdoin College, Boston 1932 (crit A Brandl, DLz 54.218; P Crowley, Commonweal 17.278; D. Everett, RES 9.468, YWES 13.102; E Fischer, AnglB 46.24; K Hammerle, Arch 165.95; J R Hulbert, MP 31.104; W E Leonard, The Nation [N Y] 136.677; K M, MLN 49.138; C S Northup, JEGP 33.116; TLS June 15 1933, p 409).

Olivero F, La Perla, poemetto in Middle English, introduzione testo traduzione e commento, Bologna 1936 (Osgood's text; richly annotated; surveys of scholarship).

Gordon E V, Pearl, London 1953 (crit D S Brewer, RES ns 6.189; L Le Grelle, EA 7.316; M P Hamilton, JEGP 54.124; B von Lindheim, Angl 72.473; D W Robertson, Spec 30.107; H L Savage, MLN 71.124; B J Timmer, YWES 34.79).

Hillman M V, The Pearl, medieval text with literal translation and interpretation, St Elizabeth's Press, N J 1961.

Cawley A C, Pearl and Sir Gawain and the Green Knight (with introd, text, appendices), Everyman Library, 1962.

Selections. Cook A S, A Literary ME Reader, Boston 1915, p 441 (Osgood's text, lines 37–300, 385–420).

Brandl A and O Zippel, Mittelenglische Sprach- und Literaturproben, Berlin 1917, p 140 (lines 1–360); 2nd edn: ME Literature, N Y 1947, p 140.

Sisam K, Fourteenth Century Verse and Prose, Oxford 1921, p 59 (lines 361–612).

Sampson G, The Cambridge Book of Prose and Verse, Cambridge 1924, p 318 (Gollancz's 1921 text with modern rendering by Coulton).

Mossé F, Manuel de l'anglais du moyen âge des origines au XIVᵉ siècle, Paris 1950, 2.279 (lines 985–1092); trans J A Walker: A Handbook of ME, Baltimore 1952, p 248.

Kaiser R, Alt- und mittelenglische Anthologie, Berlin 1955, p 245 (34 stanzas passim); 3rd edn rvsd, Medieval English, An OE and a ME Anthology, 1958, p 297.

Modernizations and Translations. Gollancz I, (1) modern unrhymed version in his edn of the text, London 1891; rvsd as (2) Pearl, An English Poem of the Fourteenth Century, Re-set in Modern English, London 1918 (British Red Cross edn); further rvsd in (3) the modern rendering in his 2nd edn of the text, London 1921.

Mitchell S W, Pearl, Rendered into Modern English Verse (46 stanzas freely rendered), N Y 1906; rptd Portland 1908; rptd in Century Readings in English Literature, ed J W Cunliffe et al, 3rd edn, N Y 1929, p 59.

Coulton G G, Pearl, A Fourteenth Century Poem, Rendered into Modern English (45 stanzas, original metre), London 1906 (crit H T Price, AnglB 17.290; 2nd edn rvsd 1907; selections rptd in Cambridge Bk of Prose and Verse, p 318).

Osgood C G, The Pearl, An Anonymous English Poem of the Fourteenth Century, rendered in prose, Cambridge 1907; Princeton 1907 (privately published; crit A M, MLR 4.132).

Jewett S, The Pearl, A ME Poem, a modern version in the metre of the original, N Y 1908; rptd in R S Loomis and R Willard, Medieval English Verse and Prose in Modernized Versions, N Y 1948, p 220.

Mead M, The Pearl, An English Vision-Poem of the Fourteenth Century, done into modern verse, Portland Me 1908.

Weston J L, Romance, Vision, and Satire, Boston 1912, p 185 (modified original meter).

Neilson W A and K G T Webster, Chief British Poets of the Fourteenth and Fifteenth Centuries, Cambridge 1916, p 6 (Webster's prose rendering).

Kirtlan E J B, Pearl, A Poem of Consolation, Rendered into Modern English Verse from the Alliterative Poem of 1360–1370 . . . with an Introduction and Theological Critique, London 1918 (modified original meter).

Chase S P, The Pearl, The Fourteenth Century English Poem Rendered in Modern Verse with an Introductory Essay, N Y and London 1932 (crit A Brandl, DLz 54.2089; C B, MLR 29.228; P Crowley, The Commonweal 17.278; D Everett, RES 9.469; E Fischer, AnglB 46.25; K Hammerle, Arch 165.95; J R Hulbert, MP 31.104; W E Leonard, The Nation [N Y] 136.677; K M, MLN 49.138; MÆ 4.239; TLS Jan 1933, p 409).

Hillman M V, The Pearl, mediaeval text with literal translation and interpretation, St. Elizabeth's Press, N J 1961.

Williams M, Glee-Wood, N Y 1949, p 402 (42 stanzas passim).

Stone B, Medieval English Verse, Penguin Classics 1964 (Pearl, Introduction and Translation, p 136).

Gardner J, The Complete Works of the Gawain-Poet in a Modern English Version with a Critical Introduction (Pearl commentary, p 55; trans, p 95), Univ of Chicago 1965.

Williams M, The Pearl Poet, His Complete Works (as above under [1]), pp 62, 267.

The Pearl, Medieval Text with Verse Translation by S de Ford et al, Crofts Classics, N Y 1967.

Olivero F, La Perla, poemetto inglese del secolo 14, traduzione, con introduzione e note, Torino 1926 (trans into Italian of Osgood's text; crit H S V Jones, JEGP 28.287); La Perla, poemetto in Middle English, introduzione testo traduzione e commento, 2nd edn, Bologna 1936 (Osgood's text).

Kalma D, De Pearel: in Visioen ut it Middel-Ingelsk oerbrocht yn it Nij-Frysk, Dokkum (Holland) 1938 (Frisian version in original meter and rime of Gollancz's 1936 text), pamphlet (crit F P Magoun, MLN 60.353).

Textual Matters. Fick, Zum me Gedicht der Perle, Part 1. Holthausen, Zur Textkritik me Dichtungen, Arch 90.144; Arch 123.241.

Skeat W W, TPSL, 1903–06, p 359 (bantelȝ, 992, 1017).

Bradley H, Acad 38.201, 249 (on lines 689–94); Gollancz, Acad 38.223, replies to Bradley.

Cook, MP 6.197.

Fehr B, Zu the Pearl z 51–56, Arch 131.154 (kynde of Kryst).

Tuttle E H, Notes on the Pearl, MLR 15.298.

Emerson, Imperfect Lines, MP 19.131; Some Notes on the Pearl, PMLA 37.52 (crit P G Thomas, YWES 3.40); More Notes, PMLA 42.807.

Whitely M, Of vyrgyn flour, TLS Jan 15 1931, p 44; Fairchild H N, TLS Mar 5, 1931, p 178 (Of vyrgyn flour); Everett D, YWES 12.10 (corroborates Whitely).

Gordon E V and C T Onions, Notes on the Text and Interpretation of Pearl, MÆ 1.126, 2.165.

Onions C T, RES 9.93 (gawle, 461).

Day M, Two Notes on Pearl, MÆ 3.241.

Bone G, A Note on Pearl and the Buke of the Howlat, MÆ 6.169 (cf MÆ 1.131).

Thomas P G, Notes on the Pearl, LMS 1².221.

Wright E M, Additional Notes on Sir Gawain and the Green Knight (actually on Pearl), JEGP 38.1; Additional Notes on the Pearl, JEGP 39.315.

Sledd J, Three Textual Notes on Fourteenth Century Poetry, MLN 55.381 (on Pearl 603–04).

Hillman M V, Diss Abstr Fordham Univ 1942, p 27 (textual notes); Pearl: Inlyche and Rewarde, MLN 56.457 (on Pearl 603–04); The Pearl: West ernays (307), Fasor (432), MLN 58.42; Pearl: Lere leke, 216, MLN 59.417; Some Debatable Words in Pearl and Its Theme, MLN 60.241.

Hamilton M P, The Orthodoxy of Pearl 603–04, MLN 58.370 (cf MLN 56.457 above and JEGP 57.177).

Savage H L, Lote, loteȝ in Sir Gawain and the Green Knight, MLN 60.492 (on Pearl 238, 896).

Everett D and N D Hurnand, Legal Phraseology in a Passage in Pearl, MÆ 16.9.

Holman C H, Marereȝ Mysse in the Pearl, MLN 66.33; Hillman M V, Pearl 382: Mare reȝ mysse? MLN 68.528 (crit B J Timmer, YWES 34.82).

Olszewska E S, Norse Alliterative Tradition in ME, Leeds SE 6.55 (Pearl 868).

Luttrell, Neophil 39.207; A Gawain Group Miscellany, N&Q ns 9.447 (Pearl: dayly, freles).

Johnston G K W, Northern Idiom in Pearl, N&Q ns 6.347 (marereȝ mysee).

Rupp H R, Word-play in Pearl 277–78, MLN 70.558.

Kellogg A L, Note on Line 274 of the Pearl, Traditio 12.406.

Visser F T, Pearl 609–11, ES 39.20 (dard).

Hamilton M P, Notes on Pearl, JEGP 57.177.

Kaske R E, Two Cruxes in Pearl: 596 and 601–10, Traditio 15.418.

Fowler D C, Pearl 558: Waning, MLN 74.581; On the Meaning of Pearl, 139–40, MLQ 21.27 (devyse).

Knightly W J, Pearl: The hyȝ Sesoun, MLN 76.97.

Revard C, A Note on Stonden, Pearl 113, N&Q ns 9.9; A Note on at þe fyrst fyne (Pearl 635), ELN 1.164.

Rathborne I E, New Light on Pearl 690 (solution to the crux), Traditio 19.467.

Mitchell B, Pearl, Lines 609–10, N&Q ns 11.47.

Barron W R J, Luf-daungere in Medieval Miscellany presented to Eugene Vinaver, ed F Whitehead et al, Manchester Univ Press, 1965.

Moorman C, Some Notes on Patience and Pearl, SoQ 4.67.

Vasta E, Pearl: Immortal Flowers and the Pearl's Decay, JEGP 66.519 (fede et al).

Davis N, A Note on Pearl (line 1208), RES ns 17.403, 18.294 (correspondence).

Language. Fick, Zum mc Gedicht von der Perle (crit Knigge, LfGRP 6.495).

Skeat W W, Some Rare Words in ME, TPSL 1891–94, pp 362, 364.

Northup C S, A Study of the Metrical Structure of the ME Poem the Pearl, PMLA 12.326 (the question of unstressed e, especially final e).

Osgood, Pearl, p xi.

Sisam K, Epenthesis in the Consonant Groups sl, sn, Arch 131.305, 309.

Stidston (see under *Language* in [1] above), pp 44, 47, 93.

Andrew, RES 5.432, 436.

Oakden J P, Alliterative Poetry in ME, vol 1, Manchester 1930, pp 72, 235, 241; vol 2 (1935), pp 168, 179, 184, 192, 343.

Serjeantson, EETS 210.xli. Cf Serjeantson, RES 3.54, 186, 319.

Chase S P et al, The Pearl (Bowdoin edn), p 68.

Gordon and Onions, Notes . . . on Pearl, MÆ 1.126 (preterites with −d omitted).

Thomas, LMS 1².221 (diction).

Dobson E J, The Etymology and Meaning of Boy, MÆ 9.121 Pearl 805–06).

Gordon, Pearl, p xliv (dialect, rhymes,

vocabulary), Appendixes II–VI (analysis of the language).

Everett D, Essays on ME Literature, ed P Kean, Oxford 1955, p 94.

See also *Language* under [1] above, *Textual Matters* under [2] above.

Versification. Trautmann, Angl 1.119.

Schipper, 1.223, 317, 421 (cf Schipper, Grundriss under [1] above).

Luick, Angl 11.572; in Paul Grundriss, 2nd edn (1905), 2².168, 239.

Kaluza, EStn 16.178.

Gollancz, Pearl, 1st and 2nd edns (1891 and 1921), p xxiii.

Northup, PMLA 12.326.

Saintsbury G, A History of English Prosody, London 1906, 1.106.

Osgood, Pearl, p xlii.

Kaluza, Englische Metrik (see under *Versification* in [1] above), §§ 163, 166, 173.

Medary M P, Stanza-linking in ME Verse, RomR 7.243.

Brown A C L, On the Origin of Stanza-linking in English Alliterative Verse, RomR 7.271.

Emerson, MP 19.131 (rhyming words).

Oakden, Allit Poetry in ME, 1.235, 240, 241.

Reese J B, Alliterative Verse in the York Cycle, SP 48.639, 646, 659, 661, 666.

Gordon, Pearl, p xxxvi and Appendix 1.

See also the more general studies under [1] above.

Authorship and Date. See [1] above for discussions of the date and chronology of the four poems in MS Cotton Nero A.x + 4.

Gollancz, Pearl (1891), p xliii (Huchown as the poet), p xlvi (hypothetical biography of the poet), p l (Strode as the poet); 2nd edn (1921), p xxxvii, xl, and xlvi respectively; date, p xxxvi.

Horstmann C, Richard Rolle, London 1895, 2.xviii, n 3 (earliest mention of Strode as the poet).

Brown J T T, The Poems of David Rate, SA July 1897 (Strode as the poet).

Gollancz I, Ralph Strode, DNB (1898), 55.57.

Neilson G, Cross-links between Pearl and the Awntyrs of Arthure, SA Oct 1901 (on Huchown as the poet).

Brown, PMLA 19.115; Note on the Question of Strode's Authorship of the Pearl, PMLA 19.146.

Osgood, Pearl, p xlvii (author), p xi (date).

Madeleva M, Pearl: A Study in Spiritual Dryness, N Y and London 1925, chap 4 (the poet a professed religious).

Cargill O and M Schlauch, The Pearl and Its Jeweler, PMLA 43.105 (Pearl and the poet, members of Pembroke's household; crit D Everett, YWES 9.101).

Oakden, Allit Poetry in ME, 1.257 (on the poet's identity).

Chapman C O, The Musical Training of the Pearl-Poet, PMLA 46.177; The Authorship of the Pearl, PMLA 47.346 (ascribed to Friar John de Erghome of York; crit A Brandl, DLz 54.218; D Everett, YWES 13.104; R W King, MLR 29.43).

Chase, The Pearl . . . in Modern Verse, p xvii and passim.

Gollancz, CHEL, 1.368.

Wellek R, The Pearl, An Interpretation, Studies in English IV by Members of the English Seminar, Charles Univ, Prague 1933, no 1, p 5.

Savage, MLN 52.432.

Olivero, La Perla, 2nd edn, p xxxvii (survey of opinion).

Day, EETS 210.xviii (identity of the poet).

Le Grelle L, La Perle, EA 6.315, 330.

Wintermute E, The Pearl's Author as Herbalist, MLN 64.83.

Gordon, Pearl, p xli (author), p xliii (date).

Spearing, Angl 84.305; Brewer, EC 17.130 (both as under Authorship in [1] above).

Sources and Literary Relations. Gollancz, Pearl (1891), pp xix, xxii; 2nd edn (1921), pp xi, xv, xx, xxvii, xxviii, xxxi, xxxii; Appendix, p 243: Boccaccio's eclogue Olympia, text and trans (analogue).

Courthope, 1.349, 350, 366 (Dante, Platonic allegory).

Neilson, SA 16.67 (Awntyrs of Arthure).

Schofield W H, The Nature . . . of the Pearl, PMLA 19.154 (relation to mystical poems, allegories); Appendix, p 203 (Boccaccio's Olympia as source); Symbolism, Allegory, and Autobiography in the Pearl, PMLA 24.585.

Osgood, Pearl, pp xiii, xix, xxi, xxiii, xxvi, xxxvii, 98.

Ricci A, Nuovi studi medievali, 2^1.192 (Olympia).

Madeleva, Pearl: A Study, chaps 2, 3, 4.

Hammerle K, Arch 165.95, 98 (Olympia, Dante); The Castle of Perseveraunce und Pearl, Angl 60.401.

Heather P J, Precious Stones in ME Verse of the Fourteenth Century (in two parts), Folklore 42.233, 241; 353, 392.

Billour E, La 14 egloga del Boccaccio: Olympia e la Perla, Estratto dall' annuario del R Ginnario Liceo Piazzi di Sondrio, 1933.

Gerould G H, The Gawain-Poet and Dante, PMLA 51.31.

Chapman C O, Numerical Symbolism in

Dante and the Pearl, MLN 54.256; Virgil and the Gawain-Poet, PMLA 60.16.

Wrenn C L, On Re-reading Spenser's Shepheardes Calender, E&S 29.30 (April Eclogue, Pearl st 4).

Gordon, Pearl, pp xxix, 165.

Conley J, Pearl and a Lost Tradition, JEGP 54.332 (Boethius).

Everett, Essays on ME Literature, pp 85, 90, 91, 95.

Ackerman R W, The Pearl Maiden and the Penny, RomP 17.615.

Kean P M, Numerical Composition in Pearl, N&Q 12.49 (cf Chapman above and Hopper below).

Pilch H, Das me Perlengedicht: sein Verhältniss zum Rosenroman, NM 65.427.

Relation to Medieval Life and Tradition. Usk T, The Testament of Love, in Complete Works of G Chaucer, ed W W Skeat, Oxford 1894, 7.1 (the pearl as symbol).

Garrett R M, The Pearl, Univ of Washington Publ 4, no 1, Appendix: St. Hilary's Epistle to Abra; cf Migne PL, 10.549 (the pearl as symbol).

Osgood, Pearl, p xxxvii.

Gollancz, Pearl (1921), pp xi, xv.

Campbell J M, Patristic Studies and ME Literature, Spec 8.472 (Pearl the poem and the pearl in Patristic tradition).

Glunz H H, Die Literarästhetik des europäischen Mittelalters, Bochum-Langendreer 1937, p 511 (relation of Pearl to Augustinian-Neo-platonic tradition, to Dante).

Hopper V F, Medieval Number Symbolism, Columbia Univ Studies in English and Comparative Lit 132, N Y 1938, p 126.

Patch H R, The Other World, Cambridge 1950, pp 190, 224; see also passim for analogues to the vision in Pearl.

Elliott R W V, Pearl and the Medieval Garden: Convention or Originality? Les langues modernes 45.85 (the gardens in Pearl compared with actual and literary gardens; crit G Willcock, YWES 32.88).

Gordon, Pearl, pp xix, xxvii, xxix.

Frank R W, The Art of Reading Medieval Personification Allegory, ELH 20.237 (also symbol-allegory).

Stern M R, An Approach to Pearl, JEGP 54.684 (through Scriptural exegesis and lapidary tradition).

Luttrell C A, The Mediaeval Tradition of the Pearl Virginity, MÆ 31.194; Pearl: Symbolism in a Garden Setting, Neophil 49.160, rptd in Sir Gawain and Pearl, Critical Essays, ed R J Blanch, Indiana Univ Press 1967, p 60.

Fisher J, Wyclif, Langland, Gower and the Pearl Poet on the Subject of Aristocracy, p 139 in Studies in Medieval Literature in Honor of Professor Albert Croll Baugh, ed MacEdward Leach, Univ of Pa Press 1961.

Hieatt C, Pearl and the Dream-Vision Tradition, SN 37.139.

Evans W O, Cortaysye in Middle English, MS 29.143.

Brewer D S, Courtesy and the Gawain-Poet, in Patterns of Love and Courtesy, Essays in Memory of C S Lewis, ed J Lawlor, London 1966, p 54.

For other discussions of Pearl in its relation to religious tradition see, listed below, the interpretations of Brown, Fletcher, Hamilton, Madeleva, Robertson, Schofield, Wellek.

Interpretations. For surveys of interpretations see Olivero, La Perla (1936), p lvi, and the studies here below by Chapman, Chase, Oakden, Wellek.

Morris, EE Alliterative Poems, EETS 1.ix; Ten Brink, 1.348; Courthope, 1.349, 366 (Pearl as Platonic allegory); Brown, PMLA 19.15.

Schofield W H, The Nature and Fabric of the Pearl, PMLA 19.154 (dissent from the elegiac, autobiographical interpretation); Symbolism, Allegory, and Autobiography in the Pearl, PMLA 24.585.

Coulton G G, In Defence of Pearl, MLR 2.39 (defends the elegiac theory vs Schofield's).

Osgood, Pearl, p xxviii.

Garrett R M, The Pearl: An Interpretation (crit C F Brown, MLN 34.42; C S Northup, JEGP 20.288).

Gollancz, Pearl (1921), pp xv, xviii.

Fletcher J B, The Allegory of the Pearl, JEGP 20.1.

Greene W K, The Pearl: A New Interpretation, PMLA 40.814 (crit D Everett, YWES 6.96).

Madeleva M, Pearl: A Study in Spiritual Dryness, N Y and London 1925 (crit R L Menner, MLN 41.411; H R Patch, Spec 3.411; TLS Jan 21 1926, p 46).

J M, A New Interpretation of Pearl, The Month 147.544 (includes criticism of Sister Madeleva above).

Hart E, The Heaven of Virgins, MLN 42.113 (refutes Sr Madeleva's view of a childless heaven of virgins).

Cargill and Schlauch, PMLA 43.105 (Pearl as granddaughter to Edward III).

Oakden, Allit Poetry in ME, 1.259; 2.69, 74.

Chase, The Pearl . . . in Modern Verse, pp xxxv, xlix.

Kuriyagawa F, Notes on the Pearl, Studies in English Lit, English Seminar of Tokyo Imperial Univ, 12.557 (in Japanese).

Ueno N, On the Pearl, Studies in English Lit, Tokyo Imperial Univ, 13.147 (in Japanese).

Wellek, Pearl, An Interpretation (crit D Everett, YWES 15.112; E Fischer, AnglB 46.24; S Potter, MLR 29.210); rptd in Sir Gawain and Pearl, Critical Essays, ed R J Blanch, Indiana Univ Press 1967, p 3.

Hillman, Diss Abstr Fordham Univ 1942, p 27; Some Debatable Words in Pearl and Its Theme, MLN 60.241 (crit D Willcock, YWES 26.66). See also Hillman's edn, 1961, as above.

Pons, Sire Gauvain et le chevalier vert, pp 48, 58.

Robertson D W, The Heresy of the Pearl, MLN 65.152 (cf PMLA 19.115, JEGP 38.1, MLN 55.381, 56.457, 58.370); The Pearl as a Symbol, MLN 65.155.

Chapman, Index of Names, under Perle, p 52.

Elliott, Les langues modernes 45.85. Cf Luttrell, Neophil 49.160.

Gordon, Pearl, pp xi, xix, xxvii.

Le Grelle L, La Perle, Essai d'interpretation nouvelle, EA 6.315.

Johnson W S, The Imagery and Diction of the Pearl: toward an Interpretation, ELH 20.161. Rptd in Middle English Survey, ed E Vasta, Notre Dame 1965, p 93.

Everett, Essays on ME Literature, p 85.

Conley, JEGP 54.332.

Moorman C, The Role of the Narrator in Pearl, MP 53.73.

Stern, JEGP 54.684. Cf also Luttrell, MÆ 31.194.

Hamilton M P, The Meaning of the Middle English Pearl, PMLA 70.805; rptd in Middle English Survey, ed E Vasta, Notre Dame 1965, p 117, and in Sir Gawain and Pearl, Critical Essays, ed R J Blanch, Indiana Univ Press 1966, p 37.

Bishop I, The Significance of the Garlande Gay in the Allegory of Pearl, RES ns 8.12.

McAndrew B, Pearl, A Catholic Paradise Lost, ABR 8.243.

Hoffman S de V, The Pearl: Notes for an Interpretation, MP 58.73.

Oiji T, The Middle English Pearl and Its Theology, Studies in English Literature, p 39, English No 1961, Tokyo.

Richardson F E, The Pearl: A Poem and Its Audience, Neophil 46.308.

Carson, Mother A, Aspects of Elegy in the Middle English Pearl, SP 62.17.

Ackerman R W, The Pearl Maiden and the Penny, RomP 18.615.

Spearing A C, Symbolic and Dramatic Development in Pearl, MP 40.1; rptd in Sir Gawain and Pearl, ed R J Blanch (as below), p 98.

Heiserman A R, The Plot of Pearl, PMLA 80.164.

Kean P M, The Pearl: An Interpretation, London and N Y 1967 (crit S S Hussey, N&Q ns 14.438).

Blanch R J, Precious Metal and Gem Symbolism in Pearl, Lock Haven Review, no 7.1; rptd in Blanch, Sir Gawain and Pearl, p 86.

Literary Criticism. Weichardt C, Die Entwicklung des Naturgefühls in der me Dichtung, Kiel 1900, p 77.

Moorman, QF 95.102.

Osgood, Pearl, p liv; Pearl . . . in Prose, Introd.

Jewett, Pearl, Introd.

Wells, p 583.

Gollancz, Pearl (1921), p xxv (diction, imagery); Hammerle, Arch 165.95; Chase, the Pearl . . . in Modern Verse, p lxi.

Oakden, Allit Poetry in ME, vol 2, chaps 13, 14 passim.

Renwick-Orton, London 1939, p 290; Pons, Sire Gauvain, pp 56, 58; Mossé, Handbook of ME, p 248; Le Grelle, EA 6.315, 324; Gordon, Pearl p xxxvi (style).

Johnson, ELH 20.161 (imagery, diction).

Everett, Essays on ME Literature, pp 85, 87.

Spearing A C, Symbolic and Dramatic Development in Pearl, MP 60.1.

Heiserman A R, The Plot of Pearl, PMLA 80.164.

Kean, The Pearl (as above under *Interpretations*).

See also J W Clark's studies of style and diction in the four poems: MLN 65.232, JEGP 49.60, MLQ 12.387, as under *Authorship* in [1] above.

General References. Ten Brink, 1.348; Brandl, §74; Courthope, 1.349, 366; Morley, 4.144; Körting, §105; Schofield, p 402 and index.

Palgrave F, Landscape in Poetry, London 1897, p 115.

Snell F J, The Age of Chaucer, London 1901, p 20.

Ker W P, English Literature: Medieval, N Y and London 1912, p 193.

Gollancz, Pearl, Enc Brit, 11th edn, vol 21; CHEL, 1.357, 370.

Thomas P G, English Literature before Chaucer, London 1924, p 136.

Baugh LHE, 1.233.

Williams, Glee-Wood, p 399.

Anderson, History of English Literature, p 114, 140.

Ackerman R W, ME Lit to 1400; The Medieval Literature of Western Europe, ed J H Fisher, N Y and London 1967, p 91.

Zesmer D M and S B Greenfield, Guide to English Literature, N Y 1961, pp 66, 86, 89, 155, 162–66.

Bibliography. Osgood, Pearl, p 101; CBEL 1.IX (b) and Supplement IX (b); Gollancz, Pearl (1921), p L; Chase et al, The Pearl (Bowdoin edn), p 69; Olivero, La Perla (1936), p 159; Renwick-Orton, London 1939, p 290; Gordon, Pearl, p liii; Ackerman, ME Lit (as above), p 91; Zesmer and Greenfield, Guide (as above), pp 322, 331, 345. See also *Bibliography* under [1] above.

[3] PATIENCE.

MS. BM Cotton Nero A.x + 4, ff 87ª–94ª. Also see *MS* under [1] above.

Brown-Robbins, no 2739; Brown Reg, 2.248, no 1690.

Bateson H, Patience, Manchester 1912 (see below under *Editions*), p 39; 2nd edn 1918, p xxxvii.

Gollancz I, Patience, London 1913 (see below under Editions), Preface, n p; 2nd edn 1924, p 3; Pearl, Cleanness, Patience and Sir Gawain, Reproduced in Facsimile with Introd by Sir I Gollancz, EETS 162, London 1923; rptd 1931; Introd passim; p 31 (scribal errors in Patience).

On the dialect of the MS see Serjeantson, under *Language* in [1] above.

Editions. Morris R, Early English Allit Poems (Pearl, Purity, Patience), EETS 1, London 1864, rvsd 1869; rptd 1885 etc; p xvi (analysis), p 92 (text).

Bateson H, Patience, A West Midland Poem of the Fourteenth Century, Manchester 1912 (crit Arch 129.516; Athen Oct 26 1912, p 477; E Ekwall, AnglB 24.133 (textual notes); O F Emerson, MLN 28.171, 232 (textual notes); S B Liljegren, EStn 49.142; G C Macaulay, MLR 8.396 [textual notes]); 2nd edn rvsd 1918 (crit The Nation [N Y] June 21 1919, p 991; O F Emerson JEGP 18.638 [textual notes]).

Gollancz I, Patience, An Alliterative Version of Jonah by the Poet of Pearl, London 1913, Select Early English Poems (crit Athen July 18 1914, p 70 [textual notes]; K Brunner, Arch 132.184 [textual notes]; E Ekwall, EStn 49.144; J H G Grattan,

MLR 9.403); 2nd edn rvsd 1924 (crit E Ekwall, AnglB 36.267).
Selections. Wülcker R P, Altenglisches Lesebuch, Halle 1879, 2.27 (lines 139–236, Morris's text).
Zupitza J, Alt- und mittelenglisches Übungsbuch, Vienna 1884, p 95 (lines 61–156, Morris's text); 1889, p 100; 1897, p 145; rvsd J Schipper, 1928, p 166.
MacLean G E, An Old and Middle English Reader, N Y and London 1893, p 101 (lines 61–156, Morris's text).
Kluge F, Mittelenglisches Lesebuch, Halle 1904, p 116 (lines 61–244, Morris's text); 2nd edn 1912, p 105.
Sampson G, Cambridge Book of Prose and Verse, London 1924, p 332 (lines 137–77, Gollancz's text).
Modernizations. Weston J L, Romance, Vision, and Satire, Boston 1912, p 173 (lines 61–344 in iambic pentameter couplets, Morris's text).
Williams M, Glee-Wood, N Y 1949, p 390 (lines 61–527 passim, unrimed quatrains, Morris's text).
Stone B, Medieval English Verse, Penguin Classics 1964 (Patience, Introduction and Translation, p 118).
Gardner J, The Complete Works of the Gawain-Poet in a Modern English Version with a Critical Introduction (Patience, commentary, p 69; trans, p 203), Univ of Chicago 1965.
Williams M, The Pearl Poet (trans with introd, as under *Modernizations* in [1] above), pp 26, 29, 101.
Textual Matters. Ekwall E, Arch 119.442 (line 159); Some Notes on the Text of the Alliterative Poem Patience, EStn 44.165.
Ritter O, Arch 119.463 (line 143).
Emerson O F, A Note on the Poem Patience, EStn 47.125.
Ekwall E, Another Note on Patience, EStn 47.313 (reply to Emerson); Zu Patience 143, EStn 49.483.
Onions C T, Professor Emerson's Note on Patience, EStn 47.316, 48.172.
Athen July 18 1914, p 70.
Emerson O F, Two Notes on Patience, MLN 29.85 (textual matters, parallels in de Patientia); More Notes on Patience, MLN 31.1 (and criticism of the OED coverage of the Pearl poet).
Greg W W, Sotteʒ for madde, MLR 20.185.
Day M, A Note on Patience, Line 54, MLR 33.564.
Savage, MLN 60.492 (Patience 161).
Moorman C, Some Notes on Patience, SoQ 4.67.

For valuable textual criticism consult also the notes in the reviews of edns as listed above.
Language. Skeat, TPSL 1891–1894, pp 370, 371.
Sisam, Arch 131.305, 309.
Bateson, Patience (1912), p 32; 2nd edn (1918), p xxxii.
Gollancz, Patience (1913), n p; 2nd edn (1924), p 6.
Day, MLR 14.413 (cf MÆ 1.132).
Andrew, RES 5.435.
Sunden K F, Etymology of ME trayþ(e)ly and runisch, renisch, SN 2.41 (line 191).
Oakden J P, Allit Poetry in ME, 1.72 and passim; 2.166, 179, 184, 187, 190, 192.
Sandahl B, ME Sea Terms, vol 1, The Ship's Hull, Essays and Studies in English Language and Lit, vol 8, Upsala and Copenhagen 1951 (crit A Macdonald, RES ns 4.277 [hurrok]).
See also *Textual Matters* above, *Language* under [1] above.
Versification. Rosenthal, Angl 1.417.
Schipper, 1.195; Schipper, Grundriss and the expanded English version: J Schipper, A History of English Versification, Oxford 1910, § 47.
Luick, Angl 11.572, 583; Paul Grundriss, 2nd edn, 2².160.
Kaluza M, Strophische Gliederung in der me rein alliterierenden Dichtung, EStn 16.169, 178 (quatrain groups); Englische Metrik (see under *Versification* in [1] above), §§ 156, 158, 159, 160, 166.
Lawrence J, Chapters on Allit Verse, London 1893, p 89 (vocalic alliteration).
Menner R J, Purity, YSE 61.xliii.
Gollancz, Patience (1913), preface, n p ; 2nd edn (1924), p 4.
Emerson, More Notes, MLN 31.1 (quatrain groups).
Medary, RomR 7.243, 264.
Oakden, Allit Poetry in ME, 1.53 and passim, 251 (metrical evidence of common authorship of Patience, Purity, Gawain).
Day, EStn 66.245, 248.
Spearing, Angl 84.305 (as under *Authorship* in [1] above).
Brewer, EC 17.130 (as under *Authorship* in [1] above).
Hulbert, MP 48.73.
See also items under [1] above.
Authorship and Date. Bateson, Patience (1912), pp 2, 19, 55; 2nd edn (1918), pp xi, xxxiii.
Gollancz, Patience (1913), n p; 2nd edn (1924), p 7.
Menner, Purity, pp xxiv, xxvii.

Kölbing E and M Day, The Siege of Jeru-
salem, EETS 188.xxx and n 1.
Day, EETS 210.xiii.
See discussions of dates, chronology and au-
thorship under [1] and [2] above and *Lit-
erary Relations* below.
Sources and Literary Relations. Trautmann
M, Über Verfasser (see under *Versification*
in [1] above) (Piers Plowman and Pa-
tience).
Thomas M C, Sir Gawayne and the Green
Knight, A Comparison with the French
Perceval, Preceded by an Investigation of
the Author's Other Works, Zurich 1883, p
24 (Piers Plowman and Patience).
Bradley, Acad 819.27 (Wars 1154 and Pa-
tience 319).
Emerson O F, A Parallel between the ME
Poem Patience and an Early Latin Poem
Attributed to Tertullian, PMLA 10.242
(de Jona; also de Patientia).
Brown, PMLA 19.119 (homiletic tradition,
Scriptures).
Bateson, Patience (1912), pp 1, 2, 19, 20, 45;
2nd edn, pp xi, xxiii, xxiv, xli; Appendix
2: source—passages from the Vulgate; de
Jona.
Gollancz, Patience (1913), n p; 2nd edn, pp
4, 7.
Liljegren S B, Has the Poet of Patience Read
de Jona? EStn 48.337 (questions Emerson
above).
Athen July 18 1914, p 70 (Biblical sources).
Emerson, MLN 29.85 (de Patientia).
Menner, Purity, pp xxiii (Patience and The
Wars of Alexander), xxix (Piers Plowman).
Kölbing and Day, EETS 188.xxx (Patience
and the Siege).
Day, EETS 210.xiii (Patience and The Wars
of Alexander).
Chapman C O, Virgil and the Gawain-Poet,
PMLA 60.16.
Hill O G, The Late Latin de Jona as a
Source for Patience, JEGP 66.21 (affirma-
tive).
Relation to Medieval Life and Tradition.
Bateson, Patience, 1918, p xxviii.
Hulbert J R, A Hypothesis concerning the
Alliterative Revival, MP 28.414, 415.
Heather P J, Seven Planets, Folklore 54.354.
Eberhard O, Der Bauernaufstand vom Jahre
1381 in der englischen Poesie, AF 51.33
(cf Bateson above).
Literary Criticism. Weichardt C, Die En-
twicklung des Naturgefühls in der me
Dichtung, Kiel 1900, p 77.
Moorman, QF 95.106.
Bateson, Patience (1912), p 40; 2nd edn, p
xxxviii.

Gollancz, Patience (1913), n p; 2nd edn, p 5.
Oakden, Allit Poetry in ME, 2.67; on style:
2.263 and passim; chaps 13, 14 passim.
Cazamian L, The Development of English
Humor, Durham 1952, p 55.
Reinhold H, Humoristische Tendenzen in
der englischen Dichtung des Mittelalters,
Tübingen 1953, Angl Buchreihe 4.67, 80nl,
87, 111, 120, 128, 149, 152, 154.
Everett, Essays on ME Literature, pp 69, 73.
Moorman C, The Rôle of the Narrator in
Patience, MP 61.90.
Spearing, Patience and the Gawain Poet,
Angl 84.305.
Brewer D S, The Gawain-Poet, EC 17.130;
Courtesy and the Gawain-Poet, in Patterns
of Love and Courtesy, ed J Lawlor, Lon-
don 1966, p 54.
Berlin N, Patience: A Study in Poetic Elab-
oration, SN 33.82.
Evans W O, Cortaysye in Middle English,
MS 29.143.
Anderson J J, The Prologue of Patience,
MP 63.283.
General References. Ten Brink, 1.348;
Brandl, § 74; Morley, 4.144; Schofield, p
378; Körting, § 105; Gollancz I, CHEL,
1.361, 370; Baugh LHE, 1.235.
Thomas P G, English Literature before
Chaucer, London 1924, p 137.
Anderson, History of English Literature, p
142.
See also *General References* under [1] above.
Bibliography. Bateson, Patience (1912), p 71;
2nd edn, p 35; Gollancz, Patience (1913),
n p; 2nd edn, p 11; CHEL 1.525; CBEL 1.
IX (c) and Supplement IX (c); Renwick-
Orton, London 1939, p 291.
Under *Bibliography* in [1] above, see also
Kennedy and bibliographies in serials.

[4] PURITY (CLANNESSE, CLEANNESS).

MS. BM Cotton Nero A x + 4, ff 61ª—86ª.
Also see *MS* under [1] above.
Brown-Robbins, no 635; Brown Reg, 2.69,
no 388.
Menner R J, Purity (see under *Editions*
below), p vii.
Gollancz I, Cleanness, vol 1 (see under *Edi-
tions* below), pp ix, 71; Pearl, Cleanness,
Patience and Sir Gawain, Reproduced in
Facsimile with Introd, EETS 162, London
1923; rptd 1931; Introd passim and p 19
(scribal errors in Purity).
On the dialect of the MS see Serjeantson
under *Language* in [1] above.
Editions. Morris R, Early English Allit
Poems (Pearl, Purity, Patience), EETS 1,

London 1864, rvsd 1869, pp xi (analysis), 38 (text).

Menner R J, Purity, A ME Poem, YSE 61, New Haven 1920 (crit G Binz, LfGRP, vol 42, col 376; O F Emerson, JEGP 20.229 [valuable original material]; F Holthausen, AnglB 34.136).

Gollancz I, Cleanness, An Alliterative Tripartite Poem, vol 1 (text); Select Early English Poems no 7, London 1921 (crit R J Menner, MLN 37.355; TLS May 18 1922, p 319 [rejoinders by Gollancz, TLS May 25 1922, p 343; June 1, p 364]).

—— and M Day, vol 2, Cleanness, Glossary and Illustrative Texts, Select Early English Poems no 9, London 1933 (crit D Everett, YWES 14.130; R J Menner, MLN 50.336 [valuable textual notes]).

Morris Spec 2.151 (lines 235–544), 161 (lines 947–972, 1009–1051), Morris' 1869 text.

Modernizations. Weston J L, Romance, Vision, and Satire, Boston and N Y 1912, p 153 (Belshazzar's Feast, lines 1357–1812; Morris's text, five-stress couplets).

Williams M, Glee-Wood, N Y 1949, p 385 (lines 601–44, 781–812, 941–68, 1805–12, Gollancz's text, unrimed quatrains).

Gardner J, The Complete Works of the Gawain-Poet in a Modern English Version with a Critical Introduction (Purity, commentary, p 61; trans, p 149, entire poem), Univ. of Chicago 1965.

Williams M, The Pearl Poet, His Complete Works (trans with introd), N Y 1966, pp 26, 34, 121.

Textual Matters. Koch E A, Interpretations and Emendations of Early English Texts, Angl 26.368.

Skeat, TPSL 1903–06, p 359 (line 1459).

Botker A T, MLN 26.127 (covacle).

Brett C, Notes on Cleanness and Sir Gawayne, MLR 10.188 (Purity 1413 ff).

Ekwall E, Zu Patience 143, EStn 49.483 (Purity 420, 956, 1476).

Emerson O F, A Note on the ME Cleanness, MLR 10.373.

Bateson H, The Text of Cleanness, MLR 13.377 (emendations).

Gollancz I, The Text of Cleanness, MLR 14.152 (opposes Bateson above).

Emerson O F, ME Clannesse, PMLA 34.494 (cf Bateson above); Some Notes on the Pearl, PMLA 37.52.

Thomas P G, Notes on Cleanness, MLR 17.64; Notes on Cleanness, MLR 24.323 (Ker's interpretation of lines 145, 375, 655, 1687).

Bateson H, Looking over the Left Shoulder,

Folklore 34.241; Three Notes on the ME Cleanness, MLR 19.95.

Luttrell C A, Baiting of Bulls and Boars in the ME Cleanness, N&Q 197.23 (line 55; see corroborative note by F C Morgan, N&Q 197.107); The Gawain Group: Cruxes, Etymologies, Interpretations, Neophil 39.207; A Gawain Group Miscellany, N&Q ns 9.447 (Pearl: dayly, freles; Cleanness: þrad).

Ackerman R W, Pared out of Paper: Gawain 802 and Purity 1408, JEGP 56.410.

See also textual notes in criticisms of edns above.

Language. Skeat, TPSL 1891–94, pp 359, 370, 371, 372, 373; Day, MLR 14.413 (cf MÆ 1.132); Menner, Purity, p lviii; Bateson, MLR 19.95 (on compounding); Andrew, RES 5.435; Sunden, SN 2.41 (lines 96, 907, 1137, 1545); Dobson, MÆ 9.134, 147.

Oakden J P, Allit Poetry in ME, 1.72 and passim; 2.166, 179, 183, 189, 190, 192.

Clark J W, Observations on Certain Differences in Vocabulary between Cleanness and Sir Gawain, PQ 28.261.

Sandahl B, Essays and Studies in English Language and Lit, vol 8, Upsala and Copenhagen 1951 (crit A Macdonald, RES ns 4.277 [hurrok]).

See also *Textual Matters* above and *Language* under [1] above.

Versification. Skeat W W, An Essay on Alliterative Poetry, PFMS, 3.xxx.

Kaluza, EStn 16.169; Englische Metrik (see under *Versification* in [1] above), §§ 156, 166.

Leonard W E, The Scansion of ME Allit Verse, Univ of Wisconsin Studies no 11, Madison 1920, p 76.

Menner, Purity, p xliii (stanzaic divisions in the MS), p liii (meter, alliteration).

Gollancz, Cleanness, l.ix (stanzaic divisions).

Under *Versification* in [3] above see further the entries by the following authors, the page-references in each case being identical for Patience and Purity: Day, Hulbert, Lawrence, Luick (2 entries), Oakden, Rosenthal, Schipper (2 entries).

Also see *Versification* under [1] above.

Authorship and Date. See [1], [2] above.

Morris Spec (Skeat, 1884), 2.151 (date: ca 1360).

Menner, Purity, p xi (common authorship of the four poems), p xxvii (dates, chronology).

Gollancz, Cleanness, l.xiii.

Day, EETS 210.xiii.

Clark, PQ 28.261. See also, under [1] above,

Clark's other studies testing common authorship.

Bennett J W, The Rediscovery of Sir John Mandeville, N Y 1954, p 221 and notes (date).

Spearing A C, Patience and the Gawain Poet, Angl 84.305.

Brewer D S, The Gawain Poet, EC 17.130.

Sources and Literary Relations. Thomas M C, Sir Gawayne and the Green Knight, Zurich 1883, p 27 (Piers Plowman and Purity); cf Trautmann, Über Verfasser, p 32.

Holthausen F, Zu dem me Gedicht Cleanness, Arch 106.349 (Comestor's Historia scholastica suggested as a source).

Neilson G, Huchown of the Awle Ryale, the Allit Poet, Glasgow 1902, p 115nl (Mandeville's Travels as a source).

Brown, PMLA 19.119 (homilies, Biblical influence), p 123n2 (P Plowman), p 149 (Mandeville's Travels).

Bateson, Patience (1912), Appendix 1, p 64 (on Purity and the poem de Sodoma).

Menner, Purity, pp xi, xxx, xix; xxviii (P Plowman), xxxix (sources); Appendix, p 221 (Vulgate sources).

Gollancz, Cleanness, l.xi (Pearl, Patience, Gawain), xiii (Mandeville's Travels; Le livre du Chevalier de la Tour Landry), xix (Scripture), xxvii; 2.75 (illustrative passages from possible sources).

Heather, Folklore 42.233.

Oakden, Allit Poetry in ME, 1.394 and passim (Death and Life), 2.98 (Wars of Alexander).

Day, EETS 210.x and passim (Purity and Gawain), xxx and passim (sources), xxxiii (Purity and Perlesvaus).

Chapman, PMLA 60.16.

Bennett, The Rediscovery of Sir John Mandeville, p 221 and notes.

Luttrell C A, Cleanness and the Knight of La Tour Landry, MÆ 29.187 (opposes Gollancz, Cleanness, xiii above).

Relation to Medieval Life and Tradition. Bateson, Patience (1918), Appendix 1, p 67 (relation of Purity to ecclesiastical traditions and reforms); Folklore 34.241.

Holmes, Spec 9.199 (penitotes, 1472, etc).

Luttrell, Baiting of Bulls and Boars, N & Q 197.23, 107.

Brewer D S, Courtesy and the Gawain Poet; Patterns of Love and Courtesy, ed J Lawlor, London 1966.

Literary Criticism. Weichardt C, Die Entwicklung des Naturgefühls in der me Dichtung, Kiel 1900, p 77.

Moorman, QF 95.104.

Menner, Purity, p xliii.

Oakden, Allit Poetry in ME, 2.68; on style: 2.263 and chaps 13, 14 passim.

Reinhold, Humoristische Tendenzen (see under [3] above), 4.87, 91, 110, 120. Tübingen 1953, Angl Buchreihe.

Everett, Essays on ME Literature, p 69, 73, 161.

See also *General References* below and J W Clark on the style and diction of the poems as listed under *Literary Criticism* in [3] above.

General References. Ten Brink, 1.350.

Anderson, History of English Literature, p 141.

For other general accounts see [3] above. The page-references for Patience and Purity are identical in the books listed there by Baldwin, Baugh, Brandl, Gollancz, Körting, Morley, Schofield, Thomas.

Bibliography. Menner, Purity, p 215; Gollancz, Cleanness, l.xxx; CHEL 1.525; CBEL, 1.IX (d) and Supplement 1.IX (d); Renwick-Orton, London 1939, p 292.

See under [1] above Kennedy and bibliographies in serials.

III. WYCLYF AND HIS FOLLOWERS

by

Ernest W. Talbert and S. Harrison Thomson

[1] LIFE AND INFLUENCE.

Lewis J, Hist of Life and Sufferings of J W, London 1720; Oxford 1820.

Gilpin W, Lives of J W and of the Most Eminent of His Disciples, London 1765.

Vaughan R, Life and Opinions of J de W, 2 vols, London 1828; 2nd edn 1831.

Le Bas C W, Life of Wiclif, London 1832.

Coxe M, Life of J W, Columbus 1840.

Vaughan R, J de W, London 1853.

Jäger O, J W und seine Bedeutung für die Reformation, Halle 1854.

Böhringer F, J von W, Zürich 1856.

Shirley W W, Fasciculi Zizaniorum (Rolls Series), London 1858, pp x–lxx (life of J W and followers).

Björnström H, Om J W och hans betydelse såsom en reformationens förelöpare, Upsala 1868.

Pages C, Wiclef, sa vie son oeuvre, Toulouse 1868.

Thorold Rogers J E, J W in Historical Gleanings, London 1870.

Lechler G, J v W und die Vorgeschichte der Reformation, 2 vols, 1873; Engl trans 1878, London 1878, rptd 1884, 1903.

Buddensieg R, J W, Patriot and Reformer, London 1884.

Burrows M, W's Place in History, London 1884.

Loserth J, Hus und Wiclif, Leipzig 1884; Engl trans, London 1884; 2nd edn, Munich 1925.

Buddensieg R, J W und seine Zeit, Halle 1885.

Stevenson J, The Truth about J W, His Life, Writings and Opinions, London 1885.

Vattier V, J W, sa vie, ses oeuvres, sa doctrine, Paris 1886.

Pressfield H, Wyclif and the Common Law, Bibliotheca Sacra 90.175.

Matthew F D, The Date of W's Attack on Transubstantiation, EHR 5.328.

Adams E H, J of W, Oakland 1890.

Wiegand F, De ecclesiae notione quid Wiclif docuerit, Leipzig 1891.

Loserth J, Neue Erscheinungen d Wiclif Literatur, Historische Zeitschrift 95.271.

Sergeant L, J W Last of the Schoolmen and First of the English Reformers, London 1893.

Petit-Dutaillis C, Les prédications populaires, Les Lollards . . . Études dédiées à Gabriel Monod, Paris 1896, p 373.

Loserth J, The Beginnings of W's Activity in Ecclesiastical Politics, EHR 11.319.

Loserth J, Studien zur Kirchenpolitik Englands im 14 Jahrhundert, 1, 2, Sitzungsberichte der Kaiserlichen Akademie der Wissenschaften in Wien, phil-hist Klasse, 136(1897), 156(1907), no 6; see also Historische Zeitschrift 99.237.

Trevelyan G M, England in the Age of Wycliffe, rptd London 1899.

Twemlow J A, W's Preferments and University Degrees, EHR 15.529.

Rashdall H, Wycliffe, DNB 63.202.

Workman H B, Dawn of the Reformation, I Age of Wyclif, London 1901.

Rae H R, J W, His Life and Writings, London 1903.

Whitney J P, Religious Movements in the Fourteenth Century, CHEL, 2.49.

Gairdner J, Lollardy and the Reformation in England, 4 vols, London 1908.

Carrick J C, Wycliffe and the Lollards, Edinburgh 1908.

Hague D, Life and Work of J W, 1909; 2nd edn, London 1935.

Figgis J N, J W in Typical English Churchmen, London 1909.

Dakin A, Die Beziehungen J W's und der Lollarden zu den Bettel-mönchen, London 1911.

Poole R L, Wycliffe and Movements for Reform, London 1911.

Cronin H S, J W the Reformer and Canterbury Hall, Trans Royal Hist Soc 8(1914).55.

Wilkins H J, Was J W a Negligent Pluralist?, London 1915.

Tatlock J S P, Chaucer and Wyclif, MP 14.65.

Cadman S P, The Three Religious Leaders of Oxford, N Y 1916.

Manning B L, The People's Faith in the Time of Wyclif, Cambridge 1919.

Martin C, J W, Les Lollards, Lausanne 1919.

Salter H E, J W Canon of Lincoln, EHR 35.98.

Cronin H S, W's Canonry at Lincoln, EHR 35.564.

Manning B L, Wyclif and the House of Herod, Cbg Hist J1 2(1926).66.

Shettle G T, J W of Wycliffe and Other Essays, Leeds 1922.

Workman H B, J W, A Study of the English Medieval Church, 2 vols, Oxford 1926 (crit S H Thomson, Princeton Theological Review 1926, p 328, A H Sweet, AHR 32.581, C. Jenkins, Church Quarterly Review Apr 1928).

Laun J F, Thomas v Bradwardin der Schüler Augustins und Lehrer Wiclifs, Zeitschrift für Kirchengeschichte 47(1928).333.

Pantin W A, A Benedictine Opponent of J W, EHR 43.74.

Odlozilík O, W's Influence upon Central and Eastern Europe, Slavonic Review 7.634.

Manning B L, Wyclif, Cambridge Medieval History, 7.486.

Smith H M, Lollardy, Church Quarterly Review 119.30.

Odlozilík O, Wyclif and Bohemia, Vestník kral české spol nauk 1936.

Thomson S H, Wyclif or Wyclyf? EHR 53.675.

Gwynn A, The English Austin Friars in the Time of Wyclif, London 1940 (crit W Pantin, EHR 60.112).

Dahmus J H, Further Evidence for the Spelling Wyclyf, Spec 16.224.

Russell H G, Lollard Opposition to Oaths by Creatures, AHR 51.668.

Dahmus J H, Did Wyclyf Recant? CHR 19.155.

Lloyd M E H, J W and the Prebend of Lincoln, EHR 41.388.

Towne F, Wyclif and Chaucer on the Contemplative Life, Essays . . . to Lily B Campbell, Berkeley 1950.

McFarlane K B, John Wycliffe and the Beginnings of English Non-Conformity, London 1952.

Dahmus J H, The Prosecution of J W, New Haven 1952 (crit S H Thomson, Spec 28.563).

Dahmus J H, Wyclyf Was a Negligent Pluralist, Spec 28.378.

Brandt M, Wyclifova hereza i socijalni pokreti u Splitu krajem XIV st, Zagreb 1955.

Aston M, John Wycliffe's Reformation Reputation, PP 18.23.

Robson J A, Wyclif and the Oxford Schools, Cambridge 1961.

Benrath G A, Wyclifs Bibelkommentar, Berlin 1966.

Leff G, John Wyclif: The Path to Dissent, Oxford 1968.

Thomson S H, John Wyclyf, Reformers in Profile, ed Gerrish, Phila 1968, pp 12–39.

[2] CRITICISM OF ENGLISH WORKS.

See below, under separate works, this chapter [6] to [101].

[3] WYCLYFITE TRANSLATION OF THE BIBLE.

See Wyclyfite Versions [52] under Biblical Translations and Paraphrases, Chapter IV below.

[4] CANON AND DOCTRINE.

Bale J, Scriptorum illustrium maioris Brytanie . . . catalogus, Basel 1557, p 450.

James T, ed, Wyclif, Two Short Treatises against the Begging Friars, Oxford 1608.

Cave W, Scriptorum ecclesiasticorum historia literaria, Cologne 1720, Appendix, p 40.

Tanner T, Bibliotheca Britannico-Hibernica sive de scriptoribus . . . , London 1748, p 767.

Todd J H, The Last Age of the Church, Dublin 1840.

Todd J H, An Apology for Lollard Doctrines Attributed to Wicliffe, London 1842.

Shirley W W, A Catalogue of the Original Works of J W, Oxford 1865.

Loserth J, Das vermeintliche Schreiben Wiclifs an Urban VI und einige verlorene Flugschriften Wiclif's aus seinen letzten Lebenstagen, Historische Zeitschrift 75 (ns 39).476.

Fürstenau H, J von Ws Lehren von der Einteilung der Kirche und von der Stellung der weltlichen Gewalt, Berlin 1900.

Heine D, Wiclifs Lehre vom Güterbesitz, Gütersloh 1903.

Jones E D, Authenticity of Some English Works Ascribed to J W, Angl 30.261.

Loserth J, Wiclifs Lehre vom wahren und falschen Papsttum, Historische Zeitschrift 99(1907).237.

Loserth J, Die ältesten Streitschriften

Wiclifs, Sitzungsberichte der Kaiserlichen Akademie der Wissenschaften in Wien, phil-hist Klasse, 160(1908), no 2.

Loserth J, J von W und Guilelmus Peraldus, Sitzungsberichte der Kaiserlichen Akademie 180(1916), no 3.

Loserth J, J von W und Robert Grosseteste, Sitzungsberichte der Kaiserlichen Akademie 186(1918), no 2.

Taylor H O, Thought and Expression in the 16 Century, 2 vols, N Y 1920.

Hearnshaw F J C, J W and Divine Dominion, Social and Political Ideas of Some Great Mediaeval Thinkers, London 1923, p 192.

Loserth J, Revision of Shirley's Catalogue of the Extant Latin Works of J W, London [1924].

McNeill J T, Some Emphases in W's Teaching, Journal of Religion 7.447.

Heitzman M, J W traktat De universalibus i jego wpływ na uniwersytet praski i krakowski, Arch Kom do badania Hist Filozofji w Polsce, 2(1926).111.

Thomson S H, Some Latin Works Erroneously Ascribed to Wyclif, Spec 3.382.

Thomson S H, A Lost Chapter of W's Summa de ente, Spec 4.339.

Thomson S H, The Order of Writing of W's Philosophical Works, Českou Minulostí, Prague 1929, p 146.

Thomson S H, The Philosophical Basis of W's Theology, Journal of Religion 11.86.

Stein I H, Two Notes on Wyclif, Spec 6.465.

Stein I H, The Vatican MS Borghese 29 and the Tractate De Versuciis Anti-Christi, EHR 47.95.

Manning B L, W's Writings (i) Latin, (ii) English, Cambridge Medieval History, 7.900.

Thomson S H, W's Lost De fide sacramentorum, Journal of Theological Studies 33.359.

Stein I H, The Latin Text of W's Complaint, Spec 7.87.

Stein I H, Another Lost Chapter of W's Summa de ente, Spec 8.254.

Stein I H, An Unpublished Fragment of W's Confessio, Spec 8.503.

Stein I H, Wyclif-Handschriften in Deutschland, Zentralblatt für Bibliothekswesen 47.625.

Thomson S H, Unnoticed MSS and Works of Wyclif, Journal of Theological Studies 38.24, 139.

Westin G, J W och hans reformidéer, Uppsala 1936.

Talbert E W, A Lollard Chronicle of the Papacy, JEGP 41.163.

Reeves W P, A Second MS of W's De dominio civili, MLN 50.96.

Thomson S H, Unnoticed MSS of W's De veritate sacre scripture, MÆ. 12.68.

McShane E D, A Critical Appraisal of the Antimendicantism of J W, Rome 1950.

For the Canon of English works see below [6]ff.

The Latin works of Wyclyf are authenticated and ascribed in the MSS, whereas the English works are almost never so authenticated. The proof for almost all of the English works must usually rest on internal evidence. It is therefore necessary to consult the Latin canon.

Latin Works

1 De logica, in three parts, ed M H Dziewicki, London 1893f.

2 De materia et forma, ed Dziewicki, London 1902.

3 De insolubilibus, edn in preparation S H Thomson.

4 Summa de ente sive Summa intellectualium.

Primus liber:

De ente in communi, ed Thomson, Oxford 1930.

De ente primo, ed Thomson, Oxford 1930.

Tractatus purgans errores circa veritates in communi, ed Dziewicki, London 1909.

De universalibus, edn in preparation Thomson.

De tempore.

Secundus liber:

De intelleccione Dei, ed Dziewicki, London 1909.

De sciencia Dei.

De volucione Dei, ed Dziewicki, London 1909.

De personarum distinccione sive De Trinitate, ed A D Breck, Boulder Colorado 1962.

De ideis, edn in preparation Thomson.

De potencia productiva Dei ad extra, partially ed Dziewicki, London 1909.

5 De ente predicamentali, ed R Beer, London 1891.

6 De composicione hominis, ed Beer, London 1884.

7 De actibus anime, ed Dziewicki, London 1902.

8 De incarnacione verbi sive De benedicta incarnacione, ed E Harris, London 1886.

9 De fide catholica, ed Loserth, Opera minora, London 1913, p 98.

10 De dominio divino, ed Poole, London 1890.

11 Summa theologiae:
De mandatis divinis, ed Loserth, London 1922.
De statu innocencie, ed Loserth and F D Matthew, London 1922.
De dominio civili, in three books, ed Poole (Lib I) and Loserth, London 1890, 1900f.
De veritate Sacre Scripture, ed R Buddensieg, London 1905f.
De Ecclesia, ed Loserth, London 1886.
De officio regis, ed A W Pollard and C Sayle, London 1887.
De potestate Pape, ed Loserth, London 1907.
De simonia, ed Dziewicki and Herzberg-Fränkel, London 1898.
De apostasia, ed Dziewicki, London 1889.
De blasphemia, ed Dziewicki, London 1893.

12 Trialogus sive Summa summe, ed Basel 1525, Frankfort and Leipzig 1754; G Lechler, Oxford 1869.

13 De dotacione Ecclesie sive Supplementum Trialogi, ed Lechler, Oxford 1869.

14 De Eucharistia tractatus maior, ed Loserth, London 1892.

15 De Eucharistia et penitencia sive De confessione, ed Loserth, London 1892.

16 De Eucharistia confessio, ed Lewis, 1820, p 323; Vaughan 2.445; Fasciculi Zizaniorum p 115.

17 De Eucharistia confessio, ed Thomson, Journal of Theological Studies 33.361.

18 De Eucharistia conclusiones quindecim, ed Lewis, 1820, p 318; Fasc Ziz, p 105.

19 Questio ad fratres de sacramento altaris, ed Loserth, 1892.

20 De vaticinacione seu prophecia, ed Loserth, Op min, London 1913, p 165.

21 De oracione et Ecclesie purgacione, ed Buddensieg, Pol Wks, London 1883, p 337.

22 De septem donis Spiritus Sancti, ed Buddensieg, Pol Wks, London 1883, p 199.

23 Differencia inter peccatum mortale et veniale, ed Loserth and Matthew, London 1922.

24 De Diabolo et membris eius, ed Buddensieg, Pol Wks, London 1883, p 355.

25 De solucione Satane, ed Buddensieg, Pol Wks, London 1883, p 385.

26 Errare in materia fidei quod potuit Ecclesia militans, ed Thomson, Spec 3.248.

Sermons and Practical Theology

27 Sermons Part 1 Super evangelia dominicalia, ed Loserth, London 1887.

28 Sermons Part 2 Super evangelia de sanctis, ed Loserth, London 1888.

29 Sermons Part 3 Super epistolas, ed Loserth, London 1889.

30 Sermons Part 4 Sermones miscellanei, ed Loserth, London 1890.

31 Exhortacio novi doctoris sive Sermo in Labora sicut bonus miles Christi, ed Loserth, Op min, London 1913, p 431.

32 Sermo pulcher, Sermo mixtus 24, ed Loserth, 1890.

33 De sex iugis, a composite sermon, ed Lechler, J W 2.591. See Sermones (30).202.

34 Opus evangelicum sive De sermone Domini in monte, in four books, ed Loserth, 2 vols, London 1895, 1896.

35 Exposicio textus Matthei 23 sive De vae octuplici, ed Loserth, Op min, London 1913, p 313.

36 Exposicio textus Matthei 24 sive De Antichristo, ed Loserth, Op min, London 1913, p 354.

37 In omnes Novi Testamenti libros preter Apocalypsin commentarius.

38 De officio pastorali, ed Lechler, Leipzig 1863.

39 De oracione dominica, ed Loserth, Op min, London 1913, p 393.

40 De triplici vinculo amoris, ed Buddensieg, Pol Wks, London 1883, p 151.

Protests, Disputations and Epistles

41 Ad parliamentum regis, ed Lewis, 1820, p 382; Fascicuoli Zizaniorum, p 245.

42 Declaraciones Johannis Wickliff, ed in Walsingham, Hist Anglicana (R S), 1.357.

43 De condemnacione xix conclusionum, ed Fasc Ziz, p 481.

44 Contra Kilingham Carmelitam, ed Fasc Ziz, p 453.

45 Determinacio ad argumenta Mag Outredi de Omesima, ed Loserth, Op min, London 1913, p 405.

46 Ad argumenta Wilelmi Vyrinham determinacio, ed Loserth, Op min, London 1913, p 415.

47 De dominio determinacio contra unum monachum, ed Lewis 1820, p 349, a part of 46.

48 Responsiones ad argumenta Radulphi Strode, ed Loserth, Op min, London 1913, p 175.

49 Responsiones ad argumenta cuiusdam emuli veritatis, ed Loserth, Op min, London 1913, p 258.

50 Responsiones ad xliv conclusiones sive Ad argucias monachales, ed Loserth, Op min, London 1913, p 201.

51 Responsio ad decem questiones, ed Loserth, Op min, London 1913, p 397.

52 Epistole novem, ed Loserth, Op min, London 1913, p 1. Ep 1 to Pope Urban VI previously ed Fasc Ziz, p 341; Lechler J W 2.633; and englished by Lewis 1820, p 283. Vaughan 2.455; Arnold, Sel Engl Wks 3.504.

On Church Government and Endowments

53 Dialogus sive Speculum Ecclesie militantis, ed A W Pollard, London 1886
54 De paupertate Christi sive xxxiii Conclusiones, ed Loserth, Op min, London 1913, p 19.
55 Ad quesita regis et concilii, ed Fox Acts and Monuments, Fasc Ziz, p 258.
56 Speculum secularium dominorum, ed Loserth, Op min, London 1913, p 74.
57 De servitute civili et dominio seculari, ed Loserth, Op min, London 1913, p 145.
58 De officio regis conclusio, ed Thomson, Spec 3.258.
59 De clavibus Ecclesie sive De clave celi, ed Thomson, Spec 3.251.
60 De iuramento Arnaldi, ed Lechler, J W 2.575.
61 De citacionibus frivolis et aliis versuciis Antichristi, ed Buddensieg, Pol Wks, London 1883, p 537.
62 De demonio meridiano, ed Buddensieg, Pol Wks, London 1886, p 413.
63 De dissensione Paparum sive de scismate, ed Buddensieg, Pol Wks, London 1886, p 565.
64 Contra cruciatam, ed Buddensieg, Pol Wks, London 1886, p 577.
65 De Christo et suo adversario Antichristo, ed Buddensieg, Gotha 1880, and Pol Wks, London 1886, p 633.

On the Monastic Orders

66 De ordine Christiano, ed Loserth, Op min, London 1913, p 129.
67 De perfeccione statuum, ed Buddensieg, Pol Wks, London 1886, p 441.
68 De nova prevaricancia mandatorum, ed Buddensieg, Pol Wks, London 1886, p 107.
69 De religionibus vanis monachorum sive De fundacione religionis, ed Buddensieg, Pol Wks, London 1886, p 433.
70 De religione privata, 2 parts, ed Buddensieg, Pol Wks, London 1886, p 483.
71 De concordancia fratrum cum secta simplici Christi sive De sectis monachorum sive De ordinacione fratrum, ed Buddensieg, Pol Wks, London 1886, p 88.
72 De quattuor sectis novellis, ed Buddensieg, Pol Wks, London 1886, p 375.
73 De deteccione perfidiarum Antichristi, ed Buddensieg, Pol Wks, London 1886, p 375.

74 De novis ordinibus, ed Buddensieg, Pol Wks, London 1886, p 317.
75 De mendaciis fratrum, ed Buddensieg, Pol Wks, London 1886, p 401.
76 Descripcio fratris, ed Buddensieg, Pol Wks, London 1886, p 407.
77 De fratribus ad scholares, ed Loserth, Op min, London 1913, p 15.
78 De fundacione sectarum, ed Buddensieg, Pol Wks, London 1886, p 1.

On the Secular Clergy

79 De prelatis contencionum sive De incarcerandis fidelibus, a part of Sermon 27 of Part 3, ed Loserth, Op min, p 209; also Op min, London 1913, p 92.
80 Quatuor imprecaciones, ed Buddensieg, Pol Wks, London 1886, p 713.
81 De graduacionibus sive De magisterio Christi, ed Loserth, Op min, London 1913, p 439.
82 De gradibus cleri Ecclesie sive De ordinibus Ecclesie, ed Loserth, Op min, London 1913, p 140.
83 De duobus generibus hereticorum, ed Buddensieg, Pol Wks, London 1886, p 427.
84 Purgatorium secte Christi, ed Buddensieg, Pol Wks, London 1886, p 291.

[5] COLLECTED EDITIONS OF ENGLISH WYCLYFITE WRITINGS.

Todd J H, Three Treatises of J W, Dublin 1851.
Arnold T, Select English Works of J W, 3 vols, Oxford 1869–71.
Matthew F D, The English Works of W Hitherto Unprinted, London 1880, EETS 74.
Winn H E, W Select English Writings, Oxford 1929 (crit H Savage, MLN 46.64; H S Bennett, RES 6.464).
For separate works see below, this chapter [6] to [101].

[6] OTHER SERMONS AND TRACTS UNEDITED BUT ASCRIBED TO WYCLYF OR HIS FOLLOWERS.

MSS. A sermon and two sermon collections: St. John's Camb 436, no 2 (M R James, A Descriptive Catalogue of the Manuscripts in the Library of St. John's College Cambridge, Cambridge 1913, p 359); BM Addit 41321 (G R Owst, Literature and Pulpit in Medieval England, Cambridge 1933, p 284); Univ Libr Edinb 93 (Laing 140), ff 1b–103b (15 cent; G R Owst, Preaching in Medieval England, Cambridge 1926, p 229). Tracts: A Letter to Poor Priests, Royal

17.B.xvii, ff 96^b–97^a (late 14 cent; G F Warner and J P Gilson, Catalogue of Western Manuscripts in the Old Royal and King's Collection, London 1921, 2.229); A Protestation, Bodl 3072 (Bodley 647), ff 70^a–70^b (late 14 cent; F Madan and H H E Craster, A Summary Catalogue of Western Manuscripts in the Bodleian Library, Oxford 1922, 21.583); A Treatise on Kingship, Bodl 21847 (Douce 273), ff 37^b–53^b (last quarter 14 cent; Madan, Summary Cat, Oxford 1897, 4.576); A Disputation between a Friar and a Priest, Trinity Dublin 244 (C.iii.12) (15 cent), no 26.

1. Works Generally Ascribed To Wyclyf

I. Sermons

[7] THE SERMONS.

MSS. All groups: Sunday Gospel, Commune sanctorum, Proprium sanctorum, Ferial Gospel, and Sunday Epistle Sermons. 1, Bodl 2628 (Bodley 788), ff 1–327 (1390–1400); 2, Bodl 21895 (Douce 321), ff 1–259 (lacking Sunday sermons from Trinity to latter part of that on 14 Sunday after, and from 21 Sunday after Trinity to the Gospel for Sexagesima; early 15 cent); 3, Bodl Don C.13, ff 1–(late 14 cent); 4, St. John's Camb 58 (C.8), ff 1–207 (at least 55 sermons missing, 15 cent); 5, Cotton Claud D.viii, ff 109–307 (imperfect at beginning, 15 cent); 6, Royal 18.B.ix, ff 1^a–176^a, 194^b–196^a (at least 10 Proprium sanctorum sermons missing, early 15 cent); 7, BM Addit 40672, ff 1^a–102^b, 107^a–185^a, 197^a–247^b (formerly Wrest Park 11, early 15 cent); 8, Lambeth 1149, pp 1–301, 329–457 (Ferial sermons end imperfect, 14, 15 cent); 9, Wrest Park 32 (offered for sale, Laurence Witten, 282 York St, New Haven, Conn; late 14 cent). All groups except Ferial Sermons. 10, Trinity Camb 134 (B.4.20), ff 1–80 (late 14, early 15 cent). All groups except Epistle Sermons. 11, Trinity Camb 60 (B.2.17), ff 1^a–180^b (early 15 cent); 12, BM Addit 40671, ff 1^a–157^a (formerly Wrest Park 38, late 15 cent). Commune sanctorum sermons complete, a majority of Proprium sanctorum and Ferial Gospel sermons. 13, Corp Christi Camb 336 (K.15), ff 1^a–241^a (early 15 cent). Ferial Sermons complete, 7 for Proprium sanctorum, 1 for Sunday Gospels. 14, New Coll Oxf 95, ff 1^a–121^b (early 15 cent). Sunday Sermons only. 15, Camb Univ 1732 (I.i I.40), ff 1–211 (14 cent). Sunday Gospel Sermons only. 16, Bodl 1279 (Laud Misc 314), ff 1– (late 15 cent); 17, Bodl 29002 (Add A.105), ff 1–95 (formerly Baroness North, early 15 cent); 18, St John's Camb 190 (G.22), ff 79^a–112^a (1st or 2nd Sunday after Epiphany to Whitsuntide only, 15 cent); 19, Sidney Sussex Camb 74 (△.4.12), ff 1^a–142^b (15 cent, see under Homilies). Sunday Epistle Sermons only. 20, Trinity Camb 322 (B.14.38), ff 1^a–121^a (15 cent); 21, Harley 1730, ff 1– (ends defective in Sermon for 22 Sunday after Trinity). Fragments. 22, Hertford 4 (binding: 5 leaves, 5 half leaves).

Arnold T, Select English Works of John Wyclif, Oxford 1869, 1.xvii (brief descriptions of 19 MSS).

Madan, Summary Cat, 5.540 (former MS Baroness North).

Friends of the Bodleian Annual Report 6.15 (MS Bodl Don C.13, Bodleian).

James, Cat MSS St John's Camb, p 226 (MS St John's Camb G 22).

BM Catalogue of Additions to the Manuscripts 1921–1925, London 1950, pp 116, 117 (former MSS Wrest Park 11, 38).

James M R and C Jenkins, A Descriptive Catalogue of the Manuscripts in the Library of Lambeth Palace, Cambridge 1930–32, p 824 (MS Lambeth 1149).

Parkes M B, Manuscript Fragments of English Sermons Attributed to John Wyclif, MÆ 24.97.

Edition. Arnold, Sel Wks, 1 and 2 (MS Bodley 788, occasionally collated with other MSS, most frequently with MS Douce 321).

Selections. Brandl A L and O Zippel, Mittelenglische Sprach–und Literaturproben, Berlin 1917, p 245 (Nativity Sermon).

Winn H E, John Wyclif, Oxford 1929, pp 18, 31, 35, 37, 42, 85, 95, 114, 115.

Date and Authorship. Deanesly M, The Lollard Bible and Other Medieval Biblical Versions, Cambridge 1920, pp 317, 249.

Talbert E W, The Authorship of the English Wyclifite Collection of Sermons, Abstracts of Dissertations, Stanford University, 11.65; The Date of the Composition of the English Wyclifite Collection of Sermons, Spec 12.464.

Ransom M W, The Chronology of Wyclif's English Sermons, Research Studies, State College of Washington, 16.67.

Sources and Literary Relations. Workman, John Wyclif, 2.175, 207.

Winn, John Wyclif, p xxx.

Atkins J W H, English Literary Criticism, Cambridge 1943, p 148.

Towne F, Wyclif and Chaucer on the Contemplative Life, Essays . . . Dedicated to Lily B Campbell, Berkeley 1950, p 3.

Rendering of Biblical Passages. Deanesly, Lollard Bible, p 317.

Fristedt S L, The Wycliffe Bible, Part 1: The Principal Problem Connected with Forshall and Madden's Edition, Stockholm Studies in English 4.106.

Smalley B, MÆ 22.52 (rev of M Deanesly, The Significance of the Lollard Bible, London 1951).

Style. Winn, John Wyclif, p 42.

Hargreaves H, Wyclif's Prose, E&S 19.1.

[8] WYCKLYFFE'S WYCKET.

Editions. Wycklyffes wycket, Norenburch [London, J Day] 1546 (STC no 25590); rptd T P Pantin, Wycklyffes Wycket, Oxford 1828.

Wicklieffes Wicket faythfully ouerseene [J Day and W Seres 1548]; another edn, . . . (by M C [overdale? 1550?]; another edn, Oxford, Jos Barnes for John Barnes, London 1612. (STC nos 25591, 25591ᵃ, 25592).

Modernizations. Writings of the Reverend and Learned John Wickliff, Religious Tract Soc, London 1831, p 152 (STC 25590 collated with STC 25592); rptd The Great Sermons of the Great Preachers, London 1858, p 111; H C Fish, History and Repository of Pulpit Eloquence, N Y 1856, 1.116 (begins with p vii of STC no 25590).

Literary Relations. Vaughn R, The Life and Opinions of John de Wycliffe D D, London 1831, 2.64.

Lechler G, Johann von Wyclif und die Vorgeschichte der Reformation, Leipzig 1873, 1.627.

Chaplin W N, Lollardy and the Great Bible, Church Quarterly Review 128.210.

[9] VÆ OCTUPLEX.

MSS. 1, Bodl 2628 (Bodley 788), ff 90ᵇ–96ᵃ (late 14 cent); 2, St John's Camb 193 (G.25), ff 97ᵃ–105ᵃ (15 cent); 3, Royal 18.B.ix, ff 191ᵇ–194ᵃ (early 15 cent); 4, BM Addit 40672, ff 102ᵇ–106ᵇ (formerly Wrest Park 11, early 15 cent); 5, Lambeth 1149, pp 320–26 (14, 15 cent); 6, Trinity Dublin 245 (C.v.6), ff 96ᵃ–101ᵃ (early 15 cent).

Arnold, Sel Wks, 1.xvii, 2.377 (the sermon appears in all MSS having the entire cycle of [7], except MS Douce 321, Bodleian; MSS St John's Camb 193, Lambeth 1149, and Trinity Dublin C.v.6 are not noted).

James, Cat MSS St John's Camb, p 229.

James and Jenkins, Cat MSS Libr Lambeth Palace, p 824.

Todd J H, An Apology for Lollard Doctrines, London 1842, Camden Soc 20.x (MS Trinity Dublin C.v.6).

Edition. Arnold, Sel Wks, 2.377 (MS Bodley 788).

[10] OF MINISTERS IN THE CHURCH.

MSS. 1, St John's Camb 193 (G.25), ff 105ᵃ–127ᵃ (15 cent); 2, Trinity Camb 60 (B.2.17), ff 112ᵇ–121ᵇ (early 15 cent); 3, Royal 18.B.ix, ff 177ᵃ–184ᵃ (early 15 cent); 4, BM Addit 40672, ff 185ᵃ–197ᵃ (formerly Wrest Park 11, early 15 cent); 5, Lambeth 1149, pp 301–320 (14, 15 cent); 6, Trinity Dublin 245 (C.v.6), ff 101ᵃ–116ᵇ (early 15 cent).

Arnold, Sel Wks, 1.xvii, 2.391 (the sermon appears in all MSS having the entire cycle of [7] plus MS Trinity Camb 60 (B.2.17); MSS St John's Camb 193, Lambeth 1149, and Trinity Dublin C.v.6 are not noted).

James, Cat MSS St John's Camb, p 229.

James and Jenkins, Cat MSS Libr Lambeth Palace, p 824.

Todd, Apology, p xi (Trinity Dublin C.v.6).

Edition. Arnold, Sel Wks, 2.391 (MS Bodley 788).

[11] ADDITIONAL SET OF 54 SERMONS.

MS. St John's Camb 190 (G.22), ff 1–78ᵇ (15 cent).

Authorship. Arnold, Sel Wks, 1.iii.

Matthew F D, The English Works of Wyclif Hitherto Unprinted, EETS 74.xlix.

II. Didactic Works

For items [12] to [23] in this section, see also under Works of Religious Instruction.

[12] THE TEN COMMANDMENTS.

MSS. Version attributed to Wyclyf. 1, Bodl 2643 (Bodley 789), no 5, ff 108ª– (early 15 cent). Expanded versions. 2, York Minster XVI.L.12, ff 1– (late 14 cent); 3, Trinity Dublin 245 (C.v.6), f. 9ᵇ–27ª (early 15 cent); 4, Harley 2398, ff 73ª– (ca 1400–10). Condensed versions. 5, Rylands English 85, ff 2ᵇ– (early 15 cent); 6, Lambeth 408 (Lay Folks Catechism), ff 6ᵇ– (15 cent); 7, M.861 Morgan Libr, ff 1ᵇ– (mid 15 cent); 8, Plimpton Addenda 3 Columbia Univ Libr, ff 241ᵇ– (ca 1400); 9, Bodl 21820 (Douce 246), ff 101ᵇ– (15 cent).
Editions. Arnold, Sel Wks, 3.82 (MS Bodley 789).
Kellogg A L and E W Talbert, The Wyclifite Pater Noster and Ten Commandments with Special Reference to English MSS 85 and 90 in the John Rylands Library, JRLB 42.345 (text of MS Rylands English 85).
Simmons and Nolloth, EETS 118.33 (Lambeth 408).
Bühler C F, The Middle English Texts of Morgan MS 861, PMLA 69.686 (text of MS M.861 Pierpont Morgan Libr).
Related Versions. Arnold, Sel Wks, 3.82; Warner and Gilson, Cat MSS Royal, 2.220; Todd, Apology, p vii.
Cumming W P, A Middle English MS in the Bibliothèque Ste Geneviève Paris, PMLA 42.862.
Ives S A, The Genuine and Unpublished Version of Wycliffe's Treatise on The Ten Commandments, Rare Books, N Y 1942, 3.3 (Codex of H P Kraus).

[13] EXPOSITION OF THE PATER NOSTER (BODLEY).

MSS. 1, Bodl 2643 (Bodley 789), no 5, ff 97ª– (early 15 cent); 2, Camb Univ 756 (Dd.xii.39), ff 72ᵇ–74ª (late 14 cent); 3, Harley 2385, ff 2ª–; 4, York Minster XVI.L.12, ff 32ᵇ– (late 14 cent, lacks final paragraph); 5, BM Addit 17013, ff 36ᵇ– (early 15 cent, lacks final paragraph); 6, Trinity Dublin 245 (C.v.6), ff 2ᵇ– (early 15 cent, lacks final paragraph); 7, Bibl Ste Geneviève Paris 3390, ff 27ᵇ– (early 15

cent, lacks final paragraph); 8, Lambeth 408, no I, I, ff 1ᵇ– (15 cent, lacks final paragraph).
Paues A C, A Fourteenth Century Biblical Version, Cambridge 1904, p xiii note (MS Camb Univ Dd. xii.39).
PMLA 42.862 (MS Bibl Ste Geneviève Paris 3390).
JRLB 42.358 (classification of MSS).
Editions. Arnold Sel Wks, 3.93 (MS Bodley 789).
See also [14] and [57] below.

[14] EXPOSITION OF THE PATER NOSTER (HARLEY).

MSS. 1, Harley 2398, ff 166ᵇ–173ª (ca 1400–10); 2, Rylands English 90 (Corser), ff 63ᵇ– (late 14 cent); 3, Bodl 3054 (Bodley 938), ff 24ᵇ– (early 15 cent); 4, Rylands English 85, ff 37ᵇ– (early 15 cent); 5, Wrest Park (unspecified, 32?, see [7] above).
JRLB 42.358.
Editions. Arnold, Sel Wks, 3.98 (MS Harley 2398 collated with MS Corser).
See also [13] above and [57] below.

[15] THE AVE MARIA.

MSS. 1, Bodl 2643 (Bodley 789), no 5, f 97ª (early 15 cent); 2, Harley 2385, ff 3ª–3ᵇ; 3, Lambeth 408, no I, I (15 cent); 4, Trinity Dublin (245 C.v.6), ff 3ᵇ–4ᵇ (early 15 cent).
Edition. Arnold, Sel Wks, 3. 111 (MS Bodl 789, Bodleian, 5 notes on readings in MS Lambeth 408, Lambeth Palace Library).
See also [57] below, and under Lyrical Pieces.

[16] EXPOSITION OF THE APOSTLES CREED.

MSS. 1, Lambeth 408, no I, I (15 cent); 2, Trinity Dublin 245 (C.v.6), ff 1ª–2ª (early 15 cent); 3, Bibl Ste Geneviève Paris 3390, f 24 (early 15 cent).
Todd, Apology, p vi (Trinity MS).
PMLA 42.862 (Ste Geneviève MS); JRLB 42.355.
Edition. Arnold, Sel Wks, 3.114 (MS Lambeth 408).

[17] EXPOSITION OF THE FIVE OUTER WITS.

MS. Lambeth 408, no I, I (15 cent).
Edition. Arnold, Sel Wks, 3.117.
Literary Relations. PMLA 69.686.

[18] EXPOSITION OF THE FIVE INNER WITS.

MS. Lambeth 408, no I, I (15 cent).
Edition. Arnold, Sel Wks, 3.117.
Literary Relations. PMLA 69.686.

[19] A COMMENT ON THE SEVEN DEADLY SINS.

MSS. 1, Bodl 3072 (Bodley 647), ff 1ᵃ–37ᵃ (late 14 cent); 2, Bodl 21847 (Douce 273), ff 53ᵇ– (late 14 cent); 3, Trinity Dublin 245 (C.v.6), ff 38ᵃ–63ᵃ (early 15 cent).
Warner and Gilson, Cat MSS Royal, 2.220.
Edition. Arnold, Sel Wks, 3.119 (MS Bodley 647, notes from MS Douce 273).
Selections. Winn, John Wyclif, p 108.
Authorship, Date. Workman, John Wyclif, 2.135; JRLB 42.350.

[20] TREATISES ON THE SEVEN WORKS OF MERCY BODILY and THE SEVEN WORKS OF MERCY GHOSTLY.

MSS. 1, New Coll Oxf 95, ff 127ᵇ–135ᵃ (early 15 cent); 2, Royal 17.A.xxvi, ff 26ᵇ–27ᵇ (portions of first chapters only, early 15 cent); 3, Trinity Dublin 245 (C.v.6), ff 30ᵇ–38ᵃ (early 15 cent); 4, H P Kraus (Rare Books, 3.3).
Warner and Gilson, Cat MSS Royal, 2.220.
Edition. Arnold, Sel Wks, 3.168 (New College MS collated with Trinity Dublin).
Related Version. PMLA 69.686.

[21] FIVE QUESTIONS ON LOVE.

MSS. 1, New College Oxford 95, ff 123ᵃ–124ᵃ (early 15 cent); 2, Trinity Dublin 155 (C.v.7), no 3 (15 cent).
Abbott T K, Catalogue of the Manuscripts in the Library of Trinity College Dublin, Dublin 1900, p 20.
Edition. Arnold, Sel Wks, 3.183 (MS New College Oxford 95).
Selections. Winn, John Wyclif, p 110.
Authorship, Source. Deanesly, Lollard Bible, p 245 (Opera minora 9).

[22] OF FAITH, HOPE, AND CHARITY.

MSS. 1, New Coll Oxf 95, ff 124ᵃ–127ᵇ (early 15 cent); 2, Royal 17.A.xxvi, ff 27ᵇ–28ᵇ (early 15 cent); 3, Trinity Dublin 245 (C.v.6), ff 27ᵃ–30ᵇ (early 15 cent).
Warner and Gilson, Cat of MSS Royal, 2.220.
Edition. Matthew, EETS 74.346 (MS New Coll Oxf 95 collated with MS Trinity Dublin C.v.6).
Related Version. PMLA 42.862; JRLB 42.353.

[23] CONFESSION AND PENITENCE.

MSS. 1, John Rylands Libr 86, ff 35ᵃ–43ᵃ

(formerly Ashburnham XXVII, early 15 cent); 2, Trinity Dublin 245 (C.v.6), ff 127ᵇ–138ᵃ (early 15 cent).
Tyson M, Handlist of . . . English Manuscripts in the John Rylands Library, JRLB 13.168.
Edition. Matthew, EETS 74.325 (Trinity Dublin MS collated with John Rylands).
Selections. Winn, John Wyclif, p 94.

[24] ON THE SUFFICIENCY OF HOLY SCRIPTURES.

MS. 1, Trinity Dublin 244 (C.iii.12), ff 210ᵇ–211ᵃ (early 15 cent).
Edition. Arnold, Sel Wks, 3.186.

[25] THE HOLI PROPHET DAVID SAITH.

MS. Camb Univ 1369 (Ff. vi.31), sect 3, ff 1ᵃ–16ᵇ (1380–1400).
Edition. Deanesly, Lollard Bible, p 445.
Date, Authorship. Deanesly, Lollard Bible, pp 268, 241n4, 274.

[26] OF WEDDID MEN AND WIFIS AND OF HERE CHILDREN ALSO.

MSS. 1, Bodl 3054 Bodley 938), ff 62ᵃ–73ᵃ (early 15 cent); 2, Camb Univ 756 (Dd.xii.39), ff 3ᵃ–16ᵃ (late 14 cent); 3, Corp Christi Camb 296 (C.6), pp 224–235 (late 14 cent); 4, BM Addit 24202, ff 29ᵃ–33ᵇ (late 14 cent).
Madan and Craster, Summary Cat, 21.578 (MS Bodley 938).
Paues, 14 Cent Biblical Version, p xiii note (MSS Camb Univ Dd.xii.39, BM Addit 24202).
Edition. Arnold, Sel Wks, 3.188 (MS Corp Christi Camb 296).
Selections. Winn, John Wyclif, pp 105, 107.

[27] DE STIPENDIIS MINISTRORUM.

MSS. 1, Corp Christi Camb 296 (C.6), pp 144–146 (late 14 cent); 2, Trinity Dublin 244 (C.iii.12), ff 124ᵃ–125ᵃ (early 15 cent).
Edition. Arnold, Sel Wks, 3.202 (MS Corp Christi Camb 296).

[28] A SHORT RULE OF LIFE.

MSS. 1, Bodl 668 (Laud Misc 174); 2, Corp Christi Camb 296 (C.6), pp 157–160 (late 14 cent).
Edition. Arnold, Sel Wks, 3.204 (MS Laud 174, 4 notes from MS Corp Christi Camb 296).
Authorship. Arnold, Sel Wks, l.vi.

III. Statements of Belief, A Letter, A Petition

[29] STATEMENT OF BELIEF CONCERNING THE EUCHARIST (KNIGHTON).

MSS. 1, Cotton Tib C.vii (15 cent); 2, Cotton Claud E.iii, no 7 (14 cent).
Editions. Arnold, Sel Wks, 3.499 (MSS Cotton Tib C.vii, Cotton Claud E.iii).
Lumby J R, Chronicon Henrici Knighton, Rolls Series 92, London 1895, 2.157 (MSS Cotton Tib C.vii, Cotton Claud E.iii).

[30] STATEMENT OF BELIEF CONCERNING THE EUCHARIST (BODLEY).

MSS. 1, Bodl 3072 (Bodley 647), f 63ª (late 14 cent); 2, Cotton Tib C.vii (15 cent); 3, Cotton Claud E.iii, no 7 (14 cent).
Editions. Arnold, Sel Wks, 3.501 (MS Bodley 647 collated with MSS Cotton Tib C.vii, Cotton Claud E.iii).
Lumby, Chron Knighton, 2.161 (MSS Cotton Tib C.vii, Cotton Claud E.iii).
Literary Relations and Historical Milieu. MacDonald A J, Berengar and the Reform of Sacramental Doctrine, London 1930, p 406.

Dahmus J H, The Prosecution of John Wyclyf, New Haven 1952, pp 137, 133.

[31] A LETTER TO POPE URBAN.

MSS. 1, Bodl 3072 (Bodley 647), f 107ª (late 14 cent); 2, New Coll Oxf 95, ff 121ᵇ–122ᵇ (early 15 cent).
Edition. Arnold, Sel Wks, 3.504 (MS Bodley 647, 8 notes from MS New Coll Oxf 95).
Winn, John Wyclif, p 75 (MS Bodley 647).
Date, Literary Relations. Dahmus, Prosecution of J W, p 139.

[32] A PETITION TO KING AND PARLIAMENT.

MSS. 1, Corp Christi Camb 296 (C.6), pp 288–298, 170–171 (late 14 cent); 2, Trinity Dublin 244 (C.iii.12), ff 141ª–148ᵇ (ends imperfect, early 15 cent); 3, (Latin version) Laurentian Libr Florence Plut XIX, cod XXIII, ff 23ᵇ–26ᵇ (late 14 cent).
Edition. Arnold, Sel Wks, 3.507 (MS Corp Christi Camb 296).
Stein I H, The Wyclif Manuscript in Florence, Spec 5.95, 7.87.

IV. Controversial Works

[33] SIMONISTS AND APOSTATES

MS. New Coll Oxf 95, ff 122ᵇ–123ª (early 15 cent).
Edition. Arnold, Sel Wks, 3.211.

[34] CHURCH TEMPORALITIES.

MSS. 1, Corp Christi Camb 296 (C.6), pp 221–224 (late 14 cent); 2, Trinity Dublin 244 (C.iii.12), ff 184ª–186ᵇ (ends imperfect, early 15 cent); 3, Huntington HM 503, ff 1ª– (15 cent).
de Ricci Census, 1.71 (HM 503).
Edition. Arnold, Sel Wks, 3.213 (Corp Christi Camb 296).

[35] DE PRECATIONIBUS SACRIS.

MSS. 1, Corp Christi Camb 296 C.6), pp 145–157 late 14 cent); 2, Trinity Dublin 244 (C.iii.12), ff 125ª–131ᵇ (early 15 cent); 3, Trinity Dublin 246 (C.i.14), ff 1– (ca 1600).

Edition. Arnold, Sel Wks, 3.219 (MS Corp Christi Camb 296).

[36] LINCOLNIENSIS.

MS. Bodl 3072 (Bodley 647), ff 62ᵇ–63ª (late 14 cent).
Edition. Arnold, Sel Wks, 3.230.
Winn, John Wyclif, p 38.
Textual Matters. Dickins B, Lincolniensis and S Maurice, Proceedings of the Leeds Philosophical Society 4².155 (*Mauris* is S Maurice, not S Maurus).
Authorship. Jones E D, The Authenticity of Some English Works Ascribed to Wycliffe, Angl 30.261.
Workman, John Wyclif, 2.133.

[37] VITA SACERDOTUM.

MS. Bodl 3072 (Bodley 647), ff 57ᵇ–62ᵇ (late 14 cent).
Edition. Arnold, Sel Wks, 3.233.
Authorship. Workman, John Wyclif, 2.133.

[38] DE PONTIFICUM ROMANORUM SCHISMATE.

MS. Trinity Dublin 244 (C.iii.12), ff 193ᵇ–208ᵃ (early 15 cent).
Edition. Arnold, Sel Wks, 3.242.

[39] THE GRETE SENTENCE OF CURS EXPOUNDED.

MS. Corp Christi Camb 296 (C.6), pp 239–288 (late 14 cent).
Edition. Arnold, Sel Wks, 3.267.
Selections. Winn, John Wyclif, pp 34, 77, 104, 109.
Authorship. Workman, John Wyclif, 1.330.
See also under Instructions for Religious.

[40] THE CHURCH AND HER MEMBERS.

MSS. 1, Bodl 2628 (Bodley 788), ff 328ᵃ–336ᵃ (late 14 cent); 2, Royal 18.B.ix, ff 185ᵃ–191ᵃ (early 15 cent); 3, BM Addit 40672, ff 247ᵇ–255ᵃ (formerly Wrest Park 11, early 15 cent); 4, Trinity Dublin 245 (C.v.6), ff 63ᵇ–75ᵇ (early 15 cent).
Warner and Gilson, Cat MSS Royal, 2.291.
Cat Addit 1921–25, p 117 (MS BM Addit 40672).
Editions. Todd J H, Three Treatises by John Wyclyffe D D, Dublin 1851, p i (MS Trinity Dublin C.v.6).
Arnold, Sel Wks, 3.338 (MS Bodley 788).
Selections, Winn, John Wyclif, p 118.
Literary Relations. Knowles D, The Religious Orders in England, Cambridge 1955, 2.104.

[41] DE BLASPHEMIA, CONTRA FRATRES.

MS. Bodl 3072 (Bodley 647), ff 37ᵃ–57ᵇ (late 14 cent).
Edition. Arnold, Sel Wks, 3.402.

[42] DE APOSTASIA CLERI.

MS. Trinity Dublin 245 (C.v.6), ff 76ᵃ–80ᵇ (early 15 cent).
Editions. Todd, Three Treatises, p lxxxi.
Arnold, Sel Wks, 3.430.

[43] SEVEN HERESIES.

MSS. 1, Bodl 21848 (Douce 274), ff 10ᵇ– (early 15 cent); 2, Harley 2385, no 2; 3,
Trinity Dublin 245 (C.v.6), ff 4ᵇ–6ᵇ (early 15 cent).
Edition. Arnold, Sel Wks, 3.441 (MS Douce 274).

[44] OCTO IN QUIBUS SEDUCUNTUR SIMPLICES CHRISTIANI.

MSS. 1, Bodl 2262 (Bodley 540), pp 117– (late 15 cent); 2, Corp Christi Camb 296 (C.6), (late 14 cent?); 3, Trinity Dublin 244 (C.iii.12), ff 131ᵇ–133ᵇ (ends imperfect, early 15 cent); 4, Trinity Dublin 246 (C.i.14), no 2 (ca 1600).
Madan and Craster, Summary Cat, 2¹.283 (MS Bodley 540).
Edition. Arnold, Sel Wks, 3.447 (MS Corp Christi Camb 296).

[45] DE DOMINIO DIVINO.

MS. Trinity Dublin 244 (C.iii.12), ff 188ᵃ–193ᵇ (early 15 cent).
Edition. Matthew, EETS 74.282.

[46] DE SACRAMENTO ALTARIS.

MSS. 1, Bodl 2628 (Bodley 788), f 96ᵇ (late 14 cent); 2, BM Addit 40672, ff 106ᵇ–107ᵃ (formerly Wrest Park 11, early 15 cent); 3, Trinity Dublin 244 (C.iii.12), f 211ᵃ (ends imperfect, early 15 cent).
Cat Addit 1921–25, p 117 (MS BM Addit 40672).
Edition. Matthew, EETS 74.356 (MS Bodley 788 collated with MS Trinity Dublin C.iii.12).
Literary Relations. McGarry Sister L, The Holy Eucharist in ME Homiletic and Devotional Verse, diss Catholic Univ, Washington D C 1936, p 62.

[47] TRACTATUS DE PSEUDO-FRERIS.

MS. Trinity Dublin 245 (C.v.6), ff 81ᵃ–95ᵇ (early 15 cent).
Edition. Matthew, EETS 74.294.

[48] DE PAPA.

MS. John Rylands Libr 86, ff 25ᵃ–34ᵇ (formerly Ashburnham XXVII, early 15 cent).
JRLB 13.168.
Edition. Matthew, EETS 74.458.
Selections. Winn, John Wyclif, pp 69, 83.

2. WORKS ASCRIBED TO PURVEY

[49] FIFTY HERESIES AND ERRORS OF FRIARS.

MSS. 1, Bodl 3072 (Bodley 647), ff 86ª–107ª (late 14 cent); 2, Corp Christi Camb 296 (C.6), pp 39–65 (late 14 cent); 3, Trinity Dublin 244 (C. iii.12), ff 32ª–54ᵇ (early 15 cent).

Edition. Arnold, Sel Wks, 3.366 (MS Bodley 647, with 26 readings from MS Corp Christi Camb 296).

Authorship. Deanesly, Lollard Bible, p 399. Workman, John Wyclif, 1.330.

[50] DE OFFICIO PASTORALI.

MS. John Rylands Libr 86, ff 1ª–21ᵇ (formerly Ashburnham XXVII, early 15 cent). JRLB 13.168.

Edition. Matthew, EETS 74.405.

Selections. Sisam K, Fourteenth Century Verse and Prose, Oxford 1921, p 115. Winn, John Wyclif, pp 19, 79, 81, 84.

Date and Authorship. Deanesly, Lollard Bible, pp 266, 268, 270, 378.

[51] TWELVE TRACTS OR SERMONS.

MSS. 1, Camb Univ 1905 (Ii.vi.26), pp 1–158 (ca 1400–30); 2, 3, not specified. Deanesly, Lollard Bible, p 270n.

Selections. Tract 1 (portions). Forshall J and K Madden, The Holy Bible . . . by John Wycliffe and His Followers, Oxford 1850, 1. xiv (MS Camb Univ Ii. vi.26).

Tract 2. Forshall and Madden, Holy Bible, 1.xiv (MS Arundel 254 collated with MS Harley 6333).

Tract 7 (portions). Forshall and Madden, Holy Bible, 1.xv (MS Camb Univ Ii.vi.26).

Tract 10. Deanesly, Lollard Bible, p 460 (MS Camb Univ Ii.vi.26, p 98).

Textual Note. Deanesly, Lollard Bible, p 273 (Purvey connects Lollard with loll).

Date, Authorship. Deanesly, Lollard Bible, pp 270, 303, 457.

See IV [37], [52].

[52] ECCLESIÆ REGIMEN (REMONSTRANCE AGAINST ROMISH CORRUPTIONS or THIRTY-SEVEN CONCLUSIONS).

MSS. 1, Bodl 2262 (Bodley 540), pp 1–100 (late 15 cent); 2, Cotton Titus D.i, ff 1ª–84ª (ca 1400); 3, Trinity Dublin 246 (C.i.14), no 3 (ca 1600).

Editions. Forshall J, Remonstrance against Romish Corruptions in the Church Addressed to the People and Parliament of England in 1395, London 1851 (MS Cotton Titus D.i, partially collated with MS Bodley 540).

Compston H F B, The Thirty-Seven Conclusions of the Lollards, EHR 26.738 (English version, MS Cotton Titus D.i; Latin version, MS J J Green, pr owned 1897).

Date, Source, Authorship. Deanesly, Lollard Bible, pp 266, 282, 374, 379, and errata for p 380.

Workman, John Wyclif, 2.392.

[53] TWELVE CONCLUSIONS OF THE LOLLARDS.

MSS. 1, Camb Univ 1800 (Ii.iv.3), ff 8–109 (15 cent); 2, Trinity Hall Camb 17, ff 1ª–158ª (late 14 cent); 3, Bibliothèque Nationale, Bibliothèque du Roy 3381, no 1 (15 cent).

Editions. English version. Cronin H S, The Twelve Conclusions of the Lollards, EHR 22.292 (MS Trinity Hall Camb 17 collated with MSS Camb Univ Ii.iv.3, Bibliothèque Nationale, Bibl du Roy 3381).

Latin version. Shirley W W, Fasciculi Zizaniorum Magistri Johannis Wyclif cum tritico ascribed to Thomas Netter of Walden, Rolls Ser 5, London 1858, p 361 (MS Cotton Cleop E.2; trans J Foxe, Acts and Monuments, ed J Pratt, London 1843, 3.203).

Entire treatise. Cronin H S, Rogeri Dymmok liber contra duodecim errores Lollardorum, Wyclif Society, London 1922 (all MSS).

Date and Authorship. Deanesly, Lollard Bible, pp 257, 282, 374. Workman, John Wyclif, 2.390.

Literary Relations. Workman, John Wyclif, 2.140.

General References. Trevelyan G M, England in the Age of Wyclyffe, London 1899, p 374.

Gairdner J, Lollardy and the Reformation in England, London 1908, 1.43.

[54] SIXTEEN POINTS BROUGHT AGAINST THE LOLLARDS.

MS. Trinity Camb 333 (B 14 50), sect II, ff 30ᵇ–34ª (early 15 cent).

Edition. Deanesly, Lollard Bible, p 461.
Date and Authorship. Deanesly, Lollard Bible, pp 284, 461.

[55] THE COMPENDYOUS TREATISE (ON TRANSLATING THE BIBLE INTO ENGLISH).

MSS. Complete. 1, Trinity Camb 333 (B.14.50), sect II, ff 26ª–30ᵇ (early 15 cent). Incomplete. 2, Corp Christi Camb 100 (Misc Q), sect 1, no 3, pp 229–234 (16 cent); 3, Corp Christi Camb 298 (N 7), sect 4, ff 64ª–67ᵇ (16 cent); 4, Trinity Camb 24 (B.1.26), f 146ª (first 31 lines only; 14, 15 cent); 5, Cotton Vitell D.vii, ff 146ª–147ᵇ; 6, Harley 325; 7, Harley 425, ff 1ª–2ᵇ (16 cent); 8, Lambeth 594, ff 57ª–59ª (17 cent); 9, Morgan Libr 648, ff 142ª–143ᵇ (early 15 cent).
Editions. A compendious olde treatyse shewynge howe that we ought to haue ye scripture in Englysshe, Marlborow in . . . Hessen, Hans Luft 1530 (lost Worcester MS with new matter by Tindale?, STC no 3021, see also no 3022); rptd F Fry, A Compendious Olde Treatyse, 1863 (Athen Nov 20 1919, p 1260).
Foxe J, Actes and Monuments, London John Day 1563 (STC no 3021 and MS Harley 425, a transcription of the MS from Worcester Cathedral, later in Westminster Chapter Libr).
Deanesly, Lollard Bible, p 437 (MS Trinity Camb 333).

Bühler C F, A Lollard Tract on Translating the Bible into English, MÆ 7.167 (all MSS except Harley 325 and Corp Christi Camb 100).
Date and Authorship. Deanesly, Lollard Bible, pp 290, 437.
Bibliography (false colophon and related matters of sixteenth century printing). Steele R, Hans Luft of Marburg, Libr 3 2.113.
Steele R, Notes on English Books Printed Abroad 1525–48, Transactions Bibliographical Soc 11.189.
Kronenberg M E, Notes on English Printing in the Low Countries, Libr 4 9.153.
Bennett H S, English Books and Readers 1475–1557, Cambridge 1952, p 209.

[56] THE LOLLARD DISENDOWMENT BILL.

MSS. 1, Cotton Julius B.ii (15 cent); 2, Harley 3775, f 120ª (Sharpe's petition only, 15 cent).
Editions. Kingsford C L, Chronicles of London, Oxford 1905, pp 65, 295 (MSS Cotton Julius B.ii and Harley 3775).
Riley H T, Annales monasterii S Albani a Johanne Amundesham monacho, London 1870, Rolls Series 28, pt 5, 1.453 (Sharpe's petition only).
Authorship and Historical Milieu. Deanesly, Lollard Bible, p 297.
Workman, John Wyclif, 2.397, 420.

3. OTHER WYCLYFITE WRITINGS

[57] AN EXPOSITION OF THE PATER NOSTER.

MS. Corp Christi Camb 296 (C.6), pp 172–175 (late 14 cent).
Edition. Matthew, EETS 74.197.
See above [13], [14]; also MS Sidney Sussex Coll Camb 74 (Δ.4.12), ff 143ª–166ᵇ (15 cent).

[58] A TRACT ON THE AVE MARIA.

MSS. 1, Corp Christi Camb 296 (C.6), pp 175–178 (late 14 cent); 2, Sidney Sussex Coll Camb 74 (△.4.12), ff 189ᵇ–191ᵇ (15 cent).
Edition. Matthew, EETS 74.203 (Corp Christi MS collated with Sidney Sussex MS).
See above [15].

[59] SPECULUM DE ANTICHRISTO.

MSS. 1, Corp Christi Camb 296 (C.6), pp 103–106 (late 14 cent); 2, Trinity Dublin 244 (C.iii.12), ff 89ª–92ª (early 15 cent).

Edition. Matthew, EETS 74.108 (Corp Christi MS collated with Trinity Dublin MS).

[60] OF FEIGNED CONTEMPLATIVE LIFE.

MSS. 1, Corp Christi Camb 296 (C.6), pp 165–170, 298–300 (late 14 cent); 2, Trinity Dublin 244 (C.iii.12), ff 136ª–141ª (early 15 cent).
Editions. Matthew, EETS 74.187 (Corp Christi MS collated with Trinity Dublin MS).
Sisam K, 14 Cent Verse and Prose, London 1955, p 119 (Corp Christi MS).
Selections. Winn, John Wyclif, p 90.
Textual Notes. Boyd B, Wiclif and the Sarum Ordinal, MÆ 28.96.

[61] OF SERVANTS AND LORDS.

MSS. 1, Corp Christi Camb 296 (C.6), pp 190–203 (late 14 cent); 2, Trinity Dublin 244 (C.iii.12), ff 156ᵇ–167ᵇ (early 15 cent).

Edition. Matthew, EETS 74.226 (Corp Christi MS collated with Trinity Dublin MS).
Selections. Winn, John Wyclif, p 100.

[62] HOW SATAN AND HIS PRIESTS . . . CAST BY THREE CURSID HERESIES TO DESTROY ALL GOOD LIVING AND MAINTAIN ALL MANNER OF SIN.

MSS. 1, Corp Christi Camb 296 (C.6), pp 213–221 (late 14 cent); 2, Trinity Dublin 244 (C.iii.12), ff 177ᵇ–184ᵃ (early 15 cent).
Edition. Matthew, EETS 74.263 (Corp Christi MS collated with Trinity Dublin MS).

[63] THE RULE AND TESTAMENT OF ST FRANCIS.

MSS. 1, Bodl 3072 (Bodley 647), ff 71ᵃ–86ᵃ (late 14 cent); 2, Corp Christi Camb 296 (C.6), pp 29–39 (late 14 cent); 3, Trinity Dublin 244 (C.iii.12), ff 23ᵃ–32ᵃ (early 15 cent).
Edition. Matthew, EETS 74.39 (Corp Christi MS collated with the other two).

[64] SPECULUM VITÆ CHRISTIANÆ.

Authorship, Literary Relations. Arnold, Sel Wks, 3.vi.
Matthew, EETS 74.xlix.
Allen H E, The Speculum Vitae Addendum, PMLA 32.133.
See Lay Folks' Catechism under Works of Religious Instruction.

[65] TRANSLATION OF FOUR PSEUDO-AUGUSTINIAN TRACTS.

MSS. 1, Camb Univ 1918 (Ii.vi.39), ff 118–120 (tract 3 only, early 15 cent); 2, Camb Univ 1934 (Ii.vi.55), ff 1–76 (early 15 cent); 3, Harley 2330, ff 1ᵃ, 66ᵇ, 97ᵇ 100ᵇ (late 14, early 15 cent).
Method of Translation. Fristedt, Wycliffe Bible, Stockholm Stud Eng 4.43.

[66] FOUR CAMBRIDGE TRACTS.

MS. Camb Univ 1369 (Ff.vi.31), sect 3, ff 16ᵇ–41ᵇ (1380–1400).
Authorship. Deanesly, Lollard Bible, p 445.

[67] THE BRITISH MUSEUM TRACTS (THE TENISON WYCLYFITE TRACTS).

These tracts are dealt with separately in the Commentary ([68] to [76]) and below ([69], [73]).
MS. BM Addit 24202, ff 1ᵃ– (late 14 cent).
Catalogue of Additions to the Manuscripts in the British Museum 1854–75, London 1877, 2.22.

[68] See [67].

[69] A TREATISE OF MIRACLIS PLEYINGE (SERMON AGAINST MIRACLE PLAYS).

Editions. Rel Ant 2.42; rptd W C Hazlitt, Drama and Stage under the Tudor and Stuart Princes, Roxburghe Club 1869, p 73. AESpr 2.222.
Selections. Cook A S, Literary Middle English Reader, Boston 1913, p 278.
Modernizations. Benham A R, English Literature from Widsith to the Death of Chaucer, New Haven 1916, p 525.
Loomis R S and R Willard, Medieval English Verse and Prose, N Y 1948, p 289.
Textual Notes. Cook A S, The Chester Plays, Nation 100.599 (possible reference to the Chester Antichrist play).
Coffman G R, The Miracle Play in England —Nomenclature, PMLA 31.456 (the terms *pleyinge* and *miracle*).
Kolve V A, The Play Called Corpus Christi, Stanford 1966, p 17.
Literary Relations. Chambers, 2.102; Schofield, p 381.

[70–72] See [67].

[73] A TRETYS OF IMAGES.

Literary Relations. James M R, The Western Manuscripts in the Library of Trinity College Cambridge, Cambridge 1900, p 458 (MS Trinity Camb 333 (B 14 50), ff 34ᵃ–35ᵃ).

[74–76] See [67].

[77] OF THE LEAVEN OF PHARISEES.

[78] OF PRELATES.

[79] DE OBEDIENTIA PRELATORUM.

[80] OF CLERKS POSSESSIONERS.

[81] HOW THE OFFICE OF CURATES IS ORDAINED BY GOD.

[82] THE ORDER OF PRIESTHOOD.

[83] THREE THINGS DESTROY THE WORLD.

[84] HOW SATAN AND HIS CHILDREN TURN WORKS OF MERCY UPSIDE DOWN.

MSS. These 8 items are all found in 1, Corp Christi Camb 296 (C.6) (late 14 cent); 2, Trinity Dublin 244 (C.iii.12) (early 15 cent), as follows: [77] 1, pp 1–22; 2, ff 1ᵃ–17ᵃ; [78] 1, pp 65–103; 2, ff 54ᵇ–89ᵃ; [79] 1, pp 23–29; 2, ff 17ᵃ–23ᵃ; [80] 1, pp 107–123; 2, ff 92ᵃ–103ᵃ; [81] 1, pp 123–136; 2, ff 103ᵇ–116ᵃ; [82] 1, pp 136–144; 2, ff 116ᵃ–124ᵃ; [83] 1, pp 160–164; 2, ff 134ᵃ–

136ª (begins imperfect); [84] 1, pp 179–185; 2, ff 149ª–152ᵇ (begins imperfect).

Edition. These 8 items are all edited by Matthew, EETS 74 (the Corp Christi MS being collated with the Trinity Dublin MS), as follows: [77] p 1; [78] p 52; [79] p 28; [80] p 114; [81] p 141; [82] p 164; [83] p 180; [84] p 209.

Selections. Bennett H S, England from Chaucer to Caxton, London 1928, as follows: [82] p 174; [83] p 123; [84] p 188.

Authorship. Angl 30.261. For [77] see also Workman, John Wiclif, 1.330.

[85] THE CLERGY MAY NOT HOLD PROPERTY.

MSS. 1, Egerton 2820, ff 1–121 (ends imperfect, ca 1400); 2, Lambeth 551, ff 2ª–59ᵇ (15 cent).

Cat Add 1894–1899, London 1901, p 564 (MS Egerton 2820).

Edition. Matthew, EETS 74.359 (MS Lambeth 551).

Authorship. Angl 30.261.

[86] HOW RELIGIOUS MEN SHOULD KEEP CERTAIN ARTICLES (HOW MEN OF PRIVATE RELIGION SHOULD LOVE MORE THE GOSPEL).

MSS. 1, Corp Christi Camb 296 (C.6), pp 185–190 (late 14 cent); 2, Trinity Dublin 244 (C.iii.12), ff 152ᵇ–156ᵇ (early 15 cent).

Edition. Matthew, EETS 74.219 (Corpus Christi MS collated with Trinity Dublin MS).

[87] OF POOR PREACHING PRIESTS.

MS. Corp Christi Camb 296 (C.6), pp 234–238 (late 14 cent).

Edition. Matthew, EETS 74.275.

[88] WHY POOR PRIESTS HAVE NO BENEFICE.

MSS. 1, Corp Christi Camb 296 (C.6), pp 203–209 (late 14 cent); 2, Trinity Dublin 244 (C.iii.12), ff 167ᵇ–173ª (early 15 cent).

Edition. Matthew, EETS 74.244 (Corp Christi MS collated with Trinity Dublin MS).

[89] HOW ANTICHRIST AND HIS CLERKS TRAVAIL TO DESTROY HOLY WRIT.

MSS. 1, Corp Christi Camb 296 (C.6), pp 209–213 (late 14 cent); 2, Trinity Dublin 244 (C.iii.12), ff 173ª–177ᵇ (early 15 cent).

Edition. Matthew, EETS 74.254 (Corp Christi MS collated with Trinity Dublin MS).

[90] ON THE TWENTY-FIVE ARTICLES.

MS. Bodl 21847 (Douce 273), ff 1ª–37ª (late 14 cent).

Edition. Arnold, Sel Wks, 3.454.

Dialect and Authorship. Deanesly, Lollard Bible, p 462.

Workman, John Wyclif, 2.136, 388.

[91] ANICHRIST AND HIS MEYNEE.

MS. Trinity Dublin 245 (C.v.6), ff 117ª–127ª (early 15 cent).

Edition. Todd, Three Treatises, p cxiii.

Authorship. Arnold, Sel Wks, 1.vii.

[92] THE LAST AGE OF THE CHURCH.

MS. Trinity Dublin 244 (C.iii.12), ff 208ª–210ᵇ (early 15 cent).

Edition. Todd J H, The Last Age of the Church by John Wyclyffe, Dublin 1840.

Literary Relations. T[odd J H], Wycliffe on the Last Age of the Church, British Magazine 8.267, 402.

Forshall and Madden, Wycliffite Bible, 1.viii.

[93] AN APOLOGY FOR LOLLARD DOCTRINES.

MS. Trinity Dublin 245 (C.v.6), ff 164ª–218ª (early 15 cent).

Edition. Todd J H, An Apology for Lollard Doctrines, Camden Society 1842, p 20.

Language, Date, Literary Relations. Siebert G, Untersuchungen über An Apology for Lollard Doctrines, Charlottenburg 1905.

[94] THE LANTERNE OF LIȝT.

MS. Harley 2324, ff 1ᵇ–128ᵇ (15 cent).

Edition. Swinburn L M, The Lanterne of Liȝt, EETS 151.

Historical Milieu. Gairdner J, Lollardy and the Reformation in England, London 1908, 1.90.

Thomson J A F, The Later Lollards 1414–1520, Oxford 1965, p 140.

[95], [96] JACK UPLAND, UPLAND'S REJOINDER.

MSS. Jack Upland: 1, Harley 6641, ff 1–25 (15 cent); 2, Camb Univ Ff.vi.2, ff 71–80 (early 16 cent). Upland's Rejoinder: 1, Bodl Digby 41, margins 2–15 (mid 15 cent).

Editions. P L Heyworth, Jack Upland Friar Daw's Reply Upland's Rejoinder, Oxford 1968, pp 1 (manuscripts), 5 (printed editions), 29 (text), 19 (language), 28 (versification).

4. Accounts of Lollard Trials and Related Writings

[97] THE CONFESSION OF JOHN ASTON.

MSS. 1, Cotton Tib C.vii (15 cent); 2, Cotton Claud E.iii, no 7 (14 cent).
Edition. Lumby, Chronicon Knighton, 2.171 (both MSS).
Date and Circumstances. Dahmus, Prosecution of J W, p 116.
General Reference and Historical Milieu. Cheyney E P, The Recantation of the Early Lollards, AHR 4.423.
Workman, John Wyclif, 2.137, 335.

[98] THE CONFESSION OF NICHOLAS OF HEREFORD.

MSS. 1, Cotton Tib C.vii (15 cent); 2, Cotton Claud E.iii, no 7 (14 cent).
Edition. Lumby, Chronicon Knighton, 2.170 (both MSS).
Date and Circumstances. Dahmus, Prosecution of J W, p 128.
Historical Milieu. Workman, John Wyclif, 2.131, 336.

[99] DOCUMENTS CONNECTED WITH WILLIAM SWYNDERBY'S TRIAL.

Edition. Capes W W, Registrum Johannis Trefnant episcopi Herefordensis, London 1916, Canterbury and York Series 20.237, 252, 262, 271.
Literary Relations and Historical Milieu. Gairdner, Lollary, 1.28.
Deanesly, Lollard Bible, pp 276, 286.
McFarlane K B, John Wycliffe and the Beginnings of English Nonconformity, London 1952, pp 123, 129.

[100] WALTER BRUTE'S SUBMISSION.

Edition. Capes, Registrum Trefnant, Cant and York Ser 20.360.
Literary Relations and Historical Milieu. Gairdner, Lollardy, 1.37.
Deanesly, Lollard Bible, p 286.
McFarlane, J Wycliffe, p 135.

[101] THE EXAMINATION AND TESTAMENT OF MASTER WILLIAM THORPE.

MS. Latin version only. Vienna Nationalbibliotek 3936.
Allen W A R, p 190n.
Edition. The examination of master W Thorpe preste, [Antwerp? 1530?] (STC no 24045).
Modernizations. Christmas H, Select Works of John Bale, Parker Society, Cambridge 1849, p 60.
Pollard A W, Fifteenth Century Prose and Verse, Arber's English Garner, N Y 1903, p 97; rptd Loomis and Willard, ME Verse and Prose, p 422.
Literary Relations and Historical Milieu. Gairdner, Lollardy, 1.57.
Deanesly, Lollard Bible, pp 228, 284, 292, 353.
Allen H E, Lollards and English Art, TLS July 18 1929, p 576.
Smith H M, Lollardy, Church Quarterly Review 119.30.
Russell H G, Lollard Opposition to Oaths by Creatures, AHR 51.668.
McFarlane, J Wycliffe, p 153.
Aston M, Lollardy and the Reformation: Survival or Revival? History 49.155.
Literary Criticism. Bennett H S, Fifteenth-Century Secular Prose, RES 21.257.
Bennett H S, Chaucer and the Fifteenth Century, Oxford 1947, pp 182, 298.

[102] THE EXAMINATION OF THE HONOURABLE KNIGHT, SIR JOHN OLDCASTLE.

Edition. The examination of master W Thorpe preste The examination of Syr J Oldcastell [Antwerp? 1530?] (STC no 24045).
Modernization. Pollard, 15 Cent Prose and Verse, p 175.
Literary Relations and Historical Milieu. Bale J, A brefe chronycle concernynge the examinacyon of Syr J Oldcastell, [Antwerp?] 1544 (STC no 1276); modernization, Christmas, Sel Wks of Bale, p 1.
Waugh W T, Sir John Oldcastle, EHR 20.434, 637.
Gairdner, Lollardy, 1.68.
Reid E J B, Lollards at Colchester in 1414, EHR 29.101.
Deanesly, Lollard Bible, pp 240, 351.
Richardson H G, John Oldcastle in Hiding August-October 1417, EHR 55.432.
McFarlane, J Wycliffe, p 160.
History 49. 155, 164.
Thomson, Later Lollards, p 5.

[103] THE RECANTATION OF ROBERT SPARKE OF RECHE.

MS. Camb Univ Mm.i.41 (Baker 30), pp 70–75 (18 cent).

A Catalogue of the Manuscripts Preserved in the Library of the University of Cambridge, Cambridge 1867, 5.318.

Literary Relations and Historical Milieu.
Deanesly, Lollard Bible, p 363.
History 49.149.
Thomson, Later Lollards, pp 20, 239.
Parker G H W, The Morning Star: Wycliffe and the Dawn of the Reformation, Exeter 1965.

IV. TRANSLATIONS AND PARAPHRASES OF THE BIBLE, AND COMMENTARIES

by

Laurence Muir

GENERAL

PRINCIPAL STUDIES.

Forshall J and F Madden, The Holy Bible . . . by John Wycliffe and His Followers, Oxford 1840, 1.iii.

Paues A C, A 14 Century English Biblical Version, Cambridge 1902, p xxi (extended discussion of ME versions, not included in later edns).

Deanesly M, The Lollard Bible and Other Medieval Biblical Versions, Cambridge 1920, p 131 and passim (crit E W Watson, MLR 16.72; SP 18.364; J M Clark, SHR 18.52; M L Lee, YWES 1.44; for list of errata see H S Bennett, The Pastons and Their England, Cambridge 1922, following Index).

BRIEF AND SPECIAL-STUDIES.

Smyth M W, Biblical Quotations in ME Literature before 1350, YSE 41, p xix (crit B Fehr, AnglB 26.296).

Krapp G P, The Rise of English Literary Prose, New York 1915, p 218.

Powell M J, The Pauline Epistles, EETSES, London 1915, 116.lxvii (appraisal of some 14 century versions).

Butterworth C C, The Literary Lineage of the King James Bible 1340–1611, Phila 1941, pp 22, 245 (crit B J Roberts, MLR 38.142; F E Hutchinson, RES 19.215).

Ekwall E, The Manuscript Collections of the Late Professor Anna Paues, SN 21.25.

Muir A L, Some Observations on the Early English Psalters and the English Vocabulary, MLQ 9.273.

Craig HEL, pp 113, 126.

Fowler D C, John Trevisa and the English Bible, MP 58.81.

Hargreaves H, From Bede to Wyclif: Medieval English Bible Translations, JRLB 48.118.

HISTORIES OF THE ENGLISH BIBLE.

(A selected list.)

Westcott B F, A General View of the History of the English Bible, 3rd edn rvsd by W A Wright, London 1905, p 11.

Mombert J I, English Versions of the Bible, rvsd edn, London 1907, p 27.

Brown J, The History of the English Bible, Cambridge 1911, p 15.

Moulton W F, The History of the English Bible, 5th edn, London 1911, p 12.

Heaton W J, Our Own English Bible: the Manuscript Period, 2nd edn, London 1913, p 207 (comprehensive but undependable).

Price I M, The Ancestry of Our English Bible, 9th edn, New York 1934, p 214.

Craigie W A, The English Versions (to Wyclyf), in H W Robinson, The Bible in Its Ancient and English Versions, Oxford 1940, p 134.

Kenyon F, Our Bible and the Ancient Manuscripts, N Y 1940, p 199.

Pope H, English Versions of the Bible, St Louis and London 1952, pp 25, 59 (crit TLS Oct 2 1953, p 633).

Bruce F F, The English Bible: A History of Translations, N Y 1961, p 1.

CYCLOPEDIAS.

[Paues A C], Enc Brit, Bible English.

[Maas A J], Catholic Enc, Versions—English Versions.

RELATED MATTERS.

Paues A C, A 14 Century English Biblical Version, Cambridge 1904, p xxiv (on reading and use of ME versions; not included in 1902 edn).

Deanesly, Lollard Bible, passim (use of vernacular Bibles on Continent and in England).

Smalley B, The Study of the Bible in the Middle Ages, Oxford 1941 (on Biblical exposition and interpretation; crit M L W Laistner, Spec 17.146; A G Little, EHR 57.267).

Kaulen F, Geschichte der Vulgata, Mainz 1868; S Berger, Histoire de la Vulgate pendent les premiers siècles du moyen âge, Paris 1893; H Glunz, History of the Vulgate in England from Alcuin to Roger Bacon: Being an Inquiry into the Text of Some English Manuscripts of the Vulgate Gospels, Cambridge 1933. (On the Latin base.)

Berger S, La Bible française au moyen âge, Paris 1884 (see chaps on Latin versions, AN, and use of French Bibles).

Kretzmann P E, The Story of the German Bible, St Louis 1934 (crit N C Brooks, JEGP 34.442).

Paul Grundriss, 2^1.1116; A S Cook, Biblical Quotations in Old English Prose Writers, London 1898, p xiii; Baugh LHE, pp 60, 85, 101; G K Anderson, The Literature of the Anglo-Saxons, Princeton 1949, pp 112, 308, 349; CBEL, 1.73, 89, 95. (On Old English Biblical translations and paraphrases.)

MANUSCRIPTS; BIBLIOGRAPHY.

Brown Reg, vol 1; Brown-Robbins. (For pieces in verse.) CBEL, 1.173–266 passim, especially 187.

1. THE OLD TESTAMENT

[1] GENESIS AND EXODUS.

MS. Corp Christi Camb 444, ff 1ᵃ–81ᵃ (1300–50).

Brown-Robbins, no 2072.

EETS 7.vi (see below under Editions).

Edition. Morris R, The Story of Genesis and Exodus, rvsd edn, EETS 7, London 1873 (crit W Schumann, AnglA 6.1).

Selections. AESpr, 1.75.

Wülcker R P, Altenglisches Lesebuch, Halle 1874, 1.1.

Morris Spec, 1.153 (see E A Koch, Angl 25.321, for a correction).

Emerson O F, A ME Reader, N Y 1909, p 21.

Zupitza J, Alt- und mittelenglisches Übungsbuch, 11th edn, Leipzig 1915, p 118.

Brandl A and O Zippel, Mittelenglische Sprach- und Literaturproben, Berlin 1917, p 89.

Hall Selections, 1.197.

Notes on Text and Interpretation. Stratmann F H, EStn 2.120; 4.98; E Kölbing, EStn 3.273; 17.292; F Holthausen, EStn 16.429; Arch 90.143, 295; 107.386; 109.126; Angl 15.191; 22.141; W Strunk, MLN 26.50; J Caro, EStn 68.6; G Linke, Arch 171.210; F J Visser, EStn 30.13; C Sisam, RES ns 13.385; O Arngart, ESts 38.169; 45(Supplement).121.

Language and Versification. EETS 7.xiv.

Hall Selections, 2.626.

Wyld H C, Southeastern and Southeast Midland Dialects in ME, E&S 6.112 (see especially pp 124, 126).

Funke O, Zur Wortgeschichte der Französischen Elemente im Englischen, EStn 55.25.

Linke G, Der Wortschatz des me Epos Genesis und Exodus mit grammatischer Einleitung, Palaes 197 (crit F Holthausen, AnglB 47.42; H Marcus, Arch 169.295).

Date. EETS 7.xiii.

Hinckley H B, The Riddle of the Ormulum, PQ 14.193.

Authorship. Fritzsche A, Ist die ae Story of Genesis and Exodus das Werk eines Verfassers?, Angl 5.43.

Sources and Literary Relations. Dürrschmidt H, Die Sage von Kain in der mittelalterlichen Literatur Englands, diss München, Bayreuth 1919, p 86 (crit Arch 141.308).

D'Evelyn C, The ME Metrical Version of the Revelations of Methodius with a Study of the Influence of Methodius in ME Writings, PMLA 33.146.

Faverty F E, Legends of Joseph in Old and Middle English, PMLA 43.80 and passim.

Bibliography. CBEL, 1.187.

[2] STROPHIC VERSION OF OLD TESTAMENT PIECES.

MSS. 1, Bodl 3440 (Arch Selden supra 52), ff 2ᵃ–168ᵃ (1425–75); 2, Longleat 257, ff 119ᵃ–212ᵃ (1425–75; many leaves missing).

Brown-Robbins, no 944.

Kalén, Metrical Paraphrase, p iii (description and relationships; see below under Editions).

Kölbing E, MS 25 der Bibliothek des Marquis of Bath, EStn 10.203 (description and excerpts); Manly & Rickert, 1.339. (On MS Longleat 257.)

Editions. Kalén H, A ME Metrical Paraphrase of the Old Testament, Göteborgs Högskolas Årsskrift 28, Göteborg 1923 (6000 lines, ca one-third of poem; crit S B Liljegren, AnglB 34.227; G Stern, EStn 59.280).

Ohlander U, A ME Metrical Paraphrase of the Old Testament, vols 2, 3, 4, Stockholm and Gothenburg 1955, 1960, 1963 (Gothenburg Studies in English nos 5, 11, 16). (Continues and completes edition begun by Kalén; crit I Brunner, Word 12.476; T F Mustanoja, NM 62.234; A C Cawley, MLR 52.454; H Käsmann, Angl 75.245; 80.326.)

Selections. Horstmann C, Nachträge zu den Legenden: 8, De matre et VII pueris, Arch 79.447 (2 Maccabees 6, 7 from MS 2).

Heuser W, Die Alttestamentlichen Dichtungen des MS Seld Supra 52 der Bodleiana, Angl 31.1 (crit A C Paues, Angl 31.256).

Language and Date. Kalén, Metrical Paraphrase, p xxxv.

Oakden J P, Alliterative Poetry in ME (Part I), Manchester 1930, p 125.

Versification. Oakden, Alliterative Poetry, p 239.

Sources and Literary Relations. Kalén, Metrical Paraphrase, p clxxviii.

Ohlander U, OF Parallels to a ME Paraphrase of the Old Testament, in Contributions to English Syntax and Philology, ed F Behre (Gothenburg 1962), p 203.

Ohlander, A Middle English Metrical Paraphrase, 4.6.

Bibliography. CBEL, 1.190.

[3] IACOB AND IOSEP.

MSS. 1, Bodl 2306 (652), ff 1ᵃ–10ᵇ (1250–1300); 2, Penrose 10 (Delamere MS), f 3ᵃ (1450–60; fragment of 44 lines).

Brown-Robbins, no 4172.

BBA 17.98 (see below under *Editions*); Napier, Iacob and Iosep, p vii (see below under *Editions*). (On MS 1.)

De Ricci Census, p 1996; R H Robbins, The Speculum Misericordie, PMLA 54.936; Manly & Rickert, 1.108. (On MS 2.)

Editions. Heuser W, Das frühmittelenglische Josephlied (MS Bodl 652), BBA 17.83.

Napier A S, Iacob and Iosep: A ME Poem of the Thirteenth Century, Oxford 1916 (crit A C Paues, MLR 13.239; J W Bright, MLN 31.510; N&Q 12s 2.160).

Selections. Dickins and Wilson, 1951, p 110.

Kaiser R, Alt- und mittelenglische Anthologie, Berlin 1955, p 186.

Language. BBA 17.106; Napier, Iacob and Iosep, p xiv.

Date. BBA 17.113; Napier, Iacob and Iosep, p xxix.

Versification. BBA 17.113; Napier, Iacob and Iosep, p xxx.

Sources and Literary Relations. BBA 17.104.

Faverty F E, Legends of Joseph in Old and Middle English, PMLA 43.79.

Sherwin O, Art's Spring-Birth: The Ballad of Iacob and Iosep, SP 42.1.

General References. Gerould S Leg, p 223; Wilson EMEL, p 180; CBEL, 1.188.

[4] JOSEPH AND ASENATH.

MS. Huntington EL.26.A.13 (formerly Ellesmere), ff 121ᵃ–132ᵃ (1400–1450).

Brown-Robbins, no 367.

JEGP 9.225 (see below under *Editions*).

Edition. MacCracken H N, The Story of Asneth, JEGP 9.226.

Discussion. JEGP 9.224; PMLA 43.92 (includes brief summary).

Sources and Literary Relations. K[ohler K], Jewish Enc, see under Asenath.

Faverty F E, The Story of Joseph and Potiphar's Wife in Mediaeval Literature, HSNPL 13.118, 126 (1931).

[5] HISTORYE OF THE PATRIARKS.

MS. St. John's Camb 198 (G.31), 112 folios (15 cent).

Discussion. Daly S R, The Historye of the Patriarks, Ohio State Univ Abstr of Diss, 1950–51, 64.137 (transcription of Historye unpublished).

[6] LESSONS OF THE DIRIGE I.

MSS. 1, Bodl 21896 (Douce 322), ff 10ᵃ–15ᵃ (15 cent); 2, Camb Un Ff 2.38, begins f 6ᵃ (1475–1525); 3, Pepys 1584, begins f 48ᵃ (15 cent); 4, Trinity Camb 601 (R.3.21), begins f 38ᵃ (15 cent); 5, Harley 1706, begins f 11ᵃ (1475–1525).

Brown-Robbins, no 1854.

Editions. Yksh Wr, 2.380 (MS 5 with variant readings from MSS 1 and 2).

Kail J, Twenty-six Political and Other Poems, EETS, London 1904, 124.120 (MS 1), xxiii (language).

Authorship. EETS 124.xxii (rejects Rolle's authorship). Allen WAR, p 369 (supports Kail).

[7] LESSONS OF THE DIRIGE II.

MS. Bodl 1703 (Digby 102), ff 124ᵇ–127ᵇ (1425–75).

Brown-Robbins, no 251.

EETS 124.vii (see below under *Edition*).

Edition. Kail J, Twenty-six Political and

Other Poems, EETS, London 1904, 124.107, vii (language, date, authorship).

Discussion. Day M, The Wheatley Manuscript, EETS, London 1921, 155.xix (Dirige II is founded largely on Dirige III).

Bibliography. CBEL, 1.186 (under Primer).

[8] LESSONS OF THE DIRIGE III.

MS. BM Addit 39574 (Wheatley MS), ff 45ᵃ–51ᵃ (early 15 cent).

EETS 155.vii (see below under Editions).

Edition. Day M, The Wheatley Manuscript, EETS, London 1921, 155.59, xviii (relationship to Wyclyfite and Primer versions).

Bibliography. CBEL, 1.186 (under Primer).

[9] METRICAL LIFE OF JOB.

MS. Huntington HM 140 (formerly Phillipps 8299), ff 93ᵇ–96ᵇ (1450–75).

Brown-Robbins, no 2208.

Arch 126.365 (see below under *Editions*); Manly and Rickert, 1.433; Garmonsway and Raymo, Metrical Life, p 77 (see below under *Editions*).

Editions. MacCracken H N, Lydgatiana: 1. The Life of Holy Job, Arch 126.366.

Garmonsway G N and R R Raymo, A ME Metrical Life of Job, in Early English and Norse Studies, ed A Brown and P Foote, London 1963, p 89 (corrects inaccuracies of MacCracken's edn), p 78 (sources and literary relations), p 88 (literary criticism).

Authorship. Arch 126.365 (attributes the work to an anonymous imitator of Lydgate).

[10] SURTEES PSALTER.

MSS. 1, Bodl 2325 (425), ff 1ᵃ–66, 72ᵃ–93ᵃ (mid 14 cent; lacks Psalms 1–15); 2, Bodl 3027 (921), ff 1ᵃ–101 (mid 14 cent); 3, Corp Christi Camb 278, ff 1ᵃ–90ᵃ (early 14 cent); 4, Cotton Vesp D.vii, ff 1ᵃ–104 (late 13 cent); 5, Egerton 614, ff 2ᵃ–99 (late 13 cent); 6, Harley 1770, ff 158ᵃ–241 (late 13 cent).

Brown-Robbins, no 3103.

Stevenson, Early English Psalter, p viii; Yksh Wr, 2.129. (Brief notes on MSS 4, 5, 6; see below under *Editions*.)

Angl 29.393 (on MS 1; see below under *Discussion*).

Editions. Stevenson J, Anglo-Saxon and Early English Psalter, Surtees Soc, London 1843 and 1847, 2 vols (text of MS 4 with readings supplied from MSS 5 and 6).

Yksh Wr, 2.129 (MS 4 with variant readings from MSS 5 and 6).

Selections. AEspr, 1.1.266; Morris Spec, 2.23.

Wülcker R P, Altenglisches Lesebuch, Halle 1874, 1.9.

Kluge F, Mittelenglisches Lesebuch, Halle 1904, p 108.

Kaiser R, Alt- und mittelenglische Anthologie, Berlin 1955, p 52.

Modernization. Hodgson G E, The Sanity of Mysticism, London 1926, p 183 (Psalm 103 Vulgate, wrongly attributed to Rolle).

Textual Notes. Browne W H, Notes on Morris and Skeat's Specimens of Early English, MLN 7.268 (interpretation of Psalm 8, lines 19–20).

Discussion. Wende E, Überlieferung und Sprache der me Version des Psalters, diss Breslau 1884.

Heuser W, Eine vergessene Handschrift des Surteespsalter und die dort eingeschalteten me Gedichte, Angl 29.385 (MS 1; origin and date of translation).

Everett D, The ME Prose Psalter of Richard Rolle of Hampole, MLR 17.337 (relationship with Rolle's Psalter and hypothesis of common source in an earlier glossed Psalter).

Bibliography. CBEL, 1.189.

[11] MIDLAND PROSE PSALTER.

MSS. 1, Pepys 2498, pp 263–370 (1375–1425); 2, BM Addit 17376, ff 1–149 (1325–75); 3, Trinity Dublin 69 (A.4.4), ff 1–55 (1375–1425).

EETS 97.v (on MSS 2 and 3; see below under *Edition*).

Paues, 14 Century English Biblical Version, p lvi (see below under *Discussion*).

Paues A C, A 14 Century Version of the Ancren Riwle, EStn 30.344 (on discovery of Pepys 2498).

Edition. Bülbring K D, The Earliest Complete English Prose Psalter, EETS 97, London 1891 (MS 2 with variant readings from MS 3).

Selections. Kluge F, Mittelenglisches Lesebuch, Halle 1912, p 28.

Emerson O F, A ME Reader, N Y 1915, p 100.

Kaiser R, Alt- und mittelenglische Anthologie, Berlin 1955, p 51.

Language and Text. EETS 97.viii (rejects authorship of William of Shoreham).

Hirst T O, The Phonology of the London MS of the Earliest Complete English Prose Psalter, diss Bonn 1907.

Serjeantson M S, The Dialect of the Earliest Complete English Prose Psalter, ESts 6.177 (dialect Central Midlands).

Serjeantson M S, The Dialects of the West Midlands in ME, RES 3.331 (connects Psalter with Northants).

Reuter O, A Study of the French Words in

the Earliest Complete English Prose Psalter, Societas scientiarum Fennica, Commentationes humanarum litterarum, 9, no 4 (1938; shows source in a French version; crit JEGP 37.448).

Reuter O, Instances of "the which" in the Glossed Prose Psalter and Their Relation to the French Original, as Represented by the MS Bibl Nat fr 6260, NM 40.75.

Logeman H, The ME West Minster Prose Psalter, Ps 90.10, Arch 134.132; O F Emerson, The West Midland Prose Psalter 90.10, MP 16.53. (Notes on interpretation.)

Butterworth C C, The Literary Lineage of the King James Bible, Phila 1941, p 34 and passim, Appendix 1 (excerpts arranged in parallel with other versions).

Anderson F B, The Latin and ME Glosses in the Psalter of MS Addit 17376, Abstr of Diss Stanford Univ 1951–52, p 209 (on the variations from the Vulgate text due to glosses, additions, etc).

Discussion. EETS 97.xi (description of the glosses in the text).

Paues A C, A 14 Century English Biblical Version, Cambridge 1902, p lvi (not included in later edns).

Dodson S, The Glosses in the Earliest Complete English Prose Psalter, Texas SE 12.5.

General References. Deanesly M, The Lollard Bible and Other Medieval Biblical Versions, Cambridge 1920, p 146; CBEL, 1.189.

[12] ROLLE'S ENGLISH PSALTER AND COMMENTARY.

MSS. A. Original Version. 1, Bodl 1413 (Laud 448), 159 folios (15 cent); 2, Bodl 2487 (467), 172 folios (15 cent); 3, Bodl 3089 (953), 504 pages (early 15 cent); 4, Bodl 3693 (Hatton 12), 211 folios (late 14 cent; Ten Commandments on last 2 folios); 5, Bodl 9821 (Tanner 1), 278 folios (early 15 cent; imperfect at end); 6, Magdalen Oxf 52, ff 1ᵃ–281ᵇ (early 15 cent; ends imperfectly in Magnificat); 7, Univ Coll Oxf 56, ff 4ᵃ–265ᵃ (early 15 cent); 8, Univ Coll Oxf 64, ff 6ᵃ–137ᵇ (15 cent; ends in Canticle of Moses after verse 61); 9, Corp Christi Camb 387, 115 folios (15 cent); 10, Sidney Sussex Coll Camb 89 (△.5.3), 186 folios (14–15 cent); 11, Arundel 158, ff 10ᵃ–222 (14–15 cent; imperfect at end); 12, Harley 1806, ff 1ᵃ–170ᵇ (14 cent; slightly imperfect at beginning); 13, Aberdeen Univ 243, ff 1ᵃ–152ᵇ (14 cent); 14, Eton Coll 10, 170 folios (1375–1425); 15, Newcastle Cath (early 15 cent; earlier Psalms missing,

shows many gaps); 16, Worcester Cath F.158 (15 cent); 17, formerly Phillipps 8884 (early 15 cent; sold at Sotheby's March 27 1905, Lot 1923); 18, Vatican Reg 320, 196 folios (1400–1450?; contains no canticles); 19, Huntington HM 148 (formerly Ingilby MS), ff 23ᵃ–202ᵇ (early 15 cent).

B. Interpolated Versions, Lollard. 20, Bodl 1195 (Laud 321), 278 folios (early 15 cent; imperfect at end); 21, Bodl 2438 (288), 272 folios (1425–75); 22, Bodl 9836 (Tanner 16), 117 folios (early 15 cent; imperfect at end); 23, Univ Coll Oxf 74, ff 2ᵃ–43ᵇ (15 cent; begins at Psalm 22.4, ends at Psalm 41.3); 24, Trinity Camb 171 (B.5.25), 290 folios (1400–50); 25, Royal 18.D.i, 137 folios (1400–50; has only Psalms 1–79.13); 26, Lambeth 34, ff 1ᵃ–215ᵇ (1400–50; has only Psalms 1–89); 27, Lincoln Cath 92 (A.5.16), 322 folios (1450–1500).

C. Other Interpolated Versions. 28, Bodl 1151 (Laud 286), 163 folios (1400–50; contains metrical prologue); 29 Bodl 3085 (877), 168 folios (1400–50); 30, Merton Oxf 94 (15 cent; fragments of 1st Psalms bound into covers); 31, Royal 18.B.xxi, 32 folios (1525–75; has only Psalms 1–8.4); 32, Royal 18.C.xxvi, 167 folios (1400–50; has only Psalms 89–117).

D. Unclassified Manuscripts. 33, Bodl 21832 (Douce 258), (15 cent; has a few Psalms only, not consecutive, without the Latin); 34, BM Addit 40769, ff 1ᵃ–113ᵇ (1400–50; begins and ends imperfectly); 35, Trinity Dublin 71 (15 cent; slightly imperfect at end); 36, Worcester Cath F.166 (17 cent; abbreviated copy of MS 16); 37, Phillipps 3849, 61 folios (14 cent; no longer in Phillipps collection); 38, Wrest Park 6 (1375–1400; ends imperfectly; sold Sotheby's June 21 1922, Lot 639).

Allen WAR, p 171 (lists and classifies the 38 MSS).

Bramley, Psalter by Richard Rolle, p xvi (see below under *Edition*); Paues, 14 Century English Biblical Version, p xxxiv (see below under *Discussion*); MLR 17.217 (see below under *Discussion*). (Partial lists, descriptions, and classifications.)

Moore S and others, ME Dialect Characteristics and Dialect Boundaries, Essays and Studies in English and Comparative Literature, Ann Arbor 1935, pp 51, 54 (localization of MSS 3 and 10).

New MS of Rolle's Psalter, BQR 1.175 (note on MS 4.).

Christ K, Zu Richard Rolle von Hampole: Eine vatikanische Handschrift des Psalmenkommentars, Arch 136.35 (describes MS 18).

MLR 18.5 (on MS 19; see below under *Sources and Relationships*).

de Ricci Census, p 59.

Edition. Bramley H R, The Psalter or Psalms of David and Certain Canticles with a Translation and Exposition in English by Richard Rolle of Hampole, Oxford 1884 (based on MS 8 collated with MS 10; crit W Bernhardt, Angl 8.170; E Kölbing, EStn 10.112).

Selections. Allen H E, English Writings of Richard Rolle, Oxford 1931, p 1.

Butterworth C C, The Literary Lineage of the King James Bible, Phila 1941, p 34 and passim, Appendix 1 (excerpts arranged in parallel with other versions).

Date. Allen WAR, p 185.

Discussion. Middendorff H, Studien über Richard Rolle von Hampole unter besonderer Berücksichtigung seiner Psalmencommentare, Magdeburg 1888.

Paues A C, A 14 Century English Biblical Version, Cambridge 1902, p xxxi (not included in later edns).

Deanesly M, The Lollard Bible and Other Medieval Biblical Versions, Cambridge 1920, p 144 and see Index.

Everett D, Study of the ME Prose Psalter of Rolle of Hampole, thesis Univ of London 1920.

Everett D, The ME Prose Psalter of Richard Rolle of Hampole, MLR 17.217; 17.337; 18.381 (crit P G Thomas, YWES 3.36; 4.49).

Hodgson G E, The Sanity of Mysticism: a Study of Richard Rolle, London 1926, p 151 (mystical elements in Rolle's Commentary, studied in light of Augustine's Enarrationes).

Allen WAR, p 169 and see Index.

Wilson R M, Three Middle English Mystics, E&S, London 1956, 9.91 (on Rolle's prose style in the Psalter).

Sources and Relationships. Allen H E, The Authorship of the Prick of Conscience, RadMon 15.146 (degree of dependence on Peter Lombard and Rolle's originality).

MLR 17.337 (relationship to Northern Verse Psalter and a hypothetical early source).

Allen H E, Some 14 Century Borrowings from Ancren Riwle, MLR 18.7 (one brief borrowing).

Allen WAR, p 177 (relationship between Rolle's English and Latin Commentaries).

Dodson S, The Glosses in the Earliest Complete English Prose Psalter, Texas SE 12.5 (comparison of renderings).

Muir A L, The Influence of the Rolle and Wyclifite Psalters upon the Psalter of the Authorized Version, MLR 30.302.

Lollard Interpolations. Paues, 14 Century English Biblical Version, p xliii.

CHEL, 2.54.

Deanesly, Lollard Bible, p 304.

MLR 17.217; 18.381 (interpolations show a number of revisers and Lollard sources).

Workman H B, John Wyclif, Oxford 1926, 2.172.

Allen WAR, pp 173, 188.

Related Matters. Oakden J P, Alliterative Poetry in ME (Part 1), Manchester 1930, pp 107, 201; Brown-Robbins, no 3576. (On metrical prologue to Rolle's Psalter in MS 28.)

Hulme W H, Richard Rolle's Mending of Life, Western Reserve Univ Bull 21, no 4, p 25 (notice of Rolle's prose prologue to the Psalter in Worcester Cath MS F.172; erroneous in identifying accompanying Later Wyclifite Psalter as Rolle's; see crit, M Deanesly, MP 17.549).

Deanesly M, Vernacular Books in England in the 14th and 15th Centuries, MLR 15.352 (notes on bequests of Rolle's Psalters).

Allen, English Writings, p lviii (prose style).

Bibliography. CBEL, 1.193.

[13] CANTICLES I (In Rolle's Psalter with Commentary).

MSS. Everett D, The ME Prose Psalter of Richard Rolle of Hampole, MLR 17.223 (occurrence and distribution of Canticles in Rolle MSS).

Bramley, Psalter by Richard Rolle, p xx (see below under *Editions*).

Arnold, Select English Works, 3.4 (see below under *Editions*).

Editions. Bramley H R, The Psalter or Psalms of David by Richard Rolle of Hampole, Oxford 1884, p 494 (the customary first seven Canticles with commentary).

Arnold T, Select English Works of John Wyclif, Oxford 1871, 3.3 (the twelve Canticles as in interpolated copies).

Modernizations. Heseltine G C, Selected Works of Richard Rolle Hermit, London 1930, p 153.

Discussion. Arnold, Select English Works, 3.3.

Paues A C, A 14 Century English Biblical Version, Cambridge 1902, p lii (not included in later edns).

MLR 17.223 (the fullest discussion).

Allen WAR, p 170.

[14] CANTICLES II (In Midland Prose Psalter without Commentary).

MSS. See above under [11] Midland Prose Psalter.

Edition. Bülbring K, The Earliest Complete English Prose Psalter, EETS 97, London 1891 (twelve Canticles).

[15] JEROME'S ABBREVIATED PSALTER.

MSS. A. 1, Bodl 2315 (416), ff 144–151 (1375–1425); 2, Bodl 4050 (Hatton 111), ff 2–11 (late 14 cent). B. 3, Huntington HM 501, ff 117ᵃ–121ᵇ (15 cent).

de Ricci Census, p 71 (MS 3).

Discussion. Paues, 14 Century English Biblical Version, p lxiii (not included in later edns; gives excerpts from MSS 1 and 2).

Related Matters. Yksh Wr. 1.392 (the Latin text from Lincoln Cath MS 91, f 258ᵇ).

General References. Black W H, A Paraphrase of the Seven Penitential Psalms, PPS, London 1842, 7.xii.

Deanesly M, The Lollard Bible and Other Medieval Biblical Versions, Cambridge 1920, p 146.

[16] ST BERNARD'S EIGHT-VERSE PSALTER.

MS. Royal 17.A.xxvii, ff 86ᵃ–88ᵇ (early 15 cent).

Brown-Robbins, no 908.

Edition. Black, A Paraphrase, PPS 7.51, xi (discussion).

[17] PRIMER VERSION OF CERTAIN PSALMS.

MS. St John's Camb 192 (G.24), passim (late 14 cent).

Edition. Littlehales H, The Prymer or Prayer-Book of the Lay People in the Middle Ages, London 1892, vol 1, passim.

Discussion. Hargreaves H, The Middle English Primers and the Wycliffite Bible, MLR 51.215.

Butterworth C C, The English Primers (1529–45), Phila 1953, pp 5, 100.

[18] MAIDSTONE PENITENTIAL PSALMS.

MSS. A. Without Introductory Stanza. 1, Bodl 1703 (Digby 102), ff 128ᵃ–135 (early 15 cent); 2, Bodl 6922 (Ashmole 61), ff 108ᵃ–119 (early 15 cent); 3, Bodl 21806 (Douce 232), begins f 1ᵃ (early 15 cent); 4, Harley 3810, Part 1, begins f 17ᵃ (1450–1500); 5, Royal 17.C.xvii, begins f 83ᵃ (early 15 cent); 6, BM Addit 11306, begins f 1ᵃ (1375–1425; incomplete); 7, BM Addit

36523, begins f 71ᵇ (1425–50); 8, BM Addit 39574 (Wheatley MS), ff 15ᵇ–45ᵃ (early 15 cent); 9, Trinity Dublin 156 (D.4.8), begins f 135ᵇ (early 15 cent; ends imperfectly); 10, Longleat 30, begins f 28ᵃ (15 cent); 11, Porkington 20, begins f 95ᵃ (15 cent; ends imperfectly at line 944); 12, Huntington HM 142 (formerly Bement), ff 22ᵇ–41ᵇ (1425–75); 13, Morgan Libr 99, ff 92ᵃ–132ᵃ (early 15 cent).

B. With Introductory Stanza. 14, Bodl 668 (Laud 174), begins f 1ᵃ (15 cent); 15, Bodl 1619 (Digby 18), ff 38ᵃ–64ᵇ (early 15 cent); 16, Bodl 11272 (Rawlinson A 389), ff 13ᵃ–20 (early 15 cent); 17, Rylands Libr 45387 (formerly Quaritch Sale Cat 328, Item 584), begins f 113ᵃ (15 cent; a defective text); 18, St George's Chapel, Windsor, E.I.I., ff 32ᵇ–53 (14 cent); 19, Ireland-Blackburne, ff 1ᵃ–14ᵇ (1375–1425).

C. Fifty-First Psalm (Vulgate 50th) Independently. 20, Bodl 3938 (Vernon MS), f 113ᵇ (1380–1400; lines 1–22 missing); 21, Bodl 21715 (Douce 141), ff 145ᵇ–148ᵃ (1400–50); 22, Camb Univ Dd.1, ff 226ᵃ–228ᵃ (1400–50); 23, BM Addit 10036, ff 96ᵇ–100ᵇ (early 15 cent); 24, Advocates 19.3.1, ff 97, 87–89ᵃ (15 cent).

Brown-Robbins, nos 1961, 3755, 2157.

MLN 66.224 (on MSS of 51st Psalm; see below under *Editions*).

EETS 155.xii (on MS 8; see below under *Editions*).

Schulz H C, ME Texts from the Bement Manuscript, HLQ 3.443, 449 (on MS 12).

Bühler C F, The Kelmscott Edn of the Psalmi Penitentiales and Morgan MS 99, MLN 60.16 (crit G D Willcock, YWES 26.73).

EStn 10.215 (on MSS 2, 15, 16; see below under *Editions*).

Tyson M, Hand-List of the Collection of English Manuscripts in the John Rylands Library 1928, JRLB, 1929, 13.163 (on MS 17).

Dickins B, The Ireland-Blackburne Manuscript of the Seven Penitential Psalms, Leeds SE, 1934, 3.30.

JRLB, 1945, 29.20 (on MS 19).

Editions. The Seven Psalms. Adler M and M Kaluza, Ueber die Richard Rolle de Hampole zugeschriebene Paraphrase der sieben Busspsalmen, EStn 10.215 (based on MS 15 collated with MSS 2 and 16).

Ellis F S, Psalmi Penitentiales, Kelmscott Press 1894 (from MS 13).

Day M, The Wheatley Manuscript, EETS, London 1921, 155.19 (from MS 8).

The Fifty-First Psalm. Furnivall F J, Polit-

ical, Religious and Love Poems, rvsd edn,
EETS, London 1903, 15.279 (from MS 23).
Horstmann C, Minor Poems of the Vernon
MS (Part 1), EETS, London 1892, 98.12
(from MS 20 with readings supplied from
MS 15).
Kreuzer J R, Richard Maidstone's Version
of the Fifty-First Psalm, MLN 66.224 (from
MS 21).
Selections. Cook A S, A Literary ME Reader,
Boston 1915, p 403.
Text. Day, Wheatley Manuscript, p xiii.
Language. EStn 10.228; Day, Wheatley Man-
uscript, p xvi. (Dialect East Midland.)
Authorship. EStn 10.231; Day, Wheatley
Manuscript, p xvi; Allen WAR, p 371.
Versification. EStn 10.226; Day, Wheatley
Manuscript, p xv.
Discussion. Deanesly M, The Lollard Bible
and Other Medieval Biblical Versions,
Cambridge 1920, p 147 (purpose seen as a
religious jeux d'esprit).
Bibliography. CBEL, 1.189.

[19] BRAMPTON'S PENITENTIAL
PSALMS.

MSS. Version A. 1, Pepys 2030, begins f 1ᵃ
(16 cent; imperfect at beginning, lacks
stanzas 121–4); 2, Harley 1704, ff 13–17 (15
cent; contains stanzas 62–116); 3, Sloane
1853, ff 3–30 (early 15 cent).
Version B. 4, Camb Univ Ff.2.38, ff 28ᵃ–31ᵇ
(15 cent; imperfect at beginning); 5, Pepys
1584, begins f 28ᵃ (15 cent); 6, Trinity
Camb 600, pp 197–232 (15 cent).
Brown-Robbins, nos 1591, 355.
Black, A Paraphrase, p v (see below under
Editions).
Trad 7.359 (see below under *Editions*).
Manly & Rickert, 1.238 (MS 2).
Editions. Black W H, A Paraphrase of the
Seven Penitential Psalms, London 1842,
PPS 7 (from MS 3).
Kreuzer J R, Thomas Brampton's Metrical
Paraphrase of the Seven Penitential
Psalms, Trad 7.359 (from MSS 5 and 4,
with variants from all others).
Selections. Wülcker R P, Altenglisches Lese-
buch, Halle 1879, 2.1.
Text. Trad 7.359 (relationship and classifica-
tion of MSS).
Simpson G C, The Manuscript Texts of the
Seven Penitential Psalms by Thomas
Brampton, Univ of Virginia Abstr of Diss
1949, p 22.
Date and Authorship. Black, A Paraphrase,
p vi; Trad 7.364.
General References. Deanesly M, The Lol-

lard Bible and Other Medieval Biblical
Versions, Cambridge 1920, p 320; CBEL,
1.264.

[20] COMMENTARY ON THE PENI-
TENTIAL PSALMS.

MS. Camb Univ Kk.1.6, ff 1ᵃ–147ᵃ (15 cent).
Discussion. Deanesly, Lollard Bible, p 341.

[21] PARAPHRASE OF FIFTY-FIRST
PSALM (VULGATE 50TH) I.

MS. Advocates 19.2.1 (Auchinleck MS), f 280ᵃˑᵇ
(1320–40).
Brown-Robbins, no 1956.
Bliss A J, Notes on the Auchinleck Manu-
script, Spec 26.652.
Editions. Laing D, A Penniworth of Witte,
Edinburgh 1857, p 76.
Kölbing E, Psalm L, EStn 9.49 (crit F Holt-
hausen, Angl 13.359).

[22] PARAPHRASE OF FIFTY-FIRST
PSALM (VULGATE 50TH) II.

MS. BM Addit 31042, f 102ᵃ (1425–75; ends
imperfectly).
Brown-Robbins, no 990.

[23] COMMENTARY ON PSALMS 91, 92
(VULGATE 90, 91).

MSS. 1, Bodl 3938 (Vernon MS), ff 338ᵇ–342ᵃ
(1380–1400); 2, Camb Univ Dd.1.1, ff 228ᵃ–
247ᵃ (15 cent; ff 237–9 missing); 3, Camb
Univ Hh.1.11, ff 69ᵃ–99ᵃ (15 cent); 4, Harley 2397, ff 85ᵇ–94ᵃ (1375–1425; Psalm 92
only); 5, Lambeth 472, ff 223ᵇ–252ᵇ (15
cent).
Wallner, An Exposition, p ix (see below
under *Edition*).
Edition. Wallner B, An Exposition of Qui
Habitat and Bonum Est in English, Lund
Studies in English 23, 1954 p xxi (textual
study), p xlv (northern original), p xxxix
(attributes Psalm 91 to Hilton, 92 doubtful)
(crit B Cottle, RES ns 6.192; H M Flasdieck, Angl 73.97; T A Kirby, MLN 70.128;
M M Morgan, MÆ 24.69; J Russell-Smith,
ESts 37.267.)
Modernization. Jones D, Minor Works of
Walter Hilton, London 1929, pp xl, 115
(crit E Underhill, Spectator, June 8 1929,
p 905).
Discussion. Paues A C, A 14 Century Eng-
lish Biblical Version, Cambridge 1902, p
liv (not included in later edns).
Allen WAR, p 196.
Ekwall E, The MS Collections of Anna
Paues, SN 21.30 (notes on a projected edn).

[24] PARAPHRASE OF PSALM 130 (VULGATE 129).

MS. Harley 2252, f 23ª (16 cent).
Brown-Robbins, no 2522.

[25] PARAPHRASE OF ECCLESIASTES.

MS. Camb Univ Kk.1.5, ff 5ª–12ª (1450–1500).
Edition. Lumby J R, Ratis Raving and Other Moral and Religious Pieces, EETS, London 1870, 43.11, x (according to J A H Murray, Lowland Scottish of 15 cent), xi (probably middle 15 cent).
CBEL, 1.260.
See also *Paraphrases of Psalms 42, 53, 102, 129* (Vulgate) under John Lydgate.

[26] SUSANNA OR THE PISTEL OF SWETE SUSAN.

MSS. 1, Bodl 3938 (Vernon MS), f 317ª,ᵇ (1380–1400); 2, Cotton Calig A.ii, begins f 3ª (late 15 cent; stanzas 1–8 missing); 3, BM Addit 22283 (Simeon MS), begins f 125ᵇ (1375–1425); 4, Huntington HM 114 (formerly Phillipps 8252), ff 184ᵇ–190ᵇ (1375–1425); 5, Morgan Libr M818 (formerly Ingilby), ff 1ª–5ª (1425–75).
Brown-Robbins, no 3553.
Köster Huchown's Pistel, p 1 (see below under *Editions*).
Amours, Scottish Alliterative Poems, p xlvi (see below under *Editions*).
Editions. Laing D, Early Popular Poetry of Scotland, 1822; rvsd by W C Hazlitt, London 1895, 1.45 (from MS 1).
Horstmann C, Celestin und Susanna, Angl 1.85 (from MS 1).
Nachträge zu den Legenden, Arch 62.406 (from MS 2 with variant readings from 3).
Nachträge zu den Legenden, Arch 74.339 (from MS 4).
Köster H, Huchown's Pistel of Swete Susan: kritische Ausgabe, QF 76 (crit E Kölbing, EStn 23.85; F Holthausen, LZ 1896.231; K D Bülbring, Museum 4.219).
Amours F J, Scottish Alliterative Poems, PSTS 1891–92 (published 1897), p 172 (MS 1, with texts of other MSS in Appendix).
Furnivall F J, Minor Poems of the Vernon MS, Part 2, EETS, London 1901, 117.626.
Discussion. Brade G, Über Huchown's Pistel of Swete Susan, diss Breslau 1892; Köster, Huchown's Pistel, p 6; Amours, Scottish Alliterative Poems, p lxxxii. (Include treatment of text, authorship, language, versification.)
Oakden J P, Alliterative Poetry in ME (Part 1), Manchester 1930, pp 112, 217 (dialect and meter).

Gerould S Leg, pp 238, 368; S O Andrew, Huchoun's Works, RES 5.12 (crit D Everett, YWES 10.132); W Craigie, The Scottish Alliterative Poems, Proc of the British Acad (Gollancz Memorial Lecture 1942), 28.4. (Include discussion of problem of Huchown's identity and authorship.)
Textual Notes. Brown J T T, The Pistill of Susan, Athen 1902.2.254 (emendation for stanza 22, line 8).
Literary Relationships. Holthausen F, Zu Huchown's Pistel of swete Susan, AnglB 7.373 (on a Swedish version).
CBEL, 1.189.

[27] HUCHOWN DISCUSSION.

Major Studies and Summaries, Since 1877. (For earlier references, see MacCracken as below, PMLA 25.513.)
Trautmann M, Der Dichter Huchown und seine Werke, Angl 1.109.
Ten Brink, 3.50; Morley, 6.237.
Amours F J, Scottish Alliterative Poems, PSTS 1891–92 (published 1897), p li.
Gollancz I, Recent Theories concerning Huchown, a paper delivered before the London Philological Soc, Nov 3 1901 (summarized Athen 1901.2.705).
Neilson G, Huchown of the Awle Ryale: The Alliterative Poet, Glasgow 1902 (crit A Schröer, AnglB 17.16; T F Henderson, EStn 32.124; Athen 1902.2.677).
Brown J T T, Huchown of the Awle Ryale and His Poems, Glasgow 1902 (crit A Schröer, AnglB 17.16; T F Henderson, EStn 32.124).
Körting, no 103.
[Giles P], CHEL, 2.133.
MacCracken H N, Concerning Huchown, PMLA 25.507.
Jusserand J J, A Literary History of the English People, 3rd edn, N Y 1925–26, 1.526.
Andrew S O, Huchoun's Works, RES 5.12 (crit D Everett, YWES 10.132).
Oakden J P, Alliterative Poetry in ME (Part 2), Manchester 1935, p 78.
Sampson G, The Concise Cambridge History of English Literature, Cambridge 1941, p 73.
Huchown's Identity. Morley, 7.142.
Neilson G, Sir Hew of Eglintoun and Huchown off the Awle Ryale, Glasgow (Proc of the Philosophical Soc) 1900–01.
Bradley H, A New Theory as to Huchown, Athen 1900.2.826.
Neilson J A, Another New Theory as to Huchown, Athen 1901.1.19.
Anderson J, Athen 1901.1.19; H Bradley, The

Theories as to Huchown, Athen 1901.1.52; G Neilson, The Theories as to Huchown, Athen 1901.1.81; Huchown, Athen 1901.1.114; I Platt, Huchown, Athen 1901.1.145; The Etymological Pedigree of Huchown, Athen 1901.1.176; Huchown, Athen 1901.1.244. (Further etymological notes on Huchown's name.)

The Huchown Canon. See also Major Studies above.)

Brandes H, Die me Destruction of Troy und ihre Quelle, EStn 8.398.

M'Neill G P, Huchown of the Awle Ryale, Scottish Review 11.266.

Morley, 3.279.

Neilson G, Huchown's (?) Codex, Athen 1900.1.591, 751; Huchown: I. Troy, Titus, and Morte Arthure, Athen 1901.1.694.

Gollancz I, Huchown, Athen 1901.1.760; H Bradley, Huchown, Athen 1901.1.760. (Replies to Neilson in Athen 1901.1.694.)

Neilson G, Huchown II, the Parlement of the Thre Ages, Athen 1901.2.559; Crosslinks between Pearl and The Awntyrs of Arthure, SA 16.67; Early Literary Manuscripts, Scottish History and Life, Glasgow 1902, p 264.

Björkman E, Zur Huchown-Frage, EStn 48.171.

Inman A H, Morte Arthure and Hucheon, Athen 1916.423.

Gollancz I, Pearl, London 1921, p xxxvii.

Craigie W, The Scottish Alliterative Poems, Proc of the British Acad (Gollancz Memorial Lecture 1942), 28.4.

Matthews W, The Tragedy of Arthur, Berkeley 1960, pp 195, 213, and see Index (refutes Huchown's authorship of Morte Arthure).

Huchown and the Date of Wynnere and Wastoure. A Note on Wynnere and Wastoure, Athen 1901.2.157, 319 (signed by G N); I Gollancz, A Note on Wynnere and Wastoure, Athen 1901.2.254, 351 (replies to G N).

Bradley H, Athen 1903.1.498, 657, 816; G Neilson Athen 1903. 1.626, 689, 754, and 1903.2.221. (Wynnere and Wastoure controversy.)

Bibliography. Geddie W, A Bibliography of Middle Scots Poets, London 1912, p 40 (summarizes Huchown discussion); CBEL, 1.137.

2. The New Testament

[28] LA ESTORIE DEL EUANGELIE.

MSS. 1, Bodl 3938 (Vernon MS), f 105[a,b] (1380–1400; ends imperfectly); 2, Bodl 30236 (Addit C.38), ff 71[b]–82[a] (1400–50); 3, Dulwich Coll XXII, ff 81[b]–84[b] (1275–1325; ends imperfectly); 4, Sir Louis Sterling (formerly Clopton; Robinson Sale Cat 62, Item 1), ff 97[b]–114[b] (1400–25).

Brown-Robbins, no 3194.

PMLA 30.530 (on MSS 2 and 3; see below under *Editions*).

Mitchell A G, A Newly Discovered Manuscript of the C-Text of Piers Plowman, MLR 36.243 (on MS 4).

Editions. Horstmann C, La Estorie de Euangelie, EStn 8.254 (from MS 1).

Horstmann C, The Minor Poems of the Vernon MS (Part 1), EETS, London 1892, 98.1 (from MS 1).

Campbell G H, The ME Evangelie, PMLA 30.529 (from MSS 2 and 3), 532 (text, sources, language).

Related Matters. Brown B D, The Southern Passion, EETS, London 1927, 169.xiii (brief comparison).

[29] FALL AND PASSION.

MS. Harley 913, begins f 29[b] (1300–25).

Brown-Robbins, no 3366.

Seymour, Anglo-Irish Literature, p 63 (see below under *Discussion*).

Editions. Furinvall EEP, p 12; AESpr, 1.124; Kild Ged, p 106.

Discussion. Seymour St J D, Anglo-Irish Literature 1200–1582, Cambridge 1929, p 63 (summary of poem).

[30] STANZAIC LIFE OF CHRIST.

MSS. 1, Harley 2250, ff 1[a]–47[b] (15 cent; lines 1–623 missing); 2, Harley 3909, ff 1[a]–151[b] (1450–1500; lines 1–66 and several leaves at end missing); 3, BM Addit 38666, ff 5[a]–173[b] (1425–75; imperfect at end).

Brown-Robbins, no 1755.

EETS 166.x (see below under *Edition*).

Edition. Foster F A, A Stanzaic Life of Christ, EETS 166, London 1926, pp xv (language), xiv (versification, date, authorship) (crit E Ekwall, AnglB 39.12; R Spindler, EStn 63.90; K Brunner, Arch 155.103; H T M Buckhurst, RES 5.339; W van der

Gaff, ESts 10.182; H Flasdieck, LfGRP 49.19).

Selections. Kaiser R, Alt- und mittelenglische Anthologie, Berlin 1955, p 279.

Moore S and others, ME Dialect Characteristics and Dialect Boundaries, Essays and Studies in English and Comparative Literature, Ann Arbor 1935, p 52 (localization of MS 1, Cheshire 1450–1500).

Preger E, Das me Stanzaic Life of Christ, eine sprachgeschichtliche Untersuchung, diss München 1938.

Sources and Literary Relationships. EETS 166.xvii (especially relationship to Chester plays).

Heuser W and F A Foster, The Northern Passion Supplement, EETS, London 1930, 183.viii (comparison of Northern and Southern Passions and Stanzaic Life).

Wilson R H, The Stanzaic Life of Christ and the Chester Plays, SP 28.413.

Craig H, English Religious Drama of the Middle Ages, Oxford 1955, p 196 (influence on Chester plays).

CBEL, 1.190.

[31] PROSE LIFE OF CHRIST.

MS. Pepys 2498, pp 1–43 (1375–1425).

Hulme W H, The ME Harrowing of Hell, EETSES, London 1908, 100.xxxiv; Påhlsson J, The Recluse, diss Lund 1918, p i; EETS 157.xi (see below under *Edition*). (Descriptions of MS.)

Edition. Goates M, The Pepysian Gospel Harmony, EETS 157, London 1922, pp xix (dialect a Southern variety of East Midland), xv (evidence of French source) (crit E Ekwall, AnglB 35.193; MLR 19.257).

Discussion. Paues A C, A 14 Century English Biblical Version, Cambridge 1902, p lxv (with excerpts; not included in later edns).

CBEL, 1.190.

[32] METRICAL LIFE OF CHRIST.

MS. BM Addit 39996 (formerly Phillipps 9803), ff 1ª–51ᵇ (1440–50 ?).

Brown-Robbins, nos *72, 2365, 1579.

Edition. Stine S P, The Metrical Life of Christ: Edited from MS BM Addit 39996, DA 23.1010.

[33] PASSION OF OUR LORD.

MS. Jesus Oxf 29, Part 2, ff 144ª–155ª (1275–1325).

Brown-Robbins, no 1441.

Edition. Morris R, An Old English Miscellany, EETS, London 1872, 49.37.

Language. Wolderich W, Über die Sprache

und Heimat einiger frühme religiöser Gedichte des Jesus und Cotton MS, diss Halle 1909.

Versification. Menthel E, Zur Geschichte des Otfridischen Verses in Englischen Part 4, Angl 10.105.

CBEL, 1.188.

[34] WALTER KENNEDY'S PASSION OF CHRIST.

MS. Arundel 285, ff 6ª–46ᵇ (1500–1525).

Brown-Robbins, no 1040.

Bennett, Devotional Pieces, p i (see below under *Editions*).

Editions. Schipper J, The Poems of Walter Kennedy (Denkschriften der kaiserlichen Akademie der Wissenschaften 48), Vienna 1902, p 25.

Bennett J A W, Devotional Pieces in Verse and Prose from MS Arundel 285 and MS Harleian 6919, PSTS 3s no 23, Edinburgh 1955, pp 7, iv (discussion), 336 (textual notes).

Selections. Laing D, The Poems of W Dunbar, Edinburgh 1834, 2.97.

[35] FIFTEENTH-CENTURY PASSION OF CHRIST.

MSS. 1, Arundel 285, ff 159ᵇ–161ª (1500–25); 2, Univ of Edinb 205, f 86ᵇ (1477); 3, Advocates 1.1.6 (Bannatyne MS), ff 33ᵇ–34ª (1568).

Brown-Robbins, no 648.

Bennett, Devotional Pieces, p i (MS 1; see below under *Editions*).

Stevenson, PSTS 1s no 65, p xiv (MS 2; see below under *Editions*).

Ritchie W T, The Bannatyne Manuscript, STS 3s no 5, Edinburgh 1934, 1.xiii (MS 3).

Editions. Murdock J B, Bannatyne Manuscript (Hunterian Club), Glasgow, 1873–1901, p 89 (from MS 3).

Stevenson G, Pieces from the Makculloch and the Gray MSS, STS 1s no 65, Edinburgh 1918, p 10 (from MS 2).

Ritchie W T, The Bannatyne Manuscript, STS 2s no 22, Edinburgh 1928, 2.83 (from MS 3).

Brown RLxvC, p 131 (from MS 1).

Bennett J A W, Devotional Pieces in Verse and Prose from MS Arundel 285 and MS Harleian 6919, STS 3s no 23, Edinburgh 1955, pp 255 (from MS 1), xvi (discussion).

[36] RESURRECTION AND APPARITIONS.

MS. Bodl 6922 (Ashmole 61), ff 138ᵇ–144ᵇ (1475–1500).

Brown-Robbins, no 3980.

Edition. Horstmann C, Romanze von Christi Auferstehung, Arch 79.441.

[37] CLEMENT OF LLANTHONY'S HARMONY OF THE GOSPELS.

MSS. (A partial list.) 1, Bodl 2553 (771), ff 1ᵃ–79ᵇ (1375–1400); 2, Arundel 254, ff 2ᵃ–86ᵃ (end of 14 cent); 3, Harley 1862, ff 7ᵃ–77ᵇ (1375–1425); 4, Harley 6333, ff 1ᵃ–138ᵇ (1425–50); 5, Royal 17.C.xxxiii, ff 2ᵃ–225ᵃ (1375–1400); 6, Royal 17.D.viii, ff 1ᵃ–171ᵃ (end of 14 cent); 7, Plimpton 268 (formerly Phillipps 7157), ff 1–225 (1400–25; folios 88, 91, 92 missing).
Forshall and Madden, Holy Bible, 1.x (see below under *Edition of Prologues*).
de Ricci Census, 2.1802 (on MS 7).
Edition of Prologues. Forshall J and F Madden, The Holy Bible by John Wycliffe, Oxford 1850, 1.xiv, 44 (Prologues from MSS 2 and 4).
Discussion. Forshall and Madden, Holy Bible, 1.x.
Deanesly M, The Lollard Bible and Other Medieval Biblical Versions, Cambridge 1920, p 303.
See III [51].

[38] COMMENTARY ON THE FOUR GOSPELS.

MSS. 1, Bodl 1580 (Laud 235), ff 1ᵃ–264ᵇ (14 cent; Matthew); 2, Bodl 1913 (143), begins f 1 (1400–50; Luke); 3, Bodl 1933 (243), begins f 1 (1350–1400; Luke and John); 4, Camb Univ Kk.2.9, begins f 1 (15 cent; Luke); 5, Trinity Camb 36 (B.1.38), ff 1ᵃ–165ᵇ (14–15 cent; Matthew and John); 6, BM Addit 28026, begins f 1 (1400–25; Matthew); 7, BM Addit 41175 (Dillon MS), ff 1ᵇ–164ᵃ (1375–1425; Matthew and Mark).
Authorship. Forshall and Madden, Holy Bible, 1.viii (attributed to Wyclyf).
Arnold T, Select English Works of John Wyclif, Oxford 1869, 1.iv (attribution to Wyclyf questioned).
Jones E D, The Authenticity of Some English Works Ascribed to Wycliffe, Angl 30.262 (Wyclyf's authorship rejected).
Deanesly M, The Lollard Bible and Other Medieval Biblical Versions, Cambridge 1920, p 275; H B Workman, John Wyclif, Oxford 1926, 2.161, 163. (Attributed to Purvey.)
Fristedt S L, The Wycliffe Bible (Part 1), Stockholm Studies in English, 1953, 4.135 (authorship undeterminable).
Discussion. Deanesly, Lollard Bible, pp 275, 456.
Fristedt, Wycliffe Bible, pp 7, 123.

Hargreaves H, The Marginal Glosses to the Wycliffite New Testament, SN 33.296.

[39] COMMENTARY ON MATTHEW, MARK, AND LUKE.

MSS. 1, Camb Univ Ii.2.12, begins f 1 (1400–50; Matthew); 2, Corp Christi Camb 32, ff 1ᵃ–154ᵇ (1400–25; Mark and Luke); 3, Egerton 842, no 1 (14 cent; Matthew).
Powell M J, The Pauline Epistles, EETSES, London 1916, 116.ix (on MS 2).
Language. Ekwall E, The MS Collections of Anna Paues, SN 21.27.
Discussion. Forshall and Madden, Holy Bible, 1.ix.
Paues A C, A 14 Century English Biblical Version, Cambridge 1904, p xxvii (on their orthodoxy; found only in 1904 edn).
Deanesly, Lollard Bible, pp 279, 310.

[40] COMMENTARY ON THE BENEDICTUS.

MSS. 1, Lambeth 472, ff 252ᵇ–259ᵇ (15 cent); 2, Newcastle Public Libr, last 2 leaves (1400–25).
Allen WAR, p 197; Wallner B, An Exposition of Qui Habitat and Bonum Est, Lund Studies in English, 1954, 23.xx. (On MS 1.)
Fowler J T, Old Northern English MS Psalter, N&Q 5s 1.41 (on MS 2).
Modernizations. Jones D, Minor Works of Walter Hilton, London 1929, p 217 (crit D Everett, YWES 10.146; E Underhill, Spectator June 8 1929, p 905; Jones ascribes work to Hilton).
Discussion. Colledge E, The English Prose Benedictus: A 2nd MS, MÆ 8.45; Allen WAR, p 197 (gives beginning and ending).

[41] BODLEY VERSE PIECES.

MSS. 1, Bodl 2325 (425), begins f 66ᵇ and repeats beginning f 106ᵇ (1325–75); 2, Camb Univ Add 6860 (formerly Gurney), begins f 99ᵃ (contains only 1st piece, In Principio).
Brown-Robbins, nos 1474, 1536, 4022, 1535.
Edition. Heuser W, Cyclus von vier Christusgedichten, Angl 29.396.
Related Matters. Law R A, In Principio, PMLA 37.211 (liturgical use of Biblical passages from which Bodley Verse Pieces derived).
CBEL, 1.190.

[42] RAWLINSON STROPHIC PIECES.

MS. Bodl 14667 (Rawlinson F.175), f 132ᵃˑᵇ (1325–75).
Edition. Heuser W, With an O and an I (Part 1), Angl 27.283.

Language, Date, Versification. Oakden J P, Alliterative Poetry in ME, Manchester 1930, p 106 (Northern, early 14 cent), pp 201–16 passim (versification).

Related Matters. Heuser, Angl 27.300; K Hammerle, With an O and an I, Angl 54.293; T F Mustanoja, ME with an O and an I, NM 56.161; R L Greene, A Middle English Love Poem and the O-and-I Refrain-Phrase, MÆ 30.171. (Theories on the significance of the O-and-I refrain.)

CBEL, 1.189.

[43] BALLAD OF TWELFTH DAY.

MS. Trinity Camb 323 (B.14.39), f 35[a,b] (1225–75).

Brown-Robbins, no 4170.

Editions. Greg W W, A Ballad of Twelfth Day, MLR 8.64; 9.235 (text, and note on variant first draft in margins of MS).

Brown ELxiiiC, p 39 (see p 184 for note on composition in relation to Trinity Poem immediately following in MS, and see [50] below).

[44] WOMAN OF SAMARIA.

MS. Jesus Oxf 29, Part 2, ff 178[b]–179[b] (1275–1325).

Brown-Robbins, no 3704.

Editions. Morris R, An Old English Miscellany, EETS, London 1872, 49.84.

MacLean G E, An Old and Middle English Reader, N Y 1898, p 78 (after Morris).

Zupitza J, Alt- und mittelenglisches Übungsbuch, 11th edn, Vienna and Leipzig 1915, p 120.

CBEL, 1.188.

[45] PARABLE OF THE LABORERS.

MS. Harley 2253, ff 70[b]–71[a] (1300–50).

Brown-Robbins, no 2604.

Editions. Wright SLP, p 41; Böddeker, p 184; Morris Spec, 2.46; Brown ELxiiiC, p 143.

[46] A LERNYNG TO GOOD LEUYNGE.

MS. Bodl 1703 (Digby 102), ff 121[b]–123[a] (1425–75).

Brown-Robbins, no 2763.

Edition. Kail J, Twenty-Six Political and Other Poems, EETS, London 1904, 124.96.

[47] PROSE VERSION OF EPISTLES, ACTS, AND MATTHEW.

MSS. A. Complete. 1, Corp Christi Camb 434 (R.9), ff 1–159 (1425–50); 2, Selwyn Camb 108 L.1, ff 1[a]–139[a] (1375–1425). (Prologue, Catholic Epistles, Pauline Epistles, Acts, Matthew 1–6.)

B. Partial. 3, Bodl 21824 (Douce 250), ff 1[a]–80[b] (1375–1425; Catholic Epistles in different version from MSS 1 and 2, Matthew 1–6, Acts—all with gaps); 4, Camb Univ Dd.12.39, ff 16[a]–72[b] (1400–50; Acts); 5, Holkham Hall 672, ff 132[a]–161[b] (1400–25; Catholic and Pauline Epistles as in MSS 1 and 2).

Paues, 14 Century Version, 1904 edn, p xi; 1902 edn, p lxx (less complete). (See below under *Editions.*)

Editions. Paues A C, A 14 Century English Biblical Version, Cambridge 1902 (with introductory chapters on ME Biblical versions); Cambridge 1904 (without these chapters but with expanded introduction to this version), pp lxviii (on text), xxxiii (language), xxi (on the Vulgate texts used).

Selections. Brandl A and O Zippel, Mittelenglische Sprach-und Literaturproben, Berlin 1917, p 242 (from MS 2, Matthew 2:1–12 arranged parallel with Earlier and Later Wyclyfite).

Literary Relations. Butterworth C C, The Literary Lineage of the King James Bible, Phila 1941, pp 49, 339 (excerpts, labeled Sou and API, arranged in parallel with other versions).

Discussion. Deanesly M, The Lollard Bible and Other Medieval Biblical Versions, Cambridge 1920, p 304.

CBEL, 1.190.

[48] NORTHERN PAULINE EPISTLES.

MS. Corp Christi Camb 32, ff 155[a]–208[b] (1400–25).

EETSES 116.ix (see below under *Edition*).

Edition. Powell M J, The Pauline Epistles, EETSES 116, London 1916, pp lxvi, lxxvi (later 14 cent, dialect mainly NE Midland).

Literary Relations. EETSES 116.lxvii (comparison with contemporary versions).

Butterworth C C, The Literary Lineage of the King James Bible, Phila 1941, pp 50, 339 (excerpts, labeled Nor and PPE, arranged in parallel with other versions).

Discussion. Forshall J and F Madden, The Holy Bible by John Wycliffe, Oxford 1850, 1.xiii.

EETSES 116.xxxiv (English rendering, origin, purpose).

Deanesly, Lollard Bible, p 312.

CBEL, 1.190.

[49] APOCALYPSE AND COMMENTARY.

MSS. 1, Bodl 661 (Laud 33), begins f 96[b] (15 cent); 2, Bodl 1580 (Laud 235), begins f 265[a] (14 cent); 3, Rawlinson C.750, 51 folios (14 cent; lacks chap 1 and last 4 verses of last chap); 4, Magdalene Camb 5 (F.4.5), ff 40ᵃ–65ᵃ (15 cent); 5, Pepys 2498, pp 226ᵇ–263ᵇ (1375–1425); 6, St John's Camb 193 (G.25), ff 17ᵃ–67ᵃ (15 cent); 7, Trinity Camb 50 (B.2.7), begins f 2ᵇ (16 cent); 8, Fitzwilliam, McClean 133 (formerly Phillipps 7219 and 10170), ff 227ᵃ–252ᵃ (16 cent); 9, Harley 171, ff 2ᵃ–109ᵃ (1375–1400); 10, Harley 874, ff 2ᵃ–31ᵇ (1350–1400); 11, Harley 1203, ff 2ᵃ–119ᵃ (1375–1425); 12, Harley 3913, ff 112ᵃ–203ᵃ (1375–1425); 13, Royal 17.A.xxvi, ff 37ᵃ–106ᵇ (1400–25); 14, BM Addit 5901, begins f 248 (18 cent; late transcript); 15, Trinity Dublin 69 (A.4.4), no 2 (1375–1425); 16, Rylands 92 (R.4988; formerly Ashburnham 26), 46 folios (1375–1425); 17, Plimpton Addit 3, ff 203ᵃ–237ᵇ (1375–1425).

Paues, 14 Century Version, 1902 edn, p xxiv (lists 16 MSS and classifies 11 according to base; see below under *Discussion*).

Forshall and Madden, Holy Bible, 1.viii (lists 9 MSS).

Paues A C, A 14 Century Version of the Ancren Riwle, EStn 30.344 (notice of MS 5).

Tyson M, Handlist of English Manuscripts

in the John Rylands Library 1928, JRLB, 1929, 13.170 (on MS 16).

Ives S A, Corrigenda and Addenda to the Plimpton Manuscripts, Spec 17.46 (on MS 17).

Authorship. Arnold T, Select English Works of John Wyclif, Oxford 1869, 1.iv (rejects Wyclyffian authorship).

Discussion. Paues A C, A 14 Century English Biblical Version, Cambridge 1902, p xxi (origin, texts, excerpts); Cambridge 1904, p xxvii (brief reference only).

Deanesly, Lollard Bible, p 302.

Related Matters. Meyer P and L Delisle, L'Apocalypse en français au 13 siècle, Paris 1901 (edn of French version).

Paues, 14 Century Version, 1902 edn, p xvii (on the Anglo-Norman versions).

Berger S, La Bible française au moyen âge, Paris 1884, p 78 (discussion of the French Apocalypse).

General References. Forshall and Madden, Holy Bible, 1.vii (ascribed to Wyclyf).

Workman H B, John Wyclif, Oxford 1926, 2.161.

Ekwall E, The MS Collections of Anna Paues, SN 21.29 (notes on a projected edn).

3. THE OLD AND NEW TESTAMENTS

[50] TRINITY POEM ON BIBLICAL HISTORY.

MS. Trinity Camb 323 (B.14.39), ff 36ᵃ–42ᵃ (1225–75).

Brown-Robbins, no 1946.

EStn 70.221 (see below under *Edition*).

Edition. Brunner K, Zwei Gedichte aus der Handschrift Trinity College Cambridge 323 (B.14.39), EStn 70.221 (brief analysis of language and versification; crit M S Serjeantson, YWES 16.133).

Selection. Brown ELxiiiC, p 184.

[51] BIBLE SUMMARY.

MS. Trinity Oxf 93, ff 1–200 (1375–1425).

MÆ 29.115 (see below under *Selection*).

Selection. Ker N R, A ME Summary of the Bible, MÆ 29.117 (Ruth, IV Ezra 15–16, Psalm 34), 115 (discussion).

[52] WYCLYFITE VERSIONS.

MSS. Forshall and Madden, Holy Bible, p xxxix (lists and describes 170 MSS; see below under *Editions*).

Fristedt, Wycliffe Bible, p 14 and passim (study of the principal manuscripts; see

below under *Text and Versions*).

Skeat, Introd to reprint of Wyclyfite New Testament, p xiv (on MS Royal 1.C.viii; see below under *Editions*).

James M R, The Manuscripts of St. George's Chapel Windsor, Libr 4s 13.75 (MS IV.Z.i.5).

Deanesly M, MP 17.549; Allen WAR, p 176. (On Worcester Cath MS F.172.)

Tyson M, Handlist of English Manuscripts in the John Rylands Library 1928, JRLB, 1929, 13.152, nos 3, 75–84, 88, 89, 91.

de Ricci Census (see Index).

Allen WAR, p 176 (notice of Huntington MS HM 501, formerly Quaritch Cat 344, 1916, no 64).

Ives S A, Corrigenda and Addenda to the Plimpton MSS, Spec 17.64 (Plimpton Addit 3).

Menner R J, A Manuscript of the First Wyclifite Translation of the Bible, Yale Univ Library Gazette 19.37 (MS at Yale, formerly Phillipps 9302).

Lindberg, MS Bodley 959, 1.7, 2.7, 3.5, 4.16 (see below under *Editions*).

Editions. Forshall J and F Madden, The Holy Bible . . . by John Wycliffe and His

Followers, Oxford 1850, 4 vols (Early and Later Versions parallel).

Early Version. Chiswick Press edn, The New Testament in English Translated by John Wycliffe, London 1848.

Bosworth J and G Waring, The Gospels: Anglo-Saxon, Wycliffe and Tyndale Arranged in Parallel Columns, London 1865 (4th edn 1907).

Lindberg C, MS Bodley 959, Genesis-Baruch 3.20 in the Earlier Version of the Wycliffite Bible: vol 1, Genesis and Exodus; vol 2, Leviticus-Judges 7.13; vol 3, Judges 7.13–II Paralipomenon; vol 4, I Esdras-Ecclesiasticus 48.6; Stockholm 1959, 1961, 1963, 1965; Stockholm Studies in English 6, 8, 10, 13 (crit E Colledge, MLR 55.588, 58.457, 59.624; B Cottle, JEGP 59.565; J H Dahmus, Spec 35.309; H Hargreaves, RES 13.437, 16.105; M Seymour, MLR 61.484). (First four parts of a critical edition of the manuscript generally held to be the earliest copy extant of the Early Version.)

Later Version. Lewis J, The New Testament by John Wiclif, London 1731.

Baber H H, The New Testament by John Wiclif, London 1810.

[Bagster S], The English Hexapla: Exhibiting the Six Important English Translations of the New Testament Scriptures: Wiclif 1380, Tyndale 1534, Cranmer 1539, Genevan 1557, Anglo-Rhemish 1582, Authorized 1611, the Original Greek Text after Scholz, London 1841.

[Skeat W W], The New Testament in English according to the Version by John Wycliffe, Oxford 1879 (rptd from Forshall and Madden edn, with introd by Skeat).

[Skeat W W], The Books of Job, Psalms, Proverbs, Ecclesiastes, and the Song of Solomon according to the Wycliffite Version, Oxford 1881 (rptd from Forshall and Madden edn, with introd by Skeat).

[Law T G and J Hall], The New Testament in Scots, Being Purvey's Revision of Wycliffe's Version Turned into Scots by Murdoch Nisbet ca 1520, PSTS 46, Edinburgh 1901–1905, 3 vols (from MS in possession of Lord Amherst of Hackney).

Selections. AESpr, 2.243 (Gospel of John).

A New Biblia Pauperum, London 1877 (rptd as The Smaller Biblia Pauperum, London 1884; selections from New Testament, accompanying pictures).

Wülcker R P, Altenglisches Lesebuch, Halle 1879, 2.144 (Ecclesiastes, Mark 1–5).

Maskell W, Monumenta ritualia Ecclesiae Anglicanae, Oxford 1882, 3.1 and passim (52 Psalms, and passages from Job, Isaiah,

Luke, as contained in ME Primer; see the Primer or Lay Folks' Prayer Book under Works of Religious Instruction).

Littlehales H, The Primer, EETS 105 (Part 1), London 1895, passim (ME Primer as under Maskell above).

Morris Spec, 2.215 (Mark 1–6; Psalms 15, 24, 103).

Smith G G, Specimens of Middle Scots, Edinburgh 1902, p 101 (Matthew 9 and Luke 16 from Nisbet's version in Scots).

Kluge F, Mittelenglisches Lesebuch, Halle 1912, p 36 (Matthew 2–4 from MS Douce 369).

Cook A S, A Literary ME Reader, Boston 1915, p 398 (from Job, John, Revelation, Psalms).

Brandl A and O Zippel, Mittelenglische Sprach- und Literaturproben, Berlin 1917, p 242 (verses from Matthew and Luke with Early and Later Versions parallel).

Winn H E, Wyclif: Select English Writings, London 1929, p 6.

Patterson R F, Six Centuries of English Literature, London 1933, 1.57 (Mark 3, 4).

Butterworth C C, The Literary Lineage of the King James Bible, Phila 1941, pp 29, 250 (passages arranged parallel with other versions).

Modernizations. Warner C D, Library of the World's Best Literature, N Y 1897, 27.16238.

Loomis R S and R Willard, Medieval English Verse and Prose in Modernized Versions, N Y 1948, p 285.

Text and Versions. Carr J, Über das Verhältnis der Wiclifitischen und der Purvey'schen Bibelübersetzung zur Vulgata and zu Einander, diss Leipzig 1902.

Talbert E W, A Note on the Wyclifite Bible Translation, Texas SE 1940, p 29 (suggests an intermediate version).

Fristedt S L, The Wycliffe Bible (Part 1), Stockholm Studies in English 4, 1953 (crit A I Doyle, RES 7.194; S Potter, Moderna Språk, Stockholm 1956, no 1, p 113; H Käsmann, Angl 74.134; S B Liljegren, NM 57.84; P Bacquet, EA 11.48; A L Muir, Spec 33.402). (Re-examination of principal MSS, indicating more complex textual evolution than represented by traditional Early and Later Versions.)

Hargreaves H, The Latin Text of Purvey's Psalter, MÆ 24.73. (Shows translator's reliance on Lyra in LV and disagrees with Fristedt's theory of two revisions.)

Fristedt S L, The Authorship of the Lollard Bible, Stockholm Studies in Modern Philology 19.28 (crit M L Samuels, RES 9.231).

(Summary and amplification of the author's Wycliffe Bible, Part 1.)

Hargreaves H, An Intermediate Version of the Wycliffite Old Testament, SN 28.130. (New evidence from another MS pointing to an intermediate version.)

Hargreaves H, The ME Primers and the Wycliffite Bible, MLR 51.215. (Relevance of Biblical passages in the Primers to the study of Wyclyfite revisions.)

Lindberg C, MS Bodley 959, 1.7, 2.7, 3.5.

Fristedt S L, The Dating of the Earliest Manuscript of the Wyclifite Bible, Stockholm Studies in Modern Philology ns 1.79. (Disagrees with Lindberg's position that Bodl 959 was copied from the original MS of the EV.)

Hargreaves H, The Marginal Glosses to the Wycliffite New Testament, SN 33.285. (A stage in the revision of the EV.)

Lindsay T M, A Literary Relic of Scottish Lollardy, SHR 1.260; G G Smith, CHEL, 2.325; G G Smith, The Transition Period, London 1900, p 343. (The Middle Scots adaptation.)

Language. Koch C F, Historische Grammatik der englischen Sprache, Weimar 1863, 1.19.

Fischer H, Über die Sprache John Wycliffes, Halle 1880.

Gasner E, Beiträge zum Entwickelungsgang der neuenglischen Schriftsprache auf Grund der me Bibel-versionen, diss Göttingen 1891.

Grimm F, Der syntactische Gebrauch der Präpositionen bei John Wycliffe und John Purvey, diss Warburg 1891.

Skeat W W, On the Dialect of Wycliffe's Bible, TPSL 1895–98, p 212 (includes list of contents of Forshall and Madden's edn).

Dibelius W, John Capgrave und die englische Schriftsprache, Angl 23.153, 323, 429; 24.211, 269 (idiom of Wyclyfite Bible defined as learned Oxford language); K Brunner, Die englische Sprache, Halle 1950, 1.95 (takes issue with Dibelius).

Ortmann F J, Formen und Syntax des Verbs bei Wycliffe und Purvey, diss Berlin 1902 (crit P F van Dratt, EStn 34.79; J E Wülfing, LfGRP 1905.403; H Füchsel, Arch 116.397; W Franz, DLz 1903.1660).

Hollack E, Vergleichende Studien zu der Hereford-Wiclif'schen und Purvey'schen Bibelübersetzung und der lateinischen Vulgata, diss Leipzig 1903.

Thamm W, Das Relativpronomen in der Bibelübersetzung Wyclifs und Purveys, diss Berlin 1908.

Tucker E C, The Later Version of the Wycliffite Epistle to the Romans Compared with the Latin Original: A Study of Wycliffite English, YSE 49, 1914.

Kox M, Studien zur Syntax des Artikels im englischen auf Grund der Bibelversionen (Neues Testament) John Wycliffes und John Purveys, diss Kiel 1922, Summary Kiel Philological Diss, vol 8.

Goss J H, Semasiological Notes on the Wycliffite Hebrews, Pittsburg M A Thesis, Abstracts of Theses, Univ of Pittsburg Bull 1932, p 387.

Lindberg, MS Bodley 959, 1.8, 2.8, 3.6, 4.6.

Date. Forshall and Madden, Holy Bible, 1.xxi.

Deanesly M, The Lollard Bible and Other Medieval Biblical Versions, Cambridge 1920, pp 262, 266.

Workman H B, John Wyclif, Oxford 1926, 2.162.

Fristedt, Wycliffe Bible, p 145.

Lindberg, MS Bodley 959, 1.31; 2.13, 24; 3.16, 33; 4.15, 31.

Fristedt, The Dating of the Earliest Manuscript, p 80.

Authorship. Forshall and Madden, Holy Bible, 1.xvi.

Matthew F D, The Authorship of the Wycliffite Bible, EHR 10.91 (refutes Gasquet's theory published under later date, see below).

Gasquet F A, The Old English Bible, London 1897, p 102 (theory that extant versions are not Wycliffite but a version authorized by the Church).

Pollard A W, 15 Century Prose and Verse, London 1903, p xx (suggests Trevisa as author of LV).

Jones E D, The Authenticity of Some English Works Ascribed to Wycliffe, Angl 30.262.

Deanesly, Lollard Bible, chaps 9, 10.

Workman, John Wyclif, 2.160.

Fristedt, Wycliffe Bible, pp 1, 103 and passim.

McFarlane K B, John Wycliffe and the Beginnings of English Nonconformity, N Y 1953, pp 118, 149.

Fristedt, Authorship of Lollard Bible, passim.

Lindberg, MS Bodley 959, 1.23, 2.30, 3.32, 4.30.

Fowler D C, John Trevisa and the English Bible, MP 58.81.

Literary Relations and Influence. Maas M, Die Wycliff'sche Bibelübersetzung im Vergleich mit der recipirten Englischen aus dem Angange des 17 Jahrhunderts, Arch 29.221.

Wager C H A, Pecock's Repressor and the

Wiclif Bible, MLN 9.193 (Pecock's use of Wyclyfite).

Paues A C, A 14 Century English Biblical Version, Cambridge 1904, p lxxii (comparison with Wyclyfite versions; not in earlier edn).

Smith H, Syntax der Wycliffe-Purveyschen Übersetzung und der Authorized Version der vier Evangelien, Angl 30.413.

Moulton W F, History of the English Bible, 5th edn, London 1911, p 91 (influence on Tyndale).

Smyth M W, Biblical Quotations in ME Literature before 1350, YSE 41, p xxi.

Westcott B F, A General View of the History of the English Bible, 3rd edn rvsd by W A Wright, N Y 1927, pp 11, 287 (opposes view of direct influence on Tyndale).

Gray M M, The Prose of Wyclif's Bible, London Quarterly & Holborn Review 159.354 (Wyclyfite's importance in establishing English Biblical style).

Muir A L, The Influence of the Rolle and Wyclifite Psalters upon the Psalter of the Authorized Version, MLR 30.302.

Cammack M M, John Wyclif and the English Bible, N Y 1938.

Chambers R W, Man's Unconquerable Mind, London 1939, p 192 (Wyclyfite influence on Tyndale negligible).

Butterworth, Literary Lineage of King James Bible, p 39 and passim.

Butterworth C C, The English Primers 1529–1545, Phila 1953, pp 100, 291, and see Index.

Special Treatments. Förster E, Wiklif als Bibelübersetzer, Zeitschrift für Kirchengeschichte 12.494.

Paues, 14 Century Version, 1902 edn, pp xxiii, xxx (not in later edn).

Krapp G P, The Rise of English Literary Prose, N Y 1915, p 224.

Deanesly, Lollard Bible, chaps 9–11 and passim (extended study of the purpose, prohibitions, and use of the Wyclyfite Bibles).

Workman, John Wyclif, 2.149.

Chambers R W, On the Continuity of English Prose, from Introd to EETS, London 1931, 186.cvii (view that quality of prose in Wyclyfite is undistinguished).

Brooks N C, An Ingolstadt Corpus Christi Procession and the Biblia Pauperum, JEGP 35.1 (describes Biblia Pauperum).

Glunz H H, Die Literarästhetik des europäischen Mittelalters, Bochum-Langendreer 1937, p 260 (on the intent behind the vernacular translations).

Deanesly M, The Significance of the Lollard Bible (Ethel M Wood Lecture, Univ of London), London 1951.

Hargreaves H, From Bede to Wyclif: Medieval English Bible Translations, JRLB 48.122 and passim (on the qualities of the Later Wyclifite).

Bibliography. CHEL, 2.499; CBEL, 1.204; Fristedt, Wycliffe Bible, p x.

4. THE SOUTHERN TEMPORALE

[53] THE SOUTHERN TEMPORALE.
MSS. See MSS of South English Legendary, under Legends.

AELeg 1881, p li; C Horstmann, The Early South-English Legendary, EETS, London 1887, 87.ix, xxiv; M E Wells, The Structural Development of the South English Legendary, JEGP 41.334. (On Temporale MSS in particular.)

Sources. Wells M E, The South English Legendary in Its Relation to the Legenda Aurea, PMLA 51.337 (crit E Fischer, AnglB 49.237).

Boyd B, New Light on the South English Legendary, Texas SE 37.187.

Discussion. Horstmann C, Die Legenden des MS Laud 108, Arch 49.395 (summary of some Temporale material).

AELeg 1881, p xliv; EETS 87.vii; Gerould S Leg, p 163; JEGP 41.327 (evolution of the Temporale).

General References. Brandl, § 71.

Wordsworth C and H Littlehales, The Old Service-Books of the English Church, London 1904, pp 90, 136 and passim.

Wilson, EMEL, p 184; CBEL, 1.173–6 passim.

I. Old Testament

[54] OLD TESTAMENT HISTORY.
MSS. Brown-Robbins, no 3973. 9 MSS. Add: 10, Winchester 33ᵃ, ff 1ᵃ–12ᵃ (15 cent).

Selections. Furnivall F J, Adam Davy's Five Dreams, EETS, London 1878, 69.82, 96 (excerpts, from Bodl 1414, ff 69ᵇ–70ᵇ and 69ᵃ).

Discussion. Wells M E, The Structural Development of the South English Legendary, JEGP 41.334.

II. New Testament

[55] LONG LIFE OF CHRIST.

MSS. Brown-Robbins, nos 3452, *15. 10 MSS.
Editions. Turnbull W B D D, Legendae catholicae, Edinburgh 1844, p 125 (a fragment, lines 1–309, in Advocates 19.2.1).
Horstmann C, Leben Jesu, ein Fragment, Münster 1873 (901 lines from Bodl 1486).
Discussion. JEGP 41.331.

[56] SHORT LIFE OF CHRIST.

MS. Egerton 1993, begins f 21ª (1350–1400).
Brown-Robbins, no 2643.
Discussion. JEGP 41.333.

[57] CONCEPCIO MARIE.

MSS. 1, Bodl 1414 (Laud 622), f 71ª (1375–1425; Prologue only); 2, Bodl 2567 (779), ff 22ª–23ᵇ, 271ᵇ–272ᵇ (1425–75; verses 495–648, 153–274); 3, Bodl 6924 (Ashmole 43), begins f 208ᵇ (1325–50); 4, Pepys 2344, begins p 353 (1300–25); 5, Trinity Camb 605 (R.3.25), begins f 261ᵇ (1400–50; a unique version); 6, Egerton 1993, begins f 27ª (1350–1400).
Brown-Robbins, nos 38, 2632 (the 80-line prologue).
Editions. AELeg 1875, p 64 (from Bodl 6924 and Egerton 1993).
Furnivall F J, Adam Davy's Five Dreams, EETS, London 1878, 69.93 (Prologue only from Bodl 1414).
Selections. Brandl A and O Zippel, ME Literature, 2nd edn, N Y 1949, p 92 (Marriage of the Virgin from Bodl 6924 and Egerton 1993); p 96 (Birth of Jesus from Egerton 1993).

Sources. Holthausen F, Zu alt- und mittelenglischen Dichtungen, Angl 14.314.
Discussion. JEGP 41.330.

[58] SOUTHERN PASSION.

MSS. Brown-Robbins, no 483. 12 MSS.
EETS 169.xvii (see below under *Edition*).
Edition. Brown B D, The Southern Passion, EETS 169, London 1927 (from Pepys 2344 with variant readings from Harley 2277; crit C Brett, MLR 23.354; F Wild, LfGRP 52.430), pp xxxi (language), lii (sources).
Selections. Morris R, Cursor Mundi, EETS, London 1876, 62.956 (excerpt of 163 lines inserted in Cotton MS of Cursor Mundi).
Brown C, The Cursor Mundi and the Southern Passion, MLN 26.15 (135 lines from Harley 2277, ff 12ª–14ª, as basis of insertion in Cursor Mundi).
Discussion. EETS 169.vii; JEGP 41.327.
Heuser W and F A Foster, The Northern Passion (Supplement), EETS, London 1930, 183.ix (compares Northern and Southern Passions).

[59] EUANGELIUM IN PRINCIPIO.

MSS. 1, Bodl 2567 (779), begins f 23ᵇ (1425–75; lacks Prologue of 26 lines); 2, Corp Christi Oxf 431, begins f 1ª (before 1350); 3, Pepys 2344, pp 93–97 (1325–50).
Brown-Robbins, no 276.
Related Matters. Law R A, In Principio, PMLA 37.211 (liturgical use of John 1.1–14).

III. Movable Feasts

[60] SEPTUAGESIMA.

MSS. Brown-Robbins, no 791. 18 MSS. Add: 19, Winchester 33ª, f 33ª (15 cent).
Edition. D'Evelyn C and A J Mill, The South English Legendary, vol 1, EETS, London 1956, 235.128 (from Corp Christi Camb 145).

[61] LENT (QUADRAGESIMA).

MSS. Brown-Robbins, no 1859. 19 MSS. Add: 20, Winchester 33ª, ff 33ª–35ᵇ (15 cent).
Edition. EETS 235.128.

[62] EASTER.

MSS. Brown-Robbins, nos 1546 (12 MSS), 2105 (6 MSS), 3384 (12 MSS). Add under no 3384: 13, Bodl 9837 (Tanner 17), f 69ᵇ

(early 15 cent); 14, Winchester 33ª, ff 35ᵇ–36ᵇ (15 cent).
Editions. Brown B D, The Southern Passion, 75); 2, Egerton 2810, begins f 176ᵇ (14 cent).
Brown-Robbins, no 3380.
Edition. Horstmann C, Des MS Bodl 779 jüngere Zusatzlegenden zur südlichen Legendensammlung, Arch 82.307.
EETS, London 1927, 169.63 (from Pepys 2344).
EETS 235.134.

[63] LETANIA MINOR (ROGATION).

MSS. Brown-Robbins, no 1911. 18 MSS. Add: 19, Winchester 33ª, ff 36ª–37ª (15 cent).
Edition. EETS 235.160.

[64] ASCENSION.

MSS. Brown-Robbins, nos 409, 4267. 11 MSS.
Edition. EETS 169.86.

[65] WHITSUNDAY.

MSS. Brown-Robbins, no 443. 11 MSS.
Edition. EETS 169.90.

]66[CORPUS CHRISTI.

MSS. 1, Bodl 2567 (779), begins f 172ᵇ (1425–
   75); 2, Egerton 2810, begins f 176ᵇ (14 cent).
Brown-Robbins, no 3380.
Edition. Horstmann C, Des MS Bodl 779
   jüngere Zusatzlegenden zur südlichen
   Legendensammlung, Arch 82.307.

IV. Immovable Feasts

[67] CIRCUMCISION (YEAR'S DAY).

MSS. Brown-Robbins, no 4266. 17 MSS. Add:
18, Bodl 1486 (Laud 108), f 88ᵇ (1275–
1325); 19, Winchester 33ª, f 49ª·ᵇ (15 cent).
Editions. D'Evelyn C and A J Mill, The
South English Legendary, vol 1, EETS,
London 1956, 235.3 (from Corp Christi
Camb 145).
Horstmann C, The Early South-English Leg-
endary, EETS, London 1887, 87.177 (from
Bodl 1486, in a different version from the
above).

[68] EPIPHANY (TWELFTH DAY).

MSS. Brown-Robbins, no 3813. 16 MSS. Add:
17, Bodl 1486 (Laud 108), f 88ᵇ (1275–
1325); 18, Winchester 33ª, f 49ᵇ (15 cent).
Editions. EETS 235.4.
EETS 87.178 (from Bodl 1486, in a different
version from the above).

[69] ANNUNCIATION.

MSS. Brown-Robbins, no 2989. 17 MSS.
Edition. EETS 235.127.

[70] LETANIA MAJOR (ST. MARK'S
DAY).

MSS. Brown-Robbins, no 1911. 18 MSS. Add:
19, Winchester 33ª, ff 36ᵇ–37ª (15 cent).
Edition. EETS 235.160.

[71] ALL SAINTS.

MSS. Brown-Robbins, no 184. 14 MSS.
Editions. EETS 87.418.
D'Evelyn C and A J Mill, The South English
Legendary, vol 2, EETS, London 1956,
236.460.

[72] ALL SOULS.

MSS. Brown-Robbins, no 201. 13 MSS.
Editions. EETS 87.420; EETS 236.463.

V. SAINTS' LEGENDS

by

Charlotte D'Evelyn and Frances A. Foster

LIST OF BACKGROUND BOOKS AND ABBREVIATED TITLES
Starred items are expanded in the complete Table of Abbreviations

Acta SS	Acta sanctorum Bollandiana, vol 1, Antwerp 1643 . . . (in progress)
*AELeg 1875	
*AELeg 1878	
*AELeg 1881	
*AESpr	
	Aigrain R, L'hagiographie: ses sources, ses méthodes, son histoire, Paris 1953
AnBol	Analecta Bollandiana, Paris, Brussels 1882 . . .
	Baring-Gould S, The Lives of the Saints, rvsd edn, 16 vols, Edinburgh 1914
*Brown-Robbins	(See also Ringler W below)
*Brown Reg	
	Butler A Lives of the Saints, see Thurston H and D Attwater below
Butler LA	Butler P, Legenda aurea—Légende dorée—Golden Legend . . . , Baltimore 1899; OP Books, Ann Arbor, Michigan 1960
Caxton GL	Caxton W, trans and ed, Legenda aurea, Westminster 1483 (STC, no 24873); see also Temple
Caxton VP	Caxton W, trans, Vitas patrum, Wynkyn de Worde, Westminster 1495 (STC, no 14507)
*CBEL	1.169, 173, 261, 266
*CBEL	Sup 119, 148, 150
	Delehaye H, Étude sur le légendier romain. Les Saints de Novembre et de Décembre, Subsidia hagiographica 23, Brussels 1936
	———————————, Les légendes hagiographiques,

	Subsidia hagiographica 18a, 4th edn, Brussels 1955
Dibdin Typo Antiq	Dibdin T F, Typographical Antiquities, 2 vols, London 1812
*EETS	
*EETSES	
*Furnivall EEP	
*Gerould S Leg	
Graesse LA	Graesse T, Jacobi a Voragine Legenda aurea . . . , Dresden 1846
*Herbert	
	Hinnebusch W A, The Early English Friars Preachers, Rome 1951
Horstmann Bokenam	Horstmann C, Osbern Bokenam's Legenden, *AEB 1, Heilbronn 1883
Horstmann ScL	Horstmann C, Barbour's des Schottischen National-dichters Legendensammlung, 2 vols, Heilbronn 1881–82
	Kapp R, Heilige und Heiligenlegenden in England, Studien zum 16 und 17 Jahrhundert 1, Halle 1934
	Kenny J F, The Sources for the Early History of Ireland . . . , Columbia Univ Records of Civilization: Sources and Studies, N Y 1929
Metcalfe STS	Metcalfe W M, Legends of the Saints in the Scottish Dialect of the Fourteenth Cent . . . , 3 vols, Scottish Text Soc, Edinburgh 1896 (originally *PSTS 13, 18, 35, 37, 1890–96)
*Migne PL	
*Rel Ant	
	Ringler W, A Bibliography and First-Line Index of English Verse Printed Through 1500; a Supplement to Brown and Robbins' Index of Middle English Verse, *PBSA 49.153
*Rolls Series	
Rosenthal Vitae patrum	Rosenthal C L, The Vitae patrum in Old and Middle English Literature, Philadelphia 1936
*Roxb Club	

	Saintyves P, Les saints céphalofores. Étude de folklore hagiographique, Revue de l'histoire des religions 99.158
Schubel Jungfrauen	Schubel F, Die südenglische Legende von den elftausend Jungfrauen, Greifswalder Beiträge zur Literatur- und Stilforschung 21, Greifswald 1938
*STC	
STS see *PSTS	
Temple	Ellis F S, The Golden Legend or Lives of the Saints as Englished by William Caxton, The Temple Classics, 7 vols, London 1900
	Thurston H and D Attwater, Butler's Lives of the Saints, complete edn, rvsd, supplemented, 4 vols, N Y 1956
Turnbull Leg cath	Turnbull D B B, Legendae catholicae, Edinburgh 1840
(La) vie des pères	La vie des anciens pères hermites, Lyon 1486–87
(de) Vignay LD	de Vignay J, Legende dorée, 1480?
Whytford	Whytford R, trans, The Martiloge in Englysshe after the Use of the Chirche of Salisbury . . . , Wynkyn de Worde, London 1526 (STC, no 17532; rptd F Procter and E S Dewick, Henry Bradshaw Soc 3, London 1893
	Wilson R M, The Lost Literature of Medieval England, London 1952, p 92
	Wolpers T, Die englischen Heiligenlegenden des Mittelalters, Tübingen 1964
Workman 15 Cent Trans	Workman S K, Fifteenth Century Translation as an Influence on English Prose, Princeton SE 18, Princeton 1940
Wülcker AELeseb	Wülcker R M, Altenglisches Lesebuch, Halle 1878
Zusatzleg 1889	Horstmann C, Des MS Bodl 779 Zusatzlegenden zur südlichen Legendensammlung, *Arch 82.307, 369

1. Collections of Saints' Legends

by

Charlotte D'Evelyn

[1] THE SOUTH ENGLISH
LEGENDARY (SEL).

MSS. 51 MSS. Brown-Robbins, no 2304, lists 14 MSS containing the formal prologue; add 15, Winchester Coll 33ᵃ, ff 48ᵃ–49ᵃ (15 cent); 16, PRO C 47 34 1 no 5, f 1ᵃ⁻ᵇ, fragm (early 14 cent). For Brown-Robbins nos of individual legends in SEL see Brown-Robbins index, p 780. To these add 184, 728, 2994, 3042, 3060; from these delete 421, 422, 1110, 1465, 1613, 2855, 2863 all of which refer to Vernon GL; see Section 2. Only material on MSS of the SEL as a whole is listed here; for MSS of individual legends see Section 3.

Horstmann C, Die Legenden des MS Laud 108, Arch 49.395.

AELeg 1875, p iv (description and relationship of Bodl 1486 (Laud Misc 108), 1596 (Laud Misc 463), 2567 (Bodley 779), 3938 (Vernon), 6924 (Ashmole 43), Trinity Oxf 57, BM Cotton Julius D.ix, Egerton 1993, Harley 2277, BM Addit 10301.

Zupitza J, Zwei mittelenglische Legendenhandschriften, Angl 1.392 (description of Bodl 9837 [Tanner 17] and Corp Christi Camb 145).

AELeg 1881, p xlv (to 10 MSS listed in AELeg 1875 adds Bodl 9837, Corp Christi Camb 145, King's Camb 13, St. John's Camb 28, Trinity Camb 605, Lambeth 223).

Stiehler E O, Altenglische Legenden, Angl 7.405 (description of BM Stowe 669=Stowe 949).

Horstmann, EETS 87.vii, xiii (list of contents of several MSS).

D'Evelyn, EETS 244.15 (relation of Corp Christi Camb 145 and Harley 2277 to Bodl 1486).

Boyd B, New Light on the SEL, Texas SE 37.187 (attempt to account for differences in order and content of early SEL MSS)

Kobayashi E, A Study of Verb Forms of the SEL in BM Harley 2277, diss Univ of Mich 1962, DA 23.230 (analysis of dialect as Southwestern).

Editions. Note: Only edns including all or

several legends from a MS are listed here; for single legends see Section 3.

Furnivall EEP (15 items, Harley 2277).

Horstmann, EETS 87 (67 items plus 2 in a later hand, Bodl 1486).

Zusatzleg 1889, (31 saints' legends peculiar to Bodl 2567 [Bodl 779] ca 1400).

D'Evelyn and Mill, EETS 235, 236, 244 (90 items, Corp Christi Camb 145 supplemented by Harley 2277; crit H D, Revue d'hist ecclés 53, no 1, p 324; Schirmer, Angl 76.299; R W Wilson, MLR 53.140; B Cottle, JEGP 59.727; G Kane, RES ns 11.311; H Käsmann, Angl 78.232).

Selections. Note: For lists of single items and brief extracts printed from Bodl 6924, Corp Christi Camb 145, Cotton Jul D.ix, Harley 2277 see EETS 244.37.

Warton T, The History of English Poetry, ed W C Hazlitt, 4 vols, London 1871, 2.57 (extracts from various MSS of legends of Christopher, Cuthbert, Margaret, Patrick, Swithin, Thomas Becket, Wulfstan).

Date. Horstmann, EETS 87.x, xiii (dates Bodl 1486 ca 1280–85 to 1290–95).

Brown B D, EETS 169.xi (internal evidence for ca 1275–85 as date of composition).

Language. Mohr F, Sprachliche Untersuchungen zu den me Legenden aus Gloucestershire, Bonn 1888 (analyzes language as Gloucestershire dialect).

Bülbring K D, Geschichte der Ablauts des starken Zeitwörter innerhalb des Südenglischen, QF 63, Strassburg 1889 (studies several SEL texts).

Serjeantson M S, The Dialects of the West Midlands in Middle English, RES 3.54, 319 (Bodl 1486, Harley 2277 assigned to Southwest Midlands).

Kaiser R, Zur Geographie des mittelenglischen Wortschatzes, Palaes 205, Leipzig 1937 (includes SEL in attempt to localize words).

Authorship. Note: See also under KENELM [160] and THOMAS BECKET [276] below.

Black W H, The Life and Martyrdom of Thomas Becket, Percy Soc 19.vii (Robert of Gloucester the author).

AELeg 1881, p xliv (SEL product of monks including Robert of Gloucester).

Wright W A, The Metrical Chronicle of Robert of Gloucester, Rolls Series 86, pt I, London 1887, pp xvi, xxxix (SEL work of monk or guild of monks in a Gloucestershire monastery).

Ellmer W, Über die Quellen des Reimchronik Robert's von Gloucester, Angl 10.1, 291 (Robert of G used SEL in various legends but himself wrote legend of Kenelm).

Brown B D, Robert of Gloucester's Chronicle and the Life of St Kenelm, MLN 41.13 (comparison with Latin sources virtually establishes priority of SEL Kenelm to Chronicle).

Brown, EETS 169.xciii (argues for Dominican authorship).

Heuser and Foster, EETS 183.viii (Dominican authorship accepted).

Wells M E, The SEL in Its Relation to the Legenda Aurea, PMLA 51.337 (no clear evidence for Franciscan or Dominican authorship).

Pfander H G, The Popular Sermon of the Medieval Friar in England, N Y 1937, p 12, note 42 (supports Dominican authorship).

Schubel Jungfrauen, p 3 (review of problem).

Wells M E, The Structural Development of the SEL, JEGP 41.323 (new arguments for Franciscan authorship).

Hinnebusch W A, The Early English Friars Preachers, Institutum historicum ff praedictorum Romae ad s Sabinae, Dissert Hist 14, Rome 1951, p 310 (supports Dominican authorship).

Sources and Literary Relations. Schmidt W, Über den Stil der Legenden des MS Laud 108, Halle 1893 (stylistic features closely similar to those of 1st part of Gloucester Chronicle).

Wells M E, PMLA 51.337 (on evidence of date, contents and textual parallels in Harley 2277 argues for LA as a principal source); JEGP 41.320 (comparison of items and arrangement of material in Pepys 2344 and Harley 2277 strengthens evidence for LA as source).

Weir E G, The Vernacular Sources of the Middle English Plays of the Blessed Virgin Mary, Abstracts of Diss, Stanford Univ 1941–42, p 45 (Mary material in SEL as possible source of Mary plays).

Manning W F, The Middle English Verse Life of St Dominic: Date and Sources, Spec 31.83 (claims 46% of legends in Bodl 1486 based on LA).

Other Scholarly Problems. Wells M E, JEGP 41.327 (traces growth of Sanctorale and

Temporale material and suggests connection with miracle play cycles).

[2] THE SCOTTISH LEGENDARY (ScL).

MS. Camb Univ Gg.2.6, ff 1a–395a (1400–50).

Brown-Robbins, no 587 (for Brown-Robbins nos of the 50 items see Brown-Robbins index, p 778).

AELeg 1881, p lxli (description, table of contents).

Horstmann ScL, 2.305 (scribal usages noted).

Bradshaw H, Collected Papers, Cambridge 1889, p 61.

Metcalfe STS, 1.vii; W M Metcalfe, The Legends of Sts Ninian and Machor, Paisley 1904, p 9.

Editions. Horstmann ScL (on Machor, see under *Selections*; crit A Brandl, LfGRP 2.397; E Schröder, AnzfDA 9.276; A Schröer, ZfÖG 36.121).

Metcalfe STS, 1, 2, 3.

Selections. Horstmann C, Nachträge zu den Legenden, Arch 62.397 (Alexis).

AELeg 1881, p lxliii (general prologue and opening lines of several legends); p 189 (Machor).

Lovewell B E, The Life of St Cecilia, YSE 3, New Haven 1898, p 92.

Metcalfe W M, Ninian and Machor, pp 44, 87; Specimens of Scottish Literature 1350–1835, London 1913, pp 29, 30 (Ninian lines 271–304; Machor lines 809–60, 1581–1610).

Language. Horstmann ScL, p 305 (MS written without doubt in Aberdeen dialect).

Fiby H F, Zur Laut- und Flexionslehre in Barbours(?) schottischen Legenden, Jahres-Bericht der deutschen Landes-Oberrealschule in Brunn fur das Schuljahr 1888/9, Brunn 1889, p 1 (South-Scottish dialect characteristics).

Bearder J W, Über den Gebrauch der Praepositionen in der alt-schottischen Poesie, diss Giessen, Halle 1894 (includes ScL John the Evangelist, Cecilia).

Date. Metcalfe, Ninian and Machor, p 18 (probably end 14 cent).

Author. Bradshaw H, On Two Hitherto Unknown Poems by John Barbour, Author of the Brus, Camb Antiquar Soc Communications, 1866, 3, 119; rptd H Bradshaw, Collected Papers, Camb 1889, p 58 (ScL ascribed to Barbour).

Buss P, Sind die von Horstmann herausgegebenen schottischen Legenden ein Werk Barber's? diss Göttingen, Halle 1886; rptd Angl 9.493 (rejection of Barbour as author on linguistic evidence).

Koeppel E, Die Fragmente von Barbour's

Trojanerkrieg, EStn 10.373 (supports Buss's conclusion).

Prothero G W, A Memoir of Henry Bradshaw, London 1888, p 134, Addend p xi (recalls Bradshaw's claim for Barbour).

Skeat W W, The Bruce, 2 vols, PSTS, Edinburgh 1894, 1.lv (summary and rejection of evidence for Barbour).

Neilson G, John Barbour, John Trumpour and a Legend of the Saints, The Scottish Antiquary 11.102 (in local subject-matter and language legend of Ninian supports Barbour's authorship).

Baudisch J, Ein Beitrag zur Kenntnis der früher Barbour zugeschriebenen Legendensammlung, Jahresberichte für die öffentlichen Unterrealschulen in Wien, 1903, p 1 (characterization of unknown author by his comments and literary habits; crit L Kellner, EStn 35.103).

Metcalfe, Ninian and Machor, p 14 (rejects Barbour's authorship).

Sources. AELeg 1881, p ci (LA chief source; for specific sources of separate legends see 3. Legends of Indiv Saints); Horstmann ScL, 1.iii (LA chief source).

Metcalfe STS, 1.xvii (LA chief source; for details see STS 3, passim).

Rosenthal Vitae patrum, p 65, index (LA as source).

General. Scott M M M, Barbour's Legends of the Saints, The Dublin Review 3s 17.265.

Gerould S Leg, p 176.

[3] OSBERN BOKENHAM, THE LIVES OF SAINTS, OR LEGENDS OF HOLY WOMEN.

MS. Arundel 327, ff 1ᵃ–192ᵇ, prologue, 13 legends (1447).

Brown-Robbins, no 3817, index p 745 under Bokenham.

AELeg 1881, p cxxviii (identifies MS as formerly in Gresham Coll; see below under *Authorship* N Toner, Augustinian Writers, p 501, who lists Gresham Coll text as a 2nd MS).

Horstmann Bokenam, p xii.

Liljegren S B, Four Middle English Versions of the Legend of the Eleven Thousand Virgins, EStn 57.86.

Serjeantson, EETS 206.xxiv.

Editions. [Bokenam O], The Lyvys of Seyntys, Roxb Club 50, London 1835.

Horstmann Bokenam (crit E Kölbing, EStn 7.142; E Schröder, AnzfDA 9.390; A Brandl, LfGRP 5.102).

Serjeantson M S, Legendys of Hooly Wummen by Osbern Bokenham, EETS 206 (crit

G D Willcock, YWES 19.93; S Potter, MLR 34.81; A Brandl, Arch 176.118; K Brunner, AnglB 50.45).

Language. Horstmann Bokenam, p xi (characteristics of Suffolk dialect).

Hoofe A, Lautuntersuchungen zu Osbern Bokenam's Legenden, EStn 8.209.

Wyld H C, Southeastern and Southeast Midland Dialects in Middle English, E&S 6.112, 126.

Serjeantson, EETS 206.xxviii (detailed analysis of language).

Versification. Horstmann Bokenam, p viii (notes kinds of verse used).

Serjeantson, EETS 206.xxvi (analysis of verse).

Date. Horstmann Bokenam, p vii (internal evidence for dating legends).

Serjeantson, EETS 206, xix (order of legends in MS probably corresponds to order of writing).

Authorship. AELeg 1881, p cxxviii (personal details from MS and text).

Horstmann Bokenam, p v (Bokeham, now Bookham Surrey, suggested as birthplace).

Horstmann C, Mappula Angliae von Osbern Bokenham, EStn 10.1 (anagram of name, references to other works noted).

Moore S, Patrons of Letters in Norfolk and Suffolk ca 1450, PMLA 28.79 (Lincolnshire suggested as birthplace).

Serjeantson, EETS 206.xiii (evidence for Old Buckenham, South Norfolk, as birthplace).

Bennett H B, The Author and His Public in the Fourteenth and Fifteenth Centuries, E&S 23.15 (Bokenham as example of practice of local patronage).

Jeremy Sister M, The English Prose Translation of the LA, MLN 59.181 (Bokenham's authorship of 1438 GL argued; see [6] below); Caxton and the Synfulle Wretche, Trad 4.427 (further evidence for B's authorship of 1438 GL).

de Meijer A, John Capgrave OESA, Augustiniana (Louvain) 5.416 note 71; 7.563 note 89 (traditional date of B's death ca 1447 queried on evidence of official documents of Order naming him under years 1463, 1464).

Toner N, Augustinian Spiritual Writers of the English Province in the 15th and 16th Cent, S Augustinus vitae spiritualis Magister, Rome 1959, 2.498 (evidence for "after 1464" as date of death; see also N&Q ns 8.246).

Sources. Horstmann Bokenam, p ix (LA as chief source).

Willenberg G, Die Quellen von Osbern Bokenham's Legenden, diss Marburg 1888, rptd EStn 12.1 (detailed study of sources).

Serjeantson, EETS 206.xxi (summary of Willenberg).

Literary Relations. Allen H E, The Manuel des Pechiez and the Scholastic Prologue, RomR 8.451 (B's prologue as example of formal opening).

General. Gerould S Leg, p 188.

Bibliography. Serjeantson, EETS 206.xi

[4] CAXTON, VITAS PATRUM
(Caxton VP).

(Note: The records of the following Desert Fathers who are represented in Caxton as in his sources only briefly by precept or incident are omitted: Ammon Abbot chap 3, Ammon Hermit 8, Ammonius 23, Benus 4, Crenius or Cronius 25, Didymus 24, Dioscorus 20, Elia or Helye 12, Eulogius 14, Evragius 27, Isidore of Alexandria 17, John of Dioclos 32, Origenes 26, Piammon 31, Serapion 18. See also under Caxton.)

Editions. [Caxton, W trans], Vitas patrum,

Wynkyn de Worde, Westminster 1495 (STC, no 14507).

Selections. Dibdin Typo Antiq 2.42 (prologue; six extracts from Caxton pt i; Caxton's conclusion, pt v).

Date. Caxton VP, heading of pt i, colophon of pt v (1491 date of translation and of Caxton's death; see Crotch, EETS 176.cxxiv).

Sources. La vie des pères, Lyon 1486.

Claudin A, Histoire de l'imprimerie en France au 15e et au 16e siècle, Paris 1904, 3.143, 467 (account of Lyon 1486 edn).

Rosenthal Vitae patrum, p 134 (relation of Caxton VP to Latin text; see Migne PL 21.col 387; 73.col 127).

Background. Williams C A, Oriental Affinities of the Legend of the Hairy Anchorite, Illinois Stud in Lang and Lit 10, No 2, May 1925; 11, No 4, Nov 1926 (connects VP with pre-Christian and Christian myth and folklore; crit M Gaster, Folklore 39.186; A Taylor, MLN 43.271; P P, AnBol 47.138).

2. ENGLISH TRANSLATIONS OF LEGENDA AUREA

by

Charlotte D'Evelyn

[5] VERNON GOLDEN LEGEND
(Vernon GL).

MS. Bodl 3938, ff 89a–103a, ca 250 lines lost at beg; 9 items, last Euphrosyne from VP (ca 1385).

Brown-Robbins, no *26.

AELeg 1875, p xxiv.

Editions. AELeg 1878 (p 3 items 1–7; p 174 item 9 Euphrosyne, prtd also EStn 1.303; item 8 Barlaam and Josaphat om here, prtd AELeg 1875, p 215; crit A Brandl, ZfÖG 31.392; E Kölbing, EStn 3.125).

Language. Horstmann C, Die Legende der Euphrosyne, EStn 1.300 (dialect of MS East Midland with northern traces).

Kölbing E, EStn 3.134 (unrecorded words in Vernon GL).

AELeg 1881, p lxl, note 1 (influence of Latin diction and construction).

Date. AELeg 1881, p lxl, note 1 (ca 1360–70).

Sources. AELeg 1878, p 3 (text of Graesse LA given for items 1–7).

AELeg 1881, p lxl, note 1 (Euphrosyne based on VP).

[6] 1438 GOLDEN LEGEND (1438 GL).

MSS. Note: Of the MSS listed here nos 1–7 are relatively complete copies of the 1438 GL; no 8 has only 19 legends. MSS containing single legends or a very small group are listed under individual saints in Section 3. For comparison of text, MSS Harley 4775 and BM Addit 35298 have been available in rotograph and microfilm. With a few exceptions information on other MSS is derived from secondary sources, notably Butler LA and A Kurvinen, NM 60.353.

1, Bodl 21947 (Douce 372), ff 1a–163b, badly mutilated (1438); 2, Egerton 876, ff 2a–320b, gaps, end lost (mid 15 cent); 3, Harley 630, ff 1a–365b, beg lost, gaps (mid 15 cent); 4, Harley 4775, ff 3a–262b, folios missing after ff 16 and 136, end lost (mid 15 cent; MLA roto 343); 5, BM Addit 11565, ff 34a–214a, gaps, end lost (the fragmentary f 1 of Lansdowne 350, identified by Butler LA, p 64, as part of BM Addit 11565, is now inserted in that MS as f 114, see below Kurvinen, NM 60.355) (mid 15 cent); 6, BM Addit 35298, formerly Ashburnham Appendix 91, ff 2ª–168ᵇ (mid 15 cent); 7, Lambeth 72, ff 1ª–420, beg lost (15 cent); 8, Trinity Coll Dublin 319, beg, end lost, 19 legends (15 cent).

Horstmann C, Barlaam and Josaphat, Sagan 1877, p 5 (description of MSS 2, 3, 4; phonetic and grammatical characteristics of MSS 2, 4).

AELeg 1881, p cxxx (description of MSS 1, 2, 3, 4; table of contents of MS 4).

Gibbs H H, The Life and Martyrdom of S Katherine of Alexandria, Roxb Club, London 1884, p xiii (MS 6).

Butler LA, pp 50, 73, 149 (description and interrelation of MSS 1–7; crit P M, Rom 29.292; H D, AnBol 22.81; H Spies, EStn 29.282; G Binz, AnglB 14.360).

Gerould S Leg, p 195 (MS 8 identified; see EStn 44.259 for earlier report of this MS).

Moore G E, The Middle English Verse Life of Edward the Confessor, Philadelphia 1942, p 72 (MS 6).

Kurvinen A, Caxton's GL and the MSS of the Gilte Legende, NM 60.353 (description and interrelation of MSS 1–7; list of contents of MSS 4 and 6 and of Caxton GL).

Selections. Butler LA, p 99 (for his selections from various 1438 GL MSS see 3. Legends of Individual Saints under ALDHELM [18], CUTHBERT [68], DUNSTAN [76], MARINA [186], SEVEN SLEEPERS [254], SWITHUN [264], THOMAS BECKET [276]; 5. Legends of the Cross under 1348 GL [308]; 7. Legends of the After-Life under St PATRICK'S PURGATORY [312]).

Authorship. Horstmann C, Mappula Angliae von Osbern Bokenham, EStn 10.2 (rejects B's authorship of 1438 GL because of absence of legends of Chad, Edward, Felix, Oswald).

Jeremy Sister M, The English Prose Translation of the LA, MLN 59.181 (B's authorship supported by presence of legends of Chad, Edward, Oswald in newly found MSS); Caxton and the Synfulle Wretche, Trad 4.427 (evidence for B's authorship restated).

Sources. AELeg 1881, p cxxxiii (verbal translation of deVignay version).

Butler LA, pp 70, 146 (evidence for use of both Latin and French texts).

Jeremy Sister M, Caxton's Golden Legend and de Vignai's Légende dorée, MS 8.97

(the 3 versions of de Vignay's text; relation of 1438 GL to last revised version).

[7] CAXTON'S GOLDEN LEGEND (Caxton GL).

Editions. Note: Only 15 cent edns are listed here; for 16 cent edns see STC, nos 24877–80. The Pierpont Morgan Library copies of the first four edns have been checked for contents; for subject-matter, references are given to F S Ellis, The Golden Legend, Temple Classics, 7 vols, London 1900.

[Caxton W, trans and pr], Westminster 1483 (STC, no 24873) (for contents see AELeg 1881, p cxxxvi).

[Caxton W, trans and pr], Westminster 1487? (STC, no 24874).

[Caxton W, trans], Here begynneth . . . the golden legende . . . , Wynkyn de Worde, Westminster 1493 (STC, no 24875).

[Caxton W, trans], Wynkyn de Worde, Westminster 1498 (STC, no 24876).

Blades W, The Biography and Typography of William Caxton, 2nd edn, London 1882, p 280 (typographical description of 1st edn).

Butler LA, p 77 (analysis of contents of 1st edn).

Seybolt R F, Fifteenth-Century Editions of the Legenda Aurea, Spec 21.327 (edns of Latin and vernacular texts).

Modernizations. Ellis F S, The Golden Legend or the Lives of the Saints as Englished by William Caxton, Temple Classics, London 1900, 7 vols.

Selections. Dibdin Typo Antiq 2.75 (1498 edn, extracts from Brendan, Eugene, George, Thomas Becket).

Aspland A, The Golden Legend, The Holbein Society's Fac-Simile Reprints, London 1878 (1483 edn, prologue, beg of table of contents, 14 complete legends and feasts, epilogue).

Madge H D, Leaves from the Golden Legend, Westminster 1898 (44 modernized selections based on 1483, 1527, and Kelmscott edns).

Pollard A W, An English Garner, 15 Century Prose and Verse, N Y 1903 (?), p 225 (1483 edn, prologue).

Shackford M S, Legends and Satires from Mediaeval Literature, Boston 1913, pp 53, 73 (Brendan, Margaret modernized).

O'Neill G V, The Golden Legend, Cambridge 1914 (Caxton's prologue, 22 legends modernized).

Aurner N S, Caxton Mirrour of Fifteenth-Century Letters, Boston 1926, p 255 (1483 edn, prologue, epilogue, Caxton's interpolations in Augustine of Hippo, Circumcision, David, George).

Crotch, EETS 176.70 (selections as in preceding entry).

Loomis R S and R Willard, Medieval English Verse and Prose in Modernized Versions, N Y 1948, p 487 (Agnes, Assumption of the Virgin, Thomas Becket).

Jeremy Sister M, Caxton's Original Additions to the Legenda Aurea, MLN 64.259 (3 additions by Caxton noted in Ursula, Nativity of Our Lady, Nativity of Our Lord).

Sources. Note: For Caxton's French source, the revised version of de Vignay's Légende dorée, Sister M Jeremy (MS 8.99) reports a 2nd MS, Fitzwilliam 22 (Camb) dated 1480, incomplete; and a 2nd printed copy, Camb Univ Libr A.B.i.17, which she claims is probably from the same press as the BM copy now marked IC 50152. The provenance of the BM copy was formerly given as Paris? It is now given as Low Countries in a handwritten note, BM Genl Cat of Printed Books (London 1962), 133.593.

AELeg 1881, p cxxxv (based on 1438 GL).

Butler LA, pp 75, 82 (review of earlier statements on sources; reappraisal of use of Latin, French, English texts, including Higden's Polychronicon).

Rosenthal Vitae patrum, p 68 (Caxton's indirect use of VP).

Jeremy Sister M, Caxton's GL and Varagine's LA, Spec 21.212 (relation between Latin and English versions in plan, contents, details); Caxton's Golden Legend and de Vignai's Légende dorée, MS 8.97 (Caxton's use of third form of de Vignay); Trad 4.423 (1438 GL closer to Latin than Caxton GL).

Kurvinen A, Caxton's Golden Legend and the MSS of the Gilte Legende, NM 60.353 (evidence from content and wording for Caxton's use of 1438 GL, possibly of BM Addit 35298 directly).

3. LEGENDS OF INDIVIDUAL SAINTS

by

Charlotte D'Evelyn

(Note: For general information on the collections in which a saint's legend occurs see Sections 1 and 2. Unless otherwise stated, dates of feast-days and of historical periods are quoted from H Thurston and D Attwater. Verse versions are identified by Brown-Robbins numbers; where the number of MSS listed in Brown-Robbins exceeds six, only the total number is quoted, e g Agatha [Brown-Robbins, no 2839] 17 MSS. In noting the sources for legends in 1438 GL and Caxton GL, the form "cf LA" or "cf de Vignay LD" is used as a convenience in locating the corresponding material rather than as a statement of direct or sole source of the legend in question; see Butler LA, p 98. Undated MSS in this section which also appear in Section 1 or 2 above are dated in Section 1 or 2.)

[8] ABDON AND SENNEN (July 30, 303?)
   a. SEL: Brown-Robbins, no 2836.
MS. Bodl 2567 (Bodley 779), f 239[a] (ca 1400).
Editions. Zusatzleg 1889, p 416.
Sources. Zusatzleg 1889, pp 416, 422 (source unidentified).

   b. 1438 GL.
MSS. 1, Harley 4775, chap 99, ff 132[b]–133[a]; MLA roto 343, 2.265; 2, BM Addit 11565, f 145[b] incomplete; 3, BM Addit 35298, f 90[a].
Sources. Cf Graesse LA, chap 106, p 447; cf de Vignay LD, f 200[b].

   c. Caxton GL.
Editions. Caxton GL, chap 139; Temple, 4.141.
Sources. See under b.

[9] ABRAHAM, HERMIT OF KIDUNAIA (March 16, 6 cent).
Editions. Caxton VP, pt 1, chap 51, ff 102[b]–110[a] (includes legend of his niece Mary the Prostitute).
Sources. Cf La vie des pères, pt 1, chap 51, ff 82[b]–87[b].

ACHILLE, ACHILLEUS: see NEREUS.

ADAUCTUS: see FELIX THE PRIEST.

ADELWOLD: see ETHELWOLD.

[10] ADRIAN AND NATALIA
(Sept 8, ca 304).

a. ScL; Brown-Robbins, no 3489.
MS. Camb Univ Gg.2.6, ff 291ª–296ᵇ (1400–50).
Editions. Horstmann ScL, 2.106; Metcalfe STS, 2.272 (notes 3.395).
Sources. Horstmann ScL, 2.106 (quotes Graesse LA, chap 134, p 597; refers to Vincent of Beauvais Spec Hist); Metcalfe STS, 3.397 (as in Horstmann).

b. 1438 GL.
MSS. 1, Harley 4775, chap 125, ff 166ª–167ª; MLA roto 343, 2.330; 2, BM Addit 11565, f 172 incomplete; 3, BM Addit 35298, ff 115ª–116ª (lost Bodl 21947).
Sources. Cf Graesse LA, chap 134, p 597.

c. Caxton GL.
Editions. Caxton GL, chap 166; Temple, 5.112.
Sources. Cf de Vignay LD, ff 266ᵇ–268ª.

AELDRI: see ETHELDREDA of ELY.
AETHELBERHT: see ETHELBERT.
AGACE, AGASE: see AGATHA.
AGAPITUS: see SIXTUS II.

[11] AGATHA (Feb 5, year?).
a. SEL; Brown-Robbins, no 2839.
MSS. 17 MSS.
Editions. Horstmann, EETS 87.193 (Bodl 1486 [Laud Misc 108], ff 94ᵇ–96ª; end 13 cent); D'Evelyn and Mill, EETS 235.54 (Corp Christi Camb 145, ff 20ᵇ–22ª; early 14 cent).

b. NHC; Brown-Robbins, no 2840.
MS. Harley 4196, ff 143ᵇ–145ᵇ (15 cent).
Edition. AELeg 1881, p 45.

c. ScL; Brown-Robbins, no 135.
MS. Camb Univ Gg.2.6, ff 351ᵇ–354ª (1400–50).
Editions. Horstmann ScL, 2.157; Metcalfe STS, 2.358 (notes 3.423).
Sources. Horstmann ScL, 2.157 (Graesse LA, chap 39, p 170 quoted); Metcalfe STS, 3.425 (see preceding entry).

d. Bokenham; Brown-Robbins, no 347.
MS. Arundel 327, ff 151ª–162ᵇ (1447).
Editions. [Bokenam O], The Lyvys of Seyntys, Roxb Club 50, London 1835; Horstmann Bokenam, p 208; Serjeantson, EETS 206.225.
Sources. Horstmann Bokenam, p ix (see under c); G Willenberg, EStn 12.15 (notes differences from Graesse LA but accepts LA as source); Serjeantson, EETS 206.xxiii (quotes Willenberg results).

e. 1438 GL.
MSS. 1, Egerton 876, f 57ᵇ incomplete; 2, Harley 4775, chap 38, ff 41ª–42ᵇ; MLA

roto 343, 1.82; 3, BM Addit 35298, f 23ª⁻ᵇ.
Sources. Cf Graesse LA, chap 39, p 170.

f. Caxton GL.
Editions. Caxton GL, chap 67; Temple, 3.32.
Sources. Cf Graesse LA, chap 39, p 170; cf de Vignay LD, f 100ᵇ; Sister M Jeremy, MS 8.105 (details from de Vignay noted).

AGATHEN: see AGATHON.

[12] AGATHON (Dec 7 [Whytford]).
a. 1438 GL.
MSS. 1, Bodl 21947 (Douce 372), f 152; 2, Harley 4775, chap 170, ff 237ᵇ–238ᵇ; MLA roto 343, 2.473; 3, BM Addit 35298, f 154ᵇ (lost BM Addit 11565).
Sources. Cf Graesse LA, chap 179, p 809.

b. Caxton GL.
Editions. Caxton GL, chap 226; Temple, 7.82.
Sources. Cf Graesse LA, chap 179, p 809; cf 1438 GL, chap 170; Rosenthal Vitae patrum, p 64 (VP as indirect source).

[13] AGNES (Jan 21, 304?).
(Note: See also EMERENTIANA [87]).

a. SEL; Brown-Robbins, nos 2850, 127.
MSS. 18 MSS; add 19, Winchester Coll 33ª, ff 51ᵇ–54ᵇ including miracle, Brown-Robbins, no 127 (15 cent).
Editions. Horstmann, EETS 87.181 (Bodl 1486 [Laud Misc 108], ff 89ᵇ–91ª, end 13 cent); D'Evelyn and Mill, EETS 235.19 (Corp Christi Camb 145, ff 7ᵇ–9ᵇ with added miracle, early 14 cent).
Sources. Denomy A J, The Old French Lives of St Agnes, HSRL 13, Cambridge 1938, p 164 note 1 (based on pseudo-Ambrosius Gesta S Agnes).

b. ScL; Brown-Robbins, no *10.
MS. Camb Univ Gg.2.6, ff 348ª–351ᵇ (1400–50); beg incomplete.
Editions. Horstmann ScL, 2.151; Metcalfe STS, 2.346 (notes 3.416).
Sources. Horstmann ScL, 2.151 (quotes Graesse LA, chap 24, p 113); Metcalfe STS, 3.419 (passages from LA); Denomy, St Agnes, p 165 (supplementary use of Gesta S Agnes; parallels with Old French poetic version).

c. Bokenham; Brown-Robbins, no 2849.
MS. Arundel 327, ff 74ª–86ᵇ.
Editions. [Bokenam O], The Lyvys of Seyntys, Roxb Club 50, London 1835, p 116; Horstmann Bokenam, p 102; Serjeantson, EETS 206.110.
Date. Horstmann Bokenam, p vii (evidence for ca 1445).
Sources. Horstmann Bokenam, p ix (LA and

Gesta S Agnes noted); G Willenberg, EStn 12.5 (detailed comparison with LA and Gesta S Agnes); Serjeantson, EETS 206.xxii (summarizes Willenberg); Denomy, St Agnes, p 173 (union of LA with close translation of Gesta).

d. 1438 GL.

MSS. 1, Harley 4775, chap 23, ff 23ᵇ–25ᵃ; MLA roto 343, 1.47; 2, BM Addit 35298, f 15ᵃ⁻ᵇ; 3, Lambeth 72, ff 41ᵃ–42ᵇ; beg incomplete; 4, Trinity Dublin 319, see Gerould S Leg, p 195.
Sources. Cf Graesse LA, chap 24, p 113.

e. Caxton GL.

Editions. Caxton GL, chap 57; Temple, 2.245.
Modernizations. Loomis R S and R Willard, Med Eng Verse and Prose in Modernized Versions, N Y 1948, p 478 (based on Temple 2.245).
Sources. Cf Graesse LA, chap 24, p 113; cf de Vignay LD, ff 83ᵃ–84ᵇ; Sister M Jeremy, MS 8.104 (details in Caxton and de Vignay not in LA).
Background. Denomy, St Agnes passim.

AGRICOLA: see VITALIS.

AILBRIȝT: see ETHELBERT.

[14] ALBAN AND AMPHIBALUS (June 22 Alban; June 25 Amphibalus [Whytford], year?).

a. SEL Alban; Brown-Robbins, no 2842.
MSS. 16 MSS.
Editions. Horstmann, EETS 87.67 (Bodl 1486 [Laud Misc 108], ff 46ᵇ–47ᵇ; end 13 cent); D'Evelyn and Mill, EETS 235.238 (Corp Christi Camb 145, ff 89ᵇ–90ᵇ; early 14 cent).

b. Lydgate; Brown-Robbins, no 3748. (Note: For Lydgate's version see under Lydgate.)

c. 1438 GL.
MSS. 1, Bodl 21947 (Douce 372), chap 78, incomplete; see Butler LA, p 60; 2, Harley 630, with inserted folio from different text between ff 169–170; see Butler LA, p 55; 3, Harley 4775, chap 78, ff 97ᵃ–104ᵇ; MLA roto 343, 1.192; 4, BM Addit 11565, see Butler LA, p 67; 5, BM Addit 35298, ff 57ᵃ–61ᵇ; 6, Lambeth 72, chap 79, f 143, see Butler LA, p 151.
Sources. Note: Not in Graesse LA or de Vignay LD; for probable ultimate sources see T D Hardy, Descriptive Cat of Materials, 1. p 6, no 9; p 18, no 33, Rolls Series, London 1862.

d. Caxton GL.
Editions. Caxton GL, chap 110; Temple, 3.236.
Sources. Butler LA, p 83 (claims 1438 GL, MS BM Addit 11565 as direct source).
Background. Meyer W, Die Legende des hl Albanus des Protomartyr Angliae in Texten vor Beda, Abh d Königl Gesell d Wissens zu Göttingen, Philolog-hist K1, NF xiii, Berlin 1904, pp 1–82; W Levison, St Alban and St Albans, Antiquity 15.337.

[15] ALBINUS, AUBIN, BISHOP OF ANGERS (March 1, ca 550).

Editions. Caxton GL, chap 247; Temple, 7.222.
Sources. Cf de Vignay LD, ff 439ᵇ–440ᵇ.

[16] ALCMUND, KING OF NORTHUMBRIA (March 19, ca 800).

MSS. Note: For Mirk Festial MSS, only MSS for which folio nos are available are listed here. See also ANDREW d MSS [25] below.
1, Bodl 17680 (Gough Eccl Top 4), ff 137ᵃ–139ᵇ (1400–50); 2, Cotton Claud A.ii, ff 102ᵇ–109ᵃ (ca 1420); (om Bodl 21634, 21682= Douce 60, 108; Harley 2247, 2391, 2403; Lansdowne 392; Durham Cosins v.iii.5).
Editions. Note: Alcmund is not included in the following 15 cent edns of Mirk Festial: Caxton 1483, STC no 17957; Ravynell 1495, STC no 17963; Hopyl 1495, STC no 17964; Wynkyn de Worde 1499, STC no 17967; Notary 1499, STC no 17968.
AELeg 1881, p cxxiv (Cotton Claud A.ii; variants Caius Camb 168, see p cxvii).
Erbe, EETSES 96.240 (Bodl 17680, variants Cotton Claud A.ii).
Sources. AELeg 1881, p cxi (possibly based on local source).

[17] ALDEGUNDIS (Jan 30, 684).

Editions. Caxton GL, chap 246; Temple, 7.218.
Sources. Cf de Vignay LD, ff 438ᵃ–439ᵇ.

[18] ALDHELM, BISHOP OF SHERBORNE (May 25, 709).

a. SEL; Brown-Robbins, no 2843.
MSS. 16 MSS.
Editions. D'Evelyn and Mill, EETS 235.211 (Corp Christi Camb 145, ff 79ᵇ–80ᵇ (early 14 cent).

b. 1438 GL.
MSS. 1, BM Addit 11565, f xxix(53)ᵇ (15 cent); 2, BM Addit 35298, chap 112, ff 77ᵇ–78ᵃ (15 cent); 3, Lambeth 72, chap 107, f

224ª (15 cent); (om Bodl 21947, Harley 630, 4775).
Editions. Butler LA, p 101 (BM Addit 11565).

c. Caxton GL.
Editions. Caxton GL, chap 99ª; Temple, 3.193 (om in Horstmann's list AELeg 1881, p cxxxvii).
Sources. Butler LA, p 83 (1438 GL as in BM Addit 11565 claimed as source).
General. Cook A S, Sources of the Biography of Aldhelm, Trans Conn Acad of Arts and Sciences 28.273 (bibliography and summaries of Latin sources).

[19] ALEXIS (July 17, 5 cent).

a. Early 6-line stanzas; Brown-Robbins, no 3156.
MSS. 1, Bodl 1486 (Laud Misc 108, pt iii), ff 233ᵇ–237ª (ca 1400); 2, Bodl 3938 (Vernon), ff 44ª, col 2–45ª, col 1 (ca 1385); 3, Durham Univ Cosin v.ii.14, f 92ª (15 cent); 4, Naples Royal Lib xiii.B.29, pp 80–86 (1457).
Rel Ant, 2.58 (description of MS 4 by D Laing).
Horstmann C, Die Legenden des MS Laud 108, Arch 49.413 (Alexis a 14–15 cent addit to MS 1).
Schipper J, Englische Alexius-legenden aus dem xiv und xv Jahrhundert, QF 20.5 (description of MSS 1, 2, 4).
Manly & Rickert, 1.376 (detailed account of MS 4).
Editions. Horstmann C, Leben des h Alexius nach MS Laud 108, Arch 51.103 (MS 1 with passages from anon Vita).
Horstmann C, Zwei Alexiuslieder, Arch 56.394 (MS 2 collated with MS 1).
Schipper, QF 20.66 (MSS 1 and 2 collated with MS 4; crit E Kölbing, EStn 2.489).
Furnivall, EETS 69.20 (MSS 1 and 2).
Selections. Laing D, Rel Ant, 2.64 (lines 1–12 of MS 4; rptd Furnivall, EETS 69.100).
Furnivall, EETS 69.99 (lines 1–42 of MS 3).
Language. Arch 51.102 (typical orthographical and grammatical forms of MS 1).
Arch 56.393 (traces of northern dialect in MS 2).
Schipper, QF 20.20 (author's dialect East Midland with northern and southern traces).
Sources. Arch 51.102 (notes correspondence with anon prose Vita in Acta SS).
Rösler M, Die Fassungen des Alexius-Legende, WBEP 21. 77.99 (classifies Alexis a with Group I of extant versions and claims LA as direct source; crit G H

Gerould, EStn 27.139, suggests Alphabetum Narrationum as source).
Literary Relations. Kötting G, Studien über altfranzösiche Bearbeitungen der Alexius-legende mit Berücksichtigung deutscher und englischer Alexiuslieder, Trier 1890, p 18 (differences between Alexis a and Latin noted).

b. Later 6-line stanzas; Brown-Robbins, no 1876.
MSS. 1, Bodl 1596 (Laud Misc 463), ff 116ª–118ᵇ (beg 15 cent); 2, Trinity Oxf 57, ff 73ª–77ᵇ (end 14 cent).
AELeg 1875, p xxx.
Schipper J, Die zweite Version der mittelengl Alexislegenden, Sitzungberichte der philoshist Classe der kaiserl Akad der Wissenschaft, Wien 1887, 114.232 (evidence for MS 1 as nearer original than MS 2).
Editions. Arch 56.404 (MSS 1 and 2).
Furnivall, EETS 69.20 (MSS 1 and 2).
Schipper, Die zweite Version, p 267 (critical edn based on MS 1; textual notes, p 293; study of accent and rime, p 264).
Language. Arch 56.401 (original dialect Southern).
Schipper, Die zweite Version, p 238 (original dialect probably Southeast Midland).
Sources. Rösler, WBEP 21.82, 99 (classifies with Group III of extant versions; no direct source given); Alexius Probleme, ZfRP 53.524 (comparison with Greek text in treatment of bride).

c. 12-line stanzas; Brown-Robbins, no 217.
MS. Bodl 1414 (Laud Misc 622), ff 21ᵇ–26ᵇ (beg 15 cent).
Editions. Furnivall, EETS 69.19; Horstmann C, Arch 59.79.
Language. Arch 59.71 (southern border of Midland with northern coloring).
MacKenzie B A, A Special Dialectal Development of OE ea in ME, EStn 61.386 (includes rime-words of Bodl 1414).
Sources. Arch 59.74 (not dependent on Alexis a or b).
Rösler, WBEP 21.85, 99 (evidence for Fr or AN source).

d. Couplets; Brown-Robbins, no 216.
MS. Cotton Titus A.xxvi, ff 145ª–152ª (15 cent).
Editions. Furnivall, EETS 69.20; Arch 59.96 (fundamentally Northern dialect, p 90).
Sources. Arch 59.94 (in content closely related to Alexis a).
Rösler, WBEP 21.90, 99 (questions Horstmann's classification); ZfRP 53.524 (com-

parison with Greek text in treatment of bride).

e. Northern Homily Cycle (NHC); Brown-Robbins, no 1525.

MSS. 1, Bodl 6923 (Ashmole 42), f 243ᵃ (early 15 cent); 2, Camb Univ Gg.5.31, f 140ᵃ (early 15 cent); 3, Huntington HM 129 (olim Phillipps 20420), f 207ᵃ (1400–50).

Editions. AELeg 1881, p 174 (MSS 1, 2; crit A Brandl, ZfÖG 33.685).

Sources. Rösler, WBEP 21.93, 99 (suggests Acta SS texts rather than LA as source of MSS 1, 2).

f. ScL; Brown-Robbins, no 4058.

MS. Camb Univ Gg.2.6, ff 163ᵃ–169ᵃ (1400–50).

Editions. Horstmann C, Nachträge zu den Legenden, Arch 62.397; Horstmann ScL, 1.210; Metcalfe STS, 1.441 (notes 3.226).

Sources. Metcalfe STS, 3.277 (Graesse LA, chap 94, not closely followed).

Rösler, WBEP 21.96, 99 (LA source; notes unique details in f).

g. Alphabet of Tales.

MS. BM Addit 25719, chap 600 (mid 15 cent).

Editions. Banks, EETS 127.399.

Sources. Herbert, pp 423, 440 (translated from Latin Alphabetum Narrationum ca 1308 attributed to Arnold of Liège).

h. 1438 GL.

MSS. 1, Bodl 21947 (Douce 372), chap 87, f 72ᵇ; 2, Harley 630, f cxcvi; 3, Harley 4775, chap 87, ff 118ᵇ–120ᵃ; MLA roto 343, 1.237; 4, BM Addit 35298, ff 69ᵇ–70ᵇ.

Edition. Rösler, WBEP 21.113 (Harley 4775 with collation of Harley 630; de Vignay LD ff 436ᵃ–438ᵃ direct source, p 105).

i. Caxton GL.

Editions. Caxton GL, chap 207; Temple 6.205; rptd Arch 59.103.

Sources. Arch 59.101 (possible use of Alexis c and de Vignay LD, ff 436ᵃ–438ᵃ).

Butler LA, p 97 (etymology from de Vignay, not LA).

Rösler, WBEP 21.106 (variations from Graesse LA perhaps due to use of other texts).

Jeremy Sister M, MS 8.105 (minor changes common to de Vignay and Caxton perhaps result of careless use of LA by de Vignay).

General. de Gaiffier B, Intactam sponsam relinquens, A propos de la vie de St Alexis, AnBol 65.156 (interpretation of marriage episode).

Bibliography. Rösler, WBEP 21.192.

ALFE, ALPHEY: see ALPHEGE.

ALKEMUND: see ALCMUND.

[20] ALPHEGE, ARCHBISHOP OF CANTERBURY (April 19, 1012).

a. SEL; Brown-Robbins, no 2844.

MSS. 17 MSS.

Edition. D'Evelyn and Mill, EETS 235.148 (Corp Christi Camb 145, ff 56ᵃ–59ᵃ; early 14 cent).

b. 1438 GL.

MSS. 1, BM Addit 35298, chap 99, f 76ᵃ⁻ᵇ (mid 15 cent); 2, Lambeth 72, chap 104, f 220 (15 cent).

Butler LA, p 149 (description and contents of both MSS).

c. Caxton GL.

Editions. Caxton GL, chap 84; Temple, 3.121.

Sources. Cf ALPHEGE b, MS BM Addit 35298.

Butler LA, p 83 (not in Latin or French texts; probably based on 1438 GL).

[21] AMAND, BISHOP (Feb 6, ca 679).

a. 1438 GL.

MSS. 1, Harley 4775, chap 40, ff 42ᵇ–43ᵃ; MLA roto 343, 1.85; 2, BM Addit 35298, f 24ᵃ (lost Egerton 876).

Sources. Cf Graesse LA, chap 41, p 174.

b. Caxton GL.

Editions. Caxton GL, chap 68; Temple, 3.40.

Sources. Cf de Vignay LD, f 102ᵇ.

[22] AMBROSE, BISHOP OF MILAN (Dec 7, 397).

a. Vernon GL; Brown-Robbins, nos 1110, 1613.

MS. Bodl 3938 (Vernon), ff 89ᵇ col 1, 91ᵃ col 2 (De Theodosio is part of Ambrose legend).

AELeg 1875, p xxiv.

Edition. AELeg 1875, pp 8, 22.

Textual Notes. Kölbing E, EStn 3.126.

Sources. AELeg 1878, p 8 (Graesse LA, chap 57, p 250 quoted).

b. 1438 GL.

MSS. 1, Bodl 21947 (Douce 372), chap 52, breaks off f 44ᵇ; 2, Harley 4775, chap 53, ff 63ᵃ–66ᵃ; MLA roto 343, 1.126; 3, BM Addit 11565, f lxxxv (97); 1st half of legend lost; 4, BM Addit 35298, ff 33ᵇ–35ᵃ.

Sources. Cf Graesse LA, chap 57, p 250.

c. Caxton GL.

Editions. Caxton GL, chap 83; Temple, 3.110.

Sources. Cf de Vignay LD, ff 121ᵇ–124ᵃ.

[23] AMMON, ABBOT IN NITRIA (Oct 4, ca 350).

Edition. Caxton VP, pt 1, chap 30, ff 26ᵇ–28ᵃ.

Selections. Dibdin Typo Antiq, 2.47 (passage on early life).
Sources. La vie des pères, pt 1, chap 30.

AMPHIBALUS: see ALBAN.

ANASTACE: see ANASTASIA.

[24] ANASTASIA (Dec 25, 304?).

  a. SEL; Brown-Robbins, no 2845.
MSS. 8 MSS.
Edition. D'Evelyn and Mill, EETS 236.586 (Corp Christi Camb 145, ff 170ᵇ–172ᵃ; early 14 cent).
Background. Duine F, Notes sur les saints bretons: S Anastase de Bretagne, Revue de Bretagne 35.81 (Anastasia as midwife of Virgin; see SEL version, line 115).

  b. NHC; Brown-Robbins, no 2846.
MS. Harley 4196, ff 15ᵃ–16; f 198ᵇ (15 cent).
Edition. AELeg 1881, p 25.

  c. ScL; Brown-Robbins, no 3441.
MS. Camb Univ Gg.2.6, ff 368ᵃ–371ᵇ (1400–50).
Editions. Horstmann ScL, 2.182; Metcalfe STS, 2.407 (notes 3.449).
Sources. Horstmann ScL, 2.182 (quotes Graesse LA, chap 7, p 47 with variants from Spec Hist); Metcalfe STS, 3.450 (see preceding entry).

  d. 1438 GL.
MSS. 1, Harley 4775, chap 6, ff 13ᵇ–14ᵇ; MLA roto 343, 1.27; 2, BM Addit 35298, f 6ᵇ (lost Bodl 21947, Lambeth 72).
Sources. Cf Graesse LA, chap 7, p 47.

  e. Caxton GL.
Editions. Caxton GL, chap 40; Temple, 2.149.
Sources. Cf de Vignay LD, f 63ᵇ.

[25] ANDREW, APOSTLE (Nov 30, 1st cent).

  a. SEL; Brown-Robbins, no 2848.
MSS. 15 MSS.
Editions. Furnivall EEP, p 98 (Harley 2277, ff 174ᵇ–176ᵃ; end imperf; ca 1300; edn om Miracle of the 3 Riddles).
D'Evelyn and Mill, EETS 236, p 543 (Harley 2277, ff 174ᵇ–176ᵇ; lines 163–238 from Bodl 6924 (Ashmole 43), ff 201ᵃ–200ᵃ; 1325–50).

  b. NHC; Brown-Robbins, no 2847.
MSS. 1, Cotton Tib E.vii, f 277ᵇ (ca 1400); 2, Harley 4196, f 133ᵃ, repeated f 197ᵇ (15 cent).
AELeg 1881, p 1, notes 1, 2 (comparison of texts).
Editions. AELeg 1881, p 1 (MS 1, text from f 133ᵃ, variants of f 197ᵇ; MS 2 text).

Sources. Retzlaff O, Untersuchungen über d nordengl Legenden-cyclus der MSS Harl 4196 und Cotton Tib E.vii, Berlin 1888, p 21 (source either LA or closely related Latin text).

  c. ScL; Brown-Robbins, no 2650.
MS. Camb Univ Gg.2.6, ff 21ᵃ–32ᵇ (1400–50).
Editions. Horstmann ScL, 1.31; Metcalfe STS, 1.63 (notes 3.50).
Sources. Horstmann ScL, 1.31 (quotes Graesse LA, chap 2, p 12).
Metcalfe STS, 3.51 (quotes LA and earlier apocryphal accounts).

  d. Mirk Festial.
MSS. Note 1: Only MSS for which folio nos can be given are listed here.
1, Bodl 17680 (Gough Eccl Top 4), ff 3ᵇ–6ᵇ (1400–50); 2, Cotton Claud A.ii, ff 4ᵃ–6ᵇ (ca 1420); 3, Harley 2247, ff 129ᵇ–133ᵃ (1450–1500); 4, Royal 18.B.xxv, ff 82ᵃ–83ᵃ; rest of fol blank (late 15 cent); 5, Durham Cosins v.iii.5, ff 52ᵃ–56ᵃ (15 cent).
Note 2: AELeg 1881, p cxx lists Harley 2247 as a much expanded version of the Festial; see also Wells, p 302. The Catalog of Western MSS, London 1921, 2.298 notes that the collection of sermons and legends in Royal 18.B.xxv "differs but slightly" from that in Harley 2247 and that about 55 items (these include the legends) "are more or less closely parallel in contents" with Bodl 17680; see EETSES 96. The Catalog also states that the variation in language between Royal 18.B.xxv and Bodl 17680 "suggests the possibility of their being another translation from a common original." This statement would apply equally to Harley 2247 and raises the question whether Harley and Royal should be included with MSS of Mirk's Festial.
Editions. [Mirk J], Liber Festiualis, Caxton pr, Westminster 1483, sig f 3ᵇ–f 4ᵃ (STC, no 17957).
Erbe, EETSES 96.6 (Bodl 17680).
Sources. Cf Graesse LA, chap 2, p 12.

  e. Speculum Sacerdotale.
MS. BM Addit 36791, ff 137ᵇ–138ᵇ (15 cent).
Edition. Weatherly, EETS 200.244 (source LA; abridgement of Passio Andreae, pp xxix, 280).

  f. 1438 GL.
MSS. 1, Harley 4775, chap 1, ff 3ᵃ–5ᵃ; MLA roto 343, 1.6; 2, BM Addit 11565, f 34ᵃ; 3, BM Addit 35298, chap 1, ff 2ᵃ–3ᵃ (Harley 630, f ii only; Egerton 876, f 1 lost; missing in Bodl 21947, Lambeth 72).
Sources. Cf Graesse LA, chap 2, p 12.

g. Caxton GL.
Editions. Caxton GL, chap 33; Temple, 2.94.
Sources. Cf de Vignay LD, ff 50ᵃ–53ᵇ.

[26] ANICET, POPE (April 17, ca 165).

SEL; Brown-Robbins, no 2852.
MS. Bodl 2567 (Bodley 779), f 231ᵃ (ca 1400).
Edition. Zusatzleg 1889, p 398 (Liber pontificalis indirect source, pp 398, 422).

[27] ANNE (July 26, 1st cent B C).
(Note: The life of Anne includes material on Mary, Joseph, and Jesus; see 6. Legends of Jesus and Mary, below.)

a. 12-line stanzas; Brown-Robbins, no 208.
MS. Minnesota Univ, Z.822.N.81 (olim Phillipps 8122), ff 185ᵇ–215ᵃ (early 15 cent).
Parker, EETS 174.xi.
Edition. Parker, EETS 174.1 (crit A C Baugh, PQ 8.414; D Everett, YWES 9.115; N&Q 155.251; E Ekwall, AnglB 40.233; P Grosjean AnBol 47.209; TLS, May 2, 1929, p 360; A Brandl, Arch 158.322; H T M Buckhurst RES 6.91; F A Foster, MLN 45.135; G H Gerould, Spec 5.121).
Textual Notes. Parker, Corrigenda for EETS 174, issued 1930, p 1.
Language. Parker, EETS 174.xii (generally Northern).
Sources. Parker, EETS 174.xxvii, 127 (based on pseudo-Matthew).
Literary Relations. Parker, EETS 174.xxxiv (probable source of Virgin plays in Coventry cycle).

b. Bokenham; Brown-Robbins, no 1414.
MS. Arundel 327, ff 27ᵃ–39ᵃ (1447).
Editions. [Bokenam O], The Lyvys of Seyntys, Roxb Club 50, London 1835, p 41; Horstmann Bokenam, p 37; Serjeantson, EETS 206.38.
Textual Notes. Toner N, Augustinian Spiritual Writers of the English Province in the 15 and 16 Cent, S Augustinus vitae spiritualis magister, Rome 1959, II.504 (possible title for Latin work on Anne referred to in EETS 206.55, line 2008).
Versification. Serjeantson, EETS 206.xxviii (prologue in 16-line stanzas, narrative in rime royal).
Sources. Willenberg G, EStn 12.32 (no direct source known); Serjeantson, EETS 206.xxii (follows Willenberg).

c. Trinity, rime royal; Brown-Robbins, no 2392.
MSS. 1, Trinity Camb 601, ff 221ᵃ–230ᵃ (1450–1500); 2, Chetham 8009, ff 19ᵃ–30ᵇ (late 15 cent).

Kölbing E, Vier Romanzen-Handschriften, EStn 7.195 (contents of MS 2).
Edition. Parker, EETS 174.90; see Corrigenda 1930, p 5 (Trinity with variants of Chetham).
Language. Parker, EETS 174.xvi, xviii (both MSS copies of Southeast Midland text).
Authorship. McCracken, EETSES cvii, pt 1, xxxviii (rejects Stowe's ascription of Life of Anne no 35 to Lydgate).
Sources. Parker, EETS 174.xxx, 134 (source unknown).
Baugh A C, Osbert of Clare, the Sarum Breviary, and the ME St Anne in Rime Royal, Spec 7.106 (English poem a paraphrase of lectiones for St Anne's day in Sarum Breviary).

d. Quatrains; Brown-Robbins, no 3207.
MSS. 1, Bodl 10234 (Tanner 407), ff 21ᵃ–29ᵃ (end 15 cent); 2, Harley 4012, f 130ᵇ (15 cent).
Parker, EETS 174.xxxii (localization of MS 1 in Accle, E Norfolk).
Edition. Parker, EETS 174.110; see Corrigenda 1930, p 6 (MS 1 with variants of MS 2; MS 1 Northeast Midland from original Northern text, MS 2 East Midland, p xxi; based on LA, p xxxiii).

e. 1438 GL.
MSS. 1, Bodl 21947 (Douce 372) beg imperf, ends f 37; 2, Harley 4775, chap 122, ff 160ᵇ–163ᵇ; MLA roto 343, 2.319; 3, BM Addit 35298, ff 111ᵇ–113ᵇ.
Sources. Cf Graesse LA, chap 131, p 585.

f. Caxton GL.
Editions. Caxton GL, chap 165; Temple, 5.96.
Sources. Cf de Vignay LD, ff 262ᵇ–266ᵇ.
Background. Förster M, Die Legende vom Trinubium der hl Anna, Probleme des engl Sprache und Kultur, Festschrift Johannes Hoops, Germanische Biblioth xx, Heidelberg 1925, p 105 (survey of Latin and vernacular versions; argument for possible origin of legend in Normandy or England).

ANNEIS: see AGNES.

ANTIOCH: see VIRGIN OF ANTIOCH.

[28] ANTONY, ABBOT (Jan 17, 356).

a. Royal 17.C.xvii, prose.
MSS. 1, Royal 17.C.xvii, ff 124ᵇ–133ᵃ (early 15 cent); 2, Trinity Camb 601, ff 257ᵃ–271ᵇ (1450–1500).
Horstmann C, Prosalegenden, Angl 4.109 (full descriptions of MS 1).

Edition. Angl 4.116 (MS 1 in 3 parts: life, invention, 1st and 2nd translations).
Textual Notes. Holthausen F, Zur mittelengl Antonius-Legende, Arch 87.61 (corrections of Horstmann's text based on comparison with Latin and French versions).
Language. Angl 4.113 (West Midland with Northern traces).
Authorship. Angl 4.113 (suggests Johannes Presbytor?; the scribe is also the compiler).
Sources. Angl 4.113 (notes incorrect ascription of Latin version to Jerome); Arch 87.60 (notes ultimate Latin sources and similarities of English and French versions).
Rosenthal Vitae patrum, p 74 (notes composite nature of this version).

b. 1438 GL.
MSS. 1, Bodl 21947 (Douce 372) first extant item; beg imperf; 2, Harley 4775, chap 20, ff 21ᵃ–22ᵃ; MLA roto 343, 1.42; 3, BM Addit 35298, ff 13ᵇ–14ᵃ; 4, Trinity Dublin 319; (lost Lambeth 72).
Sources. Cf Graesse LA, chap 21, p 104.

c. Caxton GL.
Editions. Caxton GL, chap 54; Temple, 2.224.
Sources. Cf de Vignay LD, ff 79ᵃ–80ᵇ.

d. Caxton VP.
Edition. Caxton VP, pt 1, chap 36, 32ᵃ–43ᵃ.
Sources. Cf La vie des pères, pt 1, chap 36, ff 31ᵃ–38ᵇ.

ANUPH: see SYRUS.

[29] APOLLINARIS, BISHOP OF RAVENNA (July 23, year?).

a. 1438 GL.
MSS. 1, Harley 4775, chap 90, f 123ᵃ⁻ᵇ; MLA roto 343, 1.246; 2, BM Addit 35298, f 72ᵃ⁻ᵇ; ⅔ of text of Bodl 21947 extant: see Butler LA, p 60.
Sources. Cf Graesse LA, chap 97, p 417.

b. Caxton GL.
Editions. Caxton GL, chap 130; Temple, 4.89.
Sources. Cf Graesse LA, chap 97, p 417 (legend in 1480 edn of de Vignay LD confused).

APOLLINARIS: see TIMOTHY.

[30] APOLLO, ABBOT IN HERMOPOLIS (Jan 25, ca 395).
Edition. Caxton VP, pt 1, chap 7, ff 10ᵃ–12ᵃ.
Sources. Cf La vie des pères, pt 1, chap 7, ff 13ᵇ–16ᵃ.

[31] APOLLONIUS AND PHILEMON, MM (March 8, ca 305).

Edition. Caxton VP, pt 1, chap 19, ff 21ᵇ–22ᵇ.
Sources. Cf La vie des pères, pt 1, chap 19, f 23ᵃ⁻ᵇ.

APOLLONYEN, ABBOT: see APOLLO, ABBOT IN HERMOPOLIS.

APOLLONYEN, MARTYR: see APOLLONIUS AND PHILEMON.

[32] APELLEN (Feb 23 [Whytford Add]).
Edition. Caxton VP, pt 1, chap 15, ff 18ᵇ–19ᵃ.
Sources. Cf La vie des pères, pt 1, chap 15, ff 20ᵇ–21ᵃ.

ARNOLD: see ARNULF.

[33] ARNULF, BISHOP OF METZ (July 18, ca 643).
Editions. Caxton GL, chap 234; Temple, 7.164.
Sources. Cf de Vignay LD, ff 386ᵃ–388ᵃ.

[34] ARSENIUS (July 19, ca 450).

a. 1438 GL.
MSS. 1, Bodl 21947 (Douce 372), f 151 with Moses; 2, Egerton 876, f 299 with Moses; 3, Harley 4775, chap 169, ff 236ᵇ–237ᵇ; MLA roto 343, 2.471; 4, BM Addit 35298, f 154ᵃ⁻ᵇ with Moses (lost BM Addit 11565).
Sources. Cf Graesse LA, chap 178, p 807.

b. Caxton GL.
Editions. Caxton GL, chap 225; Temple, 7.78.
Sources. Cf de Vignay LD, ff 346ᵇ–347ᵃ.
Rosenthal Vitae patrum, p 65 and index (indirect use of VP in Caxton GL).

ATHELWOLD: see ETHELWOLD, BISHOP OF WINCHESTER.

AUDEGONDE: see ALDEGUNDIS.

AUDREY: see ETHELDREDA OF ELY.

AULBYNE: see ALBINUS ((AUBIN).

[35] AUGUSTINE, ARCHBISHOP OF CANTERBURY (May 28, ca 605).

a. SEL; Brown-Robbins, no 2854.
MSS. 19 MSS.
Editions. Horstmann, EETS 87.24 (lines 1–36, Bodl 3938 (Vernon), f 31ᵃ, ca 1385; lines 37–86 Bodl 1486 (Laud Misc 108), f 31ᵃ⁻ᵇ; end 13 cent); D'Evelyn and Mill, EETS 235.214 (Corp Christi Camb 145, ff 80ᵇ–82ᵃ; early 14 cent).

b. Lydgate; Brown-Robbins, no 1875. (Note: For Lydgate's version see under Lydgate.)

c. Speculum Sacerdotale.
MS. BM Addit 36791, chap 38, f 87ᵃ (15 cent).

Edition. Weatherly, EETS 200.154 (Bede ultimate source, pp xxviii, 271).

d. 1438 GL.

MSS. 1, BM Addit 35298, chap 100, f 76ᵇ; 2, Lambeth 72, chap 130, f 220 (lost BM Addit 11565).

e. Caxton GL.

Editions. Caxton GL, chap 100; Temple, 3.194.

Sources. Butler LA, pp 83, 154 (not in Caxton's "legitimate Latin or French texts").

[36] AUGUSTINE, BISHOP OF HIPPO (Aug 28, 430).

a. Vernon GL; Brown-Robbins, no 2855.

MS. Bodl 3938 (Vernon), ff 96ᵃ–100ᵃ (ca 1385).

Edition. AELeg 1878, p 61 (Graesse LA, chap 124, p 548 rptd as source).

Textual Notes. Kölbing E, EStn 3.127.

b. Capgrave Life of St Augustine, prose.

MSS. 1, Cotton Vitell D.xiv, ff 29–35 (7 fragments); 2, BM Addit 36704, ff 5ᵃ–45ᵃ (15 cent).

Munro, EETS 140.ix (accepts MS 2 as holograph).

Bannister H B, Ye Solace of Pilgrimes by John Capgrave, ed C A Mills, Brit and Amer Archaeol Soc of Rome, London 1911, p xii (MS 2 as holograph).

Edition. Munro, EETS 140, 1 (MS 2 as example of Lynn Norfolk dialect, p xiv).

Date. Munro, EETS 140.vii (before 1451).

Arbesmann R, Jordanus of Saxony's Vita S Augustini, The Source for John Capgrave's Life of S Augustine, Trad 1.353 (connected with Capgrave's probable pilgrimage to Rome 1450).

Authorship. de Meijer A, John Capgrave OESA, Augustiniana 5.400; 7.118,531 (detailed bibliography and summary of life and works; for his St Augustine see 5.423; 7.555).

Toner N, Augustinian Spiritual Writers of the English Province in the 15 and 16 Cent, S Augustinus vitae spiritualis magister, Rome 1959, 2.507 (summary of Capgrave's life and works).

Sources. Munro, EETS 140.vii (based on writings of Augustine; possibly on Capgrave's lost Latin life).

Trad 1.341 (Capgrave's chap 5–45, om 12 and 14, are adaptation of Jordanus of Saxony's Vita).

Sanderlin G, John Capgrave Speaks up for Hermits, Spec 18.358 (Capgrave like Jor-

danus upholds priority of Aug Hermits against Aug Canons; minor divergencies from Jordanus listed).

Arbesmann R, The "Malleus" Metaphor in Medieval Characterization, Trad 3.389 (refutes Sanderlin's claim, see preceding entry p 362, that hammer figure is original with Capgrave).

c. 1438 GL.

MSS. 1, Bodl 21947 (Douce 372), gap after f 102; 2, Harley 4775, chap 116, ff 153ᵇ–157ᵇ; MLA roto 343, 2.305; 3, BM Addit 11565, ca f 158, see Butler LA, p 68; 4, BM Addit 35298, chap 138, ff 107ᵃ–109ᵇ; 5, Lambeth 72, chap 98, f 208.

Sources. Cf Graesse LA, chap 124, p 548.

d. Caxton GL.

Editions. Caxton GL, chap 158; Temple, 5.44.

Selections. Aurner N S, Caxton Mirrour of Fifteenth-Century Letters, Boston 1926, p 259 (miracle of boy's reproof, see Temple, 5.65).

Crotch, EETS 176.75 (see preceding entry).

Sources. Cf de Vignay LD, ff 247ᵃ–254ᵃ; cf 1438 GL, Harley 4775, ff 153ᵇ–157ᵇ.

Jeremy Sister M, MS 8.100 (notes Caxton's agreement with 1438 GL in omission of miracles given in de Vignay).

AUSTIN: see AUGUSTINE.

BALTHASAR: see THREE KINGS OF COLOGNE.

[37] BARBARA (Dec 4, year?).

a. SEL; Brown-Robbins, no 3994.

MS. Bodl 14716 (Rawl poet 225), f 2ᵃ (1450–1500).

b. 1438 GL.

MS. Lambeth 72, chap 118, f 251.

Butler LA, p 152.

c. Caxton GL.

Editions. Caxton GL, chap 206; Temple, 6.198; rptd separately J Notary, London 1518 (STC, no 1375).

Sources. Cf de Vignay LD, ff 434ᵃ–436ᵇ.

[38] BARLAAM AND JOSAPHAT (Nov 27, year?).

a. SEL; Brown-Robbins, no 1794.

MS. Bodl 2567 (Bodley 779), ff 288ᵇ–302ᵃ (ca 1400).

Edition. AELeg 1875, p 113.

MacDonald K S, The Story of Barlaam and Joasaph, Buddhism and Christianity, Calcutta 1895, appendix p 26, text p 113, notes by J Morrison (based on AELeg 1875).

Textual Notes. Holthausen F, Zu alt- und mittelengl Dichtungen, Angl 14.318 (emendations of Horstmann's text).
Sources. Cf Graesse LA, chap 180, p 811.

b. NHC; Brown-Robbins, no 41.
MS. Harley 4196, f 199[b]; end imperf (early 15 cent).
Editions. AELeg 1875, p 226.
MacDonald, Barlaam, appendix pp 12, 93 (based on AELeg 1875).

c. Vernon couplets; Brown-Robbins, no 39.
MS. Bodl 3938 (Vernon), f 100[b] col 2; one folio lost after line 568 (ca 1385).
Editions. AELeg 1875, p 215.
MacDonald, Barlaam, appendix pp 1, 57 (based on AELeg 1875).
Sources. Rosenthal Vitae patrum, p 79 (relation of a,b,c versions to LA).

d. Peterhouse; Brown-Robbins, no 3918.
MS. Peterhouse Camb 257, ff 1[a]–144[a] (15 cent).

e. 1438 GL.
MSS. 1, Bodl 21947 (Douce 372), ff 152–154; end imperf; 2, Egerton 876, ff 296[a]–301[b]; 3, Harley 4775, chap 171, ff 238[a]–242[b]; MLA roto 343, 2.474; 4, BM Addit 35298, ff 154[b]–157[a] (lost Harley 630, BM Addit 11565).
Edition. Horstmann C, Barlaam and Josaphat, eine Prosaversion aus MS Egerton 876, Programm . . . des konigl katholischen Gymnasiums zu Sagan, Sagan 1877, p 7 (MS 2 with variants of MS 3; crit E Kölbing, EStn 3.190).
Textual Notes. Kölbing E, EStn 3.193 (comments on Horstmann's text).
Sources. EStn 3.190 (supplements Horstmann's discussion of Graesse LA, chap 180 as source); Ward, 2.131 (de Vignay LD as source of 1438 version).

f. Caxton GL.
Editions. Caxton GL, chap 227; Temple, 7.84.
MacDonald, Barlaam, p 91, The Hystorye of the Hermyte Balaam from William Caxton's Golden Legend (rpt based on Kelmscott edn).
Jacobs J, Barlaam and Josaphat, English Lives of the Buddha, Bibliothèque de Carabas X, London 1896, p 1 (rpt of Caxton; crit F C Conybeare, Acad 49.223).
Sources. Cf Graesse LA, chap 180, p 811; cf de Vignay LD, ff 348[a]–353[a].
Literary Relations. Brotanek R, Mittelengl Dichtungen aus HS 432 des Trinity College

in Dublin, Halle 1940, p 53 (The Trumpet of Death in Balaam and Josaphat and as a separate exemplum).
General. Kuhn E, Barlaam und Joasaph, Eine bibliographisch-literargeschichliche Studie, Abhand d I Class d kaiser Akad d Wissenschaft, Munich 1893, 20, Abteil 1, p 1 (history of legend; see p 71 for English versions; crit F C Conybeare, Acad 49.223).

[39] BARNABAS (June 11, 1st cent).

a. SEL; Brown-Robbins, no 2856.
MSS. 16 MSS.
Editions. Horstmann, EETS 87.26 (Bodl 1486 (Laud Misc 108), ff 31[b]–32[b]; end 13 cent).
D'Evelyn and Mill, EETS 235.217 (Corp Christi Camb 145, ff 82[a]–83[a]; early 14 cent).

b. ScL; Brown-Robbins, no 3175.
MS. Camb Univ Gg.2.6, ff 88[b]–91[b] (1400–50).
Editions. Horstmann ScL, 1.120; Metcalfe, STS, 1.249 (notes 3.178).
Sources. Horstmann ScL, 1.120 (prints passages from Graesse LA, chap 81, p 346, but notes LA is not source).
Metcalfe STS, 3.179 (use of LA doubtful; apocryphal Acta possible source).

c. Mirk Festial.
MSS. Note: See ANDREW d *MSS* [25] above.
1, Bodl 17680 (Gough Eccl Top 4), ff 101[b]–102[b] (1400–50); 2, Cotton Claud A.ii, ff 79[b]–80[b] (ca 1420); (om Bodl 21634, 21682= Douce 60, 108; Harley 2247, 2391; Royal 18.B.xxv; Durham Cosins v.iii.5).
Editions. Note: AELeg 1881, p cxxiii, notes om of Barnabas from Caxton's edn of Mirk, 1483 (STC, no 17957) and later 15 cent edns.
Erbe, EETSES xcvi, chap 42, p 175 (Bodl 17680).

d. Speculum Sacerdotale.
MS. BM Addit 36791, f 87[a-b] (15 cent).
Edition. Weatherly, EETS 200.154 (LA similar but more detailed, pp xxviii, 271).

e. 1438 GL.
MSS. 1, Bodl 21947 (Douce 372), f 54[a]; beg imperf; 2, Harley 4775, chap 73, ff 93[b]–94[b]; MLA roto 343, 1.185; 3, BM Addit 35298, f 46[a-b] (lost BM Addit 11565).
Sources. Cf Graesse LA, chap 81, p 346.

f. Caxton GL.
Editions. Caxton GL, chap 104; Temple, 3.214.
Sources. Cf de Vignay LD, ff 140[a]–142[a].

[40] BARTHOLOMEW (Aug 24, 1st cent).

a. SEL; Brown-Robbins, no 2858.
MSS. 15 MSS.

Editions. Horstmann, EETS 87.366 (Bodl 1486 (Laud Misc 108), ff 157ᵇ–160ᵇ; end 13 cent).

D'Evelyn and Mill, EETS 236.373 (Corp Christi Camb 145, ff 138ᵇ–142ᵃ; early 14 cent).

b. NHC; Brown-Robbins, no 2857.

MSS. 1, Cotton Tib.E.vii, ff 258ᵃ–260ᵃ (ca 1400); 2, Harley 4196, ff 173ᵃ–176ᵃ (15 cent).

Edition. AELeg 1881, p 119 (Harley 4196).

c. ScL; Brown-Robbins, no 2351.

MS. Camb Univ Gg.2.6, ff 62ᵇ–66ᵇ (1400–50).

Editions. Horstmann ScL, 1.86; Metcalfe STS, 1.180 (notes 3.134).

Sources. Horstmann ScL, 1.180 (quotes Graesse LA, chap 123, p 540); Metcalfe STS, 3.135 (quotes LA).

d. Mirk Festial.

MSS. Note: See ANDREW d *MSS* [25] above.

1, Bodl 17680, ff 134ᵇ–137ᵃ (1400–50); 2, Cotton Claud A.ii, ff 101ᵃ–102ᵇ (ca 1420); 3, Harley 2247, ff 185ᵇ–187ᵃ (1450–1500); 4, Royal 18.B.xxv, ff 124ᵇ–126ᵇ (late 15 cent); 5, Durham Cosins v.iii.5, ff 131ᵇ–134ᵇ (15 cent); (om Bodl 21634, 21682; lost Lansdowne 372).

Editions. Liber Festivalis, Caxton, Westminster 1483, sig n 3ᵃ-n 5ᵇ; STC, no 17957.

Erbe, EETSES 96.235 (Bodl 17680).

e. Speculum Sacerdotale.

MS. BM Addit 36791, ff 108ᵇ–110ᵇ (15 cent).

Editions. Weatherly, EETS 200.192 (LA source, pp xxix, 274).

f. 1438 GL.

MSS. 1, Harley 4775, chap 114, ff 150ᵃ–152ᵇ; MLA roto 343, 2.300; 2, BM Addit 35298, ff 105ᵇ–107ᵃ.

Sources. Cf Graesse LA, chap 123, p 540; cf de Vignay LD, ff 243ᵇ–246ᵇ.

g. Caxton GL.

Editions. Caxton GL, chap 157; Temple, 5.31.

Sources. Cf BARTHOLOMEW [40] above.

[41] BASIL THE GREAT (June 14, 379).

a. 1438 GL.

MSS. 1, Harley 4775, chap 25, ff 26ᵃ–27ᵇ; MLA roto 343, 1.52; 2, BM Addit 35298, ff 16ᵃ–17ᵃ.

Sources. Cf Graesse LA, chap 26, p 121.

b. Caxton GL.

Editions. Caxton GL, chap 59; Temple, 2.258.

Sources. Cf de Vignay LD, ff 86ᵇ–88ᵇ; see BASIL a *Sources.*

Butler LA, p 96 (Caxton's etymology compared with French and Latin texts).

c. Caxton VP.

Edition. Caxton VP, pt 1, chaps 159–65.

Sources. Cf La vie des pères, pt 1, chaps 159–65, ff 132ᵃ–137ᵇ.

Rosenthal Vitae patrum, pp 65, 134 (legend in Caxton GL and Caxton VP from different sources).

BASTIAN: see SEBASTIAN.

BEATRICE: see SIMPLICIUS.

[42] BEDE (May 27, 735).

Editions. Caxton GL, chap 218; Temple 7.39; see 2 anecdotes of Bede in Caxton GL, Pelagius, chap 228; Temple, 7.120.

Sources. Butler LA, pp 83, 85 (Bede not in Caxton's usual Latin or French sources).

[43] BENEDICT, ABBOT (March 21, ca 547).

a. SEL; Brown-Robbins, no 2860.

MSS. 16 MSS.

Editions. McCann J, Early English Verses on St Benedict, Downside Review 41.48 (Bodl 6924 [Ashm 43], ff 46ᵃ–48ᵇ; 1325–50; corrections from Corp Christi Camb 145; crit P Grosjean, AnBol 42.196).

D'Evelyn and Mill, EETS 235.122 (Corp Christi Camb 145, ff 46ᵃ–48ᵃ; early 14 cent).

b. SEL variant; Brown-Robbins, no 2861.

MSS. 1, Bodl 3938 (Vernon), f 16ᵃ col 1 (ca 1385); 2, Fitzwilliam Mus, McClean 128, f 20ᵇ; lines 1–5 only (15 cent); 3, Lambeth 223, f 88ᵇ (end 14 cent).

Editions. DownR 41.53 (Bodl 3938, corrections from Lambeth 223).

Sources. DownR 41.48 (material of both a & b found in Gregory's Dialogues; cf Migne PL 66, col 125).

c. 1438 GL.

MSS. 1, Bodl 21947 (Douce 372); gaps after ff 30, 31; 2, Egerton 876, f 65ᵃ; beg imperf; 3, Harley 4775, chap 47, ff 51ᵇ–54ᵇ; MLA roto 343, 1.103; 4, BM Addit 35298, ff 28ᵃ–29ᵇ.

Sources. Cf Graesse LA, chap 49, p 204.

d. Caxton GL.

Editions. Caxton GL, chap 78; Temple, 3.80.

Sources. Cf de Vignay LD, ff 114ᵃ–117ᵃ.

BENET: see BENEDICT.

BERIN: see BIRINUS.

[44] BERNARD, ABBOT OF CLAIRVAUX (Aug 20, 1153).

a. Vernon GL; Brown-Robbins, no 2863.

MS. Bodl 3938 (Vernon), f 93[b] col 3 (ca 1385).
Edition. AELeg 1878, p 41.
Textual Notes. Kölbing E, EStn 3.127.
Sources. Cf Graesse LA, chap 120, p 527; rptd AELeg 1878, p 41.

b. 1438 GL.
MSS. 1, Harley 4775, chap 112, ff 146[a]–150[a]; MLA roto 343, 2.292; 2, BM Addit 35298, ff 103[a]–105[a].
Sources. Cf Graesse LA, chap 120, p 527; cf de Vignay LD, ff 239[a]–243[a].

c. Caxton GL.
Editions. Caxton GL, chap 154; Temple, 5.12.
Sources. See BERNARD b *Sources.*
Butler LA, p 91 (use of Latin and French in etymology).

BIRGITTA: see BRIDGET OF SWEDEN.

[45] BIRINUS, BISHOP OF
DORCHESTER (Dec 5, ca 650).
SEL; Brown-Robbins, no 2862.
MSS. 1, Bodl 1596 (Laud Misc 463), f 126[a] (beg 15 cent); 2, Bodl 2567 (Bodl 779), f 270[a] (ca 1400); 3, Trinity Oxf 57, f 145[b] (end 15 cent); 4, Cotton Julius.D.ix, ff 205[b]–207[a] (15 cent).

[46] BLAISE, BISHOP OF SEBASTEA
(Feb 3, 316?).
a. SEL; Brown-Robbins, no 2866.
MSS. 18 MSS.
Editions. Horstmann, EETS 87.485 (Bodl 1486 (Laud Misc 108), ff 228[b]–230[b]; add in later hand).
D'Evelyn and Mill, EETS 235.47 (Corp Christi Camb 145, ff 17[b]–20[a]; early 14 cent).

b. ScL; Brown-Robbins, no 3086.
MSS. Camb Univ Gg.2.6, ff 132[b]–137[a] (1400–50); ff 134–135 missing.
Editions. Horstmann ScL, 1.170; Metcalfe STS, 1.361 (notes 3.228).
Sources. Cf Graesse LA, chap 38, p 167; rptd Horstmann ScL, 1.70); Metcalfe STS, 3.229 (passages from LA).

c. 1438 GL.
MSS. 1, Harley 4775, chap 37, ff 40[a]–41[a]; MLA roto 343, 1.80; 2, BM Addit 11565, f 85[a]; beg imperf); 3, BM Addit 35298, ff 22[b]–23[a].
Sources. See BLAISE b *Sources.*

d. Caxton GL.
Editions. Caxton GL, chap 66; Temple, 3.27.
Sources. Cf de Vignay LD, ff 99[a]–100[b]; see also BLAISE b *Sources.*

BOTOLPH: see BOTULF.

[47] BOTULF, ABBOT (June 17, ca 680).
SEL; Brown-Robbins, no 2867.
MSS. 1, Bodl 2567 (Bodl 779), f 305[a] (ca 1400); 2, Bodl 3938 (Vernon), f 33[b] col 1 (ca 1385); 3, Trinity Camb 605, f 68[b] (early 15 cent); 4, Egerton 1993, f 161[a] (1300–50).
Background. Stevenson F S, St Botolph (Botwulf) and Iken, Suffolk Instit of Archaeol and Nat Hist, Proceedings 59.29.

BRANDAN: see BRENDAN.

[48] BRENDAN, ABBOT OF CLONFORT
(May 16, 6 cent).
a. SEL; Brown-Robbins, no 2868.
MSS. 15 MSS.
Bälz M, Die ME Brendanlegende des Gloucesterlegendars, Berlin 1909, p i (relationship of 12 MSS).
Editions. Wright T, St Brandan, A Medieval Legend of the Sea in English Verse and Prose, Percy Soc 14, London 1844; rptd D O'Donoghue, Brendaniana, Dublin 1893, p 359 (Harley 2277, ff 41[b]–51[a]; ca 1300).
Horstmann C, Die altenglische Legende von St Brendan, Arch 53.17 (Bodl 6924 [Ashm 43], ff 71[b]–80[b]; 1325–50).
Horstmann, EETS 87.220 (Bodl 1486 [Laud Misc 108], ff 104[a]–110[a]; end 13 cent).
Bälz, Brendanlegende, p 1 (Bodl 6924 with variants of 11 MSS).
D'Evelyn and Mill, EETS 235.180 (Corp Christi Camb 145, ff 67[b]–77[a]; early 14 cent).
Selections. Sampson G, The Cambridge Bk of Prose and Verse, Camb 1924, p 345 (Great Fish and Paradise of Birds, Harley 2277, lines 151–222 from Wright, Percy Soc 14.7; followed by corresponding passage from Caxton GL, cf Temple, 7.51).
Modernizations. Weston J L, The Chief ME Poets, Boston 1914, p 57 (based on Horstmann, EETS 87.220).
Language. Bälz, Brendanlegende, p xxvii (SW dialect characteristics noted).
Versification. Bälz, Brendanlegende, p xii (by analysis of versification of Brendan and other SEL items attempts to show common authorship of SEL and Poema Morale).
Sources. Wright, Percy Soc 14.viii (abridged indirectly from Navigatio S Brandani).
Schirmer G, Zur Brendanus-Legende, Leipzig 1888, p 56 (Navigatio as direct source).
Bälz, Brendanlegende, p v (textual evidence for Navigatio, French and AN versions as sources).
Literary Relations. Ker W P, The Craven Angels, MLR 6.85 (compares neutral angels in SEL Brendan and Michael legends with classic daemons).

b. 1438 GL.
MSS. 1, BM Addit 11565, ff 59ᵃ–61ᵇ; breaks off in Judas incident; 2, BM Addit 35298, ff 81ᵇ–84ᵃ; 3, Lambeth 72, chap 97, f 202ᵃ.
Ward, 2.555 (description of MS 1).
Sources. Ward, 2.556 (based on SEL).

c. Caxton GL.
Editions. Caxton GL, chap 220, ff 394ᵇ–398ᵇ; Temple, 7.48; rptd separately Wynkyn de Worde, London (1520? STC, no 3600); rptd from 1527 edn of GL (STC, no 24880) Wright, Percy Soc 14.35; rptd from Wright, O'Donoghue, Brendiana, p 380.
Selections: See also above under a *Selections*. Dibdin Typo Antiq, 2.78 (account of Earthly Paradise from 1498 edn, f 357 [STC, no 24876]).
Modernization. Shackford M H, Legends and Satires from Mediaeval Literature, Boston 1913, p 53.
Sources. Ward, 2.556 (based on 1438 GL with slight changes and omissions).
Butler LA, p 83 (claims positive evidence for 1438 GL as source).
Background. Suchier H, Brandans Seefahrt, RomanSt 1, no 5, p 558 (brief account of Eng material).
Schirmer G, Zur Brendanus-Legende, Leipzig 1888 (relationship of extant versions; p 56 Eng material).
Zimmer H, Brendans Meerfahrt, ZfDA 33.129,257 (evidence for Imram Maelduin as source of Navigatio B; latter's place in spread of legend).
Ward, 2.516 (Latin, French and Eng versions).
Plummer C, Vitae sanctorum hiberniae, 2 vols, Oxford 1910, 1.xxxvi (detailed study of Brendan's life and legend).
Kenny J F, The Legend of St Brendan, Proc and Transact Royal Soc of Canada 3s 14.51 (life, legend, versions, sources).
Baum P F, Judas' Sunday Rest, MLR 18.168 (treatment of incident in various versions).
Bibliography. Dunn J, The Brendan Problem, CHR 6.471.
Selmer C, The Vernacular Translations of the Navigatio S Brendani: A Bibliographical Study, MS 18.145 (English listed under Germanic versions); Navigatio S Brendani Abbatis from Early Latin MSS, Univ Notre Dame Publ in Mediaeval Studies 16.117 (includes work on ME versions).

[49] BRICE, BISHOP OF TOURS (Nov 13, 444).

a. SEL; Brown-Robbins, no 2870.
MSS. 11 MSS.

b. NHC; Brown-Robbins, no 2869.
MSS. 1, Cotton Tib.E.vii, ff 269ᵇ–271ᵃ (ca 1400); 2, Harley 4196, ff 189ᵇ–190ᵇ (15 cent).
Edition. AELeg 1881, p 156 (Harley 4196).
Sources. Retzlaff O, Untersuchungen über den nordenglischen Legendencyklus der MSS Harley 4196 und Cotton Tib.E.vii, Berlin 1888, p 16 (no essential variations from LA).

c. 1438 GL.
MSS. 1, Harley 4775, chap 159, ff 216ᵇ–217ᵃ; MLA roto 343, 2.431; 2, BM Addit 35298, f 143ᵇ.
Sources. Cf Graesse LA, chap 167, p 751.

d. Caxton GL.
Editions. Caxton GL, chap 204; Temple, 6.158.
Sources. Cf de Vignay LD, ff 329ᵇ–330ᵃ; Butler LA, p 89 (etymology only in French version).

BRIDE: see BRIDGET OF IRELAND.

[50] BRIDGET OF IRELAND (Feb 1, ca 525).

a. SEL short version; Brown-Robbins, no 2871.
MSS. 1, Bodl 1486 (Laud Misc 108), ff 93ᵇ–94ᵇ (end 13 cent); 2, Bodl 3938 (Vernon), f 16ᵃ col 2 (ca 1385); 3, Lambeth 223, f 62ᵃ (end 14 cent).
Edition. Horstmann, EETS 87.192 (Bodl 1486).

b. SEL long version; Brown-Robbins, no 2872.
MSS. 15 MSS; add 16, PRO C.47.34.1 no 5, f 4ᵃ; lines 1–82 (early 14 cent).
Report on the MSS of Lord Middleton, Hist MSS Com, London 1911, p 622 (identification and text of MS 15, olim Wollaston Hall, fragments, ca 1300).
D'Evelyn, EETS 244.1n5 (contents of MS 16).
Edition. D'Evelyn and Mill, EETS 235.37 (Corp Christi Camb 145, ff 14ᵃ–17ᵇ; early 14 cent).

c. 1438 GL.
MSS. 1, BM Addit 35298, chap 95, ff 74ᵇ–75ᵃ; 2, Lambeth 72, chap 100, f 216.

[51] BRIDGET, BIRGITTA, OF SWEDEN (Oct 8, 1373).

(Note: See also Audelay's Salutatio S Brigitte).

a. Cotton Claud B.i, prose.
MS. Cotton Claud B.i, ff 2–4; beg, end imperf (15 cent).

Cumming, EETS 178.xvii, xxx note 2 (description of MS).

b. Cotton Jul F.ii, prose.

MS. Cotton Jul F.ii, f 254ᵃ (15 cent; brief account of death, writings, canonization).
Cumming, EETS 178.xvi, xxx note 2 (description of MS).
Selections. Aungier G J, History and Antiquities of Syon Monastery, London 1840, p 19 (account of her death).

c. Gascoigne? Life of St Bridget, prose.

Editions. The lyfe of St Birgette, Pynson 1516 (STC, no 4602); rptd Blunt, EETSES 19.xlvii.
Authorship. Blunt, EETSES 19.ix (accepts Thomas Gascoigne as author).
Cumming, EETS 178.xxx note 2 (evidence against Gascoigne as author).
Pronger W A, Thomas Gascoigne, EHR 53.625 (Gascoigne not author).
Bibliography. Cumming, EETS 178.xxiii note 1 (chief medieval and modern authorities for life).
Redpath H M D, God's Ambassadress St Bridget of Sweden, Milwaukee 1947, p 208 (Latin and vernacular versions noted).

CALIXT, KALIXT: see ALEXIS g.

CALIXT: see CALIXTUS I.

[52] CALIXTUS I, POPE (Oct 14, ca 222).

a. SEL; Brown-Robbins, no 1553.

MS. Bodl 2567 (Bodl 779), ff 187ᵃ–188ᵇ (ca 1400).
Edition. Zusatzleg 1889, p 328 (source uncertain, pp 328n1, 422).

b. 1438 GL.

MSS. 1, Harley 630, f 314; 2, Harley 4775, chap 146, f 193ᵃ⁻ᵇ; MLA roto 343, 2.386; 3, BM Addit 35298, f 131ᵃ⁻ᵇ; (om Lambeth 72).
Sources. Cf Graesse LA, chap 154, p 686.

c. Caxton GL.

Editions. Caxton GL, chap 188; Temple, 5.255.
Sources. Cf de Vignay LD, f 303ᵃ⁻ᵇ; Butler LA, p 89 (etymology as evidence for French source).

CALSTON: see CALIXTUS I.

CARPOFORUS: see FOUR CROWNED MARTYRS.

CASPAR: see THREE KINGS OF COLOGNE.

CATHERINE: see KATHERINE.

[53] CECILIA (Nov 22, year?).

a. SEL; Brown-Robbins, no 2873.

MSS. 12 MSS.
Editions. Furnivall F J, Originals and Analogues of Some of Chaucer's CT, pt ii.12, ChS 2s, no 10, p 208 (Bodl 6924 [Ashm 43], ff 185ᵇ–188ᵇ; 1325–50).
Horstmann, EETS 87.490 (Bodl 1486 [Laud Misc 108], ff 230ᵇ–233ᵇ; appendix, in later hand).
Lovewell B E, The Life of St Cecilia, YSE 3, Boston 1898 (1, p 73, Bodl 2567 [Bodl 779], ff 286ᵃ–288ᵇ; ca 1400; 2, p 72, Bodl 6924, ff 185ᵇ–188ᵇ; 3, p 3, Cotton Cleop D.ix, ff 155ᵇ–158ᵇ; 14 cent) (crit E Kölbing, EStn 26.394; A Brandl, Arch 103.177).
Sources. Kölbing E, Zu Chaucer's Caecilien-Legende, EStn 1.229 (textual evidence that SEL and NHC versions depend on different texts of LA and were not used by Chaucer).
Holthausen F, Zu Chaucer's Caecilien-Legende, Arch 87.270 (further comparison of SEL and NHC with LA; similar comparison of ScL and Bokenham).

b. NHC; Brown-Robbins, no 1671.

MSS. 1, Cotton Tib E.vii, ff 271ᵃ–274ᵇ (ca 1400); 2, Harley 4196, ff 191ᵃ–193ᵇ (15 cent).
Editions. Kölbing E, EStn 1.235 (Harley 4196; crit J Zupitza, AfDA, 4.251).
AELeg 1881, p 159 (Harley 4196).
Lovewell, St Cecilia, p 92 (Cotton Tib E.vii).
Modernizations. Weston J L, The Chief ME Poets, Boston 1914, p 72 (based on AELeg 1881, p 159).
Textual Notes. AfDA 4.252 (emendations of Kölbing's text); EStn 26.397 (emendations of Lovewell's text).
Sources. See CECILIA a *Sources.*

c. Chaucer CT; Brown-Robbins, no 4019.
(Note: See SECOND NUN'S TALE under Chaucer.)

d. ScL; Brown-Robbins, no 3765.

MS. Camb Univ Gg.2.6, ff 354ᵃ–360ᵇ (1400–50).
Editions. Horstmann ScL, 2.162; Metcalfe STS, 2.368 (notes 3.429); Lovewell, St Cecilia, p 92.
Sources. Horstmann ScL, 2.162 (quotes Graesse LA, chap 169, p 771); Metcalfe STS, 3.431 (see preceding entry); Arch 87.272 (ScL and Bokenham compared with LA).

e. Bokenham; Brown-Robbins, no 589.

MS. Arundel 327, ff 134ᵇ–150ᵇ (1447).

Editions. [Bokenam O,] The Lyvys of Seyntys, Roxb Club 50, London 1835, p 212; Horstmann Bokenam, p 186; Serjeantson, EETS 206.201.

Sources. See CECILIA d *Sources.*

Kölbing E, EStn 7.143 (agreements with Chaucer due to common use of longer version of LA).

Willenberg G, Die Quellen von Osbern Bokenham's Legenden, EStn 12.17; see EETS 206.xxiii (source LA but not Graesse's text).

f. 1438 GL.

MSS. 1, Bodl 21947, chap 24 = 124, f 37ª, repeated f 141ª, beg imperf; 2, Harley 4775, chap 124, ff 163ᵇ–166ª repeated chap 161, ff 219ᵇ–221ᵇ; MLA roto 343, 2.325, 439; 3, BM Addit 11565, f 172; 4, BM Addit 35298, ff 113ᵇ–115ª.

Sources. Cf Graesse LA, chap 169, p 771.

g. Caxton GL.

Editions. Caxton GL, chap 212; Temple, 6.247; rptd Furnivall, Originals and Analogues, p 207.

Sources. Cf de Vignay LD, ff 373ᵇ–374ª; rptd from 1513 edn, Furnivall, Originals and Analogues, p 193; EStn 1.240 (evidence for Caxton's direct use of Chaucer's text); Butler LA, p 91 (LA as source of etymology).

CECILY: see CECILIA.

[54] CELESTINE I, POPE (April 6, 432).

Stanzas; Brown-Robbins, no 195.

MS. Bodl 1596 (Laud Misc 463), ff 118ᵇ–124ᵇ (beg 15 cent).

Edition. Horstmann C, Die Legenden von Celestin und Susanna, Angl 1.67.

Textual Notes. Holthausen F, Zu alt- und mittelengl Dichtungen, Angl 14:310 (emendations of Horstmann's text).

Language. Angl 1.56 (East Midland with northern traces).

Versification. Angl 1.62 (stanza form aaabb unique); Gerould S Leg, p 229 (stanza form aaabcb).

Date, Authorship. Angl 1.63 (possibly written by author of Gregorius legend, see Brown-Robbins, nos 204, 209).

CELSE, CELSUS: see NAZARIUS.

CEMON: see ABDON and SENNEN.

[55] CHAD, BISHOP OF LICHFIELD (March 2, 672).

(Note: See WULFHAD AND RUFFIN [294].)

a. SEL; Brown-Robbins, no 2874.

MSS. 13 MSS.

Edition. D'Evelyn and Mill, EETS 235.78 (Corp Christi Camb 145, ff 29ᵇ–30ᵇ; early 14 cent).

Sources. Cf Bede, Historia ecclesiastica gentis Anglorum, bk 3, chap 28; bk 4, chap 3 (ultimate source).

b. 1438 GL.

MSS. 1, BM Addit 11565; see Butler LA, p 66; 2, BM Addit 35298, f 79ᵇ; 3, Lambeth 72, chap 111, f 230.

Background. Warner R H, Life and Legends of St Chad, Wisbech 1871 (includes modernized passages from SEL Chad).

[56] CHRISTIAN OF MAINE (CENOMANENSIS) (ca 1160?).

Edition. Caxton VP, pt 1, chap 105, ff 133ᵇ–134ª.

Sources. Cf La vie des pères, p 1, chap 105, f 105ᵃ⁻ᵇ; see Migne PL, 73.77.

[57] CHRISTINA OF BOLSENA (July 24, year?).

a. SEL; Brown-Robbins, no 2876.

MSS. 14 MSS.

Edition. D'Evelyn and Mill, EETS 235.315 (Corp Christi Camb 145, ff 117ᵇ–122ª; early 14 cent).

b. NHC; Brown-Robbins, no 1006.

MS. Harley 4196, ff 162ᵇ–164ª (15 cent).

Edition. AELeg 1881, p 93.

Sources. See CHRISTINA d *Sources.*

c. ScL; Brown-Robbins, no 3358.

MS. Camb Univ Gg.2.6, ff 364ᵇ–368ª (1400–50).

Editions. Horstmann ScL, 2.177; Metcalfe STS, 2.398 (notes 3.444).

Sources. See CHRISTINA d *Sources.*

d. William Paris, 8-line stanzas; Brown-Robbins, no 2877.

MS. Arundel 168, ff 2ª–4ᵇ (15 cent).

Edition. AELeg 1878, p 183.

Textual Notes. Kölbing E, EStn 3.132 (emendations of Horstmann's text).

Date. Gerould G H, The Legend of St Christina by William Paris, MLN 29.129 (written ca 1398–99 during imprisonment of Thomas Earl of Warwick).

Sources and Literary Relations. MLN 29.131 (like Christina a,b,c, based independently on some version of LA; influenced by Chaucer's St Cecilia).

e. Bokenham; Brown-Robbins, no 4073.

MS. Arundel 327, ff 39ᵇ–58ª (1447).

Editions. [Bokenam O,] The Lyvys of Seyntys,

Roxb Club 50, London 1835, p 61; Horstmann Bokenham, p 54; Serjeantson, EETS
206.58.
Sources. See CHRISTINA d under *Sources.*
Willenberg G, Die Quellen von Osbern
Bokenham's Legenden, EStn 12.34 (exact
source undetermined).

f. 1438 GL.
MSS. 1, Harley 4775, chap 91, ff 123ᵇ–124ᵇ;
MLA roto 343, 1.249; 2, BM Addit 35298,
f 84ᵃ⁻ᵇ.
Sources. Cf Graesse LA, chap 98, p 419.

g. Caxton GL.
Editions. Caxton GL, chap 131; Temple, 4.93.
Sources. Butler LA, p 90 (Caxton's etymology
not in agreement with known LA or de
Vignay texts).

[58] CHRISTINA MIRABILIS OF ST
TRUDONS (July 24, 1224).
MS. Bodl 21688 (Douce 114), ff 12ᵃ–26ᵇ (15
cent).
Horstmann C, Prosalegenden. Die Legenden
des MS Douce 114, Angl 8.102.
Editions. Angl 8.119 (Nottinghamshire dia-
lect?, p 106).
Sources. Angl 8.104 (translation of Vita S
Christinae by Thomas Cantimpre, OP).
Background. Thurston H, The Transition
Period of Catholic Mysticism II, The
Month 140.122 (psychological explanation
of Christina's marvels).

[59] CHRISTOPHER (July 25, year?).
(Note: Brown-Robbins, no 3545, 26 lines
in 19 cent hand om).

a. SEL; Brown-Robbins, no 2878.
MSS. 16 MSS.
Editions. Furnivall EEP, p 59 (Harley 2277,
ff 101ᵇ–104ᵃ, ca 1300; AESpr 1.194 (Harley
2277 from Furnivall).
Horstmann C, JfRESL 14.35 (Bodl 1486
[Laud Misc 108], ff 121ᵇ–124ᵃ, end 13 cent).
Horstmann, EETS 87.271 (Bodl 1486).
D'Evelyn and Mill, EETS 235.340 (Corp
Christi Camb 145, ff 127ᵃ–130ᵃ, early 14
cent).

b. ScL; Brown-Robbins, no 793.
MS. Camb Univ Gg.2.6, ff 124ᵇ–132ᵇ (1400–
50).
Editions. Horstmann ScL, 1.160; Metcalfe
STS, 1.340 (notes 3.216).
Sources. Horstmann ScL, 1.160 (quotes
Graesse LA, chap 100, p 430, though per-
haps not source).
Metcalfe STS, 3.218 (quotes LA; refers also
to Petrus de Natalibus Cat SS).

c. Thornton couplets; Brown-Robbins,
no 1990.
MS. Lincoln Cath 91 (Thornton MS), ff 122ᵇ–
129ᵇ (ca 1440); material missing between ff
122–3.
AELeg 1881, p 454 (notes date, dialect and
contents of MS).
Editions. AELeg 1881, p 454.

d. 1438 GL.
MSS. 1, Bodl 21947 (Douce 372), f 78ᵇ, end
imperfect; 2, Harley 4775, chap 93, ff 127ᵃ–
128ᵇ; MLA roto 343, 1.254; 3, BM Addit
35298, ff 86ᵇ–87ᵇ; 4, Trinity Coll Dublin
319; see Gerould S Leg, p 195.
Sources. Cf Graesse LA, chap 100, p 430.

e. Caxton GL.
Editions. Caxton GL, chap 133; Temple,
4.111; rptd with slight changes H Thurs-
ton and D Attwater, Butler's Lives of the
Saints, 3.184.
Sources. Cf de Vignay LD, ff 196ᵃ–198ᵃ.

[60] CHRYSOGONUS (Nov 24, 304?).
(Note: See ANASTASIA [24]).

a. 1438 GL.
MSS. 1, Harley 4775, chap 163, f 225ᵃ⁻ᵇ;
MLA roto 343, 2.450; 2, BM Addit 35298,
ff 147ᵇ–148ᵃ. Lost Bodl 21947; omitted
Lambeth 72.
Sources. Cf Graesse LA, chap 171, p 788.

b. Caxton GL.
Editions. Caxton GL, chap 214; Temple,
6.270.
Sources. Cf de Vignay LD, f 338ᵃ⁻ᵇ.

CIRIACUS, CIRIAK: see CYRIACUS.

CISINE, SISINNIUS: see SATURNINUS
and CISINE.

[61] CLARE OF ASSISI (Aug 12, 1253).
Editions. Caxton GL, chap 205; Temple
6.161. Omitted in index of 1483 edn.
Sources. Cf de Vignay LD, ff 162ᵃ–169ᵇ (omits
appendix with miracles).

[62] CLEMENT I, POPE (Nov 23, ca 99).

a. SEL; Brown-Robbins, no 2875.
MSS. 17 MSS.
Editions. Horstmann, EETS 87.322 (Bodl 1486
[Laud Misc 108], ff 141ᵃ–147ᵃ, end 13 cent).
D'Evelyn and Mill, EETS 236.515 (Harley
2277, ff 164ᵃ–171ᵃ, ca 1300).

b. ScL; Brown-Robbins, no 3781.
MS. Camb Univ Gg.2.6, ff 137ᵃ–148ᵇ (1400–
50).
Editions. Horstmann ScL, 1.175; Metcalfe
STS, 1.373 (notes 3.234).

Sources. Horstmann ScL, 1.175 (quotes Graesse LA, chap 170, p 777).

Metcalfe STS, 3.236 (passages from LA; references to "Homilies" and "Recognitions" of Clement).

c. Speculum Sacerdotale.

MSS. BM Addit 36791, ff 135^b–137^a (15 cent).

Editions. Weatherly, EETS 200.240 (LA, chap 170, as source, pp xxix, 279).

d. 1438 GL.

MSS. 1, Bodl 21947 (Douce 372), f 143, end imperfect; 2, Harley 4775, chap 162, ff 221^b–225^a; MLA roto 343, 2.443; 3, BM Addit 11565, follows Elizabeth f 215, see Butler LA, p 69; 4, BM Addit 35298, ff 145^b–147^b; 5, Lambeth 72, corresponds to chap 163 of Harley 4775, see Butler LA, p 152.

Sources. Cf Graesse LA, chap 170, p 777.

e. Caxton GL.

Editions. Caxton GL, chap 213; Temple, 6.253.

Sources. Cf de Vignay LD, ff 334^a–338^a; Butler LA, p 92 (evidence for use of de Vignay but not in 1480 edn).

COPRES: see COPRETT.

[63] COPRETT AND MUTIUS (May 25?).

(Note: see Rosweyd's comment, Migne PL 21.422, note a; for date see Whytford Martiloge, p. 82.)

Editions. Caxton VP, pt 1, chap 9, ff 13^b–15^b.

Sources. La vie des pères, pt 1, chap 9, ff 16^b–18^a; cf Migne PL 21.422.

CORNELIEN: see CORNELIUS AND CYPRIAN.

[64] CORNELIUS, POPE, AND CYPRIAN, BISHOP OF CARTHAGE (Sept 16, 253, 258).

a. 1438 GL.

MSS. 1, Harley 4775, chap 130, f 171^a–b; MLA roto 343, 2.342; 2, BM Addit 35298, f 119^a.

Sources. Cf Graesse LA, chap 132, p 595.

b. Caxton GL.

Editions. Caxton GL, chap 171; Temple, 5.142.

Sources. Cf de Vignay LD, ff 275^b–276^a.

CORONA: see VICTOR WITH CORONA.

[65] COSMAS AND DAMIAN (Sept 27, year?).

a. ScL; Brown-Robbins, no 2629.

MS. Camb Univ Gg.2.6, ff 298^a–332^a (1400–

50; after f 300 folios are misnumbered in MS).

Editions. Horstmann ScL, 2.116; Metcalfe STS, 2.292 (notes 3.403).

Sources. Cf Graesse LA, chap 143, p 636 (passages rptd by both Horstmann and Metcalfe).

b. 1438 GL.

MSS. 1, Harley 4775, chap 136, f 178^a–b; MLA roto 343, 2.356; 2, BM Addit 35298, ff 122^b–123^a (om Lambeth 72).

Sources. Cf Graesse LA, chap 143, p 636.

c. Caxton GL.

Editions. Caxton GL, chap 177; Temple, 5.172.

Sources. Cf de Vignay LD, ff 283^a–284^a; Butler LA, p 91 (comparison with French and Latin etymologies).

Background. Deubner L, Kosmas und Damian, Texte und Einleitung, Leipzig 1907, p 38 (materials on which facts and theories of development of cult are based).

[66] CRISAUNT AND DARIA (Oct 25, year?).

a. SEL; Brown-Robbins, no 2761.

MS. Bodl 2567 (Bodley 779), ff 192^a–195^a (15 cent).

Editions. Zusatzleg 1889, p 336 (version in Acta SS not the source, p 336n1).

b. 1438 GL.

MSS. 1, Harley 4775, chap 150, ff 197^b–198^a; MLA roto 343, 2.395; 2, BM Addit 35298, ff 133^b–134^a (om Lambeth 72).

Sources. Cf Graesse LA, chap 157, p 700.

c. Caxton GL.

Editions. Caxton GL, chap 191; Temple, 6.59.

Sources. Cf de Vignay LD, f 309^a–b.

[67] CRISPIN AND CRISPINIAN (Oct 25, year?).

a. SEL; Brown-Robbins, no 2225.

MS. Bodl 2567 (Bodley 779), ff 197^a–198^b (ca 1400).

Edition. Zusatzleg 1889, p 343 (general reference to Acta SS, Oct 25, p 343n1).

b. Caxton GL.

Editions. Caxton GL, chap 193; Temple, 6.69.

Sources. Note: This legend, which stands between Ursula and Simon and Jude, is not included in the BM copy of the 1480 edn of de Vignay LD (see Butler LA, p 43) nor in Graesse LA. Caxton's vocabulary suggests a French source.

[68] CUTHBERT, BISHOP OF LINDISFARNE (March 20, 687).

a. SEL; Brown-Robbins, no 2880.
MSS. 19 MSS; add 20, Winchester Coll 33ª, ff 24ª–25ª (15 cent).
Editions. Horstmann, EETS 87.359 (Bodl 1486 [Laud Misc 108], ff 154ᵇ–155ᵇ, end 13 cent).
Fowler J T, The Life of St Cuthbert in English Verse, Durham 1891, Surtees Soc 87 (Bodl 1486).
Fowler, Surtees Soc 87 (Bodl 2567 [Bodley 779], f 134ª, ca 1400).
D'Evelyn and Mill, EETS 235.118 (Corp Christi Camb 145, ff 44ᵇ–46ª, early 14 cent).

　　b. Castle Howard couplets; Brown-Robbins, no 2879.
MS. Castle Howard, pp 1–203 (ca 1450).
Editions. Fowler, Surtees Soc 87.1 (crit E Kölbing, EStn 19.121; emendations of lines 1–3000, EStn 19.122).
Lessmann H, Studien zu dem mittelengl Life of St Cuthbert I, Darmstadt 1896; rptd EStn 23.345 (emendations of Fowler's complete text).
Language. Lessmann H, St Cuthbert II, p 26, Darmstadt 1896; rptd with additions EStn 24.176 (analysis of northern features and ON loan words).
Sources and Literary Relations. Fowler, Surtees Soc 87 (compilation of legendary and historical material, p vi and marginal notes in text; miracle of Cuthbert and King Alfred, lines 4333–4571, p x, also in Chronicon Vilodunense, see EDITH OF WILTON [78] below).
McKeehan I P, The Book of the Nativity of St Cuthbert, PMLA 48.981 (12th cent source of romantic details of saint's early life; crit P Grosjean, AnBol 54.206).
Colgrave B, The Post-Bedan Miracles and Translations of St Cuthbert, in The Early Culture of North-West Europe, ed C Fox and B Dickins, Cambridge 1950, p 307 (source material for miracles of bk iii).

　　c. 1438 GL.
MSS. 1, BM Addit 11565, f 56ᵇ; 2, BM Addit 35298, ff 79ᵇ–80ª; 3, Lambeth 72, chap 112, f 230ᵇ.
Editions. Butler LA, p 99 (BM Addit 11565).

　　d. Caxton GL.
Editions. Caxton GL, chap 79; Temple, 3.94.
Sources. Butler LA, pp 83, 99 (1438 GL as in BM Addit 11565).
Background. McKeehan I P, Contemporary Life in Two Twelfth-Century Saints' Legends, Univ Col Stud in Lang and Lit 22.289.
Colgrave B, Two Lives of St Cuthbert, A Life by an Anonymous Monk of Lindisfarne and Bede's Prose Life, Cambridge

1940 (crit P G, AnBol 59.324; F M Stenton, RES 16.460).

CYPRIAN OF CARTHAGE: see **CORNELIUS AND CYPRIAN.**

CYPRIAN: see **JUSTINA.**

CYR, CYRUS: see **SYRUS.**

CYRIACUS: see **QUIRIAC (JUDAS).**

[69] **CYRIACUS WITH COMPANIONS** (Aug 8, year?).

　　a. 1438 GL.
MS. BM Addit 35298, ff 95ᵇ–96ª (lost Harley 4775, BM Addit 11565; om Lambeth 72).
Sources. Cf Graesse LA, chap 116, p 486.

　　b. Caxton GL.
Editions. Caxton GL, chap 149; Temple, 4.205.
Sources. Cf de Vignay LD, ff 222ᵇ–223ª.

[70] **DAMASUS, POPE** (Dec 11, 384).
　　SEL; Brown-Robbins, no 2881.
MS. Bodl 2567 (Bodley 779), f 235ª⁻ᵇ (15 cent).
Editions. Zusatzleg 1889, p 407 (refers to Anastasius, Liber pontificalis, p 407n1).

DAMIAN: see **COSMAS AND DAMIAN.**

DARIA, DARIƷE: see **CRISAUNT AND DARIA.**

[71] **DEMETRIUS** (Oct 8, year?).
　　Caxton GL.
Editions. Caxton GL, chap 238; Temple, 7.182.
Sources. Cf de Vignay LD, ff 395ᵇ–396ª; Delehaye H, Les légendes grecques des saints militaires, Paris 1909, p 103 (on sources mentioned in French and English texts).

[72] **DENIS, BISHOP OF PARIS** (Oct 9, 258?).

　　a. SEL; Brown-Robbins, no 2882.
MSS. 13 MSS.
Edition. D'Evelyn and Mill, EETS 236.434 (Corp Christi Camb 145, ff 161ª–163ª, early 14 cent).

　　b. 1438 GL.
MSS. 1, Bodl 21947 (Douce 372), f 123; beg imperfect; 2, Harley 630, f 313; 3, Harley 4775, chap 145–146, ff 191ª–193ª; MLA roto 343, 2.382; 4, BM Addit 35298, ff 130ª–131ª; 5, Trinity Dublin 319; see Gerould S Leg, p 195.
Sources. Cf Graesse LA, chap 153, p 680.

c. Caxton GL.
Editions. Caxton GL, chap 187; Temple, 5.244.
Sources. Cf de Vignay LD, ff 300[b]–303[a].
Background. Loenertz R J, La légende parisienne de St Denys l'Aréopagite, AnBol 69.217.

[73] DOMINIC (Aug 4, 1221).

a. SEL; Brown-Robbins, no 2883.
MSS. 1, Bodl 1486 (Laud Misc 108), ff 124[a]–127[b] (end 13 cent); 2, Bodl 2567 (Bodley 779), f 167[a] (ca 1400); 3, Bodl 3938 (Vernon), f 47[b] (ca 1385); 4, Trinity Camb 605, f 137[a] (early 14 cent); 5, Egerton 1993, f 206[a] (1300–50); 6, Lambeth 223, f 155[a] (end 14 cent).
Editions. Horstmann, EETS 87.278 (Bodl 1486).
Date. Manning W F, The ME Verse Life of St Dominic: Date and Source, Spec 31.90 (evidence for 1280–90 as date of Dominic a; evidence for Dominican authorship and for LA as source, Spec 31.82,83).

b. 1438 GL.
MSS. 1, Bodl 21947 (Douce 372), ff 88[b]; end imperfect; 2, Egerton 876, f 178 end; 3, Harley 630, f 226 end; 4, BM Addit 35298, ff 93[a]–95[a] (lost Harley 4775, BM Addit 11565; om Lambeth 72).
Sources. Cf Graesse LA, chap 113, p 466; cf de Vignay LD, ff 214[b]–221[a]; Butler LA, p 146 (notes reference to name de Vignay in 1438 MSS of Dominic).

c. Caxton GL.
Editions. Caxton GL, chap 146; Temple, 4.172.
Sources. See DOMINIC b above.

DOMITILLA: see NEREUS.

[74] DONATUS, BISHOP OF AREZZO (Aug 7, 362).

a. 1438 GL.
MSS. 1, Bodl 21947 (Douce 372), f 89[a], beg imperfect; 2, BM Addit 35298, f 95[a–b] (lost Harley 4775, BM Addit 11565; om Lambeth 72).
Sources. Cf Graesse LA, chap 115, p 484.

b. Caxton GL.
Editions. Caxton GL, chap 148; Temple, 4.202.
Sources. Cf de Vignay LD, ff 221[b]–222[b].

DOROTHEA: see DOROTHY.

DOROTHEUS: see GORGONIUS.

[75] DOROTHY (Feb 6, ca303?).

a. Bokenham; Brown-Robbins, no 3936.
MSS. 1, Arundel 327, ff 87[a]–90[a] (1447); 2, BM Addit 36983, f 305[b], lines 1–35 (ca 1442).
Editions. [Bokenam O,] The Lyvys of Seyntys, Roxb Club 50, London 1835, p 137; Horstmann Bokenam, p 120; Serjeantson, EETS 206.130.
Sources. Horstmann Bokenam, p ix (LA chief source).
Willenberg G, Die Quellen von Osbern Bokenham's Legenden, EStn 12.25 (agreements with Lambeth 432, see version d; source an unknown Latin text).
Peterson J M, The Dorothea Legend: Its Earliest Records, ME Versions, and Influence on Massinger's Virgin Martyr, Heidelberg 1910, p 45 (metrical versions independently derived from Latin source similar to LA; crit G H Gerould, EStn 44.25).

b. 8-line stanzas; Brown-Robbins, no 2447.
MSS. 1, Camb Univ Add 4122, f 145[b]; 2, Arundel 168, f 5[a] (15 cent); 3, Harley 5272, f 99[a], end imperfect.
Editions. AELeg 1878, p 191 (Harley 5272; conclusion and variants from Arundel 168; crit E Kölbing, EStn 3.133).
Authorship. EStn 3.133 (William Paris suggested as author; see CHRISTINA OF BOLSENA d [57]).
Sources. AELeg 1878, p 191 (free translation of Graesse LA, chap 210, p 910); Peterson, Dorothea Legend, p 45 (see under DOROTHY a *Sources*).

c. Royal 2.A.xviii, prose.
MS. BM Royal 2.A.xviii, f 236 (ca 1425).
Sources. Peterson, Dorothea Legend, p 27 (prose versions independently derived from Latin text similar to LA).

d. Lambeth 432, prose.
MS. Lambeth 432, ff 90–94 (ca 1425).
Horstmann C, Prosalegenden, Angl 3.319.
Edition. Angl 3.325.
Sources. Angl 3.320 (Lambeth 432 a re-working of DOROTHY b Harley 5272 text); Peterson, Dorothea Legend, p 27 (see DOROTHY c *Sources*); Workman, 15th Cent Translation, p 192 (supports Peterson against Horstmann).

e. Chetham 8009, prose.
MS. Chetham Manchester 8009, ff 1–2, f 3 missing (15 cent).
Kölbing E, Vier Romanzen-Handschriften, EStn 7.195.

f. 1438 GL.
MSS. 1, BM Addit 11565, ff 57[b]–58[b]; 2, BM Addit 35298, ff 80[b]–81[a]; 3, Lambeth 72, ff

232–233; 4, Trinity Dublin 319, ff 2[b]–4[b], repeated ff 15[a]–16[b].

Butler LA, pp 70, 152 (on MSS 1,2,3); Peterson, Dorothea Legend, p 27 (on MSS 1,2,3 following Butler).

Gerould G H, EStn 44.259 (life of Dorothy reported in Trinity MS but not identified certainly as 1438 GL text); Gerould S Leg, p 195 (Trinity MS identified as 1438 GL).

Sources. Peterson, Dorothea Legend, p 27 (see DOROTHY c *Sources*; crit EStn 44.258).

     g. Caxton GL.

Editions. Caxton GL, chap 219; Temple, 7.42.

Sources. Butler LA, p 85 (apparently derived from Graesse LA, chap 210, p 910).

[76] DUNSTAN, ARCHBISHOP OF CANTERBURY (May 19, 988).

     a. SEL; Brown-Robbins, no 2884.

MSS. 21 MSS.

Editions. Furnivall EEP, p 34 (Harley 2277, ff 51[a]–54[a]; ca 1300).

AESpr 1.171 (Harley 2277 from Furnivall).

Horstmann C, JfRESL 14.32 (Bodl 1486 [Laud Misc 108], ff 29[b]–30[b]; lines 107–160 missing; end 13 cent).

Horstmann, EETS 87.19 (Bodl 1486 completed from Bodl 3938).

D'Evelyn and Mill, EETS 235.204 (Corp Christi Camb 145, ff 77[a]–79[b]; early 14 cent).

Selections. Morris Spec 2.19 (Harley 2277, lines 1–92).

Modernizations. Weston J L, The Chief ME Poets, Boston 1914, p 37 (based on AESpr).

     b. 1438 GL.

MSS. 1, BM Addit 11565, f 53[a–b], beg imperfect; 2, BM Addit 35298, f 77[a–b]; 3, Lambeth 72, chap 106, f 222[b].

Selections. Butler LA, p 105 (BM Addit 11565, f 53[a], § 1).

     c. Caxton GL.

Editions. Caxton GL, chap 99; Temple, 3.188.

Sources. Butler LA, p 83 (1438 GL as in MS 2 the source).

EADBURG: see EDBURGA.

ECGWINE: see EGWINE.

[77] EDBURGA OF WINCHESTER (June 15, 960).

     SEL; Brown-Robbins, no 2885.

MSS. 1, Bodl 2567 (Bodley 779), f 282[a] (ca 1400); 2, Bodl 3938 (Vernon), f 32[a] col 2 (ca 1385); 3, Egerton 1993, f 160[a–b] (1300–50).

[78] EDITH OF WILTON (Sept 16, 984).

Quatrains; Brown-Robbins, no 243.

MS. Cotton Faustina B.iii, ff 194[a]–258[a]; loss of ca 980 lines between ff 205–6 (ca 1420).

Black W H, Chronicon Vilodunense; sive de Vita et Miraculis S Edithae, London 1830, p viii.

Horstmann C, S Editha sive Chronicon Vilodunense, Heilbronn 1883, p vii.

Editions. Black, Chronicon Vilodunense (with Latin prose supplement on Wilton).

Horstmann, S Editha, p 1 (crit L Morsbach, AnglA 7.31; E Schröder AfDA 10.391; H Varnhagen DLz 5, no 17, p 616).

Selections. Dugdale W, Monast Angl, London 1846, II. 315,316 notes (lines 318–366, 604–7, 614–629, 1586–1617; see Horstmann's text).

Language. Horstmann, S Editha, p vii (literary Wiltshire dialect).

Heuser W, Die me Legenden von S Editha und S Etheldreda, eine Untersuchung über Sprache und Autorschaft, Göttingen 1887 (linguistic differences between pts i and ii as indication of different authors).

Bülbring K, QF 63.45 (on strong verbs).

Fischer R, Zur Sprache und Autorschaft der me Legenden S Editha und S Etheldreda, Angl 11.175 (questions Heuser's claim on basis of language for 2 authors).

Heuser W, Zu Fischer, Sprache und Autorschaft, Angl 12.578 (correction and rebuttal of Fischer).

Date. Horstmann, S Editha, p v (with Black accepts ca 1420 for English text).

Gerould S Leg, p 276 (evidence for ca 1450 as earliest date).

Sources. Black, Chronicon Vilodunense, p v (primary source Latin life by Goscelin, ca 1058).

Horstmann, S Editha, p vi (rpt of Goscelin from Acta SS; not direct source).

Wilmart A, La légende de Ste Edith en prose et vers par le moine Goscelin, AnBol 56. 5,265 (analysis of long and short versions of Goscelin's Vita S Edithae; classification of Eng Chron Vilod as short version with common source for pts i and ii; see p 18 for criticism of Horstmann and Schröder).

Literary Relations. Schröder E, Die Tänzer von Kölbigk, ein Mirakel des 11 Jahrhunderts, Perthes 1896; rptd ZKG 17.94 (history of legend of the accursed dancers; crit G Paris, JS, 1899, p 733); AnBol 56. 20,285 (summary of research on the accursed dancers; comment on Schröder and G Paris).

[79] EDMUND RICH OF ABINGDON, ARCHBISHOP OF CANTERBURY (Nov 16, 1240).

a. SEL; Brown-Robbins, no 2886.
MSS. 16 MSS.
Editions. Furnivall EEP, p 71, Harley 2277,
ff 155ª–162ᵇ; ca 1300).
Horstmann, EETS 87.431 (Bodl 1486 [Laud
Misc 108], ff 179ᵇ–185ª; end 13 cent).
D'Evelyn and Mill, EETS 236.492 (Harley
2277).
Sources. Lawrence C H, St Edmund of
Abingdon, Oxford 1960, p 60 (Anon A,
Vita, ca 1244–46, basis of SEL).

b. 1438 GL.
MSS. 1, BM Addit 35298, chap 94, ff 73ª–
74ᵇ; 2, Lambeth 72, chap 99, f 213ª.

c. Caxton GL.
Editions. Caxton GL, chap 209; Temple,
6.230.
Sources. Butler LA, p 83 (not in usual French
or Latin sources).
Background. Wallace W, Life of St Edmund
of Canterbury from Original Sources, London 1893.
Lawrence, St Edmund, Oxford 1960.

[80] EDMUND, KING OF EAST ANGLIA
(Nov 20, 870).

(Note: See also FREMUND [111].)

a. SEL; Brown-Robbins, no 2887.
MSS. 14 MSS.
Editions. Furnivall EEP, p 87 (Harley 2277,
ff 162ᵇ–164ª; ca 1300).
Horstmann, EETS 87.296 (Bodl 1486 [Laud
Misc 108], ff 131ª–132ª; end 13 cent); rptd
.F Hervey, Corolla S Eadmundi, London
1907, p 362.
D'Evelyn and Mill, EETS 236.511 (Harley
2277).

b. Life, Lydgate, rime royal; Brown-
Robbins, no 3440.

c. Miracles, Lydgate, 8-line stanzas;
Brown-Robbins, no 1843.

Note: For b and c see under Lydgate.

d. Speculum Sacerdotale.
MS. BM Addit 36791, ff 134ᵇ–135ᵇ (15 cent).
Editions. Weatherly, EETS 200.239.
Sources. Weatherly, EETS 200.xxix, 279
(claims LA as source; not in Graesse LA).

e. 1438 GL.
MSS. 1, BM Addit 35298, chap 96, f 75ª; 2,
Lambeth 72, chap 101, f 217ᵇ.

f. Caxton GL.
Editions. Caxton GL, chap 211; Temple,
6.243.
Background. Hervey, Corolla S Eadmundi.
McKeehan I P, St Edmund of East Anglia:

The Development of a Romantic Legend,
Univ of Col Stud in Lang and Lit 25.13.
Loomis G, The Growth of the St Edmund
Legend, HSNPL 14.83.
Wright C E, The Cultivation of Saga in
Anglo-Saxon England, London 1939, pp
58, 117.

[81] EDWARD THE CONFESSOR (Oct
13, 1066).

a. SEL; Brown-Robbins, no 2888.
MSS. 1, Bodl 2567 (Bodley 779), ff 273ª–279ᵇ
(ca 1400); 2, Bodl 6924 (Ashmole 43), ff
260ª–269ᵇ (1325–50); 3, Cotton Julius D.ix,
ff 281ª–297ᵇ (15 cent).
Moore G E, The ME Verse Life of Edward
the Confessor, Phila 1942, p iii.
Editions. Moore, Edward the Confessor, p 1
(Cotton Julius D.ix; crit YWES 23.74; P G,
AnBol 65.302; K Brunner, Angl 69.74).
Language. Moore, Edward the Confessor, p
lxxii (dialect of MS 3 southern bordering
on Southwest-Midland), p lvii (Robert of
Gloucester's Chronicle dependent on SEL;
common source back of SEL and Trinity
Oxford prose version).

b. Trinity Oxford, prose.
MS. Trinity Oxf 11, ff 1ª–51ᵇ (15 cent).
Moore, Edward the Confessor, p 73.
Editions. Moore, Edward the Confessor, p
108.
Sources. See EDWARD THE CONFESSOR
a *Sources.*

c. 1438 GL.
MS. BM Addit 35298, chap 79, ff 48ª–53ª.
Butler LA, p 150; Moore, Edward the Con-
fessor, p 72.
Editions. Moore, Edward the Confessor, p 75
(for the text of a separate item, Vision of
St Edward and Earl Leofric in Camb Univ
Ii.iv.9, 15 cent, prose, see pp 73, 132).

d. Caxton GL.
Editions. Caxton GL, chap 189; Temple, 6.1.
Sources. Butler LA, pp 83, 151 (not in Latin
or French sources).
Moore, Edward the Confessor, p 134 (1438
GL as in BM Addit 35298 Caxton's source).
Literary Relations. Moore, Edward the Con-
fessor, p xix (comparison of legendary ma-
terial in verse and prose texts).

[82] EDWARD THE ELDER (March 18,
979).

a. SEL; Brown-Robbins, nos 2889, 2890.
MSS. 18 MSS; add 19, Winchester Coll 33ª,
ff 20ᵇ–23ᵇ (15 cent).
D'Evelyn, EETS 244.1n4 17 (on MS 19 and

difference between Laud and Harley texts).
Editions. Horstmann, EETS 87.47 (Bodl 1486 [Laud Misc 108], ff 39ᵃ–41ᵇ, end 13 cent).
D'Evelyn and Mill, EETS 235.110 (Corp Christi Camb 145, ff 41ᵇ–44ᵇ, early 14 cent).

b. 1438 GL.
MSS. 1, BM Addit 35298, chap 98, ff 75ᵇ–76ᵃ; 2, Lambeth 72, chap 103, f 219ᵃ.

c. Caxton GL.
Editions. Caxton GL, chap 109; Temple, 3.233.
Sources. Cf BM Addit 35298 (Caxton briefer); Butler LA, p 83 (not in usual Latin or French sources).

EFFAM: see EUPHEMIA.

EFFREM, EPHRAEM: see BASIL c.

[83] EGWIN, BISHOP OF WORCESTER (Dec 30, 717).

SEL, Brown-Robbins, no 2891.
MSS. 1, Bodl 3938 (Vernon), f 52ᵇ col 2 (ca 1385); 2, Cotton Julius D.ix, ff 266ᵇ–268ᵇ (15 cent); 3, Egerton 1993, f 221ᵇ (1300–50); 4, Stowe 949, f 142ᵇ (late 14 cent); 5, BM Addit 10626, f 7ᵃ, lines 1–46 (14 cent).
Editions. Brown L, in Benedictines of Stanbrook, St Egwin and His Abbey of Evesham, London 1904, p 167 (Stowe 949, 128 lines).

ELENE: see HELENA.

ELEVEN THOUSAND VIRGINS: see URSULA.

[84] ELIGIUS, ELOI, LOYE, BISHOP OF NOYON (Dec 1, 660).

Caxton GL.
Editions. Caxton GL, chap 112; Temple 3.261.
Sources. Cf de Vignay LD, ff 367ᵃ–368ᵃ.

ELIZABETH OF ERKENRODE: see ELIZABETH OF SPALBECK.

[85] ELIZABETH OF HUNGARY (Nov 19, 1231).

a. Bokenham; Brown-Robbins, no 3509.
MS. Arundel 327, ff 172ᵃ–192ᵇ (1447).
Editions. [Bokenam O,] The Lyvys of Seyntys, Roxb Club 50, London 1835, p 271.
Horstmann Bokenam, p 237; Serjeantson, EETS 206.257.
Selections. Wülcker AELeseb 2.15; notes, p 232 (lines 10075–10192 parting of Elizabeth and Louis; see EETS 206.274).

Sources. Willenberg G, Die Quellen von Osbern Bokenham's Legenden, EStn 12.11 (LA but not Graesse text).

b. 1438 GL.
MSS. 1, Bodl 21947 (Douce 372), f 140, end imperf; 2, Harley 4775, chap 160, ff 216ᵃ–219ᵇ; MLA roto 343, 2.432; 3, BM Addit 11565, ends f 215; 4, BM Addit 35298, ff 143ᵇ–145ᵇ.
Sources. Cf Graesse LA, chap 168, p 752.

c. Caxton GL.
Editions. Caxton GL, chap 208; Temple, 6.213.
Sources. Cf de Vignay LD, ff 330ᵃ–334ᵃ.

[86] ELIZABETH OF SPALBECK OR ERKENRODE (Oct 19, 1266?).

Anon, þe lyfe of s Elizabeth of Spalbeck, prose.
MS. Bodl 21688 (Douce 114), ff 1–12 (15 cent).
Horstmann C, Prosalegenden: Die Legenden des MS Douce 114, Angl 8.102.
Editions. Angl 8.107.
Textual Notes. Gerould G H, The Source of the ME Prose S Elizabeth of Spalbeck, Angl 39.357 (Horstmann's text and notes compared with Latin).
Language. Angl 8.106 (MS probably written in Nottinghamshire dialect).
Sources. Angl 39.356 (translation of Latin life by Philip of Clairvaux, 1st prtd 1889).
Literary Style. Angl 39.357; Workman 15 Cent Trans, pp 76, 91, 133.

ELMO: see ERASMUS.

ELOI: see ELIGIUS.

[87] EMERENTIANA (Jan 23, ca304).

a. SEL; Brown-Robbins, no 2851.
MS. Bodl 2567 (Bodley 799), f 233ᵃ⁻ᵇ (ca 1400).
Edition. Zusatzleg 1889, p 403; p 403, note 1 (independently developed from Vita S Agnetis).
Literary Relations. Denomy A J, The OF Lives of St Agnes . . . , Harvard Stud in Rom Lang 13, Cambridge 1938, p 164 (relation to SEL Agnes).

b. 1438 GL.
MSS. 1, Harley 4775, chap 23, ff 24ᵇ–25ᵃ; MLA roto 343, 1.49; 2, BM Addit 35298, f 15ᵃ⁻ᵇ; 3, Lambeth 72, ends f 42ᵇ.

c. Caxton GL.
Editions. Caxton GL, chap 57; Temple, 2.250.
Sources. See AGNES d, e [13] *Sources.*
Background. Denomy, St Agnes, p 32 (relation of Emerentiana and Agnes legends).

EPIMACHUS: see GORDIAN.

[88] ERASMUS, ELMO, BISHOP OF FORMIAE (June 2, 303?).

a. Passio S Erasmi, couplets; Brown-Robbins, no 173.
MSS. 1, Bodl 14528 (Rawl poet 34), f 6ª (15 cent); 2, Camb Univ Dd.I.1, f 295ª (1400–50); 3, Harley 1671, f 1*ª, prologue only beg line 5 (mid 15 cent); 4, Harley 2382, ff 109ª–111ª (1470–1500); 5, Royal 8.C.xii, f 2ª, prologue only (15 cent); 6, BM Addit 36983 (formerly Bedford MS), f 279ᵇ, lines 1–50, followed by 52 "passions" in prose (ca 1442).
Horstmann C, Nachträge zu den Legenden, Arch 62.413 (comparison of MSS 4,5,6).
Manly & Rickert, 1.245 (description of MS 4).
Editions. AELeg 1878, p 198, MS 4; p 201, MS 6 (crit E Kölbing, EStn 3.133; Arch 62.414, MS 2).
Authorship. MacCracken, EETSES 107.xlvi and note 2 (Lydgate not author).

b. Caxton GL.
Editions. Caxton GL, edns 1487, 1493, 1498 last item; Temple, 7.267 (rptd from 1527 edn).
Sources. Cf Graesse LA, chap 199, p 890 (not direct source).

[89] ERKENWALD, BISHOP OF LONDON (May 13, ca 686).

a. Alliterative verse; Brown-Robbins, no 428.
Note: For related material on the Alliterative School, see elsewhere in the Manual.)
MS. Harley 2250, ff 72ᵇ–75ª (end 15 cent).
Gollancz I, St Erkenwald, Select Early English Poems 4, London 1922, p v.
Savage H L, St Erkenwald, YSE 72, New Haven 1926, p ix.
Editions. AELeg 1881, p 266; notes p 527 (crit M Trautmann, AnglA 5.23).
Gollancz, St Erkenwald, p 1 (crit TLS, Aug 24, 1922, p 541; F Holthausen, AnglB 34.17; P G Thomas, YWES 3.39; H S V Jones, JEGP 24.284).
Savage, St Erkenwald, p 1 (crit F W B, MLR 22.487; M Day, RES 3.490 and 4.90; O F Emerson, Spec 2.224; F Holthausen, AnglB 38.193; N&Q 152.143; C S Northup, JEGP 27.402; P G, AnBol 46.405; J Mansion, Bulletin Bibliographique et Pédagogique du Musée Belge, Revue de Philologie Classique 32.333).
Modernizations. Loomis R S and R Willard, Medieval Engl Verse and Prose in Mod-

ernized Versions, N Y 1948, p 239 (based on Savage edn).
Language. Knigge F, Die Sprache des Dichters v Sir Gawain and the Green Knight, der sogenannten Early English Alliterative Poems u De Erkenwalde, Marburg 1886 (phonetic system of Erkenwald agrees with that of Gawain poet but shows traces of East Midland).
Savage, St Erkenwald, p xxi (dialect of MS and of author probably Northwest Midland).
Serjeantson M S, The Dialects of the West Midlands in Middle English, RES 3.326 (dialect of Erkenwald North Midland).
Oakden J P, Alliterative Poetry in ME, MUPES 18, Manchester 1930, p 87 (comparison of dialect with that of Gawain poet inconclusive as to authorship).
Moore S, S B Meech, H Whitehall, ME Dialect Characteristics . . . , Univ of Mich Pub in Lang and Lit 13.52 (Harley 2250 associated with Dunham Massey, Cheshire).
Versification. Luick K, Die engl Stabreimzeile im xiv, xv and xvi Jahrh, Angl 11.584 (alliterative usage of Erkenwald agrees with that of Gawain poet).
Kaluza M, Strophische Gliederung in der mittelengl rein alliter Dichtung, EStn 16.174 (scheme for division of text into strophes and quatrains).
Savage, St Erkenwald, p xliii (discussion of quatrain arrangement).
Oakden, Alliterative Poetry, 1930, p 253 (metrical evidence for identification of author with Gawain poet).
Day M, Strophic Division in ME Alliterative Verse, EStn 66.245 (MS evidence for quatrain as basic unit of text).
Clark, J W, On Certain Alliterative and Poetic Words in the Poems Attributed to the Gawain-Poet, MLQ 12.387 (questions Oakden's claim for common authorship of Gawain poems based on groups of alliterative words).
Date. Gollancz, St Erkenwald, p lvi (suggests ca 1386 date of re-establishment of saint's feast).
Savage, St Erkenwald, p lxxv (accepts ca 1386).
Authorship. AELeg 1881, pp 266, 527 (groups Erkenwald with alliterative poems claimed for Huchown).
Neilson G, Huchown of the Awle Ryale . . . , Glasgow 1902, p 105 (parallels between Erkenwald and Huchown's supposed poems).
Gollancz, St Erkenwald, p lvi (suggests Ralph Strode).

Savage, St Erkenwald, p xlviii (review of evidence for Gawain poet as author).

Koziol H, Zur Frage der Verfasserschaft einiger mittelenglischen Stabreimdichtungen, EStn 67.170 (grammatical evidence for Erkenwald as work of Gawain poet).

Clark J W, The Gawain-Poet and the Substantival Adjective, JEGP 49.60 (use of subst adjective tells against common authorship).

Clark J W, Paraphrases for God in the Poems Attributed to the Gawain-Poet, MLN 65.232 (paraphrases offer further evidence for multiple authorship).

Sources. AELeg 1881, p 527 (Bede, Historia ecclesiastica gentis Anglorum, bk 4, chap 6 as main source).

Hulbert J R, The Sources of St Erkenwald and the Trental of Gregory, MP 16.485 (traces connection between miracle of pagan judge and Trajan legend).

Hibbard L A, Erkenwald the Belgian: A Study in Medieval Exempla of Justice, MP 17.669; rprt Adventures in the Middle Ages, N Y 1962, p 41. (Bromyard's Summa and exemplum of Belgian judge as links in growth of Erkenwald legend).

Gollancz, St Erkenwald, pp xiii, xxxiv (prologue based on Bede and Geoffrey of Monmouth; no direct source for miracle of pagan judge).

Jones H S V, JEGP 24.284 (supports Hibbard's interpretation of links between Trajan and Erkenwald legends).

Savage, St Erkenwald, p xii (argues for chronicle, not yet discovered, as single source).

Literary Relations. Chambers R W, Long Will, Dante and the Righteous Heathen, E&S 9.64 (connection of Erkenwald with theological aspects of Trajan legend).

Oakden, Alliterative Poetry, MUPES 22, Manchester 1935, p 76 (literary features compared with those of Gawain poet).

Bibliography. Savage, St Erkenwald, p 85.

b. 1438 GL.

MS. BM Addit 35298, chap 81, ff 53ᵃ–57ᵇ (includes miracles).

Butler LA, p 151.

c. Caxton GL.

Editions. Caxton GL, chap 221; Temple, 7.67.

Sources. AELeg 1881, p 527 (Latin versions noted).

Butler LA, pp 83, 85 (legend not in usual Latin or French sources; questions Caxton's use of Capgrave; see Horstmann, Nova legenda Angliae 1.391).

ERMENILDA, ERMENGILDA: see WERBURGA.

[90] ETHELBERT,   AETHELBERHT, AILBRIȝT (May 20, 794).

SEL; Brown-Robbins, no 2841.

MSS. 1, Bodl 3938 (Vernon), f 33ᵃ col 1 (ca 1385); 2, Trinity Camb 605, f 254ᵃ (early 15 cent); 3, Cotton Julius D.ix, chap 73, ff 160ᵇ–161ᵇ, repeated chap 97, ff 271ᵇ–272ᵇ (15 cent); 4, Egerton 1993, f 154ᵃ (1300–50).

Sources. James M R, Two Lives of St Ethelbert, King and Martyr, EHR 32.214 (review of Latin lives; Hereford version traced back to Corp Christi Camb 308 Passio, early 12 cent, perhaps itself based on vernacular material).

Wright C E, The Cultivation of Saga in Anglo-Saxon England, Edinburgh 1939, p 95 (comparison of Hereford and St Albans versions; evidence for vernacular traditions as basis of Hereford version).

Background. Wilson R W, The Lost Literature of Medieval England, London 1952, p 106.

[91] ETHELDREDA, AUDREY, ABBESS OF ELY (June 23, 679).

a. SEL; Brown-Robbins, no 2838.

MSS. 1, Bodl 2567 (Bodley 779), f 279ᵇ (ca 1400); 2, Bodl 3938 (Vernon), f 33ᵃ col 2 (ca 1385); 3, Egerton 1993, f 163ᵃ (1300–50).

b. Quatrains; Brown-Robbins, no 3090.

MS. Cotton Faust B.iii, f 265ᵃ, end imperfect (ca 1420).

Editions. AELeg 1881, p 282; notes p 528.

Language. Note: for Language, Date, Author, Sources see also EDITH OF WILTON [78] above.

Brandl A, LfGRP 2.398 (dialect probably Wiltshire; MS not a holograph).

Bülbring K, QF 63.45 (on strong verbs).

c. Bradshaw, rime royal.

Editions. Bradshaw H, A lytell treatyse of the lyfe of Saynt Audry abbesse of Ely, chap xviii in The Holy Lyfe and History of Saynt Werburge, Pynson, London 1521; STC no 3506; see WERBURGA [288].

[92] ETHELWOLD, BISHOP OF WINCHESTER (Aug 1, 984).

SEL; Brown-Robbins, nos 446, 2837.

MSS. 1, Bodl 2567 (Bodley 799), f 241*ᵃ, variant text (ca 1400); 2, Bodl 3938 (Vernon), f 38ᵇ col 2 (ca 1385); 3, Trinity Camb 605, f 136ᵇ, repeated f 235ᵃ (early 15 cent); 4,

BM Addit 10626, f 5ᵇ (14 cent); 5, Lambeth 223, f 153ᵇ (end 14 cent).

EUFEMIE: see EUPHEMIA.

EUFRAXE: see EUPHRASIA.

EUGENE: see EUGENIA.

[93] EUGENIA WITH PROTUS AND HYACINTH (JACINCTUS) (Sept 11, Dec 25, year?).

a. ScL; Brown-Robbins, no 307.
MS. Camb Univ Gg.2.6, ff 236ᵇ–247ᵇ (1400-50).
Editions. Horstmann ScL, 2.38; Metcalfe STS, 2.124, notes 3.344.
Sources. Horstmann ScL, 2.38 (cites Graesse LA, chap 136, p 602; notes fewer details in LA).
Metcalfe STS, 3.345 (passages from LA).
Rosenthal Vitae patrum, p 83 (comparison with LA).

b. Alphabet of Tales.
MS. BM Addit 25719, no 318 (mid 15 cent).
Edition. Banks, EETS 126, pt 1, p 218.
Sources. Herbert, pp 423, 440 (translation of Arnold of Liège, Alphabetum narrationum, ca 1308).
Rosenthal Vitae patrum pp 82, 146 (VP and LA as ultimate sources).

c. 1438 GL.
MSS. 1, Harley 630, f 278ᵇ; 2, Harley 4775, chap 127, ff 166ᵇ–168ᵃ; MLA roto 343, 2.333; 3, BM Addit 11565, f 174, beg imperfect; 4, BM Addit 35298, f 116ᵃ⁻ᵇ (om Lambeth 72).
Sources. Cf Graesse LA, chap 136, p 602.

d. Caxton GL.
Editions. Caxton GL, (1) chap 41, Temple, 2.151, short version under Eugenia; (2) chap 168, Temple, 5.120, long version under Prothus, Jacinctus and Eugenia.
Selections. Dibdin Typo Antiq, 2.77 (incident of Eugenia and Melancye from 1498 edn, long version).
Sources. Cf de Vignay LD, f 64ᵃ⁻ᵇ short version; ff 268ᵃ–269ᵇ long version).
Rosenthal Vitae patrum, p 71 (claims VP as source of short version).
Jeremy Sister M, Caxton's Golden Legend and de Vignai's Légende dorée, MS 8.103 (revised de Vignay, not VP, Caxton's source for both versions).

e. Caxton VP.
Edition. Caxton VP, pt 1, chap 158.
Sources. Cf La vie des pères, pt 1, chap 158, ff 126ᵃ–132ᵃ.

Background. Delehaye H, Étude sur le légendier romain, Brussells 1936, p 171.

[94] EUPHEMIA, EFFAME (Sept 16, ca 303?).

a. ScL; Brown-Robbins, no 712.
MS. Camb Univ Gg.2.6, ff 371ᵇ–373ᵇ (1400-50).
Editions. Horstmann ScL, 2.186; Metcalfe STS, 2.417, notes 3.453.
Sources. Horstmann ScL, 2.186 (quotes Graesse LA, chap 139, p 620); Metcalfe STS, 3.454 (passages from LA).

b. 1438 GL.
MSS. 1, Bodl 21947 (Douce 372), f 110, end imperfect; 2, Harley 4775, chap 31, ff 171ᵇ–172ᵇ; MLA roto 343, 2.343; 3, BM Addit 35298, f 119ᵃ⁻ᵇ (om Lambeth 72).
Sources. Cf Graesse LA, chap 139, p 620.

c. Caxton GL.
Editions. Caxton GL, chap 172; Temple, 5.143.
Sources. Cf de Vignay LD, ff 276ᵃ–277ᵃ.

[95] EUPHRASIA (March 13, ca 420).

Editions. Caxton VP, pt 1, chap 47.
Sources. Cf La vie des pères, pt 1, chap 47, ff 67ᵇ–73ᵃ.

[96] EUPHROSYNE (Jan 1, 5 cent?).

a. Vernon GL; Brown-Robbins, no 1465.
MS. Bodl 3938 (Vernon), f 103ᵃ col 3 (ca 1385).
Editions. Horstmann C, Die Legende der Eufrosyne, EStn 1.303.
AELeg 1878, p 174.
Textual Notes. Kölbing E, EStn 3.131 (comments based on comparison with Latin text).
Language. EStn 1.300 (East Midland with Northern and Southern forms).
Sources. AELeg 1881, p lxl, note 1 (based on VP).
Gerould S Leg, p 229 (apparently translation from OF).
Rosenthal Vitae patrum, p 85 (Latin VP as source).

b. Caxton VP.
Editions. Caxton VP, pt 1, chap 44.
Sources. Cf La vie des pères, pt 1, chap 44, ff 61ᵃ–62ᵃ.

[97] EUSEBIUS, BISHOP OF VERCELLI (Dec 16, 371).

a. 1438 GL.
MSS. 1, Harley 4775, chap 101, ff 134ᵃ–135ᵃ;

MLA roto 343, 2.268; 2, BM Addit 35298, ff 90ᵇ–91ᵃ (lost BM Addit 11565).
Sources. Cf Graesse LA, chap 108, p 452.

b. Caxton GL.
Editions. Caxton GL, chap 141; Temple, 4.149.
Sources. Cf de Vignay LD, ff 208ᵇ–209ᵇ.

[98] EUSTACE, PLACIDAS (Sept 20, year?).

(Note: See also Romances. For a late verse version see John Partridge, The worthie Hystorie of . . . Plasidas, London 1566; STC, no 19438; rptd AELeg 1881, p 472.)

a. Stanzas; Brown-Robbins, no 211.
MSS. 1, Bodl 1687 (Digby 86), f 122ᵇ (ca 1275); 2, Bodl 6922* (Ashmole 61), f 1ᵃ (15 cent).
Edition. AELeg 1881, p 211 (Bodl 1687).
Modernizations. Weston J L, The Chief ME Poets, Boston 1914, p 78 (based on AELeg 1881, p 211).
Language. AELeg 1881, p 211 (dialect Southern).
Brandl A, LfGRP 2.398 (author's language Midland, copyist's Southern).

b. SEL; Brown-Robbins, no 2894.
MSS. 13 MSS.
Edition. Horstmann, EETS 87.393 (Bodl 1486 [Laud Misc 108], ff 167ᵃ–169ᵇ, end 13 cent, damaged folio lines 86–179, supplied from Cotton Julius D.ix, 15 cent).
Sources. Monteverdi A, I testi della leggenda di S Eustachio, Studi medievali 3.490 (claims Latin version rather than OF as source).

c. NHC; Brown-Robbins, no 43.
MSS. 8 MSS.
Edition. Horstmann C, Die Evangelien-Geschichten des MS Vernon, Arch 52.262 (Bodl 3938 [Vernon], f 181ᵃ col 2, ca 1385).
Sources. See EUSTACE b *Sources.*

c* NHC, variant; Brown-Robbins, no 3544.
MS. Bodl 3440 (Arch Selden supra 52), f 209ᵃ (mid 15 cent).

d. ScL; Brown-Robbins, no 326.
MS. Camb Univ Gg.2.6, ff 217ᵃ–227ᵃ (1400–50).
Editions. Horstmann ScL, 2.12; Metcalfe STS, 2.69, notes 3.326.
Sources. Horstmann ScL, 2.12 (cites Graesse LA, chap 161, p 712; notes closer agreement in some details with texts in Acta SS, Sept vi, pp 123–137).
Metcalfe STS, 3.328 (see preceding entry).

e. 1438 GL.
MSS. 1, Harley 4775, chap 153, ff 202ᵃ–204ᵃ; MLA roto 343, 2.404; 2, BM Addit 35298, ff 136ᵃ–137ᵇ.
Sources. Cf Graesse LA, chap 161, p 712.

f. Caxton GL.
Editions. Caxton GL, chap 196; Temple, 6.83.
Sources. Cf de Vignay LD, ff 313ᵇ–316ᵇ.
Background. Murray J, The Eustace Legend in Medieval England, MHRA 1.35.

[99] EUTROPIUS, BISHOP OF SAINTES (April 30, 3 cent).

Editions. Caxton GL, chap 114; Temple, 3.269.
Sources. Cf de Vignay LD, ff 379ᵃ–380ᵇ.
de Gaiffier B, Les sources de la passion de S Eutrope de Saintes dans le Liber s Jacobi, AnBol 69.57 (development of version of legend probably used by Caxton).

[100] EVARISTUS, POPE (Oct 26, ca 107).
SEL; Brown-Robbins, no 733.
MS. Bodl 2567 (Bodley 779), f 198ᵇ (ca 1400).
Edition. Zusatzleg 1889, p 346; p 422 (ultimate source Liber pontificalis).

[101] FABIAN, POPE (Jan 20, 250).

a. SEL; Brown-Robbins, nos 2895, 2896.
MSS. Note: The lives of Fabian and Sebastian united in Brown-Robbins as one legend are separated here. F is either 4 or 24 lines long; S is consistently 90 lines; see SEBASTIAN a *MSS* [251] below and EETS 244.23.
Brown-Robbins, no 2896, 4 lines. 4 MSS; add 5, Lambeth 223, f 53ᵃ (end 14 cent).
Brown-Robbins, no 2895, 24 lines. 14 MSS; delete Lambeth 223; add 14, Winchester Coll 33ᵃ ff 48ᵇ–49ᵃ (15 cent).
Editions. Horstmann C, Die Legenden des MS Laud 108, Arch 49.405 (Bodl 1486 [Laud Misc 108], f 88ᵇ, end 13 cent, short life).
Horstmann, EETS 87.178 (Bodl 1486).
D'Evelyn and Mill, EETS 235.15 (Corp Christi Camb 145, f 6ᵃ⁻ᵇ, early 14 cent, long life).

b. 1438 GL.
MSS. 1, Harley 4775, chap 21, f 22ᵃ; MLA roto 343, 1.44; 2, BM Addit 11565, f 48; 3, BM Addit 35298, f 14ᵃ (in Trinity Dublin 319, lost Lambeth 72: see [6] above, under *MSS*).
Sources. Cf Graesse LA, chap 22, p 108.

c. Caxton GL.
Editions. Caxton GL, chap 55; Temple, 2.231.
Sources. Cf de Vignay LD, f 80ᵃ.

[102] FAITH (Oct 6, 3 cent?).

    a. SEL; Brown-Robbins, no 2897.

    a.* SEL, variant; Brown-Robbins, no 1397.

MSS. a. 10 MSS.

Edition. Horstmann, EETS 87.83 (Bodl 1486 [Laud Misc 108], ff 52ᵇ–54ᵃ, end 13 cent).

MS. a.* Bodl 2564 [Bodley 779], ff 183ᵇ–184ᵇ (ca 1400).

Edition. Zusatzleg 1889, p 323.

    b. Bokenham; Brown-Robbins, no 4086.

MS. Arundel 327, ff 66ᵃ–74ᵇ (1447).

Editions. [Bokenam O,] The Lyvys of Seyntys, Roxb Club 50, London 1835, p 103.

Horstmann Bokenam, p 91.

Serjeantson, EETS 206.98.

Sources. Horstmann Bokenam, p x (based on account of St Caprasius in Surius, De probatis ss historiis).

Willenberg G, Die Quellen v Osbern Bokenham's Legenden, EStn 12.27 (notes differences between Surius and Bokenham).

Serjeantson, EETS 206.xxii (summarizes Willenberg).

    c. 1438 GL.

MSS. 1, BM Addit 11565 (see Butler LA, pp 66, 70); 2, BM Addit 35298, f 80ᵃ⁻ᵇ; 3, Lambeth 72, chap 113, f 231ᵇ.

FAUSTINUS: see SIMPLICIUS.

FELICIAN: see PRIMUS.

FELICISSIMUS: see SIXTUS II.

FELICITY: see PERPETUA.

[103] FELIX OF NOLA (Jan 14, ca 260):
    a. 1438 GL.

MSS. 1, Harley 4775, chap 18, f 20ᵃ⁻ᵇ; MLA roto 343, 1.40; 2, BM Addit 35298, f 13ᵃ⁻ᵇ (lost Bodl 21947, Lambeth 72).

Sources. Cf Graesse GL, chap 19, p 102.

    b. Caxton GL.

Editions. Caxton GL, chap 52; Temple, 2.221.

Sources. Cf de Vignay LD, ff 77ᵇ–78ᵃ.

[104] FELIX "II," POPE (July 29, 365).

(Note: On confusion of Felix "II" and "III" see FELIX "III" *Editions* [105] below.)

    a. 1438 GL.

MSS. 1, Harley 4775, chap 96, f 131ᵃ; MLA roto 343, 1.262; 2, BM Addit 35298, f 89ᵃ.

Sources. Cf Graesse LA, chap 103, p 442.

    b. Caxton GL.

Editions. Caxton GL, chap 136; Temple, 4.132.

Sources. Cf de Vignay LD, f 200ᵃ.

Butler LA, p 92 (evidence from etymology of use of revised de Vignay).

[105] FELIX "III," POPE (March 1, 492). SEL; Brown-Robbins, no 794.

MS. Bodl 2567 (Bodley 779), ff 237ᵇ–238ᵃ (ca 1400).

Editions. Zusatzleg 1889, p 413 (lines 51–74 refer to Felix "II"); p 413, note 1, p 422 (ultimate source Liber pontificalis).

[106] FELIX, PRIEST, AND ADAUCTUS (Aug 30, 304?).

    a. 1438 GL.

MSS. 1, Harley 4775, chap 116, f 156ᵇ; MLA roto 343, 2.313; 2, BM Addit 35298, f 109ᵃ (om Lambeth 72).

Sources. Cf Graesse LA, chap 126, p 575.

    b. Caxton GL.

Editions. Caxton GL, chap 160; Temple, 5.78; rptd A Aspland, The Golden Legend . . . , Holbein Soc Fac-Simile Reprints, London 1878.

Sources. Cf de Vignay LD, ff 257ᵇ–258ᵃ.

Butler LA, p 92 (Caxton's etymology compared with revisions of de Vignay).

FEY: see FAITH.

[107] FIACRE (Sept 1, 670?).

Editions. Caxton GL, chap 236; Temple, 7.173.

Sources. Cf de Vignay LD, ff 390ᵃ–392ᵃ.

Porter M E and J H Baltzell, The Medieval French Lives of St Fiacre, MLQ 17.25, note 20 (de Vignay as source).

Background and Bibliography. MLQ 17.21.

[108] FIRMIN, BISHOP OF TOULOUSE ? (Sept 25, 4 cent?).

    a. SEL; Brown-Robbins, no 2898.

MS. Bodl 2567 (Bodley 779), ff 201ᵇ–202ᵇ (ca 1400).

Editions. Zusatzleg 1889, p 348; p 348, note 1 (English varies frequently from Vita in Acta SS).

    b. Caxton GL.

Editions. Caxton GL, chap 50; Temple, 2.216 (Invention only).

Sources. Cf de Vignay LD, f 76ᵇ.

Background. Salmon C, Histoire de St Firmin . . . , Amiens 1861, p 198 (cult in England).

[109] FOUR CROWNED MARTYRS: SEVERUS, SEVERIANUS, CARPOPHORUS, VICTORINUS (Nov 8, 306?).

a. Short couplets; Brown-Robbins, no 4149.

MS. Royal 17.A.i, f 1ᵃ (ca 1400).

Note: 397 couplets on masonic craft of which lines 497–535 give the legend under the title Ars quatuor coronatorum. A prose text in BM Addit 23198 (ca 1400), ed M Cooke, The History and Articles of Masonry, London 1861, does not include the legend.

See Whymper H J under *Editions* below.

Knoop D and G P Jones, The Mediaeval Mason, Manchester Univ Publ Ec Hist Series, no viii, Manchester 1933, p 169.

Editions. Halliwell [Phillipps] J O, The Early History of Free Masonry in England, London 1840, 1844, p 28.

Whymper H J, Constituciones artis gemetriae secundum Euclydem . . . , Quatuor Coronati Lodge, London 1891, p 8 (facsimile of Royal 17.A.i).

b. 1438 GL.

MSS. 1, Harley 4775, chap 156, f 211ᵇ; MLA roto 343, 2.423; 2, BM Addit 11565, f ccix; 3, BM Addit 35298, f 141ᵃ (lost Egerton 876; om Lambeth 72).

Sources. Cf Graesse LA, chap 164, p 739.

c. Caxton GL.

Editions. Caxton GL, chap 201; Temple, 6.139.

Sources. Cf de Vignay LD, f 325ᵃ.

Background. Kirsch J P, Die Passio der heil Vier Gekrönten in Rom, Hist Jahrbuch, Görres Gesellschaft, 38.72 (review of problems connected with legend).

du Colombier P, Les Quatre-Couronnés, patrons des tailleurs de pierre, La Revue des Arts 2.216 (cult in England).

[110] FRANCIS OF ASSISI (Oct 4, 1226).

a. SEL, regular text; Brown-Robbins, no 2899.

a*. SEL, variant; Brown-Robbins, no 3494.

MSS. a. 11 MSS.

Edition. a. Horstmann, EETS 87.53 (Bodl 1486 [Laud Misc 108], ff 41ᵇ–46ᵇ, end 13 cent); p 53, note 1 (based on Vita by Bonaventura).

MS. a*. Bodl 2567 (Bodley 779), ff 177ᵃ–183ᵃ, end imperfect (ca 1400).

Edition. a*. Zusatzleg 1889, p 312 and note 1 (a* completely different from a).

b. 1438 GL.

MSS. 1, Bodl 21947 (Douce 372), f 121, end imperfect; 2, Egerton 876, f 245, end imperfect; 3, Harley 4775, chap 142, ff 184ᵇ–

189ᵃ; MLA roto 343, 2.369; 4, BM Addit 35298, ff 126ᵇ–129ᵃ; 5, Lambeth 72, chap 137; see Butler LA, p 152.

Sources. Cf Graesse LA, chap 149, p 662.

c. Caxton GL.

Editions. Caxton GL, chap 183; Temple, 5.214.

Sources. Cf de Vignay LD, ff 293ᵃ–298ᵇ.

d. Anon Translation of Bonaventura.

Edition. Here begynneth the lyfe of . . . s Frauncis, Pynson, London 1515 ? STC, no 3270.

Sources. Cf Bonaventura, Legendae duae de vita S Francisci, 1263; Engl trans E G Salter, The Life of St Francis, Everyman Library, London 1914, 1944, p 303 (ultimate source).

[111] FREMUND, KING (May 11?, year?).

(Note: See also EDMUND, KING [80].)

a. SEL; Brown-Robbins, no 3192.

MS. Stowe 949, f 145ᵇ (late 14 cent).

Note: For record of legend included in Index of Bodl 3938 but missing in text, see M S Serjeantson, MLR 32.233, 254.

b. Lydgate; Brown-Robbins, no 3440.
See under Lydgate.

[112] FRIDESWIDE (Oct 19, ca 735).

a. SEL; Brown-Robbins, no 2900.

MSS. 1, Bodl 2567 (Bodley 779), f 280ᵇ (ca 1400); 2, Bodl 6924 (Ashmole 43), ff 155ᵇ–157ᵇ (1325–50); 3, Pepys 2344, p 430 (1325–50); 4, Trinity Camb 605, f 247ᵃ (early 14 cent); 5, Cotton Julius D.ix, ff 273ᵇ–275ᵇ (15 cent); 6, Stowe 949, f 144ᵃ (late 14 cent).

b. 1438 GL.

MSS. 1, BM Addit 35298, chap 97, f 75ᵃ⁻ᵇ; 2, Lambeth 72, chap 102, f 218.

Sources. Parker J, The Early History of Oxford, Oxford 1885, p 93 (analysis of earliest Latin lives).

[113] FRONTINIAN, ABBOT (April 14, 2 cent).

Edition. Caxton VP, pt 1, chap 45.

Sources. Cf La vie des pères, pt 1, chap 45, ff 63ᵃ–64ᵇ.

[114] FRONTON, BISHOP (Oct 25, year?).

(Note: See also MARTHA [189].)

SEL; Brown-Robbins, no 2901.

MS. Bodl 1596 (Laud Misc 463), f 61ᵃ (beg 15 cent).

Background. Coens M, La vie ancienne de St Front de Pèriguese, AnBol 48.324 (Latin text BHL 3182 given and early references noted).

[115] GAIUS, POPE (April 22, 296).

   a. SEL; Brown-Robbins, no 901.
MS. Bodl 2567 (Bodley 779), ff 232ᵃ–233ᵃ (ca 1400).
Edition. Zusatzleg 1889, p 401; p 401 note 1, and p 422 (ultimate source Liber pontificalis).
   b. Caxton GL.
Editions. Caxton GL, chap 233; Temple, 7.161.
Sources. Cf de Vignay LD, ff 385ᵇ–386ᵃ.

GAYE: see GAIUS.

GENEUESE: see GENEVIEVE.

[116] GENEVIEVE (Jan 3, ca 500).
Editions. Caxton GL, chap 116; Temple, 3.284.
Sources. Cf de Vignay LD, ff 424ᵃ–434ᵃ (Caxton om later miracles ff 429ᵇ–434ᵃ).

[117] GEORGE (April 23, ca 303).

   a. SEL, martyrdom; Brown-Robbins, no 2905.
MSS. 19 MSS.
Editions. Horstmann, EETS 87.294 (Bodl 1486 [Laud Misc 108], ff 130ᵃ–131ᵃ, end 13 cent).
D'Evelyn and Mill, EETS 235.155 (Corp Christi Camb 145, ff 59ᵃ–60ᵃ, early 14 cent).

   a*. SEL, dragon story; Brown-Robbins, no 2904.
MSS. 1, Lambeth 223, f 94ᵃ (end 14 cent); 2, Minnesota Univ Z.822,N.81 (formerly Phillipps 8122), ff 215ᵇ–216ᵇ, end imperfect (ca 1400).
Edition. Parker R E, A Northern Fragment of the Life of St George, MLN 38.97 (Minn Univ MS).
Sources. MLN 38.97 (Graesse LA, chap 58, pp 260–61).

   b. ScL; Brown-Robbins, no 4269.
MS. Camb Univ Gg.2.6, ff 257ᵃ–267ᵇ (1400–50).
Editions. Horstmann ScL, 2.61; Metcalfe STS, 2.176, notes 3.359.
Sources. Horstmann ScL, 2.61 (quotes Graesse LA, chap 58, p 259, noting variations).
Metcalfe STS, 3.362 (see preceding entry).

   c. Lydgate; Brown-Robbins, no 2592. See under Lydgate.

   d. Mirk Festial.
MSS. Note: See ANDREW d *MSS* [25] above.
1, Bodl 17680 (Gough Eccl Top 4), ff 77ᵃ–

78ᵇ (1400–50); 2, Cotton Claud A.ii, ff 59ᵃ–60ᵇ (ca 1420); 3, Harley 2247, ff 155ᵃ–156ᵃ (1450–1500); 4, Royal 18.B.xxv, ff 97ᵃ–99ᵇ (late 15 cent); 5, Durham Cosins v.iii.5, ff 96ᵃ–98ᵇ (15 cent).
Editions. Liber Festiualis, Caxton, Westminster 1483, sig k iiᵃ– k ivᵇ (STC, no 17957). Erbe, EETSES 96.132 (Bodl 17680).

   e. Speculum Sacerdotale.
MS. BM Addit 36791, ff 72ᵇ–75ᵃ (15 cent).
Editions. Weatherly, EETS 200.129; pp xxviii, 268 (similar to LA).

   f. 1438 GL.
MSS. 1, Harley 4775, chap 54, ff 66ᵃ–68ᵃ; MLA roto 343, 1.132; 2, BM Addit 35298, ff 35ᵃ–36ᵃ (in Trinity Dublin 319, lost Bodl 21947: see [6] above, under *MSS*).
Sources. Cf Graesse LA, chap 58, p 259.

   g. Caxton GL.
Editions. Caxton GL, chap 85; Temple, 3.125; rptd separately De la Mare Press, London 1920; W Nelson, EETS 230.112; Bruce Rogers, New Fairfield, Conn 1957.
Sources. Cf de Vignay LD, ff 124ᵃ–126ᵃ.

   h. Barclay Life of St George.
Editions. Barclay A, The Lyfe of Saynt George, Pynson, London 1515; rptd W Nelson, EETS 230 from unique copy in Trinity Coll Camb; p xii (dedication dated 1515); p xi (new biographical details), pp ix, xvi (translation in rime royal from Latin prose of Baptista Spagnuoli the Mantuan), p xix (analysis of translator's treatment of subject matter and style of source).
Literary Relations. Matzke J E, The Legend of St George: Its Development into a Roman d'Aventure, PMLA 19.449 (relation of legend to Bevis of Hamtoun and Seven Champions of Christendom).
Padelford F M and M O'Connor, Spenser's Use of the St George Legend, SP 23.142; rptd Variorum Spenser, Baltimore 1932, 1.379 (Caxton, Mirk, Lydgate as background for Spenser).

GERMAIN: see GERMANUS.

[118] GERMANUS, BISHOP OF AUXERRE (Aug 3, 448).

   a. SEL; Brown-Robbins, no 2919.
MS. Bodl 2567 (Bodley 779), ff 240ᵇ–241ᵃ (ca 1400).
Edition. Zusatzleg 1889, p 419; p 419, note 1 (abridged from Constantius, Vita Germani).
   b. 1438 GL.
MSS. 1, Egerton 876, f 175ᵇ; 2, Harley 630,

f 219[b]; 3, Harley 4775, chap 100, ff 133[a]–134[a]; MLA roto 343, 2.266; 4, BM Addit 11565, f 145[b] end; 5, BM Addit 35298, f 90[a–b].
Sources. Cf Graesse LA, chap 107, p 448.

c. Caxton GL.
Editions. Caxton GL, 1, chap 101; Temple, 3.203; 2, chap 140, Temple, 4.142.
Sources. Cf Graesse LA, chap 107, p 448; cf de Vignay LD, ff 207[a]–208[b].
Butler LA, p 84 (claims chap 101 based on 1438 GL, chap 140 on de Vignay LD).

[119] GERVASE AND PROTASE (June 19, year?).
a. 1438 GL.
MSS. 1, Harley 4775, chap 77, ff 96[a]–97[a]; MLA roto 343, 1.190; 2, BM Addit 35298, f 47[b].
Sources. Cf Graesse LA, chap 85, p 354.

b. Caxton GL.
Editions. Caxton GL, chap 108; Temple, 3.228.
Sources. Cf de Vignay LD, ff 176[b]–177[b].

[120] GILBERT OF SEMPRINGHAM (Feb 16, 1189).
Capgrave Life of St Gilbert, prose.
MSS. 1, Cotton Vitell D.xv, ff 24[a]–35[b], 7 fragments (15 cent); 2, BM Addit 36704, ff 46[a]–116[a] (mid 15 cent).
Munro, EETS 140.ix.
Bannister H B, Ye Solace of Pilgrimes by John Capgrave . . . , ed C A Mills, Brit and Amer Archaeol Soc of Rome, London 1911, p xii (BM Addit 36704 a Capgrave holograph).
Edition. Munro, EETS 140.61 (BM Addit 36704).
Modernizations. Ross J B and M M McLaughlin, The Portable Medieval Reader, New York 1949, p 73 (parts of chaps i, ii, iii from EETS 140.62).
Language. Munro, EETS 140.xiv (MS an example of dated and localized East Midland usage).
Authorship. Hingeston F C, The Chronicles of England by John Capgrave, Rolls Series, London 1858, pp i, ix, 321 (records of life and works).
Furnivall F J, The Life of St Katharine of Alexandria by John Capgrave, EETS 100.v.
Munro, EETS 140.v.
de Meijer A, John Capgrave OESA . . . , Augustiniana 5.400; 7.118, 531 (detailed bibliography and summary of life and works; for St Gilbert see 5.423; 7.556).
Toner N, Augustinian Spiritual Writers of the Eng Province in the 15th and 16th Cent, S Augustinus vitae spiritualis magister, Rome 1956, 2.509 (summary of Capgrave's life and works).
Sources. Munro, EETS 140.ix (based on Latin life written under direction of Abbot Roger, Gilbert's successor).

[121] GILES, ABBOT (Sept 1, year?).
a. SEL; Brown-Robbins, no 2906.
MSS. 12 MSS.
Edition. D'Evelyn and Mill, EETS 236.384 (Corp Christi Camb 145, ff 142[a]–144[a]; early 14 cent).

b. Lydgate; Brown-Robbins, no 2606; see under Lydgate.

c. 1438 GL.
MSS. 1, Bodl 21947 (Douce 372), f 105; end imperf; 2, Harley 4775, chap 120, ff 158[b]–159[b]; MLA roto 343, 2.317; 3, BM Addit 35298, ff 110[b]–111[b].
Sources. Cf Graesse LA, chap 130, p 582.

d. Caxton GL.
Editions. Caxton GL, chap 164; Temple, 5.91.
Sources. Cf de Vignay LD, ff 261[a]–262[a].

[122] GORDIAN AND EPIMACHUS (May 10, 250?).
a. 1438 GL.
MSS. 1, Bodl 21947 (Douce 372), chap 61, f 53; 2, Harley 4775, chap 66, f 91[a]; MLA roto 343, 1.180; 3, BM Addit 35298, f 45[a] (lost BM Addit 11565).
Sources. Cf Graesse LA, chap 74, p 337.

b. Caxton GL.
Editions. Caxton GL, chap 94; Temple, 3.178.
Sources. See GORDIAN a *Sources.*
Butler LA, p 87 (de Vignay version longer than LA or Caxton texts).

GORGONE, GORGONIEN: see GORGONIUS AND DOROTHEUS.

[123] GORGONIUS AND DOROTHEUS (Sept 9, year?).
a. 1438 GL.
MSS. 1, Bodl 21947 (Douce 372), f 106[a]; 2, Harley 4775, chap 126, f 166[b]; MLA roto 343, 2.333; 3, BM Addit 35298, f 115[a] (om Lambeth 72).
Sources. Cf Graesse LA, chap 135, p 601.

b. Caxton GL.
Editions. Caxton GL, chap 167; Temple, 5.119.
Sources. Cf de Vignay LD, f 268[a].

[124] GREGORY THE GREAT, POPE (March 12, 604).

(Note: The Gregorius Legend [Brown-Robbins, nos 204, 209] and the Trental of St Gregory [Brown-Robbins, nos 83, 1653, 3184] are not included here.)

a. SEL; Brown-Robbins, no 2910.
MSS. 18 MSS; add 19, Winchester Coll 33ª, ff 30ª–31ᵇ (15 cent).
Editions. Horstmann, EETS 87.355 (Bodl 1486 [Laud Misc 108], ff 153ª–154ᵇ; end 13 cent).
D'Evelyn and Mill, EETS 235.81 (Corp Christi Camb 145, ff 30ᵇ–32ª; early 14 cent).

b. Speculum Sacerdotale.
MS. BM Addit 36791, ff 21ᵇ–23ª (15 cent).
Edition. Weatherly, EETS 200.36 (sources, pp xxvii, 259; no direct source given).

c. 1438 GL.
MSS. 1, Bodl 21947 (Douce 372), f 27ª; beg imperf; 2, Egerton 876, f 64ᵇ; end imperf; 3, Harley 4775, chap 45, ff 47ª–51ᵇ; MLA roto 343, 1.94; 4, BM Addit 35298, ff 26ª–28ª.
Sources. Cf Graesse LA, chap 46, p 188.

d. Caxton GL.
Editions. Caxton GL, chap 74; Temple, 3.60.
Sources. Cf de Vignay LD, ff 108ᵇ–111ª.
Jeremy Sister M, Caxton's Golden Legend and de Vignai's Légende dorée, MS .8.105 (paraphrase of sermon, Temple, 3.63, based on de Vignay).

GRYSOGONE: see CHRYSOGONUS.

[125] GUTHLAC (April 11, 714).

SEL; Brown-Robbins, no 2911.
MSS. 1, Bodl 2567 (Bodley 779), 163ª–164ª (ca 1400); 2, Corp Christi Camb 145, ff 210ᵇ–213ª (in 2nd hand, later than early 14 cent); 3, Cotton Jul D.ix, ff 297ᵇ–301ᵇ (15 cent).
Editions. Forstmann H, Untersuchungen zur Guthlac-Legende, BBA 12.23 (Bodl 2567), p 22 (Corp Christi Camb 145).
Bolton W F, The ME and Latin Poems of St Guthlac, diss Princeton 1954, Microfilm Publ no 13669; see DA xv, no 11, p 2201 (p 210, Bodl 2567; p 221, Corp Christi Camb 145; p 184, Cotton Jul D.ix).
Selections. Birch W de G, Memorials of St Guthlac of Crowland, Wisbech 1881, p xxix (Corp Christi Camb 145, lines 1–24; Cotton Jul D.ix, lines 1–24, 105–24).
Forstmann H, BBA 12.32 (Corp Christi Camb 145, lines 1–24 from Birch).
Background. Colgrave B, Felix's Life of St Guthlac, Cambridge 1956.

HELAYN: see HELENUS.

[126] HELENA (Aug 18, ca 330).
(Note: See also Invention of the Cross [302] below.)
SEL; Brown-Robbins, no 2893.
MSS. 1, Harley 2250, f 50ᵇ (end 15 cent); 2, Lambeth 223, f 102ᵇ (end 14 cent).
Sources. Wilson R M, Some Lost Saints' Lives in O and ME, MLR 36.163 (Jocelyn of Furness' use of English life for his Vita of Helena).
Wilson R M, The Lost Literature of Medieval England, London 1952, p 93.

[127] HELENUS, ABBOT (April 17, [Whytford Add]).
Edition. Caxton VP, pt 1, chap 11.
Sources. Cf La vie des pères, pt 1, chap 11.

[128] HILARION, ABBOT (Oct 21, ca 371).

a. SEL; Brown-Robbins, no 902.
MS. Bodl 2567 (Bodl 779), ff 190ᵇ–192ª (ca 1400).
Edition. Zusatzleg 1889, p 333.
Sources. Zusatzleg 1889, p 333 (refers to Vita by St Jerome).
Rosenthal Vitae pàtrum, p 87 (Vita by St Jerome possibly direct source).

b. Caxton VP.
Edition. Caxton VP, pt 1, chap 37.
Sources. Cf La vie des pères, pt 1, chap 37, ff 38ᵇ–44ᵇ.
Background. Williams C A, Oriental Affinities of the Legend of the Hairy Anchorite, part II, Illinois Studies in Lang and Lit xi, no 4, p 100 (traditional elements in the ascetic practices of Hilarion).

[129] HILARY, BISHOP OF POITIERS (Jan 14, ca 368).

a. SEL; Brown-Robbins, no 2912.
MSS. 15 MSS; add 16, PRO c.47.34.1 no 5, f 2ª⁻ᵇ; end imperf (early 14 cent).
Edition. D'Evelyn and Mill, EETS 235.5 (Corp Christi Camb 145, ff 2ª–3ᵇ; early 14 cent).

b. 1438 GL.
MSS. 1, Harley 4775, chap 16, f 19ª⁻ᵇ; MLA root 343, 1.38; 2, BM Addit 35298, ff 12ᵇ–13ª (lost Lambeth 72).
Sources. Cf Graesse LA, chap 17, p 98.

c. Caxton GL.
Editions. Caxton GL, chap 49; Temple, 2.213.
Sources. Cf de Vignay LD, ff 75ᵇ–76ᵇ.

[130] HIPPOLYTUS OF ROME (Aug 13, ca 235).

a. SEL; Brown-Robbins, no 2915.
MSS. 9 MSS.
Edition. Horstmann, EETS 87.480 (Bodl 1486 [Laud Misc 108], ff 197ᵃ–198ᵃ; end 13 cent).

b. 1438 GL.
MSS. 1, Harley 4775, chap 110, ff 138ᵇ–139ᵃ; MLA roto 343, 2.277; 2, BM Addit 35298, f 97ᵃ⁻ᵇ (in Trinity Dublin 319; lost Bodl 21947, BM Addit 11565; om Lambeth 72).
Sources. Cf Graesse LA, chap 118, p 501.

c. Caxton GL.
Editions. Caxton GL, chap 151; Temple, 4.228.
Sources. Cf de Vignay LD, ff 228ᵃ–229ᵇ; Butler LA, p 90 (etymology from LA).

[131] HOR, ABBOT (March 29 [Whytford Add], ca 400).
Edition. Caxton VP, pt 1, chap 2.
Sources. La vie des pères, pt 1, chap 2, ff 11ᵇ–12ᵃ.

[132] HUGH, BISHOP OF LINCOLN (Nov 17, 1200).
Editions. Caxton GL, chap 210; Temple, 6.241.
Sources. Dimock J F, Magna vita S Hugonis, Rolls Series, London 1864, p xiv, note 1 (Caxton's version a derivative of liturgical Legenda in MS Lansdowne 436; for text of Lansdowne see Dimock, Giraldi Cambrensis Opera VII, Rolls Series, London 1877, p 172).
Butler LA, pp 83, 85, 154 (legend not in known texts of Latin or French sources used by Caxton; probably in some text of 1438 GL).

HYACINTH: see EUGENIA.

[133] HYGINUS, POPE (Jan 11, ca 142).
SEL; Brown-Robbins, no 2913.
MS. Bodl 2567 (Bodley 779), ff 233ᵇ–234ᵃ (ca 1400).
Edition. Zusatzleg 1889, p 404 (source uncertain, pp 404n1, 422).

IGIN: see HYGINUS.

[134] IGNATIUS, BISHOP OF ANTIOCH (Feb 1, ca 107).
a. SEL; Brown-Robbins, no 2914.
MS. Cotton Jul D.ix, chap 98, ff 272ᵃ–273ᵇ (15 cent).

b. 1438 GL.
MSS. 1, Harley 4775, chap 35, ff 36ᵇ–37ᵇ; MLA roto 343, 1.73; 2, BM Addit 35298, f 21ᵃ⁻ᵇ.

Sources. Cf Graesse LA, chap 36, p 155.
c. Caxton GL.
Editions. Caxton GL, chap 64; Temple, 3.16.
Sources. Cf de Vignay LD, ff 96ᵇ–97ᵃ.
Jeremy Sister M, Caxton's GL and de Vignai's LD, MS 8.106 (de Vignay source of details not in LA).

ILLARION: see HILARION.

ILLURIN: see SILVERIUS.

[135] INNOCENT I, POPE (July 28, 417).
SEL; Brown-Robbins, no 3386.
MS. Bodl 2567 (Bodl 779), ff 236ᵇ–237ᵇ (15 cent).
Edition. Zusatzleg 1889, p 411 (sources, pp 411n1, 422; refers to Liber pontificalis).

ISAIS: see SYRUS.

[136] IVES OF KERMARTIN (May 19, 1303).
Editions. Caxton GL, chap 242; Temple, 7.191.
Sources. Cf de Vignay LD, ff 414ᵃ–417ᵃ.
Butler LA, pp 39, 44 (legend in revised de Vignay texts).
Background. De la Borderie A, J Daniel, R P Perquis, and D Tempier, Monuments originaux de l'histoire de St Yves, Saint-Brieuc 1887.

JACINCTUS, JACINTH: see EUGENIA.

JACQUES, JAKES: see JAMES THE MARTYR.

[137] JAMES THE GREATER (July 25, 44).
a. SEL; Brown-Robbins, no 2918.
MSS. 16 MSS.
Editions. Horstmann, EETS 87.33 (Bodl 1486 [Laud Misc 108], ff 34ᵃ–38ᵇ; end 13 cent).
D'Evelyn and Mill, EETS 235.327 (Corp Christi Camb 145, ff 122ᵃ–127ᵃ; early 14 cent).
Selections. Furnivall EEP, pp 57–59 (Harley 2277, ff 100ᵇ–101ᵇ; miracle of the Deceived Pilgrim).

b. NHC; Brown-Robbins, no 2917.
(Note: For the miracle of the Deceived Pilgrim not included in the NHC legend of St James but used as a separate exemplum see Brown-Robbins, no 1642).
MSS. 1, Cotton Tib E.vii, f 248ᵇ col 1 (ca 1400); 2, Harley 4196, ff 164ᵃ–166ᵃ 15 cent).
Edition. AELeg 1881, p 96 (Harley 4196).

c. ScL; Brown-Robbins, no 2659.
MS. Camb Univ Gg.2.6, ff 32ᵇ–37ᵃ (1400–50).

Editions. Horstmann ScL, 1.47; Metcalfe STS, 1.97 (notes 3.72).
Sources. Horstmann ScL, 1.47 (quotes Graesse LA, chap 99, p 421); Metcalfe STS, 3.73 (quotes LA; notes other parallels).

d. Mirk Festial.

MSS. Note: See ANDREW d *MSS* [25] above.
1, Bodl 17680 (Gough Eccl Top 4), ff 119ᵇ–122ᵃ (1400–50); 2, Cotton Claud A.ii, ff 91ᵇ–93ᵇ (ca 1420); 3, Harley 2247, ff 174ᵃ–175ᵇ (1450–1500); 4, Harley 2391, f 103 (1450–1500); 5, Royal 18.B.xxv, ff 114ᵃ–115ᵇ (late 15 cent); 6, Durham Cosins v.iii.5, ff 121ᵇ–123ᵇ (15 cent). (Om Bodl 21634, 21682 [Douce 60, 108].)
Editions. Liber Festiualis, Caxton, Westminster 1483, sig m iiᵇ–m ivᵇ (STC, no 17957). Erbe, EETSES 96.208 (Bodl 17680).

e. Speculum Sacerdotale.

MS. BM Addit 36791, ff 98ᵃ–100ᵇ (15 cent).
Edition. Weatherly, EETS 200.174 (sources, pp xxviii, 272; Belethus Rationale Divinorum Offic; LA; notes other versions of miracles).

f. 1438 GL.

MSS. 1, Harley 4775, chap 92, ff 124ᵇ–127ᵃ; MLA roto 343, 1.249; 2, BM Addit 35298, ff 84ᵇ–86ᵃ.
Sources. Cf Graesse LA, chap 99, p 421.

g. Caxton GL.

Editions. Caxton GL, chap 132; Temple, 4.97.
Sources. Cf de Vignay LD, ff 192ᵃ–196ᵃ.

[138] JAMES THE LESS (May 1, 1st cent).

(Note: See also PHILIP AND JAMES [232]; for the "romance" of Titus and Vespasian included in the present legend see I (Romances) [107].)

a. ScL; Brown-Robbins, no 2353.

MS. Camb Univ Gg.2.6, ff 52ᵃ–61ᵇ (1400–50).
Editions. Horstmann ScL, 1.72; Metcalfe STS, 1.150 (notes 3.110).
Sources. Horstmann ScL, 1.72 (quotes Graesse LA, chap 67, p 295); Metcalfe STS, 3.112 (LA quoted; other accounts referred to).

b. 1438 GL.

MSS. 1, Harley 4775, chap 60, ff 74ᵇ–77ᵇ; MLA roto 343, 1.149; 2, BM Addit 35298, ff 38ᵇ–40ᵃ (lost Bodl 21947).
Sources. Cf Graesse LA, chap 67, p 295.

c. Caxton GL.

Editions. Caxton GL, chap 91; Temple, 3.158.
Sources. Cf de Vignay LD, ff 132ᵃ–134ᵃ (some material missing in this text of de Vignay).

[139] JAMES THE MARTYR, INTERCISUS (Nov 27, ca 421).

a. SEL; Brown-Robbins, no 2916.

MSS. 1, Bodl 2567 (Bodl 779,), f 113ᵃ (ca 1400); 2, Cotton Jul D.ix, chap 85, ff 201ᵇ–202ᵇ (15 cent); 3, Egerton 2810, f 122ᵇ (14 cent). (Note: Listed in Bodl 3938 [Vernon] Index, but lost in text; see M S Serjeantson, MLR 32.233).

b. 1438 GL.

MSS. 1, Harley 4775, chap 166, ff 234ᵇ–235ᵇ; MLA roto 343, 2.467; 2, BM Addit 35298, ff 152ᵇ–153ᵇ (in Lambeth 72, chap 166; see Butler LA, p 152; om Harley 630; lost BM Addit 11565).
Sources. Cf Graesse LA, chap 174, p 799.

c. Caxton GL.

Editions. Caxton GL, chap 217; Temple, 7.34.
Sources. Cf de Vignay LD, ff 343ᵃ–344ᵃ.

JASPAR: see THREE KINGS OF COLOGNE.

JERMAN: see GERMANUS.

[140] JEROME (Sept 30, 420).

a. SEL; Brown-Robbins, no 2922.

MSS. 14 MSS; add 15, Cotton Jul D.ix, chap 63, ff 137ᵃ–139ᵃ (15 cent).
Edition. D'Evelyn and Mill, EETS 236.428 (Corp Christi Camb 145, ff 159ᵃ–161ᵃ; early 14 cent).

b. The Life of St Jerome, prose (intro, 19 chaps).

MSS. 1, St John's Camb 250, ff 2ᵇ–35ᵇ (15 cent); 2, Lambeth 432, ff 1–37 (15 cent). James M R and C Jenkins, Descript Catalog of the MSS . . . in Lambeth Palace, Cambridge 1930, p 599 (identification of MSS 1 and 2 as copies of the same text; for companion pieces in St John's Camb 249 on John the Baptist and John the Evangelist see also James, Descript Cata of the MSS . . . of St John's Coll Camb, Cambridge 1913, p 285).
Editions. [Vita beati Jeronimi confessoris,] Wynkyn de Worde 1500? (STC, no 14508; intro om).
Horstmann C, Prosalegenden iv, Angl 3.328 (Lambeth 432).
Selections. Workman 15 Cent Trans, p 154 (chap 4, vision of J's death from Horstmann).
Textual Notes. Holthausen F, Zu Alt- und Mittelengl Dichtungen, Angl 14.311 (on Lambeth 432).
Authorship. Gerould S Leg, p 288 (Thomas

Gascoigne, 1403–58, possible author).
Sources. Angl 3.319 (as stated in MS, chap 1 from LA; chaps 6–18 from letters of Augustine and Cyrillus; chap 19 from Revelations of St Bridget).
Workman 15 Cent Trans, p 194 (more exact identification of sources).
Literary Criticism. Workman 15 Cent Trans, p 154 (analysis of style of chap 4).

c. 1438 GL.

MSS. 1, Bodl 21947 (Douce 372), f 117ᵃ; beg imperf; 2, Harley 4775, chap 139, ff 181ᵇ–183ᵃ; MLA roto 343, 2.363. (Note: Chap 66, entitled Jerome in MS 2, is the legend of Malchus ascribed to Jerome); 3, BM Addit 35298, ff 124ᵇ–125ᵇ (in BM Addit 11565; see Butler LA, p 69).
Sources. Cf Graesse LA, chap 146, p 653.

d. Caxton GL.

Editions. Caxton GL, chap 180; Temple, 5.199.
Sources. Cf de Vignay LD, ff 289ᵇ–291ᵇ.

[141] JOHN, ABBOT (Feb 28 [Whytford Add]).

a. 1438 GL.

MSS. 1, Harley 4775, chap 168, f 235ᵃ⁻ᵇ; MLA roto 343, 2.470; 2, BM Addit 35298, ff 153ᵇ–154ᵃ (lost BM Addit 11565).
Sources. Cf Graesse LA, chap 176, p 805.

b. Caxton GL.

Editions. Caxton GL, chap 223; Temple, 7.75.
Sources. Cf de Vignay LD, ff 345ᵇ–346ᵃ.
Rosenthal Vitae patrum, p 66 (relation of Vitae patrum version to LA and Caxton).

[142] JOHN THE ALMONER, PATRIARCH OF ALEXANDRIA (Jan 23, 619?).

a. 1438 GL.

MSS. 1, Harley 4775, chap 26, ff 27ᵇ–30ᵃ; MLA roto 343, 1.55; 2, BM Addit 35298, ff 17ᵃ–18ᵃ.
Sources. Cf Graesse LA, chap 27, p 126.

b. Caxton GL.

Editions. Caxton GL, chap 60; Temple, 2.268.
Sources. Cf de Vignay LD, ff 88ᵇ–91ᵇ.

c. Caxton VP.

Edition. Caxton VP, pt 1, chaps 106–57.
Selections. Dibdin Typo Antiq, 2.48 (from chap 117).
Sources. La vie des pères, pt 1, chaps 106–51, ff 105ᵇ–126ᵃ.

[143] JOHN THE BAPTIST (1, Nativity June 24; 2, Beheading Aug 29, ca 30).

a. SEL (2 only); Brown-Robbins, no 2945.

MSS. 17 MSS.
Editions. Horstmann, EETS 87.29 (Bodl 1486 [Laud Misc 108], ff 32ᵇ–34ᵃ; end 13 cent).
D'Evelyn and Mill, EETS 235.241 (Corp Christi Camb 145, ff 90ᵇ–92ᵇ; early 14 cent).

b. ScL (1, 2 combined); Brown-Robbins, no 1499.

MS. Camb Univ Gg.2.6, ff 274ᵃ–287ᵃ (1400–50).
Editions. Horstmann ScL, 2.83; Metcalfe STS, 2.223 (notes 3.377).
Sources. Horstmann ScL, 2.83 (quotes LA; refers to Speculum Hist and Gospels); Metcalfe STS, 3.378 (see preceding entry).

c. Mirk Festial (1, 2 combined).

MSS. Note: See ANDREW d *MSS* [25] above.
1, Bodl 17680 (Gough Eccl Top 4), ff 105ᵃ–107ᵃ (1400–50); 2, Cotton Claud A.ii, ff 82ᵃ–84ᵃ (ca 1420); 3, Harley 2247, ff 162ᵇ–166ᵃ (1450–1500); 4, Royal 18.B.xxv, ff 105ᵃ–108ᵃ (late 15 cent); 5, Durham Cosins v.iii.5, ff 107ᵇ–111ᵃ (15 cent). (Om Bodl 21634 = Douce 60.)
Editions. Liber Festiualis, Caxton, Westminster 1483, sig l iᵇ–l iiiᵃ (STC, no 17957).
Erbe, EETSES 96, chap 44, p 182 (Bodl 17680).

d. Speculum Sacerdotale (1, 2 separated).

MS. BM Addit 36791, ff 92ᵇ–95ᵃ; ff 110ᵇ–112ᵃ (15 cent).
Edition. Weatherly, EETS 200.164, 195 (sources, pp xxviii, xxix, 271, 274; lists Belethus Rationale Div Off, LA, and Gospels as sources).

e. 1438 GL (1, 2 combined).

MSS. 1, Bodl 21947 (Douce 372) ff 63–64; fragment; 2, Harley 4775, chap 79, ff 104ᵇ–107ᵃ; MLA roto 343, 1.209; 3, BM Addit 35298, ff 61ᵇ–62ᵇ (in Trinity Dublin 319; see Gerould S Leg, p 195).
Sources. Cf Graesse LA, chap 86, p 356; chap 125, p 566.

f. Caxton GL (1, 2 separated).

Editions. Caxton GL, chap 111; Temple, 3.253; chap 159, Temple, 5.67; rptd A Aspland, The GL, Holbein Soc Fac-simile Reprints, London 1878.
Sources. Cf de Vignay LD, ff 177ᵇ–180ᵃ; ff 254ᵃ–257ᵇ.

g. Life and Miracles, prose (intro, 18 chaps).

MS. St John's Camb 249, ff 1–29 (15 cent); for companion pieces see JEROME b *MSS* [140], JOHN THE EVANGELIST i *MS* [146].

[144] JOHN CHRYSOSTOM, ARCH-
BISHOP OF CONSTANTINOPLE (Jan
27, 407).

a. 1438 GL.
MSS. 1, Harley 4775, chap 129, ff 170ª–171ª;
MLA roto 343, 2.340; 2, BM Addit 35298,
ff 118ª–119ª; 3, Lambeth 72, chap 135.
Sources. Cf Graesse LA, chap 138, p 611.

b. Caxton GL.
Editions. Caxton GL, chap 170; Temple,
5.136.
Sources. Cf de Vignay LD, ff 272ª–275ᵇ.
Jeremy Sister M, Caxton's GL and de Vignai's LD, MS 8.100 (notes Caxton's omission of Arian passage given in LA and LD).

[145] JOHN OF EGYPT (March 27, 394).
Editions. Caxton VP, pt 1, chap 1, ff iiª–viiª.
Selections. Dibdin Typo Antiq, 2.45.
Sources. La vie des pères, pt 1, chap 1, ff
8ª–11ᵇ.

[146] JOHN THE EVANGELIST (1, Port
Latin May 6; 2, Life Dec 27, ca 100).

a. SEL (1, 2 combined); Brown-
Robbins, no 2932.
MSS. 21 MSS
Editions. Horstmann, EETS 87.402 (Bodl
1486 [Laud Misc 108], ff 169ᵇ–174ª; end
13 cent).
D'Evelyn and Mill, EETS 236.594 (Corp
Christi Camb 145, ff 173ᵇ–180ª; early 14
cent).
Selections. Furnivall EEP, p 106 (Harley
2277, f 195ᵇ; miracle of St Edward's ring).

b. NHC (1, 2 combined); Brown-
Robbins, no 2923.
MS. Harley 4196, ff 20ª–23ᵇ (15 cent).
Edition. AELeg 1881, p 35.

c. ScL (1, 2 combined); Brown-
Robbins, no 3769.
MS. Camb Univ Gg.2.6, ff 37ª–44ª (1400–50).
Editions. Horstmann ScL, 1.53; Metcalfe STS,
1.109 (notes 3.79).
Language. Bearder J W, Über dem Gebrauch
der Praepositionen in der altschottischen
Poesie, Halle 1894 (Horstmann's text of
John used).
Sources. Horstmann ScL, 1.53 (quotes Graesse
LA, chap 9, p 56); Metcalfe STS, 3.81
(quotes LA; refers to other versions).

d. Thornton, stanzas (1, 2 combined);
Brown-Robbins, no 2608.
MS. Lincoln Cath 91 (Thornton), ff 231ª–
233ᵇ (ca 1440); AELeg 1881, p 454 (description, contents).

Editions. Perry, EETS 26, 1867; rvsd 1889;
rvsd, enlarged 1913, p 97; AELeg 1881, p
467.
Language. Oakden J P, Alliterative Poetry
in ME, 2 vols, Manchester 1930, 1935; 1.115
(evidence for Northern dialect); 2.217, 226,
231 (versification); 2.79 (literary criticism).

e. Mirk Festial (1, 2 separate).
MSS. Note: See ANDREW d *MSS* [25] above.
1, Bodl 17680 (Gough Eccl Top 4), ff 18ª–
20ᵇ; ff 85ª–86ᵇ (1400–50); 2, Cotton Claud
A.ii, ff 18ᵇ–21ª; ff 68ᵇ–69ᵇ (ca 1420); 3,
Harley 2247, ff 17ᵇ–20ª, 1 om (1450–1500);
4, Royal 18.B.xxv, ff 2ᵇ–4ª, 1 om (late 15
cent); 5, Durham Cosins v.iii.5, ff 71ᵇ–73ᵇ;
ff 106ª–107ᵇ (15 cent).
Editions. Liber Festiualis, Caxton, Westminster 1483, sig g viiiᵇ–h iiiᵇ; sig k iiiª–l iª
(STC, no 17957).
Erbe, EETSES 96, chap 8, p 30; chap 35, p
146 (Bodl 17680).
Sources. Cf Graesse LA, chap 9, p 56; chap
69, p 311.

f. Speculum Sacerdotale (1, 2 separate).
MS. BM Addit 36791, ff 7ª–8ª; ff 86ª–
87ª (15 cent).
Edition. Weatherly, EETS 200.11, 152 (sources,
pp xxvii, xxviii, 256, 271; Belethus Rationale Div Off; LA; references to other versions).

g. 1438 GL (1, 2 separate).
MSS. 1, Harley 4775, chap 8, f 16ª⁻ᵇ, end
imperf; chap 62, f 80ᵇ; MLA roto 343, 1.32,
161; 2, BM 11565, f 44, life, end imperf;
3, BM Addit 35298, chap 7 (= 8), ff 7ᵇ–8ª;
f 41ª⁻ᵇ (both parts lost, Bodl 21947; life
lost, Lambeth 72).
Sources. Cf Graesse LA, chap 9, p 56; chap
69, p 311.

h. Caxton GL (1, 2 separate).
Editions. Caxton GL, chap 43; Temple, 2.161;
chap 93, Temple, 3.176.
Sources. Cf de Vignay LD, ff 66ᵇ–69ª; f 136ª.
(Note: The 1480 copy of de Vignay omits
several incidents and the miracle of St
Edward's ring.)
Jeremy Sister M, Caxton's GL and de Vig-
nai's LD, MS 8.104 (details not in LA sup-
plied from de Vignay).

i. Life and Miracles, prose (intro, 18
chaps).
MS. St John's Camb 249, ff 23ᵇ–44 (15 cent);
for companion pieces see JEROME b *MSS*
[140], JOHN THE BAPTIST g *MS* [143].

JOHN GRISOSTOME:
see JOHN CHRYSOSTOM.

[147] JOHN AND PAUL OF ROME (June 26, 362?).

a. SEL; Brown-Robbins, no 1790.
MS. Bodl 2567 (Bodley 779), f 216ᵃ (ca 1400).
Edition. Zusatzleg 1889, p 379 (sources, p 379n1; refers to Vita in Acta SS).

b. 1438 GL.
MSS. 1, Bodl 21947 (Douce 372), f 64ᵇ; fragment; 2, Egerton 876, f 141; 3, Harley 4775, chap 80, ff 107ᵃ–108ᵃ; MLA roto 343, 1.214; 4, BM Addit 35298, ff 62ᵇ–63ᵇ.
Sources. Cf Graesse LA, chap 87, p 364.

c. Caxton GL.
Editions. Caxton GL, chap 119; Temple, 4.6; rptd A Aspland, The GL, Holbein Soc Fac-simile Reprints, London 1878.
Sources. Cf de Vignay LD, ff 180ᵃ–181ᵃ.

JOSAPHAT: see BARLAAM.

[148] JOSEPH OF ARIMATHEA (March 17, 1st cent).

(Note: See also I [Romances] [40], [42]; IV [Translations and Paraphrases of the Bible] [33].)

a. Stanzaic version; Brown-Robbins, no 1778.
Editions. Lyfe of Joseph of Armathia, Pynson, London 1520, pp 1–8 (STC, no 14807); rptd Skeat, EETS 44.37.
Date. Skeat, EETS 44.xxii, 73 (written ca 1502).
Sources. Skeat, EETS 44.xxii, 72 (based on Capgrave, Nova legenda Angliae 2.78, and local tradition).

b. Life of Joseph of Armathy, prose.
Editions. A treatyse . . . of Joseph of Armathy, Wynkyn de Worde, London 1510?, pp 1–15 (STC, no 14806); rptd Skeat, EETS 44.27.
Sources. Skeat, EETS 44.xx, 68 (based on Capgrave).
Background. Robinson J A, St Joseph of Arimathea in Two Glastonbury Legends, Cambridge 1926, p 28 (local tradition on legend).

JUDAS: see QUIRIAC.

JUDAS: see SIMON AND JUDE.

[149] JUDAS ISCARIOT.
(Note: The legend of Judas is included (1) in some MSS of Titus and Vespasian (Brown-Robbins, no 1881; see also I (Romances) [107]; for text see J A Herbert, Titus and Vespasian, Roxb Club, London 1905, pp xli, 202, lines 4487–4885); (2) in the legend

of Matthias, see [196 b, c, d, e] below. Huntington HM 144, ff 57ᵃ–58ᵃ (15 cent) contains a prose life of Judas somewhat similar to that in 1438 GL and Caxton GL. For the ballad of Judas see under Ballads.)

MSS. 11 MSS; add 12, Winchester Coll 33ᵃ, ff 15ᵇ–17ᵇ (15 cent).
Editions. Furnivall EEP, p 107 (Harley 2277, ff 227ᵃ–229ᵃ; ca 1300).
Wülcker AELeseb, Halle 1874, 1.18 (notes p 132; Harley 2277 based on Furnivall).
D'Evelyn and Mill, EETS 236.692 (Corp Christi Camb 145, ff 214ᵃ–215ᵃ; addition in later hand).
Sources. Rand E K, Mediaeval Lives of Judas Iscariot, Kittredge Anniv Papers, Boston 1913, p 305 (early Latin versions of possible significance for LA and vernacular accounts of Judas).
Baum P F, The Mediaeval Legend of Judas Iscariot, PMLA 31.526 (exact relation to Latin versions including LA not determinable).
Wells M E, The SEL and Its Relation to the LA, PMLA 51.337 (evidence for LA rather than common source as direct basis for SEL Judas).
Literary Relations. Baum P F, Judas' Sunday Rest, MLR 18.172 (meeting of Judas and Brendan in SEL and Caxton GL versions of BRENDAN [48]).
Background. Creizenach W, Judas Ischarioth in Legende und Sage des Mittelalters, BGDSL 2.176 (brief reference to English material, p 193).

JUDE: see SIMON.

JULIAN THE APOSTATE. (Note: An account of Julian the Apostate, not listed separately here, is included with four other Julians in ScL, 1438 GL, Caxton GL; see following entries.)

JULIAN OF AUVERGNE: see JULIAN OF BRIOUDE.

[150] JULIAN OF BRIOUDE (OR AUVERGNE) (Aug 28, 3 cent?).

a. ScL; Brown-Robbins, no 4028.
MS. Camb Univ Gg.2.6, ff 170ᵃ–171ᵃ (1400–50).
Editions. Horstmann ScL, 1.219; Metcalfe STS, 1.460 (notes 3.285).
Sources. Horstmann ScL, 1.218 (passages from Graesse LA, chap 30, p 140); Metcalfe STS, 3.288 (passages from LA).

b. 1438 GL.
MSS. 1, Harley 4775, chap 29, f 32ᵃ⁻ᵇ; MLA

roto 343, 1.64; 2, BM Addit 35298, ff 19ᵃ–20ᵃ.
Sources. Cf Graesse LA, chap 30, p 141.

c. Caxton GL.
Editions. Caxton GL, chap 63; Temple, 3.9.
Sources. Cf de Vignay LD, ff 94ᵇ–95ᵃ.

JULIAN THE CONFESSOR: see JULIAN OF LE MANS.

[151] JULIAN THE HOSPITALLER (Feb 12, year?).

a. SEL; Brown-Robbins, no 2950.
MSS. 19 MSS; add 20, PRO c.47.34.1 no 5, ff 3ᵃ–4ᵇ; fragmentary lines 44–152 (early 14 cent); 21, Cotton Titus A.xxvi, ff 204ᵇ–207ᵃ; garbled, written as prose (15 cent).
Editions. Horstmann, EETS 87.256 (Bodl 1486 [Laud Misc 108], ff 116ᵃ–117ᵇ; end 13 cent).
D'Evelyn and Mill, EETS 235.32 (Corp Christi Camb 145, ff 12ᵇ–14ᵇ; early 14 cent).

b. ScL; Brown-Robbins, no 4028.
MS. Camb Univ Gg.2.6, ff 171ᵇ–174ᵇ (1400–50).
Editions. Horstmann ScL, 1.221; Metcalfe STS, 1.464 (notes 3.285).
Sources. Horstmann ScL, 1.121 (passages from Graesse LA, chap 30, p 142); Metcalfe STS, 3.291 (passages from LA).

c. 1438 GL.
MSS. 1, Harley 4775, chap 29, f 33ᵃ; MLA roto 343, 1.66; 2, BM Addit 35298, f 19ᵇ.
Sources. Cf Graesse LA, chap 30, p 142.

d. Caxton GL.
Editions. Caxton GL, chap 63; Temple, 3.11.
Sources. Cf de Vignay LD, f 95ᵃ⁻ᵇ.
Background. De Gaiffier B, La légende de St Julien l'Hospitalier, AnBol 63.145 (origin and diffusion of legend, with Latin text).

[152] JULIAN, BROTHER OF JULIUS (date?).

a. ScL; Brown-Robbins, no 4028.
MS. Camb Univ Gg.2.6, f 171ᵃ⁻ᵇ (1400–50).
Editions. Horstmann ScL, 1.220; Metcalfe STS, 1.462 (notes 3.290).
Sources. See JULIAN OF BRIOUDE a *Sources* [150].

b. 1438 GL.
MSS. 1, Harley 4775, chap 29, ff 32ᵇ–33ᵃ; MLA roto 343, 1.65; 2, BM Addit 35298, f 19ᵃ⁻ᵇ.
Sources. Cf Graesse LA, chap 30, p 141.

c. Caxton GL.
Editions. Caxton GL, chap 63; Temple, 3.10.
Sources. Cf de Vignay LD, f 95ᵇ.

[153] JULIAN OF LE MANS (Jan 27, year?).

a. SEL; Brown-Robbins, no 2949.
MSS. 18 MSS.
Editions. Horstmann, EETS 87.255 (Bodl 1486 [Laud Misc 108], ff 115ᵇ–116ᵃ; end 13 cent).
D'Evelyn and Mill, EETS 235.31 (Corp Christi Camb 145, f 12ᵃ⁻ᵇ; early 14 cent).

b. ScL; Brown-Robbins, no 4028.
MS. Camb Univ Gg.2.6; ff 169ᵃ–170ᵃ (1400–50).
Editions. Horstmann ScL , 1.218; Metcalfe STS, 1.458 (notes 3.285).
Sources. Horstmann ScL, 1.218 (passages from Graesse LA, chap 30, p 140); Metcalfe STS, 3.288 (passages from LA).

c. 1438 GL.
MSS. 1, Harley 4775, chap 29, f 32ᵃ; MLA roto 343, 1.64; 2, BM Addit 35298, f 19ᵃ.
Sources. Cf Graesse LA, chap 30, p 140.

d. Caxton GL.
Editions. Caxton GL, chap 63; Temple, 3.8.
Sources. Cf de Vignay LD, f 94ᵇ.

[154] JULIANA OF CUMAE (Feb 16, ca 305?).

a. Liflade of St Juliene, alliterative prose.
(Note: See also KATHERINE OF ALEXANDRIA a [157], MARGARET OF ANTIOCH a [184].)
MSS. 1, Bodl 1883 [Bodl 34], ff 36ᵇ–52ᵇ (early 13 cent); 2, Royal 17.A.xxvii, ff 56ᵃ–70ᵃ (early 13 cent).
Hall Selections, 2.492.
D'Ardenne, edn, p xv.
Wilson R M, Sawles Warde, Leeds Texts and Monographs 3.xxx.
Editions. Cockayne, EETS 51; rptd 1957 (both MSS with translation).
D'Ardenne S R T O, An Edition of þe Liflade ant te Passiun of Seinte Julienne, Bibl de la Faculté de Philos et Lettres de l'Univ de Liège, 64, Liège 1936; rptd EETS 248 (both MSS; crit E V Gordon, MÆ 5.131; P G, AnBol 55.150; K Malone, MLN 53.313; E Ekwall, EStn 21.125).
Selections. Morris Spec, 1.96 (passages from both MSS in EETS 51.4–21, 30–35; crit Angl 25.319; MLN 7.267).
Emerson O F, A Middle English Reader, N Y 1905, p 191 (passages from Royal MS, EETS 51).
Hall Selections, 1.138 (notes 2.543; passages from both MSS).

Textual Notes. Stratmann F H, Verbesserungen zu me Schrift-stellern, EStn 4.94 (emendations of EETS 51 text).
Language. Bülbring K D, QF 63, pp 3.21; Hall Selections, 2.543; D'Ardenne, edn, pp xxvii, xxix (comparison of language of both MSS).
Literary Form. Hall Selections, 2.505 (written in rhythmic prose).
D'Ardenne, edn, p xxviii (summary of controversy with further support for prose).
Hotchner C A, A Note on Dux Vitae and Lifes Lattiow, PMLA 57.572 (use of prose in Juliene).
Authorship. Cockagne, EETS 51.vii (suggests Richard Poor, Bishop of Salisbury).
Einenkel E, Über die Verfasser einiger neuangelsächischer Schriften, Leipzig 1881, pt I, pp 1–86 (comparison of Bodl 34 text of Jul with Hali Meidenhad disproves common authorship; crit W Merkes, AnglA 5.86).
Einenkel E, Über den Verfasser der neuangelsäch Legende von Katharina, Angl 5.91 (Jul probably not by author of Kath; restated EETS 80.xix).
Hall Selections, 2.505 (suggests unity of authorship and Gilbertine origin for Katherine Group).
Wilson R M, A Note on the Authorship of the Katherine Group, Leeds SE 1.24 (unity of authorship improbable).
D'Ardenne, edn, p xl (Katherine Group product of a school rather than of a single author).
Sources. Einenkel, Über die Verfasser, p 65 (comparison with Latin version, Acta SS, Feb, II.873).
Backhaus O, Über die Quellen der mittelengl Legende von heilige Juliane und ihr Verhältnis zu Cynewulfs Juliana, Halle 1899 (no direct dependence of Jul on Acta SS Latin or on Cynewulf).
Hall Selections, 2.545 (Latin life basis of English).
D'Ardenne, edn, p xxii, 2 (Bodl 2430 [Bodley 285] printed as closest Latin source yet noted).

b. SEL; Brown-Robbins, no 2951.
MSS. 16 MSS; Arch 151.19 (description and interrelation of 7 MSS).
Editions. Cockayne, EETS 51.81 (Bodl 6924 [Ashm 43], ff 25ᵃ–28ᵃ; 1325–50).
Schleich G, Die Gloucestershire-Legende der heiligen Juliane, Arch 151.25 (Bodl 6924).
D'Evelyn and Mill, EETS 235.62 (Corp Christi Camb 145, ff 23ᵇ–26ᵃ; early 14 cent).
Language and Sources. Arch 151.34 (language supports claims for Gloucestershire origin), p 41 (comparison with other versions inconclusive for direct source).

c. ScL; Brown-Robbins, no 2952.
MS. Camb Univ Gg.2.6, ff 373ᵇ–376ᵃ (1400–50).
Editions. Horstmann ScL, 2.190; Metcalfe STS, 2.424 (notes 3.457).
Sources. Horstmann ScL, 2.190 (cites Graesse LA, chap 43, p 177).
Metcalfe STS, 3.458 (cites LA).
Brunöhler E, Über einige lateinische, englische, französische und deutsche Fassungen der Julianenlegende, Bonn 1912 (attempt to show relation of vernacular versions a, b, and c to each other and to Latin in Acta SS).

d. 1438 GL.
MSS. 1, Harley 4775, chap 42, f 43ᵃ⁻ᵇ; MLA roto 343, 1.86; 2, BM Addit 35298, f 24ᵃ⁻ᵇ (lost Egerton 876, BM Addit 11565).
Sources. Cf Graesse LA, chap 43, p 177.

e. Caxton GL.
Editions. Caxton GL, chap 71; Temple, 3.45.
Sources. Cf de Vignay LD, ff 104ᵇ–106ᵃ.
Jeremy Sister M, Caxton's GL and de Vignai's LD, MS 8.105 (fuller dialogue with devil not in LA but in de Vignay and Caxton).

JULIANA OF NICOMEDIA: see JULIANA OF CUMAE.

JULITTA, JULITTE: see QUIRINE AND JULITTA.

[155] JUSTIN, MARTYR (April 14, ca 165).
Editions. Caxton GL, chap 237; Temple, 7.181.
Sources. Cf de Vignay LD, f 392ᵃ⁻ᵇ

[156] JUSTINA AND CYPRIAN OF ANTIOCH (Sept 26, year?).
(Note: For use of legend as exemplum under Lechery, see Handlyng Synne, EETS 123.258.)

a. SEL; Brown-Robbins, no 2953.
MSS. 1, Bodl 2567 (Bodley 779), f 161ᵃ (ca 1400); 2, Bodl 3938 (Vernon), f 55ᵃ col 1 (ca 1385); 3, Bodl 6924 (Ashm 43), ff 137ᵇ–138ᵃ (1325–50); 4, Pepys 2344, p 485 (1325–50); 5, Cotton Jul D.ix, ff 135ᵃ–136ᵃ (15 cent); 6, Egerton 1993, f 203ᵇ (1300–50).

b. ScL; Brown-Robbins, no 3490.
MS. Camb Univ Gg.2.6, ff 247ᵇ–257ᵃ (1400–50).

Editions. Horstmann ScL, 2.50; Metcalfe STS, 2.152 (notes 3.351).

Sources. Horstmann ScL, 2.50 (cites Graesse LA, chap 142, p 632); Metcalfe STS, 3.353 (cites LA but notes author had fuller source).

c. 1438 GL.

MSS. 1, Harley 4775, chap 135, ff 176ᵇ–177ᵇ; MLA roto 343, 2.353; 2, BM Addit 11565, f 173; 3, BM Addit 35298, f 122ᵃ⁻ᵇ (om Lambeth 72).

Sources. Cf Graesse LA, chap 142, p 632.

d. Caxton GL.

Editions. Caxton GL, chap 176; Temple, 5.165.

Sources. Cf de Vignay LD, ff 281ᵇ–283ᵃ.

Background. D[elehaye] H, Cyprien d'Antioche et Cyprien de Carthage, AnBol 39.314 (summary of Greek text; development of legend).

[157] KATHERINE OF ALEXANDRIA (Nov 25, year?).

(Note: For a 15 cent lyrical treatment by Richard Spalding, see Brown-Robbins, no 1813.)

a. Katerine, alliterative prose.

(Note: See also JULIANA OF CUMAE [154] and MARGARET OF ANTIOCH [184].)

MSS. 1, Bodl 1883 (Bodl 34), ff 1ᵃ–17ᵇ (early 13 cent); 2, Cotton Titus D.xviii, ff 133ᵇ–147ᵇ (ca 1220); 3, Royal 17.A.xxvii, ff 11ᵃ–37ᵃ (early 13 cent).

Furuskog R, A Collation of the Katherine Group (MS Bodl 34), SN 19.119 (latest edn of each text compared with rotograph).

D'Ardenne S R T O and J R R Tolkien, MS Bodl 34: A Re-collation of a Collation, SN 20.65 (crit of Furuskog's readings).

Editions. Morton J, The Legend of St Katherine of Alexandria, Abbotsford Club, London 1841 (Cotton Titus D.xviii).

Hardwick C, An Historical Inquiry Touching St Catharine of Alexandria, Camb Antiq Soc, Cambridge 1849, p 21 (Cotton Titus D.xviii).

Einenkel, EETS 80.1 (Royal 17.A.xxvii; Morton's translation of Cotton Titus D.xviii; Latin text of Cotton Calig A.viii; crit E Förster, AnglA 8.175).

Einenkel E, The Life of St Katherine, Hertford 1884 (EETS 80 edn printed in quarto as Appendix of Roxb Club edn; see KATHERINE 1 *Editions* below).

Selections. Kluge F, Mittelengl Leseb, Halle 1904, p 73 (Royal MS lines 1–305; see EETS 80.2).

Victor O, Zur Textkritik und Metrik der früh-mittelengl Katherinen-legende (EETS 80), Bonn 1912, p 71 (crit edn of lines 1501–2001).

Hall Selections, 1.128 (notes 2.524; Royal MS, ff 11ᵃ–14ᵃ).

Kaiser R, Medieval English: An OE and ME Anthology, 3rd edn, in English, Berlin 1958, no 85, p 185 (2 selections from Bodl 34, see EETS 80.95, 115; not included in original German edns Berlin 1954, 1955).

Modernizations. Morton, St Katherine, p 1 (rptd EETS 80.2 and Gibbs, Roxb Club edn, Appendix, p 2; see KATHERINE 1 *Editions* below).

Textual Notes. Hall J, Note on St Katherine, line 1690, EStn 9.174 (sedewal for batewil); Victor, Zur Textkritik, p 11.

Language. Einenkel, EETS 80.xxxix, lvii ("written somewhere between Worcestershire and Dorsetshire").

Bülbring, QF 63.3 (on strong verbs).

Stodte H, Über die Sprache u Heimat der Katherine-Gruppe: Ein Beitrag zur mittelengl Dialectkunde, Göttingen 1896 (evidence for Southern dialect).

Funke O, Zur Wortgeschichte der französichen Elemente im Englischen, EStn 55.22 (additions to Mettig's list of French loan words in Katherine Group; see EStn 41.191, 252).

Serjeantson M S, The Dialects in the West Midlands in Middle English, RES 3.323 (Royal MS assigned to North Herefordshire).

Tolkien J R R, Ancrene Wisse and Hali Meiþhad, E&S 14.104 (identity of language in AW and Katherine Group Bodl 34 as evidence for probable localization in Herefordshire).

Allen H E, The Localisation of Bodl MS 34, MLR 28.485 (no evidence for localization in Herefordshire before 16 cent; see Moore Meech and Whitehall, 13.56).

Smithers G V, Ten Cruces in ME Texts, EGS 3.72 (derivation of nurþ; see Hall Selections, 2.528, for note on Katherine line 47).

Bliss A J, A Note on the Language of AB, EGS 5.1 (see YWES 34.77).

Van Wijngaarden, Syntactical Studies on the Language of the Katherine Group MS Bodley 34, Oxford, diss Univ of Gent 1953.

Literary Form. Note: For bibliography and summary of the early controversy over the form, prose or poetry, of the Katherine Group see W Wagner, Sawles Warde, Bonn 1908, p xiv, and Victor, Zur Textkritik, p 37.

Einenkel E, Über die Verfasser einiger neu-angelsächischer Schriften, Leipzig 1881 (use of alliterative couplet as test of authorship; crit W Merkes, AnglA 5.86).

Einenkel E, Über den Verfasser der neuan-gelsächsischen Legende von Katharina, Angl 5.105 (comparison of metrical usage in Katherine Group).

Einenkel, EETS 80.xxi (restatement of case for metrical form; see reviews noted under *Editions*).

Schipper, 1.195; see also Eng edn, A History of English Versification, Oxford 1910, p 85 (bibliography of argument between Schipper and Einenkel)

Victor, Zur Textkritik, p 42 (crit K Luick, AnglB 23.226).

Bethurum D, The Connection of the Katherine Group with OE Prose, JEGP 34.533 (Aelfric's Lives as model for Katherine Group in rhythm and alliteration).

Authorship. Morton, St Katherine, p ix (Richard Poor, Bishop of Salisbury, as author).

Angl 5.91 (author of Katherine not author of Juliana and Margaret; see also EETS 80.xix).

Wilson R M, A Note on the Authorship of the Katherine Group, Leeds SE 1.24 (unity of authorship possible but unprovable).

Sources. Hardwick, edn, p 4 (free paraphrase of Latin text in Cotton Calig A.viii and Camb Univ Gg.1.26; for Cotton text see EETS 80.1); Angl 5.109 (detailed comparison with Cotton Calig A.viii; see also EETS 80.xii, 1).

     b. SEL; Brown-Robbins, no 2954.

MSS. 17 MSS.

Editions. Furnivall EEP, p 90 (Harley 2277, ff 171ᵃ–174ᵇ; ca 1300).

Horstmann, EETS 87.92 (Bodl 1486 [Laud Misc 108], ff 56ᵃ–59ᵃ; end 13 cent).

Wülcker AELeseb, 1.12 (notes p 128; Harley 2277 from Furnivall).

D'Evelyn and Mill, EETS 236.533 (Harley 2277).

     c. NHC; Brown-Robbins, no 3177.

MSS. 1, Cotton Tib E.vii, ff 273ᵇ–277ᵇ; lines 1–8 lost (ca 1400); 2, Harley 4196, ff 193ᵇ–197ᵃ (15 cent).

Editions. AELeg 1881, p 165 (Harley 4196).

     d. ScL; Brown-Robbins, no *14.

MS. Camb Univ Gg.2.6, ff 380ᵃ–395ᵃ; beg lost (1400–50).

Horstmann ScL, 2.197 (Kath written in 2 hands; see AELeg 1881, p lxlii).

Editions. Horstmann ScL, 2.197; Metcalfe STS, 2.442 (notes 3.463).

Sources. Horstmann ScL, 2.197 (quotes Graesse LA, chap 172, p 789, but claims author used fuller source); Metcalfe STS, 3.465 (quotes LA).

     e. Auchinleck, quatrains; Brown-Robbins, no 1159.

MS. Advocates 19.2 (Auchinleck), ff 21ᵃ–24ᵇ; end imperf (1300–25).

Editions. Turnbull Leg cath, p 167; AELeg 1881, p 242 (crit A Brandl, ZfÖG 33.687).

Textual Notes. Bliss A J, N&Q 201.186 (coments on oliue, gouȝ, wiȝtine); Sisam K, N&Q 201.317 (treatment of oliue in OED).

Authorship. Bliss A J, The Auchinleck St Margaret and St Katherine, N&Q 201.186 (use of oliue = dead as evidence of common authorship).

     f. Eight-line stanzas; Brown-Robbins, no 1158.

MS. Caius Camb 175, p 107 (rvsd version of e; 15 cent).

Editions. AELeg 1881, p 242 (crit A Brandl, ZfÖG 33.687; Brandl claims f, not e, is original text).

     g. Short couplets; Brown-Robbins, no 227.

MSS. 1, Bodl 14528 (Rawl poet 34), f 7ᵃ (15 cent); 2, Camb Univ Ff.2.38, f 45ᵃ (mid 15 cent).

Editions. Halliwell J O, Contributions to Early English Literature, London 1849, pt 2, p 1; originally published separately, Brixton Hill 1848 (Camb Univ Ff.2.38).

AELeg 1881, p 260 (Camb Univ Ff.2.38; crit A Brandl, ZfÖG 33.687).

     g*. Longleat, couplets; Brown-Robbins, no 3205.

MS. Longleat (Red Book of Bath), f 55ᵃ (1428; Brown-Robbins queries whether this is same as version g, no 227).

     h. Capgrave, rime royal; Brown-Robbins, no 6.

MSS. 1, Bodl 14611 (Rawl poet 118), ff 1ᵃ–113 (1450–75); 2, Arundel 20, ff 1ᵃ–42ᵇ; lacks prologue (late 15 cent); 3, Arundel 168, ff 15ᵃ–65ᵇ (15 cent); 4, Arundel 396, ff 1ᵃ–117ᵇ (ca 1440).

Hingeston, p xxviii; see below under *Selections*.

Furnivall, EETS 100.xxix.

Editions. Horstmann, EETS 100.2 (Forewords, p v, by F J Furnivall; Bodl 14611, bks 1–3; Arundel 396, bks 1–5).

Selections. Hingeston F C, The Chronicle of England by John Capgrave, Rolls Series, London 1858, p 337 (Arundel 396, prologue).

Knust, Geschichte der h Katharine, p 96; see below under *General Background and Literary Relations* (selections from prologue, Rolls Series edn; selections from legend in Arundel 396).

Language. Debelius W, John Capgrave u die engl Schriftsprache, diss Berlin 1899 (see next entry).

Debelius W, John Capgrave, Angl 23.153, 323, 427; 24.211, 269 (expansion of diss Berlin 1899; on basis of Katherine legend and Chronicle of England, attempts to show Capgrave's place in development of written language from Wyclif to Caxton).

Date. De Meijer A, John Capgrave, Augustiniana 5.416n71 (on evidence of Bokenham's reference to Katherine [see EETS 206.173, line 6354], dates Capgrave version ca 1445).

Authorship. Augustiniana 5.400; 7.118, 531 (detailed bibliography and summary of life and works; for Katherine see 5.416; 7.563).

Toner N, Augustinian Spiritual Writers of the English Province in the 15 and 16 Centuries, Rome 1956, 2.507 (summary of Capgrave's life and works).

Sources. Furnivall, EETS 100.xxiii, xxxv (on Arrek, Capgrave's alleged source).

Varnhagen H, Zur Geschichte der Legende der Katharina von Alexandrien, Erlangen 1891, pp 2, 5, 10 (discussion and edn of Latin version of Arrechis).

Hilka A, Zur Katharinenlegende: Die Quelle der Jugendgeschichte Katharinas, Arch 140.171 (notes Capgrave's variations from Latin sources).

i. Bokenham; Brown-Robbins, no 1812.

MS. Arundel 327, ff 115^b–134^b (1447).

Editions. [Bokenam O,] The Lyvys of Seyntys, Roxb Club 50, London 1835, p 182; Horstmann Bokenam, p 159; Serjeantson, EETS 206.172.

Sources. Horstmann Bokenam, p ix (notes passages not in LA).

Willenberg G, Die Quellen von Osbern Bokenham's Legenden, EStn 12.22 (source LA but not Graesse's text; see Serjeantson, EETS 206.xxiii).

Varnhagen, Festschrift, p 71; see below under *General Background and Literary Relations* (suggests Bokenham combined Latin versions).

Background. Moore S, Patrons of Letters in Norfolk and Suffolk, ca 1450, PMLA 28.84.

j. Mirk Festial.

MSS. Note: See ANDREW d *MSS* [25] above.
1, Bodl 17680 (Gough Eccl Top 4), ff 156^b–

158^a (1400–50); 2, Cotton Claud A.ii, ff 114^a–115^a (ca 1420); 3, Lansdowne 372, f 95; end imperf (1400–50); 4, Durham Cosins v.iii.5, ff 152^a–154^a (15 cent). (Om Harley 2247, Royal 18.B.xxv.)

Editions. Liber Festiualis, Caxton, Westminster 1483, sig p iii^b–p v^b; rptd Hardwick, edn (see above under a), p 9.

Erbe, EETSES 96.275 (Bodl 17680).

k. Speculum Sacerdotale.

MS. BM Addit 36791, f 137^a−b (15 cent).

Edition. Weatherly, EETS 200.243 (source unknown, pp xxix, 279).

l. 1438 GL.

MSS. Note: For more complete information on MSS see A Kurvinen, Two Sixteenth-Cent Editions of the Life of St Catharine, in Eng and Med Studies Presented to J R R Tolkien, London 1962, p 269.

1, Bodl 21947 (Douce 372), f 144^a; beg imperf; 2, Egerton 876, f 286^b; 3, Harley 630, f 359^b; 4, Harley 4775, chap 164, ff 225^b–233^a; MLA roto 343, 2.451; 5, BM Addit 11565, ff 210–213; end imperf; 6, BM Addit 35298, ff 148^a–152^b. (In Trinity Dublin 319.)

Note: The following MSS, 7–12, contain single items or a very small number of items; their exact relation to the text of the collected 1438 GL has not been determined.

7, Cotton Titus A.xxvi, ff 180^a–202^b (15 cent); see Arch 56.392; 8, Harley 2559, ff 126–138 (early 15 cent); 9, Chetham 8009, ff 31^a–48^a (15 cent); see EStn 7.196; 10, Stonyhurst B.xliii, ff 83^a–96^a (ca 1460); see EETSES 100.xxxiii, xxxvii, note 1; 11, Gibbs MS, ff 22^a–125^a (ca 1430); see below under *Editions*; 12, Porkington 10, ff 91^a–129^a (15 cent); see Hist MSS Com, 2nd report, London 1871, p 84.

Rudd H, reviser, Catalogue of the Aldenham Library Mainly Collected by Henry Hucks Gibbs, First Lord Aldenham, Privately Printed, Letchworth 1914, p 228 (description of Gibbs MS).

Editions. Note: For the announcement of a forthcoming edn of the life of St Katherine, see A Kurvinen, NM 60.364 and Eng and Med Studies Presented to J R R Tolkien, p 272n1.

Gibbs H H, The Life and Martyrdom of St Katherine of Alexandria, Roxb Club, London 1884 (Gibbs MS with readings from prose versions in Cotton Titus A.xxvi, BM Addit 35298, and Caxton GL; from English verse versions; from Greek and Latin texts; Appendix reprints EETS 80 edn; see above under KATHERINE a *Editions*).

Selections. Knust, Geschichte, p 66; see below under *General Background and Literary Relations* (Cotton Titus A.xxvi, ff 180ª–193ᵇ, conversion and marriage).

Sources. Gibbs, Life and Martyrdom of St Katherine, pp vii, xiv ("in great part a translation" of Latin version in Cotton Calig A.viii; see EETS 80.xii, 1).

Butler LA, p 70 (1438 Katherine not based on LA).

Knust, Geschichte, p 78; see below under *General Background and Literary Relations* (comparison of English martyrdom in Cotton Titus A.xxvi with LA).

m. Caxton GL.

Editions. Caxton GL, chap 215; Temple, 7.1.

Sources. Cf Graesse LA, chap 172, p 789; de Vignay LD, ff 339ª–342ª; 1438 GL, Harley 4775, ff 225ᵇ–233ª.

Gibbs, Life and Martyrdom of St Katherine, p xiv (notes similarity of wording in Caxton, Cotton Titus A.xxvi, and BM Addit 35298).

Knust, Geschichte, p 231; see below (prints Latin text of Cotton Calig A.viii, ff 169ª–191ª; 11 cent; includes references to English versions).

Kurvinen A, Caxton's GL and the MSS of the Gilte Legende, NM 60.364 (evidence for BM Addit 35298 as extant MS of 1438 GL nearest to Caxton in Katherine legend).

General Background and Literary Relations. Knust H, Geschichte der Legenden der h Katharina von Alexandrien und der h Maria Aegyptiaca, Halle 1890 (chronological survey of versions in several languages; for English see pp 11, 64, 92, 110; see p 231 for English references in notes on Latin text Cotton Calig A.viii; crit H Varnhagen, Göttingische Gelehrte Anzeigen, 1890, no 15, p 593).

Varnhagen H, Zur Geschichte der Legende der Katharina von Alexandrien nebst latein Texten, Erlangen 1891 (survey of Greek and Latin versions with edition of Latin Passion of 12 cent and of Latin Conversion of 1337).

Varnhagen H, Zur Geschichte der Legende der Katharina von Alexandrien, in Festschrift . . . dem Prinzregenten Luitpold von Bayern . . . dargebracht von der Univ Erlangen, Erlangen 1901, p 60 (includes summary of sources of 7 English versions [KATHERINE a, b, c, d, e, g, i] not containing the Conversion episode).

[158] KATHERINE OF SIENA (April 30, 1380).

a. A Letter Touching the Life of St Kateryn of Senys, prose.

MS. Bodl 21688 (Douce 114), ff 76ª–89ᵇ (15 cent).

Horstmann C, Prosalegenden: Die Legenden des MS Douce 114, Angl 8.102.

Editions. Horstmann, Angl 8.184; sources, p 105 (translation of Latin letter by Stephen of Siena; see Acta SS, April 3, 961).

Prose Style. Workman 15 Cent Trans, p 114 (prologue compared with Latin).

b. The Life of St Katherine of Senis, prose.

Editions. The Lyf of s Katherin of Senis, Wynkyn de Worde, 1493? (STC, no 24766).

Horstmann C, The Lyf of s Katherin of Senis, Arch 76.33, 265, 353 (based on 1493? edn).

Sources. Arch 76.33n (condensed mid 15 cent translation of Raymundus de Vineis = Raymond of Capua, Vita s Catharinae Senensis, ca 1390).

Prose Style. Workman 15 Cent Trans, pp 24, 110, 159 (structure and syntax compared with Latin).

[159] KATHERINE OF SWEDEN OR OF VADSTENA (Mar 24, 1381).

Digby Life of St Katherine, prose.

MS. Bodl 1773 (Digby 172) (15 cent).

Authorship. Blunt, EETSES 19.ix (Thomas Gascoigne accepted as author); Gerould S Leg, p 288 (denies Gascoigne's authorship).

[160] KENELM (July 17, ca 812).

a. SEL; Brown- Robbins, no 2956.

MSS. 11 MSS.

Editions. Furnivall EEP, p 47 (Harley 2277, ff 80ª–84ᵇ; ca 1300).

Horstmann, EETS 87.345 (Bodl 1486 [Laud Misc 108], ff 149ª–153ª; end 13 cent).

D'Evelyn and Mill, EETS 235.279 (Corp Christi Camb 145, ff 104ᵇ–109ª; early 14 cent).

a*. SEL variant; Brown-Robbins, no 2955.

MSS. 1, Bodl 3938 (Vernon), f 39ᵇ col 1 (ca 1385); 2, Lambeth 223, f 132ª (end 14 cent).

Literary Relations. Brown B D, Robert of Gloucester's Chronicle and the Life of St Kenelm, MLN 41.13 (SEL text not dependent on Robert; crit YWES 7.93).

b. 1438 GL.

MSS. 1, BM Addit 11565; see Butler LA, p 66; 2, BM Addit 35298, ff 78ᵇ–79ᵇ; 3, Lambeth 72, chap 110, ff 228ᵇ–230ª. (Om Bodl 21947, Egerton 876, Harley 630, Harley 4775.)

c. Caxton GL.

Editions. Caxton GL, chap 127; Temple, 4.60; rptd Goudy, Village Press, N Y 1905.

Sources. Butler LA, p 83 (not found in Latin or French sources; expanded version of 1438 GL probable source).

General Background. Levison W, England and the Continent in the Eighth Century, Oxford 1946, p 249 (historic and legendary Kenelm).

[161] LAMBERT, BISHOP OF MAESTRICHT (Sept 17, ca 705).

a. 1438 GL.

MSS. 1, Harley 4775, chap 132, f 172[b]; MLA roto 343, 2.345; 2, BM Addit 35298, f 119[b]. (Lost Bodl 21947; om Lambeth 72.)

Sources. Cf Graesse LA, chap 133, p 596.

b. Caxton GL.

Editions. Caxton GL, chap 173; Temple, 5.147.

Sources. Cf de Vignay LD, f 277[a-b].

[162] LANDRY, BISHOP OF PARIS (June 10, ca 660).

Editions. Caxton GL, chap 240; Temple, 7.187.

Sources. Cf de Vignay LD, f 397[a-b].

LARGUS: see CYRIACUS WITH COMPANIONS.

[163] LAWRENCE (Aug 10, 258).

a. SEL; Brown-Robbins, no 2957.

MSS. 16 MSS.

Editions. Horstmann, EETS 87.340 (Bodl 1486 [Laud Misc 108], ff 147[a]–149[a]; end 13 cent).

D'Evelyn and Mill, EETS 236.358 (Corp Christi Camb 145, ff 133[a]–135[a]; early 14 cent).

b. ScL; Brown-Robbins, no 1844.

MS. Camb Univ Gg.2.6, ff 148[b]–157[b] (1400–50).

Editions. Horstmann ScL, 1.191; Metcalfe STS, 1.403 (notes 3.251).

Sources. Horstmann ScL, 1.191 (quotes Graesse LA, chap 117, p 468); Metcalfe STS, 3.254 (quotes parallels from LA, Vincent of Beauvais Spec Hist, Ado Martyrolog).

c. Mirk Festial.

MSS. Note: See ANDREW d *MSS* [25] above. 1, Bodl 17680 (Gough Eccl Top 4), ff 123[b]–126[b] (1400–50); 2, Cotton Claud A.ii, ff 94[b]–96[a] (ca 1420); 3, Harley 2247, ff 177[a]–179[b] (1450–1500); 4, Royal 18.B.xxv, ff 116[a]–118[b] (late 15 cent); 5, Durham Cosins

v.iii.5, ff 125[a]–128[a] (15 cent). (Om Bodl 21634, 21682 = Douce 60, 108.)

Editions. Liber Festiualis, Caxton, Westminster 1483, sig m vi, (STC, no 17957).

Erbe, EETSES 96.216 (Bodl 17680).

d. Speculum Sacerdotale.

MS. BM Addit 36791, ff 101[b]–103[b] (15 cent).

Edition. Weatherly, EETS 200.179 (sources, pp xxix, 273; extremely similar to LA and Ado Martyrolog).

e. 1438 GL.

MSS. 1, Bodl 21947 (Douce 372), f 90; end imperf; 2, Harley 4775, chap 109, ff 137[a]–138[b]; beg imperf; 3, BM Addit 11565, f 146[a]; beg imperf, miracles only; 4, BM Addit 35298, ff 96[a]–97[a]. (In Lambeth 72, see Butler LA, p 152; Trinity Dublin 319, see Gerould S Leg, p 195.)

Sources. Cf Graesse LA, chap 117, p 488.

f. Caxton GL.

Editions. Caxton GL, chap 150; Temple, 4.208.

Sources. Cf de Vignay LD, ff 223[a]–228[a].

[164] LEGER, BISHOP OF AUTUN (Oct 2, 679).

a. SEL; Brown-Robbins, no 2958.

MSS. 11 MSS.

Editions. Horstmann, EETS 87.81 (Bodl 1486 [Laud Misc 108], f 52[a-b]; end 13 cent).

b. 1438 GL.

MSS. 1, Harley 4775, chap 141, f 184[a-b]; MLA roto 343, 2.368; 2, BM Addit 11565; given twice: after St Dorothy and at f 180; see Butler LA, p 66; 3, BM Addit 35298; given twice: f 81[a-b] under Leger; f 126[a-b] under Leodegarie; subject same, texts different; 4, Lambeth 72, chap 115, f 232[b].

Sources. Cf Graesse LA, chap 148, p 660, De S Leodegario.

c. Caxton GL.

Editions. Caxton GL, chap 182; Temple, 5.211.

Sources. Cf de Vignay LD, ff 292[b]–293[a].

[165] LEO THE GREAT, POPE (April 11, 461).

a. 1438 GL.

MS. 1, Bodl 21947 (Douce 372), f 65? (see Butler LA, p 60); 2, Harley 4775, chap 81, f 108[a-b]; MLA roto 343, 1.216; 3, BM Addit 35298, ff 47[b]–48[a].

Sources. Cf Graesse LA, chap 88, p 367.

b. Caxton GL.

Editions. Caxton GL, chap 120; Temple,

4.10; rptd A Aspland, The GL, Holbein Soc Fac-Simile Reprints, London 1878.
Sources. Note: Leo the Great not in de Vignay LD, Paris 1480 edn, but is in MSS; see Butler LA, p 89.

[166] LEO II, POPE (July 3, 683).
MS. Bodl 2567 (Bodley 779), f 217ª (ca 1400).
Editions. Zusatzleg 1889, p 381.

LEODEGARIE: see LEGER.

[167] LEONARD OF NOBLAC (Nov 6, 6 cent?).
    a. SEL; Brown-Robbins, no 2959.
MSS. 12 MSS.
Editions. Horstmann, EETS 87.456 (Bodl 1486 [Laud Misc 108], ff 188ª–190ª; end 13 cent).
D'Evelyn and Mill, EETS 236.476 (Harley 2277, ff 149ᵇ–152ª; ca 1300).
    b. 1438 GL.
MSS. 1, Bodl 21947 (Douce 372), f 125; end imperf; 2, Harley 630, f 315; 3, Harley 4775, chap 147, ff 193ᵇ–195ª; MLA roto 343, 2.387; 4, BM Addit 35298, ff 131ᵇ–132ª. (In Trinity Dublin 319, see Gerould S Leg, p 195.)
Sources. Cf Graesse LA, chap 155, p 687.
    c. Caxton GL.
Editions. Caxton GL, chap 200; Temple, 6.132.
Sources. Cf de Vignay LD, ff 303ᵇ–305ª.

[168] LEONARD OF VANDOEUVRE, ABBOT (Oct 15, ca 570).

(Note: An account of this second Leonard is added to the legend of Leonard of Noblac in both 1438 GL and Caxton GL and in their sources, LA and de Vignay; see entries above under [167] b, c.)

LION, LYON: see LEO II, POPE.

LOGYER: see LEGER.

[169] LONGINUS (March 15, 1st cent).
    a. SEL; Brown-Robbins, no 2960.
MSS. 11 MSS.
Editions. Peebles R J, The Legend of Longinus in Ecclesiastical Tradition and in English Literature and Its Connection with the Grail, Bryn Mawr Mon 9, Baltimore 1911, p 94 (Bodl 1596 [Laud Misc 463], f 16ᵇ; beg 15 cent).
D'Evelyn and Mill, EETS 235.84 (Corp Christi Camb 145, f 32ª⁻ᵇ; early 14 cent).

    b. 1438 GL.
MSS. 1, Harley 4775, chap 46, f 51ᵇ; MLA roto 343, 1.103; 2, BM Addit 35298, f 28ª (lost Egerton 876).
Sources. Cf Graesse LA, chap 47, p 202.
    c. Caxton GL.
Editions. Caxton GL, chap 75; Temple, 3.70.
Sources. Cf de Vignay LD, f 111ª⁻ᵇ.
Jeremy Sister M, Caxton's GL and de Vignai's LD, MS 8.105 (details in Caxton also in rvsd de Vignay).
General Sources and Literary Relations. Peebles, edn, passim (crit B Fehr, AnglB 24.29).

LONGIUS: see LONGINUS.

LOUIS OF ANJOU: see LOUIS OF MARSEILLES.

[170] LOUIS IX, KING OF FRANCE (Aug 25, 1270).
Editions. Caxton GL, chap 244; Temple, 7.204.
Sources. Cf de Vignay LD, ff 417ᵇ–422ª.

[171] LOUIS OF MARSEILLES, BISHOP OF TOULOUSE (Aug 19, 1297).
Editions. Caxton GL, chap 245; Temple, 7.215.
Sources. Cf de Vignay LD, ff 422ᵇ–424ª.

LOWE: see LUPUS, BISHOP OF SENS.

LOYE: see ELIGIUS.

[172] LUCY (Dec 13, 304).
    a. SEL; Brown-Robbins, no 2961.
MSS. 16 MSS.
Editions. Furnivall EEP, p 101 (Harley 2277, ff 183ª–185ª; ca 1300).
Horstmann, EETS 87.101 (Bodl 1486 [Laud Misc 108], ff 59ª–60ᵇ; end 13 cent).
D'Evelyn and Mill, EETS 236.566 (Harley 2277).
    b. NHC; Brown-Robbins, no 2962.
MS. Harley 4196, ff 138ª–139ᵇ (15 cent).
Edition. AELeg 1881, p 17.
    c. ScL; Brown-Robbins, no 4272.
MS. Camb Univ Gg.2.6, ff 361ª–364ᵇ (1400–50).
Editions. Horstmann ScL, 2.172; Metcalfe STS, 2.387 (notes 3.439).
Sources. Horstmann ScL, 2.172 (quotes passages from Graesse LA, chap 4, p 29); Metcalfe STS, 3.441 (passages from LA).
    d. Bokenham; Brown-Robbins, no 2019.

MS. Arundel 327, ff 163ᵃ–172ᵃ (1447).
Editions. [Bokenam O,] The Lyvys of Seyntys, Roxb Club 50, London 1835, p 257; Horstmann Bokenam, p 225; Serjeantson, EETS 206.243.
Sources. Willenberg G, Die Quellen von Osbern Bokenham's Legenden, EStn 12.21 (LA but not Graesse's text as source). Serjeantson, EETS 206.xxiii (summary of Willenberg).

e. 1438 GL.

MSS. 1, Harley 4775, chap 3, ff 8ᵃ–9ᵃ; MLA roto 343, 1.16; 2, BM Addit 35298, chap 3, f 4ᵃ⁻ᵇ (lost Bodl 21947 [Douce 372], Egerton 876, Lambeth 72).
Sources. Cf Graesse LA, chap 4, p 29.

f. Caxton GL.

Editions. Caxton GL, chap 37; Temple, 2.130.
Sources. Cf de Vignay LD, ff 59ᵃ–60ᵇ.
Jeremy Sister M, Caxton's GL and de Vignai's LD, MS 8.104 (notes details from rvsd de Vignay text).

[173] LUKE (Oct 18, 1st cent).

(Note: The legend of St Luke takes two forms: (1) an exposition of the symbolism of his character and work with a minimum of narrative; (2) an account of his conversion, travels, death. The first type is represented by LA and its derivatives, the second by SEL and its undetermined sources.)

a. SEL; Brown-Robbins, no 2973.

MSS. 13 MSS.
Edition. D'Evelyn and Mill, EETS 236.439 (Corp Christi Camb 145, ff 163ᵃ–164ᵃ; early 14 cent).

a*. SEL variant; Brown-Robbins no 2974.

MS. Camb Univ Addit 3039, f 16ᵇ.

b. ScL; Brown-Robbins, no 630.

MS. Camb Univ Gg.2.6, ff 87ᵇ–88ᵇ (1400–50).
Editions. Horstmann ScL, 1.119; Metcalfe STS, 1.246.
Sources. Horstmann ScL, l.v note (combination of Vincent of Beauvais Spec Hist and LA); Metcalfe STS, 3.176 (parallels from LA and Peter de Natalibus Cat SS).

c. Mirk Festial.

MSS. Note: See ANDREW d *MSS* [25] above.
1, Bodl 17680 (Gough Eccl Top 4), ff 148ᵇ–149ᵇ (1400–50); 2, Cotton Claud A.ii, ff 109ᵇ–110ᵃ (ca 1420); 3, Harley 2247, ff 197ᵇ–199ᵃ (1450–1500); 4, Royal 18.B.xxv, ff 134ᵃ–135ᵃ (late 15 cent); 5, Durham Cosins v.iii.5, ff 143ᵇ–145ᵃ (15 cent). (Om Bodl 21632, 21684 = Douce 60, 108.)

Editions. Liber Festiualis, Caxton, Westminster 1483, sig O ivᵃ⁻ᵇ (STC, no 17957).
Erbe, EETSES 96.260 (Bodl 17680).

d. Speculum Sacerdotale.

MS. BM Addit 36791, ff 121ᵇ–122ᵃ (15 cent).
Edition. Weatherly, EETS 200.215 (sources, pp xxix, 276; refers to Belethus Rationale Div Off and La).

e. 1438 GL.

MSS. 1, Bodl 21947 (Douce 372), f 120; beg imperf; 2, Harley 4775, chap 149, ff 195ᵃ–197ᵇ; MLA roto 343, 2.390; 3, BM Addit 35298, ff 132ᵃ–133ᵇ.
Sources. Cf Graesse LA, chap 156, p 692.

f. Caxton GL.

Editions. Caxton GL, chap 190; Temple, 6.46; rptd A Aspland, The GL, Holbein Soc Fac-Simile Reprints, London 1878.
Sources. Cf de Vignay LD, ff 305ᵇ–308ᵇ.

LUPE: see LUPUS, BISHOP OF SENS.

[174] LUPUS, BISHOP OF SENS (Sept 1, 623).

a. 1438 GL.

MSS. 1, Bodl 21947 (Douce 372), f 105; 2, Harley 4775, chap 118, ff 157ᵇ–158ᵃ; MLA roto 343, 2.315; 3, BM Addit 35298, f 110ᵃ⁻ᵇ.
Sources. Cf Graesse LA, chap 128, p 579.

b. Caxton GL.

Editions. Caxton GL, chap 162; Temple, 5.85.
Sources. Cf de Vignay LD, ff 259ᵇ–260ᵇ; Butler LA, p 89 (no etymology in Graesse LA).

[175] MACARIUS OF ALEXANDRIA (Jan 2, ca 394).

a. 1438 GL.

MSS. 1, Harley 4775, chap 17, ff 19ᵇ–20ᵃ; MLA roto 343, 1.39; 2, BM Addit 35298, f 13ᵃ (lost Bodl 21947, Lambeth 72).
Sources. Cf Graesse LA, chap 18, p 100.

b. Caxton GL.

Editions. Caxton GL, chap 51; Temple, 2.218.
Sources. Cf de Vignay LD, f 77.

c. Caxton VP.

Edition. Caxton VP, pt 1, chap 29, ff 25ᵃ–26ᵃ.
Sources. Cf La vie des pères, pt 1, chap 29, ff 25ᵇ–26ᵇ.

[176] MACARIUS THE ELDER OF EGYPT (Jan 15, 390).

Edition. Caxton VP, pt 1, chap 28, ff 24ᵃ–25ᵃ.
Sources. Cf La vie des pères, pt 1, chap 28, f 25ᵃ⁻ᵇ.

[177] MACARIUS OF ROME (Oct 23 [Greek Menolog]).
Edition. Caxton VP, pt 1, chap 48, ff 90ᵇ–95ᵃ.
Sources. Cf La vie des pères, pt 1, chap 48, ff 73ᵃ–77ᵃ; see also Migne PL, 73.415.
Literary Relations. Williams C A, Affinities of the Legend of the Hairy Anchorite, Illinois Studies in Lang and Lit 11, no 4, p 101 (typical and unusual features of Macarius legend).

MACHAIRE, MAKARIE: see MACARIUS OF ALEXANDRIA.

[178] MACHOR, BISHOP OF ABERDEEN (Nov 12, 6 cent).
    ScL; Brown-Robbins, no 842.
MS. Camb Univ Gg.2.6, ff 190ᵇ–208ᵇ (1400–50).
Editions. AELeg 1881, p 189; Metcalfe STS, 2.1 (notes 3.308); Metcalfe W M, The Legends of Sts Ninian and Machor, Paisley 1904, p 87.
Selections. Metcalfe W M, Specimens of Scottish Literature 1325–1835, Glascow 1913, p 30 (lines 809–860, 1581–1610).
Sources. AELeg 1881, pp xviii, ci and note 1 (based on lost Latin life also used in Office for saint's feast Nov 12 in Aberdeen Breviary and in O'Donnell's Vita S Columbae; text of Breviary ptd p xix; summary of Vita given p cii, note); Metcalfe STS, 3.310 (see preceding entry); Metcalfe, Sts Ninian and Machor, pp 4, 31, 210 (gives translation of O'Donnell, Vita S Columbae, chaps xxiii–xxx on Machor, ptd by John Colgan, Trias Thaumaturgae, Louvain 1647, p 345).
Background. Ferguson A S, The Bull of Hadrian IV and the Northern Marches, Scottish Gaelic Studies 5.80 (names and local cult of Machor).

MALACHY: see MALCHUS.

[179] MALCHUS (Oct 21, 4 cent).
    a. 1438 GL (under title of St Jerome).
MSS. 1, Bodl 21947 (Douce 372), f 51ᵃ; 2, Harley 4775, chap 66, ff 88ᵃ–90ᵃ; MLA roto 343, 1.176 (om BM Addit 35298; lost BM Addit 11565).
    b. Caxton VP.
Edition. Caxton VP, pt 1, chap 38, ff 51ᵃ–53ᵃ.
Sources. La vie des pères, pt 1, chap 38, ff 44ᵇ–46ᵃ; see Migne PL, 23.55.
Literary Relations. Duckworth G E, Classical

Echoes in St Jerome's Life of Malchus, The Classical Bulletin, Univ of St Louis, 24.28.

MALLONIN: see MALLONUS, BISHOP OF ROUEN.

[180] MALLONUS, BISHOP OF ROUEN (Oct 22, 4 cent?).
Editions. Caxton GL, chap 241; Temple, 7.189.
Sources. Cf de Vignay LD, ff 397ᵇ–398ᵃ.

[181] MAMERTIN, ABBOT (March 30 [Whytford Add], 5 cent?).
    a. 1438 GL.
MSS. 1, Harley 4775, chap 119, f 158ᵃ–ᵇ; MLA roto 343, 2.316; 2, BM Addit 35298, f 110ᵇ.
Sources. Cf Graesse LA, chap 129, p 580.
    b. Caxton GL.
Editions. Caxton GL, chap 163; Temple, 5.88.
Sources. Cf de Vignay LD, ff 260ᵇ–261ᵃ.

MARCEL, MARCELLE: see MARCELLUS I, POPE.

MARCELIN: see MARCELLINUS, POPE.

MARCELLINUS, MARTYR: see PETER THE DEACON.

[182] MARCELLINUS, POPE (April 26, 304).
    a. 1438 GL.
MSS. 1, Harley 4775, chap 56, f 70ᵃ–ᵇ; MLA roto 343, 1.140; 2, BM Addit 35298, f 36ᵃ (lost Bodl 21947).
Sources. Cf Graesse LA, chap 60, p 271.
    b. Caxton GL.
Editions. Caxton GL, chap 87; Temple, 3.143.
Sources. Cf de Vignay LD, f 128ᵃ–ᵇ.

[183] MARCELLUS I, POPE (Jan 16, 309).
    a. 1438 GL.
MSS. 1, Harley 4775, chap 19, f 20ᵇ; MLA roto 343, 1.41; 2, BM Addit 35298, f 12ᵇ (lost Bodl 21947, Lambeth 72).
Sources. Cf Graesse LA, chap 20, p 103.
    b. Caxton GL.
Editions. Caxton GL, chap 53; Temple, 2.223.
Sources. Cf de Vignay LD, f 78ᵇ.

[184] MARGARET OF ANTIOCH (July 20, year?).
    a. Marherete, alliterative prose.
(Note: For additional references, see JULI-

ANA OF CUMAE a [154] and KATHERINE OF ALEXANDRIA a [157].)

MSS. 1, Bodl 1883 (Bodley 34), ff 18ᵃ–36ᵇ (early 13 cent); 2, Royal 17.A.xxvii, ff 37ᵃ–56ᵃ (early 13 cent).
Mack, EETS 193.xiii; rptd 1958.
Editions. Cockayne O, St Marherete The Meiden ant Martyr in OE, 1862, p 1; re-issued 1866 as EETS 13 (Royal 17.A.xxvii).
Mack, EETS 193.2; (both MSS; crit D Everett, YWES 15.131; E V Gordon, MÆ 6.131; TLS Dec 13 1934, p 894; N&Q 167.141; D Everett, RES 11.337; R M Wilson, MLR 31.73).
Selections. Dickins and Wilson, p 96 (Bodl 1883, dragon episode; see EETS 193.20).
Kaiser R, Medieval English, An OE and ME Anthology, 3rd edn (in English), Berlin 1958, no 86, p 186 (Bodl 1883; see EETS 193.4, 20, 30, 32, 36; selections not included in 1st and 2nd edns, in German, Berlin 1954, 1955).
Modernizations. Cockayne, EETS 13.51.
Textual Notes. Stratmann F H, Corrections, N&Q 59 (4s 11). 381 (notes on EETS 13, p 9/14 crenchenut; p 14/11 leinen; rptd EStn 2.119).
Stratmann F H, Verbesserungen zu mittelengl Schriftstellern, EStn 4.93 (further corrections of EETS 13).
Language. Bülbring, QF 63.3; Mack, EETS 193.xxxv; Dickins and Wilson, p 210.
Authorship. Mack, EETS 193.xxii (common authorship of the Katherine Group and AR possible).
Sources. Vogt F, Über die Margarentenlegenden, BGDSL 1.263 (for Latin sources of MARGARET a and b see p 281).
Krahl E, Untersuchungen über vier Versionen der mittelengl Margaretenlegende, Berlin 1889 (4 versions d'scussed are a, b, c and d as one version, e; Mombritius Latin text accepted as basic source; crit F Holthausen, LfGRP 12.158).
Mack, EETS 193.xxiv, 127 (comparison of English and Latin in content and style; Latin text of Harley 2801, ca 1200, ptd).
Gerould G H, A New Text of the Passio S Margaretae with Some Account of Its Latin and English Relations, PMLA 39.525 (comparison of 4 Latin versions of Mombritius text shows none is direct source of MARGARET a).

b. SEL; Brown-Robbins, no 2987.
MSS. 17 MSS.
Editions. Cockayne, EETS 13.24 (Harley 2277, ff 84ᵇ–88ᵇ; ca 1300).
AESpr, 1.200 (Harley 2277 from Cockayne).

D'Evelyn and Mill, EETS 235.291 (Corp Christi Camb 145, ff 109ᵃ–113ᵃ; early 14 cent).
Language. Bülbring, QF 63.22.
Sources. BGDSL 1.263 (SEL a combination of sources).
Krahl, Untersuchungen, p 60 (direct use of LA and Mombritius probable).

c. Early quatrains; Brown-Robbins, no 2672.
MSS. 1, Bodl 2567 (Bodley 779), f 204ᵇ (ca 1400); 2, Bodl 14528 (Rawl poet 34), f 1ᵃ (15 cent); 3, Camb Univ Add 4122, f 6ᵃ; 4, Trinity Camb 323, f 20ᵃ (13 cent); 5, olim Petworth 3, f 167ᵃ (15 cent; Francis Edwards, Sale Cat 619, London 1932, Item 147).
Editions. Hickes G, Linguarum veterum septentrionalium thesaurus, Oxford 1705, 1.224 (Trinity Camb 323); rptd Cockayne, EETS 13.34; rptd AELeg 1881, p 489 (crit A Brandl, ZfÖG 33.686).
Horstmann C, Nachträge zu den Legenden, Arch 79.411 (Bodl 2567).
Language. Bülbring, QF 63.16.
Sources. Krahl, Untersuchungen, pp 18, 24, 53 (versions c and d derived through common source from Mombritius).

d. Auchinleck, quatrains; Brown-Robbins, no 203.
MS. Advocates 19.2.1 (Auchinleck), ff 16ᵇ–21ᵃ (1300–25).
Editions. Turnbull Leg cath, p 71; AELeg 1881, p 226 (crit A Brandl, ZfÖG 33.686; textual notes).
Textual Notes. Bliss A J, The Auchinleck St Margaret and St Katherine, N&Q 201.186 (see also KATHERINE OF ALEXANDRIA a *Textual Notes, Authorship* [157]).
Sources. Krahl, Untersuchungen, pp 18, 24, 53.

e. Short couplets; Brown-Robbins, nos 2673, 1192.
MSS. 1, Bodl 6922* (Ashm 61), f 145ᵃ (15 cent); 2, Hamilton (olim Brome), f 39ᵃ; ends line 365 (1450–1500).
Editions. Here begynneth of S Margarete, Pynson, ca 1493 (STC, no 17325; with new prologue of 6 lines; 2 fragments; see AELeg 1881, p 236, lines 1–44, 136–241).
Here begynneth of S Margarete, R Redman, London ca 1530 (STC, no 17326, Brown-Robbins, no 1192; with new prologue of 6 lines; complete; 3 extracts rptd T Corser, Collectanea anglo-poetica, pt viii, Chetham Soc 102, Manchester 1878,

p 385; see AELeg 1881, p 236, lines 1–24, 302–403, 582–618; see W Ringler, PBSA 49.164, item 23; note: STC, no 17327, listed as same text as no 17326, is the life of Margaret of Scotland [June 10, 1093], beg, end imperf).

AELeg 1881, p 236 (Bodl 6922*; crit A Brandl, ZfÖG 33.686).

Smith L T, A Commonplace Book of the Fifteenth Century, Norwich 1886, p 107 (Hamilton MS).

Sources. Krahl, Untersuchungen, pp 31, 54 (based on version c).

    f. ScL; Brown-Robbins, no 4114.

MS. Camb Univ Gg.2.6, ff 209ᵃ–217ᵃ (1400–50).

Editions. Horstmann ScL, 2.3; Metcalfe STS, 2.47 (notes 3.319).

Sources. Horstmann ScL, 2.3 (quotes Graesse LA, chap 93, p 400, but notes differences); Metcalfe STS, 3.321 (see preceding entry); Krahl, Untersuchungen, p 75 (stemma of Margaret texts).

    g. Mirk Festial.

MSS. Note: See ANDREW d *MSS* [25] above. 1, Bodl 17680 (Gough Eccl Top 4), ff 114ᵃ–116ᵇ (1400–50); 2, Cotton Claud A.ii, ff 88ᵇ–89ᵇ (ca 1420); 3, Durham Cosins v.iii.5, ff 116ᵇ–118ᵃ (15 cent). (Om Harley 2247, Royal 18.B.xxv.)

Editions. Liber Festiualis, Caxton, Westminster 1483, sig l viiᵃ – l viiiᵃ.

Erbe, EETSES 96.199 (Bodl 17680).

    h. Lydgate; Brown-Robbins, no 439.

(Note: See also under Lydgate.)

    i. Bokenham; Brown-Robbins, no 2651.

MS. Arundel 327, ff 5ᵃ–26ᵃ (1447).

Editions. [Bokenam O,] The Lyvys of Seyntys, Roxb Club 50, London 1835, p 8; Horstmann Bokenam, p 7; Serjeantson, EETS 206.7.

Sources. Horstmann Bokenam, p ix (etymology from LA; life similar to Mombritius text; translation similar to Acta SS text).

Willenberg G, Die Quellen von Osbert Bokenham's Legenden, EStn 12.29 (fuller comparison of sources noted by Horstmann).

Serjeantson, EETS 206.xxii (summary of Willenberg).

    j. 1438 GL.

MSS. 1, Harley 4775, chap 86, f 118ᵃ⁻ᵇ; MLA roto 343, 1.236; 2, BM Addit 35298, f 69ᵇ.

Sources. Cf Graesse LA, chap 93, p 400.

    k. Caxton GL.

Editions. Caxton GL, chap 128; Temple, 4.66.

Modernizations. Shackford M H, Legends and Satires, Boston 1913, p 73.

Sources. Butler LA, p 43 (includes Margaret at f 188 in the list of contents of de Vignay LD, 1480? edn, but the legend is not in that edn; see next entry).

Jeremy Sister M, Caxton's GL and de Vignai's LD, MS 8.100, 105 (legend not in known MSS or edns of rvsd de Vignay; Caxton may be using undiscovered MS).

General Background. Spencer F, The Legend of Margaret, MLN 4.197 (sketch of development of legend in England and other countries).

Francis E A, A Hitherto Unprinted Version of the Passio S Margaritae with Some Observations on Vernacular Derivatives, PMLA 42.87 (includes discussion of type of Latin version used in English texts).

MARGARET CALLED PELAGIA: see PELAGIA OF ANTIOCH, THE PENITENT.

[185] MARGARET CALLED PELAGIEN OR REPARATA (Oct 8, year?).

(Note: See H Delehaye, Les Légendes hagiographiques, 4th edn, Brussels 1955, p 188.)

    a. 1438 GL.

MSS. 1, Bodl 21947 (Douce 372), f 122, end imperf; 2, Harley 630, 308ᵇ–309ᵃ; 3, Harley 4775, chap 144, ff 189ᵇ–190ᵃ; MLA roto 343, 2.379; 4, BM Addit 35298, f 129ᵃ⁻ᵇ (om Lambeth 72; lost Egerton 876).

Sources. Cf Graesse LA, chap 151, p 676.

    b. Caxton GL.

Editions. Caxton GL, chap 185; Temple, 5.238.

Sources. Cf de Vignay LD, f 299ᵃ⁻ᵇ.

[186] MARINA (Feb 12, year?).

    a. NHC; Brown-Robbins, no 89.

MSS. 10 MSS.

Editions. Horstmann C, Die Evangelien-Geschichten der Homiliensammlung des MS Vernon, Arch 57.259 (Bodl 3938 [Vernon], f 179ᵇ; ca 1385).

Sources. Kölbing E, EStn 2.509 (comparison of versions a and b with Vitae patrum).

Gerould G H, The North-English Homily Collection, 1902, p 44 (Vitae patrum probable source).

Rosenthal Vitae patrum, p 93 (based on Vitae patrum).

    b. Harley, couplets; Brown-Robbins, no 1104.

MS. Harley 2253, f 64ᵇ (ca 1310).

Editions. AELeg 1878, p 171; K Böddeker, Altengl Dichtungen des MS Harl 2253,

Berlin 1878, p 256 (crit E Kölbing, EStn 2.509).
Textual Notes. EStn 2.511.
Sources. Böddeker, p 255 (versions a and b independently based on a Latin source); EStn 2.509 (comparison of versions a and b with Vitae patrum); Rosenthal Vitae patrum, p 94 (based on Vitae patrum).

c. Alphabet of Tales, prose.
MS. BM Addit 25719, chap 32 (mid 15 cent).
Edition. Banks, EETS 126, pt 1, p 22.
Sources. Rosenthal Vitae patrum, p 93 (directly from Vitae patrum).

d. 1438 GL.
MSS. 1, Bodl 21947 (Douce 372), chap 76, f 55b; 2, Egerton 876, f 124b; 3, Harley 4775, chap 76, ff 95b–96a; MLA roto 343, 1.189; 4, BM Addit 11565, f 114; 5, BM Addit 35298, f 47a–b.
Selections. Butler LA, p 114 (1st half of legend from BM Addit 11565 with variants of MSS 1, 2 and passage from de Vignay LD).
Sources. Cf Graesse LA, chap 84, p 353; Butler LA, p 71 (favors LA over de Vignay as source).

e. Caxton GL.
Editions. Caxton GL, chap 107; Temple, 3.226.
Sources. Butler LA, pp 87, 93, 144 (LA probable source); Rosenthal Vitae patrum, p 92 (both LA and de Vignay used).

f. Caxton VP.
Edition. Caxton VP, pt 1, chap 43.
Sources. Cf La vie des pères, pt 1, chap 43, ff 60a–61a.

MARINE, MAWRYNE: see MARINA.

[187] MARIUS WITH MARTHA (Jan 19, ca 260).

SEL; Brown-Robbins, no 2126.
MS. Bodl 2567 (Bodl 779), f 217b (ca 1400).
Edition. Zusatzleg 1889, p 382.
Sources. Zusatzleg 1889, p 382n1 (differs from account in Acta SS).

[188] MARK (April 25, ca 74).

a. SEL; Brown-Robbins, no 3004.
MSS. 18 MSS.
Editions. Horstmann, EETS 87.362 (Bodl 1486 [Laud Misc 108], ff 155b–156a; end 13 cent).
D'Evelyn and Mill, EETS 235.159 (Corp Christi Camb 145, f 60a–b; early 14 cent).

b. ScL; Brown-Robbins, no 4270.
MS. Camb Univ Gg.2.6, ff 84a–87b; with prologue on the 4 Evangelists (1400–50).

Editions. Horstmann ScL, 1.114; Metcalfe STS, 1.236 (notes 3.169).
Sources. Horstmann ScL, 1.114 (refers prologue to Graesse LA, chap 156, p 692; legend to chap 59, p 265); Metcalfe STS, 3.170 (to LA adds Peter de Natalibus Cat SS 4.86).

c. Mirk Festial.
MSS. Note: See ANDREW d *MSS* [25] above.
1, Bodl 17680 (Gough Eccl Top 4), ff 78b–80b (1400–50); 2, Cotton Claud A.ii, ff 60b–61b (ca 1420); 3, Harley 2247, ff 156a–157b (1450–1500); 4, Royal 18.B.xxv, ff 99b–100a (late 15 cent); 5, Durham Cosins v.iii.5, ff 98b–100a (15 cent).
Editions. Liber Festiualis, Caxton, Westminster 1483, sig k iiib–k iiiia.
Erbe, EETSES 96, p 135 (Bodl 17680).

d. Speculum Sacerdotale.
MS. BM Addit 36791, ff 75a–76b (15 cent).
Edition. Weatherly, EETS 200.133. (sources pp xxviii, 268; LA in part).

e. 1438 GL.
MSS. 1, Egerton 876, ff 85b–86; fragment; 2, Harley 4775, chap 55, ff 68a–70a; MLA roto 343, 1.136; 3, BM Addit 35298, ff 36a–37a (lost Bodl 21947).
Sources. Cf Graesse LA, chap 59, p 265.

f. Caxton GL.
Editions. Caxton GL, chap 86; Temple, 3.134.
Sources. Cf de Vignay LD, ff 126a–128a.

[189] MARTHA (July 29, 1st cent).

a. SEL; Brown-Robbins, no 2127.
MSS. 11 MSS.
Editions. D'Evelyn and Mill, EETS 235.348 (Corp Christi Camb 145, ff 130a–132b (early 14 cent).

b. ScL; Brown-Robbins, no 3295.
MS. Camb Univ Gg.2.6, ff 103b–107b; lines 289–344 an appended miracle of Mary Magdalen (1400–50).
Editions. Horstmann ScL, 1.137; Metcalfe STS, 1.285 (notes 3.198).
Sources. Horstmann ScL, 1.137 (passages from Graesse LA, chap 105, p 444 and chap 96, p 416); Metcalfe STS, 3.199 (LA quoted; Peter de Natalibus Cat SS referred to).

c. 1438 GL.
MSS. 1, Harley 4775, chap 98, ff 131b–132b; MLA roto 343, 1.263; 2, BM Addit 11565, ends f 145b; 3, BM Addit 35298, ff 89a–90a; 4, Lambeth 72, chap 119.
Sources. Cf Graesse LA, chap 105, p 444.

d. Caxton GL.
Editions. Caxton GL, chap 138; Temple, 4.135.

Sources. Cf Graesse LA, chap 105, p 444; de Vignay LD, ff 160ᵇ–162ᵃ.

Jeremy Sister M, Caxton GL and de Vignai's LD, MS 8.105 (details in Caxton not in LA go back to Metaphrastes version and probably reach Caxton through French).

MARTHA OF CAPPADOCIA: see MARIUS WITH MARTHA.

[190] MARTIAL, BISHOP OF LIMOGES (June 30, ca 250).
Editions. Caxton GL, chap 115; Temple, 3.275.
Sources. Cf de Vignay LD, ff 393ᵇ–395ᵇ.

[191] MARTIN, BISHOP OF TOURS (Nov 11, 397).

a. SEL; Brown-Robbins, no 3005.
MSS. 16 MSS.
Editions. Horstmann, EETS 87.449 (Bodl 1486 [Laud Misc 108], ff 185ᵃ–188ᵃ; end 13 cent).
D'Evelyn and Mill, EETS 236.483 (Harley 2277, ff 152ᵃ–155ᵃ; ca 1300).

b. Mirk Festial.
MSS. Note: See ANDREW d *MSS* [25] above.
1, Bodl 17680 (Gough Eccl Top 4), ff 154ᵇ–156ᵇ (1400–50); 2, Cotton Claud A.ii, ff 113ᵃ–114ᵃ (ca 1420); 3, Durham Cosins v.iii.5, ff 150ᵃ–152ᵃ (15 cent). (Om Bodl 21634, 21682=Douce 60, 108; Harley 2247; Royal 18.B.xxv.)
Editions. Liber Festiualis, Caxton, Westminster 1483, sig p iiᵇ – p iiiᵇ.
Erbe, EETSES 96.272 (Bodl 17680).

c. Speculum Sacerdotale.
MS. BM Addit 36791, ff 132ᵇ–134ᵇ (15 cent).
Edition. Weatherly, EETS 200.235 (source chiefly LA, pp xxix, 278).

d. 1438 GL.
MSS. 1, Bodl 21947 (Douce 372), f 135; beg lost; 2, Harley 4775, chap 158, ff 212ᵃ–215ᵇ; MLA roto 343, 2.424; 3, BM Addit 35298, ff 141ᵇ–143ᵇ.
Sources. Cf Graesse LA, chap 166, p 741.

e. Caxton GL.
Editions. Caxton GL, chap 203; Temple, 6.141.
Sources. Cf de Vignay LD, ff 325ᵇ–329ᵇ.

[192] MARY MAGDALEN July 22, 1st cent).

(Note: For the Lamentation of Mary Magdalen, Brown-Robbins, no 2759, formerly attributed to Lydgate, see under Lydgate. Brown-Robbins, nos 859, 2102, 4226, which

give the Gospel story of Mary Magdalen, are omitted here.)

a. SEL, stanzaic variant; Brown-Robbins, no 3159.
MSS. 1, Bodl 1486 (Laud Misc 108), ff 190ᵃ–197ᵃ (end 13 cent); 2, Trinity Camb 605, ff 127ᵇ–133ᵃ (early 15 cent); 3, Lambeth 223, f 137ᵇ (end 14 cent).
Knörk O, Untersuchungen über die mittelengl Magdalenenlegende des MS Laud 108, Berlin 1889, p 8 (notes Laud as fuller text than Trinity and Lambeth; regards Trinity as best text).
Editions. AELeg 1878, p 148 (Bodl 1486; crit E Kölbing, EStn 3.130).
Horstmann C, Nachträge zu den Legenden, Arch 68.52 (Trinity, Lambeth MSS).
Horstmann, EETS 87.462 (Bodl 1486).
Textual Notes. EStn 3.130 (on AELeg 1878 text).
Versification. Knörk, Untersuchungen, p 49 (notes variations in meter; frequency of caesural rime; grouping of lines in quatrains and larger units).
Sources. Knörk, Untersuchungen, p 30 (comparison with LA as Latin version nearest in content to Bodl 1486).

b. SEL; Brown-Robbins, no 2994.
MSS. 15 MSS.
Editions. D'Evelyn and Mill, EETS 235.302 (Corp Christi Camb 145, ff 113ᵃ–117ᵇ; early 14 cent).

c. NHC, expanded version; Brown-Robbins, no 2637.
MS. Harley 4196, ff 157ᵃ–162ᵃ (15 cent).
Edition. AELeg 1881, p 81.

d. Auchinleck, couplets; Brown-Robbins, no *12.
MS. Advocates 19.2.1 (Auchinleck), ff 62ᵃ–65; beg imperf (1300–25).
Editions. Turnbull Leg cath, p 213; AELeg 1878, p 163 (crit E Kölbing, EStn 3.130).

e. ScL; Brown-Robbins, no 1683.
MS. Camb Univ Gg.2.6, ff 91ᵇ–103ᵇ (1400–50).
Editions. Horstmann ScL, 1.123; Metcalfe STS, 1.256 (notes 3.182).
Sources. Horstmann ScL, 1.123 (passages from Graesse LA, chap 96, p 407); Metcalfe STS, 3.185 (passages from LA; references to Bible and Peter de Natalibus Cat SS).

f. Mirk Festial.
MSS. Note: See ANDREW d *MSS* [25] above.
1, Bodl 17680 (Gough Eccl Top 4), ff 116ᵃ–119ᵃ (1400–50); 2, Camb Univ Ff.ii.38, f 35 (1400–50); 3, Cotton Claud A.ii, ff 89ᵇ–91ᵇ (ca 1420); 4, Cotton Titus A.xxvi, ff 174ᵃ–179ᵃ (15 cent); 5, Harley 2247, ff 169ᵇ–

173ª (1450–1500); 6, Harley 2391, f 101; beg imperf (1450–1500); 7, Royal 18.B.xxv, ff 111ᵇ–113ᵇ (late 15 cent); 8, Durham Cosins v.iii.5, ff 118ª–121ᵇ (15 cent).
Editions. Liber Festiualis, Caxton, Westminster 1483, sig 1 viiiᵇ–m iiᵇ.
Erbe, EETSES 96.203 (Bodl 17680).

g. Bokenham; Brown-Robbins, no 3508.
MS. Arundel 327, ff 91ᵇ–115ª (1447).
Editions. [Bokenam O,] The Lyvys of Seyntys, Roxb Club 50, London 1835, p 144; Horstmann Bokenam, p 126; Serjeantson, EETS 206.136.
Sources. Willenberg G, Die Quellen von Osbern Bokenham's Legenden, EStn 12.7 (intermingling of Biblical accounts and Graesse LA, chap 96, p 407); Serjeantson, EETS 206.xxiii (summary of Willenberg).

h. Speculum Sacerdotale.
MS. BM Addit 36791, ff 96ª–98ª (15 cent).
Edition. Weatherly, EETS 200.170 (source LA, pp xxviii, 272).

i. 1438 GL.
MSS. 1, Bodl 21947 (Douce 372); frag only; see Butler LA, p 60; 2, Harley 4775, chap 89, ff 120ª–123ª; MLA roto 343, 1.240; 3, BM Addit 35298, ff 70ᵇ–72ª; 4, Durham Cosins v.ii.14, ff 106ª–111ᵇ; end lost; single item of 1438 GL (15 cent); 5, Trinity Dublin 319 (15 cent); see Gerould S Leg, p 195.
Zupitza J, Das Leben der h Maria Magdalena, Arch 91.207 (description of MS 4).
Edition. Arch 91.210 (Durham Cosins v.ii.14).
Sources. Arch 91.207 (de Vignay direct source; see also Arch 95.439).

j. Caxton GL.
Editions. Caxton GL, chap 129; Temple, 4.72; rptd A Aspland, The GL, Holbein Soc Fac-Simile Reprints, London 1878.
Sources. Cf de Vignay LD, ff 188ª–192ᵇ.
General Background. Knörk, Untersuchungen, p 18 (development of Mary Magdalen saga).
Garth H M, St Mary Magdalene in Mediaeval Literature, Johns Hopkins Univ Studies in Hist and Pol Sci 67, no 3, Baltimore 1950 (Engl versions among others used to illustrate features of legend; crit B de Gaiffier, AnBol 70.420; Ævum (Milan) 28.388; J Misraeli, Spec 27.383).

[193] MARY OF EGYPT (April 2, 5 cent?).
a. SEL; Brown-Robbins, no 2990.
MSS. 20 MSS; add 21, Winchester Coll 33a, ff 25ª–30ª (15 cent).
Editions. Horstmann, EETS 87.260 (Bodl 1486 [Laud Misc 108], ff 117ᵇ–121ᵇ; end 13 cent).
D'Evelyn and Mill, EETS 235.136 (Corp Christi Camb 145, ff 51ᵇ–56ª; early 14 cent).
Sources and Literary Relations. Knust H, Geschichte der Legenden der h Katherina von Alexandrien und der h Maria Aegyptiaca, Halle 1890, p 219 (sketch of English versions with passages from Harley 2277 and Trinity Oxf 57).
Baker A T, La vie de Ste Marie l'Egyptienne, RLR 59.158 (SEL version probably based on abbreviation of Paul the Deacon's Latin text).
Rosenthal Vitae patrum, p 97 (summary of Baker).

b. ScL; Brown-Robbins, no 1651.
MSS. Camb Univ Gg.2.6, ff 107ᵇ–124ᵇ (1400–50).
Editions. Horstmann ScL, 1.143; Metcalfe STS, 1.296 (notes 3.205).
Sources. Horstmann ScL, 1.143 (source not LA but Latin text as in Acta SS April 2, i e Vita by Paul the Deacon).
Metcalfe STS, 3.205, 207 (specifies Latin source as Paul the Deacon's translation of Greek text of Sophronius, Bishop of Jerusalem; see Migne PL 73.671).
Rosenthal Vitae patrum, pp 24, 43, 96 (summary of Metcalfe).

c. 1438 GL.
MSS. 1, Bodl 21947 (Douce 372), chap 51; 2, Harley 4775, chap 52, ff 62ª–63ª; MLA roto 343, 1.124; 3, BM Addit 35298, f 33ª⁻ᵇ (lost BM Addit 11565).
Sources. Cf Graesse LA, chap 56, p 247.

d. Caxton GL.
Editions. Caxton GL, chap 82; Temple, 3.106.
Sources. Cf de Vignay LD, ff 120ᵇ–121ᵇ.
Rosenthal Vitae patrum, p 69 (comparison of Caxton and LA).
Jeremy Sister M, Caxton's GL and de Vignai's LD, MS 8.103 (details in Caxton, not in LA, derived from rvsd de Vignay).

e. Caxton VP.
Edition. Caxton VP, pt 1, chap 42, ff 65ᵇ–71ᵇ.
Sources. Cf La vie des pères, pt 1, chap 42, ff 55ᵇ–59ᵇ.

[194] MARY OF OIGNIES, prose (June 23, 1213).
MS. Bodl 21688 (Douce 114), ff 26ᵇ–76ª (15 cent).
Horstmann C, Prosalegenden: Die Legenden des MS Douce 114, Angl 8.102 (contents, script).
Edition. Angl 8.134 (authorship, p 105; notes

passages referring to anon monk as translator).

Sources. Angl 8.104 (Latin life by Jacques de Vitry, 1215).

Funk P, Jakob von Vitry Leben und Werke, Beitr zur Kulturgeschichte des Mittelalters und der Renaissance 3, Leipzig 1909, p 113 (traditional hagiographical and typical 13 cent mystical elements in Vita Mariae).

Literary Criticism. Workman 15 Cent Trans, pp 104, 133, 156 (comparison of Latin and English).

MARY THE PROSTITUTE: see ABRAHAM, HERMIT.

MARY THE VIRGIN: for Lydgate's LIFE OF THE VIRGIN see under Lydgate.

[195] MATTHEW (Sept 21, 1st cent).

     a. SEL; Brown-Robbins, no 3017.

MSS. 14 MSS.

Editions. Horstmann, EETS 87.77 (Bodl 1486 [Laud Misc 108], ff 50ᵇ–52ᵃ; end 13 cent).

D'Evelyn and Mill, EETS 236.397 (Corp Christi Camb 145, ff 147ᵃ–149ᵃ; early 14 cent).

     b. NHC, expanded; Brown-Robbins, no 3016.

MSS. 1, Cotton Tib E.vii, ff 263ᵇ–266ᵃ (ca 1400); 2, Harley 4196, ff 179ᵃ–181ᵃ (early 15 cent).

Edition. AELeg 1881, p 131 (Harley 4196; lines 1–406, legend; lines 407–500, exposition of Gospel).

     c. ScL; Brown-Robbins, no 2325.

MS. Camb Univ Gg.2.6, ff 66ᵇ–73ᵃ (1400–50).

Editions. Horstmann ScL, 1.92; Metcalfe STS, 1.190 (notes 3.141).

Sources. Horstmann ScL, 1.93 (passages from Graesse LA, chap 140, p 622 cited; LA not direct source); Metcalfe STS, 3.143 (passages from LA given; Abdias Vita S Matt cited as possible source).

     d. Mirk Festial.

MSS. Note: See ANDREW d *MSS* [25] above.

1, Bodl 17680 (Gough Eccl Top 4), ff 145ᵃ–146ᵇ (1400–50); 2, Cotton Claud A.ii, ff 107ᵇ–108ᵇ (ca 1420); 3, Harley 2247, ff 193ᵃ–194ᵇ (1400–50); 4, Royal 18.B.xxv, ff 131ᵃ–132ᵇ (late 15 cent); 5, Durham Cosins v.iii.5, ff 140ᵇ–142ᵃ (15 cent). (Om Bodl 21634, 21682 = Douce 60, 108.)

Editions. Liber Festiualis, Caxton, Westminster 1483, sig Oiᵇ–Oiiᵇ.

Erbe, EETSES 96.254 (Bodl 17680).

     e. Speculum Sacerdotale.

MS. BM Addit 36791, ff 117ᵇ–118ᵇ (15 cent).

Edition. Weatherly, EETS 200.208 (source, pp xxix, 276; LA condensed).

     f. 1438 GL.

MSS. 1, Bodl 21947 (Douce 372), f 111; end lost; 2, Harley 4775, chap 133, ff 173ᵇ–176ᵃ; MLA roto 343, 2.345; 3, BM Addit 11565, ends f 172ᵇ; 4, BM Addit 35298, ff 119ᵇ–121ᵃ; 5, Lambeth 72, chap 136.

Sources. Cf Graesse LA, chap 140, p 622.

     g. Caxton GL.

Editions. Caxton GL, chap 174; Temple, 5.149; rptd A Aspland, The GL, Holbein Soc Fac-Simile Reprints, London 1878.

Sources. Cf de Vignay LD, ff 277ᵇ–279ᵇ.

[196] MATTHIAS (Feb 24, 1st cent).

(Note: See also JUDAS ISCARIOT [149].)

     a. SEL; Brown-Robbins, no 3026.

MSS. 17 MSS; add 18, Winchester Coll 33a, f 39ᵃ⁻ᵇ (15 cent).

Editions. Horstmann, EETS 87.389 (Bodl 1486 [Laud Misc 108], ff 165ᵇ–166ᵃ; end 13 cent).

D'Evelyn and Mill, EETS 235.70 (Corp Christi Camb 145, f 26ᵃ⁻ᵇ; early 14 cent).

     b. ScL; Brown-Robbins, no 1191.

MS. Camb Univ Gg.2.6, ff 78ᵇ–84ᵃ (1400–50).

Editions. Horstmann ScL, 1.107; Metcalfe STS, 1.222 (notes 3.160).

Sources. Horstmann ScL, 1.107 (passages from Graesse LA, chap 45, p 183); Metcalfe STS, 3.161 (LA quoted).

     c. Mirk Festial.

MSS. Note: See ANDREW d *MSS* [25] above.

1, Bodl 17680 (Gough Eccl Top 4), ff 47ᵃ–48ᵇ (1400–50); 2, Cotton Claud A.ii, ff 41ᵇ–43ᵃ (ca 1420); 3, Harley 2247, ff 149ᵃ–151ᵃ (1450–1500); 4, Lansdowne 392, f 30 (1400–50); 5, Royal 18.B.xxv, ff 93ᵇ–95ᵃ (late 15 cent); 6, Durham Cosins v.iii.5, ff 91ᵇ–94ᵃ (15 cent).

Editions. Liber Festiualis, Caxton, Westminster 1483, sig i viᵇ–i viiiᵃ.

Erbe, EETSES 96.79 (Bodl 17680).

Literary Relations. Baum P F, The Mediaeval Legend of Judas Iscariot, PMLA 31.531 (connection of Mirk and ScL versions with Judas legend).

     d. Speculum Sacerdotale.

MS. BM Addit 36791, ff 20ᵃ–21ᵇ (15 cent).

Edition. Weatherly, EETS 200.34 (sources, pp xxvii, 259; based on LA).

     e. 1438 GL.

MSS. 1, Bodl 21947 (Douce 372), f 26ᵇ; end lost; 2, Egerton 876, f 58ᵃ; beg lost; 3, Harley 4775, chap 44, ff 45ᵃ–46ᵇ; MLA roto 343, 1.90; 4, BM Addit 11565, f 89ᵃ; beg lost; 5, BM Addit 39298, 25ᵃ–26ᵃ.
Sources. Cf Graesse LA, chap 45, p 183.

    f. Caxton GL.
Editions. Caxton GL, chap 73; Temple, 3.54.
Sources. Cf de Vignay LD, ff 107ᵃ–108ᵇ.

[197] MATURIN (Nov 1, 4 cent?).
Editions. Caxton GL, chap 117; Temple, 4.1.
Sources. Cf de Vignay LD, ff 384ᵇ–385ᵃ.

MAUR(E): see MAURUS, ABBOT.

[198] MAURICE AND COMPANIONS OF THE THEBAN LEGION (Sept 22, ca 287?).
    a. 1438 GL.
MSS. 1, Harley 4775, chap 134, ff 175ᵃ–176ᵇ; MLA roto 343, 2.350; 2, BM Addit 11565, f 172ᵇ; end lost; 3, BM Addit 35298, ff 121ᵃ–122ᵃ.
Sources. Cf Graesse LA, chap 141, p 628.

    b. Caxton GL.
Editions. Caxton GL, chap 175; Temple, 5.158.
Sources. Cf de Vignay LD, ff 279ᵇ–281ᵃ.
Background. Van Berchen D, Le martyre de la Legion Thébaine, Essai sur le formation d'une légende, Schweizerische Beitr zur Altertumswissenschaft 8, Basel 1956 (analysis of earliest known account on basis of historical, topographical, and archaeological evidence).

MAURICIUS: see MAURICE AND COMPANIONS.

[199] MAURUNTIUS, ABBOT OF BREUIL (May 5, 701).
Editions. Caxton GL, chap 243; Temple, 7.201.
Sources. Cf de Vignay LD, f 417ᵃ⁻ᵇ.

[200] MAURUS, ABBOT (Jan 15, 6 cent).
Editions. Caxton GL, chap 76; Temple, 3.73.
Sources. Cf de Vignay LD, ff 111ᵇ–112ᵇ (Note: de Vignay has incorrect title, De saint benoit, followed by etymology of Benoit; see Graesse LA, chap 49, p 204).

MAWRINE: see MARINA.

[201] MELCHIADES, POPE (Dec 10, 314).
    SEL: Brown-Robbins, no 2143.
MS. Bodl 2567 (Bodley 779), ff 234ᵃ–235ᵃ (ca 1400).

Edition. Zusatzleg 1889, p 405 (ultimate source Liber Pontificalis, p 405n1).

MELCHIOR: see THREE KINGS OF COLOGNE.

MELLON, MELLONIN: see MALLONUS.

[202] MICHAEL, ARCHANGEL (Sept 29 Michaelmas, May 8 Mt Garganus).
    a. SEL; Brown-Robbins, no 3029.
MSS. Note: Under this number are listed (1) MSS containing pt I in monte Gargano, pt II in monte Tomba, and pt III, pseudo-scientific information on the natural world and man; (2) MSS containing only pts I and II. (1) 14 MSS; add 15, Corp Christi Camb 145, ff 149ᵃ–158ᵇ (early 14 cent). (2) 4 MSS; delete no 5. For pt III occurring separately see Brown-Robbins, no 3453 and Arch 98.401.
Editions. Horstmann C, Die Legende des hl Michael nach MS Laud 108, JfRESL 13.154 (Bodl 1486, ff 132ᵃ–140ᵇ; end 13 cent).
Horstmann, EETS 87.299 (Bodl 1486).
D'Evelyn and Mill, EETS 236.402 (Corp Christi Camb 145).
Language. JfRESL 13.150 (phonology, grammar of Bodl 1486).
Literary Relations. Ker W P, The Craven Angels, MLR 6.85 (neutral angels of medieval folklore and classic daemons).

    b. Mirk Festial.
MSS. Note: See ANDREW d MSS [25] above.
1, Bodl 17680 (Gough Eccl Top 4), ff 146ᵇ–148ᵇ (1400–50); 2, Cotton Claud A.ii, ff 108ᵇ–109ᵇ (ca 1420); 3, Harley 2247, ff 194ᵇ–197ᵇ (1450–1500); 4, Royal 18.B.xxv, ff 132ᵇ–134ᵃ (late 15 cent); 5, Durham Cosins v.iii.5, ff 142ᵃ–143ᵇ (15 cent). (Om Bodl 21634, 21682 = Douce 60, 108.)
Editions. Liber Festiualis, Caxton, Westminster 1483, sig o iiᵇ–o iiiᵃ.
Erbe, EETSES 96.257 (Bodl 17680).

    c. Speculum Sacerdotale.
MS. BM Addit 36791, ff 118ᵇ–121ᵇ (15 cent).
Edition. Weatherly, EETS 200.210 (source, pp xxix, 276; apparently from LA with details from Belethus Rationale Div Off).

    d. 1438 GL.
MSS. 1, Bodl 21947 (Douce 372), f 116; frag; 2, Harley 4775, chap 138, ff 179ᵇ–181ᵇ; MLA roto 343, 2.359; 3, BM Addit 11565, f 175ᵇ (contains material of pt III; see Butler LA, p 68); 4, BM Addit 35298, f 124ᵃ⁻ᵇ; 5, Lambeth 72, chap 116, f 234.
Sources. Cf Graesse LA, chap 145, p 642.

e. Caxton GL.

Editions. Caxton GL, chap 179; Temple, 5.180.

Sources. Cf de Vignay LD, ff 285ª–289ᵇ.

[203] MILDRED, ABBESS OF MINSTER-IN-THANET (July 13, ca 700).

SEL; Brown-Robbins, no 3030.

MSS. 1, Bodl 2567 (Bodley 779), f 302ª (ca 1400); 2, Bodl 3938 (Vernon), f 41ᵇ col 2 (ca 1385); 3, Egerton 1993, f 176ª (1300–50).

MILTIADES: see MELCHIADES, POPE.

MOCHUMMA: see MACHOR.

MODESTUS: see VITUS.

MORA(U)NT: see MAURUNTIUS, ABBOT.

MORICE: see MACHOR.

MORIS: see MAURICE AND COMPANIONS.

[204] MOSES (MOYSES), ABBOT (Aug 28, ca 405).

(Note: See also ARSENIUS [34].)

a. 1438 GL.

MSS. 1, Bodl 21947 (Douce 372), f 151 (with Arsenius); 2, Egerton 876, f 299; 3, Harley 4775, chap 169, f 235ᵇ; MLA roto 343, 2.471; 4, BM Addit 35298, f 154ª⁻ᵇ (with Arsenius); 5, Lambeth 72, chap 170 (with Arsenius).

Sources. Cf Graesse LA, chap 177, p 806.

b. Caxton GL.

Editions. Caxton GL, chap 224; Temple, 7.76.

Sources. Cf de Vignay LD, f 346ª⁻ᵇ; Rosenthal Vitae patrum, p 66, index (Vitae patrum named as source in LA, 1438 GL, and Caxton GL; content not from any known text of Vitae patrum).

MUTIUS: see COPRETT.

NATALIA: see ADRIAN.

NAVINIEN: see SAVINIAN AND SAVINA.

NAZARIEN: see NAZARIUS.

[205] NAZARIUS AND CELSUS (July 28, year?).

a. 1438 GL.

MSS. 1, Harley 4775, chap 95, ff 130ª–131ª; MLA roto 343, 1.260; 2, BM Addit 35298, ff 88ᵇ–89ª.

Sources. Cf Graesse LA, chap 102, p 439.

b. Caxton GL.

Editions. Caxton GL, chap 135; Temple, 4.127.

Sources. Cf de Vignay LD, ff 381ᵇ–383ª.

[206] NEREUS AND ACHILLEUS (May 12, 1st cent?).

a. 1438 GL.

MSS. 1, Bodl 21947 (Douce 372), f 53; 2, Harley 4775, chap 67, ff 91ª–92ª; MLA roto 343, 1.180; 3, BM Addit 35298, f 45ª (lost BM Addit 11565).

Sources. Cf Graesse LA, chap 75, p 338.

b. Caxton GL.

Editions. Caxton GL, chap 95; Temple, 3.179.

Sources. Cf de Vignay LD, ff 136ᵇ–137ª.

NEREYNE: see NEREUS.

[207] NICASIUS, BISHOP OF RHEIMS (Dec 14, 451?).

a. SEL; Brown-Robbins, no 125.

MS. Bodl 2567 (Bodley 779), ff 186ª–187ª (ca 1400).

Edition. Zusatzleg 1889, p 326 (sources, p 326n1; refers to Acta SS).

b. Caxton GL.

Editions. Caxton GL, chap 38; Temple, 2.136.

Sources. Cf de Vignay LD, f 60ᵇ.

[208] NICHOLAS, BISHOP OF MYRA (Dec 6, 4 cent).

a. SEL; Brown-Robbins, no 3033.

MSS. 18 MSS.

Editions. Horstmann, EETS 87.240 (Bodl 1486 [Laud Misc 108], ff 111ª–115ᵇ; end 13 cent; lines 361–448 from Harley 2277, ff 181ª–182ª; ca 1300).

D'Evelyn and Mill, EETS 236.550 (Harley 2277, ff 177ª–182ᵇ; ca 1300; lines 1–4 from Bodl 6924 [Ashm 43], f 202ª; (1325–50).

Textual Notes. Seybolt R F, The Adriatic Port in the LA, Spec 21.500 (identification of place-name; see Graesse LA, chap 3, p 25; Horstmann, EETS 87.246, line 218).

b. NHC expanded; Brown-Robbins, no 3032.

MSS. 1, Cotton Tib E.vii, f 278ᵇ (ca 1400); 2, Harley 4196, f 135ᵇ (early 15 cent).

Edition. AELeg 1881, p 11 (Harley 4196).

c. ScL; Brown-Robbins, no 1631.

MS. Camb Univ Gg.2.6, ff 178ª–190ᵇ (1400–50).

Editions. Horstmann ScL, 1.229; Metcalfe STS, 1.481 (notes 3.296).

Textual Notes. Seybolt R F, A Troublesome Mediaeval Greek Word, Spec 21.38 (oleum mydiacon, Greek fire, in LA and translations).

Sources. Horstmann ScL, 1.229 (quotes Graesse

LA, chap 3, p 22 but claims use of second source); Metcalfe STS, 3.298 (follows Horstmann).

d. Mirk Festial.

MSS. Note: See ANDREW d *MSS* [25] above. 1, Bodl 17680 (Gough Eccl Top 4), ff 6ᵇ–8ᵇ (1400–50); 2, Cotton Claud A.ii, ff 6ᵇ–9ᵇ (ca 1420); 3, Harley 2247, ff 134ᵃ–137ᵇ (1450–1500); 4, Royal 18.B.xxv, ff 86ᵃ–87ᵃ; beg lost (late 15 cent); 5, Durham Cosins v.iii.5, ff 56ᵃ–61ᵃ (15 cent).
Editions. Liber Festiualis, Caxton, Westminster 1483, sig f viᵃ–f viiiᵇ.
Erbe, EETSES 96.11 (Bodl 17680).

e. Speculum Sacerdotale.

MS. BM Addit 36791, ff 138ᵇ–140ᵇ (15 cent).
Edition. Weatherly, EETS 200.246 (sources, pp xxix, 280; LA with details possibly from Vita by Johannes Diaconus).

f. 1438 GL.

MSS. 1, Egerton 876, f 6ᵇ; end lost; 2, Harley 630, f 7ᵇ; 1st half of legend lost; 3, Harley 4775, chap 2, ff 5ᵇ–8ᵃ; MLA roto 343, 1.11; 4, BM Addit 35298, chap 2, ff 3ᵃ–4ᵃ (in Trinity Dublin 319; see Gerould S Leg, p 195; lost Bodl 21947, Lambeth 72).
Sources. Cf Graesse LA, chap 3, p 22.

g. Caxton GL.

Editions. Caxton GL, chap 34; Temple, 2.109.
Sources. Cf de Vignay LD, ff 43ᵇ–56ᵇ.

[209] NICHOLAS OF TOLENTINO (Sept 10, 1305).

St Nycholas of Tollentyne, prose.
Editions. S Nycholas of tollentyne, Wynkyn de Worde, London 1520? (STC, no 18528).
Date. Bennett H S, English Books and Readers 1475–1557, Cambridge 1952, p 261 (dates edn 1525?).

[210] NINIAN, BISHOP (Sept 16, 432?).

ScL; Brown-Robbins, no 3639.
MS. Camb Univ Gg.2.6, ff 332ᵃ–349ᵇ; end lost (1400–50).
Editions. Horstmann ScL, 2.121.
Metcalfe STS, 2.304 (notes 3.409).
Metcalfe W M, The Legends of Sts Ninian and Machor, Paisley 1904, p 41.
Selections. Metcalfe W M, Specimens of Scottish Literature 1325–1835, Glascow 1913, p 29 (lines 271–304, episode of rebellious king converted).
Authorship. Metcalfe, Ninian and Machor, pp 18, 153 (refutes Neilson's argument for Barbour as author).
Sources. AELeg 1881, p cii (lines 1–814 based on Ailred of Rievaulx, Vita S Niniani; lines 815–1447 based on local and traditional material).
Horstmann ScL, 2.138 (Ailred's text rptd from J Pinkerton, Vitae . . . sanctorum Scotiae, London 1789).
Metcalfe, Ninian and Machor, pp 14, 22, 187 (gives translation of Ailred of Rievaulx, Vita S Niniani).
Chadwick N K, St Ninian: A Preliminary Study, Trans and Journal of Proceedings, Dumfriesshire and Galloway Nat Hist and Antiq Soc, 3s, 27.9 (relation of lost Latin life to Bede's and Ailred's accounts).
Background. Neilson G, John Barbour, John Trumpour and a Legend of the Saints, 11.102 (identification of Fergus Macdowal, cf line 815).

[211] NORBERT, ARCHBISHOP OF MAGDEBURG (June 6, 1134).

Capgrave, rime royal; Brown-Robbins, no 1805.
MS. Huntington HM 55 (formerly Phillipps 24309), ff 1ᵃ–59ᵇ (1440 holograph).
Furnivall F J, Forewords, EETS 100.xliv (description from Sotheby Sale Cat, Feb 6 1861).
Munro, EETS 140.xi (includes H N McCracken's notes on MS).
Editions. Colvin H M, The White Canons in England, Oxford 1951, p 322n (refers to an edition in preparation for EETS by Prof W H Clawson, Univ of Toronto; see also below under *Authorship*, A de Meijer, Augustiniana 5.413n58; in July 1960, the edn is reported as still expected).
Selections. Furnivall, EETS 100.xliv (opening stanza, 2-stanza envoy).
Munro, EETS 140.xii (stanzas 1–4, envoy).
Kirkfleet C J, The White Canons of St Norbert, West DePere, Wisconsin 1943, p 119 (stanzas 1–5, envoy; slightly modernized).
Colvin H M, The White Canons in England, Oxford 1951, p 322 (envoy from EETS 140).
Language. Munro, EETS 140.xiv (holograph an example of 15 cent Norfolk dialect).
Authorship. De Meijer A, John Capgrave, Augustiniana 5.400; 7.118, 531 (detailed bibliography and summary of life and works; for St Norbert see 5.413; 7.569).
Toner N, Augustinian Spiritual Writers of the Eng Province in the 15 and 16 Centuries, S Augustinus vitae spiritualis magister, Rome 1956, 2.507 (summary of Capgrave's life and works).
Sources. Kirkfleet C J, History of St Norbert, St Louis and London 1916, p vi (account of early Latin lives).

Kirkfleet, The White Canons of St Norbert, p 121 (Capgrave text based on Vita B by Hugh of Fosse; see Migne PL, 170.1257).

NYCASIE: see NICASIUS.

ONUFFRYEN: see ONUPHRIUS.

[212] ONUPHRIUS, HERMIT (June 12, ca 400?).
Editions. Caxton VP, pt 1, chap 50, ff 49ª–52ᵇ.
Sources. Cf La vie des pères, pt 1, chap 50, ff 80ª–82ª.
Background. Williams C A, Oriental Affinities of the Legend of the Hairy Anchorite, Illinois Studies in Lang and Lit 10, no 2; 11, no 4 (crit AnBol 47.138).

[213] OSWALD, BISHOP OF WORCESTER (Feb 28, 992).
a. SEL; Brown-Robbins, no 3035.
MSS. 18 MSS; add 19, Winchester Coll 33a, ff 17ᵇ–20ᵇ (15 cent).
Edition. D'Evelyn and Mill, EETS 235.71 (Corp Christi Camb 145, ff 26ᵇ–29ᵇ; early 14 cent).

b. 1438 GL.
MSS. 1, BM Addit 35298, ff 76ᵇ–77ª (15 cent); 2, Lambeth 72, chap 105, f 221ª (mid 15 cent). (Lost BM Addit 11565; om Harley 4775.)

[214] OSWALD, KING OF NORTHUMBRIA (Aug 9, 642).
SEL; Brown-Robbins, no 3036.
MSS. 11 MSS.
Editions. Horstmann, EETS 87.45 (Bodl 1486 [Laud Misc 108], f 38ᵇ; end 13 cent). D'Evelyn and Mill, EETS 236.357 (Corp Christi Camb 145, ff 132ᵇ–133ª; early 14 cent).

[215] OSWIN, KING OF DEIRA (Aug 20, 651).
SEL; Brown-Robbins, no 1531.
MS. Bodl 2567 (Bodley 779), ff 208ª–212ᵇ (ca 1400).
Edition. Zusatzleg 1889, p 369 (sources, p 309n2; refers to Bede, Historia ecclesiastica gentis Anglorum, bk iii, chap 14 and John of Tynemouth; cf Nova legenda Angliae 2.268).

[216] PACHOMIUS, ABBOT (May 9, 348).
Edition. Caxton VP, pt 1, chaps 52–104, ff 110ª–133ᵇ.
Sources. Cf La vie des pères, pt 1, chaps 52–104, ff 87ᵇ–105ª.

[217] PANCRAS (May 12, 304?).
a. 1438 GL.
MSS. 1, Harley 4775, chap 68, f 92ª; MLA roto 343, 1.182; 2, BM Addit 35298, f 45ᵇ (lost Bodl 21947, BM Addit 11565).
Sources. Cf Graesse LA, chap 76, p 340.

b. Caxton GL.
Editions. Caxton GL, chap 96; Temple, 3.182.
Sources. Cf de Vignay LD, f 137ª⁻ᵇ.

PAPHNUCE: see PAPHNUTIUS.

[218] PAPHNUTIUS, ABBOT (Nov 29 [Whytford Add], 4 cent).
Edition. Caxton VP, pt 1, chap 16, ff 19ª–21ª.
Sources. Cf La vie des pères, pt 1, chap 16, ff 21ª–22ᵇ.

[219] PASTOR, ABBOT (Jan 12 [Whytford Add], year?).
a. 1438 GL.
MSS. 1, Harley 4775, chap 167, ff 234ᵇ–235ª; MLA roto 343, 2.469; 2, BM Addit 35298, f 153ᵇ.
Sources. Cf Graesse LA, chap 175, p 803.

b. Caxton GL.
Editions. Caxton GL, chap 222; Temple, 7.71.
Sources. Cf de Vignay LD, f 345ª⁻ᵇ.
Butler LA, p 89 (etymology in de Vignay).
Rosenthal Vitae patrum, p 66 (relation of Vincent of Beauvais Spec Hist, LA, and Caxton to Vitae patrum).

PASTUMYEN: see POSTHUMIUS.

[220] PATRICK, ARCHBISHOP OF ARMAGH (March 17, 461).

(Note: Versions a, b, c include an account of St Patrick's Purgatory; version d refers to that legend but connects it with the second Patrick, the Abbot. For separate treatment of St. Patrick's Purgatory see [321] below.)
a. SEL; Brown-Robbins, no 3037.
MSS. 17 MSS.
Editions. AELeg 1881, p 151 (Bodl 6924 [Ashm 43], ff 34ª–41ᵇ; 1325–50). D'Evelyn and Mill, EETS 235.85 (Corp Christi Camb 145, ff 32ª–41ᵇ; early 14 cent).
Selections. AELeg 1875, p 175 (Egerton 1993, ff 119ᵇ–120ᵇ, lines 1–74; 1300–50).

b. Quatrains; Brown-Robbins, no 3038.
MS. Harley 4012, ff 140ª–151ᵇ; incomplete; based on SEL (15 cent).

c. 1438 GL.
MSS. 1, Egerton 876, f 69; 2, Harley 630, f 94; 3, Harley 4775, chap 48, ff 54ᵇ–55ᵇ; MLA roto 343, 1.109; 4, BM Addit 11565,

f 95; 5, BM Addit 35298, ff 29ᵇ–30ᵃ (lost Bodl 21947).
Edition. Butler LA, p 116 (Harley 4775).
Sources. Cf Graesse LA, chap 50, p 213.

d. Caxton GL.

Editions. Caxton GL, chap 77; Temple, 3.76.
Sources. Cf de Vignay LD, ff 112ᵇ–114ᵃ; rptd Butler LA, p 125.
Babington C, ed, Polychronicon, R Higden, Rolls Series, London 1865, 1.lxi (part of Caxton's statement of his own work on LA and on Trevisa's translation of Higden; for full statement see Crotch, EETS 176.66; rptd 1956).
Lumby R J, ed, Polychronicon, R Higden, Rolls Series, London 1874, 5.187, 303 (Trevisa's translation of Higden's account of Patrick).
Butler LA, p 86 (use of Trevisa).
Language. Babington, Polychronicon 1.lxiii (Caxton's rewriting of Trevisa).

PAUL: see SYRUS, ABBOT, AND COMPANIONS.

[221] PAUL (SAUL), APOSTLE (Jan 25 Conversion, June 30 Commemoration, 67?).
(Note: See also PETER, APOSTLE [227]; for VISIO PAULI, see [320] below.)

a. SEL; Brown-Robbins, no 3041.

MSS. 16 MSS; add 17, Winchester Coll 33ᵃ, ff 38ᵃ–39ᵃ (15 cent); MSS 1, 16, 17 contain Conversion only, lines 1–74).
D'Evelyn, EETS 244.18 (relation of long and short versions).
Editions. Horstmann, EETS 87.189 (Bodl 1486 [Laud Misc 108], f 93ᵃ⁻ᵇ; Conversion only; end 13 cent).
D'Evelyn and Mill, EETS 235.264 (Corp Christi Camb 145, ff 90ᵃ–102ᵇ; early 14 cent).

b. ScL; Brown-Robbins, no 308.

MS. Camb Univ Gg.2.6, ff 9ᵃ–20ᵇ (1400–50).
Editions. Horstmann ScL, 1.15; Metcalfe STS, 1.29 (notes 3.30).
Sources. Horstmann ScL, 1.15 (quotes Graesse LA, chap 90, p 380; chap 28, p 133; chap 89, p 376); Metcalfe STS, 3.30 (passages from LA; references to and passages from Vulgate and apocryphal Acts).

c. Mirk Festial.

MSS. Note: See ANDREW d *MSS* [25] above.
1, Bodl 17680 (Gough Eccl Top 4), ff 31ᵇ–34ᵃ (1400–50); 2, Cotton Claud A.ii, ff 30ᵇ–33ᵃ (ca 1420); 3, Harley 2247, ff 143ᵃ–145ᵇ (1450–1500); 4, Royal 18.B.xxv, ff 91ᵃ–92ᵇ

late 15 cent); 5, Durham Cosins v.iii.5, ff 86ᵃ–88ᵇ (15 cent). (Om Bodl 21682=Douce 108.)
Editions. Liber Festiualis, Caxton, Westminster 1483, sig i iiᵇ–i iiiiᵃ (Conversion).
Erbe, EETSES 96.52 (Bodl 17680).

d. Speculum Sacerdotale.

MS. BM Addit 36791, ff 12ᵇ–14ᵃ (Conversion); ff 95ᵃ–96ᵃ (Commemoration; 15 cent).
Edition. Weatherly, EETS 200.21, 168 (sources, pp xxvii, xxviii, 257, 271; chiefly from LA and Belethus Rationale Div Offic).

e. 1438 GL.

MSS. 1, Harley 4775, chap 27, f 30ᵃ⁻ᵇ (Conversion); chap 83, ff 112ᵇ–116ᵇ (Commemoration); MLA roto 343, 1.60, 225; 2, BM Addit 35298, f 18ᵃ⁻ᵇ (Conversion); ff 66ᵇ–68ᵇ (Commemoration). (In Trinity Dublin 319, see Gerould S Leg, p 195.)
Sources. Cf Graesse LA, chap 28, p 133; chap 90, p 380.

f. Caxton GL.

Editions. Caxton GL, chap 61 (Conversion), chap 122 (Commemoration); Temple, 2.279; 4.27; rptd A Aspland, The GL, Holbein Soc Fac-Simile Reprints, London 1878 (Commemoration).
Sources. Cf de Vignay LD, ff 91ᵇ–92ᵇ; ff 185ᵃ–187ᵇ.

[222] PAUL, HERMIT (Jan 15, 342).

a. SEL; Brown-Robbins, no 2679.

MS. Bodl 2567 (Bodley 779), f 226ᵃ (ca 1400).
Edition. Zusatzleg 1889, p 386.
Sources. Zusatzleg 1889, p 386 (based on Jerome's Vita, see Acta SS); Rosenthal Vitae patrum, p 98 (LA as source).

b. 1438 GL.

MSS. 1, Harley 4775, chap 14, f 18ᵃ⁻ᵇ; MLA roto 343, 1.36; 2, BM Addit 35298, f 12ᵃ (lost Bodl 21947, Lambeth 72).
Sources. Cf Graesse LA, chap 15, p 94.

c. Caxton GL.

Editions. Caxton GL, chap 47; Temple, 2.204.
Sources. Cf de Vignay LD, ff 73ᵇ–75ᵃ.
Rosenthal Vitae patrum, p 69 and index based on LA supplemented by Jerome's Vita).
Jeremy Sister M, Caxton GL and de Vignai's LD, MS 8.103 (de Vignay direct source).

d. Caxton VP.

Edition. Caxton VP, pt 1, chap 34–35, ff 28ᵇ–32ᵃ.
Sources. Cf La vie des pères, pt 1, chap 34–35, ff 28ᵃ–31ᵃ.

[223] PAUL THE SIMPLE (March 7, ca 339).
Edition. Caxton VP, pt 1, chap 39, ff 53ª–54ª.
Sources. Cf La vie des pères, pt 1, chap 39, ff 46ᵇ–47ª.

PAUL OF ROME: see JOHN AND PAUL OF ROME.

[224] PAULA (PAULINE) (Jan 26, 404).

a. Vernon GL; Brown-Robbins, no *26.
MS. Bodl 3938 (Vernon), f 89ª col 1; approx 250 lines lost at beg (ca 1385).
Edition. AELeg 1878, p 3.
Textual Notes. Kölbing E, EStn 3.126.
Sources. AELeg 1878, p 3 (Graesse LA, chap 29, p 138 quoted); Rosenthal Vitae patrum, p 98 (comparison with LA).

b. 1438 GL.
MSS. 1, Harley 4775, chap 28, ff 30ᵇ–32ª; MLA roto 343, 1.61; 2, BM Addit 35298, ff 18ª–19ª.
Sources. Cf Graesse LA, chap 29, p 135.

c. Caxton GL.
Editions. Caxton GL, chap 62; Temple, 3.1.
Sources. Cf de Vignay LD, ff 92ᵇ–94ᵇ; Sister M Jeremy, MS 8.103 (correspondences with de Vignay noted).

d. Caxton VP.
Edition. Caxton VP, pt 1, chap 40, ff 51ª–62ª.
Selections. Dibdin Typo Antiq, 2.45 (on Paula's austerities).
Sources. Cf La vie des pères, pt 1, chap 40, ff 47ª–53ª.

PAULIN: see PAUL, HERMIT.

PAULINE: see PAULA.

[225] PELAGIA (MARGARET) OF ANTI-OCH, THE PENITENT (Oct 8, year?).

a. NHC; Brown-Robbins, no 1469.
MSS. 8 MSS.
Edition. Horstmann C, Die Evangelien-Geschichten der Homiliensammlung des MS Vernon, Arch 57.300 (Bodl 3938 [Vernon], f 208ᵇ col 2; ca 1385).
Sources and Literary Relations. Gerould G H, The North-English Homily Collection, 1902, p 83 (source probably Jacobus Diaconus; see Acta SS); Rosenthal Vitae patrum, p 101 (except for prologue follows VP).

b. ScL; Brown-Robbins, no 4271.
MS. Camb Univ Gg.2.6, ff 267ᵇ–271ᵇ (1400–50).

Editions. Horstmann ScL, 2.74; Metcalfe STS, 2.204 (notes 3.369).
Sources. Horstmann ScL, 2.74 (quotes Graesse LA, chap 150, p 674); Metcalfe STS, 3.370 (quotes LA; refers to Vincent of Beauvais Spec Hist 11.41); Rosenthal Vitae patrum, p 101 (LA source).

c. 1438 GL.
MSS. 1, Bodl 21947 (Douce 372), f 122ª; beg lost; 2, Harley 630, ff 308ᵇ–309ᵇ; 3, Harley 4775, chap 143, f 189ª⁻ᵇ; 4, BM Addit 35298, f 129ª. (Lost Egerton 876; om Lambeth 72.)
Sources. Cf Graesse LA, chap 150, p 674.

d. Caxton GL.
Editions. Caxton GL, chap 184; Temple, 5.234.
Sources. Cf de Vignay LD, ff 298ª–299ª.

e. Caxton VP.
Edition. Caxton VP, pt 1, chap 41, ff 62ª–65ᵇ.
Sources. Cf La vie des pères, pt 1, chap 41, ff 53ª–55ᵇ.

PELAGIEN(NE): see PELAGIA OF ANTI-OCH, THE PENITENT.

PELAGIEN(NE): see MARGARET CALLED PELAGIEN OR REPARATA.

PELAGIUS I, POPE. (Note: This pope's name heads the title of chap 172 in 1438 GL [Harley 4775] and of chap 228 in Caxton GL, but his legend does not follow. The subtitle in each case, "Gests of Lombardy" and "History of the Lombards," indicates the general content of these chapters, which include extracts from Paul the Deacon, Historia Lombardica; see Graesse LA, chap 181, p 824.)

PERES THE PREACHER: see PETER THE DOMINICAN.

PERNEL: see PETRONILLA.

[226] PERPETUA, FELICITY, AND SATURNINUS (Mar 6, 203).

(Note: Both versions list the Perpetua legend under Saturnine.)

a. 1438 GL.
MSS. 1, Harley 630, f 364, end lost; 2, Harley 4775, chap 165, f 233ª⁻ᵇ; MLA roto 343, 2.466; 3, BM Addit 35298, f 152ᵇ.
Sources. Cf Graesse LA, chap 173, p 797.

b. Caxton GL.
Editions. Caxton GL, chap 216; Temple, 7.30.
Sources. Cf de Vignay LD, ff 342ª–343ª.

[227] PETER, APOSTLE (64?).

(Note: The legend of Peter is told either in consecutive narrative, as in SEL, the unexpanded NHC, ScL, and Mirk Festial, or in three sections under the three feasts, (1) Cathedra Petri Jan 18, Feb 22, (2) Vita June 29, (3) Ad Vincula Aug 1, as in the expanded NHC, Speculum Sacerdotale, 1438 GL, and Caxton GL.)

a. SEL; Brown-Robbins, no 3046.
MSS. 15 MSS; add 16, Winchester Coll 33ª, ff 37ª–38ª (15 cent).
Editions. D'Evelyn and Mill, EETS 235.246 (Corp Christi Camb 145, ff 92ᵇ–99ª; early 14 cent).

b1. NHC unexpanded; Brown-Robbins, nos 3560, 3815, 1538.
MSS. Note: The material covered in these 3 Brown-Robbins nos forms one continuous narrative in the 4 MSS listed below; Brown-Robbins, no 3815 separates MS Camb Univ Dd.1.1 from the other 3 MSS only because it lacks their opening couplet.
1. Bodl 6923 (Ashm 42), ff 251ᵇ–257ᵇ (early 15 cent); 2, Camb Univ Dd.1.1, f 145ª; lines 1–2 om (1400–50); 3, Camb Univ Gg.5.31, f 144ᵇ (early 15 cent); 4, Huntington HM 129 (olim Phillipps 20420), f 213ᵇ (1400–50).
Edition. AELeg 1881, p 77 (Bodl 6923).

b2. NHC expanded; Brown-Robbins, nos 3043, 3044, 3045.
MSS. 1, Cotton Tib E.vii, f 243ᵇ, Vita; ff 251ª–252ª, Ad Vincula, Cathedra missing (ca 1400); 2, Harley 4196, f 145ª, Cathedra; f 152ᵇ, Vita; ff 166ª–167ᵇ, Ad Vincula (15 cent).
Editions. AELeg 1881, p 49, Cathedra; p 62, Vita; p 102, Ad Vincula (Harley 4196).
Sources (b1 and b2). Gerould G H, The North-English Homily Collection, 1902, p 98 (LA probable source of Simon Magus material).

c. ScL; Brown-Robbins, no 2748.
MS. Camb Univ Gg.2.6, ff 2ᵇ–9ª (1400–50).
Editions. Horstmann ScL, 1.5; Metcalfe STS, 1.7 (notes 3.10).
Sources. Horstmann ScL, 1.5 (quotes Graesse LA, chap 44, p 178; chap 89, p 368; Metcalfe STS, 3.10 (quotes LA; refers to indirect sources).

d. Mirk Festial.
MSS. Note: See ANDREW d *MSS* [25] above.
1, Bodl 17680 (Gough Eccl Top 4), ff 107ª–109ᵇ (1400–50). 2; Cotton Claud A.ii, ff 84ª–85ᵇ (ca 1420); 3, Harley 2247, ff 166ᵇ–

169ª (1450–1500); 4, Harley 2391, f 100ᵇ; end lost (1450–1500); 5, Royal 18.B.xxv, ff 108ᵇ–111ª (late 15 cent); 6, Durham Cosins v.iii.5, ff 111ª–114ª (late 15 cent). (Om Bodl 21634, 21682 = Douce 60, 108.)
Editions. Liber Festiualis, Caxton, Westminster 1483, sig l iiiª – l vª.
Erbe, EETSES 96.186 (Bodl 17680).

e. Speculum Sacerdotale.
MS. BM Addit 36791, ff 17ᵇ–20ª, Cathedra; ff 95ª–96ª, Vita; ff 100ᵇ–101ᵇ, Ad Vincula (15 cent).
Edition. Weatherly, EETS 200.29, 168, 178 (sources, pp xxvii, xxviii, xxix, 259, 271, 273; variety of parallels, chiefly LA, noted).

f. 1438 GL.
MSS. 1, Harley 4775, chap 43, ff 43ᵇ–45ª, Cathedra; chap 82, ff 108ᵇ–112ᵇ, Vita; chap 103, ff 135ª–136ᵇ, Ad Vincula; MLA roto 343, 1.87, 217; 2.270; 2, BM Addit 11565, f 88ᵇ, Cathedra, end lost; Ad Vincula lost; 3, BM Addit 35298, ff 24ᵇ–25ª, Cathedra; ff 62ᵇ–64ª, Vita; ff 91ª–92ᵇ, Ad Vincula. (In Trinity Dublin 319, feast not identified; lost Egerton 876, Cathedra.)
Sources. Cf Graesse LA, chap 44, p 178; chap 89, p 368; chap 110, p 455.

g. Caxton GL.
Editions. Caxton GL, chap 72, Cathedra; chap 121, Vita; chap 143, Ad Vincula; Temple, 3.50; 4.12, 154; rptd A Aspland, The GL, Holbein Soc Fac-Simile Reprints, London 1878 (Vita, Ad Vincula).
Sources. Cf de Vignay LD, ff 106ª–107ª, Cathedra; ff 181ª–185ª, Vita; ff 210ª–212ᵇ, Ad Vincula.

[228] PETER, DEACON, AND MARCELLINUS (June 2, 304).

a. 1438 GL.
MSS. 1, Harley 4775, chap 71, f 93ª; MLA roto 343, 1.183; 2, Lansdowne 350 frag; 3, BM Addit 35298, ff 45ᵇ–46ª (lost Bodl 21947, BM Addit 11565).
Sources. Cf Graesse LA, chap 79, p 343.

b. Caxton GL.
Editions. Caxton GL, chap 102; Temple, 3.210.
Sources. Cf de Vignay LD, f 139ª–ᵇ.

[229] PETER THE DOMINICAN (April 29, 1252).

a. SEL; Brown-Robbins, no 3042.
MSS. 14 MSS.
Edition. D'Evelyn and Mill, EETS 235.162 (Corp Christi Camb 145, f 61ᵇ; early 14 cent).

b. 1438 GL.
MSS. 1, Harley 4775, chap 58, ff 70ᵇ–71ᵇ; MLA roto 343, 1.141; 2, BM Addit 35298, ff 37ᵃ–38ᵇ (lost Bodl 21947).
Sources. Cf Graesse LA, chap 63, p 277.

c. Caxton GL.
Editions. Caxton GL, chap 89; Temple, 3.146.
Sources. Cf de Vignay LD, ff 129ᵃ–131ᵇ.

PETER OF MILAN: see PETER THE DOMINICAN.

PETER OF VERONA: see PETER THE DOMINICAN.

[230] PETRONILLA (May 31, 251?).
(Note: For Brown-Robbins, no 3446, a stanzaic version probably by Lydgate, see under Lydgate.)

a. SEL; Brown-Robbins, no 3049.
MSS. 1, Bodl 2567 (Bodley 779), f 304ᵃ (ca 1400); 2, Bodl 3938 (Vernon), f 31ᵇ col 2 (ca 1385); 3, Egerton 1993, f 157ᵇ (1400–50); 4, Stowe 949, f 154ᵃ (late 14 cent).

b. 1438 GL.
MSS. 1, Harley 4775, chap 70, f 92ᵇ; MLA roto 343, 1.183; 2, Lansdowne 350 frag; 3, BM Addit 35298, f 45ᵇ (lost Bodl 21947, BM Addit 11565).
Sources. Cf Graesse LA, chap 78, p 343.

c. Caxton GL.
Editions. Caxton GL, chap 78; Temple, 3.186.
Sources. Cf Graesse LA, chap 78, p 343.

PHILEMON: see APOLLONIUS.

[231] PHILIP, APOSTLE (May 1, 1st cent).
(Note: See also PHILIP AND JAMES THE LESS [232]).

a. ScL; Brown-Robbins, no 2652.
MSS. Camb Univ Gg.2.6, ff 61ᵇ–62ᵇ (1400–50).
Editions. Horstmann ScL. 1.85; Metcalfe STS, 1.176; notes 3.129.
Sources. Horstmann ScL, 1.85 (quotes Graesse LA, chap 65, p 292); Metcalfe STS, 3.131 (quotes LA; refers to other Latin accounts).

b. 1438 GL.
MSS. 1, Harley 4775, chap 59, f 74ᵇ; MLA roto 343, 1.149; 2, BM Addit 35298, f 38ᵇ (lost Bodl 21947).
Sources. Cf Graesse LA, chap 65, p 292.

c. Caxton GL.
Editions. Caxton GL, chap 90; Temple, 3.155.
Sources. Cf de Vignay LD, ff 131ᵇ–132ᵃ.

[232] PHILIP AND JAMES THE LESS, APOSTLES (May 1, 1st cent).

(Note: See also the separate legends JAMES THE LESS [138] and PHILIP [231].)

a. SEL; Brown-Robbins, no 3048.
MSS. 19 MSS; add 20, Winchester Coll 33ᵃ, ff 31ᵇ–33ᵃ (15 cent).
Editions. Horstmann, EETS 87.364 (Bodl 1486 [Laud Misc 108], ff 156ᵃ–157ᵃ; end 13 cent).
D'Evelyn and Mill, EETS 235.164 (Corp Christi Camb 145, ff 62ᵃ–63ᵃ; early 14 cent).

b. NHC expanded; Brown-Robbins, no 3047.
MSS. 1, Cotton Tib E.vii, f 240ᵇ (ca 1400); 2, Harley 4196, ff 148ᵃ–149ᵇ (15 cent).
Edition. AELeg 1881, p 52 (Harley 4196).

c. Mirk Festial.
MSS. Note: See ANDREW d *MSS* [25] above.
1, Bodl 17680 (Gough Eccl Top 4), ff 80ᵇ–82ᵇ (1400–50); 2, Cotton Claud A.ii, ff 61ᵇ–63ᵇ (ca 1420); 3, Harley 2247, ff 157ᵇ–159ᵇ (1450–1500); 4, Royal 18.B.xxv, ff 101ᵃ–103ᵃ (late 15 cent); 5, Durham Cosins v.iii.5, ff 101ᵃ–103ᵃ (15 cent).
Editions. Liber Festiualis, Caxton, Westminster 1483, sig k iiiiᵇ–viᵃ.
Erbe, EETSES 96.138 (Bodl 17680).

d. Speculum Sacerdotale.
MS. BM Addit 36791, ff 80ᵇ–81ᵃ (15 cent).
Edition. Weatherly, EETS 200.143.
Sources. Weatherly, EETS 200.xxviii, 269 (based on Ado Martyrol and LA).

[233] PILATE.

(Note: The story of Pilate forms part of the "romance" of Titus and Vespasian, see Romances I [107]; but only the couplet version of this account [Brown-Robbins, no 1881] includes the story of Pilate's early years; for the text see R Fischer, Vindicta Salvatoris, Arch 111.295, lines 673–788; J A Herbert, Titus and Vespasian, Roxb Club, London 1905, p 69, lines 1489–1607.)

a. SEL; Brown-Robbins, no 2755.
MSS. 12 MSS; add 13, Winchester Coll 33ᵃ, ff 12ᵃ–15ᵇ (15 cent).
Editions. Furnivall EEP, p 111 (Harley 2277, ff 229ᵃ–232ᵃ; ca 1300).
D'Evelyn and Mill, EETS 236.697 (Corp Christi Camb 145, ff 215ᵃ–217ᵇ; early 14 cent).
Sources. Day, EETS 188.xx (probable sources of details of Pilate's suicide).

b. 1438 GL.
MSS. 1, Bodl 21947 (Douce 372), f 40; end

lost; 2, Harley 4775, chap 50, ff 60ᵇ–61ᵇ; MLA roto 343, 1.121; 3, BM Addit 35298, ff 32ᵃ–33ᵃ (lost BM Addit 11565).

Note: Huntington HM 144, ff 21ᵃ–64ᵃ (15 cent) contains a series of chapters in prose covering the Passion and the Destruction of Jerusalem; ff 54ᵃ–56ᵃ give a life of Pilate not yet identified but similar to that in 1438 and Caxton GL.

Sources. Cf Graesse LA, chap 50, p 231.

c. Caxton GL.

Editions. Caxton GL, chap 10; Temple, 1.80.
Sources. Cf de Vignay LD, ff 20ᵃ–21ᵇ.
General Background. Creizenach W, Legenden und Sagen von Pilatus BGDSL 1.89 (development of characterization of Pilate; local legends and parallels).

Dobschütz E von, Christusbilder, Untersuchungen zur Christlichen Legende, Texte und Untersuchungen zur Geschichte der altchristlichen Literatur, III, Leipzig 1899, p 197 (detailed account and bibliography of Veronica-Pilate legend; p 305* SEL version referred to LA).

Bergau F, Untersuchungen über Quellen und Verfasser des mittelengl Reimgedicht: The Vengeaunce of Goddes Deth (The Bataile of Jerusalem), Königsberg 1901 (material on Pilate included in discussion of dependence of alliterative Titus and Vespasian [Brown-Robbins 1583] on couplet version [Brown-Robbins 1881]).

Day, EETS 188.xix, xxiv (refutation of Bergau).

[234] PITHIRION, ABBOT (April 8 [Whytford]).

Edition. Caxton VP, pt 1, chap 13, ff 17ᵇ–18ᵃ.
Sources. La vie des pères, pt 1, chap 13, f 20ᵃ.

PLACIDAS: see EUSTACE.

[235] POLYCARP, BISHOP OF SMYRNA (Jan 26, 155?).

Editions. Caxton GL, chap 230; Temple, 7.146.
Sources. Cf de Vignay LD, ff 71ᵇ–72ᵇ.

[236] POSTHUMIUS (PASTUMYEN) (date?).

(Note: Rosweyd [Migne PL, 73, col 437, note 1] states that some editions of VP give the name as Pasthumius; he suspects confusion of this Pasthumius with Pachomius; see [216] above.)

Edition. Caxton VP, pt 1, chap 49, ff 95ᵃ–99ᵃ (f 98 should be numbered 97; material is missing between ff 96ᵃ and 96ᵇ).

Sources. La vie des pères, pt 1, chap 49, ff 77ᵇ–80ᵃ.

[237] PRAXEDES (July 21, year?).

a. 1438 GL.

MSS. 1, Harley 4775, chap 88, f 120ᵃ; MLA roto 343, 1.140; 2, BM Addit 35298, f 70ᵇ.
Sources. Cf Graesse LA, chap 95, p 407.

b. Caxton GL.

Editions. Caxton GL, chap 128; Temple, 4.72. Note: AELeg 1881, p cxxxviii, om this legend from Table of Contents.
Sources. Cf de Vignay LD, f 188ᵃ.

[238] PRIMUS AND FELICIAN (June 9, ca 297).

a. 1438 GL.

MSS. 1, Harley 4775, chap 72, f 93ᵃ⁻ᵇ; MLA roto 343, 1.184; 2, BM Addit 35298, f 46ᵃ (lost Bodl 21947, BM Addit 11565).
Sources. Cf Graesse LA, chap 80, p 345.

b. Caxton GL.

Editions. Caxton GL, chap 103; Temple, 3.212.
Sources. Cf de Vignay LD, ff 139ᵇ–140ᵃ.

PROTASE: see GERVASE.

PROTUS: see EUGENIA.

PURNELE: see PETRONILLA.

[239] QUENTIN (Oct 31, year?).

a. SEL; Brown-Robbins, no 3050.

MSS. 12 MSS.
Edition. D'Evelyn and Mill, EETS 236.456 (Harley 2277, ff 142ᵃ–143ᵇ; ca 1300).

b. 1438 GL.

MSS. 1, Harley 4775, chap 152, ff 201ᵇ–202ᵃ; MLA roto 343, 2.403; 2, BM Addit 35298, f 136ᵃ (lost Bodl 21947; om Lambeth 72).
Sources. Cf Graesse LA, chap 160, p 711.

c. Caxton GL.

Editions. Caxton GL, chap 195; Temple, 6.81.
Sources. Cf de Vignay LD, f 311ᵇ.

[240] QUIRIAC (JUDAS), BISHOP (May 4, 133?).

(Note: See also [302] under Legends of the Cross.)

SEL; Brown-Robbins, no 3051.

MSS. 16 MSS; add 17, Bodl 1486 (Laud Misc 108), ff 26ᵇ–27ᵃ (end 13 cent); 18, Winchester Coll 33ᵃ, ff 44ᵇ–45ᵃ (15 cent).
Editions. Morris, EETS 46.58, 59 (Bodl 3938 [Vernon], f 30ᵃ, ca 1385; Bodl 6924 [Ashm 43], f 71ᵃ⁻ᵇ, 1425–50).

Horstmann, EETS 87.11 (Bodl 1486).

D'Evelyn and Mill, EETS 235.179 (Corp Christi Camb 145, f 67[b]; early 14 cent).

[241] QUIRINE AND JULITTA (June 16, 304?).

    a. 1438 GL.
MSS. 1, Bodl 21947 (Douce 372), chap 75; 2, Harley 4775, chap 75, f 95[a-b]; MLA roto 343, 1.188; 3, BM Addit 11565, f cx(114); beg lost; 4, BM Addit 35298, f 46[a].
Sources. Cf Graesse LA, chap 83, p 351.

    b. Caxton GL.
Editions. Caxton GL, chap 106; Temple, 3.225.
Sources. Note: Om de Vignay LD, 1480 edn; see Butler LA, p 25 for record of legend in MS BN fr 185, f 233[b].

[242] RADEGUND (Aug 13, 587).
Editions. The Lyfe of saynt Radegunde, Pynson, 1521? (STC, no 3507).
Brittain F, The Lyfe of Saynt Radegunde Edited from the Copy in Jesus College Library, Cambridge 1926 (204 stanzas in 26 sections, rime royal, except sect xxv in 8-line stanzas).
Date. Brittain, St Radegunde, pp vi, viii (ptd probably between 1508 and 1527; written ca 1500).
Author. Dibdin Typo Antiq, 2.599 (evidence for Bradshaw as author; see [291] below).
Hawkins E, Bradshaw's Life of Werburge, Chetham Soc 15, p xvii (repeats Dibdin).
Horstmann, EETS 88.vii (reports Dibdin's source of evidence now inaccessible).
Brittain, St Radegunde, p vi (accepts Bradshaw as author).
Sources. Brittain, St Radegunde, p xiii (based on Chronica of Antoninus of Florence, d 1459).
Bibliography. Brittain F, St Radegund Patroness of Jesus College Cambridge, Cambridge 1925, p 85.

[243] REMIGIUS, BISHOP OF RHEIMS (Oct 1 Life, Jan 13 Transl, ca 530).

    a. SEL Life; Brown-Robbins, no 3383.
MS. Bodl 2567 (Bodley 779), ff 229[b]–231[a] (ca 1400).
Edition. Zusatzleg 1889, p 394.
Sources. Zusatzleg 1889, p 394 note 1 (includes extract from Hincmar, Vita; see Acta SS Oct 1).

    b. 1438 GL Life and Translation.
MSS. 1, Harley 4775, Life chap 15, ff 18[b]–19[a]; Transl chap 140, ff 183[a]–184[a]; MLA roto 343, 1.37; 2.266; 2, BM Addit 35298,

Life f 12[b]; Transl ff 125[b]–126[a] (Life lost Bodl 21947, BM Addit 11565, Lambeth 72; Transl om Lambeth 72).
Sources. Cf Graesse LA, Life chap 16, p 95; Transl chap 147, p 659.

    c. Caxton GL.
Editions. Caxton GL, Life chap 48, Transl chap 181; Temple, 2.209; 5.208.
Sources. Cf de Vignay LD, Life f 75[a-b]; Transl ff 291[b]–292[a].

[244] RIGOBERT, ARCHBISHOP OF RHEIMS (Jan 4, ca 745).
Editions. Caxton GL, chap 239; Temple, 7.185.
Sources. Cf de Vignay LD, ff 396[b]–397[a].

[245] ROBERT OF KNARESBOROUGH (Sept 24, 1218?).

    Egerton couplets; Brown-Robbins, no 3677.
(Note: See also FOUNDING OF THE ORDER OF HOLY TRINITY (VI [17]).
MS. Egerton 3143, ff 39[b]–60[b] (late 15 cent).
Haslewood J, ed, The Metrical Life of St Robert of Knaresborough, Roxb Club, London 1824 (gives description and history of MS by F Douce now preserved on front flyleaf of modern binding of MS).
Flower R, Manuscripts from the Clumber Collection, BMQ 12.79 (provenance and contents).
Bazire, EETS 228.1 (full description; p 8 rpt of Douce note).
Editions. Haslewood, St Robert, p 1 (35 copies only).
Bazire, EETS 228.42 (crit B Colgrove, Durham Univ Jour 47.33.
D S Brewer, MLR 50.239; P Hodgson, REL ns 6.191; B J Timmer, YWES 34.87).
Language. Bazire J, The Vocabulary of the Metrical Life of St Robert of Knaresborough, Leeds SE 7–8.39 (words and meanings antedating OED quotations or not recorded).
Bazire, EETS 228.9 15 (apparently belongs to northern dialect area).
Date. Bazire, EETS 228.14 (on internal and linguistic evidence ca 1350–1450).
Authorship. Bazire, EETS 228.26 (possibly written by brother of Trinitarian house at Walknoll, Newcastle).
Sources and Literary Relations. Bazire, EETS 228.27 (related to Latin prose lives ptd pp 113, 129; see P G, AnBol 57.364).
Literary Criticism. Gerould S Leg, p 249.
Background. Clay R M, The Hermits and

Anchorites of England, London 1914, p 40.
Bibliography. Bazire, EETS 280.40.

[246] ROCK (Aug 16, ca 1378).
Editions. Caxton GL, chap 153; Temple, 5.1.
Sources. Butler LA, pp 83, 85 (not in Caxton's usual French or Latin sources).
Fliche A, Le problème de St Roch, AnBol 68.343 (relation of three earliest Latin lives including Caxton's possible source).
Jeremy Sister M, Caxton's Life of St Rocke, MLN 67.313 (probable source a text similar to Acta breviora in Acta SS, August, III.407).
Literary Relations. MLN 67.314 (characteristic features of Caxton's method of translation in whole GL as illustrated in his St Rocke).

RUFFIN: see WULFHAD AND RUFFIN.

SATURNINUS OF AFRICA: see PERPETUA.

[247] SATURNINUS AND SISINNIUS OF ROME (Nov 29, ca 309).
a. SEL; Brown-Robbins, no 87.
MS. Bodl 2567 (Bodley 779), ff 235ᵇ–236ᵇ; end lost (ca 1400).
Edition. Zusatzleg 1889, p 408.
Sources. Zusatzleg 1889, p 408 (refers to Acta S Marcelli papae; see Acta SS, Jan 16).

b. 1438 GL.
Note: Both 1438 and Caxton GL and their sources om Sisinnius.
MSS. 1, Harley 630, f 364; 2, Harley 4775, chap 165, f 233ᵃ; MLA roto 343, 2.466; 3, BM Addit 35298, f 152ᵇ (lost BM Addit 11565).
Sources. Cf Graesse LA, chap 173, p 798.

c. Caxton GL.
Editions. Caxton GL, chap 216; Temple, 7.30.
Sources. Cf de Vignay LD, f 342ᵃ⁻ᵇ

[248] SATURNINUS, BISHOP OF TOULOUSE (Nov 29, 3 cent?).
a. 1438 GL.
MSS. 1, Harley 630, f 152ᵇ; 2, Harley 4775, chap 165, f 233ᵃ; MLA roto 343, 2.466; 3, BM Addit 35298, f 152ᵇ.
Sources. Cf Graesse LA, chap 173, p 797.

b. Caxton GL.
Editions. Caxton GL, chap 216; Temple, 7.30.
Sources. Cf de Vignay LD, f 342ᵃ.

SAVINA: see SAVINIAN AND SAVINA.

[249] SAVINIAN AND SAVINA (Jan 29, year?).
a. Vernon GL; Brown-Robbins, no 3188.
MS. Bodl 3938 (Vernon), f 100ᵃ col 2 (ca 1385).
Edition. AELeg 1878, p 93.
Textual Notes. Kölbing E, EStn 3.128.
Sources. Cf Graesse LA, chap 127, p 576, rptd AELeg 1878, p 93.

b. 1438 GL.
Note: This version substitutes Navinien for Savinian.
MSS. 1, Bodl 21947 (Douce 372), ff 103–104; 2, Harley 4775, chap 117, ff 156ᵇ–157ᵇ; MLA roto 343, 2.313; 3, BM Addit 35298, ff 109ᵇ–110ᵃ.
Sources. Cf Graesse LA, chap 127, p 576.

c. Caxton GL.
Editions. Caxton GL, chap 161; Temple, 5.79.
Sources. Cf de Vignay LD, ff 258ᵃ–259ᵇ.

[250] SCHOLASTICA (Feb 10, 543).
a. SEL; Brown-Robbins, no 3052.
MSS. 15 MSS.
Editions. Horstmann, EETS 87.197 (Bodl 1486 [Laud Misc 108], f 96ᵃ⁻ᵇ; end 13 cent).
D'Evelyn and Mill, EETS 235.59 (Corp Christi Camb 145, f 22ᵃ⁻ᵇ; early 14 cent).

b. 1438 GL.
Note: In 1438 and Caxton GL, Scholastica is included in the legend of Benedict.
MSS. 1, Egerton 876, f 65; beg lost; 2, Harley 4775, chap 47, f 54ᵃ⁻ᵇ; MLA roto 343, 1.108; 3, BM Addit 35298, f 29ᵃ⁻ᵇ.
Sources. Cf Graesse LA, chap 49, p 212, de s Benedicto; see also Appendix, chap 198, p 885 for separate account of Scholastica.

c. Caxton GL.
Editions. Caxton GL, chap 78, s Benet; Temple, 3.92.
Sources. Cf de Vignay LD, f 117ᵃ.

[251] SEBASTIAN (Jan 20, 288?).
a. SEL; Brown-Robbins, nos 2895, 2896.
MSS. Note: See FABIAN a *MSS* [101] above. 18 MSS; add 19, Winchester Coll 33ᵃ, ff 50ᵃ–51ᵇ (15 cent).
Editions. Horstmann, EETS 87.178 (Bodl 1486 [Laud Misc 108], ff 88ᵇ–89ᵇ; end 13 cent).
D'Evelyn and Mill, EETS 235.16 (Corp Christi Camb 145, ff 6ᵇ–7ᵇ; early 14 cent).

b. 1438 GL.
MSS. 1, Harley 4775, chap 22, ff 22ᵃ–23ᵇ;

MLA roto 343, 1.44; 2, BM Addit 11565, f 48; 3, BM Addit 35298, f 14ᵃ⁻ᵇ (in Trinity Dublin 319; lost Lambeth 72).
Sources. Cf Graesse LA, chap 23, p 108.

c. Caxton GL.
Editions. Caxton GL, chap 56; Temple, 2.232.
Sources. Cf de Vignay LD, ff 80ᵇ–83ᵃ.
Butler LA, p 90 (etymology, incomplete in Caxton, not decisive of source).
Jeremy Sister M, Caxton's GL and de Vignai's LD, MS 8.104 (additions in Caxton from revised de Vignay).

[252] SECUNDUS OF ASTI (March 30 [Whytford], 119).
a. 1438 GL.
MSS. 1, Bodl 21947 (Douce 372), f 41ᵃ; 2, Harley 4775, chap 51, ff 61ᵃ–62ᵃ; MLA roto 343, 1.123; 3, BM Addit 35298, f 33ᵃ (lost BM Addit 11565).
Sources. Cf Graesse LA, chap 55, p 245.

b. Caxton GL.
Editions. Caxton GL, chap 81; Temple, 3.102.
Sources. Cf de Vignay LD, f 138ᵃ⁻ᵇ.

SENNAN: see ABDON.

[253] SEVEN BROTHERS, SONS OF FELICITY (July 10, 2 cent?).
a. 1438 GL.
MSS. 1, Harley 4775, chap 84, f 116ᵇ; MLA roto 343, 1.233; 2, BM Addit 35298, f 68ᵃ.
Sources. Cf Graesse LA, chap 91, p 396.

b. Caxton GL.
Editions. Caxton GL, chap 123; Temple, 4.46.
Sources. Cf de Vignay LD, f 188ᵃ.

[254] SEVEN SLEEPERS OF EPHESUS (July 27, year?).
a. SEL; Brown-Robbins, no 3091.
MSS. 8 MSS; add 9, Cotton Titus A.xxvi, ff 202ᵇ–204ᵇ, 1 fol lost (15 cent).
Edition. Huber M, Die Wanderlegende von den Siebenschläfern, Leipzig 1910, p 165 (Cotton Titus A.xxvi ptd as prose).
Textual Notes. Koch J, Chardry's Josaphaz, Set Dormanz und Petit Plet, Altfranz Bibl I, Heilbronn 1879, pp xvii, 190 (parallels between AN text and SEL Egerton 1993; Huber, Siebenschläfern, p 165 (quotes Koch's passages from Egerton 1993).
Sources. Huber, Siebenschläfern, p 168 (in general agrees with LA).

b. ScL; Brown-Robbins, no 415.
MS. Camb Univ Gg.2.6, ff 157ᵇ–163ᵃ (1400–50).

Editions. Horstmann ScL, 1.203; Metcalfe STS, 1.426; notes 3.265.
Sources. Horstmann ScL, 1.203 (quotes Graesse LA, chap 101, p 435); Metcalfe STS, 3.269 (quotes LA).

c. 1438 GL.
MSS. 1, Bodl 21947 (Douce 372), f 79; beg lost; 2, Egerton 876, f 169ᵇ; 3, Harley 630, f 213; 4, Harley 4775, chap 94, ff 128ᵇ–130ᵃ; MLA roto 343, 1.257; 5, BM Addit 11565, f 141ᵇ; 6, BM Addit 35298, ff 87ᵇ–88ᵇ.
Edition. Butler LA, p 107 (Harley 4775).
Sources. Cf Graesse LA, chap 101, p 435.

d. Caxton GL.
Editions. Caxton GL, chap 134; Temple, 4.120.
Sources. Cf de Vignay LD, ff 198ᵃ–200ᵃ.
General. Huber, Siebenschläfern, p 164 (material on Eng versions a, b, c).

SEVERIANUS, SERVERUS: see FOUR CROWNED MARTYRS.

SEXBURGA: see WERBURGA.

[255] SILVERIUS (ILLURIN), POPE (June 20, ca 537).
SEL; Brown-Robbins, no 1445.
MS. Bodl 2567 (Bodley 779), ff 225ᵃ–226ᵃ (ca 1400). Note: Initial S- is dropped only in title and line 1.
Edition. Zusatzleg 1889, p 384 (note 1 refers to Acta SS, June 20).

[256] SILVESTER I, POPE (Dec 31, 335).
a1. SEL; Brown-Robbins, no 3053.
MSS. 1, Bodl 1486 (Laud Misc 108), ff 166ᵃ–167ᵃ; om 308 lines on dispute with Jews (end 13 cent); 2, Trinity Camb 605, f 269ᵇ (early 15 cent); 3, Cotton Jul D.ix, ff 268ᵇ–271ᵇ (15 cent); 4, Egerton 2810, f 164ᵇ (14 cent); 5 Lambeth 223, f 290ᵇ (end 14 cent).
Edition. Horstmann, EETS 87.391 (Bodl 1486).

a2. SEL variant; Brown-Robbins, no 318.
MS. Bodl 2567 (Bodley 779), ff 227ᵃ–229ᵇ; only incident of dispute with Jews (ca 1400).
Edition. Zusatzleg 1889, p 388 (note 1, ultimate source Mombritius, Sanctuarium II.283).

b. 1438 GL.
Note: 1438 and Caxton GL combine material of SEL 1, 2.
MSS. 1, BM Addit 11565, f 40; 2, BM Addit 35298, ff 9ᵇ–11ᵃ (lost Bodl 21947, Harley 4775, Lambeth 72).

Sources. Cf Graesse LA, chap 12, p 70.

c. Caxton GL.
Editions. Caxton GL, chap 46; Temple, 2.197.
Sources. Cf de Vignay LD, ff 72ª–73ᵇ.

[257] SIMEON STYLITES (Jan 5, 459).

a. Caxton GL.
Editions. Caxton GL, chap 229, Temple, 7.139.
Sources. Cf de Vignay LD, ff 368ª–370ª.

b. Caxton VP.
Edition. Caxton VP, pt 1, chap 46, ff 78ª–82ᵇ.
Sources. Cf La vie des pères, pt 1, chap 46, ff 64ᵇ–67ᵇ.
General Background. Delehaye H, Les Saints Stylites, Subsidia hagiographica 14, Brussels 1923.

[258] SIMON AND JUDE, APOSTLES (Oct 28, 1st cent).

a. SEL; Brown-Robbins, no 3055.
MSS. 15 MSS.
Edition. D'Evelyn and Mill, EETS 236.448 (Corp Christi Camb 145, ff 166ᵇ–168ᵇ; early 14 cent; completed by Harley 2277, f 142ª; ca 1300).

b. NHC; Brown-Robbins, no 3054.
MSS. 1, Cotton Tib E.vii, ff 266ª–268ª (ca 1400); 2, Harley 4196, ff 181ᵇ–183ᵇ (15 cent).
Edition. AELeg 1881, p 138 (Harley 4196).

c. ScL; Brown-Robbins, no 2655.
MS. Camb Univ Gg.2.6, ff 73ª–78ᵇ (1400–50).
Editions. Horstmann ScL, 1.100; Metcalfe STS 1.208; notes 3.150.
Sources. Horstmann ScL, 1.100 (quotes Graesse LA, chap 159, p 705); Metcalfe STS, 3.152 (quotes LA with supplementary sources).

d. Mirk Festial.
MSS. Note: See ANDREW d MSS [25] above. 1, Bodl 17680 (Gough Eccl Top 4), ff 149ᵇ–151ᵇ (1400–50); 2, Cotton Claud A.ii, ff 110ª–111ª (ca 1420); 3, Harley 2247, ff 199ª–202ª (1450–1500); 4, Royal 18.B.xxv, ff 135ª–137ª (late 15 cent); 5, Durham Cosins v.iii.5, ff 145ª–146ᵇ (15 cent) (om Bodl 21634, 21682 = Douce 60, 108).
Editions. Liber Festiuialis, Caxton, Westminster 1483, sig o vª–o viª (STC, no 17957).
Erbe, EETSES 96.263 (Bodl 17680).

e. Speculum Sacerdotale.
MS. BM Addit 36791, ff 122ª–123ª (15 cent).
Edition. Weatherly, EETS 200.216 (probably from LA, pp xxix, 276).

f. 1438 GL.
MSS 1 Bodl 21947 (Douce 372), f 128; beg

lost; 2, Harley 4775, chap 153, ff 199ᵇ–201ᵇ; MLA roto 343, 2.399; 3, BM Addit 35298, ff 135ª–136ª.
Sources. Cf Graesse LA, chap 159, p 705.

g. Caxton GL.
Editions. Caxton GL, chap 194; Temple, 6.72.
Sources. Cf de Vignay LD, ff 311ª–313ᵇ.

[259] SIMPLICIUS AND FAUSTINUS (July 29, 304?).

a. SEL; Brown-Robbins, no 3814.
MS. Bodl 2567 (Bodley 779), ff 238ª–239ª (ca 1400).
Edition. Zusatzleg 1889, p 414 (note 1, Engl is fuller than account in Acta SS July 29).

b. 1438 GL.
MSS. 1, Harley 4775, chap 97, f 131ᵇ; MLA roto 343, 1.263; 2, BM Addit 35298, f 89ª.
Sources. Cf Graesse LA, chap 104, p 443.

c. Caxton GL.
Editions. Caxton GL, chap 137; Temple, 4.133.
Sources. Cf de Vignay LD, f 200ª⁻ᵇ.

[260] SIXTUS II, POPE, FELICISSIMUS, AGAPITUS (Aug 6, 258).

a. NHC; Brown-Robbins, no 1584.
MSS. 1, Cotton Tib E.vii, ff 252ª–253ª (ca 1400); 2, Harley 4196, ff 167ᵇ–168 (15 cent).
Edition. AELeg 1881, p 105 (Harley 4196).
Sources. Retzlaff O, Untersuchungen über den nordenglischen Legendencyclus der MSS Harl 4196 und Cotton Tib E.vii, Berlin 1888, p 27 (suggests source more detailed than LA, chap 114).

b. 1438 GL.
MS. BM Addit 35298, f 95ª (lost Bodl 21947, Harley 4775, BM Addit 11565; om Lambeth 72).
Sources. Cf Graesse LA, chap 114, p 483.

c. Caxton GL.
Editions. Caxton GL, chap 147; Temple, 4.200.
Sources. Cf de Vignay LD, f 221ᵇ.

SMARAGDUS: see CYRIACUS AND COMPANIONS.

[261] SOTHER, POPE (April 22, 174).

SEL; Brown-Robbins, no 3202.
MS. Bodl 2567 (Bodley 779), ff 231ᵇ–232ª (ca 1400).
Edition. Zusatzleg 1889, p 400.

[262] STEPHEN, FIRST MARTYR (Aug 3 Invention, Dec 26 Life, ca 34).

(Note: For the ballad of St Stephen [Brown-Robbins, no 3058] see under Ballads.)

a. SEL; Brown-Robbins, no 3059.
MSS. 18 MSS.
Edition. D'Evelyn and Mill, EETS 236.590 (Corp Christi Camb 145, ff 172ª–173ᵇ; early 14 cent).

b. NHC; Brown-Robbins, no 3056.
MS. Harley 4196, ff 17ª–20ª (early 15 cent).
Edition. AELeg 1881, p 28.

c. Mirk Festial.
MSS. Note: See ANDREW d *MSS* [25] above.
1, Bodl 17680 (Gough Eccl Top 4), ff 15ᵇ–18ª (1400–50); 2, Cotton Claud A.ii, ff 16ᵇ–18ᵇ (ca 1420); 3, Harley 2247, ff 129ᵇ–133ª (1450–1500); 4, Royal 18.B.xxv, ff 13ᵇ, 62ª⁻ᵇ (late 15 cent); 5, Durham Cosins v.iii.5, ff 69ª–71ᵇ (15 cent).
Editions. Liber Festiualis, Caxton, Westminster 1483, sig g 6ᵇ–g 8ᵇ (STC, no 17957).
Erbe, EETSES 96.26 (Bodl 17680).

d. Speculum Sacerdotale.
MS. BM Addit 36791, ff 6ª–7ª (15 cent).
Edition. Weatherly, EETS 200.9 (refers to Biblical account, pp xxvii, 256).

e. 1438 GL.
MSS. 1, Harley 4775, Life chap 7, ff 14ᵇ–16ª; Invention chap 104, f 136ᵇ, incompl; MLA roto 343, 1.29; 2.273; 2, BM Addit 35298, Life chap 7, ff 6ᵇ–7ª; Invention ff 92ᵇ–93ª (Life lost Bodl 21947, Lambeth 72; Invention lost BM Addit 11565).
Sources. Cf Graesse LA, chap 8, p 49; chap 112, p 461.

f. Caxton GL.
Editions. Caxton GL, Life chap 42, Invention chap 145; Temple, 2.152, 4.165.
Sources. Cf de Vignay LD, Life ff 64ᵇ–66ᵇ, Invention ff 212ᵇ–214ᵇ.

[263] STEPHEN I, POPE (Aug 2, 257).
Editions. Caxton GL, chap 144; Temple, 4.164; rptd A Aspland, The GL, Holbein Soc Fac-Simile Reprints, London 1878.
Sources. Cf de Vignay LD, f 212ᵇ.

[264] SWITHUN, BISHOP OF WINCHESTER (July 15, 862).

a. SEL; Brown-Robbins, no 3060.
MSS. 11 MSS.
Editions. Earle J, Gloucester Fragments I, London 1861, p 78 (Bodl 1596 [Laud Misc 463], f 63ª; beg 15 cent).

Furnivall EEP, p 43 (Harley 2277, ff 78ª–80ª; ca 1300).
D'Evelyn and Mill, EETS 235.274 (Corp Christi Camb 145, ff 102ᵇ–104ᵇ; early 14 cent).

b. 1438 GL.
MSS. 1, BM Addit 11565, f xxxii(55); 2, BM Addit 35298, f 78ᵇ; 3, Lambeth 72, chap 109, f 227ᵇ (om Egerton 876, Harley 630, Harley 4775).
Edition. Butler LA, p 103 (BM Addit 11565).

c. Caxton GL.
Editions. Caxton GL, chap 125; Temple, 4.53.
Sources. Butler LA, p 83 (claims BM Addit 11565 as source).

SYMONDE: see SIMON AND JUDE.

[265] SYMPHORIAN (Aug 22, 2 or 3 cent).

a. 1438 GL.
MSS. 1, Harley 4775, chap 114, f 151ª; MLA roto 343, 2.300; 2, BM Addit 35298, f 105ᵇ (om Lambeth 72).
Sources. Cf Graesse LA, chap 122, p 539.

b. Caxton GL.
Editions. Caxton GL, chap 156; Temple, 5.30.
Sources. Cf de Vignay LD, f 243ª⁻ᵇ.

[266] SYRUS, ABBOT, AND COMPANIONS (Feb 26 [Whytford]).
Edition. Caxton VP, pt 1, chap 10.
Sources. La vie des pères, pt 1, chap 10, f 18ª⁻ᵇ.

TAISIS, THADEE: see THAIS.

TECLA: see THECLA.

[267] TEILO, BISHOP (Feb 9, 6 cent).

SEL; Brown-Robbins, no 3061.
MS. Egerton 2810, f 94ª (14 cent).

TELYOU: see TEILO.

TEOFLE: see THEOPHILUS.

THADDEUS: see SIMON AND JUDE.

[268] THAIS (Oct 8, year?).

a. NHC; Brown-Robbins, nos 40, 3178, 3547.
MSS. Note: Whether it appears in expanded or unexpanded texts of the NHC, this form of the Thais legend should be considered as a single version. 15 MSS.
Editions. Horstmann C, Die Evangelien-Geschichten der Homiliensammlung des

MS Vernon, Arch 57.279 (Brown-Robbins, no 40; Bodl 3938 [Vernon], f 195ᵇ; ca 1385).

Rosenthal Vitae patrum, p 159 (Brown-Robbins, no 3178; Harley 4196, ff 96ᵇ–97ᵃ; 15 cent).

Rosenthal Vitae patrum, p 158 (Brown-Robbins, no 3547; BM Addit 38010, ff 96ᵃ–97ᵃ; mid 15 cent).

Sources. Gerould G H, The North-English Homily Collection, Lancaster Pa 1902, p 70 (ultimate source VP, see Migne PL, 72.661).

b. ScL; Brown-Robbins, no 2628.

MS. Camb Univ Gg.2.6, ff 271ᵇ–274ᵃ (1400–50).

Editions. Horstmann ScL, 2.79; Metcalfe STS, 2.215; notes 3.373.

Sources. Horstmann ScL, 2.79 (quotes Graesse LA, chap 152, p 677, noting variations from VP); Metcalfe STS, 3.374 (quotes LA).

c. Alphabet of Tales.

MS. BM Addit 25719, no 3 (mid 15 cent). Herbert, p 440.

Edition. Banks, EETS 126.2, no 3.

Sources. Herbert, p 423 (direct Latin source Alphabetum Narrationum probably by Arnold of Liège).

d. Jacob's Well.

MS. Salisbury Cath 103, f 12ᵃ⁻ᵇ (1445–55).

Edition. Brandeis, EETS 115, pt 1, p 22.

Date. Brandeis, EETS 115, pt 1, p x (date of MS 1445–55; of text 1400–50).

Authorship. Brandeis, EETS 115, pt 1, p ix (unidentified churchman).

Sources and Literary Relations. Rosenthal Vitae patrum, p 104 (notes variations from other versions).

e. 1438 GL.

MSS. 1, Bodl 21947 (Douce 372), f 122 fragment; 2, Egerton 876, f 246; beg lost; 3, Harley 4775, chap 145, ff 190ᵃ–191ᵃ; MLA roto 343, 2.380; 4, BM Addit 35298, ff 129ᵇ–130ᵃ.

Sources. Cf Graesse LA, chap 152, p 677.

f. Caxton GL.

Editions. Caxton GL, chap 186; Temple, 5.240.

Sources. Cf de Vignay LD, ff 229ᵇ–300ᵃ.

[269] THECLA OF ICONIUM (Sept 23, 1st cent?).

ScL; Brown-Robbins, no 4003.

MS. Camb Univ Gg.2.6, ff 376ᵃ–379ᵇ (1400–50).

Editions. Horstmann ScL, 2.193; Metcalfe STS, 2.432; notes 3.460.

Sources. Horstmann ScL, 2.193 (notes Acta Pauli as ultimate source).

Metcalfe STS, 3.461 (refers to Acta Pauli).

[270] THEODORA OF ALEXANDRIA (Sept 11, year?).

a. Vernon GL; Brown-Robbins, no 421.

MS. Bodl 3938 (Vernon), f 91ᵇ col 1 (ca 1385).

Edition. AELeg 1878, p 35.

Sources. AELeg 1878, p 35 (quotes Graesse LA, chap 92, p 397).

b. ScL; Brown-Robbins, no 2151.

MS. Camb Univ Gg.2.6, ff 227ᵃ–236ᵇ (1400–50).

Editions. Horstmann ScL, 2.27; Metcalfe STS, 2.99; notes 3.337.

Sources. Horstmann ScL, 2.27 (quotes Graesse LA, chap 92, p 397 as much shortened source).

Metcalfe STS, 3.337 (notes author had longer version than that in LA).

c. Alphabet of Tales.

MS. BM Addit 25719, no 599 (mid 15 cent). Herbert, p 440.

Edition. Banks, EETS 127.397, no 599.

Sources. Herbert, p 423 (Latin Alphabetum Narr direct source).

d. 1438 GL.

MSS. 1, Harley 4775, chap 85, ff 116ᵇ–117ᵇ; MLA roto 343, 1.233; 2, BM Addit 35298, ff 67ᵇ–68ᵃ.

Sources. Cf Graesse LA, chap 92, p 397.

e. Caxton GL.

Editions. Caxton GL, chap 124; Temple, 4.48.

Sources. Note: Legend om in de Vignay LD, 1480 edn, but is in MS copies; see Butler LA, p 89.

[271] THEODORE TIRO (Nov 9, ca 306).

a. 1438 GL.

MSS. 1, Bodl 21947 (Douce 372), f 135; beg lost; 2, Egerton 876, f 270 fragment; 3, Harley 4775, chap 157, ff 212ᵇ–213ᵃ; MLA roto 343, 2.423; 4, BM Addit 35298, f 141ᵃ⁻ᵇ.

Sources. Cf Graesse LA, chap 165, p 740.

b. Caxton GL.

Editions. Caxton GL, chap 202; Temple, 6.140.

Sources. Cf de Vignay LD, f 325ᵃ⁻ᵇ.

THEODOSIUS I: see AMBROSE.

[272] THEON, ABBOT (April 23 [Whytford], year?).

Edition. Caxton VP, pt 1, chap 6, ff 9ᵇ–10ᵃ.

Sources. Cf La vie des pères, pt 1, chap 6, f 13[a–b].

[273] THEOPHILUS (Feb 4, year?).

　　a. SEL; Brown-Robbins, no 3266.
MSS. 13 MSS.
Editions. Horstmann, EETS 87.288 (Bodl 1486 [Laud Misc 108], ff 128[a]–130[a]; end 13 cent).
D'Evelyn and Mill, EETS 235.221 (Corp Christi Camb 145, ff 83[a]–89[b]; with 6 Mary miracles; early 14 cent).

　　b. NHC; Brown-Robbins, no 25.
MSS. 14 MSS.
Editions. Kölbing E, Die jüngere englische Fassung der Theophilussage, EStn 1.38 (Bodl 3938 [Vernon], f 203[b] col 3; ca 1385; Harley 4196, ff 113[a]–117[b], 15 cent).
Horstmann C, Die Evangelien-Geschichten der Homiliensammlung des MS Vernon, Arch 57.290 (Bodl 3938 [Vernon] om lines 687–726 of Kölbing text).
Textual Notes. Kölbing E, Nachtrag zur Theophilussage, EStn 1.186 (disclaimer of attempt at critical text in his edn).
Zupitza J, ZfDA 22.248 (corrections of Kölbing, EStn 1.38).
Language. EStn 1.33 (linguistic evidence for Northern origin).
Sources and Literary Relations. Kölbing E, Über die englischen Fassung der Theophilussage, Beiträge z vergleichenden Geschichte der romantischen Poesie u Prosa des MA, Breslau 1876, p 1 (similarity of treatment noted in NHC and German and Icelandic versions).
EStn 1.16 (relation of Latin prose and French verse versions).

　　c. Stanzaic; Brown-Robbins, no 1883.
MS. Bodl 14716 (Rawl poet 225), ff 11[a]–15 (1450–1500).
Editions. Heuser W, Eine neue mittelenglische Version der Theophilussage, EStn 32.5; see correction EStn 33.335 (crit G H Gerould, MLN 18.145).
Boyd B M, Middle English Miracles of the Virgin: Independent Tales in Verse, diss Columbia 1955, Univ Microf 15622, p 75; see DA 16.334.
Textual Notes. Holthausen F, Zu mittelenglischen Romanzen, Angl 43.313.
Sources and Literary Relations. Boyd, ME Miracles of the Virgin, p 66 (tail-rime romance rather than miracle play as model).
Boyd B M, The Rawlinson Version of Theophilus, MLN 71.556 (restatement of romantic conventions in c version).

　　d. 1438 GL.
Note: In both 1438 and Caxton GL the legend of Theophilus is included in Nativity of Our Lady.
MSS. 1, Bodl 21947 (Douce 372), chap 23, f 37; 2, Harley 4775, chap 122, f 162[b]; MLA roto 343, 2.325; 3, BM Addit 11565 twice: f xxx(54) followed by Mary miracles; f clxx(164) under Nativity; see Butler LA, p 66; 4, BM Addit 35298 twice: f 78[a–b] no other Mary miracles; f 113[a–b] under Nativity; 5, Lambeth 72, chap 108, f 224[b] with 6 Mary miracles: presumably under Nativity, see Butler LA, p 152.
Sources. Cf Graesse LA, chap 113 (Nativity), p 593.

　　e. Caxton GL.
Editions. Caxton GL, chap 165 (Nativity); Temple, 5.109.
Sources. Cf de Vignay LD, ff 265[b]–266[a].
General Background. Gerould G H, The North-English Homily Collection, Lancaster Pa 1902, p 75.
Plenzat K, Die Theophuslegende in den Dichtungen des Mittelalters, Germanische Studien 43, Berlin 1926 (English versions a,b,c discussed p 75; bibliography p 253; crit W Golther, Euphorion 28.624; R Petsch, ZfDP 53.406).

[274] THOMAS, APOSTLE (Dec 21, 1st cent).

　　a. SEL; Brown-Robbins, no 3063.
MSS. 17 MSS.
Editions. Horstmann, EETS 87.376 (Bodl 1486 [Laud Misc 108], ff 161[a]–165[b]; end 13 cent).
D'Evelyn and Mill, EETS 236.571 (Harley 2277, ff 185[a]–188[b]; ca 1300; completed by Corp Christi Camb 145, ff 169[a]–170[b]; early 14 cent).

　　b. NHC expanded; Brown-Robbins, no 3062.
MSS. 1, Cotton Tib E.vii, f 279[b] (ca 1400); 2, Harley 4196, ff 139[b]–140[b] (early 15 cent).
Edition. AELeg 1881, p 19 (Harley 4196).

　　c. ScL; Brown-Robbins, no 2653.
MS. Camb Univ Gg.2.6, ff 44[b]–52[a] (1400–50).
Editions. Horstmann ScL, 1.62; Metcalfe STS, 1.129; notes 3.98.
Sources. Horstmann ScL, 1.62 (quotes Graesse LA, chap 5, p 32).
Metcalfe STS, 3.99 (quotes LA; refers to other Latin versions).

　　d. Mirk Festial.
MSS. Note: See also ANDREW d *MSS* [25] above.

1, Bodl 17680 (Gough Eccl Top 4), ff 15ᵇ–18ᵃ (1400–50); 2, Cotton Claud A.ii, ff 11ᵃ–13ᵃ (ca 1420); 3, Harley 2247, ff 140ᵇ–143ᵃ (1450–1500); 4, Royal 18.B.xxv, ff 88ᵇ–91ᵃ (late 15 cent); 5, Durham Cosins v.iii.5, ff 63ᵃ–65ᵇ (15 cent).
Editions. Liber Festiualis, Caxton 1483, sig g iiᵇ – g ivᵇ.
Erbe, EETSES 96.18 (Bodl 17680).

e. Speculum Sacerdotale.
MS. BM Addit 36791, ff 141ᵇ–142ᵇ (15 cent).
Edition. Weatherly, EETS 200.251 (chief sources Gospel of St John, LA, pp xxix, 280).

f. 1438 GL.
MSS. 1, Egerton 876, f 7ᵃ fragment; 2, Harley 4775, chap 4, ff 9ᵃ–11ᵃ; MLA roto 343, 1.18; 3, BM Addit 11565, f 39ᵃ; beg lost; 4, BM Addit 35298, ff 4ᵇ–5ᵃ (lost Bodl 21947, Lambeth 72).
Sources. Cf Graesse LA, chap 5, p 32.

g. Caxton GL.
Editions. Caxton GL, chap 39; Temple, 2.138.
Sources. Cf de Vignay LD, ff 61ᵃ–63ᵇ.
[275] THOMAS AQUINAS (March 7, 1274).
Editions. Caxton GL, chap 232; Temple, 7.154.
Sources. Cf de Vignay LD, ff 400ᵃ–402ᵃ.

[276] THOMAS BECKET, ARCHBISHOP OF CANTERBURY (Dec 29, 1170).
(Note: For the prophecies ascribed to Thomas Becket see under Works on Contemporary Conditions.)

a. SEL; Brown-Robbins, nos 728, 907, 3064, 4171.
MSS. Note: The classification of SEL MSS as Laud and Harley versions of the Legend is misleading. The Legend of Thomas is practically the same text whatever introductory material precedes it. Only the story of Gilbert, Thomas's father, offers somewhat variant texts; see EETS 244.20. In summary the total number of MSS of the Thomas Legend—20 if the fragmentary BM Addit 24078 (under Brown-Robbins, no 907) is omitted—divides as follows: Harley Gilbert, 13 MSS; Laud Gilbert, 4 MSS; neutral omitting Gilbert story, 3 MSS. The regrouping under Brown-Robbins nos is as follows:
Brown-Robbins, no 728; neutral texts om Gilbert story.
1, Bodl 1596 (Laud Misc 463), f 141ᵃ (early 15 cent); 2, Bodl 29430 (MS Add C.220), ff 8ᵇ–18ᵇ; end lost (early 15 cent); 3, Camb Univ Add 3039, f 79ᵇ.

Brown-Robbins, no 907; Harley Gilbert.
12 MSS; add 13, Bodl 6924 (Ashmole 43), ff 228ᵇ–260ᵃ (1325–50); 14, Cotton Julius D.ix, ff 232ᵇ–266ᵇ (15 cent).
Brown-Robbins, no 3064. Note: The Translation of Thomas follows the Legend directly except in Corp Christi Camb 145 and Pepys 2344.
10 MSS; add 11, Bodl 1596 (Laud Misc 463) (beg 15 cent); 12, Bodl 6924 (Ashmole 43), ff 259ᵃ–260ᵃ (1325–50); 13, Camb Univ Add 3039; 14, Corp Christi Camb 145 c¹, ff 217ᵇ–218ᵃ (early 14 cent); 15, Cotton Julius D.ix, ff 265ᵇ–266ᵇ (15 cent); 16, Lambeth 223 (end 14 cent).
Brown-Robbins, no 4171; Laud Gilbert.
1, Bodl 1486 (Laud Misc 108), ff 61ᵃ–88ᵃ (end 13 cent); 2, Bodl 3938 (Vernon), ff 73ᵃ col 2–80ᵇ; end lost (ca 1385); 3, Lambeth 223, f 256ᵇ (end 14 cent); 4, Stowe 949, f 110ᵇ (late 14 cent) under different opening, see Brown-Robbins, no 728.
Thiemke H, Die ME Thomas Beket-legende des Gloucesterlegendar, Palaes 131.i (interrelation of 13 MSS).
D'Evelyn, EETS 244.20 (Laud and Harley texts).
Editions. Black W H, Percy Soc xix, London 1845 (Harley 2277).
Horstmann, EETS 87.106 (Bodl 1486).
Thiemke, Beket-legende, p 14 (critical edn based on Bodl 6924 with collation of 12 MSS; crit K Brunner, Arch 140.270; W Fischer, EStn 54.408; G Hübener, DLz 42.276; M Weyrauch, LZ 74.385).
D'Evelyn and Mill, EETS 236.610 (Corp Christi Camb 145).
Selections. AESpr, p 177 (Harley 227, lines 1787–2398 Martyrdom and Translation, from Black, Percy Soc xix).
Thiemke, Beket-legende, p 1 (Bodl 1486, lines 1–210 Gilbert story).
Funke O, A ME Reader, Bibliotheca Anglicana 7, Bern 1944, p 56 (Bodl 6924, lines 2103–2190 Martyrdom from Thiemke, Beket-legende).
Kaiser R, Alt- und Mittelenglische Anthologie, 2nd edn, Berlin 1955, p 328 (Bodl 1486, 4 selections, 314 lines from Horstmann, EETS 87, pp 117, 157, 161, 163; rptd English edn, Medieval English, Berlin 1958, p 341).
Modernizations. Weston J L, The Chief ME Poets, Boston 1914, p 41 (Martyrdom and Translation based on AESpr, p 177).
Authorship. Ellmer W, Über die Quellen der Reimchronik Robert's von Gloucester, Angl 10.308 (argument against Robert's authorship).

Thiemke, Beket-legende, p liii (claims for and against Robert of Gloucester judged indecisive).

Sources. Thiemke, Beket-legende, p x (evidence for Latin compilation Quadrilogus as direct source).

    b. NHC; Brown-Robbins, no 2639.

MSS. Harley 4196, ff 23ᵇ–24ᵃ; fol missing after line 70 (15 cent); for exemplum Dream of St Thomas's Mother in NHC see Brown-Robbins, nos 2930, 3299.

Edition. AELeg 1881, p 42.

    c. Quatrains and couplets; Brown-Robbins, no 1756.

MS. Bodl 14716 (Rawl poet 225), ff 53ᵃ–84ᵇ; 93**–94 (1450–1500).

Selections. Brown P A, The Development of the Legend of Thomas Becket, Philadelphia 1930, p 262 (lines 1–248, story of Thomas's parents).

Sources and Literary Relations. Brown, Thomas Becket, pp 28, 51 (appraisal of various accounts of Thomas's parents).

    d. Mirk Festial.

MSS. Note: See ANDREW d *MSS* [25] above. 1, Bodl 17680 (Gough Eccl Top 4), Life ff 22ᵇ–27ᵃ; Transl ff 112ᵃ–114ᵃ (1400–50); 2, Camb Univ Ff.2.38, after f 35 (ca 1420–30); see AELeg 1881, p cxiii note 1; 3, Cotton Claud A.ii, Life ff 22ᵇ–26ᵇ; Transl ff 87ᵃ–88ᵇ (ca 1420); 4, Harley 2247, Life ff 22ᵃ–25ᵃ; Transl note only f 169ᵃ (1450–1500); 5, Royal 18.B.xxv, Life ff 5ᵇ–ᵃ; Transl om (late 15 cent); 6, Durham Cosins v.iii.5, Life ff 75ᵇ–80ᵇ; Transl ff 114ᵃ–116ᵇ (15 cent).

Editions. Liber Festiualis, Caxton, 1483, Life sig h 4ᵃ–6ᵇ, Transl sig 1 5ᵇ–7ᵃ (STC, no 17957).

Erbe, EETSES 96, Life p 98, Transl p 196 (Bodl 17680).

    e. Speculum Sacerdotale.

MS. BM Addit 36791, Life ff 7ᵇ–9ᵇ (15 cent).

Edition. Weatherly, EETS 200.13 (sources undetermined, pp xxvii, 256).

    f. 1438 GL.

MSS. 1, BM Addit 11565, ff 45ᵇ–52ᵇ; end lost; 2, BM Addit 35298, f 9ᵃ–ᵇ (lost Harley 4775, Lambeth 72).

Selections. Butler LA, p 105 (BM Addit 11565, f 45ᵇ, story of parents through Thomas's appointment as Chancellor, with omissions).

Brown, Thomas Becket, p 271 (BM Addit 11565, ff 45ᵇ–46ᵃ, story of parents through Gilbert's second return from Holy Land).

Sources. Butler LA, p 65 (version in BM Addit 11565, with Gilbert story, not from LA or de Vignay).

    g. Caxton GL.

Editions. Caxton GL, Life chap 45; Transl chap 126; Temple, 2.182; 4.56; rptd Pynson 1520? (STC, no 23954), see Brown, Thomas Becket, p 37.

Selections. Dibdin Typo Antiq, 2.75 (1498 edn, f lxiᵛ, miracle of flesh turned to fish).

Modernizations. Loomis R S and R Willard, Med Eng Verse and Prose in Modernized Versions, N Y 1948, p 487 (Life and Transl from Temple, 2.182; 4.56).

Sources. Butler LA, pp 65, 83, 174 (Life based on 1438 GL, BM Addit 11565; Transl possibly).

    h. Wade, rime royal; Brown-Robbins, no 2601.

MS. Corp Christi Camb 298, f 2ᵃ (early 16 cent).

Edition. Horstmann C, Thomas Beket, epische Legende, von Laurentius Wade (1497), EStn 3.411.

Sources. EStn 3.409, 411 (author notes sources: for Gilbert story and 2 miracles, Vita by John Grandison Bishop of Exeter, d 1369; for Life of Thomas, Herbert of Bosham Vita, wr 1184–86).

Brown, Thomas Becket passim (for parallels in material in Grandison, Herbert of Bosham and L Wade, see index under these names).

General Background and Bibliography. Brown, Thomas Becket, p 278 (crit TLS Dec 18, 1930, p 1090; G H Gerould, JEGP 31.147; P G, AnBol 50.204).

[277[THREE KINGS OF COLOGNE: BALTHASAR, MELCHIOR, CASPAR OR JASPER (July 23, 1st cent).

(Note: Details of this legend occur under the Feast of Epiphany Jan 6 in NHC, Mirk Festial, Speculum Sacerdotale, and more fully in 1438 and Caxton GL; but since in all these versions exposition outweighs narrative, they are omitted here.)

    a. Three Kings, rime royal; Brown-Robbins, no *31.

MS. BM Addit 31042, 111ᵃ–119ᵇ; ca 100 lines lost at beg (mid 15 cent).

Edition. MacCracken H N, Lydgatiana III, The Three Kings of Cologne, Arch 129.51 (rimes suggest Scottish origin; author is a northern imitator of Lydgate; work is based on John of Hildesheim, Historia Trium Regum, p 50).

b. Three Kings of Cologne, prose.

MSS. 1, Bodl 6943 (Ashmole 59), f 100 (mid 15 cent); 2, Bodl 21875 (Douce 301), 29 ff; beg imperf (15 cent); 3, Camb Univ Ee.4.32, ff 1ᵃ–23ᵇ (15 cent); 4, Camb Univ Kk.1.3 (15 cent); 5, Cotton Titus A.xxv, f 35 (15 cent); 6, Cotton Vesp E.xvi, f 38; end lost (15 cent); 7, Harley 1704, f 49ᵇ (15 cent); 8, Royal A.x, f 87ᵃ (beg 15 cent); 9, Lambeth 491, ff 228ᵇ–274ᵇ (1400–50); 10, Bedford MS (1442); 11, Patrik Papers 43 (15 cent).

AELeg 1881, p cxxxii note 2 (9 MSS reported).

Horstmann, EETS 85.v (10 MSS classified).

Bülbring K D, Über die HS Nr 491 der Lambeth-Bibliothek, Arch 86.384 (evidence for Lambeth as independent translation).

Editions. Heere begynnyth the lyfe of the thre kynges of Coleyn, Wynkyn de Worde, Westminster 1496; STC, no 5572.

The moost excellent treatise of the thre kynges of Coleyne, Wynkyn de Worde, Westminster [after July 1499]; STC, no 5573 (for 16 cent edns, see STC).

Horstmann, EETS 85.2 (Camb Univ Ee.4.32 and Royal 18.A.x; p 159 variants; p 266 Latin text).

Language. Horstmann, EETS 85.viii (South Midland dialect of earliest MSS probably represents that of original).

Date. Horstmann, EETS 85.viii (on date of MSS, translation written ca 1400).

Authorship. Horstmann, EETS 85.vi, ix translator unknown; anagrams in Royal MS may represent rearrangers of text).

Sources. Horstmann, EETS 85.ix (abridged from Historia Trium Regum of John of Hildesheim, d 1375).

Literary Criticism. Workman 15th Cent Trans, p 151 (effect of close translation on narrative structure).

[278] TIMOTHY WITH APOLLINARIS (Aug 23 [Whytford], 1st cent).

a. 1438 GL.

MSS. 1, Harley 4775, chap 113, f 150ᵃ; MLA roto 343, 2.300; 2, BM Addit 35298, f 105ᵃ⁻ᵇ (om Lambeth 72).

Sources. Cf Graesse LA, chap 121, p 538.

b. Caxton GL.

Editions. Caxton GL, chap 155; Temple, 5.29.

Sources. Cf de Vignay LD, f 243ᵃ; Butler LA, pp 89, 91 (comparison of etymology in Caxton, de Vignay, and LA indecisive).

[279] TURIEN OF BRITTANY (July 13 [Whytford], 6 cent?).

Editions. Caxton GL, chap 235; Temple, 7.171.

Sources. Cf de Vignay LD, ff 389ᵇ–390ᵃ.

[280] URBAN I, POPE (May 25, ca 230).

a. 1438 GL.

MSS. 1, Harley 4775, chap 70, f 92ᵃ⁻ᵇ; MLA roto 343, 1.182; 2, Lansdowne 350 fragment; 3, BM Addit 35298, f 45ᵇ (lost Bodl 21947, BM Addit 11565).

Sources. Cf Graesse LA, chap 77, p 341.

b. Caxton GL.

Editions. Caxton GL, chap 97; Temple, 3.184.

Sources. Cf de Vignay LD, ff 138ᵇ–139ᵃ.

[281] URSULA AND THE 11000 VIRGINS (Oct 21, year?).

a. SEL; Brown-Robbins, no 721.

MSS. 14 MSS.

Schubel F, Die südenglische Legende von den elftausend Jungfrauen, Greifswalder Beiträge 21, Greifswald 1928, p 140 (interrelation of 12 MSS).

Editions. Furnivall EEP, p 66 (Harley 2277, ff 137ᵃ–139ᵇ; ca 1300).

Horstmann, EETS 87.86 (Bodl 1486 [Laud Misc 108], ff 54ᵃ–55ᵇ; end 13 cent).

Liljegren S B, Four ME Versions of the Legend of the Eleven Thousand Virgins, EStn 57.98, 103, 108 (Cotton Julius D.ix, ff 153ᵇ–156ᵃ; 15 cent; Harley 2277; Stowe 949, ff 29ᵇ–32ᵃ; late 14 cent).

Schubel, Jungfrauen, p 140 (12 texts om MSS 6 and 14 of Brown-Robbins, no 721; crit G Linke, Arch 174.259; K Wittig, AnglB 50.41, see reply AnglB 50.157; M C, AnBol 57.431; J P Oakden, MLR 34.257; H Marcus, EStn 74.112).

D'Evelyn and Mill, EETS 236.443 (Corp Christi Camb 145, ff 164ᵃ–166ᵇ; early 14 cent).

Sources. Schubel, Jungfrauen, pp 7, 104 (study of motifs of SEL version points to LA as source).

b. Bokenham; Brown-Robbins, no 2621.

MS. Arundel 327, ff 58ᵃ–65ᵇ (1447).

Editions. [Bokenam O,] The Lyvys of Seyntys, Roxb Club 50, London 1835, p 90.

Horstmann Bokenam, p 80; Liljegren, EStn 57.87.

Serjeantson, EETS 206.86.

Sources. Willenberg G, Die Quellen von Osbern Bokenham's Legenden, EStn 12.10; also diss Marburg 1888 (notes variations from alleged source; see Graesse LA, chap 158, p 701).

Serjeantson, EETS 206.xxii (suggests source similar to LA).

c. 1438 GL.
MSS. 1, Bodl 21947 (Douce 372), f 127ᵇ; end lost; 2, Harley 4775, chap 151, ff 198ᵃ–199ᵇ; MLA roto 343, 2.396; 3, BM Addit 35298, ff 134ᵃ–135ᵃ (also in Trinity Dublin 319, see Gerould S Leg, p 195).
Sources. Cf Graesse LA, chap 158, p 701.

d. Huntington 140, prose.
MS. Huntington HM 140 (olim Phillipps 8299), ff 154ᵃ–155ᵇ (1450–75).
Manly & Rickert, 1.433.
Edition. Garmonsway G N and R R Raymo, A ME Prose Life of St Ursula, RES ns 9.355.
Sources. RES ns 9.354 (based on LA; possible influence of Bokenham).

e. Caxton GL.
Editions. Caxton GL, chap 192; Temple, 6.62.
Sources. Cf de Vignay LD, ff 309ᵇ–311ᵃ.

f. Hatfield, stanzaic.
Editions. [Hatfield Edmund], Here begynneth þᵉ lyf of Saynt Ursula after þᵉ cronycles of engelonde, Wynkyn de Worde, London [no date]; rptd facsimile Roxb Club, London 1818 [32 copies].
The Legend of St Ursula and the Virgin Martyrs of Cologne, London 1862, pt II, p 72 (black letter rpt of Roxb Club 1818 text).
Authorship. Bennett H S, English Books and Readers, 1475 to 1557, Cambridge 1952, p 317 (works of Hatfield noted).
General Background. Tout M, The Legend of St Ursula and the Eleven Thousand Virgins, Hist Essays by Members of the Owens College, Manchester, ed by T F Tout and James Tait, London 1902, p 17 (for Caxton and Hatfield versions see p 47; crit A P, AnBol 22.109).
Bibliography. Schubel, Jungfrauen, p 245.

[282] VALENTINE (Feb 14, ca 269).
a. SEL; Brown-Robbins, no 3066.
MSS. 15 MSS.
Edition. D'Evelyn and Mill, EETS 235.61 (Corp Christi Camb 145, f 23ᵃ⁻ᵇ; early 14 cent).

b. 1438 GL.
MSS. 1, Harley 4775, chap 41, f 43ᵃ; MLA roto 343, 1.86; 2, BM Addit 35298, f 24ᵃ.
Sources. Cf Graesse LA, chap 42, p 176.

c. Caxton GL.
Editions. Caxton GL, chap 70; Temple, 3.43.
Sources. Cf de Vignay LD, f 104ᵃ⁻ᵇ.

VALERIA: see VITAL.

[283] VEDAST, BISHOP OF ARRAS (Feb 6, 539).
a. 1438 GL.
MSS. 1, Harley 4775, chap 39, f 42ᵇ; MLA roto 343, 1.85; 2, BM Addit 35298, f 24ᵃ.
Sources. Cf Graesse LA, chap 40, p 174.

b. Caxton GL.
Editions. Caxton GL, chap 69; Temple, 3.42.
Sources. Cf de Vignay LD, f 103ᵃ.

[284] VICTOR WITH CORONA (May 14 [Whytford], 177?).
Editions. Caxton GL, chap 118; Temple, 4.3.
Sources. Cf de Vignay LD, ff 392ᵇ–393ᵃ.

VICTORIANUS: see FOUR CROWNED MARTYRS.

[285] VINCENT OF SARAGOSSA (Jan 22, 304).
a. SEL; Brown-Robbins, no 3067.
MSS. 18 MSS.
Editions. Horstmann, EETS 87.184 (Bodl 1486 [Laud Misc 108], ff 91ᵃ–93ᵃ; end 13 cent.
D'Evelyn and Mill, EETS 235.25 (Corp Christi Camb 145, ff 9ᵇ–12ᵃ; early 14 cent).

b. ScL; Brown-Robbins, no 3634.
MS. Camb Univ Gg.2.6, ff 287ᵃ–291ᵃ (1400–50).
Editions. Horstmann ScL, 2.100; Metcalfe STS, 2.259; notes 3.388.
Sources. Horstmann ScL, 2.100 (source not LA, but nearer Vincent of Beauvais Spec Hist; passages from both prtd).
Metcalfe STS, 3.390 (probable source Spec Hist).

c. 1438 GL.
MSS. 1, Harley 4775, chap 24, ff 25ᵃ–26ᵃ; MLA roto 343, 1.50; 2, BM Addit 35298, ff 15ᵇ–16ᵃ.
Sources. Cf Graesse LA, chap 25, p 117.

d. Caxton GL.
Editions. Caxton GL, chap 58; Temple, 2.252.
Sources. Cf de Vignay LD, ff 85ᵃ–86ᵇ.

[286] VIRGIN OF ANTIOCH (Oct 8, year?).
Vernon GL; Brown-Robbins, nos 422, 3186.
(Note: These texts are one legend.)
MS. Bodl 3938 (Vernon), ff 91ᵇ col 3–92ᵇ col 3 (ca 1385).
Edition. AELeg 1878, p 26.
Textual Notes. Kölbing E, EStn 3.127.

Sources. AELeg 1878, p 26 (Graesse LA, chap 62, p 273 quoted).
General Background. Delehaye H, Les légendes hagiographiques, 4th edn, Brussels 1955, p 186.

[287] VITALIS AND AGRICOLA (Nov 4, year?).

SEL; Brown-Robbins, no 3855.
MS. Bodl 2567 (Bodley 779), f 203ª⁻ᵇ (ca 1400).
Edition. Zusatzleg 1889, p 351 (source uncertain, p 351n1).

[288] VITALIS AND VALERIA (April 28, 2 cent?).

a. 1438 GL.
MSS. 1, Harley 4775, chap 57, f 70ᵇ; MLA roto 343, 1.141; 2, BM Addit 35298, f 37ª (lost BM Addit 11565).
Sources. Cf Graesse LA, chap 61, p 272.

b. Caxton GL.
Editions. Caxton GL, chap 88; Temple, 3.144.
Sources. Cf de Vignay LD, ff 128ᵇ–129ᵇ.

VITE, VUTE: see VITUS.

[289] VITUS AND MODESTUS (June 15, ca 300?).

a. 1438 GL.
MSS. 1, Bodl 21947 (Douce 372), chap 74; see Butler LA, p 60; 2, Harley 4775, chap 74, ff 94ᵇ–95ª; MLA roto 343, 1.187; 3, BM Addit 35298, ff 46ᵇ–47ª.
Sources. Cf Graesse LA, chap 82, p 350.

b. Caxton GL.
Editions. Caxton GL, chap 105; Temple, 3.221.
Sources. Cf de Vignay LD, ff 151ª–152ª.

[290] WALSTAN OF BAWBURGH (May 30, 1016).

Lambeth, rime royal; Brown-Robbins, no 242.
MS. Lambeth 935, Art 8 (1658 transcript of life on parchment attached to triptych).
Edition. James M R, Lives of St Walstan, Norfolk and Norwich Archae Soc 19.250 (late 15 cent; notes differences between English text and Latin life in Nova legenda Anglie, 2.412; p 241).
Selections. Pamphlet prtd by Thomas Jones, 13 Paternoster Row, 1859, 4 stanzas; see James, St Walstan, p 238.
Background. Blomefield F, An Essay towards a Topographical History of the County of Norfolk, London 1805, 2.387 (local traditions about Walstan).

[291] WERBURGA (Feb 3, ca 700).
Bradshaw, Life of St Werburga, stanzaic.

Editions. Bradshaw H, . . . the holy lyfe and history of S Werburge, R Pynson, London 1521; STC, no 3506. (Note: For account of St Ermenilda see bk I, chap 20; for St Sexburga, bk I, chap 19).
Hawkins E, Bradshaw's Life of Werburge, Chetham Soc 15, London 1848 (black-letter rpt of Pynson).
Horstmann C, The Life of St Werburge of Chester by Henry Bradshaw, EETS 88 (re-edition of Pynson; crit R W, Angl 11.543).
Selections. Wood A à, Athenae Oxoniensis, ed P Bliss, London 1813, 1.col 18 (3 stanzas from Prologue; bk 2, lines 2013–2031).
Warton T, History of English Poetry, ed W C Hazlitt, London 1871, 3.144 (bk I, sta 38–40, 222–248).
Dibdin Typo Antiq, 2.491 (various passages).
Language. Horstmann, EETS 88.xxxvi.
Versification. Hawkins, Chetham Soc 15.vi; Horstmann, EETS 88.xxxi.
Authorship. Wood A à, Athenae Oxon, 1.col 18 (life and works).
Warton T, Hist of Eng Poetry 3.140.
Hawkins, Chetham Soc 15.x (summary of earlier accounts).
Horstmann, EETS 88.v (dates birth ca 1465).
Bühler C, A Note on the Balade to St Werburge, MLN 68.538 (evidence for C Buckley as author of concluding balade in Life; crit B J Timmer, YWES 34.92).
Sources. Horstmann, EETS 88.xvi (source Vita S Werburgae ascribed to Goscelin).
Literary Relations. Byrne M, The Tradition of the Nun in Medieval England, Washington D C, 1932, p 130 (new and conventional elements in portrayal of nun).
Literary Criticism. Horstmann, EETS 88. xxvii (appraisals of Bradshaw as poet); Gerould S Leg, p 278.
Bibliography. CBEL, 1.253.

[292] WILLIAM, ARCHBISHOP OF BOURGES (Jan 10, 1209).

Editions. Caxton GL, chap 113; Temple, 3.266.
Sources. Cf de Vignay LD, ff 378ᵇ–379ª.

[293] WINIFRED (Nov 3, ca 650).

(Note: See also Audelay's lyrics addressed to Winifred.)

a. SEL; Brown-Robbins, no 4176.

MS. Bodl 2567 (Bodley 779), f 189ª (ca 1400).

Edition. Zusatzleg 1889, p 331 (refers to Vita in Acta SS).

b. Mirk Festial.

MSS. Note: See ANDREW d *MSS* [25] above. 1, Bodl 17680 (Gough Eccl Top 4), ff 102ª–105ª (1400–50); 2, Cotton Claud A.ii, ff 80ᵇ–82ª (ca 1420) (om Bodl 21634, 21682, Harley 2247, 2391, Royal 18.B.xxv, Durham Cosins v.iii.5).

Editions. Note: Winifred om in the following available 15 cent edns: STC, nos 17957, 17960, 17963, 17964, 17967, 17968.

Horstmann C, Prosalegenden, Angl 3.314 (Cotton Claud A.ii).

Erbe, EETSES 96.177 (Bodl 17680).

Selections. Wright T, The History and Antiquities of the Town of Ludlow, 2nd edn, Ludlow 1826, p 181 (miracle of spider-bite from a Shrewsbury MS; see AELeg 1881, p cxii note 1).

Textual Notes. Holthausen F, Zu AE und ME Dichtungen, Angl 14.310 (correction of text, Angl 3.316).

c. 1438 GL.

MS. BM Addit 35298, chap 80, f 53ª (om in all other recorded MSS).

d. Caxton GL.

Editions. Caxton GL, chap 199; Temple, 6.127.

Sources. Butler LA, p 83 ("not in his legitimate Latin or French texts." Ed note: clearly related to text of 1438 GL in BM Addit 35298).

e. Caxton Life 1485.

Edition. [Caxton W, tr,] Here begynneth the lyf of . . . saynt Wenefrede, [Westminster 1485]; rptd C Horstmann, Prosalegenden, Angl 3.295, from Lambeth copy, STC, no 25853.

Sources. Angl 3.294 (Latin life by Robert of Shrewsbury ca 1140 suggested).

AELeg 1881, p cxi (Mirk Festial version not used or printed by Caxton).

WOLFADE AND RUFFYN: see WULFHAD AND RUFFIN.

WOLSTAN, WULSTAN: see WULFSTAN OF WORCESTER.

[294] WULFHAD AND RUFFIN (July 24 or 31, 650–700).

(Note: See [55] above.)

a. Stone Priory couplets; Brown-Robbins, no *36.

MS. Cotton Nero c.xii, ff 182ª–187ª; lines 1–69 defective (ca 1450).

Edition. AELeg 1881, p 308 (Staffordshire dialect).

Date. Gerould G H, The Legend of St Wulfhad and St Ruffin at Stone Priory, PMLA 32.331 (contemporary references suggest ca 1425).

Authorship. PMLA 32.323 (evidence for co-authorship of these verses and of verses on Founders of Stone Priory; see Dugdale, Monast Angl, edn 1846, 6.230).

Sources. AELeg 1881, p 529 (rejects Latin Passio, Acta SS, July, V.571 as source; suggests Peterborough Chron and verses on Founders; see Dugdale, Monast Angl, 1.375; 6.230).

PMLA 32.324 (accepts Passio as presumably the Chronicle referred to in English text line 155 as source. For another text of the Passio see W T Mellows, The Chronicle of Hugh Candidus, London 1949, p 140.)

Other Scholarly Problems. PMLA 32.334 (technical and social factors involved in practice of engraving verses).

b. Peterborough, couplets.

Note: Version b is not strictly a legend but a series of couplets explaining scenes pictured in glass formerly in Peterborough Monastery cloisers; for the story see also [55] above.

Editions. Dugdale Monast Angl, edn 1846, 1.377.

Note: In PMLA 32.334 Gerould says these verses are printed from Cotton Claudius A.v. Dugdale's preceding Latin extracts on the history of Peterborough are taken, as he notes, from that MS; but recent search has not discovered the English verses in Cotton Claudius. Probably Dugdale, like his contemporary Gunton, made his own copy of the verses. Gunton's editor, Simon Patrick, Preface, § 1, says that in 1641 Dugdale took "Draughts of inscriptions" and monuments in various cathedral churches including Peterborough; see Dugdale Monast Angl, 1.344, note d; see also WULFHAD b *Tetual Notes* below.

Gunton S, The History of the Church of Peterburgh, rvsd and ed by Simon Patrick, London 1686, p 104. Note: text apparently copied from verses explaining the legend pictured in the cloister windows later destroyed; rptd R H Warner, Life and Legend of St Chad, Wisbech 1871, p 96.

Textual Notes. Warner, St Chad, p 99 (general comment on differences between Dugdale and Gunton texts).

[295] WULFRIC OF HASELBURY (Feb 20, 1154).

Rime royal; Brown-Robbins, no 1590.
MS. Harley 2251, f 77^b (1450–1500).
Edition. Halliwell J O, A Selection from the Minor Poems of Lydgate, London 1840, Percy Soc 2.72.
Authorship. MacCracken, EETSES 107.xlvii (no evidence for Lydgate as author).
Background. Clay R M, The Hermits and Anchorites of England, London 1914, pp 74, 150, index.
Bell Dom M, Wulfric of Haselbury by John, Abbot of Ford, London 1933, Somerset Record Soc 47 (history of legend; texts of contemporary Latin life and 17 cent English life).
Bibliography. Bell, Wulfric of Haselbury, p 186.

[296] WULFSTAN, BISHOP OF WOR-CESTER (Jan 19, 1095).

a. SEL; Brown-Robbins, no 3068.
MSS. 19 MSS.
Editions. Horstmann, EETS 87.70 (Bodl 1486 [Laud Misc 108], ff 48^a–50^b; end 13 cent).

D'Evelyn and Mill, EETS 235.8 (Corp Christi Camb 145, ff 3^b–6^a; early 14 cent).

b. 1438 GL.
Note: In 1438 and Caxton GL the account of Wulfstan is included in the legend of Edward the Confessor, see [81] b, c, above.
MS. BM Addit 35298, ff 51^b–52^a (incident of the Pastoral Staff; not in other recorded MSS of 1438 GL).
Edition. Moore G E, The ME Verse Life of Edward the Confessor, Philadelphia 1942, p 99.

c. Caxton GL.
Editions. Caxton GL, chap 189; Temple, 6.36.
Sources. Moore, Edward the Confessor, p 134 (evidence for BM Addit 35298 as direct source).
Background. Lamb J W, St Wulfstan Prelate and Patriot, Church Hist Soc, London 1933; for Pastoral Staff incident, see p 101.

YPOLIT: see HIPPOLYTUS.

YVES, YVO: see IVES OF KERMARTIN.

4. LEGENDS OF ADAM AND EVE

by

Frances A. Foster

GENERAL REFERENCES.

Meyer W, Vita Adae et Evae, Abhandl d könig Bayer Akad d Wiss, philos-philol Cl, München 1878, 14, pt 3, p 187.
Day M, The Wheatley MS, EETS 155.xxii.
Mozley J H, The Vita Adae, Journal of Theological Studies, 30.121.
Quinn E C, The Quest of Seth, Chicago 1962 (general bibl, p 165).

OTHER VERSIONS.

See Translations and Paraphrases of the Bible (IV above); Cursor Mundi, lines 1237–1432; Legends of the Cross, SEL ([302] below); Northern Passion ([303] below); Northern Homily Collection ([304] below); Questiones by tweene the Maister of Oxenford and his Clerke (under Catechisms); Homiletic versions, SEL; and Caxton GL, Temple, 1.168.

[297] AUCHINLECK COUPLETS.

MS. Two fragments: Edinburgh Univ 218, Div II, 2 leaves, formerly Advocates 19.2.1 (Auchinleck MS), ff 14–15; and Advocates 19.2.1, ff 14^a–16^b (1330–40).
Brown-Robbins, no *43.
Kölbing E, Vier Romanzen-Handschriften, EStn 7.180.
Bliss A J, Notes on the Auchinleck Manuscript, Spec 26.652; The Auchinleck Life of Adam and Eve, RES 1956, p 406 (collation under ultra-violet rays with Horstmann's text).
Carr M B, Notes on a Middle English Scribe's Method, Univ of Wisconsin Studies in Lang and Lit, Madison 1918, 2.153 (on the scribe's presentation of OE ā.
Editions. Laing D, A Penni Worth of Witte, Abbotsford Club, 1857, p 49.
AELeg 1878, p 139 (lines 1–352 rptd from

Laing, lines 353–780 from transcript of L Toulmin Smith; crit E Kölbing, EStn 3.129).
Selection. Emerson O F, A Middle English Reader, rvsd ed, N Y 1915, p 64 (lines 445–780).
Language. Bachmann F, Die beiden Versionen, des me Canticum de Creatione, Eine Untersuchung über Sprache, Dialekt, Metrik und Verhältnis der beiden Versionen zu einander und zu ihrer Quelle (diss Rostock Univ), Hamburg 1891, p 17 (crit E Kölbing, EStn 16.304; AnglB 2.243).
Emerson, A Middle English Reader, p 270.
Versification. Bachmann, Die beiden Versionen des me Canticum, p 18.
Sources and Literary Relations. Meyer, Vita Adae et Evae, p 212.
Bachmann, Die Beiden Versionen des me Canticum, p 43.
Day, EETS 155.xxvi, xxviii.
Mozley J H, Journal of Theological Studies, 30.121.
Dunstan A C, The ME Canticum de Creatione and the Latin Vita Adae et Evae, Angl 55.431.

[298] CANTICUM DE CREATIONE.

MS. Trinity Ox 57, ff 157^b–164^b (end 14 cent).
Brown-Robbins, no 1676.
Editions. Horstmann C, Canticum de Creatione, Angl 1.303.
AELeg 1878, p 124 (crit E Kölbing, EStn 3.129).
Language. Horstmann C, Angl 1.287 (crit E Kölbing, EStn 2.269).
Bachmann, Die beiden Versionen des me Canticum, p 1 (crit E Kölbing, EStn 16.304; AnglB 2.243).
Versification. Bachmann, Die beiden Versionen des me Canticum, p 18.
Sources and Literary Relations. Meyer, Vita Adae et Evae, p 211.
Kölbing E, EStn, 2.270.
Meyer W, Die Geschichte des Kreuzholzes vor Christus, Abandl d König Bayer Akad d Wissenschaften, Philos-Philol Cl, 16, pt II, p 151.
Bachmann, Die beiden Versionen des me Canticum, p 43.
Foster F A, The Northern Passion, EETS 147.8.
Day, EETS 155.xxviii.
Mozley, Journal of Theological Studies 30.121.
Dunstan A C, The ME Canticum de Creatione and the Latin Vita Adae et Evae, Angl 55.431.

[299] THE VERNON PROSE NARRATIVE.

MS. Bodl 3938 (Vernon), ff 393^a–394^b (1380–90).
Edition. AELeg 1878, p 220.
Sources and Literary Relations. Meyer, Vita Adae et Evae, p 312; Die Geschichte des Kreuzholzes, Abhandl d König Bayer Akad d Wissenschaften, Philos-Philol Cl, 16, pt II, p 151.
Horstmann C, Nachträge zu den Legenden, Arch 79.469.
Emerson O F, Legends of Cain, PMLA 21.831.
Förster M, Adams Erschaffung und Namengebung; ein lateinisches Fragment des sog Slawischen Henoch, Archiv f Religions-Wissenschaft, 11.477.
Day, EETS 155.xxvi (suggests text was originally a poem in long lines like SEL).
Bonnell J R, Cain's Jaw-Bone, PMLA 39.142.
Crawford S J, The Influence of the Ancren Riwle on the Late Fourteenth Century, MLF 25.191.
Heather P J, Seven Planets, Folklore 54.355 (on loss of light after Adam's fall).
Wells M E, The Structural Development of the South English Legendary, JEGP 41.320 (14 lines adapted from SEL, Trinity Camb MS 605).

[300] THE BODLEIAN 2376 PROSE VERSION.

MSS. 1, Bodl 2376 (Bodley 596), ff 1^a–12^a (early 15 cent); 2, Trinity Camb 601 (R.3.21), ff 249^a–256^b (1450–1500).
James M R, The Western MSS in Trinity College Cambridge, Cambridge 1901, 2.83, 90.
Edition. Horstmann C, Nachträge zu den Legenden, Arch 74.345 (text of Bodl 2376).
Sources and Literary Relations. Day, EETS 155.xxix.
Mozley, Journal of Theological Studies 30.125.

[301] 1438 GOLDEN LEGEND ADAM AND EVE.

MSS. 1, Bodl 6909 (Ashmole 802), ff 19^a–48^a (1599); 2, Bodl 7419 (Ashmole 244), f 187^{a-b} (1600–20); 3, Bodl 21589 (Douce 15), ff 8^b–77^a (1438–50); 4, Bodl 21947 (Douce 372), chap 176, ff 158^a–161^b (one leaf lost, 1438); 5, Egerton 876, begins f 321^a (incomplete, mid 15 cent); 6, Harley 1704, ff 18^a–26^b (15 cent, ff 19–22 a 16 cent replacement); 7, Harley 2388, ff 20^a–35^b (15 cent); 8, Harley 4775, chap 178, ff 258^b–264^a

(mid 15 cent), MLA Rot no 343, 2.513; 9, BM Addit 35298 (formerly Ashburnham), ff 162ª–165ª (mid 15 cent); 10, BM Addit 39574 (Wheatley MS), ff 59ᵇ–88ª (beg 15 cent); 11, Lambeth 72, ff 423ᵇ–431ª (15 cent).

AELeg 1878, p 227 note; Butler Legenda Aurea, p 49; Manly & Rickert, 1.238 (on Harley 1704); Day, EETS 155.xxix (on BM Addit 39574).

Editions. Horstmann C, Nachträge zu den Legenden, Arch 74.353 (text of Harley 4775).

Day, EETS 155.76 (text of BM Addit 39574).

Sources. Day, EETS 155.xxii; Mozley, Journal of Theological Studies 30.125.

5. LEGENDS OF THE CROSS

by

Frances A. Foster

GENERAL REFERENCES.

Mussafia A, Sulla Leggenda del legno della Croce, Sitzb d Kaiser Akad d Wiss Philos-Hist Cl, LXIII, pt II, p 165.

Morris R, Legends of the Holy Rood, EETS 46.xi.

Meyer W, Die Geschichte des Kreuzholtzes vor Christus, Abhandl d König Bayer Akad d Wiss, Philos-Philol Cl, XVI, pt II, p 101.

Horstmann C, Nachträge zu den Legenden, Arch 79.465.

Napier A S, History of the Holy-Rood Tree, EETS 103.x.

Peebles R J, The Dry Tree, Vassar Medieval Studies, New Haven 1923, p 63.

Lascelles M, Alexander and the Earthly Paradise in Mediaeval English Writings, MÆ 5.175.

Greenhill E S, The Child in the Tree, A Study of the Cosmological Tree in Christion Tradition, Traditio 10.323.

Quinn E C, The Quest of Seth, Chicago 1962.

OTHER VERSIONS.

Cynewulf, Elene, Vercelli Book, ff 121ª–133ᵇ; Cursor Mundi, Early History beginning line 1237, Invention beginning line 21347; Legends of Adam and Eve (see above); Travels of Sir John Mandeville, Early History, EETS 153.6, Invention, EETS 6, 51.

GENERAL BIBLIOGRAPHY.

Horstmann, Arch 79.465 note; Napier, EETS 103.x; Quinn, The Quest of Seth, p 165.

[302] SOUTH ENGLISH LEGENDARY.
Early History.
MSS. 20 MSS and Brotherton 501.

Brown-Robbins, no 3389.

Editions. Morris, EETS 46.18 (from Bodl 6924, ff 63ᵇ–66ª, and Bodl 3938, ff 28ᵇ col 2– 29ª col 2).

D'Evelyn C and A J Mill, The South English Legendary, EETS 235.167 (from Corp Christ Camb 145, ff 63ª–65ᵇ).

Toomey J P, edn from Brotherton, MA thesis Leeds 1957.

Sources and Literary Relations. Napier, EETS 103.xxxiv.

Wells M E, The Structural Development of the South English Legendary, JEGP 41.320.

Invention.

MSS. 17 MSS and Brotherton 501.

Brown-Robbins, no 82.

Editions. Morris, EETS 46.36 (from Bodl 6924, ff 65ª–68ª and Bodl 3938, f 29).

D'Evelyn and Mill, EETS 235.174 (from Corp Christ Camb 145, ff 65ᵇ–67ª).

Toomey (see above).

Exaltation.

MSS. 17 MSS and Brotherton 501.

Brown-Robbins, no 3388.

Editions. Morris, EETS 46.48 (from Bodl 6924, ff 68ª–69ᵇ, and Bodl 3938, f 30ª).

D'Evelyn and Mill, EETS 236.390 (from Corp Christ Camb 145, ff 144ª–147ª).

Toomey (see above).

Historia Sancte Crucis.

MSS. 1, Bodl 1486 (Laud 108), ff 23ª–29ᵇ (end 13 cent); 2, Winchester Cath 33ª, ff 39ᵇ–47ª (15 cent).

Brown-Robbins, no 3387.

AELeg 1875, p xi and C Horstmann, The Early South English Legendary, EETS 87.VII (on Bodl 1486).

D'Evelyn, The South English Legendary, EETS 244.1.
Edition. Horstmann, EETS 87.1 (from Bodl 1486).
Selection. Horstmann C, Die Legenden der MS Laud 108, Arch 49.401 (lines 1–10, 613–614).
General References. See under SOUTH ENGLISH LEGENDARY ([1] above) and under ST QUIRIAC ([240] above).

[303] NORTHERN PASSION.

a. Original Version.
MSS. 1, Bodl 6922* (Ashmole 61), ff 99ᵇ–100ᵇ (end 15 cent); 2, Bodl 11951 (Rawlinson C.86), ff 19ᵇ–21ᵃ (end 15 cent); 3, Bodl 15481 (Rawlinson C.655), ff 33ᵃ–35ᵃ (middle 15 cent); 4, Camb Univ Dd.1.1, ff 14ᵃ–14ᵇ (1400–1450, incomplete); 5, Camb Univ Ff.5.48 ff 30ᵃ–31ᵇ (15 cent); 6, Camb Univ Gg.1.1, ff 129ᵇ–130ᵇ (1300–30); 7, Camb Univ Ii.4.9, ff 26ᵇ–29ᵇ (15 cent).

b. Camb Univ Gg.5.31.
MS. Camb Univ Gg.5.31, ff 161ᵇ–164ᵇ (end 14 cent).

c. Thornton.
MS. BM Addit 31042 (Thornton MS), ff 40ᵇ–45ᵇ (middle 15 cent).
Editions. Foster F A, The Northern Passion, EETS 145.134 (from Camb Univ Dd.1.1, Gg.1.1, Ii.4.9, Gg.5.31, BM Addit 31042).
Heuser W and F A Foster, The Northern Passion (Supplement), EETS 183.30 (from Camb Univ Gg.1.1).
Language. Foster, EETS 147.18.
Sources and Literary Relations. Foster, EETS 147.8 and 67.

[304] NORTHERN HOMILY COLLECTION.

MSS. 1, Bodl 14667 (Rawlinson Poetry 175, 1340–60), Early History, ff 65ᵇ–70ᵇ; 2, BM Cotton Tib E.vii (1390–1410), Early History, ff 174ᵇ–179ᵃ, Invention, beg fol 241ᵇ, Exaltation, ff 262ᵃ–263ᵃ; 3, Harley 4196 (beg 15 cent), Early History, ff 76ᵇ–81ᵃ, Invention, ff 149ᵇ–151ᵇ, Exaltation, ff 177ᵃ–179ᵃ.
Brown-Robbins, p 628.
Foster, EETS 147.17.
Editions. Morris, EETS 46, Early History, p 62, Invention, p 87, Exaltation, p 122.
AELeg 1881, Invention, p 56, Exaltation, p 128.
Foster, EETS 145.146, Early History (all from Harley); Heuser and Foster, The

Northern Passion (Supplement), EETS 183.95, Early History (from Bodl 14667).
Language. Foster, EETS 147.36.
Sources and Literary Relations. Meyer W, Vita Adae et Evae, Abhandlungen 14.III.211; and Geschichte des Kreuzholzes, Abhandlungen 16.II.150.
Napier, EETS 103.xxxiii.

[305] HISTORY OF THE ROOD-TREE.

MS. Bodl 2406 (Bodley 343), ff 14ᵇ–20ᵇ (1150–75).
Napier A S, EETS 103.ix.
Edition. Napier, EETS 103.2 (crit J Zupitza, Arch 92.94).
Date. Napier, EETS 103.xli.
Language. Napier, EETS 103.xlvii.
Sources and Literary Relations. Mussafia, Sitzungsb LXIII, pt II, p 197.
Meyer, Abhandl XVI, pt II, p 131.
Napier A S, EETS 103.xi and xxxi.
Bibliography. Napier, EETS 103.x.

[306] MIRK'S FESTIAL.
MSS. Only MSS checked for the Cross legend are noted here. 1, Bodl 17680 (Gough Eccl Top 4), Invention, ff 83ᵃ–85ᵃ, Exaltation, ff 142ᵇ–144ᵃ (15 cent); 2, Cotton Claud A.ii, Invention, ff 63ᵇ–64ᵇ, 68ᵃ–68ᵇ, Exaltation, ff 105ᵇ–106ᵇ (15 cent), MLA Film 449; 3, Harley 2247, Invention, ff 158ᵇ–161ᵇ (159ᵇ–162ᵇ in modern paging), Exaltation, ff 188ᵇ–191ᵃ (189ᵇ–192ᵃ in modern paging) (late 15 cent), MLA Film 254; 4, BM Royal 18.B.xxv, Invention, ff 102ᵇ–105ᵃ, Exaltation, ff 128ᵃ–129ᵇ (late 15 cent), MLA Film 211; 5, Durham Univ Cosin V.iii.5, Invention, ff 103ᵃ–107ᵇ, Exaltation, ff 138ᵃ–139ᵇ (15 cent), MLA Film 544.
AELeg 1881, p cxii.
Editions. See E Gordon Duff, Fifteenth Century English Books, Bibliographical Soc, Oxford 1917, Illustrated Monographs no XVIII, p 84. Only 15 cent editions of Festial available in microfilm owned by Hampshire Interlibrary Center are listed here.
Caxton W, Liber Festivalis, Westminster 1483, Invention, sig k, Exaltation, sig n, Duff no 298, Film 525, BM copy; R Pynson, Liber Festiualis, London 1493, Invention, sig k, Exaltation, sig m, Duff no 303, Film 547, Pepys copy; J Ravynell, Liber Festivalis, Rouen 1495, Invention, ff cxxviiᵇ–cxxxᵃ, Exaltation, ff clxxviiᵇ–clxxixᵃ, incomplete, Duff no 309, Film 531, BM copy; W Hopyl, Liber Festivalis, Paris 1495, Invention, ff lxxx–lxxxvii, Exaltation, ff

cxi[b]–cxii[b], Duff no 311, Film 532, BM copy; W de Worde, Liber Festiualis, Westminster 1499, Invention, ff cxxvii[b]–clxxx[a], Exaltation, ff clxxvii[a]–clxxix[a], Duff no 317, Film 535, BM copy; J Notary, Liber Festiualis, Westminster 1499 [1500], Invention, ff lxxxxiii[a]–c[a], Exaltation, ff cxxxvi[b]–cxxxvii[b], Duff no 319, Film 536, BM copy.

Erbe T, Mirk's Festial, EETSES 96, Invention, p 142, Exaltation, p 249 (from Gough MS).

Sources. See Graesse LA, pp 303, 605.

[307] SPECULUM SACERDOTALE.

MS. BM Addit 36791, Invention ff 82[b]–86[a], Exaltation ff 115[a]–117[b] (15 cent).

Weatherly E H, Speculum Sacerdotale, EETS 200.xv.

Edition. Weatherly, EETS 200, Invention, p 146, Exaltation, p 203 (language, p xx; source, pp 270, 275).

[308] 1438 GOLDEN LEGEND.

MSS. 1, Bodl 21947 (Douce 372), Exaltation, ff 107[a]–109[a] (1438); 2, Egerton 876, Invention, ff 102[a]–105[b], Exaltation, ff 223[a]–225[a] (middle 15 cent); 3, Harley 630, Invention, ff 124[a]–128[a], Exaltation, ff 274[a]–277[a] (15 cent); 4, Harley 4775, Invention, ff 77[b]–80[b], Exaltation, ff 169[b]–171[a] (middle 15 cent), MLA Rot no 343, vol 1.155 and 2.336; 5, BM Addit 11565, Invention, ff 107[b]–109[b], Exaltation, ff 168[a]–170[a] (middle 15 cent); 6, BM Addit 35298 (formerly Ashburnham), Invention, ff 40[a]–41[a], Exaltation, ff 116[b]–118[a] (middle 15 cent); 7, Lambeth 72, Invention, ff 118[a]–121[b], Exaltation, ff 330[b]–333[b] (middle 15 cent).

AELeg 1881, p cxxx; Butler LA, pp 50, 149 (on BM Addit 35298 and Lambeth MSS).

Edition. Butler LA, p 130 (Invention from Harley 4775).

Sources and Literary Relations. Butler LA, pp 28, 72, 145 (on Invention); Graesse LA, p 605 (Exaltation).

[309] CAXTON'S GOLDEN LEGEND.

Editions. Caxton GL, Westminster 1483, Invention, chap 92, Exaltation, chap 169; Temple, Invention, 3.169, Exaltation, 5.125; for other editions see under English Translations of Legenda Aurea, [7] above.

Morris, EETS 46, Invention, p 154, Exaltation, p 161 (text of 1493).

Ashton J, The Legendary History of the Cross, A Series of Sixty-four Woodcuts from a Dutch Book published by Veldemer A D 1483, London 1887, Invention, p xxii, Exaltation, p xli (rptd from Caxton 1483).

AELeg 1881, p cxxxv.

Sources and Literary Relations. Butler LA, p 145.

Sister Mary Jeremy, Caxton's Golden Legend and Varagine's Legenda Aurea, Spec 21.216 (both on Invention).

[310] WORCESTER EARLY HISTORY.

MS. Worcester Cath F.172, ff 13[a]–16[a] (late 15 cent).

Hulme W H, A Valuable Middle English Manuscript, MP 4.70; The Middle-English Harrowing of Hell and Gospel of Nicodemus, EETSES 100.1.

Edition. Hill B, The Fifteenth-Century Prose Legend of the Cross before Christ, MÆ 34.203.

6. LEGENDS OF JESUS AND MARY

by

Frances A. Foster

[311] THE CHILDHOOD OF JESUS.

a. Couplet; Brown-Robbins, no 1550.

MS. Bodl 1486 (Laud Misc 108), ff 11[a]–22[a] (end 13 cent).

Horstmann C, Die Legenden des MS Laud 108, Arch 49.397; AELeg 1875, p x.

Edition. AELeg 1875, p 3 (crit R P Wülcker, Jenaer Literaturzeitung 2.871).

Textual Notes. Holthausen F, Zu alt- und mittelenglischen Dichtungen, Angl 14.312; Zum mittelenglischen Gedicht Kindheit Jesu, Arch 127.319.

Versification. AELeg 1875, p xlii.

Sources and Literary Relations. Horstmann, Arch 49.398; AELeg 1875, p xxxviii.

Reinsch R, Die Pseudo-Evangelien von Jesu und Maria's Kindheit in der romanischen und germanischen Literatur mit Mittheilungen aus Pariser und Londoner Handschriften, Halle 1879, p 129.

Köhler R, Zu einer Stelle des altenglischen Gedichts von der Kindheit Jesu, EStn 2.115.

P M[eyer], Version anglaise du Poème français des Enfances Jésus Christ, Rom 18.128.

Hänisch H C W, Inquiry into the Sources of the Cursor Mundi EETS 99.31*.

Gast E, Die beiden Redaktionen des Évangile de l'Enfance, diss Greifswald 1909, p xxvii.

Holthausen F, Arch 127.318.

James M R, The Apocryphal New Testament, Oxford 1926, p 38.

b. Stanzaic; Brown-Robbins, no 250.

MSS. 1, Harley 2399, begins f 47ᵇ (15 cent); 2, Harley 3954, begins f 70ᵃ (ca 1420); 3, BM Addit 31042, begins f 163ᵇ (mid 15 cent).

Editions. AELeg 1878, p 101 (text of Harley 3954 and Harley 2399; [C Horstmann], Nachträge zu den Legenden, Arch 74.327 (text of BM Addit 31042).

Selections. Kölbing E, EStn 2.117 (lines 345–380 from Harley 3954).

James M R, The Apocryphal New Testament, Oxford 1926, p 69 (lines 531–574 rptd from AELeg 1878, p 108).

Textual Notes. Landshoff H, Kindheit Jesu, Ein englisches Gedicht aus dem 14 Jahrhundert, I, Verhältnis der Handschriften, Berlin 1889.

Sources and Literary Relations. AELeg 1878, p 103n (lines 25–182 taken from lines 1–215 of A Disputisoun in Bodley 3938, f 301*).

Reinsch, Die Pseudo-Evangelien, p 129.

Gast, Die beiden Redaktionen des Évangile de l'Enfance, p xxxviii.

Gerould S Leg, p 226 (crit G L Hamilton, MLN 36.239).

General. James, The Apocryphal New Testament, p 38.

[312] THE GOSPEL OF NICODEMUS.

General References. Wülcker R P, Das Evangelium Nicodemi in der abländischen Literatur, Paderborn 1872; Jenaer Literaturzeitung, 2.872.

Hulme W H, The Middle English Harrowing of Hell and Gospel of Nicodemus, EETSES 100.xv.

James M R, The Apocryphal New Testament, Oxford 1926, p 94.

See also under THE SIEGE OF JERUSALEM (I [107]); HARROWING OF HELL [313] below; CURSOR MUNDI (lines 17271–18638); PRICK OF CONSCIENCE (lines 6529–6546).

General Bibliography. CBEL 1.188.

a. Stanzaic; Brown-Robbins, no 312.

MSS. 1, Cotton Galba E.ix, ff 57ᵇ–66ᵇ (1400–50); 2, Harley 4196, ff 206ᵃ–215ᵃ (1400–50); 3, BM Addit 32578, ff 116ᵇ–140ᵇ (1405); 4, Sion Coll Arc L 40.2/E.25, ff 13ᵃ–38ᵇ (14 cent).

AELeg 1881, p lxxviii (on Harley MS); J Hall, The Poems of Laurence Minot, 2nd edn, Oxford 1897, p vii (on Cotton MS); W H Hulme, EETSES 100.viii.

Editions. Horstmann C, Evangelium Nicodemi, Arch 53.391 (text of Harley); Nachträge zu den Legenden, Arch 68.207 (text of Sion).

Hulme, EETSES 100.22 (all MSS; crit A Schröer, EStn 40.263).

Klotz F, Das mittelenglische strophische Evangelium Nicodemi mit einer Einleitung kritisch herausgegeben, diss Königsberg 1913 (text of Sion).

Textual Notes. Horstmann C, Zum Evangelium Nicodemi, Arch 57.74.

Language. Klotz, Das mittelenglische strophische Evangelium Nicodemi, p 29.

Versification. Hulme, EETSES 100.xvi.

Klotz, Das mittelenglische strophische Evangelium Nicodemi, p 26.

Date. Craigie W A, The Gospel of Nicodemus and the York Mystery Plays, An English Miscellany, Oxford 1901, p 61.

Hulme, EETSES 100.xviii.

Sources and Literary Relations. Horstmann, Archiv 53.391; Arch 57.78.

Hulme, EETSES 100.xviii.

Foster F A, The Northern Passion, EETS 147.77.

Miller F H, The Northern Passion and the Mysteries, MLN 34.88.

Lyle M C, The Original Identity of the York and Towneley Cycles, Research Publications of the Univ of Minnesota, 8 no 3, Studies in Language and Literature no 6, Madison 1919, p 30 (crit G Frank, MLN 35.45).

Clark E G, The York Plays and the Gospel Nicodemus, PMLA 43.153.

Frank G, On the relation between the York and Towneley Plays, PMLA 44.313; crit M C Lyle, The Original Identity of the York and Towneley Cycles—A Rejoinder, PMLA 44.326.

Curtis C G, The York and Towneley Plays on the Harrowing of Hell, SP 30.24.

b. Couplet; Brown-Robbins, no 130.

MS. BM Addit 39996 (formerly Phillips 9803), begins f 52ᵇ (1440–1550).

c. Prose.

MSS. 1, Bodl 2021 (Bodley 207), ff 120ᵇ–124

(ca 1470); 2, Camb Univ Mm.1.29, ff 8–16 (1490–1510); 3, Magdalene Camb Pepys 2498, pp 459, col 2—463 (beginning 15 cent); 4, Egerton 2658, ff 15ᵇ–18 (ca 1450); 5, Harley 149, ff 255–276 (1450–1500); 6, BM Addit 16165, ff 94ᵇ–114ᵇ (middle 15 cent); 7, Salisbury Cath 39, ff 129ᵇ–147 (15 cent); 8, Worcester Cath F.172, ff 4–16 (late 15 cent); 9, Stonyhurst Coll B.xliii, ff 83–96 (ca 1460); 10, Libr of Congress 4, ff 37ᵇ–63ᵇ (early 15 cent).

Paues A C, A Fourteenth Century Version of the Ancren Riwle, EStn 30.344; A Fourteenth Century English Biblical Version, Cambridge, 1902, p lvii (on Pepys 2498); W H Hulme, A Valuable Middle English Manuscript, MP 4.65 (on Worcester MS); EETSES 100.xxxiv; B Hill, A Newly-identified Middle English Prose Version of the Gospel of Nicodemus, N&Q 204.243 (on Libr of Congress MS).

Editions. Only early editions available on University Microfilm are listed. Julyan Notary, Nycodemus gospell, London 1507, Film 2705 (case 26, carton 152), STC no 18565, Marsh Library Dublin Z 4.1.14 (1); Wynkyn de Worde, Nycodemus gospell, London 1509, Film 2706 (case 23, carton 138), STC no 18566, Bodl Tanner 206 (2); Wynkyn de Worde, Nychodemus gospell, London 1512 (fragment, 4 pages), Film 2708 (case 21, carton 121), STC no 18567ᵃ, Bodl Tanner 206. See also H C Kim, DA XXV.1893.

Hulme, EETSES 100.lvii (on early prints).

Authorship. Wülcker, Das Evangelium Nicodemi, p 20; M Förster, Zum altenglischen Nicodemus-Evangelium, Arch 107.321; Hulme, EETSES 100.xxxv, note 2, lviii.

[313] THE HARROWING OF HELL.

General References. James M R, The Apocryphal New Testament, Oxford 1926, p 117.

Burstein S R, The Harrowing of Hell, Folklore 39.113.

MacCulloch J A, The Harrowing of Hell, A Comparative Study of an Early Christian Doctrine, Edinburgh 1930.

Cahaniss A, The Harrowing of Hell, Psalm 24, and Pliny the Younger, Vigiliae Christianae 7.64.

General Bibliography. MacCulloch, The Harrowing of Hell, p xi; CBEL 1.188.

a. Short couplet; Brown-Robbins, nos 1258, 185.

MSS. 1, Bodl 1687 (Digby 86), ff 119ᵃ–120ᵇ (ca 1275); 2, Harley 2253, ff 55ᵇ–56ᵇ (ca

1310); 3, Advocates 19.2.1 (Auchinleck), ff 36ᵃ–37ᵃ, lines 1–28 and end lacking, (1300–40).

Böddeker, p 265; E Kölbing, Vier Romanzen-Handschriften, EStn 7.178, 182 (on Advocates MS); Varnhagen (see under *Editions*), p 2; Hulme (see under *Editions*), EETSES. viii; A J Bliss, Notes on the Auchinleck Manuscript, Spec 26.652.

Editions. Collier J P, Five Miracle Plays or Scriptural Dramas, London 1836 (text of Harley).

Laing O, Owain Miles and Other Inedited Fragments of Ancient English Poetry, Edinburgh 1837 (text of Auchinleck).

Halliwell-[Phillipps] J O, The Harrowing of Hell, A Miracle Play, London 1840 (text of Harley).

Mall E, The Harrowing of Hell. Das altenglische Spiel von Christi Höllenfahrt, Breslau 1871 (text of Harley); and Zu Harrowing of Hell, JfRESL 13.217; crit Wülcker R P, Das Evangelium Nicodemi in der abendländischen Literatur, Paderborn 1872, p 76; Varnhagen (see below), p 3.

Böddeker, p 270 (text of Harley).

Pollard A W, English Miracle Plays, Moralities and Interludes, Oxford 1890, p 106 (rptd from Mall).

Varnhagen H, Praemissa est editionis criticae vetustissimi quod sermone anglico conscriptum est dramatis pars prior, Erlangen 1898 (facsimiles of all MSS).

Hulme W H, The Middle-English Harrowing of Hell and Gospel of Nicodemus, EETSES 100.2 (all MSS).

Selections. Rel Ant 1.253 (Prologue from Bodley MS); J O Halliwell-[Phillipps], A Dictionary of Archaic and Provincial Words, 10th edn London 1881, 2.958 (Prologue from Bodley).

Textual Notes. Zupitza J, Zu dem altenglischen Spiel The Harrowing of Hell, Wagner's Archiv für die Geschichte deutscher Sprache und Dichtung, Wien 1874, 1.190.

Language. Mall, The Harrowing of Hell, p 10; Böddeker, p 265; S Moore, S B Meech, H Whitehall, Middle English Dialect Characteristics and Dialect Boundaries, Univ of Michigan Essays and Studies in English and Comparative Literature, Ann Arbor 1935, 13.54.

Date. Hulme, EETSES 100.vii.

Literary Relations. Mall, The Harrowing of Hell, p 47; Böddeker, p 264; Ten Brink, 2.242; Ward Hist, 1.89; Chambers, 2.74; K Young, The Harrowing of Hell in Liturgical Drama, Transactions of the Wisconsin Academy of Sciences, Art, and Letters, 16.889; crit P E Kretzmann, A Few Notes on the Harrowing of Hell, MP 13.49; Gerould S Leg, p 214.

b. Septenary; Brown-Robbins, no 3706.
MS. St Johns Camb 28, begins f 73ª (late 14 cent).
Horstmann C, Early English Verse Lives of the Saints, EETS 87.xxiv.

[314] THE DEVILS' PARLIAMENT.
MSS. 1, BM Addit 15225, begins f 48ª (1350–1400); 2, BM Addit 37492, begins f 83ª (1450–1500); 3, Lambeth 853, pp 157–182 (ca 1430).
Brown-Robbins, no 3992.
Editions. De Worde W, Parlyament of deuylles, London 1509 (STC, no 19305).
Furnivall F J, Hymns to the Virgin and Christ, The Parliament of Devils, &c, EETS 24.41 (text of Lambeth).

[315] THE HOLY BLOOD OF HAYLES.
MS. Royal 17.C.xvii, ff 147ª–152ᵇ (early 15 cent).
Brown-Robbins, no 3153.
Horstmann C, Prosalegenden, Angl 4.109; AELeg 1881, p cx, note 2.
Editions. AELeg 1881, p 275 (notes p 528; crit A Brandl, LfGRP 2.398).
Duff E G, The Library of Richard Smith, The Library New Series 8.127.
Source. Gerould S Leg, p 272.
Background. Skeat W W, The Works of Geoffrey Chaucer, Oxford 1894, 5.284 (on line 652 of the Pardoner's Tale); W St J Baddeley, A Cotteswold Shrine, being a Contribution to the History of Hailes County Gloucester Manor, Parish and Abbey, Gloucester 1908; and see under JOSEPH OF ARIMATHIE (I [40]).

[316] THE MIRROR OF MAN'S SALVATION.
MS. Foyle (Mr W A Foyle, Beeleigh Abbey, Maldon, Essex, formerly Huth MS, 1400–50).
Roxburghe Club (see *Edition*), p xii; O Brix, Über die me Übersetzung des Speculum humanae salvationis, Berlin und Leipzig 1900 (Anastatischer Neudruck 1922), Palaes 7.101 (language, p 101; versification, p 95; source, p 4).
Edition. Huth A H, The Miroure of Man's Saluacioune, A fifteenth Century Translation into English of the Speculum Humanae Salvationis and now for the first

time printed from a MS in the possession of Alfred Henry Huth with Preface and Glossary, Roxburghe Club 1888.

[317] THE LIFE OF THE VIRGIN MARY AND THE CHRIST.
MS. Trinity Coll Dublin 423, ff 123ª–146ᵇ (15 cent).
Abbott T K, Cat of the MSS in the Library of Trinity Coll Dublin, London 1900, p 65.
Edition. McQuillan P A, A Critical Edition of the Life of the Virgin Mary and the Christ (Trinity College Dublin MS 423), M A Thesis, Duquesne Univ, Pittsburgh 1951 (unprinted).
Selection. Klinefelter R A, The Four Daughters of God, A New Version, JEGP 52.92 (ff 128ª–129ᵇ).
Sources. McQuillan, A Critical Edition, p 4; R A Klinefelter, Lydgate's Life of our Lady and the Chetham MS 6709, PBSA 46.274; Four Daughters of God, JEGP 52.90.

[318] THE ASSUMPTION OF THE VIRGIN.
General References. Lumby J R and G H McKnight, Kyng Horn, Floris and Blancheflour, etc, EETS 14.xlix.
Ryan N J, The Assumption in the Early English Pulpit, Theological Studies 11.477.
General Bibliography. CBEL 1.175; Ryan, Theological Studies 11.522; H Lansberg, Zur literarischen Gestaltung des Transitus Beatae Mariae, Historisches Jahrbuch 72.25.

a. Early couplet; Brown-Robbins, no 2165.
MSS. 1, Camb Univ Dd.1.1, begins f 175ª (1400–50); 2, Camb Univ Ff.2.38, begins f 40ᵇ (mid 15 cent); 3, Camb Univ Gg 4.27.2 (lines 1–240, end 13 cent); 4, Harley 2382, ff 75ª–86ª (1470–1500); 5, BM Addit 10036, ff 62ª–80ᵇ (beginning 15 cent); 6, Chetham 8009, begins f 4ª (late 15 cent).
Halliwell J O, An Account of the European Manuscripts in the Chetham Library, Manchester 1842, p 16; Lumby and McKnight, EETS 14.liv; F Gierth, Über die älteste mittelenglische Version der Assumptio Marie, EStn 7.12; E Kölbing, Vier romanzenhandschriften, EStn 7.195 (on Chetham MS); M Swarz, Kleine Publicationen aus der Auchinleck-HS, IV. Die Assumptio Mariae in der Schweifreimstrophe, EStn 8.427, 457; E Hackauf (see under *Editions*), ETB 8.I; Manly & Rickert 1.245 (on Harley MS).
Editions. Lumby and McKnight, EETS 14.111

(text of Camb Univ GG.4.27.2; Harley, lines 241–716; BM Addit MSS).

Morris R, Cursor Mundi, EETS 68.1638 (text of BM Addit).

Hackauf E, Die älteste mittelenglische Version der Assumptio Mariae, ETB 8 (lines 1–250 from Camb Univ Gg.4.27.2, lines 251 on from Harley); language, p xxii; versification, p xxiii; date and authorship, p xi (crit W M, LZ 54, no 25, p 851; W Heuser, EStn 33.255).

Selections. Ryan, Theological Studies 11.491 (Harley MS rptd from EETS 14.133).

Textual Criticism. Kölbing E, Kleine Beiträge zur Erklärung und Text-kritik englischer Dichter, EStn 3.93; E Kölbing, Collationen, EStn 7.348; Hackauf, EStn 33.179 (new collation of BM Addit and Harley).

Sources and Literary Relations. Cursor Mundi, lines 20011–20848, EETS 65.1146 (Brown-Robbins, no 3976).

Gierth, EStn 7.3.

Lumby and McKnight, EETS, 14.1.

Retzlaff O, Untersuchungen über den nordenglischen Legenden-cyclus des MSS Harl 4196 und Cotton Tib.E.vii, Berlin 1888, p 37.

Leendertz P jr, Die Quellen der ältesten mittelenglischen Version der Assumptio Mariae, EStn 35.350.

    b. Stanzaic; Brown-Robbins, no *75.

MS. Advocates 19.2.1 (Auchinleck MS), ff 73ª–78ª (1330–40).

Kölbing E, Vier Romanzen-Handschriften, EStn 7.178, 185.

Bliss A J, Notes on the Auchinleck Manuscript, Spec 26.652.

Edition. Schwarz M, Kleine Publicationen aus der Auchinleck-MS, EStn 8.448 (language, p 444; versification, p 437; literary relations, p 428).

Textual Notes. Holthausen F, Zu alt und mittelengl Dichtungen, Angl 13.358.

    c. South English Legendary; Brown-Robbins, nos 2991, 1092.

MSS. 14 MSS (Brown-Robbins, no 2991), and (15) Lambeth 223 (Brown-Robbins, no 1092), begins f 43ª (end 14 cent, unique text).

AELeg 1875, p xxxiv; Lumby and McKnight, EETS 14 (rvsd), p lii; AELeg 1881, p xlvii (on Lambeth).

Edition. D'Evelyn C and A J Mill, The South English Legendary, EETS 236.365 (text of Corp Christi Camb 145).

Source and Literary Relations. Swarz M, Die Assumptio Mariae in der Fassung des MS Bodl 779, EStn 8.461.

Gierth F, Über die älteste mittelenglische Version der Assumptio Mariae, EStn 7.28.

Wells M E, Structural Development of the South English Legendary, JEGF 41.336 (parallel of Lambeth to Vernon Life of Mary).

    d. Northern Homily Collection; Brown-Robbins, nos 2638, 2191.

MSS. 1, Cotton Tib E.vii, ff 255ª–258ª (1390–1400); 2, Harley 4196, ff 170ᵇ–173ª (beginning 15 cent); 3, Huntingdon HM 129, ff 218ª–220ᵇ (unique version, formerly Phillipps 20420, 1400–50). One NHC MS, Camb Univ Dd.1.1, has the Early Couplet Assumption, see under a. above.

Edition. AELeg 1881, p 112 (text of Harley).

Sources and Literary Relations. Gierth, EStn 7.12; O Retzlaff, Untersuchungen über den nordenglischen Legenden-cyclus der MSS Harl 4196 u Cotton Tib E.vii, Berlin 1888, p 37.

    e. Late couplet; Brown-Robbins, no 315.

MS. BM Addit 39996 (formerly Phillipps 9803), ff 61ª–69ᵇ (1440–50).

    f. Mirk Festial.

MSS. 1, Bodley 17680 (Gough Eccl Top 4), ff 126ᵇ–130ª (15 cent); 2, Cotton Claud A.ii, ff 96ª–98ᵇ (15 cent, MLA Film 449); 3, Harley 2247, ff 179ᵇ–182ᵇ (late 15 cent, MLA Film 254); 4, BM Royal 18.B.xxv, ff 118ª–121ᵇ (late 15 cent, MLA Film 211).

Erbe T, Mirk's Festial, EETSES 96.xcvi.

Editions. See E Gordon Duff, Fifteenth Century English Books, Bibliographical Soc, Oxford 1917, Illustrated Monographs no XVIII, p 84. Only 15 cent editions available in microfilm owned by Hampshire Interlibrary Center are listed.

Caxton W, Liber Festivalis, Westminster 1483, sig n iª–n iiiª, Duff no 298, Film 525, BM copy.

Pynson R, Liber Festiualis, London 1493, sig l vᵇ–l viiᵇ, Duff no 303, Film 547, Pepys copy.

Ravynell J, Liber Festivalis, Rouen 1495, ff clxviᵇ–clxxª, Duff no 309, Film 531, BM copy.

Hopyl W, Liber Festivalis, Paris 1495, ff cvª–cviiᵇ, Duff no 311, Film 532, BM copy.

de Worde W, Liber Festiualis, Westminster 1499, ff clxviᵇ–clxxª, Duff no 317, Film 535, BM copy.

Notary J, Liber Festiualis, Westminster 1499 [1500], ff cxxviiiª–cxxxiª, Duff no 319, Film 536, BM copy.

Erbe T, EETSES 96.221 (text of Gough MS).

Selection. Ryan N J, Theological Studies 11.497 (rptd from EETSES 96.221).

Source. Graesse LA, cap CXIX, p 504.

Style. Long M M, Undetected Verse in Mirk's Festial, MLN 70.14.

g. Speculum Sacerdotale.

MS. BM Addit 36791, ff 103ᵇ–108ᵇ (15 cent).

Weatherly E H, Speculum Sacerdotale, EETS 200.xv.

Edition. Weatherly, EETS 200.182 (language, p xvii; sources, pp xxix, 273).

h. 1438 Golden Legend.

MSS. 1, Bodl 21947 (Douce 372), imperfect, begins f 91 (1438); 2, Egerton 876 (mid 15 cent); 3, Harley 630 (15 cent); 4, Harley 4775, ff 139ᵃ–147ᵃ (one folio lacking, 15 cent), MLA Roto 343, vol 2, p 278; 5, BM Addit 11565 (15 cent); 6, BM Addit 35298 (formerly Ashburnham) (mid 15 cent); 7, Lambeth 72 (mid 15 cent).

Butler LA, pp 51, 150.

i. Caxton Golden Legend.

Editions. Caxton W, Golden Legende, Westminster 1483, chap 152; Temple, 4.234 (also in 1487, 1493, 1498 edns).

Modernization. Loomis R S and R Willard, Medieval English Verse and Prose, N Y 1948, p 482, notes p 557.

Literary Criticism. Ryan, Theological Studies, 11.64n.

[319] THE ORIGIN OF THE FESTIVAL OF THE CONCEPTION OF MARY.

General Sources and Literary Relations. Pseudo-Anselm, Miraculum de Conceptione Sanctae Mariae, Migne PL, 159.323.

Wace, L'Établissement de la Fête de la Conception Notre-Dame, Caen 1842, p 91.

Cursor Mundi, lines 24731–24972, EETS 68.1416.

a. South English Legendary; Brown-Robbins, no 104.

MSS. 1, Bodl 2567 (Bodley 799), begins f 244ᵇ, with 114-line Prologue (Brown-Robbins, no 4173) (ca 1400); 2, Bodl 3938 (Vernon), begins f 6ᵇ with Head-link (Brown-Robbins, no 213) and 114-line Prologue (Brown-Robbins, no 4173) (ca 1385).

Wells M E, Structural Development of the South English Legendary, JEGP 41.336.

b. Mirk Festial.

MSS. 1, Bodl 17680 (Gough Eccl Top 4), begins f 10ᵃ (15 cent); Cotton Claud A.ii, ff 10ᵇ–11ᵃ (15 cent), MLA film 449; 3, Harley 2247, ff 139ᵃ–140ᵇ (late 15 cent), MLA film 254; 4, BM Royal 19.B.xxv, ff 87ᵃ–88ᵃ (late 15 cent), MLA film 211; 5, Durham Univ Cosin V.iii.5, ff 62ᵃ–63ᵃ (15 cent), MLA film 544.

AELeg 1881, p cxx.

Editions. Of early editions, only those available on Edwards Bros film, Case III, Carton 14, are listed here.

Caxton W, Liber Festivalis, Westminster 1483, sig gii, Duff no 298, Film order no 525, BM copy.

Pynson R, Liber Festiualis, London 1493, p liiiᵇ, Duff no 303, Film order no 547, Pepys copy.

Ravynell J, Liber Festivalis, Rouen 1495, p lxxixᵃ, Duff no 309, Film order no 531, BM copy.

Hopyl W, Liber Festiualis, Paris 1495, f 1ᵇ, Duff no 311, Film order no 532, BM copy.

de Worde W, Liber Festiualis, Westminster 1499, p lxxixᵃ Duff no 317, Film order no 535, BM copy.

Notary J, Liber Festiualis, Westminster 1499 [1500], p lxᵇ, Duff no 319, Film order no 536, BM copy.

Erbe T, Mirk's Festial, EETSES 96.17 (text of Bodl 17680).

c. Speculum Sacerdotale.

MS. BM Addit 36791, ff 140ᵇ–141ᵇ (15 cent).

Weatherly E H, Speculum Sacerdotale, EETS 200.xv.

Edition. Weatherly, EETS 200.250 (sources, pp xxix, 280).

d. 1438 Golden Legend.

MS. 1, Bodl 21947 (Douce 372), ff 157ᵃ–158ᵃ (fragment of 20 lines, 1438); 2, Harley 4775, ff 257ᵃ–258ᵇ (mid 15 cent), MLA Roto 343, vol 2.510; 3, Lambeth 72, begins f 421ᵇ (mid 15 cent).

AELeg 1881, p cxxx; Butler LA, pp 49, 149.

e. Caxton Golden Legend.

Editions. Caxton W, Westminster 1483, chap 35; Temple 2.126.

Source. See Graesse LA, chap 189, p 869.

7. Legends of the After-Life

by   ▪

Francis A. Foster

GENERAL REFERENCES.

Wright T, St Patrick's Purgatory: An Essay on the Legends of Purgatory, Hell, and Paradise current during the Middle Ages, London 1844.

Becker E J, A Contribution to the Comparative Study of the Medieval Visions of Heaven and Hell, with Special Reference to the Middle English Versions, diss Johns Hopkins, Baltimore 1899.

Boswell C S, An Irish Precursor of Dante, Grimm Library 18, London 1908.

Landau M, Hölle und Fegfeuer in Volksglauben, Dichtung und Kirchenlehre, Heidelberg 1909.

Verdeyen R and J Endepols, Tondalus' Visioen en St Patricius' Vagevuur, Koninklijke Vlaamsche Academie voon Taal en Letterkunde, Ghent 1914.

Willson E, The Middle English Legends of Visits to the Other World and Their Relation to the Metrical Romances, Chicago 1917.

Voight M, Beiträge zur Geschichte der Visions-literatur im Mittelalter, Palaes 146.

Brotanek R, Refrigerium damnatorum, Festgabe der philos Fakultät der Friederich-Alexander-Univ Erlangen zur 55 Versammlung deutscher Philologen u Schulmänner, Erlangen 1925, p 77.

Seymour St J D, Irish Visions of the Other-World, London 1930.

Os A B van, Religious Visions, The Development of the Eschatological Elements in Mediaeval English Religious Literature, Amsterdam 1932.

Patch H R, The Other World according to Descriptions in Medieval Literature, Cambridge Mass 1950.

See also under HARROWING OF HELL ([313] above); CURSOR MUNDI, lines 23195–23652; PRICKE OF CONSCIENCE, lines 6411–9532; ADULTEROUS FALMOUTH SQUIRE; ST BRENDAN ([48] above); VISION OF DRIHTHELM, Bede Ecclesiastical History, bk XL, chap 12; VISION OF THURCILL, Roger of Wendover Chronicle, ed H O Coxe, 1843, 3.190; VISION OF THE BOY WILLIAM, Vincent de Beauvais, Speculum historiale, Venice 1591, p 1126.

GENERAL BIBLIOGRAPHY.

Landau, Hölle u Fegfeuer in Volksglauben, p xii.

Patch, The Other World, p 329.

[320] THE VISION OF ST PAUL OR THE ELEVEN PAINS OF HELL.

General References. Wright, St Patrick's Purgatory, p 7.

Brandes H, Über die Quellen der me Versionen der Paulusvision, EStn 7.34; rptd Visio S Pauli, Ein Beitrag zur Visionsliteratur mit einem deutschen und zwei lateinischen Texten, Halle 1885.

James M R, Apocrypha anecdota, Texts and Studies, ed J A Robinson, II no 3, Cambridge 1893, p 11; The Apocryphal New Testament, Oxford 1926, p 525.

Ward, 2.397.

Becker, Medieval Visions, p 78.

Willson, Middle English Legends, p 26.

Os, Religious Visions, pp 40, 202.

Silverstein T, Visio Sancti Pauli, The History of the Apocalypse in Latin together with Nine Texts, Studies & Documents, ed K & S Lake, IV, London 1935.

Willard R, The Latin Texts of the Three Utterances of the Soul, Spec 12.147; Two Apocrypha in OE Homilies, Beiträge zur Englische Philologie, 30.38.

Patch, The Other World, p. 91.

General Bibliography. Becker, Medieval Visions, p 74.

Hall Selections, 2.407.

Silverstein, Visio Sancti Pauli, p 219.

CBEL 1.176; 5.120.

    a. Early couplet; Brown-Robbins, no 3828.

MSS. 1, Bodl 1687 (Digby 86), ff 132ᵃ–134ᵇ (1275–1300); 2, Jesus Oxf 29, Part II, f 198ᵃ (1250–1300).

Editions. Morris R, An Old English Miscellany, EETS 49.147 (text of Jesus).
Horstmann C, Nachträge zu den Legenden, Arch 62.403 (text of Digby).
Textual Notes. Brandes, EStn 7.34; F Holthausen, Zu Morris OE Miscellany, Arch 88.372.
Literary Relations. Batiouchkof T, Le Débat de l'Âme et du Corps, Rom 20.17.
Stanley E G, Die anglonormannischer Verse in dem mittelenglischen Gedicht Die elf Höllenpeinen, Arch 192.21.

    b. Early stanzaic; Brown-Robbins, no 3089.
MS. Bodl 1486 (Laud Misc 108), ff 199ª–200ᵇ (end 13 cent).
Horstmann C, Die Legenden des MS Laud 108, Arch 49.397, AELeg 1875, p x.
Edition. Horstmann C, Die Vision des h Paulus, Arch 52.35.
Authorship. Kölbing E, Zwei mittelenglische Bearbeitungen der Sage von St Patrick's Purgatorium, EStn 1.91; crit H Varnhagen, Zu mittelenglischen Gedichten, Angl 3.60.
Literary Relations. Brandes EStn 7.34 .

    c. Vernon couplet; Brown-Robbins no 1898.
MSS. 1, Bodl 3938 (Vernon), ff 230ª–231ª (ca 1385); 2, BM Addit 22283 (Simeon), f 32ᵇ (lines 1–124 only, late 14 cent).
Ward, 2.415 (on BM Addit MS).
Editions. Horstmann C, Die Vision der heiligen Paulus, EStn 1.295 (text of Bodl 3938).
Morris R, An Old English Miscellany, EETS 49.223 (text of Bodl 3938).
Horstmann C, The Minor Poems of the Vernon MS, Part I, EETS 98.251; Part II (ed F J Furnivall), EETS 117.750 (variants of BM Addit).
Textual Notes. Holthausen F, Arch 88.373.
Language. Horstmann, EStn 1.293.
Literary Relations. Brandes, EStn 7.34.

    d. Audelay stanzaic; Brown-Robbins, no 3481.
MS. Bodl 21876 (Douce 302), ff 17ª–18ᵇ (1425–50).
Whiting E K, The Poems of John Audelay, EETS 184.vii.
Editions. Morris R, An Old English Miscellany, EETS 49.210; crit F Holthausen, Arch 88.373.
Whiting, EETS 184.111.
Language. Whiting, EETS 184.xxviii.
Source and Literary Relations. Brandes, EStn 7.34.

Priebsch R, John Audelay's Poem on the Observance of Sunday, An Old English

Miscellany Presented to Dr Furnivall, Oxford 1901, p 398.
Whiting, EETS 184.241.

    e. Lambeth early prose.
MS. Lambeth 487, ff 15ᵇ–18ª (before 1200).
Editions. Morris R, Old English Homilies and Homiletic Treatises of the Twelfth and Thirteenth Centuries, Series I, Part I, EETS 29.41; rptd Morris Spec, Part I, 2nd edn, Oxford 1885, p 17; and J Zupitza, Alt- und Mittelenglisches Übungsbuch, 4th edn, Wien 1889, p 69; and G E MacLean, An Old and Middle English Reader, N Y 1896, p 59.
Hall Selections, 1.76.
Modernizations. Morris, EETS 29.40.
Loomis R S and R Willard, Mediaeval English Verse and Prose in Modernized Versions, N Y 1948, p 32.
Language. Morris, EETS 29.xviii; Hall Selections, 2.407.
Sources and Literary Relations. Brandes, EStn 7.34; Hall Selections, 2.413.
General. Os, Religious Visions, p 137; and see under LAMBETH HOMILIES.
Bibliography. Hall Selections, 2.407.

    f. Late prose.
MS. BM Addit 10036, ff 81ª–85ª (14 cent).
Edition. Kölbing E, Eine bisher unbekannte me Version von Pauli Höllenfahrt, EStn 22.134 (sources, p 134).

[321] ST PATRICK'S PURGATORY.
General References. Wright, St Patrick's Purgatory, p 60.
Kölbing E, Zwei mittelenglische Bearbeitungen der Sage von St Patrick's Purgatorium, EStn 1.60.
Eckleben S, Die älteste Schilderung vom Fegefeuer des Heiligen Patricius, Eine literarische Untersuchung, Halle 1885.
Ward, 2.435, 468.
Krapp G P, The Legend of Saint Patrick's Purgatory: Its Later History, Baltimore 1900.
Horstmann C, Nova legenda Anglie, Oxford 1901, 2.293.
Delehaye H, Le Pèlerinage de Larent de Pasȝthe au Purgatoire de St Patrice, Analecta Bollandiana, 27.35.
Verdeyen and Endepols, Tondalus' Visioen, 1.294.
Willson, Middle English Legends, pp 5, 19, 25.
Seymour St J D, St Patrick's Purgatory, A Mediaeval Pilgrimage in Ireland, Dundalk 1918.
van der Zanden C M, Étude sur le Purga-

toire de saint Patrice, accompagnée du
texte latin d'Utrecht et du texte anglo-
normand de Cambridge, Amsterdam 1927.
Leslie S, Saint Patrick's Purgatory, a Record
from History and Literature, London 1932.
Os, Religious Visions, p 58.
Other English notices of St Patrick's Purga-
tory are in Trevisa's Polychronicon, bk 1,
chap 35; Caxton's Mirror of the World,
part 2, chap 14; and his Golden Legend,
Life of St Patrick, Temple edn, 3.79.
General Bibliography. Becker, Mediaeval Vi-
sions, p 87.
van der Zanden, Étude sur le Purgatoire de
St Patrice, p 155.
Leslie, St Patrick's Purgatory, p 95.
Patch, The Other World, p 115n.
CBEL, 1.177.

a. South English Legendary; Brown-
Robbins, nos 3037, 3039.
MSS. 10 MSS, of which two, Bodl 1486 (Laud
Misc 108) and Lambeth 223, omit lines
1–54.
Ward, 2.478, 480 (on Egerton 1993, Cotton
Julius D.ix, and BM Addit 10301).
Editions. AELeg 1875, pp 151, 175 (texts of
Bodl 1486 and 6924, Egerton 1993).
Horstmann C, The Early South-English Leg-
endary, EETS 87.199 (text of Bodl 1486).
D'Evelyn C and A J Mill, The South English
Legendary, EETS 235.85 (text of Corp
Christi Camb 145 and Cotton Julius C.ix).
Literary Relations. Stanford M A, The Sum-
ner's Tale and Saint Patrick's Purgatory,
JEGP 19.377.

b. Stanzaic; Brown-Robbins, no *11.
MS. Advocates 19.2.1 (Auchinleck), ff 25ª–31ª
(1330–40).
Editions. Turnbull W D B B and D Laing,
Owain Miles, Edinburgh 1837.
Kölbing, EStn 1.98 (crit J Zupitza, ZfDA
22.248).
Selections. Scott W, Minstrelsy of the Scot-
tish Border, ed T F Henderson, Edin-
burgh 1902, 3.165 (stanzas 116–126 rptd
from EStn 1.106).
Wright, St Patrick's Purgatory, p 64.
Modernizations. Shackford M H, Legends
and Satires from Mediaeval Literature,
Boston 1913, p 33 (prose).
Wetson J L, The Chief Middle English
Poets, Boston 1914, p 83 (verse, stanzas
116–98).
Leslie, St Patrick's Purgatory, p 149 (stanzas
51–73, 120–49).
Language. Mackenzie B A, A Special Dia-
lectal Development of OE ea in Middle
English, EStn 61.386.

Authorship. Kölbing, EStn 1.90; crit H Varnhagen, Zu mittelenglischen Gedichten,
Angl 3.60.
Sources. Willson, Middle English Legends,
pp 5, 34.

c. Early couplet; Brown-Robbins, no
982.
MS. Cotton Calig A.ii, ff 91ᵇ–95ᵇ (1400–50).
Ward, 2.482.
Edition. Kölbing, EStn 1.113.
Selections. Wright, St Patrick's Purgatory, p
64; R P Wülcker, Altenglisches Lesebuch,
Halle 1874, 1879, 2.22 (lines 250–460).
Textual Notes. Kölbing E, Nachträge und
Besserungen zu den englischen Studien,
EStn 5.493.

d. Late couplet; Brown-Robbins, no
1767.
MS. Hamilton (formerly Brome), ff 28ª–38ª
(1450–1500).
Smith L T, Abraham and Isaac, A Mystery
Play; from a private MS of the 15th Cen-
tury, Angl 7.316.
Editions. Smith L T, St Patrick's Purgatory,
and the Knight, Sir Owen, EStn 9.3; A
Commonplace Book of the Fifteenth Cen-
tury, Norwich 1886, p 82 (collation of
Cotton Calig A.ii).
Modernizations. Leslie, St Patrick's Purga-
tory, p 145 (lines 65–118, 203–56, 545–614).

e. Harley fragment; Brown-Robbins,
no 3038.
MS. Harley 4012, ff 140ª–151ᵇ (15 cent, incomplete).
Source. St Patrick's Purgatory a.

f. Hearne fragment.
Edition. Hearne T, Joannis de Fordun Scoti-
Chronicon genuinum . . . e codibus MSS
eruit ediditque T H, Oxford 1722, p xxxiii
(9 quatrains from a MS of T Rawlinson);
rptd Leslie, St Patrick's Purgatory, p 158.

g. 1438 Golden Legend.
MSS. 1, Egerton 876, begins f 69 (15 cent);
2, Harley 630, begins f 94 (15 cent); 3,
Harley 4775, ff 54ᵇ–55ᵇ (15 cent, MLA Roto
343, 1.109); 4, BM Addit 11565, begins f
95 (mid 15 cent); 5, BM Addit 35298, ff
29ᵇ col 1 – 30ª col 1 (formerly Ashburnham, mid 15 cent); 6, Lambeth 72 (mid
15 cent).
AELeg 1881, p cxxx; Ward 2.467; Butler LA,
pp 50, 149.
Edition. Butler LA, p 116 (text of Harley
4775 with collation of Egerton, Harley 630,
BM Addit 11565).

h. Staunton prose.

MSS. 1, Royal 17.B.xliii, ff 133ᵃ–148ᵇ (15 cent); 2, BM Addit 34193, ff 99ᵃ col 2 – 100ᵇ col 2, 106ᵃ col 1 – 106ᵇ col 2, 119ᵇ col 1 – 125ᵇ col 2; end missing (late 15 cent). Ward, 2.484, 487; Krapp, The Legend of St Patrick's Purgatory, p 54.

Edition. Krapp, The Legend of St Patrick's Purgatory, p 58 (text of Royal MS).

Selections. Wright, St Patrick's Purgatory, p 140 (summary with quotations from Royal MS).

Leslie, St Patrick's Purgatory, p 28 (selections from Royal MS slightly modernized).

Literary Relations. Verdeyen en Endepols, Tondalus' Visioen, 1.267.

[322] THE VISION OF TUNDALE.

MSS. 1, Bodl 7656 (Ashmole 1491), 5 vellum leaves at the end of the book, lines 2307–2326, 115–386, 700–1165 (beginning 15 cent); 2, Cotton Calig A.ii, ff 95ᵇ–107ᵇ (1400–50); 3, Royal 17.B.xliii, ff 150ᵃ–184ᵃ, lines 1–63 missing (mid 15 cent); 4, Advocates 19.3.1, ff 98ᵃ–157ᵃ (15 cent); 5, Penrose 10 (formerly Delamere), ff 166ᵇ–175ᵇ, lines 1482–2000 (1450–60).

Brown-Robbins, no 1724.

Furnivall F J, Lord Delamere's MS of the Canterbury Tales, N&Q 4s 9.353; Ward, 2.428, 433 (on Cotton and Royal MSS); Wagner, Tundale (see below under *Editions*) p ix (on Bodley, Cotton, Royal and Advocates MSS); R H Robbins, The Speculum Misericordie, PMLA 54.935; de Ricci Census, 2.1996; and Manly and Rickert, 1.108 (on Penrose MS).

Editions. Turnbull W B D D, The Visions of Tundale; together with Metrical Moralizations and Other Fragments of Early Poetry Hitherto Inedited, Edinburgh 1843, p 1 (text of Advocates MS).

Wagner A, Tundale, das mittelenglische Gedicht über die Vision des Tundalus auf Grund von vier Handschriften mit Einleitung und Anmerkungen, Halle 1893 (crit K D Bülbringe, LfGRP 15.259; M Kaluza, EStn 19.268; F Holthausen, AnglB1 4.129) (language, p xvi; versification, p xxxvii; authorship and date, pp xxxii, xxxviii).

Selections. Wülcker R P, Altenglisches Lesebuch, Halle 1879, 2.17 (210 lines of Cotton MS).

Ward, 2.428, 433 (62 lines from Cotton MS, 32 lines from Royal MS).

General. Wright, St Patrick's Purgatory, p 32; Wagner, Tundale, p xxxii; Becker, Medieval Visions, p 85; Verdeyen en Ende-

pols, Tondalus' Visioen, 1.118, 294; Willson, Middle English Legends, pp 8, 37; Seymour, Irish Visions, p 124; Os, Religious Visions, p 46.

Bibliography. Becker, Medieval Visions, p 81; CBEL, 1.177.

[323] THE VISION OF FURSEY.

Old English versions in (1) Bede's Ecclesiastical History of the English People, III.19 (EETS 95.210); (2) Aelfric's Sermones catholicae, chap 36 (EETS 152.109).

An exemplum on the subject is in (1) the prose translation of Manuel des Péchés in St Johns Coll Camb 197; (2) An Alphabet of Tales in BM Addit 25719 (EETS 27.208); (3) The Floure of the Commandementes of God, Wynkyn de Worde, 1510.

a. Handlyng Synne, lines 2473–2590.

MSS. Brown-Robbins, no 778.

Editions. Furnivall F J, Robert of Brunne's Handlyng Synne, Roxburghe Club, London 1862, p 79 (text of Harley 1701); Robert of Brunne's Handlyng Synne (1303) and Its French Original, EETS 119.88 (text of Bodley 2313, variants of Dulwich Coll XXIV).

Sources. Herbert, p 280, no 15.

b. 1438 Golden Legend.

MSS. 1, Bodl 21947 (Douce 372) (15 cent); 2, Egerton 876 (15 cent); 3, Harley 630 (15 cent); 4, Harley 4775, chap 137, ff 179ᵇ–180ᵇ (mid 15 cent), MLA Roto 343, vol 2.357; 5, BM Addit 11565 (mid 15 cent); 6, BM Addit 35298 (formerly Ashburnham) (mid 15 cent).

AELeg 1881, p cxxx; Butler LA, pp 51, 149.

Source. Graesse LA, p 639.

c. Caxton Golden Legend.

Editions. Caxton GL, Westminster 1483, chap 178; Temple, 5.177 (also in 1487, 1493, 1498 edns).

[324] THE VISIONS OF LEOFRIC.

MS. Corp Christi Camb 367, ff 1ᵇ–3ᵇ of part V (ff 48ᵇ–50ᵇ of complete volume, ca 1100).

Napier A S, An Old English Vision of Leofric, Earl of Mercia, TPSL 26.180.

Edition. Napier, TPSL 26.182.

Source. Gerould S Leg, p 126.

Silverstein H T, The Vision of Leofric and Gregory's Dialogues, RES 9.186.

[325] A REVELATION OF PURGATORY.

MSS. 1, Bodl Eng Th c.58, begins f 10 (15 cent); 2, Lincoln Cath 91 (Thornton MS), ff 250ᵇ–257ᵃ, leaf missing after f 253 (ca

1446); 3, Longleat 29, ff 155ᵃ–165ᵇ (15 cent).

Halliwell J O, The Thornton Romances, Camden Soc 30, pp xxv, xxxiv.

Allen WAR, pp 34, 36n1; Manly and Rickert, 1.343 (on Longleat).

The Bodleian Library Record 2, no 25, p 169 (on Bodley).

Edition. Yksh Wr, 1.383 (from Lincoln Cath MS).

[326] THE VISION OF THE MONK OF EYNSHAM.

Editions. William de Machlinia . . . a maruelous reuelacion . . . to a monk of Euyshamme, London 1485 (MLA Film, order no 577).

Arber E, The Revelation to the Monk of Evesham 1196, English Reprints, London 1869, 1901.

Duff E G, Fifteenth Century Books, Bibliographical Soc Illustrated Monographs no XVIII, London 1917, p 99, no 357.

Language. Oliphant T L K, The New English, London 1886, 1.321.

Royster J F and J M Stedman Jr, The "Going-to" Future, Manly Anniversary Studies, Chicago 1923, p 398.

Source. Ward, 2.493.

Becker, Mediaeval Visions, p 95.

Thurston H, Visio Monachi de Eynsham, Analecta Bollandiana 22.236.

Huber M, Beitrag zur Visionsliteratur und Siebenschläferlegende des Mittelalters, 1 Teil, Texte, Beilage zum Jarhesbericht der humanistischen Gymnasium Metten für das Schuljahr 1902/1903, p iii; Visio Monachi de Eynsham, RF 16.644.

Salter H E, Eynsham Cartulary, Oxford Hist Soc, Oxford 1908, 2.285.

Os, Religious Visions, p 68.

Author of Latin Text. Dimock J F, Magna vita S Hugonis Episcopi Lincolniensis, Rolls Series, London 1864, p xxxiv.

Luard H F, Matthew Paris, Chronica majora, Rolls Series, London 1874, 2.xiii.

Ward, 2.493, 502, and 512.

Thurston, Analecta Bollandiana, 22.226.

Salter, Eynsham Cartulary, 2.258.

Identity of Monk. Luard, Rolls Series, London 1874, 2.423, note 1.

Hewlet H G, Roger of Wendover, Rolls Series, London 1889, 2.xlvi, 187.

Ward, 2.494, 502.

Thurston H, The Vision of the Monk of Eynsham, The Month 90.49; Analecta Bollandiana 22.232; A Conjectural Chapter in the Life of St Edmund of Canterbury, The Dublin Review 135.229.

Salter, Eynsham Cartulary, 2.260.

Davies C, The Revelation to the Monk of Evesham, RES 11.182 (crit E K Chambers, RES 11.330).

General. Os, Religious Visions, p 68.

Bibliography. Becker, Mediaeval Visions, p 93.

VI. INSTRUCTIONS FOR RELIGIOUS

by

Charlotte D'Evelyn

Note: Epistola ad simplices sacerdotes (Wells VI [44]) is here omitted because it is a fragment on secular, not regular, clergy.

1. ANCRENE RIWLE

[1] ANCRENE RIWLE.

MSS. English: 1, Bodl 3938 (Vernon), ff 371ᵇ–391ᵇ (ca 1385); 2, Gonville and Caius Camb 234/120, pp 1–185 (1250–1300); 3, Corp Christi Camb 402, ff 1ᵃ–117ᵃ (ca 1230); 4, Magdalen Camb Pepys 2498, pp 371–449 (14 cent); 5, Cotton Cleop C.vi, ff 3ᵃ–197ᵃ (13 cent); 6, Cotton Nero A.xiv, ff 1ᵃ–120ᵇ (1225–50); 7, Cotton Titus D.xviii, ff 14ᵃ–105ᵃ (ca 1230–40); 8, BM Royal 8.C.i, ff 122ᵇ–143ᵇ (15 cent); 9, Lanhydrock Fragment (formerly Robartes MS), Bodl MS Eng th.c.70, 1 leaf (1300–50).

French: 1, Bodl 1887 (Bodley 90), ff 1–77 (1250–1300); 2, Trinity Camb 883 R.14.7, ff 124ᵇ–154ᵇ (late 13—early 14 cent); 3, Cotton Vitell F.vii, ff 2ᵃ–70ᵃ (early 14 cent); 4, BN fr 6276, ff 3–127ᵃ/36 (late 13—early 14 cent).

Latin: 1, Magdalen Oxf Latin 67, ff 1ᵃ–95ᵃ (ca 1400); 2, Merton Oxf c.1.5, ff 90ᵃ–165ᵇ (1300–50); 3, Cotton Vitell E.vii, fragments (early 14 cent); 4, BM Royal 7.C.x, ff 69ᵇ–124ᵇ (beg 16 cent).

For fuller description of published MSS or parts of MSS see below under *Editions* and *Selections.*

Items following give various information about the MSS in the order listed above.

English: Allen H E, MSS of the AR, TLS Feb 1936, p 116 (clues to provenance of several MSS); M S Serjeantson, The Index of the Vernon MS, MLR 32.222; J Zupitza, Eine unbekannte HS der AR, Angl 3.34 (Caius); E Kölbing, Eine unbekannte HS der AR, EStn 3.535 (correction of Zupitza); M R James, Supplement to the Catalogue of MSS in the Library of Gonville and Caius College, Cambridge 1914, p xix (description and discussion of Caius MS); Moore Meech and Whitehall, p 56 (localization of Corpus in Herefordshire uncertain); M S Serjeantson, The Dialect of the Corpus MS of the AR, LMS 1².225 (dialect "most probably that of Herefordshire"); J R R Tolkien, Ancrene Wisse and Hali Meiþhad, E&S 14.105 (comparison of language of Corpus and Bodl 34); H E Allen, The Localization of Bodl MS 34, MLR 28.485 (suggests origin of Corpus in Shropshire); A C Paues, A 14-Century Version of the AR, EStn 30.344 (description of Pepys); J Påhlsson, Zur AR-Frage, EStn 38.453 (dialect and revisions in Pepys); E Colledge, The Recluse, A Lollard-Interpolated Version of the AR, RES 15.1, 129 (lists interpolations); T Mühe, Über den im MS Cotton Titus Text der AR, diss Göttingen 1901.

French: Liddell M, The Source of Chaucer's Person's Tale, Acad 49.447, 509 (description of Bodl 90); H E Allen, E&S Brown, p 207 (identification of Bodl 90 as part of French AR); H E Allen, The AR, TLS Oct 24 1936, p 863 (identification of Trinity Camb 883 as part of French AR); H E Allen, E&S Brown, pp 182, 193 (discussion of Trinity Camb 883); H E Allen, Eleanor Cobham, TLS March 22 1934, p 214 (Cotton Vitell F.vii owned by Eleanor); C Marson, TLS April 12 1934, p 262 (anagram for Eleanor).

Latin: Allen H E, A New Latin MS of the AR, MLR 14.209 (identification of Merton c.1.5 = Merton 44); H E Allen, Another

Latin MS of the AR, MLR 17.403 (identification of BM Royal 7.C.x).

Interrelation of MSS. Macaulay G C, The Ancren Riwle, MLR 9.145, 326 (collation of 13-cent Eng MSS).

D'Evelyn C, Notes on Some Interrelations between the Latin and English Texts of the AR, PMLA 64.1164 (comparison of Latin particularly with "additions" of Corpus).

Trethewey, EETS 240.xvi, xxv (French and English texts compared).

Stevens W J, The Titles of MSS AB, MLN 76.443 (evidence for close relation between Corpus 402 and Bodl 34).

Dobson E J, The Affiliations of the MSS of Ancrene Wisse, in English and Medieval Studies, London 1962, p 128 (comparison of English, French, and Latin texts, supporting Corpus 402 as close copy of author's revision).

Editions. Morton J, The AR, Camden Soc 57, London 1853 (text of Cotton Nero with variants of Titus and Cleop; crit Archaeological Journal of the Arch Instit of Gt Britain and Ireland 11.194; E Kölbing, JfRESL 15.179).

Napier A S, A Fragment of the AR, JEGP 2.199 (Robartes MS; see English MS 9 above, and Zettersten, edn, below).

Påhlsson J, The Recluse, A 14-Cent Version of the AR, Lund 1911; rptd in 2 pts with notes 1918 (text of Pepys; crit R Jordan, EStn 51.255; B Fehr, AnglB 25.75; Arch 140.314).

Jewitt A R, Ancrene Wisse, Edited with Introduction and Notes, diss Cornell 1936, Abstract, Ithaca 1936 (text of Corpus).

Day M, The English Text of the AR, BM Cotton Nero A.xiv, EETS 225, London 1952, rptd 1957 (crit E Colledge, RES ns 4.275; H D, Revue d'histoire ecclésiastique 48.484; T F Mustanoja, NM 56.72).

Wilson R M, The English Text of the AR, Gonville and Caius College MS 234/120, EETS 229, London 1954 (crit S R T O D'Ardenne, RES 9.56; G L Brooks, MÆ 26.58).

Baugh A C, The English Text of the AR, BM Royal 8.C.i, EETS 232, London 1956 (crit T F Mustanoja, NM 58.118; G Shepherd, MÆ 27.44; R M Wilson, MLR 52.625; S I Tucker, RES 9.116).

Tolkien J R R, The English Text of the AR, Ancrene Wisse, EETS 249, London 1962 (Corp Christi Camb 402).

Mack F M, The English Text of the AR MS Cotton Titus D.xviii, EETS 252, London 1963.

Zettersten A, The English Text of the AR,

The Lanhydrock Fragment, EETS 252.166 (with facsimile).

Herbert J A, The French Text of the AR, BM Cotton Vitell F.vii, EETS 219, London 1944 (crit TLS June 23 1945, p 297; L Oliger, Apollinaris [Rome] 19.289).

Trethewey W H, The French Text of the AR, Trinity Camb R.14.7, EETS 240, London 1958 (crit R M Wilson, MLR 54.627; A C Baugh, Spec 35.156).

D'Evelyn C, The Latin Text of the AR, Merton MS 44 and BM Cotton Vitell E.vii, EETS 216, London 1944, rptd 1957 (for criticism see entries under J A Herbert above).

Selections. Fosbroke T D, British Monachism, 3rd edn London 1843, p 374 (brief extracts from Cotton Nero).

Rel Ant (4 passages) 1.65 (from Nero, 7 sins, see EETS 225.86); 2.1 (from Cleop, Greek fire etc, see EETS 225.183, 188); 2.4 (from Titus, practical rules and conclusion, see EETS 225.192).

AESpr, Berlin 1869, 2.5 (pt 2 of AR based on Morton, edn, pp 48–116).

Morris Spec, 1.110, 321 (see Morton, edn, pp 208–16, 416–30).

Sweet H, First Middle English Primer, 1st edn Oxford 1884, cited 2nd edn 1891, p 19 (see Morton, edn, pp 64–80, 118–28, 384–402, 416–18).

Kluge F, Mittelenglische Lesebuch, Halle 1904, p 15 (Nero, pt 8; see Morton, edn, pp 416–30).

Heuser W, Die AR—Ein aus angelsachischer Zeit überliefertes Denkmal, Angl 30.108 (from Corpus; see Morton, edn, p 26).

Emerson O E, A Middle English Reader, rvsd edn, N Y 1915, p 197 (see Morton, edn, pp 64–72, 414–18).

Macaulay G C, The AR, MLR 9.463 ("additions" in Corpus).

Cook A S, A Literary Middle English Reader, Boston 1915, p 269 (see Morton, edn, pp 50–52, 72, 132–34, 388–90, 416–24).

Brandl A and O Zippel, Mittelenglische Sprach- und Literaturproben, Berlin 1917; 2nd edn, Middle English Literature, N Y 1949, p 223 (see Morton, edn, pp 198–216).

Hall Selections, 1.54, 2.354 (the 7 Deadly Sins from Corpus and Caius, the Outer Rule from Corpus and Nero).

Sampson G, The Cambridge Book of Prose and Verse, Cambridge 1924, p 179 (text and translation from Morton, edn, pp 388–91).

Funke O, A Middle English Reader, Bibliotheca Anglicana 7, Bern 1944, p 19 (see Morton, edn, pp 12, 64, 218, 314, 388).

Dickins and Wilson, p 91 (flatterers from Nero; see Morton, edn, pp 86–90; "dog of hell" from Corpus; crit MÆ 22.121, 123).

Mossé F, A Handbook of Middle English, trans J A Walker, Baltimore 1952, p 139 (4 selections from Corpus with parallel passages from French, EETS 219, and Latin, EETS 216).

Kaiser R, Alt- und mittelenglische Anthologie, 2nd edn, Berlin 1955, p 157 (5 passages from Nero).

Shepherd G, Ancrene Wisse, Pts 6 and 7, Nelson's Medieval and Renaissance Library, London 1959 (text of Corpus; crit C D'Evelyn, Spec 35.324; G H Russell, MP 58.270; M Salu, MÆ 29.205; R Woolf, EC 11.210).

Allen H E, E&S Brown, p 209 (extracts from French Trinity Camb 883).

Dempster G, The Parson's Tale, Bryan-Dempster, p 748 (passages from Trinity Camb 883).

Trethewey W H, The Seven Deadly Sins, PMLA 65.1235 (passage from Trinity Camb 883; see EETS 240.39).

Modernizations. Morton J, The AR, London 1853; rptd as The Nun's Rule, King's Classics, London 1907; rptd in The Mediaeval Library, London 1924.

Salu M B, The AR (The Corpus MS: Ancrene Wisse), pref by J R R Tolkien, intro by Dom G Sitwell, The Orchard Books, London 1955; rptd Notre Dame, Indiana 1956 (crit P F C, AJ 61.95; J Russell-Smith, RES 8.424; M W Bloomfield, Spec 33.128; B Cottle, JEGP 57.117; J H Fisher, MLN 73.639).

Textual Notes. Stratmann F H, Notes on the AR, N&Q 48(4s 12).224.

Stratmann F H, Verbesserungen zu altenglischen Texten, EStn 2.119.

Kenyon J S, A Syntactical Note, MLN 29.127.

Onions C T, Middle English (i) wite God, wite Crist, (ii) God it wite, RES 4.334.

Colledge E, "The Hours of the Planets": An Obscure Passage in The Recluse, MLN 54.442.

Russell-Smith J, Ridiculosae Sternutationes (o nore in AW), RES 8.266 (practice of augury by sneezing).

Bennett J A W, Lefunge o swefne, o nore, RES ns 9.280.

Language. Brock E, The Grammatical Forms of Southern English (about 1220–30 AD) Occurring in the AR, TPSL 1865, p 150.

Wülcker R, Über die Sprache der AR und die Homilie Hali Meidenhad, PBBeitr 1.209.

Kölbing E, JfRESL 15.190 (dialect of Nero, Titus, Cleop, Corpus).

Bülbring K D, Geschichte des Ablauts der starken Zeitwörter innerhalb des Südenglischen, QF 63.6.

Ostermann H, Lautlehre des german Wortschatzes in der von Morton herausgegebenen Hds der AR, BBA 19.1 (crit H Middendorff, AnglB 18.108; Neue Philolog Rundschau, 1906, p 331).

Williams I F, The Language of the Cleopatra MS of the AR, Angl 28.300.

Redepenning H, Syntaktische Kapitel aus der AR, Berlin 1906.

Påhlsson J, Zur AR-Frage, EStn 38.453 (dialect and revisions in Pepys).

Püttmann A, Die Syntax der sogenannten progressiven Form in Alt- und Frühmittelenglischen, Angl 31.405 (for AR see p 450).

Landwehr M, Das gram Geschlecht in der AR, diss Heidelberg 1911.

Dieth E, Flexivisches u Syntaktisches über das Pronomen in der AR, diss Zürich 1919.

Hall Selections, 2.357 (phonology of Caius, Corpus, Cleop, Nero, Titus), 2.372 (dialect of AR).

Funke O, Zur Wortgeschichte der französischen Elemente im Englischen, EStn 55.17, 24.

Zeise A, Der Wortschatz der AR, diss Jena, Summary 1923.

Serjeantson M S, The Dialects of the West Midlands in Middle English, RES 3.323 (Nero assigned to southeast Worcestershire).

Tolkien J R R, Ancrene Wisse and Hali Meiþhad, E&S 14.104 (language of Corpus).

Cravens M J, Designations and Treatment of the Holy Eucharist in Old and Middle English before 1300, diss Catholic Univ of America 1932, p 61 (technical vocabulary of Mass).

Serjeantson M S, A History of Foreign Words in English, London 1935, pp 84, 121 (Scandinavian and French words in Nero).

Grosse E, Die neuenglische ea-Schreibung. Ein Beitrag zur Geschichte der engl Orthographie, Palaes 208.37 (Nero discussed).

Füller L, Das Verbum in der AR, diss Jena 1937.

Hulbert J R, A 13-Century English Literary Standard, JEGP 45.411 (opposes Tolkien on language of Corpus).

Bliss A J, A Note on the Language of AB, EGS 5.1 (review and discussion of theory of "standard language" in Corpus and Bodl 34).

Salu M B, Some Obscure Words in Ancrene

Wisse (MS Corp Christi Camb 402), EGS 5.100 (criblin, taueles riuin, riuunges).

Ladd C A, A Note on the Language of the AR, N&Q 206.288 (archaisms in Nero).

Original Language of AR. Morton, edn, p vii (English).

Bramlette E E, The Original Language of the AR, Angl 15.478 (Latin).

Mühe T, Über die AR, Angl 31.399 (Latin).

Macaulay G C, The AR, MLR 9.63 (French).

Hall Selections, 2.377 (English).

Dymes D M E, The Original Language of the AR, E&S 9.31 (English; crit G Hübener, AnglB 35.367).

Chambers R W, Recent Research upon the AR, RES 1.6 (English).

Samuels M L, AR Studies, MÆ 22.1 (English).

Käsmann H, Zur Frage der ursprünglichen Fassung der AR, Angl 75.134 (further textual evidence for English).

Fisher J H, The French Versions of the AR, Univ of N C Stud in Germ Langs and Lits 26.65 (AR excerpts in Tretyce of Loue, EETS 223, as supporting English original).

Date and Origin. Heuser W, Die AR—ein aus angelsächischer Zeit überliefertes Denkmal, Angl 30.103 (argues for lost OE original of Corpus; crit T Mühe, Angl 31.399; A S Napier, MLR 4.434).

Allen H E, The Origin of the AR, PMLA 33.474 (AR written for three 12-cent recluses of Kilburn Priory; crit G G Coulton, MLR 15.99; V McNabb, MLR 15.406).

Allen H E, The AR and Kilburn Priory, MLR 16.316 (questions McNabb's theory of Dominican origin; crit G G Coulton, MLR 17.66; V McNabb, RES 2.84; H Thurston, RES 2.199).

Chambers R W, Further Research upon the AR, RES 2.85, 198 (evidence for date after 1153).

Allen H E, The Three Daughters of Deorman, PMLA 50.899 (would identify 3 recluses of Kilburn with daughters of Deorman, temp Henry I).

Allen H E, The Tortington Cartulary, TLS Feb 14 1935, p 92 (notice of brother of Deorman).

White B, The Barnacle Goose and the Date of the AR: Three Notes on Old and Middle English, MLR 40.206 (crucifix described in Morton, edn, p 390, suggests date after 1200).

Bloomfield SDS, p 148 (treatment of sins suggests date ca 1225).

Kirchberger C, Some Notes on the AR, DomS 7.215 (evidence for early 13-cent date and Dominican influence).

Talbot C H, The De institutis inclusarum of Ailred of Rievaulx, Analecta s o Cisterciensis 7.169 (error in AR of assigning Ailred's treatise to Anselm, see EETS 225.137, as evidence of date).

Talbot C H, Some Notes on the Dating of the AR, Neophil 40.38 (liturgical evidence for 12- or 13-cent date).

Brewer D S, Two Notes on the Augustinian and Possibly West Midland Origin of the AR, N&Q 201.232 (traces in the AR of Augustinian practices and of Herefordshire culture).

Author. Einenkel E, Eine englische Schriftstellerin aus dem Anfanges des 12 Jahrhunderts, Angl 5.265 (suggests nun of AR as author of Wohung; crit W Vollhardt, Einfluss der lateinischen geistlichen Litteratur, diss Leipzig 1888, p 44).

McNabb V, The Authorship of the AR, MLR 11.1 (proposes Dominican Robert Bacon; crit H E Allen, PMLA 33.538; G G Coulton, MLR 17.66).

Hall Selections, 2.375 (suggests Gilbert of Sempringham; crit R M Wilson, Leeds SE 1.24).

Chambers R W, Recent Research upon the AR, RES 1.14 (review of authorship proposals).

Chambers R W, Further Research upon the AR, RES 2.87 (problems involved in proposal of Dominican authorship).

McNabb V, Further Research on the AR, RES 2.197 (answers objections to his theory).

Allen H E, On the Author of the AR, PMLA 44.635 (suggests Godwin hermit of Kilburn as author).

McNabb V, The Authorship of the AR, Archivum fratrum praedicatorum (Rome) 4.49 (restatement of his proposal; crit E J Arnould, MLR 31.463).

Kirchberger C, Some Notes on the AR, DomS 7.220 (argues for Robert Bacon).

Talbot C H, Some Notes on the Dating of the AR, Neophil 40.38 (secular priest rather than monk as author).

Brewer D S, N&Q 201.232 (evidence for Augustinian canon as author).

Title. Magoun F P, Ancrene Wisse vs Ancren Riwle, ELH 4.112 (favors AW).

Sources and Literary Relations. Vollhardt W, Einfluss der lateinischen geistlichen Litteratur, diss Leipzig 1888.

Allen H E, Mystical Lyrics of the Manual des Pechiez, RomR 9.189 (connection of AR with mystical tradition in England).

Allen H E, Some 14-Century Borrowings

from AR, MLR 18.1 (corrected MLR 19.95).

Chambers R W, Recent Research upon the AR, RES 1.17 (connection with Ailred's Rule and Bernard's Sententiae).

Oliger L, Regulae tres reclusorum et eremitarum Angliae saec xiii–xiv, Antonianum 3.151, 299 (links of AR with Dublin, Cambridge, and Oxford Rules; see following item and also H E Allen, PMLA 44.663).

Allen H E, Further Borrowings from AR, MLR 24.1.

D'Ardenne S R T O, An Edition of þe Liflade ant te Passiun of seinte Iuliene, Liège 1936, rptd EETS 248.x1 (literary tradition as link between Katherine group and AR).

Gardner H L, Walter Hilton and the Mystical Tradition in England, E&S 22.103 (no direct borrowing from AR).

Colledge E, The Recluse, RES 15.1, 129 (Lollard and mystical writings reflected in Pepys MS).

Fisher J H, Continental Associations for the AR, PMLA 64.1180 (relation to Tretys of Love [1493] and associated tracts).

Trethewey W H, The Seven Deadly Sins, PMLA 65.1233 (relation of French Trinity Camb 883 to English AR).

Fisher J H, The Tretyse of Love, EETS 223.xvi (words and subject matter borrowed from AR; crit N&Q 197.86; H R Patch, Spec 27.106).

Brady M T, The Pore Caitif: An Introductory Study, Trad 10.529 (use of AR following H E Allen).

Kaske R E, Eve's Leaps in the AR, MÆ 29.22 (connection with medieval interpretations of Cant C.2.8).

Biblical Quotations and Proverbs. Smyth M W, Biblical Quotations in Middle English Literature before 1350, YSE, N Y 1911, 41.85.

Brown ELxiiiC, p xi, n 2 ("Euer is þe eie," Morton, edn, p 96; crit B J Whiting, Spec 9.219; B J Whiting, Proverbs in the AR and the Recluse, MLR 30.502n3).

Clark C, A Mediaeval Proverb, ESts 35.11.

Ives D V, The Proverbs in the AR, MLR 29.257 (crit D Everett, YWES 15.130; B J Whiting, MLR 30.502).

Prins A A, On Two Proverbs in the AR, ESts 29.146 (1, high wind allayed by dust; 2, after rain, sun).

Shepherd G, "All the Wealth of Croesus,": a Topic in the AR, MLR 51.161.

Style. Dahlstedt A, The Word-Order of the AR with Special Reference to the Word-Order in Anglo-Saxon and Modern English, Sundsvall 1903 (crit E A Koch, EStn 34.78).

Chambers R W, On the Continuity of English Prose, EETS 186.xc, separately ptd London 1932.

Bethurum D, The Connection of the Katherine Group with Old English Prose, JEGP 34.553.

Bogholm N, Vocabulary and Style of the ME AR, ESts 19.113.

Humbert A M, Verbal Repetition in the AR, diss Catholic Univ of America 1944 (crit G D Willcox, YWES 26.71).

General Discussion and Bibliography. Wilson EMEL, p 128; Baugh LHE, p 127; Hall Selections, 2.357; CBEL, 1.179, 5.121; Renwick-Orton, rvsd edn 1952, p 276; G Shepherd, *Ancrene Wisse,* London 1959, p 73.

2. BENEDICTINE ORDER

[2] RULE OF ST BENET.

(Note: OE versions are not included.)

Version a (Winteney, Prose):

MS. Cotton Claud D.iii, ff 52ª–138ª (1200–25).

Schröer M M A, Die Winteney-Version der Regula S Benedicti lateinish und englisch, Halle 1888, p lx.

Edition. Schröer, Winteney-Version, p 3 (crit L Morsbach, Götting Gelehrte Anz, 1888, p 1013; E Kölbing, EStn 16.152).

Language. Schröer, Winteney-Version, p xiv (Winteney as representing transition from OE to ME).

Morsbach L, Götting Gelehrte Anz, 1888, p 1014 (objection to Schröer's linguistic analysis).

Schröer, EStn 14.243 (fuller statement on transitional nature of language).

Tachauer J, Die Laute und Flexionen (Winteney), Warzburg 1900.

Funke O, Zur Wortgeschichte der französiche Elemente im Englischen, EStn 55.4 (French words in Winteney).

Moore Meech and Whitehall, p 53 (Hampshire dialect characteristics in Winteney).

Sources. Schröer, Winteney-Version, pp xii, 2 (original Winteney version based directly on OE "common version"; extant version based on Latin text Cotton Claud D.iii, ff 50ª–137ᵇ).

Version b (Northern Prose):
MS. Lansdowne 378, ff 1ᵇ–42ᵇ (early 15 cent).
Koch, EETS 120.xvi.
Edition. Koch, EETS 120.1.
Language. Koch, EETS 120.xix, xl (phonology and grammar of Northern Prose and Verse versions.
Heuser W, Die ältesten Denkmäler und die Dialekte des Nordenglischen, Angl 31.276 (archaic elements in language of Lansdowne; for controversy over this article see Angl 31.398, 543).
Hagel F, Zur Sprache der Nordenglischen Prosaversion der Benediktiner-regel, Angl 44.1 (fuller evidence for two layers of language in Lansdowne).
Versification. Koch, EETS 120.xii (scraps of verse in text).

Version c (Northern Verse, Couplets):
MS. Cotton Vesp A.xxv, ff 66ᵃ–119ᵇ (early 15 cent).
Brown-Robbins, no 218.
Koch, EETS 120.xvii (description).
Editions. Böddeker K, Versifizirte Benediktinerregel im Northern Dialect, EStn 2.61; corrections, p 384.
Koch, EETS 120.48.
Selections. Cook A S, A Literary ME Reader, Boston 1915, p 293 (from EETS 120.95, 99, 102, 115).
Kaiser R, Medieval English, Berlin 1958, p 534 (134 scattered lines from EETS 120.93, 104, 97, 81, 105, 99, 89, 95, 102).
Textual Notes. Holthausen F, Zu alt- und mittelenglischen Dichtungen, Angl 14.302.
Kölbing E, Beiträge zur Textkritik und Erklärung, EStn 23.284.
Language. Böddeker K, Über die Sprache der Benediktinerregel: Ein Beitrag zur Kenntniss des nordhumbrischen Dialekts, EStn 2.344 (see Koch, EETS 120.x, xlv).
Koch, EETS 120.xix, xlv (phonology, grammar).
Versification. Koch, EETS 120.xiii, xxxv (meter, index of rimes).

Version d (Prose Rule for Women):
MS. Libr Congress MS 4, ff 1ᵃ–36ᵃ (15 cent).
de Ricci Census, 1.180.
Dean R J and M D Legge, The Rule of St Benedict, A Norman Prose Version, MÆ Mon 7, Oxford 1964, pp xi, 105. (I am grateful to Miss Dean for information about this version and for the loan of rotographs.)
Version e (Caxton Print, Prose):
Editions. [A] compendious abstracte . . . of the holy rule of S Benet, Caxton, Westminster 1490?; rptd Koch, EETS 120.119; STC, no 3305.
Dibdin Typo Antiq 1.331 (description of Caxton edn).
Koch, EETS 120.xvii (description).
Sources. Koch, EETS 120.xiv (relation to Latin text).

Version f (Fox Translation, Prose):
Edition. [Fox R,] Here begynneth the Rule of S Benet, Pynson, Westminster 1516; STC, no 1859.
Dibdin Typo Antiq 2.463 (description of edn).
Bibliography. CBEL, 1.178.

[3] RITUAL FOR ORDINATION OF NUNS.
MSS. 1, Camb Univ Mm.3.13, 16 ff (ca 1500; rubrics in English, service in Latin); 2, Cotton Vesp A.xxv, ff 120ᵃ–124ᵇ (early 15 cent; English); 3, Lansdowne 378, ff 43ᵃ–46ᵇ (early 15 cent; Latin and English); 4, Lansdowne 388 (ca 1480; Latin and English).
Koch, EETS 120.x (notes on MSS).
Editions. Maskell W, Monumenta ritualia ecclesiae Anglicanae, 2nd edn, Oxford 1882, 3.333 (Camb Univ Mm with extracts in notes from Lansdowne 388), p 360 (Cotton Vesp).
Henderson W G, Liber pontificalis Chr Bainbridge archiep Ebor, Surtees Soc 61, Durham 1875, p 237 (Lansdowne 388 with Benedictio abbatissae electae, p 248).
Koch, EETS 120.141, 145 (Lansdowne 378, Cotton Vesp).

3. AILRED OF RIEVAULX, INFORMACIO

[4] AILRED OF RIEVAULX, INFORMACIO AD SOROREM SUAM INCLUSAM.
MSS. 1, Bodl 2322 (Bodl 423), ff 178–192 (ca 1430–40); 2, Bodl 3938 (Vernon), ff iiiᵇ–viᵃ (early 15 cent).

AELeg 1875, p xix, n 1 (description and opening lines of Bodl 3938).
Serjeantson M S, The Index of the Vernon MS, MLR 32.222 (Informatio in same hand as Index, early 15 cent).

Edition. Horstmann C, Informacio Alredi abbatis . . . ad sororem suam inclusam, EStn 7.304 (Bodl 3938 with Latin rptd from Migne PL, 32, col 1457).

Selections. Fosbroke T D, British Monachism, 3rd edn, London 1843, p 376 (brief extracts from Bodl 2322 with Latin from Cotton Nero A.iii).

Modernizations. Webb G and A Walker, A Letter to His Sister by St Aelred of Rievaulx, London 1957 (follows Horstmann's text).

Author. Horstmann, EStn 7.305 (Thomas N, named in Bodl 3938, not identified).

Sources and Literary Relations. Horstmann, EStn 7.304 (literal translation beginning at chap 21 of Ailred's De vita eremetica ad sororem liber.

Allen H E, The Origin of the AR, PMLA 33.529 and n 85 (links between AR and Ailred's rule; see Chambers, RES 1.17).

Powicke F M, Ailred of Rievaulx and His Biographer Walter Daniel, JRLB 6.509n3 (English translation made from fuller text than that in Migne).

Allen H E, On the Author of the AR, PMLA 44.653 (possible borrowing from AR in fuller Latin text of Ailred).

Powicke F M, The Life of Ailred of Rievaulx, London 1951, pp xcii, xcvii, xcix (on date and character of Ailred's text).

Talbot C H, The De institutis inclusarum of Ailred of Rievaulx, Analecta sacris ordinis Cisterciensis 7.177 (edn of fuller Latin text from Cotton Nero A.iii, prob 13 cent; see p 169 for borrowings from and by Ailred).

4. ENGLISH BRIGITTINE ORDER

[5] RULE OF ST AUGUSTINE.

MSS. 1, Camb Univ Ff.vi.33, ff 88ᵃ–98ᵇ (15 cent); 2, St Paul's Cath Libr MS, ff 84ᵃ– 88ᵇ (15 cent).

Waltzer H S, An Edition of the ME Translation of the Regula S Salvatoris, unptd diss Yale 1950, pp ii, iv, clxxxvi (relation of MSS in contents, date, source).

Editions. Note: References are to the Bodley copy Douce A.277, in microfilm, which contains both the undated edn of the Rule in English alone and the Nov 28 1525 edn of the Rule with two expositions.

Whytforde R, Saynt Augustyns Rule in englysshe alone, Wynkyn de Worde, London nd; STC, no 13925 (in 7 chaps).

Whytforde R, The rule of Saynt Augustyne/ bothe in latyn and englysshe/with two exposicyons. And also yᵉ same rule agayn onely in englysshe without latyn or exposicyon, Wynkyn de Worde, London Nov 28 1525; STC, no 25417.

Dibdin Typo Antiq 2.256 (description of both edns).

Boardman C, A Catalogue of Books Printed Either in Gothic Letter or Before the Year 1551, Forming Part of the Library of Stonyhurst College, London 1862, p 4 (description of Stonyhurst copy which, like Oxford copy, has both edns bound together).

Duff E G, Hand-lists of Books Printed by London Printers, 1501-56, Biblio Soc, London 1913, Wynkyn de Worde, p 16.

Waltzer, Regula S Salvatoris, p 182 (notes both edns).

Author. For Richard Whytford (fl 1495– 1555?) see DNB and Waltzer, Regula S Salvatoris, p 182.

Sources. St Augustine, Regula ad servos Dei, Migne PL, 32, col 1377 (translated and expounded by Whytford).

Aungier G J, The History and Antiquities of Syon Monastery, London 1840, p 246 (English summary of Latin Rule from BM Addit 5208).

Hugo of St Victor, Expositio in regulam beati Augustini, Migne PL, 176, col 881 (translated by Whytford).

General Background. Gwynn A, The English Austin Friars in the Time of Wyclyf, Oxford 1940.

[6] RULE OF ST SAVIOUR.

MSS. 1, Camb Univ Ff.vi.33, ff 38ᵇ–67ᵃ (15 cent); 2, St Paul's Cath Libr MS, ff 75ᵇ– 84ᵃ (1450–1500).

Waltzer, Regula S Salvatoris, pp i, clxxxvi (evidence for St Paul MS as later than Camb MS; both from common source).

Edition. Waltzer, Regula S Salvatoris, pp 2, 6 (table of contents from St Paul MS, f 75ᵃ; preface, prologue, rule from Camb MS, f 38ᵇ; Latin text on facing pages), p ccxvii (language), p 192 (bibliography).

Sources. Aungier G J, The History and Antiquities of Syon Monastery, London 1840, pp 243, 246 (summary of Latin text from BM Addit 5208, ca 1450).

Waltzer, Regula S Salvatoris, p vi (MSS of Latin texts owned in England).
Background. Deanesly M, The Incendium Amoris of Richard Rolle of Hampole, Manchester Univ Publ Hist Ser 26, Manchester 1915, p 91 and index.
Waltzer, Regula S Salvatoris, p cxlii.

[7] ADDITIONS TO THE RULE OF ST SAVIOUR.

MSS. 1, BM Arundel 146 (15 cent; beg, end imperf; for Sisters); 2, St Paul's Cath Libr MS, ff 6ᵃ–55ᵇ (1450–1500; for Brothers).
Edition. Aungier, History and Antiquities of Syon Monastery, p 249 (MS 1 supplemented by MS 2).
Date. Deanesly M, Incendium amoris of Richard Rolle, p 130 (ca 1431 for Additions in extant form).
Other Literary Problems. Blunt, EETSES 19.xx (summary of Additions with material from other Syon documents).
Deanesly M, Incendium amoris of Richard Rolle, p 113 (history of compilation).
Waltzer, Regula S Salvatoris, p clxiii (relation of Additions to other rules).

[8] MIRROR OF OUR LADY.

MSS. 1, Aberdeen Univ WPR.4.18 (1450–1500; extends through Part II, Sunday services); 2, Bodl 12772 (Rawl C.941), ff 1–139 (begins Part II, Monday services).
Blunt, EETSES 19.vii (description and history of Aberdeen MS).
Macray W D, Cat Codd MSS Bibl Bodl, Oxford 1878, Part V, 2, col 511 (Aberdeen and Rawl MSS "form but one book").
Waltzer, Regula S Salvatoris, p 189n1 (quotes colophon of Rawl MS).

Editions. Here after folowith the boke callyd the Myrroure of Oure Lady, ptd R Fawkes, London 1530; STC, no 17542.
Blunt, EETSES 19, 1873, rptd 1898 (text based on Durham Univ copy; p x, copies known to Blunt; for correction of STC and Blunt see BM Cat of Printed Books, 1962 edn, 154, col 506).
Selections. Blunt, EETSES 19.lx (pp 1 and 2 of Aberdeen MS).
Power E, Medieval English Nunneries, ca 1275 to 1535, Cambridge 1922, p 531 (passage on attendance at services).
Date. Deanesly M, The Lollard Bible, Cambridge 1920, p 339 (written 1421–50).
50).
Author. Blunt, EETSES 19.viii (suggests Thomas Gascoigne, 1403–58, of Merton Coll).
Wylie J H, History of England under Henry the Fourth, London 1894, 2.363n3 (Clement Maidstone, fl 1410, possible author).
Deanesly, Lollard Bible, p 340n3 (Maidstone, Brother of Syon, more probable compiler than Gascoigne).
Waltzer, Regula S Salvatoris, p 188 (summary of acceptance or rejection of Mirror in canon of Gascoigne's works).
Sources and Literary Relations. Blunt, EETSES 19.xl (translation of Latin Offices of Syon with comment).
Mosher J A, The Exemplum in the Early Religious and Didactic Literature of England, N Y 1911, p 128 (type of exempla in Mirror).
For its relation to the English Brigittine Order, see also P Hodgson and G M Liégey, The Orcherd of Syon, EETS 258, 1966.

5. Franciscan Order

[9] RULE OF ST FRANCIS (First Order of St Francis).

Version a (Wyclyfite):
MSS. 1, Bodl 3072 (Bodley 647), ff 71ᵃ–74ᵃ (late 14 cent); 2, Corp Christi Camb 296, pp 29–39 (1375–1425); 3, Trinity Dublin C.iii.12 (15 cent).
Arnold T, Select English Works of John Wyclyf, Oxford 1871, 3.xiii (description of MSS 1, 2, 3).
Edition. Matthew F D, The English Works of Wyclyf, EETS 74.40 (text of Corp Christi with collation of Bodley and Trinity).

Author. Arnold, Select Eng Works of Wyclyf, 3.xx (no 21 under Doubtful Works).
Sources. Sabatier P, Vie de St François d'Assise, Paris 1899, p 288 (development of Latin Rule).
Butler C, Life of St Francis of Assisi, London 1938, p 90 (on Latin Rule).
Background. Moorman J R H, The Sources for the Life of St Francis of Assisi, Manchester 1940, p 12.

Version b (Howell):
MS. Cotton Faust D.iv, ff 10ᵃ–24ᵇ (text), ff 34ᵃ, 42ᵃ, 56ᵃ (Howell notes; 15 cent).
Editions. Howlett R, Monumenta Francis-

cana, Rolls Series, London 1882, 2.65 (text).

Brewer J S, Monu Franc, London 1858, 1.567 (Howell notes).

Sources. See above under *Sources* for *Version a.*

[10] TESTAMENT OF ST. FRANCIS.

Version a (Wyclyfite):

MSS. 1, Bodl 3072 (Bodley 647), ff 74ᵇ–78ᵇ (late 14 cent); 2, Corp Christi Camb 296 (1375–1425); 3, Trinity Dublin C.III.12 (15 cent).

Arnold T, Select English Works of John Wyclyf, Oxford 1871, 3.xiii.

Matthew, EETS 74.vii.

Edition. Matthew, EETS 74.45 (chap 13 of Rule; text of Corp Christi collated with Trinity and Bodley).

Author. Arnold, Select Eng Works of Wyclyf, 3.xx (no 25 under Doubtful Works).

Sources. Matthew, EETS 74.497 (extracts from Latin text quoted).

Sabatier P, Vie de St François d'Assise, Paris 1899, pp xxxviii, 385.

Butler C, Life of St Francis of Assisi, London 1938, p 449.

Version b (Howell):

MS. Cotton Faust D.iv, ff 25ᵃ–33ᵃ (15 cent).

Brewer, Monu Franc 1.562 (MS a portuary owned by Franciscan James Howell).

Edition. Brewer, Monu Franc 1.562.

Sources. See above under *Sources* for *Version a.*

[11] RULE OF ST CLARE (Second Order of St Francis).

MS. Bodl 2357 (Bodley 585), ff 48ᵃ–72ᵃ (Rule), ff 72ᵃ–101ᵃ (additions to Rule; 15 cent).

Seton, EETS 148.71 (history and description of MS).

Edition. Seton, EETS 148.81 (Rule), 98 (additions to Rule).

Language. Chambers R W and M Daunt, A Book of London English, Oxford 1931, p 9 (very probably written by a Londoner, but too literally translated to represent London English).

Sources. Seton, EETS 148.69, 76 (English probably a translation of French version of Latin Rule).

Background. Fly H, Some Account of an Abbey of Nuns . . . in the Street Called the Minories, Archaeol 15.92.

Seton, EETS 148.72 (history of first house of Poor Clares in England).

Bourdillon A F C, The Order of Minoresses in England, Manchester 1926.

Bibliography. Seton, EETS 148.78; Bourdillon, Minoresses, p 103.

[12] RULE OF THE ORDER OF PENITENTS (Third Order of St Francis).

MS. Pennant MS, ff 2ᵃ–15ᵇ (1450–1500); Seton, EETS 148.38 (Note: Pennant MS owned by Seton in 1914 listed for sale in Rosenbach Cat 1937, item 157; present location not discovered).

Edition. Seton, EETS 148.45 (crit B Fehr, AnglB 31.146), p 27 (sources, Eng translation based on 3rd version of Latin Rule, 1289), p 41, (bibliography).

[13] RULE OF THE OBSERVANTS (First Order of St Francis, Reformed).

MS. Cotton Faust D.iv, item 6 (15 cent; Howell summary of Statutes of Barcelona, 1451).

Edition. Brewer, Monu Franc 1.574.

Sources. Howlett, Monu Franc 2.xlviii, 81 (text of Abbreviatio statutorum of Barcelona, 1451, basis of Eng translation).

6. Rules for Hermits and Recluses

[14] RULE OF ST CELESTINE.

MSS. 1, BM Sloane 1584, ff 89ᵃ–95ᵇ (early 16 cent; MLA roto 213); 2, BM Addit 34193, ff 131ᵃ–136ᵇ (late 15 cent; MLA roto 213); 3, Bristol Reference Libr No 6*, ff 137ᵇ–140ᵇ (1502).

Clay R M, The Hermits and Anchorites of England, London 1914, p 87.

Allen WAR, p 330.

Oliger L, Regulae tres reclusorum et eremitarum Angliae saec xiii-xiv, Antonianum 3.156.

Date. Oliger, Antonianum 3.161 (Latin source dated probably 1350–1400).

Author. Allen WAR, p 331 (evidence against St Celestine as author of Latin source).

Oliger, Antonianum 3.165 (further evidence against St Celestine).

Sources. Clay, Hermits, p 87 (similarity of Eng text Bristol MS to Latin text Bodl 11937).

Allen WAR, p 329 (comparison between English and Latin texts).

Sources and Literary Relations. Oliger, Antonianum 3.158 (direct and indirect sources of Latin version, Oxford Rule, on which English translation is based; for Latin text see pp 299, 312).

Allen H E, Further Borrowings from Ancren Riwle, MLR 24.10 (relation of Latin source of Celestine Rule to Cambridge Rule and AR).

Talbot C H, The De institutis inclusarum of Ailred of Rievaulx, Analecta sacris ordinis Cisterciensis 7.170 (influence of Ailred on later rules including St Celestine's).

[15] RULE OF ST LINUS.

MS. Lambeth 192, f 46ᵃ (15 cent).

Clay, Hermits, p 88.

Oliger L, Regula reclusorum Angliae saec xiii–xiv, Antonianum 9.48, 260.

Edition. Oliger, Antonianum 9.263 (with facsimile of Lambeth and parallel Latin text), p 262 (date; on liturgical grounds Latin source dated 1275–1325; Eng text dated by MS 15 cent), p 261 (author; no

evidence for Linus as author of Latin source; Thomas Scrope probably translator or transcriber of Eng text).

[16] SPECULUM INCLUSORUM.

MS. Harley 2372, ff 1ᵃ–37ᵇ (mid 15 cent; imperf).

Clay, Hermits, p 99.

Oliger L, Speculum inclusorum, Lateranum ns 4, no 1, Rome 1938, p 28 (condition of MS: prol om; parts I and II imperf; part III, 2 fragments; part IV lost).

Editions. No ptd edn; for summary of contents see Clay, Hermits, p 99; for incipits of chapters see Oliger, Lateranum 4.26; Oliger, p 23, reports edn by Lilian E Rogers presented to Univ of Oxford for BA degree 1933.

Author. Oliger, Lateranum 4.31 (unknown author writing before end of 15 cent).

Sources. Oliger, Lateranum 4.63 (edn of Latin source from BM Royal A.V, beg 15 cent, with corrections from St John's Oxford MS 177, beg 16 cent).

7. OTHER ORDERS

[17] FOUNDING OF THE ORDER OF HOLY TRINITY.

(Note: See above, V [245], St Robert of Knaresborough.)

MS. BM Egerton 3143, formerly Newcastle Clumber, ff 60ᵇ–63ᵃ (late 15 cent).

Brown-Robbins, no 261.

Bazire, EETS 228.1.

Editions. Bazire, EETS 228.72 (ptd text numbered consecutively with metrical Life of St Robert), p 9 (language; Northern dialect with occasional Southern forms), p 23 (author; possibly by author of metrical Life), p 34 (sources and literary relations; English version of Founding possibly source of Latin version in same MS), p 140 (bibliography).

[18] FOUNDING OF THE CARTHUSIAN ORDER.

MS. BM Addit 37049, f 22ᵃ (1400–50; 29 couplets).

Brown-Robbins, no 435.

Allen WAR, p 306 (scribe probably a Carthusian; dialect Northern).

[19] ORDINANCE AND CUSTOMS OF THE HOSPITAL OF ST LAWRENCE, CANTERBURY.

MSS. 1, Camb Univ Add 6845, formerly Phillipps 6845 (14 cent); 2, Clumber Libr MS (sold Sotheby Feb 15 1938, lot 1143).

[20] SCROPE T, INSTITUTIONS AND SPECIAL DEEDS OF RELIGIOUS CARMELITES.

MS. Lambeth 192, ff 47ᵃ–153ᵇ (15 cent).

Oliger L, Regula reclusorum Angliae, Antonianum 9.260.

Sources. James M R, Descriptive Cat of the MSS in the Library of Lambeth Palace, Cambridge 1932, 2.300 (translation of P Ribot, Speculum Carmelitarum in Lambeth 192, ff 1ᵃ–40ᵇ).

Index

A bold-face number indicates the main reference in the Commentary; a number preceded by B indicates the reference in the Bibliography. Titles are indexed under the first word following an article. Indexed are all literary works and their authors, names of early printers, and main subdivisions. Saints are indexed for the Commentary only; for the Bibliography, the reader should refer to B561–B635, where the saints are listed alphabetically. No attempt has been made to index the names of characters and places in the literary works nor the names of scholars.